A HISTORY OF CANADIAN LITERATURE

A History of
Canadian Literature

W.H. New

SECOND EDITION

McGill-Queen's University Press
Montreal & Kingston • London • Ithaca

Legal deposit third quarter 2003
Bibliothèque nationale du Québec

Printed in Canada on acid-free paper

First edition published by New Amsterdam Books of New York,
1989. Reprinted in paperback by McGill-Queen's University Press,
2001.

McGill-Queen's University Press acknowledges the financial support
of the Government of Canada through the Book Publishing Industry
Development Program (BPIDP) for its publishing activities. It also
acknowledges the support of the Canada Council for the Arts for its
publishing program.

National Library of Canada Cataloguing in Publication

New, W.H. (William Herbert), 1938–
A history of Canadian literature / W.H. New. – 2nd ed.

Includes bibliographical references and index.
ISBN 0–7735–2597–1

1. Canadian literature – History and criticism.   I. Title.

PS8061.N48 2003   C810.9   C2003–901300–6
PR9184.3.N48 2003

Typeset in 10/12 Palatino by True to Type

For Peggy

Contents

Introduction; Aboriginal cultures; Aboriginal texts; Aboriginal
mythology; Inuit culture; Inuit mythology; European myth and
cultural context

Backgrounds; Journalism and cultural politics; Exploration
journals; Missionary journals; Travel, captivity and settlement
journals; Letters and epistolary form; Satire and speech; Politics
and poetry; Romantic documentary; Documentary romance

Anglo-protestant, ultramontane, prairie; Currents of ideas;
Historical tales; Sentimentality, satire and social reform; Social
and literary resistance; Nature stories; Confederation Poets;
The Nelligan symbol; Sketches of reality

National romance and the land; Painters and the Montreal
Group; Social protest and social change; Realism; The politics
of literary form; Literature and war; Voice and point of view;

Plates

Acknowledgments

I should like to thank several colleagues who read parts of this book and offered helpful advice: Alan Lawson of the University of Queensland, and Diana Brydon, Eva-Marie Kröller, and Laurie Ricou of the University of British Columbia. Many others willingly answered particular questions. Jon Nightingale and Victoria Lyon-Lamb provided guidance with computer programming; Lilita Rodman located some statistical data; Robin Bellamy helped find some of the illustrations, and along with Diane Thomson and numerous other people, helped verify authors' dates; Richard Ruggles, Michael Ames and Conrad Heidenreich answered questions about ethnographic and cartographic history. Doreen Todhunter, Debbi Onbirbak and Beverly Westbrook typed sections of the manuscript. To all of them, and to A.N. Jeffares and Beverley Tarquini, for their editorial suggestions, I am grateful.

My greatest debt is to Peggy, my wife, and our two sons, David and Peter. As always, they generously encouraged me. I want especially to thank Peggy for her constructive comments on the typescript, and for the twenty years of conversation that helped in no small way to shape this book.

The author and publisher also wish to express their appreciation to the following, for permission to quote from material in copyright:

David Arnason, excerpt from *The Circus Performers' Bar*: Talonbooks; Margaret Atwood, excerpts from poems: the author; Margaret Avison, excerpts from poems from *The Dumbfounding*: the author; Earle Birney, excerpts from poems: the author; George Bowering, excerpt from *Burning Water*: the author; Morley Callaghan, excerpt from 'A Girl with Ambition': Don Congdon Associates Inc.; Emily Carr, from FRESH SEEING by Emily Carr © 1972 Clarke Irwin & Co. Ltd: used by permission of Irwin Publishing Inc.; Rienzi Crusz, excerpt from poem:

Porcupine's Quill; Raymond Filip, excerpt from poem: reprinted with permission from *Somebody Told Me I Look Like Everyman*, by Raymond Filip: Arsenal Pulp Press, 1150 Homer St, Vancouver, Canada, V6B 2X6; Mavis Gallant, excerpts from stories: Macmillan of Canada; John Glassco, excerpt from *Memoirs of Montparnasse*: © Oxford University Press, Canada, 1970; Barbara Thompson Godard, excerpt from introduction to Nicole Brossard's *These Our Mothers*: the author; Ralph Gustafson, excerpt from 'Partial Argument' (*Corners in the Glass*, published by McClelland & Stewart): the author; A.M. Klein, excerpts from poems: McGraw-Hill Ryerson Ltd; Robert Kroetsch, excerpt from *Seed Catalogue*: the author; Margaret Laurence, excerpt from 'The Sound of the Singing' (*A Bird in the House*): reprinted by permission of The Canadian Publishers, McClelland & Stewart, Toronto; Irving Layton, excerpts from *Darkening Fire* by Irving Layton: used by permission of The Canadian Publishers, McClelland & Stewart, Toronto, and the author; Dennis Lee, excerpt from *Civil Energies*: the author; Dorothy Livesay, excerpts from *Collected Poems: The Two Seasons*: the author; Jay Macpherson, excerpts from *Welcoming Disaster*: the author; Eli Mandel, excerpt from 'The Double' (*Out of Place*, 1977): Press Porcépic; Gaston Miron, excerpts from *Embers and Earth*: Les Editions Guernica Editions; John Newlove, excerpts from poems: the author; bp Nichol, 'Blues' (typography by Vivien Halas): the author; Michael Ondaatje, excerpt from 'White Dwarfs' (*There's a Trick with a Knife I'm Learning to Do*, McClelland & Stewart, © Michael Ondaatje): the author; P.K. Page, excerpts from 'Photos of a Salt Mine' and 'Cook's Mountains': the author; Al Purdy, excerpts from *Cariboo Horses* by Al Purdy: used by permission of The Canadian Publishers, McClelland & Stewart, Toronto, and the author; Bill Reid and Robert Bringhurst, excerpt from *Raven Steals the Light*: Douglas & McIntyre; C.G.D. Roberts, excerpts from 'The Prisoners of the Pitcher Plant', *Kindred of the Wild*, and *Poems*: used by permission of The Canadian Publishers, McClelland & Stewart, Toronto; Hector de Saint-Denys Garneau, excerpts from 'Le Jeu', 'Accompagnement', 'Cage d'or' (*Poésies Complètes*): Éditions Fides; D.C. Scott, excerpts from *Selected Poems*: used by permission of The Canadian Publishers, McClelland & Stewart, Toronto; F.R. Scott, excerpts from *Collected Poems* by F.R. Scott: used by permission of The Canadian Publishers, McClelland & Stewart, Toronto; Lola Lemire Tostevin, excerpts from *Color of Her Speech*: the author; Sheila Watson, excerpt from *The Double Hook* by Sheila Watson: used by permission of The Canadian Publishers, McClelland & Stewart, Toronto; Phyllis Webb, excerpts from poems: the author; Ethel Wilson, excerpts from *Swamp Angel* and *The Innocent Traveller*: the University of British Columbia Library.

Preface to the Second Edition

The first edition of this book ended with the following sentence: 'Given the context of the closing chapter ... it is well to regard this entire book as a history-in-process.' It still is. To look back at 1987 from the year 2002 is to see that the process of cultural change has continued in Canada and that the first edition's dialogue with the future has already begun. Political events have reshaped Canadians' sense of themselves; critical fashions have altered, reassessing reputations, reconstructing canons, and reacting to modified social priorities and preoccupations. New literary voices are also being heard; the sheer number of publications has increased multifold; technological changes have altered both the manner of literary production and the patterns and methods of dissemination; and such issues as ethnicity, ecology, economics, social status, gender, copyright, and sexuality all vie for further attention. To survey literature in Canada during the last decade of the twentieth century, therefore, is still to be selective, charting trends and relationships, and hinting at the further complexities that closer criticism will reveal.

This second edition of *A History of Canadian Literature* differs from the first primarily by the addition of a chapter on literary developments following 1988 and the social contexts in which they took place. There are additions, too, to the chronology, changes in the suggestions for further reading, and biographical updates whenever they could be verified.

I have, however, except for correcting some typographical mistakes and a few errors of fact, largely left the first five chapters intact. As will be clear from Chapter 6, new research, changing taste, and changing views of history all modified, during the 1990s, some of the judgments that are recorded in earlier chapters. The politics of naming also substantially changed the terms that are used in relation to the Native peoples. Hence the term 'Indian' is now used here when historical or textual context demands it, but otherwise has been altered to read 'Native' or 'Aboriginal,' in accordance with current practice. The spelling of Aboriginal tribal names and languages has also been updated ('Mi'kmaq' instead of 'Micmac,' for example). The critical recuperation of earlier writers, however – whether Native or not: George Copway and Pauline Johnson, Eudore Évanturel and Marcel Dugas – is addressed in Chapter 6, as a feature of 1990s commentary, as is the late-twentieth-century emergence of contemporary 'First Nations' writers.

Once again I am indebted to the many people who patiently answered my questions, made suggestions, and read preliminary drafts of the new chapter, especially Joseph Jones of the UBC Library and my colleagues and friends Sherrill Grace, Laurie Ricou, Margery Fee, Gabi Helms, Jerry Wasserman, Jane Flick, James Doyle, John O'Brian, and Richard Cavell. The Canadian Museum of Civilization searched their archives for answers to some biographical questions, and I am grateful for their cooperation and time. I am also deeply indebted to my research assistant René Brisebois for his care with detail and for long and absorbing conversations about contemporary francophone writing in Canada, and to Kathryn Grafton for preparing the website list in the Further Reading section. I wish also to thank Shelley MacDonald and David Andrien for technical assistance, and my editors at McGill-Queen's University Press, Philip Cercone, Joan McGilvray, and Elizabeth Hulse. Special thanks, as always, to Peggy.

WHN

Vancouver

October 2002

1. *Talelayu* (1979), by Kenojuak Ashevak, represents Sedna, the sea-woman
   in Inuit mythology. (By kind permission of Dorset Fine Arts Division of
   West Baffin Eskimo Co-operative Ltd., Toronto, Ontario)

2. *My Dream* (1975), by Carl Ray, shows the characteristic Ojibway shamanistic or 'X-ray' design. (Courtesy of the McMichael Canadian Art Collection, Purchase 1975)

BRITISH
AMERICAN
JOINT OCCUPATION
DANISH
SPANISH
RUSSIAN

1825

The international boundary is extended westward along the 49th parallel to the Rocky Mountains (1818). The Oregon Territory is occupied jointly by Britain and U.S.A. Reannexation: Cape Breton Island to Nova Scotia (1820); Île d'Anticosti and part of the coast of Labrador to Lower Canada (1825). Agreement between Russia and Britain on the description of Alaska boundary (1825).

3. & 4. Upper and Lower Canada join to become Canada in 1840; The Oregon Treaty (1846) extends the international boundary to the west coast along the 49th parallel; Vancouver's Island becomes a colony in 1849; the colony of British Columbia (est. 1858; formerly New Caledonia) unites with Vancouver's Island and the Stickeen Territory in 1866.

1867

New Brunswick, Nova Scotia and Canada are united in a federal state, the Dominion of Canada, by the British North America Act (July 1, 1867). The province of Canada is divided into Ontario and Quebec. The United States of America proclaims the purchase of Alaska from Russia (June 20).

Ungava, Mackenzie, Yukon, and Franklin are established as Districts in the North-West Territories. The creation of the District of Franklin acknowledges the inclusion of the arctic islands in Canada. The Districts of Athabaska and Keewatin are enlarged.

5. & 6. Manitoba joins Confederation in 1870, British Columbia in 1871, Prince Edward Island in 1873, Alberta and Saskatchewan in 1905; Ontario, Manitoba, and Quebec are extended northward in 1912; Canada's boundary is extended to the North Pole in 1927.

(Plates 3–6 courtesy of Macmillan Co. of Canada Ltd and Information Canada. Crown copyright, Information Canada, 1974)

At its own request, after a plebiscite, Newfoundland enters the Confederation as the tenth and most recent province of the Dominion of Canada.

7. *The Emigrant's Welcome to Canada* (c. 1820) emphasizes the unpreparedness of many European immigrants for the wilderness, and exaggerates its difficulties. (© Public Archives of Canada, c41067)

8. *Hommage à Nelligan*, by Jean-Paul Lemieux, suggests the poet's isolation and also his figurative importance in modern Quebec. (Collection Université de Montréal)

9. *The Jack Pine* (1916), by Tom Thomson, a precursor of the Group of Seven; all were concerned with representing images of the natural wilderness. (National Gallery of Canada, Ottawa)

10. *Big Raven* (1931), by Emily Carr, one of the first painters to recognise the spiritual significance of native Indian art. (Courtesy of the Collection of the Vancouver Art Gallery; photo: Robert Keziere/VAG)

11. *Young Canadian* (1932), by Charles Comfort, suggests the emotional and economic deprivations of the Depression. (© Hart House Permanent Collection, University of Toronto)

12. *Reason Over Passion* (1968), a quilt design by Joyce Wieland, satirizes Pierre Elliott Trudeau's political maxim, and challenges male systems of aesthetic authority. (National Gallery of Canada, Ottawa. © Joyce Wieland)

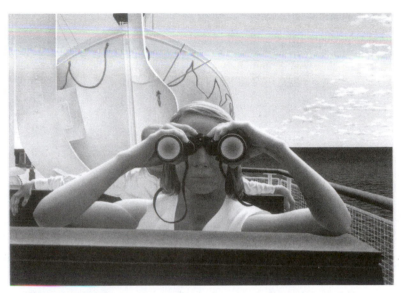

13. *To Prince Edward Island* (1965), by Alex Colville, an example in
    acrylic of the techniques of 'Magic Realism'. (National Gallery of
    Canada, Ottawa)

14 & 15. *Susanna Moodie* and *Margaret Atwood* (1982), cartoons by Isaac
    Bickerstaff, examples of contemporary playful parody. (By cour-
    tesy of Isaac Bickerstaff, from the Don Evans Papers, Special Col-
    lections Division, University of Calgary Library)

16. This detail from *A Group of Sixty-Seven* (1966) by Jin-me Yoon, is one of 138 photographs (each 40 x 50 cm) in an arranged patchwork design. A picture of Yoon's mother in front of a characteristic "Group of Seven" wilderness scene, it reimagines the Canadian cultural landscape by positioning a minority face visibly within it. (Cibachrome photograph, courtesy Vancouver Art Gallery, VAG 97.2a-ZZZZ, photo by Trevor Mills)

17. *Cola Wars* (1993) by Chris Woods represents the commercial rivalry between the giants in the Cola industry by drawing on a familiar scene from the Leonard Bernstein musical *West Side Story* (itself based on Shakespeare's *Romeo and Juliet*) in which two New York street gangs face off against each other in a potentially violent 'rumble.' (Oil on canvas, 76" x 114". Courtesy Chris Woods and the Diane Farris Gallery; www.dianefarrisgallery.com)

A HISTORY OF CANADIAN LITERATURE

CHAPTER ONE

Mythmakers: early literature

INTRODUCTION

Snow, North, Wilderness: these stereotypes of Canada suggest a fierce uniformity – but even from earliest times, such generalizations have been inaccurate. To read Canadian literature attentively is to realise how diverse Canadian culture is – how marked by politics and religion, how influenced by differences of language and geography, how preoccupied (apparently) by the empirical world, but how fascinated by the mysterious and the uncertain. 'Apparent' is important: illusion is everywhere. For repeatedly Canadian history has designed images of continuity and order, which the social realities touch, but only sometimes reconfirm.

French before it was British, Aboriginal and Inuit before that, when 'The Dominion of Canada' became independent on 1 July 1867 – by an Act of the British Parliament (the British North America Act) – the nation was nonetheless established on the British model. It was a constitutional monarchy with a bicameral parliamentary system; 'peace, order, and good government' was to be its watchword; English was the official language. But other languages and cultures persisted. The fact that the nation was also a secular state, preserving in some measure the status of the four confederating colonies (Nova Scotia, New Brunswick, Canada East and Canada West), hints at the changes to come.

Though Canada was a secular state, religion was everywhere in its history and language. The first prime minister, Sir John A. Macdonald (1815–91) (apparently at the suggestion of the New Brunswick politician Samuel Tilley, 1818–96), drew the name 'Dominion' from Psalm 72 – 'He shall have dominion from sea to sea, and from the river unto the ends of the earth' – finding the phrase appropriate to

the geography and ambitions of the new country. The phrase still survives, truncated in the national motto (*A mari usque ad mare*: from sea
to sea), first used about 1906. Several decades into the twentieth century the source was generally forgotten, and the term 'dominion' was
abandoned when people took it to denote merely a continuing colonial servility. Clearly, politics was everywhere in the language, too.
The biases of region, religion, class, gender, race – noted or unnoted,
conscious or unconscious – these all conditioned the way people
viewed the world. In Canada they helped to shape the expectations
of the new society and its patterns of expression. As the new nation
expanded to occupy most of the northern half of North America,
these perspectives altered. A history of literature in Canada is of
necessity, then, a record not only of specific literary accomplishments
over space and through time, but also an account of ways in which
the shaping contexts also changed, and of the interconnections
between context and language.

The term 'literature in Canada' poses a problem: 'Canadian literature' is not bounded by citizenship (there were writers before there
was a 'Canada', and there have been immigrants and long-term visitors since, for whom Canada has been home). It is not restricted to
Canadian settings. Neither does it imply some single nationalist
thesis. There are exiles and expatriates whose work still connects
with writing in Canada; and there are many Canadian-born writers
(Wyndham Lewis, 1886–1957; Saul Bellow, b. 1915; John Hearne,
1926–95; A.E. Van Vogt, 1912–2000) whose work bears no obvious
connection to Canada. Yet within the country, despite these apparent
inconsistencies, a community of understanding has developed. A
shared familiarity with popular culture, a localized adaptation to
space and distance, a reliance on common civil rights and expectations of behaviour, and a recognition of local forms of speech and
intonation (often ironic and often indirect) all underlie the more
immediately observable regional and linguistic disparities. Literature
in Canada grows from these social attitudes held in common, as well
as from historical antecedents and extranational models. But definitions of a single Canadian identity are suspect. It is the cultural plurality inside the country that most fundamentally shapes the way
Canadians define their political character, draw the dimensions of
their literature, and voice their commitment to causes, institutions
and individuality.

The word 'Canada' eludes precise translation: it has variously been
taken as the Spanish for 'nothing here' (*a ca nada*), the Portuguese for
'narrow road', the Montagnais Cree for 'clean land', the Mohawk
word for 'castle' (*canadaghi*) and a word meaning 'the mouth of the

country' or 'hunting land' or 'province'. The people of the North
Shore of the St Lawrence, wrote François de Belleforest (1530–83) in
1575, were 'Canadeen'. The most common contemporary view
accepts the early observation of Jacques Cartier (1491–1557): that the
Iroquois referred to their 'village' as *ka-na-ta*, the Hurons as *an-da-ta*.
Some of these interpretations indicate guesswork and simple ignorance; a few reflect the strange cringe that betrays an embarrassment
at colonial origins. Some hint at a determination to locate European
connections; some suggest a desire for a romantic history or a desperate need to fix a certainty. Some seem ironic. Some are undoubtedly wrong. Certainty is probably beyond reach.

These several translations also suggest the ambivalent position
that the Native peoples occupy in Canada. 'Indians' were displaced,
assigned Reserves, presumed to be a dying race – the Beothuks of
Newfoundland were even the victims of genocide (the last known
surviving tribe member, a woman named Shawnadithit, or Shanan-
ditti, c. 1801–29, died of tuberculosis in St John's). Yet they also
retained and actively exert a number of powerful claims on land,
resources and cultural traditions. European settlers largely misun-
derstood Native cultures, yet accepted many indigenous names for
the places they later claimed as home. Totems and headdresses also
appear routinely as tokens of Canadiana: writers and image-makers
have drawn repeatedly on Aboriginal and Inuit motifs to declare the
distinctiveness of things Canadian. This notion of indigenous art as
simply 'decorative', however, obliterates the religious and social
function that Native myths, poems, totemic designs, dances, rites and
shamanistic practices had within traditional culture. Only in the
twentieth century did the sophistication of the oral cultures come to
be more generally appreciated. Only then did Canadian writers of
other ethnic backgrounds abandon the twin stereotypes of 'savage'
and 'primitive noble', and come both to respect indigenous cultures
and to absorb some of the essential character of the indigenous myths
into the argument and design of their own art.

ABORIGINAL CULTURES

The notion of a uniform 'Red Indian' culture is a false one, just as the
term 'Red Indian' itself – perhaps deriving from the Beothuk practice
of painting the body in ochre (an insect repellent) – is also a mis-
nomer. In Canada, the usual reference is simply 'Indian', although
during the 1980s the word 'aboriginal' began to replace it – a change
which rhetorically asserts the freedom of indigenous cultures from
the historical mistakes of European definition.

Some sense of the variety of cultures present in North America when the first Europeans arrived in the sixteenth century is apparent from the sheer number of separate language families even now in existence – families quite different from each other in structure, syntax and vocabulary. There are ten separate language groups, some of them constituted by the existence of a single language, others embracing as many as sixteen separate languages, several with recognizable dialect subgroups, spoken in turn by an even greater number of individual bands. Inuktitut, the language of the Inuit, belongs to an eleventh language group, Eskimo–Aleut. The extinct Beothuk language may have been an Algonquian tongue, or may have been a twelfth separate language. Other languages already extinct include the Salishan language Pentlatch, and two Athapaskan languages, Tsetsaut and Nicola. It is difficult to predict the continuing survival of particular tongues: there are more than 100,000 speakers of Algonquian languages today, and fewer than 50 speakers of Kutenai. The size of the indigenous population, decimated by disease (a smallpox epidemic in 1823 almost halved the number of Blackfoot, and the 1917 flu epidemic diminished populations all across the country), is again increasing. Table 1 shows the distribution of Aboriginal languages.

By the end of the nineteenth century, it seemed that native cultures would entirely disappear, to be replaced by Christianity, schoolbooks and a metal technology. It was against such a background that the work of Franz Boas (1858–1942) and those he influenced – Edward Sapir (1884–1939), and later the folklorist Marius Barbeau (1883–1969) – assumes such importance. Their investigations attempted not simply to record vocabulary, seeking equivalents in English or French, but to preserve patterns of talk – the myths and stories – and thereby to understand the inner workings of custom and belief.

Sapir, the linguist who headed the anthropology division of the National Museum of Canada between 1910 and 1925, constructed the broad outlines of the pattern of classification in Table 1. The author of *Language* (1921), Sapir studied anthopology under Boas at Columbia University (New York), and developed the idea that language and cultural psychology intricately connect. Prior to his day numerous writers had attempted to produce Indian dictionaries and to record trade languages. As early as 1615, Gabriel Sagard (d. c. 1636) was at work on his *Dictionnaire de la langue Huronne*. In the 1830s the missionary James Evans (1801–46) developed a written form for Ojibway, and in 1840 devised Cree syllabics – a system later adapted in Inuktitut in the Central Arctic, even though Inuktitut does not operate by

Table 1   Aboriginal language groups

Language family	Territory		Number of member languages
Algonquian	Widespread, from Northern Alberta through Ontario and Quebec to the Maritimes	10	Abenaki, Blackfoot, Cree (six dialects), Delaware, Maliseet (Malecite), Micmac (Mi'kmaq), Montagnais, Ojibwa (five dialects, including Chippewa, Ottawa, and Mississauga), Potawatomi, Delaware
Athapaskan	Central interior of British Columbia, northern prairies, Yukon and Mackenzie Valley	16	Babine, Beaver, Carrier, Chilcotin (Tsilqot'in), Chipewyan, Dogrib, Han, Hare, Kaska, Kutchin (Gwich'in), Sarcee, Sekani, Slave (Slavey), Tagish, Tahltan, Tutchone
Haida	Queen Charlotte Islands (Haida Gwaii)	1	Haida
Iroquoian	St Lawrence lowlands	6	Cayuga, Mohawk, Oneida, Onondaga, Seneca, Tuscarora
Kutenai (Ktunaxa)	S E British Columbia	1	Kutenai (Ktunaxa)
Salishan	Southern coast and interior of British Columbia	12	Bella Coola (Nuxalk), Comox-Sliammon, Hakomelem, Klallam, Lillooet (Lil'wet), Okanagan, Sechelt (Tse'Shaht), Shuswap, Squamish, Straits, Thompson (Nlaka'pamux)
Siouan	Southern prairies	1	(in Canada): Dakota
Tlingit	Yukon-B.C. border	1	Tlingit
Tsimshian	Northern B.C. coast and Nass Valley	3	Nass-Gitksan, two versions of Tsimshian
Wakashan	Vancouver Island and central B.C. coast	6	(in Canada): Haisla, Heiltsuk, Nootka (Nuu-chah-nulth), Nitinat, Kwak'wala, Oowekeeno

the same syllabic structures as Cree. By means of their systems, however, Evans and the other lexicographers were, perhaps unknowingly, effecting another kind of translation. They were helping to turn an oral culture into a written one, hence markedly altering some of the basic presumptions within indigenous societies about the role of language as a medium of power. Such changes reinforced what traders and other missionaries had begun in the 1500s – a slow process of reshaping cultural norms.

While Boas's work primarily contributed to the shape of an academic discipline, it had other, less constructive results. For some readers, the appearance in English of the myths and tales merely reconfirmed their belief that 'Indians' were a simple primitive people. European presumptions about culture and reality produced an illogical syllogism: the myths were told simply – therefore mythmaking could not have a complex function. Hence 'Indian' myths, considered colourful and quaint, were frequently consigned to books of stories for European children, made into entertainments alone. Publishers often deemed contrary judgments unacceptable. T. M. McIlwraith's (1899–1964) *The Bella Coola Indians* (1948) was kept out of print for twenty years because the author refused to remove or rewrite the earthy tales it contained. Unlike some earlier collectors, McIlwraith would not bend Aboriginal myth to fit conventional Victorian propriety; he was an anthropologist first, a writer second, a censor not at all. He realised that myths were not mere entertainments but a functional part of indigenous religion, an issue which the missionary-translators had resisted. And he knew that rewriting the myths to fit a European notion of fairytale had altered both their character and their function.

ABORIGINAL TEXTS

The texts of Aboriginal tales appear in about four separate forms: as anecdotes retold within the context of the Jesuit *Relations* and in missionary journals, often as cautionary stories; as documentary records, in the pages of scholarly bulletins, complete with annotations and footnoted variants; as child narratives, with any earthiness removed; and as literary or religious narratives, anthologized first for nineteenth-century readers, and retold for modern readers often by contemporary native writers. Sometimes the narratives were single stories; sometimes they connected into a longer sequence – John Swanton (1873–1958) recorded two hundred and fifty episodes of the Raven story from a single tale-teller, Charles Edenshaw (1839–1920) – and there have been suggestions that these 'collective epics' constituted a form of New World history which is still not adequately understood.

Among scholarly texts, Franz Boas's *Tsimshian Mythology* (1916) and *Kutenai Tales* (1918) appeared in an ethnological series from the Smithsonian Institution; his *Kwakiutl Texts* (1905–6) and John Swanton's *Haida Texts* (1908) were publications of the American Museum of Natural History; Boas's *Bella Bella Tales* (1932) and such volumes as Douglas Leechman's (1890–1980) *Loucheux Tales* (1950) were published in the memoirs of the American Folklore Society; and W.H. Mechling's (1888–1953) *Malecite Tales* (1914) and Marius Barbeau's *Huron and Wyandot Mythology* (1915) – the latter showing how European fable had already marked Indian tales by the early twentieth century – appeared under the auspices of the anthropological division of the Geological Survey of Canada. Horatio Hale's (1817–96) *The Iroquois Book of Rites* appeared as a separate anthropological volume in 1883. Stith Thompson's (1885–1976) *Tales of the North American Indians* (1929) and William Bright's (b. 1928) *Coyote Stories* (1978) emphasize the fact that indigenous tales cross the contemporary political boundary between Canada and the USA. Thompson also attempts to produce a taxonomy of tale-telling motifs.

Collections designed for (non-native) children include Cyrus Macmillan's (1880–1953) *Canadian Wonder Tales* (1918), largely about Glooscap and Gitchi-Manitou; Ella Elizabeth Clark's (1896–1984) *Indian Legends of Canada* (1960); and Harold Horwood's (b. 1912) *Tales of the Labrador Indians* (1981), a collection from Nascapi sources. Among the earliest of the literary volumes are Émile Petitot's (1838–1917) *Traditions indiennes du Canada nord-ouest* (1886), George Bird Grinnell's (1849–1938) *Blackfoot Lodge Tales* (1892), Silas T. Rand's *Legends of the Micmacs* (1894), Egerton Ryerson Young's *Stories from Indian Wigwams and Northern Campfires* (1893) and *Algonquin Indian Tales* (1903), and Pauline Johnson's *Legends of Vancouver* (1911). Rand (1810–89) was the compiler of a Micmac–English dictionary, a linguist in search of Classical parallels, whose folktale collections began in the 1840s. Young (1840–99) was a Methodist minister whose versions of Indian mythology were coloured by his desire to use wilderness settings as conventional proving-grounds of Christian moralism, much in the manner of his contemporary Ralph Connor (1860–1937); Pauline Johnson (1861–1913) was the Mohawk poet Tekahionwake, whose verse and stories ('The Song My Paddle Sings' and the Squamish 'Vancouver' legends, which she adapted from Chief Joseph Capilano (1850–1910) were – as her 1982 biographer Betty Keller (b. 1930) establishes – deliberately designed to appeal to the expectations of a European audience.

Several later books also responded personally to Indian culture, among them Emily Carr's (1871–1945) *Klee Wyck* (1941); Diamond Jenness's (1886–1969) *The Corn Goddess* (1956); Claude Melançon's (1895–1973) *Légendes indiennes du Canada* (1967); the New Brunswick poet Alden Nowlan's (1933–83) *Nine Micmac Legends* (1983); a collection by the gifted Haida artist Bill Reid (1920–98) and the poet Robert Bringhurst (b. 1946) called *The Raven Steals the Light* (1984); Herbert Schwarz's (b. 1921) anthology of erotic stories called *Tales from the*

Smokehouse (1974); and an absorbing semi-fictionalized 'discovery' of a secret matrilineal heritage of stories, *Daughters of Copper Woman* (1981), by the poet and dramatist Anne Cameron (b. 1938) (author of *Dreamspeaker* and other works). Two other anthologies – Kent Gooderham's (b. 1927) *I Am an Indian* (1969) and Penny Petrone's (b. 1923) *First People, First Voices* (1983) – survey early literary practice by Native writers.

Several more recent writers, such as the outspoken essayist Harold Cardinal (b. 1945) and the poet Duke Redbird (b. 1939), have concerned themselves primarily with political and social issues. Many others have sought to reclaim cultural dignity by other means, by reiterating their tradition through song (the 1977 anthology *Many Voices*, ed. David Day, b. 1947, and Marilyn Bowering, b. 1949, provides current examples); through journalism (as in the periodical *Tawow*); through oratory (the eloquence of Chief Dan George, 1899–1981, will be remembered also from his career as a film actor); through drama (as in the plays of Bernard Assiniwi, 1935–2000); through fiction (the most telling examples being Basil Johnston's, b. 1929, comic stories, *Moose Meat & Wild Rice*, 1978, novels by Yves Thériault, 1915–83, and Jovette Marchessault, b. 1938, and Beatrice Culleton's, b. 1949, indictment of the foster home system, *In Search of April Raintree*, 1983); through myth and through memoir. George Clutesi's (1905–88) *Son of Raven, Son of Deer* (1967) tells Tse-Shaht stories for Native children and others; Clutesi asserts the oneness of human and nature, and rejects the explicit divisiveness he finds characteristic of European fairytale. Edward Ahenakew's (1885–1961) legends appeared as *Voices of the Plains Cree* (1973). Basil Johnston's *Tales the Elders Told* (1981) recalls Ojibway legends of Nanabush and other culture figures; Norval Morriseau (b. 1932) wrote *Legends of My People: the Great Ojibway* (1975). In *Visitors Who Never Left* (1974), Chief Ken Harris (1906–83) translated the sequence of Ksan creation myths. These evoke Damelahamid (sometimes recorded as Temlaham), a Utopian paradise in the Upper Nass Valley, said to have been made when the Father-Creator opened heaven and put 'visitors' on earth, visitors from whom the Gitksan are descended (and, say the myths – though ethnologists disagree – also the Sali*shan*, the Waka*shan*, people who have 'wandered from the Ksan'), visitors who are still conceived to be present at tribal gatherings whenever myths are told.

ABORIGINAL MYTHOLOGY

The emergence in the 1960s and 1970s of the Woodlands painters – Norval Morriseau, Carl Ray (1943–78), Daphne Odjig (b. 1919), Jack-

son Beardy (1944–84) and Benjamin Chee Chee (1944–77), for example – also contributed to this process of reinterpretation. As Mary
Southcott's (b. 1923) *The Sound of the Drum* (1984) indicates, Anishinabe art (Cree/Ojibway) is religious in origin; the Ojibway word for
art means 'made by hands' – but for special, not commercial purposes. Painting or drawing, on birchbark scrolls, was the gift and prerogative of the shaman, who used linear images to record sacred ceremonies. This 'X-ray' or outline technique was a way of representing
the shaman's ability to see past surfaces into the core of human experience. Morriseau, who claims a contemporary role as shaman, in
both his painting and his writings, is not unaware of the dilemma created by recording his culture in print and by selling what he draws:
it breaks with certain basic customs. Yet it also extends the possibility that these customs might come to be more widely recognized, and
serves a larger purpose, using contemporary media to continue the
practice of 'making scrolls'. Traditionally, shamanism was the power
attributed to a select group of individuals in Aboriginal and Inuit
societies. Initiation rituals set these individuals apart, giving them a
curative and sustaining social role. Particular ceremonies vary from
culture to culture; they range from trances and drum dances to medicine cures and the conjuring of spirits. Among the Huron, for example, the members of the society called the Awataerohi were admired
for their skill in handling fire and hot coals to effect cures. Among the
Ojibway, initiates joined the Midewiwin or Great Medicine Society; in
their 'shaking tent' ceremony, a group of people, fortified with tobac-
co, would gather in a circle around the shaman – whose tent would
begin to shake as soon as he entered it, and from which would
emerge the voice of the spirits with whom the shaman connected.
Mikkinuk, the great turtle, was one of these voices; Mikkinuk
answered questions, solved problems, predicted the future. The ritual primarily reinforced the group's sense of its own community. The
role of the society's art – whether in myths or in drawings – was to
record the ritual, hence to recover or reassert this collective sense of
the world's wholeness.

Though individual beliefs and practices differ, several elements
appear to be common to Native religions, many with their basis in
the fact that these were hunting and trapping cultures: the animism
(or belief that all nature possesses conscious life, and that animals, for
instance, are connected with humans and must be propitiated); the
existence of shamanism in some form; a belief in processes of renew-
ing the world (myths of transformation frequently assert both the
connection between human beings and nature and the aspirations of
humankind for revival or restoration); and some reliance on guardian

spirits (represented through totems, masks, songs). Totems function in different ways. House poles were outward indications of the contact that existed between the human world and the afterworld. Other poles were commemorative tributes to illustrious ancestors or records of lineage; still others served as signs of welcome, and as grave-markers. Among the Neutral tribes of southwestern Ontario, a mask was carved into a tree while the tree was still rooted, in order to impart life directly from nature into the mask. On the West Coast, the animal figures on the totems (the clan figure occupying the topmost position on a 'talking stick') frequently blended into each other, the design itself suggesting the unity of nature. Several works provide further information on Aboriginal design, among them Marjorie Halpin's (1937–2000) *Totem Poles* (1983), George MacDonald's (b. 1938) *Haida Monumental Art* (1983), and Selwyn Dewdney's (1909–79) *Indian Rock Paintings of the Great Lakes* (1967).

Many motifs in the myths confirmed these same attitudes to nature, kinship and morality. They involve objects (animals, plants, body parts, canoes, dishes, fire, water, sky, stars), ideas (deception, trickery, punishment, rewards for modesty), actions (descent, ascent, drowning, eating), events (sex, marriage, death, ceremonies, battles, contests), persons (twins, helpers, siblings, shadows, gods), magic and taboos. The myths divide into approximately four kinds: tales of creation and other explanations of natural and supernatural phenomena, tales of tricksters, tales of transformation, and tales of culture heroes – but these four forms overlap. Among the Malecite, Mi'kmaq and Abenaki, the tales of Glooscap concern both a culture hero and transformation. The Nanabush (Nanabozo, Manabozho) stories among Algonquian speakers combine creation, transformation, and trickster patterns, as do many of the Raven stories told in British Columbia. Explanation stories, too, frequently draw on other patterns to reinforce their message. The culture hero passes tests and performs heroic feats, generally affirming in some way the survival of the tribe; the trickster gives things to mankind, but often does so at once as a trick against the gods or authorities and as a joke against humans. A recurrent creation pattern (told among the Ojibway and other) involves the figure of the Diver, the Great Spirit who dives into primeval water for mud with which to shape a new earth. The number of variations on these themes, and the number of extant stories, testifies not to a sameness of cultures, but to the imaginative richness of the differences.

A Seneca creation story tells of a woman who falls from a hole in the sky, landing in this world, which is all water at the time, and who is helped up on the back of the great turtle. When the turtle gets tired, the animals decide to create an earth for the woman to stand on; the toad brings mud up from the bottom and builds land on the turtle's back. The woman becomes impregnated by the West Wind, and in time gives birth to twins. One twin cultivates the earth and makes it fertile; the other (who is the colour of flint) makes animals and land more difficult for humans to deal with, then quarrels with his brother and kills him. It is from the surviving brother that human beings have descended. Another diver story was told by the Ojibway chief Buhkwujjenene (c. 1815–1900) at a garden party in England in 1878, apparently causing a stir of recognition; the story was first printed in an Algoma missionary journal the following year. It tells of Nanabush killing two gods who have drowned his son, only to have the waters of the lake rise up in turn against him, leaving him stranded at the top of the highest tree on the top of the highest mountain. He saves himself by making a raft from the branches of this tree, then sends the beaver, the otter, and the muskrat under water, each in turn, to bring up a bit of earth from which to create the world anew. Nanabush blows the earth over the water, and the tale ends this way:

A new world was thus formed, and Nanaboozhoo and all the animals landed. Nanaboozhoo sent out a wolf to see how big the world was. He was gone a month. Again he sent him out and he was gone a year. Then he sent out a very young wolf. The young wolf died of old age before it could get back. So Nanaboozhoo said the world was big enough, and might stop growing.

Such stories usually end with a formal phrase of closure: 'That is all', 'There is no more', or 'I have said it'. The creation stories, moreover, characteristically begin with a single word, or a wordless cry. The aim of the creator (Nanabush, Raven, the arch-shaman) was to fashion order out of darkness, to release the moon and the sun from the boxes in which they had been hidden. The act of utterance was an act of shaping, reiterated in the telling of the tale.

The Raven creation story told among the Haida is earthier and more obviously a trickster story than is this tale of Nanabush. As Reid and Bringhurst tell of 'Raven and the First Men', Raven discovers a clamshell one day when he is flying overhead, idly looking for something to do (having already stolen light from the old man who kept it hidden in a box, and scattered it across the sky). The clamshell contains many timid small creatures whom Raven coaxes out into the sunshine; discovering that they are all male, Raven mates them (much to their surprise) with molluscs. From this union emerge both men and women, 'children of the wild coast, born between the sea and the land', who become the powerful Haida of history and legend. This version of the story closes with a contemporary moral: 'the sea has lost much of its richness, and great areas of the land ... lie in waste. Perhaps it's time the Raven started looking for another clamshell.'

The moral didacticism of much of the tale-telling is more apparent in the explanation stories, many of which follow the simple fabular pattern which is familiar to European readers of Aesop and Kipling. In the Chippewa story, 'How Buffalo Got His Hump', Nanabush punishes the buffalo and the foxes for being unkind to birds: the foxes must henceforth live in the cold ground, the bison carry a hump on his back. Similarly, Nanabush attaches thorns to the porcupine's back to protect him from wolves and bears. and the oriole's colour and particular habit of nest-building are a reward for singing each morning to the sun. In a Mi'kmaq tale, replete with a different kind of moral warning, a young woman who has been taken as the bride of a star regrets her decision to move to the sky, asks to return home, is allowed to do so providing that she waits for a number of conditions to be fulfilled, but is transformed forever into a falling star when (impatient for the result) she does not wait long enough. These are stories told as behavioural models as well as explanations of natural events; the myths embodied a distinct view of good and evil, to be communicated intact from one generation to the next, confirming the established order. Any transgression against the taboos invited punishment.

Such models also codified the social roles of male and female. Alternative declarations of lineage and inheritance were sometimes oral, secret and female. The Nootka myth of D'Sonoqua, the wild woman of the woods, the cannibal woman who consumes children but is simultaneously associated with fertility, suggests a covert recognition of femaleness – made into a spirit of wilderness perennially unfathomable and unconquerable (at least to men). The Algonkin myth of the Wendigo (or windigo) expresses a more violent wilderness vision; it tells of a spirit that drives men monstrous, even turns them cannibalistic, especially when they are isolated in the woods. It, too, however, in a wide variety of forms, serves as a cautionary check on individual conduct.

The quest stories involving culture heroes and trials – such as Morriseau's tale of good and evil brothers who must prove their value to society – further emphasize the preservation of community standards. In another way, so do the humorous stories of tricksters. While Raven and Nanabush frequently turn up as tricksters as well as creators, it is the Hare and especially Coyote who most clearly fulfil this role in Canadian Native mythology. Coyote (a name conventionally given three syllables) in different tales brings light, steals fire, filches salmon from the people who have it and releases it so that it swims upstream, and performs other feats both beneficial and bothersome to people. In the Thompson tale of Coyote and the salmon, Coyote not only breaks the dam that keep the salmon downstream, he also opens the four boxes kept by the people of the Coast; but when he opens them, out come smoke, wasps, blowflies and meat-beetles, which have followed the salmon-run upriver every season since. Coyote is an ancestor-figure; he is the teacher who trains people to hunt, cook and sew; he is the miraculous transformer, who alters mosquitoes from huge animals into small pests; he is the seasonal transformer, who cyclically turns twigs into fruit-bearing berry bushes. He dies in one tale, revives in another. He is the subject of ribaldry and mirth. Sometimes his ingenuity and irrepressible curiosity get him into predicaments that he cannot solve, and the tales then close with the trickster tricked. Such trickster tales serve a further purpose. The creator and hero tales, while they provide models, also constitute ideal, even absolute versions of behaviour, realistically out of ordinary human reach. The trickster tales, by contrast, demonstrate the human, imperfect side of the gods and the godly aspirations of human beings, with which people can identify. In Coyote, as in other tricksters, lies the character of the human world and the promise of equilibrium.

INUIT CULTURE

It is difficult to date the origins of Aboriginal societies in Canada. Native claims to have been present 'from the beginning' (evidenced by the creation myths) underlie current disputes over land ownership. Empirical ethnologists assert that Aboriginal groups immigrated separately, over long periods of time, from Siberia, when the Bering land bridge still existed, and also moved north as the ice sheets receded. Stone tools from c. 11000 BC have been found in lacustrine deposits at the Bluefish Cave sites in the Yukon; the Fluted Point people lived in Ontario about 9000 BC. Recent evidence points to continuous Tsimshian habitation on Prince Rupert harbour for five thousand years.

There are more exact surviving data concerning the early peoples of the Arctic. The Dorset culture evolved about 500 BC; the Thule culture that replaced it moved from Alaska to Greenland sometime between AD 1000 and AD 1200, declining in power in about the sixteenth century. The Inuit in Canada – some 20,000 people, occupying over a million square miles in the Arctic, an area roughly the size of Europe – now divide into eight main tribal groups. (the word 'Eskimo' (meaning 'eater of raw flesh') is Athapaskan in origin, not Inuktitut, and has now largely fallen from use in Canada, except as an historical reference; in Alaska the Arctic peoples call themselves Yuit, and speak Yupik, and in Greenland they use the term Katladit.) The Inuit tribal divisions are: Labrador, Ungava, Baffin Island, Iglulik, Caribou, Netsilik, Copper and Western Arctic. These essentially geographic groupings also show up in art and mythology, in differences in nomenclature, dialect and artistic medium. Archeological finds indicate that the practice of carving in antler and whale bone is of long standing – the Hudson's Bay Company traded in artifacts for some decades – but forms of Inuit art that are now considered 'characteristic' have a much more recent history. They date effectively from 1948, when James Houston (b. 1921) the author of several popular novels, art books, and a 1972 anthology, *Songs of the Dream People*, helped to set up artists' cooperatives in the Arctic. Out of this contact emerged such talented artists as the Cape Dorset printmakers Pitseolak (1907–83) and Kenojuak Ashevak (b. 1927), and the Baker Lake soapstone carver Makpaaq (1922–78). The Inuit Tapirisat or brotherhood was founded in 1971 to promote the people's language and culture. The first novel by an Inuit writer appeared in 1970: Markoosie's (b. 1942) *Harpoon of the Hunter*, now translated into several languages.

Traditional writings were recorded first in expedition reports – in Knud Rasmussen's (1879–1933) ten-volume account of a Danish expedition to the North (1921–4), published over the succeeding twenty-five years, and in *Songs of the Copper Eskimo*, a 1925 report of the 1913–18 Canadian Arctic Expedition. Some of the poetry in these volumes has been reprinted and adapted in more recent anthologies – for example, Edmund Carpenter's (b. 1922) *Anerca* (1959) and John Robert Colombo's (b. 1936) *Poems of the Inuit* (1981). Robin Gedalof's (b. 1949) *Paper Stays Put* (1980) collects Inuit writings both traditional and contemporary, in a variety of genres. 'Anerca', as Carpenter points out, is the Inuktitut word both for 'poetry' and for 'breath'; to breathe was to utter poetry. This identity is nowhere clearer than in 'Umahaq's Song', a moving lament, anthologized by Colombo: 'I was idle', sings the poet, 'When the season turned again to spring. / My fishhook, since it pulled up nothing, / I was idle /   / I was idle / When the season turned turned again to summer. / My husband, since he caught no caribou, / I was idle.'

INUIT MYTHOLOGY

'The poet, as a shaman, is a spirit-maker', Colombo remarks; the singer, the drawer of breath, believes in 'the power of words to transform attitudes, if not realities'. Hence in Inuit as in Aboriginal cultures, at least in the past, shamanism connected the world of the people with the world of animals and spirits. The shaman, or angakok, was believed to possess the power of journeying great distances in trance or in dream, and the ability to connect with the spirits of good and evil (who are not gods so much as personifications of forces of nature). The people (as is characteristic of an oral culture) stressed the power of utterance, which the shaman in particular enjoyed. To name was to invoke – hence story-tellers (like hunters) often referred to animals by other than their real names, in order not to frighten them. To tell stories was to invoke past exploits, explain the workings of the world, and propitiate the spirits that might affect the future. The myths were often blunt, bloody and (to an English ear) repetitious. But the repetitions worked in context as a kind of choric song. The myths, as Zebedee Nungak (b. 1950) and Eugene Arima (b. 1938) observe in *Eskimo Stories from Povungnituk, Quebec* (1969), collectively reaffirmed cultural norms. All stories were 'unikkaatuat', that is 'traditions'; and all stories spoken were deemed to be about real things, and therefore true. Central to the whole mythology is the story of Sedna (to use the Baffin Land name), the woman of the sea. She also goes by such names as Nuliayuk (Netsilik = 'the poor wife'), Arnaaluk takaannaaluk (Iglulik = 'the woman down there'), Takannakapsaaluk (Iglulik = 'the terrible one down there'), Kavna (Iglulik = 'she down there'), Nerrivigssuaq (Polar = 'the great meat dish'), Arnakapshaaluk (Netsilik = 'the big bad woman') and Nakorut (Netsilik = 'giver of strength'). The obliqueness of reference and the different kinds of identification suggest both the spirit's power and the need to avoid her displeasure. Indeed, the myth is at once an explanation of origins and a mode of propitiation before the sea hunt might begin. In one version of the story, a woman is banished to an ice island because her father suspects she has mated with his lead dog; the dog, however, swims out to her with food to keep her alive; later she gives birth to three Inuit (deemed to be ancestors of 'the people') and three dogs (deemed to be ancestors of Europeans and others). In a separate story the father throws his daughter overboard to get rid of her; when she tries to hang on to the boat he cuts off her fingers, then her hands, then her forearms, which severally turn into seals, walruses and whales; she then sinks to the bottom, becomes Sedna, half-woman and half-fish, the spirit of the sea who controls the presence of the creatures of the sea and who must henceforth continuously be fed.

To hear the ritual in such stories requires the listener to respond to the system of signs that the stories employ. The shamanism is embodied in the images of bone, and in the act of paring back from flesh to spirit. The contemporary art of the Woodlands Indians, following the scroll signs of an earlier period, uses a heavy outline technique of representation to 'pierce' the coverings of the flesh, and so reveal by special sight the structure of spirit contained within. In this respect the Inuit myth-making is comparable: the shaman was to be thought of as purely skeleton, who was enabled by this absence of flesh and blood to connect with the spirit forces of nature. The tales told of the processes of connection. But the early European explorers and missionaries did not recognize such patterns in the indigenous myth-making; they heard only violence, saw only blood and gore, identified what they heard and saw only as pagan superstition. They sometimes sold off Indian artifacts in order to finance the work of the missions. They prohibited the gift-giving and name validation ceremonies, such as the West Coast potlatch (legally banned between 1874 and 1951) and the Prairie sundance, declaring such rituals to be uncivilized and unchristian. And they set about telling their own stories, putting into motion an inexorable system of conversion. When European boats first arrived on the Pacific Coast, the Natives regarded them as sea creatures and saw the white faces of ghosts. By the 1820s Christian symbolism was already marking Aboriginal myth-making in British Columbia. By the 1920s trade art in the Arctic had effectively lost all trace of its original power of religious significance. It was replaced by Christian design and by the notion that art was crafted simply as plaything or souvenir.

EUROPEAN MYTH AND CULTURAL CONTACT

The stories and expectations that the Europeans brought with them to Canada were also, however, coloured by a deep-seated, perhaps no longer even conscious mythology. They were embodied in the narrative structures and the moral and social attitudes of Judaeo-Christian rituals, of riddle and folksong, of formal literary models, Renaissance customs, and the stories and fairytales that traditionally derived from Classical, Germanic, French and Celtic sources. The terms of European expectation, that is, strongly influenced the terms of European representation, with ramifications in art, literature, geography, politics and religion. Of key significance was the image of the land and its inhabitants – the inaccuracy of which forms the subject of Olive Dickason's (b. 1920) *The Myth of the Savage* (1984). Inaccuracy is apparent in sixteenth-century cartography, in explorers' anecdotes, in cartouches and other designs. Their images tell of ignorance and exaggeration, of the desire and daring that take people into unknown territory and of the susceptibility of people to believe what they are

told. The new world is ideal, because different – or the new world is
barbaric, because different. The fact of difference is what is open to
interpretation – and hence to distortion – whether pertaining to food
customs, manners, dress, behaviour or belief. Nudity seems particularly to have offended the earliest Europeans to arrive in the Americas; the difficulty (Classical art and history aside) lay in reconciling the
offensive nakedness with the apparent presence of an Amerindian
civilization. Civilization, therefore, was presumed not to exist:
Amerindian nakedness was taken as a sign of an animal nature and
accepted as a stimulus to conversion, or it was seen as a sign of
defencelessness and accepted as an invitation to conquest. This paradigm surfaced repeatedly in European–Indian contacts. At the outset
it presumed European superiority in the world (a view that did not
adequately acknowledge Asian philosophy, Moghul art or Chinese
exploration and technology either: evidence now suggests that Chinese explorers might well have circumnavigated the world, reaching
the Americas before Columbus); the exclusiveness of Christianity
reinforced it. Yet for many Europeans the paradigm was confirmed
most not by documentary evidence, but by fable.

The fifteenth-century development of the printing press, together
with the first European voyages of discovery, resulted in numerous
woodblock and copperplate maps; by the early sixteenth century
these were still as governed by myth as by knowledge, and are now
more informative for what the ornamentation and political presumptions tell than for their cartography. Columbus (1451–1506) apparently accepted stories that people on some islands were born with tails
(this apocryphal story turns up again in the later sixteenth century,
when the Récollet missionary Father Louis Hennepin (1626–c. 1705)
reported that the Indians thought that Europeans had tails and European women but one breast). Even in the seventeenth century a belief
in monsters and humanoids persisted (as it perhaps persists today, in
the stories of the Loch Ness Monster and the Yeti, or their Canadian
equivalents Ogopogo and the Sasquatch). The German geographer
Levinus Hulsius (d. 1606) produced in 1623 an engraving of 'blem-
myae', men with their heads in their chests; *Le mercure galant* reported in 1683 that literal half-men (men with only one leg and one foot)
lived in the Arctic. The belief in monsters coalesced with a belief in
demons: a Giacomo Gastaldi (fl. 16th century) map of 1556 depicts
the 'Isola de Demoni' north of Newfoundland, ornamenting it with a
humanoid creature with wings and a tail. Onshore and off, these
maps filled blank spaces with lizards, sea monsters, beasts and beast-
men. (They become the subject of a twentieth-century poem, Earle
Birney's (1904–95) 'Mappemounde'. A long-standing myth in Europe

claimed that dog-headed monsters lived in Asia. As America was considered an extension of Asia (Gastaldi first made it an Asian peninsula, and a 1535 map inserted names from Ptolemy (90–168) and Marco Polo (1254–1324) – 'Thebet', 'Cathay' – off the coast of Mexico; the mistaken identification of indigenous North Americans as 'Indians' is a continuing reminder of the Asian expectations), what could be more 'natural' than to find comparable creatures in America, too? These expectations, rendered into maps, gave myths the cachet of reality; they also turned documentary forms into mythological narratives. When *Gulliver's Travels* (1726) placed the world of the Brobdingnagian giants somewhere in the neighbourhood of British Columbia, Jonathan Swift (1667–1745) was not only alluding to unknown, imaginary territory; he was also satirizing the impulse to exaggeration that continued to lead people from ignorance to ignorance.

It might have been possible to dismiss these images and icons of monstrosity as idle flights of decorative fancy, were it not for the way in which they also embody religious and political attitudes. Implicitly hierarchical, they argue the precedence of man over nature rather than a unity between the two, and they describe a centralist view of the world. Beasts were implicitly lesser creatures, and because lesser, they were closer to the demonic, more deprived of godliness. Such creatures, moreover, lay at the periphery of Europe, and were more 'likely' to exist the farther one moved from Europe. While the beasts and the ornaments began to disappear from reputable maps during the sixteenth century, the political presumptiveness of this position did not. Many labels were vague: 'Anian regnum' – Mercator (1512–94) in the 1590s still located mythical kingdoms approximately in Alaska. 'Terra Septentrionalis' (northern territory) was a gesture rather than an identification. 'Terra incognita' was so because it was unknown *to Europeans*; the act of naming even the unknown was a way of claiming it for European intellectual possession. The wars and the voyages of exploration that occupied the sixteenth, seventeenth and eighteenth centuries were attempts then to turn an intellectual construct into an economic fact. The opposition between Protestant and Roman Catholic denominations only fortified the militant quest for a sphere of European influence – over territory as over soul.

History furnishes a number of examples of the European view of Canada as a negligible commodity: it was savage, it was cold, it was barren, it was less economically valuable than Guadeloupe (until a taste for fur fashions gave it a marketable resource). Most of all, the early maps made it a barrier, an obstruction in the way of the real goal, Asia. Hence the desire for an Asian connection led European map-makers artificially to open a space through Canada, to draw a mythical Northwest Passage. While physically joining North America to Asia had been a way of making the New World merely an extension of the old, making Canada a 'gulf' through which imperial ships could sail to Asia was a way of refusing to recognize the unexpected empirical realities of the land itself. Admittedly, by the eighteenth century the new continent was better known. John Harrison's (1693–1776) perfection of the chronometer in 1772 enabled Captain James Cook (1728–79) to take exact readings of longitude at sea, further enhancing the science of cartography. But mapping was still an adjunct of ownership. And there remained the question of who was the owner and who or what was owned. Political mapping in the late eighteenth century accompanied territorial disputes between military powers; township mapping in the nineteenth century reflected urban growth, civil measurement of property, a system of buying and selling real estate; claim mapping delimited the ownership of mineral resources; aerial survey mapping developed when defence plans required it, when distances were great and manpower was small. Many of these developments were taking place, moreover, before uniform treaties had been signed between Europeans and Indians, and in some cases before land rights had been negotiated at all. In the eighteenth and nineteenth centuries, European expansion was not to European eyes seen even as a potential problem. It had the inertia of imperial politics behind it; perhaps more fundamentally, it had the unstated moral confirmation of Christian belief. Christianity decreed that the world existed for man's use (with the result that, for some people, using nature became more of a prerogative than managing it). Compared with some Eastern religions (which urged the preservation of nature, so that it would still be available in a future reincarnation), Christianity was a philosophy that at once encouraged independent initiative, and allowed uncommon waste. Compared with native Indian religions, which identified the human with the natural world, it drew boundary lines that the Indians did not at once comprehend. In attitudes to land, in other words, lay a confrontation between systems of belief as well as between structures of ownership.

There is a danger of romanticizing Aboriginal and denigrating European culture. The two systems do not divide into the good and the bad. Native societies did set land apart for particular uses, did recognize zones of territorial influence, did (like Europeans) sometimes act cruelly and go to war, and did possess a kinetic rather than a static culture. In *Moon of Wintertime* (1984), John Webster Grant (b. 1919) suggests that Indian cultures were resistant to

Christianity primarily as a way of countering potential cultural dissolution – that is, they resisted the politics of sectarian rule more than the symbols of doctrine, and they absorbed Christianity from the missionaries less as a direct acceptance of a dualistic doctrine than on their own metaphoric terms. Further, the arrival of Christianity exacerbated changes already taking place. Sectarian rivalry is a key element in understanding the effects of this process of intercultural contact. Bruce Trigger (b. 1937), in *The Children of Aataentsic* (1976), an ethnographic history of the Huron peoples to 1660, comments that the Hurons recurrently renegotiated their political alliances with their neighbours, and that some of the source of their decline lay in the way they responded to the two major Christian missionary forces, the Récollets and the Jesuits. The Récollets insisted on making the Natives French before converting them – language and manners coming before religion. The Jesuits insisted on religious conversion quickly, not realizing that for the Hurons religion permeated many aspects of life that Europeans did not connect with religious belief at all. Because the Hurons were culturally willing to borrow rituals from neighbouring societies, and because they saw Christianity not as a theology but as another ritual system (transubstantiation seemed not unlike ritual cannibalism, the priests' celibacy seemed equivalent to the shamans' practice of seeking extrahuman power through sexual abstinence), the Huron interpreted the Jesuits according to their own patterns of expectation. If the Jesuits were shamans, then adopting Christianity must be a way of participating in the supernatural. During a time of epidemic, the corollary was that the Jesuit priests were suspected of being evil sorcerers. There were in consequence many degrees of conversion and apostasy. Not all villages were affected – or responded – the same way. But because religious belief permeated the entire social structure, disrupting the commonality of the Native religion meant disrupting the whole alliance. And disrupting the alliance meant opening the Hurons to internal divisiveness and weakening their defence against the Iroquois – and, through them, the English.

The Hurons failed to appreciate completely the character of the culture the missionaries wished to share; the missionaries, for their part, interpreted the Native religions as signs of the devil's kingdom and accepted Huron deference to their own stories not as cultural politeness (the Hurons avoided open disagreements on social occasions) but as signs that the Hurons recognized the superiority of the European message. On both sides, the codes of manners and the stereotypes about others intervened between their actions and their understanding.

One set of European myths was thus operating to extend Europe institutionally to Canada – identifying wilderness and savagery as the demonic characteristics of the new world, and combating them with religion and a written language, the agents of European civilization. Simultaneously, another set of myths was locating manners, culture and civility among New World Natives, whether in Canada or in other societies lately discovered by European expeditions. Michel de Montaigne (1533–92) had named them 'noble savages', thus setting into motion a parallel convention that would distort New World realities as much as the myths of monstrosity did. The Montaigne message was directed, of course, at Europe rather than at North America: it was a plea for independence in the face of current European fashion, and an attempt to reclaim as 'natural' a kind of behaviour untainted by the political and moral corruption he located in European society. Perhaps ironically, the taste for his message translated into a new fashion – real natives (of North America and the South Pacific) became de rigueur features of European salons. European paintings of the seventeenth and eighteenth centuries also followed the 'noble' model, depicting North American 'Indians' as Roman centurions and in Classical Greek pose. To European observers, Amerindian 'nobility' had European antecedents. Classical myth thus became a normative standard by which to imagine the New World, whether in literature or in painting – and the myths of nobility, just as much as the doctrines of economics and religion, came to dominate the way in which Europeans thought of Canada.

As part of the American continent, Canada was an impediment to reaching Asia, a land of demons awaiting enlightenment, a land of Classical virtues like honesty and self-reliance – or in Voltaire's (1694–1778) devastating aside in Candide (1759), it was 'quelques arpents de neige', a few acres of snow. The last image persisted. But all these images were extensions of empire, controls which the European imagination exerted over both the status of the new territory and acceptable ways of representing it. For the writers and artists who would subsequently emerge in Canada, one of the greatest challenges they would face was to work out their own connection with these stereotypes. They could accept the implicit (and often explicit) hierarchies of culture that derived from Europe – accept the idea that European standards were universal, and write or paint or compose in a way that would primarily seek European approval. They could claim indigenous cultures as their true cultural roots. In time, they could mimic other models, borrow American culture, and seek American approval as an alternative to things European. Or they could, whether consciously or not, adapt their art to their own place and time, devise methods of telling their own stories, and develop an eclectic culture of their own.

CHAPTER TWO

Reporters: literature to 1867

BACKGROUNDS

Tracing Canadian literature from the beginnings through to 1867 requires the reader to think along two political planes: one observing writers sequentially against a set of events, the other observing written works as formal embodiments of separate attitudes and expectations. The terminus date 1867 illustrates the distinction; it is a year not of great publications but of political Confederation – an event which would not immediately transform literature but which would entirely change the political context within which *colonial* and subsequently *Canadian* writers wrote. Before 1867 there was no Canadian *nation*. There were outposts and colonies instead, and the distance of these places and the people in them from the centres of empire to which they felt connected left its mark upon their writing. Many literary efforts were formal imitations; whether able or amateur, they reflected what was understood to be (or at least to have been) fashionable elsewhere – in Paris, London, or later Boston and Philadelphia. Some were expressions of exile – songs, plaints, descriptions of loss. The dominant literary forms of the period were loosely reportorial in mode – journals, letters, chronicles, documentary records – all of them designed to send impressions from the edge of civilization to an authority who stayed back home.

An outline of the historical events affecting this period has to take into account four connected socio-political issues: discovery, trade, governmental conflict and the tensions of settlement.

1 Discovery

Aside from the putative visits to North America by early Chinese sailors, by St Brendan (d. 577?) in the sixth century, Leif Ericsson

(d. c. 1020) in the eleventh, and black mariners from Mali in the early fifteenth, the record of the reach to America is one of English, French, Spanish and Russian expeditions: from Italian-born John Cabot (c. 1449–99), reaching Newfoundland in 1497, to John Franklin (1786–1847), exploring the Arctic Coast in 1823 and 1827. In between are the finders, claimers and multiple mapmakers who left their names on Canadian geography:

- the French explorer Jacques Cartier reached the Gulf of Saint Lawrence in 1534 and on separate trips over the next twelve years sailed 1600 kilometres into the continent, to Stadacona and Hochelaga, now Quebec and Montreal;
- the British sailors John Davis (c. 1550–1605), William Baffin (c. 1584–1622), Martin Frobisher (c. 1535–94), Henry Hudson (d. 1611), and Luke Foxe (1586–1635) established the size and shape of Hudson's Bay in the years after 1570;
- the Greek sailor Juan de Fuca (1536–1602), in the service of Spain (perhaps) reached the West Coast in 1592;
- Samuel de Champlain (c. 1570–1635) mapped Acadia, the Saguenay and the Richelieu in the first thirty years of the seventeenth century;
- the Jesuits (Joliet, 1645–1700, and Marquette, 1637–75, for example) reached the Sault in the 1640s, and travelled south into the Mississippi Basin;
- the Russian Vitus Bering (1681–1741) reached Alaska in 1741;
- the land explorers – Henry Kelsey (c. 1667–1724), La Vérendrye (1685–1749) and his sons, Anthony Henday (fl. 1750–62), Samuel Hearne (1745–92), Peter Pond (c. 1739–1807), Peter Fidler (1769–1822), Alexander Mackenzie (1764–1820), Simon Fraser (1776–1862), David Thompson (1770–1857) – located the river routes to the north and the west: Henday traced the Saskatchewan in 1754, Hearne reached the mouth of the Coppermine in 1771, Mackenzie followed the Mackenzie River to the Arctic in 1789 and reached the West Coast in 1793, Fraser followed the Fraser River in 1808, Thompson the Columbia in 1811;
- the Spanish Captain Bodega y Quadra (1743–94) surveyed 'Quadra's and Vancouver's Island' in the 1770s;
- the English Captains James Cook and George Vancouver (1757–98) mapped the West Coast, Nootka Sound and the Strait of Georgia in 1778 and 1793.

Almost all these explorers left observations and records. (Cartier's are not extant, although a work attributed to him does exist: Giovanni Ramusio's, 1485–1557, narrative Italian translation of Cartier's account of his navigations to New France appeared in 1556, and John Florio's, c. 1553–1625, English translation from Ramusio's Italian came out in 1580.) Such records vary markedly in literary quality. The exploration narratives collectively indicate not just that the explorers thrived on their enjoyment of adventure, but also that the explorations were less a demonstration of Renaissance curiosity than offshoots of a desire for political control, whether economic, religious or simply territorial. Exploration, therefore, linked with combat, settlement and trade.

2 Trade

The earlier European settlements on the East Coast all functioned as trading posts. There were fishing harbours in Newfoundland and the Maritimes, and Halifax was early involved in the sugar trade with the West Indies (as during the Napeolonic wars it was a centre of privateering). Inland, New France lay in the control of Cardinal Richelieu's (1585–1642) 'Company of 100 Associates' until 1663, and the outposts of French penetration into the continent were the Jesuit and Récollet missions to the Hurons. To speak of the sectarian Christian rivalries as a trade in souls is to distort the passion of belief which motivated individual priests, but the competitiveness of the missions has in some degree to be related to the competition for land and trade goods. The stories of the Jesuits moving out into the Great Lakes, for example, are coupled with stories of the early *coureurs-de-bois* daring the river systems in search of furs, bending their strength in a race against freeze-up and winter. Both were deemed heroic; both also served more mundane territorial functions.

A larger economic rivalry existed between the French and the English, between the St Lawrence trade route and the Hudson's Bay route, the latter constituting the shorter distance between furs and Europe. When the English established the Hudson's Bay Company 'of Adventurers' in 1670 and granted it 'Rupert's Land' – some thousands of acres of trading territory, the lands draining into Hudson's Bay – it was setting up an economic fiefdom that was to last about two hundred years; but this structure was constantly under pressure, from the French rival (the North-West Company, established in 1783), from Native resistance, and from the encroachments of settlers, such as the Scots who founded the Selkirk Settlement in the Red River Valley in 1812.

Explorations were as often quests for new trading territory as they were the results of a simple thirst for excitement. The wanderings of two *coureurs-de-bois*, Radisson (c. 1632–1710) and Groseilliers (c. 1618–c. 1690), had led to the establishment of the Hudson's Bay Company in the first place; the North-West Company followed; and new trading posts sprang up wherever company employees – Pond, Mackenzie, Fidler and Thompson – subsequently moved. (After Hearne had explored the Coppermine River he became head of the Hudson's Bay Company post at Cumberland House.) Government by company was a standard pattern, one later repeated in the story of the Canadian Pacific Railway. The Napoleonic wars had meanwhile established the Maritimes in the timber trade (New Brunswick was a source for sailing ship spars). By the mid nineteenth century, when the Palliser (1817–87) and Hind (1823–1908) expeditions crossed the prairies, however, the impulse of exploration was to establish the commercial viability of using the land in other ways: for settlement. for farming. The new nation was expanding, and urban centres in Ontario and Quebec were seeking to become not just transit points on the way to Europe but manufacturing centres in their own right. Toronto and Montreal had become commercial as well as cultural rivals, which in a fundamental way reiterated the long-standing political tensions between England and France that punctuated their shared history.

3 Conflict

Government rivalries served to counterpoint those involving religion and trade, taking place sometimes on Canadian territory, sometimes elsewhere. Cartier's attempt to make translators out of Chief Donnaconna's (d. 1539?) two sons, by kidnapping them on board ship, earned the French the subsequent enmity of the Iroquois when the two young men died; the French, Dutch and English then came to blows in Canada, drawing on different tribal alliances for local support. Most often, the colonies in North America were mere pawns in the give-and-take of European power games. Sir Humphrey Gilbert (1537–83) set up an English colony in Newfoundland in 1583; Pierre le Moyne d'Iberville (1661–1706) attempted to destroy this English settlement in the 1660s and settle the French there instead. Three times during the seventeenth century, the British conquered parts of Nova Scotia only to return them to French control.

The eighteenth century saw several more military upheavals and distant political agreements. The Peace of Utrecht in 1713 gave Acadia (the French colony in the Maritimes) to England; in 1755 the English expelled the Acadians from their homeland, dispersing them to 'Cajun' country in Louisiana, whence many slowly returned. In 1759 the English general Wolfe (1727–59) defeated the French general Montcalm (1712–59) at Quebec, in the Battle of the Plains of Abraham, a victory made possible in part because James Cook had skilfully charted the St Lawrence shore. The Treaty of Paris in 1763 (closing the Seven Years' War) gave all of New France to England, yet reconfirmed the existing economic fishing rights, paradoxically leaving the islands of St Pierre and Miquelon in French control. Political actions frequently seemed arbitrary. Territory was won and lost in actual battle, but then renegotiated and exchanged at thousands of miles' remove. 'Settlement' came to imply the temporary truce as well as the colonial community.

Inevitably, tensions increased between colonists and Europe, even among the colonists themselves, over the issues that divided them: language, religion, political structure, freedom. These were coloured, in Eastern North America, by two opposing political attitudes that prevailed at the time of settlement. Both absolutist, one was dualistic, the other pluralistic. In the colonies of the seventeenth and early eighteenth centuries – New France, the American colonies – notions of absolutism found expression in Utopian aspirations, in Jansenist Catholicism, and in a centralist political structure: in 1663 New France came under direct royal rule, for example, the absolute monarchy reinforced locally by the commands of the military *Gouverneur* and the *Intendant* or civil governor. Dualistic attitudes prevailed. In 1763, the Protestant English combated Catholicism just as absolutely, disbanding the Jesuit order and confiscating Jesuit lands (the order was re-established in Canada only in 1842). In the colonies of the later eighteenth and nineteenth centuries, however – perhaps especially in the west – pluralistic notions came to prevail, reflecting the growing relativism that accompanied a belief that the world was imperfect, regional, ethnically diverse, and, by the twentieth century, insecure. No easy transition led from one set of attitudes to the other, either in daily life or in civil political structure. The revolutions in America (1776) and France (1789) overturned two absolute systems, only to instal implicitly Utopian (hence also absolute) systems in their place, in the name of freedom. The one drew several hundred thousand American Tories (or United Empire Loyalists) to Canada; the other effectively divided Quebec from Royal France.

Because Republican America and Republican France were alike alien structures for *Canadiens* in Quebec and the Tory Loyalists, their hold on tradition came to depend on their connection with each other. When the United States subsequently invaded Canada in 1812, presuming that the colonists of British North America would join in the rebellion against Europe, the Canadians repelled the Americans at Queenston Heights, Châteauguay, Lundy's Lane, Crysler's Farm. Isaac Brock (1769–1812), Tecumseh (c. 1768–1813) and Laura Secord (1775–1868) all became culture heroes. The colonists of northern

North America were separating from the new United States even as they were slowly separating from Europe, establishing themselves as a third option (neither Europe nor America: a direct rejection of political dualism). Tories and *Canadiens* were not identical, but they possessed a will to claim some attitudes in common.

Working towards this political conclusion required several constitutional adaptations along the way: the Quebec Act in 1774, which ratified specific protection for French language and civil law in Quebec, effectively introducing into Canadian governance a system that would house and allow alternatives; the establishment of local legislatures (1758 in Nova Scotia, 1769 in Prince Edward Island, 1791 in Upper and Lower Canada – the colony of Cape Breton, which joined Nova Scotia in 1820, never had a separate legislature, and Newfoundland did not get a general assembly till 1820); the several Acts (the Constitutional Act of 1792, the Act of Union in 1840) which separated and linked Upper and Lower Canada, transformed them into 'Canada East' and 'Canada West', and ultimately though indirectly shaped language policy; and the official responses to the failed rebellions in Upper and Lower Canada in 1837, which led to a system called Responsible Government (whereby, in theory, the political leaders are selected from and responsible to the House rather than to governmental or other authorities outside it).

The last two issues interconnect. By 1837 the traditional hierarchical political structures had resulted in several families self-interestedly manipulating power: the Council of Twelve in Nova Scotia, the Château Clique in Lower Canada, the Family Compact in Upper Canada. Reform was in order, and two newspapermen and a Quebec lawyer led the fight for it: Joseph Howe (1804–73), Louis-Joseph Papineau (1786–1871) and William Lyon Mackenzie (1795–1861). In the two Canadas, an actual combat was quickly put down. Many of the 'rebels' ('radicals', *'patriotes'*: the terms are highly charged) left more or less voluntarily for exile in the USA; others were forcibly transported to Australia. Fearful of another American Revolution, the British sent Lord Durham (1792–1840) to investigate. Only about half the reforms he recommended were enacted.

Emerging from the Union of the two Canadas in 1840 was a political collaboration between Robert Baldwin (1804–58), Francis Hincks (1807–85) and Louis-Hippolyte Lafontaine (1807–64); it survived opposition (from Governor-General Metcalfe (1785–1846) and from various special interest groups) long enough to ratify English-French collaboration in the legislature and to make the civil legislature politically effective. In the term that began in 1848 (with Lord Elgin, 1811–63, Durham's son-in-law, as the new Governor-General), this

administration passed the Rebellion Losses Bill, compensating people on both sides of the 1837 dispute for property losses; passed the
Amnesty Act, allowing the activist reformers back in the colony; sec-
ularized King's College (Halifax) and brought the state into public
education, creating both the University of Toronto and the Université
Laval; and passed laws that reformed judicial and economic policy.
Through it all, Lafontaine repeatedly spoke French. The Act of Union
had made English the sole language of House debate, but such a law
ran counter to custom and the political reality. Because of Lafontaine,
Canadian practice took precedence over the letter of the British parliamentary law, and by the time of the 'Great Coalition' (George
Brown, 1818–80; George-Étienne Cartier, 1814–73; and John A. Macdonald) in 1864 – although cultural and economic rivalry had not
ceased – an English–French political connection had become a viable
possibility. Confederation was at hand.

4 Settlement

In the various settlements, people's desire for reform in the political
structure was secondary to their need to deal with more basic questions: fire, hunger, weather, the needs and niceties of neighbourhood,
all of which frequently get ignored in the quest for grander explanations of political events. In large part the history of Canada is a history of imagination, incompetence, faction, affection, prejudice, faith,
industry, child labour, sport, slavery, food, unions, childbirth and epidemic: all affected literary endeavour, which was itself a feature of
settlement. As early as 1605, when Champlain founded Port-Royal
(now Annapolis-Royal), his few settlers had to combat cold and
scurvy if they were to last long enough to construct a society at all.
Faced with isolation and winter, Champlain established 'l'Ordre du
Bon Temps' – the Order of Good Cheer – which raised community
spirits through festive ceremonies. Reputedly the first theatrical performance anywhere in North America, Marc Lescarbot's (1570–1642)
'Le Théâtre de Neptune en la Nouvelle-France', was a spectacle performed in 1606 at one of these occasions. Lescarbot's *Une Histoire de
la Nouvelle-France* (1607) describes the event taking place on a flotilla
in the harbour – Neptune, Diana, Cupid and Amerindian 'sauvages'
all speaking in rhymed couplets, ship to ship, as they advanced in
regal procession to welcome the Sieur de Potrincourt (1577–1615)
back from his overseas exploration. In its verse regularity, its royalist
appeal, and its Classical allusion, the play was, like many early Canadian literary works, a form of escape from extremities of climate, vast
distances and difficult wilderness terrain.

Robert Hayman (1575–1629), the English governor of a colony at Harbour Grace, penned verses *praising* the country; his 'Quodlibets' (1628) read in part:

The Aire in Newfound-land is wholesome, good;
The Fire as sweet as any made of wood;
The Waters, very rich, both salt and fresh;
The Earth more rich, you know it is no lesse.
Where all are good, *Fire*, *Water*, *Earth*, and *Air*,
What man made of these four would not live there?

The sentiment conventionally adapts the Renaissance elemental world-view; the expression is neat, lodged in the end-words. Politically, one has to balance it against the views of a later writer, the Irish-born Donnchadh Rua MacConmara (c. 1716–1810), whose poem of Newfoundland in the 1740s alternates English lines with Irish Gaelic ones. The English lines declare the attractions of Newfoundland ('Newfoundland is a fine plantation, / It shall be my station till I die'); the succeeding Irish lines immediately counter them ('Mo Chrádh! go m'fhearr liom a bheith a n-Eire': 'I'd rather be in Ireland'). The contrasts extend from daily life ([From] 'Drinking, raking and playing cards / ... / Then I turned a jolly tradesman' / ... / 'S bioch ar m'fallaing-si gur mór an bhréag sin' [By my soul, that's a great lie]) to government. English lines praising 'Royal George' and his might are succeeded by Jacobite epithets ('A Chriast go bhfeiceadh mé an bhrúid da chárnadh' ['Oh Christ! may I see the brute defeated']). The English words voice the prevailing convention; the other-language words declare the political reality, whose presence at once satirizes the dominant culture and undermines its easy social generalizations.

Just as Canadian literature acquired ways of dealing with its political diversity, so did it develop ways of responding adequately to wilderness. Wilderness both of natural circumstance and human construction were facts of life. People could escape these empirical realities in fantasy, but ignore them only at their own peril. Later writers would find ways of accepting them as normative settings and symbols: they were part of the experience that people shared, if they survived. As of course many did. The initial period of French settlement in North America (1534–1608) was one of discovery; the second period (to 1663) established the Church in the territory that was already becoming modern Quebec; the third (to 1763) saw an increase in immigration and (as in the English colonies) the emergence of a laic, urban culture. Norman French became the dominant speech, largely because it was literally a 'mother-tongue', the speech of the largest number of women; and the seigneurial system (which lasted officially until 1834) codified the connection between land and culture which underscores Quebec's particular sense of nationhood.

Immigration had its problems. It took an average of sixty-two days for a sailing ship to cross from France to Quebec City in the eighteenth century (and some thirty-six days in return). Some people were born at sea; many died. Smallpox, typhus, cholera and influenza raged through the ships and the settlements, often following European outbreaks by the matter of months it would take to transport the disease across the ocean. In 1746, two-thirds of the French soldiers sent to retake Port-Royal died of typhus, as did one third of the Mi'kmaq population. A hundred years later the disease was still rampant: in 1847 almost 10,000 died of typhus on the Atlantic crossing, another 10,000 on the quarantine station of Grosse-Ile, and almost another 4,000 in Montreal. Cholera hit in 1832, and four times more between 1849 and 1854. Vaccination for smallpox was not to become mandatory till 1885.

Freedom in the new country did not imply classless egalitarianism. Statistical evidence indicates that there were some 3,600 slaves in New France in 1759, of whom nearly a third were black, and also that 3,000 of the Loyalists who moved north to Nova Scotia in 1783 were black, many of them slaves who had been promised their freedom if they supported the Loyalist cause. Canada was used at one point as a kind of holding ground to solve an uprising among the Maroons in Jamaica; and though in the Canadas the legislature had outlawed the importation of slaves by 1800, ownership did not stop until the British parliament abolished it in 1833. Canada subsequently became the free land at the end of the 'underground railroad' that allowed American slaves to escape from the United States until the end of the American Civil War in the 1860s (many of their stories are collected in Benjamin Drew's (1812–1903) 1856 anthology *The Refugee*) but neither this fact nor abolition erased prejudice, and certain black stereotypes continued during the nineteenth century to be the subjects of humour in Canadian writing.

As the French and English colonies approached each other politically, prejudice reared up in other domains as well: in the so-called 'Shiners' Wars', which pitted Irish against French–Canadian between 1837 and 1845 in the Ottawa Valley; in the conflicts between Catholics and Orangemen in Western Ontario, from the 1830s on; in the Fenian Raids following 1857; and in various acts of ethnic and gender discrimination since. Ironies abound. A commitment to religious causes led frequently to intolerant behaviour, just as the commitment to technological progress in the nineteenth century led concurrently to child labour and restrictive legislation – an 1816 Nova Scotia law prohibited collective negotiations for wages, for example. Craft unions developed in Quebec in the 1820s and elsewhere in the 1850s as a way of combating social inequities. The rivalries that affected trade and politics often had an insidious parallel in the daily distinctions of class, creed and colour. These distinctions showed up in literature as well, in the trappings of romance, the objects of satire, the absolutes of doctrinaire non-fiction and the hierarchical estimations of style and taste which continued to divide educated (or European) speech and literary models from vernacular usage and local innovations.

JOURNALISM AND CULTURAL POLITICS

As educational institutions came into being (Anglican King's College Halifax in 1789; Dalhousie University in 1818, based on Edinburgh University; McGill in Montreal in 1821; Presbyterian Queen's in Kingston in 1827) the reliance on received norms seemed to be setting even harder. In Quebec the *collège classique* system, which would continue well into the twentieth century, could trace its roots to the seventeenth-century Jesuit colleges for boys and to Marie de l'Incarnation's Ursuline schools for girls. These schools tended to be agents of tradition, not of reform. But cultural change was under way, and many changes derived from the newly-founded newspapers and magazines. There had been no newspapers in New France, because the governor had opposed there being any printing presses in the colony. This restriction on the printed word confirmed the centralist authority; it also meant that the developing oral and theatrical tradition in Quebec would call for intellectual reforms in other ways. Thus while the Jesuit and Ursuline colleges sponsored performances of allegories of saints' lives, groups of the laity performed plays by Racine (1639–99) and Corneille (1606–84). Civil and religious authorities even came to some dispute over performances of Molière (1622–73) – was this work ethical or revolutionary, they asked. While francophone political protest took *oral* forms (drama, folk tale, speech and song), anglophone protest was *written*, given journalistic shape by the emergence of the newspapers.

The first Nova Scotia paper was John Bushell's (1715–61) *Halifax Gazette* (1752). In 1764 the bilingual *Quebec Gazette* came into existence, followed in due course by other newspapers: *The Quebec Mercury* in 1805, *Le Canadien* in 1806, Samuel Hull Wilcocke's (c. 1766–1833) gossipy *Scribbler* (1821–7), Joseph Howe's *Novascotian* and W.L. Mackenzie's *Colonial Advocate* both in 1824, Thomas

McCulloch's *Colonial Patriot* in Pictou in 1827, George Brown's reformist *Globe* in Toronto in 1844, and the *British Colonist* in Victoria in 1858. Some were more conservative than others: *Le Nouveau Monde* (est. 1867) was the mouthpiece for ultramontane Catholicism, but *Le Canadien*, under the editorship of Étienne Parent (1802–74), had supported Papineau. Meanwhile literary magazines were developing: David Chisholme's (c. 1796–1842) *The Canadian Magazine* in 1823; *L'Ami du Peuple* in Montreal, which published the first Quebec tales and legends in 1835, forms which in 1861 were revived as the voice and soul of the people in *Les soirées canadiennes*; John Lovell's (d. 1893) *Literary Garland* in Montreal, which ran from 1838 to 1851, publishing Susanna Moodie (1803–85) and other significant anglophone colonial writers; the Moodies' own *Victoria Magazine*, which ran for the year 1847–8; the Saint John *Amaranth* (1841–3); *The Casket* of Antigonish (est. 1852), which published Gaelic verse; and others. The basic contrast between the papers and the magazines, one which affected both topic and form, is apparent from the editorial comments Mr and Mrs Moodie wrote for their own magazine. They had at heart 'the general good of mankind', the 'hope of inducing a taste for polite literature among the working classes', a view which they opined might be 'too liberal for many of our readers'. But (as with the Workers' Libraries that appeared later in the century) the result was different from the expectation. Public taste did not become uniform; education challenged more than it confirmed the status quo, and people used their newly acquired literacy for entertainments of their own devising and for political ends. The Moodies had 'endeavoured to ... banish from the pages of the Victoria all subjects, however interesting, that might lead to angry discussion' – in other words they omitted the very subjects that gave the newspapers their readership. The *Victoria Magazine* sought to uplift the populace by training readers to English manners; the newspapers sought to enflame the ways to change. In the name of truth, both shaped the world as fiction, and in this division lie some of the basic conflicting impulses in pre-Confederation writing.

As the colonies grew in size and substance, literature was to respond to political and social issues in a variety of ways – sometimes personally and indirectly, lamenting the distance from loved ones or praising the opportunities of the new land, and sometimes openly, in public treatise and occasional verse. In 1711, for example, recording the failure of a large English and Iroquois army from Boston to take Quebec, Paul-Augustin Juchereau (1658–1714) composed an ironic song that played off the English military aspiration against the army's actual accomplishment; the ridiculing rhythm tell all:

Walker, Vetch et Nicholson
Par une matinée
Prirent résolution
De lever deux armées.
Ah! que de besogne à leur fusée,
    Elle est mêlée.

Walker, Vetch and Nicholson
Resolved one morning
to raise two armies.
Oh what a job they had on their hands!
    (*lit*: what a lot of wool on their spindle:
    it's a real tangle.)

To the same event, François Mariauchau d'Esgly (c. 1670–1730) tried his hand at the mock epic catalogue, while Joseph de la Colombière (1651–1723) resoundingly attributed the French victory to the intervention of the Mother of God. Their writings declare the public response to the British and also suggest the extent to which the entire community employed literature as a weapon of cultural defence. De la Colombière was a noted preacher, Mariauchau d'Esgly a military man, Juchereau a Quebec-born businessman: the heart of the society was not without sophistication, even in earliest times, and the military, religious and civil arms of the administration united not to use a uniform literary method but to establish a common attitude toward the world of others, the world that was not themselves.

In later years, following the American Revolution, Loyalist poets such as Joseph Stansbury (c. 1742–1809), Jonathan Odell (1737–1818) and the Reverend Jacob Bailey (1731–1808) set themselves apart in comparable ways. Stansbury, who spent a bare two years in exile in Nova Scotia (1783–5) before being allowed to return to the new United States, variously thundered his disapproval of republican politics ('The helm of the State they have clutched in their grasp / When American Treason is at its last gasp'), announced his personal unhappiness ('Believe me, Love, this vagrant life / O'er Nova Scotia's wilds to roam ... / Delights not me'), and recognized his political dilemma ('ah! how hard to reconcile / The foes who once were friends'). More vitriolically, the outspoken Odell, who had fled New Jersey in 1776, would pillory American skills and American ambitions in the heroic couplets of *The American Times* (1780):

... what if Washington should close his scene,
Could none succeed him? – Is there not a Greene?

Knave after knave as easy we could join,
As new emissions of the paper coin.
When it became the high United States
To send their envoys to Versailles' proud gates,
Were not three ministers produced at once? –
Delicious group, fanatic, deist, dunce!
And what if Lee, and what if Silas fell,
Or what if Franklin should go down to hell,
Why should we grieve? – the land 'tis understood,
Can furnish hundreds equally as good.

This work forms part of a political literary dialogue, to which the American poet Philip Freneau's (1752–1832) work constitutes the 'rebel' side. Freneau attacked the Tories and praised action. Odell and Bailey, true to the Augustan traditions of satire, praised the virtues of orderliness, Anglicanism and loyalty, and attacked what they saw as aimless action, godless fights and misuses of power. Bailey's 'Character of a Trimmer' (1779) and his best-known poem 'The Adventures of Jack Ramble, the Methodist Preacher' (composed in the early 1790s) combine his opposition to rebel politics with his doctrinal opposition to the zealous 'enthusiasms' of dissenting preachers. To Bailey, both were emotional and non-rational – hence they were betrayals of established order, inviting indirect and dismissive exposure through narrative satire. That Methodism would nonetheless appeal in Canada is an irony Bailey could perhaps not foresee; in due course, many of the fiercest social tensions of the nineteenth century (those involving the existence of a state church and the role of any church in educating the young) would derive from precisely this tension between Anglicans and Dissenters. By that time, too, the satire would be overtaken by the literary fashion for sentimentalism. Satire would not disappear – indeed in the Maritimes it continued strong, particularly in prose – but attacks on political positions would begin to take other literary forms.

Odell's 'The Agonizing Dilemma', for example, is an octosyllabic burlesque of the report written by the American General, Stephen Van Rensselaer (1765–1839), who was defeated at the Battle of Queenston Heights in the War of 1812. This report had been published by the American Department of War as the official history; Odell transformed it into a story of incompetence and self-justification, turning the language of the original into the voice of a narrator who defends himself with empty rhetoric and bathos:

Our gallant lads, with burning liver,
Were now so keen to cross the River,

And bring their courage to the trial,
They would no longer brook denial.
Each found himself so stout and clever,
They, one and all, cried now or never.
Give orders now to act – or know,
Pack up's the word – and home we go.
Had I refus'd, would not this army
Have all agreed – to feather-and-tar me?

By the time of Margaret Blennerhasset's (c. 1778–1842) *The Widow of the Rock and Other Poems* (1824), a shift in poetic form reveals a shift in political priorities; her attack upon Jeffersonian democracy appears side-by-side with a sentimental tale about a pioneer woman who goes mad when rattlesnakes attack her husband.

After the Rebellions of 1837, literary commentary takes primarily journalistic and lyric forms; political analysis appears in essays, political experience in song. Joseph Howe's political commentary provides an example of the essay; and the songs of Pierre Falcon (1793–1876) were sung throughout the North-West – 'The Battle of Seven Oaks' celebrating the 1816 victory of the 'Bois-Brûlés' (or Métis) over the Hudson's Bay Company settlers in an area that is now Winnipeg. One of the most famous of all Quebec songs was written in 1842 by Antoine Gérin-Lajoie (1824–82); it conveys the unhappiness felt by those who were exiled from Quebec after their 1837 uprising failed: 'Un canadien errant, / Banni de ses foyers, / Parcourait en pleurant / Des pays étrangers.' [A wandering Canadian, banished from his hearth, travelled through foreign lands, weeping.] Set to the moody rhythm of a familiar folk tune ('Si tu te mets anguille'), the song rapidly became more than a record of immediate history; it turned into a tacit declaration of cultural survival. Henry Wadsworth Longfellow's (1805–82) *Evangeline* (1847; translated into French by Pamphile Le May (1837–1918) between 1862 and 1910) was to become (for all its literary sentimentality and the plain fact of its American origin) a kind of talisman for the Acadians, who still resented the expulsion of 1755 and still preserved their separate culture. Similarly, 'Un canadien errant' came to embody the continuing resistance in Quebec to the surrounding English culture. Because of the deeply-felt equation between culture and place, 'exile' represented an extraordinary alienation, felt as communal rather than just as individual suffering.

By the nineteenth century the persistent declarations of exile were more and more frequently coupled with assertions of rootedness or commitments to the new home. Behind them, however, lay a long line of songs and reportorial narratives that acknowledge and even claim the New World but leave their political and emotional commitments elsewhere. The early journals divide initially into narratives of different kinds: those that record exploration, conversion, captivity, travel, trade and settlement. These differ in the perspective they bring to observation, though the forms overlap in practice; they also differ radically in the character and quality of detail they record, in style and in interest.

EXPLORATION JOURNALS

The French language journal attributed to Cartier, that upon which several translations were based, is noteworthy for its details of language, landscape and observed custom, and for its casualness. It is orthographically a record of a provincial sixteenth-century French prose, and also an unwitting revelation of the character of the writer, who, like Adam in the garden, gave names to the land.

The fact of naming is itself significant; implicity, the places have no names to these navigators until they are claimed by European custom. Indigenous names are occasionally learned, but more or less summarily dismissed, as though of casual interest only. Cartier's ego shows even more brazenly in the way he names wilderness areas after various saints, but names 'the best harbour in the world' after himself. John Florio's 1580 translation emphasizes this issue even more by adding an intrusive 'therefore' – 'which I take to be one of the beste in all the Worlde, and therefore wee named it James Carthiers Sound'. Florio's version rather freely goes on:

If the soile were as good as the harboroughes are, it were a great commoditie: but it is not to be called the new Land, but rather Stones, and wilde Furres and a place fitte for wilde beastes [the French reads 'pierres et rochiers effrables et mal rabottez'] for in all the Northe Ilande I didde not see a Carloade of good earth; yet went I on shoare in many places, and in the Iland of White Sandes, there is nothyng else but Mosse, and small Thornes scattered here and there, withered and drye. To be shorte, I believe that this was the lande that God allotted to Caine.

The 1,480 pages that Samuel de Champlain wrote about his own voyages, and about life in New France between 1603 and 1632 (the edited *Oeuvres de Champlain* appeared in 1870), are at once more exact and full of more narrative anecdotes. Champlain's tale of 'Le gougou' is an early account of a Wendigo figure among the Huron – he tells of a trip to an island full of noises, which 'les sauvages' say are the

sounds of a great monster who comes and carries them off. His conclusion is interesting both for what it presumes and for what it
declares; if he were to report everything about the monster he has
been told, he avers, his readers would dismiss the stories as fables,
but he himself believes the place is the residence of some devil who
torments the Indians this way.

The writers were torn, in other words, between devils and fables;
between a belief in an active, effective spirit world that interfered in
human behaviour, and a rationalist desire for more tangible explanations. The great wave of Jesuit conversions was at hand, but so was a
different great wave of scientific exploration and discovery. The first
travellers' reports of the frightful and the wondrous were about to
give way to the journals of generations of mapmakers.

The age of marvels did not cease. Neither did the age of ordeals-
transformed-into-story: reading that Henry Hudson's men cast him
adrift in an open boat creates a potent symbol for a troubled life.
Thomas James's (c. 1593–c. 1635) *The Strange and Dangerous Voyage*
(1633), telling piously of Arctic trial, turned through Coleridge's
(1772–1834) imagination into 'The Ancient Mariner'. The travels of
Récollet Father Louis Hennepin led to best-selling volumes of adventure and discovery, published in French in 1697 and English in 1698
(*A New Discovery of a Vast Country in America*). These journals are a
tangle of truths, half-truths, plagiarized adventures and wholesale
fictions. Hennepin did accompany La Salle (1643–87) on his Mississippi explorations, but Hennepin not only claims La Salle's exploits
as his own but also goes on to embroider the trip with tales he has
been told of places he never visited at all. The journal form gave the
marvellous adventure credence (Daniel Defoe's (1660–1731) *Robinson
Crusoe* appeared in 1719). More sceptical readers treated all travel literature as invention, and demanded evidence. By the 1760s Cook's
expeditions were sponsored by the Royal Society as well as by the
Admiralty; their function was to chart coastlines accurately, claim territory for the empire, and also collect, describe and classify the flora
and fauna they found. Science was the watchword. Sir Joseph Banks
(1744–1820) was on Cook's first main voyage; and Banks's botany
kept in motion the line of scientific thinking that led to the publication of Darwin's (1809–82) *Origin of Species* in 1859. Scientific accuracy and some sympathy towards Nootka culture also mark the journal
of Quadra's botanist José Mariano Moziño (1757–1820), whose *Noti-
cias de Nutka* was translated from the Spanish in 1970.

With Cook on his third and last voyage (which reached Nootka
Sound in 1778) was a seaman named George Vancouver, who subsequently commanded a return expedition to the area in 1793. Vancou-

ver's journal, more directly titled *Voyage of Discovery to the North Pacific Ocean and Round the World in the Years 1790–1795* (1798) – no 'vast', no 'strange' – not only furnishes an instructive contrast with Cartier's as far as formal style is concerned, It also shows the continuing force of European perspective in governing the representation of the Canadian wilderness. Vancouver charted more ably than Cartier – he had more accurate instruments of measurement – but he still named in order to claim, and (conscious of his readership, perhaps) he still imposed a European style on the landscape by means of the verbal conventions he employed.

Almost exactly contemporaneously (from the 1750s through to 1790) Thomas Davies (c. 1737–1812) in Eastern Canada faced a similar dilemma in a different medium; a military draughtsman, he recorded landscapes with great fidelity, then ornamented them in water colour with stylized vegetation and picturesque natives.

The passage describing Vancouver's landing at the site of the city that now bears his own name shows the tension of the times: made clear is the distinction between location and place, the one measurable, the other to be appreciated less by empirical description than by familiar trope. Captain Vancouver could be as exact as the land surveyors then dividing the eastern wilderness into properties:

The observed latitude here was 49°19′, longitude 237°6′, making this point (which, in compliment to my friend Captain George Grey of the navy, was called POINT GREY) 7 leagues from Point Roberts.

He could even go on with some descriptive detail:

The intermediate space is occupied by very low land, apparently a swampy flat, that retires several miles, before the country rises to meet the rugged snowy mountains, which we found still continuing in a direction nearly along the coast.

But for key points of contact or moments of intense experience he required the elevating conventions of a generalized diction. On meeting fifty 'Indians,' he writes that they 'conducted themselves with the greatest decorum and civility', such phrasing extending the highest of current European compliments. As with civil scenes, so with scenes which fascinated and horrified because of their very lack of decorum:

The low fertile shores we had been accustomed to see, though lately with some interruption, here no longer existed; their place was now occupied by the base of the stupendous snowy barrier, thinly wooded, and rising from the sea abruptly to the clouds; from whose frigid summit, the dissolving snow in foaming torrents rushed down the sides and chasms of its rugged surface, exhibiting altogether a sublime, though gloomy spectacle, which animated nature seemed to have deserted. Not a bird, nor a living creature was to be seen, and the roaring of the falling cataracts in every direction precluded their being heard, had any been in our neighbourhood.

That word 'abrupt' may have been most horrific of all; this was an age that admired degree; and the notion of degree – the European sense of distance and dimension – was precisely what northern North America challenged. Able to accept empirical reality as science but not yet as art, European artists deemed the uncontrolled wilderness uninhabited, uninhabitable, austere – and, if compelling anyway, sublime. A sense of neighbourhood that could embrace the rugged, the frigid, the deserted (or the inarticulate) was beyond comprehension.

The explorers' journals thus offer several ways in which to observe the socio-cultural implications of documents, and opportunities to trace the transformation of simple documentation into narrative literature. There are journals which are tiresome to read because of their verbosity or their pious moralizing; others rely on the current conventions of high style; others fascinate more for their story than their method; still others cannot suppress the personality of their writer. Those of Henry Kelsey (published in 1929) and Anthony Henday (published in 1907) appeal most for their antiquarian value; conventional logbooks, they record time and place but little of character and episode. Simon Fraser's *Journals and Letters* (edited in 1960) pays more attention to incidents. Alexander Henry's (1739–1824) *Travels and Adventures in Canada and the Indian Territories between the Years 1760 and 1776* (1809) is most impressive for the author's suspenseful handling of events, his control over effective detail, his incidental revelation of political attitude, his unconsciousness of self, especially in an episode recounting the Indian attack on the English at Fort Michilimackinac in 1763 and a game of baggataway (lacrosse). Alexander Ross's (1783–1856) *The Fur Hunters of the Far West* (1855) appeals because of its barbed biases, its social comment, its satiric dismissal of the comfortable bureaucrats of the North-West Company who enjoy the results of exploration and hard-headed trading but scarcely appreciate the skills involved or the deprivations of frontier living. John Franklin's two journals *Journey to the Polar Sea* (1823, 1828) tell of the hardships of navigation and survival. Several other books tell the even more stirring stories of the efforts of subsequent expeditions to find lost explorers – John Ross (1777–1856), in George

Back's (1796–1878) *Narrative of the Arctic Land Expedition to the Mouth of the Great Fish River* (1836); and John Franklin himself, in Elisha Kent Kane's (1820–57) *The Grinnell Expedition* (1854) and Leopold M'Clintock's (1819–1907) *The Voyage of the 'Fox' in the Arctic Seas* (1859).

These contrasts derive both from the character of the original expedition and from the image projected by the character of the prose form. T.D. MacLulich (b. 1943), writing in *Canadian Literature* (1979), delineates three categories in a continuum of exploration narratives: quest, odyssey, ordeal – each of which transforms the central explorer-character into a narrative hero of a different kind: tragic, romantic, picaresque, realistic. In some sense these divisions simply record the growing shift in eighteenth-century style from so-called Ciceronian or ornate rhetorical norms to Senecan or plain ones. While writers drew on their own experience, they shaped their words to meet their audience's expectations, which between Samuel Hearne's and Alexander Mackenzie's work (published respectively in 1795 and 1801) and David Thompson's (rewritten three times between 1846 and 1851, later edited for publication by Victor Hopwood (b. 1918) in 1972) had substantially changed. The differences in documentary record also distinguish between European social expectations of wilderness and those that began to emerge in Canada in the nineteenth century.

The three major journals of Canadian land exploration are Thompson's *Travels in Western North America 1784–1812*, Hearne's *Journey from Prince of Wales's Fort in Hudson's Bay to the Northern Ocean*, and Mackenzie's *Voyages from Montreal, on the River St. Laurence, Through the Continent of North America, to the Frozen and Pacific Oceans; In the Years 1789 and 1793*. I.S. MacLaren (b. 1951), in *Canadian Literature* (1984), characterizes the features of Hearne's prose, its rootedness in eighteenth-century notions of nature as a set of composed scenes: vistas of the vast, uniform, uninhabitable sublime and prospects of the particular, variegated, habitable picturesque. Hearne undertook his three trips in his mid-twenties, between 1769 and 1772, at precisely the time Captain Cook was emerging as a scientific cartographer. The habitual characterization of unfamiliar terrain in the familiar terms of landscape aesthetics, argues MacLaren, constitutes an equivalent cartography of imaginative attitude. Hearne uses the vocabulary of current conventions so that the reader expects the Arctic Barrens to take on the character they do. Hence in his script, details of topographic measurement north of the treeline turn repeatedly for aesthetic corroboration to conventional images of ruin, of 'some convulsion of nature', of desolation and barbarity – associations which contrast with the particular details picked out in his southern forest scenes.

Hearne uses the preposition 'through' to describe his southern travels, but 'onto' and 'across' to take him over the treeless north, which reinforces for the reader familiar with the conventions his alienation from the trackless sublime. It is no surprise then that in his descriptions of persons and events, especially his dramatic rendering of an Indian attack upon an Esquimaux camp, Hearne should also preserve his distance; he would prevent the massacre if he could, he writes, but he cannot be obliged to be involved, so he takes on the role of the compassionate observer and reporter. Yet his vocabulary transforms the scene conventionally: the Esquimaux are 'poor unsuspecting creatures', unfortunate victims', 'poor expiring wretches'. For one victim, a young girl, Hearne pleads not that she be spared but that she be dispatched quickly; he records that this 'friendly blow' – a spear through the heart – still 'seemed to be unwelcome' to her, for she tried to ward it off, and he then goes on to add that he still cannot remember 'that horrid day without shedding tears'. The reader does not doubt that the event took place, but the passage draws attention to its own rhetoric; the scene turns into a pathetic interlude of the kind that punctuated the fiction of the day, one which gives a tearful, moral fillip to the main narrative.

To turn to Mackenzie and Thompson is to see style changing. Mackenzie was an observant but succinct recorder; his travels had a commercial purpose; the terms of his observation combine the exact and the colloquial. He worked for the North-West Company; the very title of *Voyages from Montreal* reads lke a sly gesture towards the Hudson's Bay Company allusion in the title of Hearne's *Journey from Prince of Wales's Fort*. When he arrived at the Pacific Coast, inscribing on rock the phrase 'Alexander Mackenzie, from Canada, by land, the twenty-second of July, one thousand seven hundred and ninety-three', he missed seeing George Vancouver in the same harbour by a scant six weeks. Vancouver had recorded the sublimity of heights and cataracts; Mackenzie imposed himself and the world of commercial realities upon the landscape. Imposing itself upon the style of Alexander Mackenzie, however, is the style of the English writer William Combe (1741–1823). It was Combe who transformed Mackenzie's journals into what has become the printed text, in the process elevating Mackenzie's vocabulary, altering and sometimes correcting syntax, and occasionally inserting presumptive statements about the landscape. MacLulich points to the changes in this passage, for example:

Close by the land is high and covered with short Grass and many plants, which are in Blossom, and has a beautiful appearance, tho' an odd contrast, the Hills covered with Flowers and Verdure, and Vallies full of Ice and Snow. The Earth is not thawed above 4 inches from the Surface, below is a solid Body of Ice. The Soil is Yellow Clay mixed with Stones. (Mackenzie)

The adjacent land is high and covered with short grass and flowers, though the earth was not thawed above four inches from the surface; beneath which was a solid body of ice. This beautiful appearance, however, was strangely contrasted with the ice and snow that are seen in the valleys. The soil, where there is any, is a yellow clay mixed with stones. (Combe)

Editorial practice thus turned Mackenzie-the-recorder-of-observations-and-events into Mackenzie-the-conveyer-of-more-conventional, less-personal-aesthetic-judgments. When, as Victor Hopwood observes, the *Edinburgh Review* praised the Mackenzie journals in 1802 (the great nineteenth-century reviews, the *Edinburgh*, *Blackwoods*, and the *Fortnightly*, were widely read and highly influential in Canada), the terms of its judgment were themselves coloured by European expectations:

There is something in the idea of traversing a vast and unknown continent, that gives an agreeable expansion to our conceptions; and the imagination is insensibly engaged and inflamed by the spirit of adventure, and the perils and the novelties that are implied in a voyage of discovery.

The review goes on to praise the 'veracity' of the writer, but the reality of Mackenzie's experience – the realities of mud, muscle, and months of endurance – somehow disappears into the romantic idea of adventure.

Not so with Thompson, the practical geographer, who remained in Canada, writing his memoirs in retirement. Although he never entirely shed his puritanical upbringing (to a contemporary reader some of his versions of his own role as a force of enlightenment in the wilderness seem like mere posturing), he brought an exact numerical curiosity to his observations of nature and human custom. He also brought a sympathy to Native cultures generated in part by his own knowledge of Native languages. He reports the experience of his own travels with sufficient plain detail that the scenes can be envisioned rather than 'insensibly inflamed', and counts speech with an idiomatic fidelity. He can catch the features of the ptarmigan:

The willow Grouse has a red stripe round the upper eyelid, is a finer bird than the rock grouse, and one fifth larger: they are both well feathered to the very toe nails; all their feathers are double, lie close on each other, two in one quill, or socket, and appear as one feather; the under side of the foot, have hard, rough, elastic feathers like bristles.

And he can record in the single speech of a Native a moment of change in a whole way of life; the Native tells him one of the Cree diver stories, of the recreation of the world after the flood, then goes on:

We are now killing the Beaver without any labor, we are now rich, but shall soon be poor, for when the Beaver are destroyed we have nothing to depend on to purchase what we want for our families, strangers now overrun the country with their iron traps, and we, and they will soon be poor.

The fur trade was altering how people perceived the continent, and changing the speech they used to come to terms with it. Thompson appreciated the degree of change involved; he was part of it, and he became, in Hopwood's phrase, 'one of the mapmakers of the Canadian mind'.

Such a phrase does not imply the emergence of some monolithic national sensibility; Thompson's was a Protestant vision, for all its familiarity with indigenous cultures, and could never encompass the whole society. The phrase refers more to the growing signs of shared memories inside Canada, and of memories shared through the art of literary allusion. Increasingly, landscape and even historical figures became familiar. Samuel Hearne was to become a kind of icon inside Canadian culture; so were a number of other historical figures: Father Jean de Brébeuf (1593–1649), Susanna Moodie, Louis Riel (1844–85), Emily Carr, Émile Nelligan (1879–1941), Mackenzie King (1874–1950). Such figures became the subjects of literature as well as of historical treatise; they became embodiments of shared cultural predicaments, representatives of cultural value, legends of a later time if not of their own, myths of persistence and circumstance. They became stories, in other words, and stopped being documentable persons alone.

MISSIONARY JOURNALS

The stories of Brébeuf and the other priests among the Huron are told in the Jesuit *Relations*, the set of annual reports sent from the Jesuit superior in New France to the provincial Society of Jesus in Paris, between 1611 and 1768. Those from the period 1632–73, published in France, served to publicize the missions; together with a number of other documents, they were translated by the American historian Reuben Gold Thwaites (1853–1913) and published in 73 volumes between 1896 and 1901, an edition that serves as the basis for later editions by Edna Kenton (1876–1954) in 1925 and S.R. Mealing (b. 1924) in 1963. The *Relations* were the prime source for Francis Parkman's (1823–93) seven-volume history, *France and England in North America* (1865–92), an heroic and Protestant version of the times which in turn was to dominate English-language thinking about *l'ancien régime* for years to come. Read attentively, the *Relations* are indeed full of incident; they are also markedly varied in style, full of mundane details about crops and daily routine, and sometimes transparent in their exhaustion and frustration – with the work of the missions and with the political tensions of colonial life. About crops, Father Paul le Jeune (1591–1664) writes in 1634 about the 'eight or ten rows' of apple and pear trees they have planted: 'I have an idea that cold is very injurious to the fruit', he observes ingenuously, adding: 'As to the Indian corn, it ripened very nicely the past year, but this year it is not so fine'. Like any annual letter, the report ranges over details both significant and not. What often comes through to the reader is less a coherent analysis of the society than a sense of the mixed emotions of the letter-writers.

Some of the phrasing is casual and unornamented; some is clearly contrived, with balanced clauses and climactic arrangement. The sentences severally convey tiredness, surprise, total conviction, conventional expressions of duty, covert pride. 'I have become teacher in Canada', writes le Jeune, in 1632, delighting in his new-found role, the fulfilment of a commitment apparently at hand, yet two years later he is wearily listing the causes of discontent in the settlement (crowded conditions and dissimilar personalities, the hardships of work, the differences in wages), adding 'notwithstanding all this, we have not failed to pass the year peacefully, reprimanding some, punishing others, though rarely – very often pretending not to see. ...' *We have not failed*: the very phrasing reveals the deliberate mind – the commitment to the cause, the pragmatic diplomacy, the refusal to proclaim oneself successful, the pleasure nonetheless in the degree of success attained. Other letters tell plaintively of things desired and needed: cloth, slippers, thread, prunes. Father François du Peron (1610–65) writes in 1639: 'As for the delicacies of France, we have none of them here; the usual sauce with the food is pure water, juice of corn or squashes.' It is hard to divorce the plain observation from the implicit comparison; the celebration of 'what is' constitutes at the same time a recognition of 'what is not'. Canada was not France.

The *Relations* report on events, language, customs, things seen and heard; they record explorations to Illinois and the Sault, offer advice on military tactics, plan the system that would establish the missions or safe houses for converts and assert a deference to authority. At the same time they are revelations of human character. In the Jesuit order the hierarchy of Authority never commands, always suggests possibilities for service; always, however, it is the duty of the humble to accept the opportunities thus provided, to find happiness in service. These men are not larger-than-life. While the documents often inadvertently reveal their human dimensions, the embedded narratives carry a different message altogether, one suffused with visions of an absolute salvation, visions at once of the heroic and the holy.

The simplest kinds of stylistic contrast underlie this distinction. In 1637, when Brébeuf penned a series of careful statements to guide other missionaries' connections with the Huron, he began with a single absolute ('You must have sincere affection for the Savages') then went on to a whole series of qualifiers:

You should try to eat their ... salmagundi in the way they prepare it, although it may be dirty. ...

It is well at first to take everything they offer, although you may not be able to eat it all; for, when one becomes somewhat accustomed to it, there is not too much.

But in 1639, Father du Peron couched his observations in a catalogue of epithets more pronounced for their theatricality than their quiet diplomacy:

The nature of the Savage is patient, liberal, hospitable; but importunate, visionary, childish, thieving, lying, deceitful, licentious, proud, lazy; they have among them many fools, or rather lunatics and insane people. ... All their actions are dictated to them directly by the devil, who speaks to them, now in the form of a crow ..., now in the form of a flame or ghost, and all this in dreams.

It is impossible to say that either priest was the more devoted to God and the mission; the firm manner of expression differs from the other not in severity, not by suppressing a desire to convert, but in the degree to which it recognizes that to reach the people they had to accommodate to existing customs. Against the language of prejudgment, Brébeuf was counselling practical politics. Ironically, it was in the electrifying language of narrative that Brébeuf's own death came to be reported in the *Relations* of 1649, by Christophe Regnaut (c. 1613–?). Regnaut constructed a story of 'martyrdom', a charged moral lesson, carefully designed.

A context for reading Regnaut's history of Brébeuf and Gabriel Lalemant (1610–49) is supplied by Father Paul Ragueneau's (1608–80) description of the death that same year of Father Charles Garnier (1606–49). Ragueneau reports him wounded, struggling to help others ('Love of God, and zeal for souls, were even stronger than death'), falling once, twice, then again a third time ('Further than this we have not been able to ascertain'). The character of the report does not deny the fact of death, nether does it undercut the will to be of service; but by appealing to the conventional rhythms of parable, it turns the particular event into a didactic moral drama. So with Brébeuf: Regnaut produces a litany of tortures Brébeuf suffered, each more horrific than the last: removing of clothes, binding, tearing of nails, cudgelling, mock baptism by boiling water, a red-hot collar of hatchets, a resin-filled belt set aflame to roast the flesh, cutting off of the tongue to deny the power of speech, stripping of the flesh from the bone and eating it, scalping, tearing out of the beating heart to be roasted and consumed. Regnaut's account is 'veritable' he claims, learned from 'several Christian savages worthy of belief'. Regnaut writes that he finds Brébeuf's body next morning, then reinforces what he has written by reiterating a single phrase: 'I saw and touched' – saw and touched blisters, wounds, cuts, marks of burns, the opening where the heart had been removed. It is the disciple's role he performs, reinvokes in the prose, giving sanctity to Brébeuf by narrative association as well as by the documentary record, turning Brébeuf's bones into relics and Brébeuf's story into another instructive lesson. 'I saw and touched' are the words of physical 'proof', functioning here to reinforce a principle of Christian faith, just as Thomas's actions do in the New Testament; the narrative of physical proof demonstrates that believers are specially favoured when they do not require it, when their belief transcends the constraints of the physical world.

Priests died from many more causes than martyrdom: exposure to the elements, drowning, disease, exhaustion, and the corrosive pressures of humiliation and discouragement. The Jesuit day journals also record many colony deaths with the same dispassion that they bring to records of the grinding of grain. It was not death alone that led to narrative, it was the idea of martyrdom.

The writings of three Catholic nuns of the seventeenth and early eighteenth centuries reinforce this distinction between daily survival and the aspirations of the spirit. Mère Marie Morin (1649–1730), in her 'Annales de l'Hôtel-Dieu de Montréal', recorded the history of the times with a clear eye for individual character. Marguerite Bourgeoys (1620–1700), the founder of the Congrégation de Notre-Dame in Ville-Marie (now Montreal), wrote autobiographically about her service to teaching and to God. Along with Jeanne Mance (c. 1606–73) and others she became a Christian model for subsequent generations. Marie de l'Incarnation (1599–1672), who left marriage and children (as Marie Guyart) to enter a French convent, only to leave again for Canada and found the Ursuline school there, wrote out her familiarity with the secular world in clear documentary history and her vision of God in a prose ripe with passion. Bossuet, the seventeenth-century French orator (1627–1704), called her the 'Teresa of New France'. Chateaubriand (1768–1848) found her fascinating. Her interior life was preoccupied with the presence of God, she wrote, and she made plain in a luxuriant rhetoric the mystic's paradox – her desire to be consumed by the presence of love in order to find abiding life:

Mon cher Bien-Aimé, qu'en un instant votre amour me consomme! Je ne puis plus me supporter, tant vous avez charmé mon âme. Venez donc, que je vous embrasse et je vous baise à mon souhait, et que je meure entre vos bras sacrés, sans faire du retour au monde, là où l'on ne vous connaît point!

My dear and most Beloved, within a moment your love consumes me! I can sustain myself no longer, so deeply have you charmed my soul. Come, that I may embrace you, and kiss you as I would wish, and die in your holy arms, never to return to this world, where one can know you not at all.

The work of the Maritime divine Henry Alline (1748–84) offers something of a protestant parallel. *Life and Journal* (1806) and *Hymns and Spiritual Songs* (1802) combine to portray the evangelical energy and doctrinal commitment of an itinerant preacher. Combining both Calvinist fatalism and Anglican ritual, Alline lays the groundwork for the Baptist church in the Atlantic provinces.

TRAVEL, CAPTIVITY AND SETTLEMENT JOURNALS

Early Canadian documentary writing also used narrative episodes for secular purposes. Many journal-writers reported on the wonders and exigencies of Canada, some alert to empirical reality and some, following in the line of sixteenth-century marvel-merchants, alert only to exotic invention. The lively episodes of John Gyles' *Memoirs of Odd Adventures* (1736) tell of the author's life while a boy captive of the Malecites in the Saint John Valley between 1689 and 1698. But the episodes are of suspect accuracy. Gyles (1677–1755) spent much of his adult life selling his story, making himself more the publicist and performer than the observer and diarist. Among later captivity stories is the narrative of the *Adventures and Sufferings of John R. Jewitt* (1815), based on a secret diary Jewitt kept while a prisoner of Chief Maquinna (fl. 1778–95) of the Nootka. Jewitt (1783–1821), one of two survivors of the *Boston* when the Nootka took the ship in 1803, reportedly developed a strong affinity for his captors; he depicts their behaviour with a shrewd if biased eye. But the prime appeal of both these books lay in their tales of strangeness and fortitude; whatever accuracy of detail they possessed was secondary, serving mainly to reinforce the narrators' claims to be telling the truth.

Like the authors of captivity narratives, various travel writers also subjectively interpreted what they saw. Diary writers foremost, they seldom claim objectivity. Their purpose lay in conveying the flavour of their personal experience to armchair travellers at home, if they intended their work for publication at all. For some, the diary was mostly a medium for daily reflection, a jotting of notes against some future need of reference or consolation.

There was the Swede Peter Kalm (1715–79), whose *Travels into North America* date from 1749; the artist Paul Kane (1810–71), whose *Wanderings of an Artist* (attributed to him, 1859) judgmentally contrasts the lives of Coastal and Plains Indians; the Methodist missionary Joshua Marsden (1777–1837), whose poem *The Mission* (1816) uses the 'horrid shore' of Labrador as a sign of God's intent that the land be converted to enlightenment; the English gentlewoman Anna Brownell Jameson (1794–1860), who turned her unclouded eye and uncluttered pen to record the risks of travel and the foibles of person that she encountered in *Winter Studies and Summer Rambles in Canada* (1838). George Heriot's (1759–1839) *Travels Through the Canadas* appeared in 1807, Frederic Marryat's (1792–1848) *A Diary in America* in 1839, Charles Dickens's (1812–70) *American Notes* in 1842, Anthony Trollope's (1815–82) *North America* in 1862. Juliana Horatia Ewing (1841–85) wrote domestic letters from Fredericton in the 1860s (*Canada Home*, 1983, ed. T.E. Blom, b. 1933, and M.H. Blom, b. 1934). *Lady Franklin Visits the Pacific Northwest* (ed. Dorothy Blakey Smith (1899–1983), 1974) excerpts the descriptive letters that Sophia Cracroft (1855–92), Sir John Franklin's niece, wrote while visiting Vancouver Island in 1861 and 1870. Rudyard Kipling (1865–1936) and Samuel Butler (1835–1902) were to follow – Kipling eager to invest in the real estate market in the West, and Butler condensing his judgment to a single choric phrase: 'O God! O Montreal!' (1878). The American writers Walt Whitman (1819–92) in *Diary in Canada* (1870, published posthumously in 1904), Henry David Thoreau (1817–62) in *A Yankee in Canada* (1866), and Henry James (1843–1916) in 'Quebec'

(1871) were to visit, to puzzle over Canada's seeming difference from the United States and its seeming sameness, and to anticipate the eventual union of the two societies. (James Doyle's (b. 1837) *Yankees in Canada*, 1980, anthologizes several American travel essays; E.-M. Kröller's *Canadian Travelers in Europe 1851–1900* (1987) studies the observations and impressions of nineteenth-century Canadian travel writers.) Lady Monck (d. 1892) and Lady Dufferin (1843–1936) would record journals of residence in the 1870s; Mary Eliza Herbert (fl. 1859–65) would adapt the journal as a fictional form in *The Amaranth* in the 1850s; and travellers and long-term settlers were to continue to visit Canada through the twentieth century – R.M. Patterson (1898–1984), Richmond P. Hobson (1907–66), Eric Collier (1903–66), Edward Hoagland (b. 1932) – the British still finding in Canada the bracing challenges of the manly wilderness and the Americans still locating in Canada the last frontier and the lost innocence of their own world. 'Canada' had become a symbol; but it had still to become, for the immigrant populations, a home in its own right.

The quest for a home in Canada led to many more diaries and journals from the 1790s on, particularly in Upper Canada and the Maritimes, where the arrival of the Loyalists led to formalized settlements and established systems of government. It led also, not altogether indirectly, to a number of forms of social tension. Power was an accoutrement of class, especially in the towns, and class an effective arbiter of taste. When Elizabeth Posthuma Simcoe (c. 1762–1850), the wife of John Graves Simcoe (1752–1806), the first Lieutenant-Governor of Upper Canada, arrived in 1791, she came with attitudes intact. Her diary (1911, re-edited in 1965, as *Mrs. Simcoe's Diary*, by Mary Quayle Innis, 1899–1972), records many details of household duties and scenic observations, but judges them sharply against an English norm. Her discriminations led many of her subordinates to resent her presence and influence. As a sketcher and observer, she adopted the attitudes of the time: the 'peasants' were attractive to her because they were 'picturesque', but their language was not. Her presence stirred up a feud, which another diary reveals; Hannah Jarvis (d. 1845), the wife of the Provincial Secretary, sharply wrote: 'I am sorry the Governor did not come out solo as the People seem not to like our Petecoat Laws'.

Like the other women who kept diaries in these decades, Mrs Simcoe and Mrs Jarvis were privileged people; they had an education (which shaped their expectations) and through their husbands they had access to land. Women alone had no recognized position; a lack of education often meant a life of domestic service; and the governor's effort to set huge tracts aside as estates for the privileged –

especially when there were colonists already occupying, farming, and claiming these lands – was one of the several irritants that in time provoked the 1837 rebellion against the Family Compact. The British compounded these problems of land ownership when, attempting to reduce the size of the army they had assembled to fight Napoleon (1769–1821), they gave their soldiers half pay and a grant of Canadian wilderness.

The wilderness also attracted many people with more practical than formal schooling – Irish and Scots, Yankees, Canadians – who valued their independence and in the new land considered themselves anyone's equal. ('Yankees' referred to the uneducated Loyalists, 'Canadians' largely to people with French background.) Conventional European expectations of domestic service could not survive such a climate, nor could clichés about class. (Hannah Jarvis complained: 'This is one of the worst places for Servants that can be – they are not to be on any Terms. ... We cannot get a Woman who can cook a Joint of Meat unless I am at her Heels. ... I have a Scotch girl from the Highlands, Nasty, Sulky, Ill Tempered Creture.') When longterm residents, having settled the community, recognized that they and, crucially, their children, had to live together, they began to construct a new set of values. They then stopped relying exclusively on their memory of the expectations of the old community for the standards by which they lived and wrote. Approvingly, Anne Langton (c. 1804–93) described Upper Canada, Mrs Frederick Beavan (fl. 1838–45) the Maritimes. In the West and the North, settler narratives appeared rather later, detailing hardships of experience but in general fewer problems in accepting the environment, perhaps because many of these settlers were Canadians already. John Keast Lord's (1818–72) *At Home in the Wilderness* (1867), Susan Allison's (1845–1937) *A Pioneer Gentlewoman in British Columbia* (1976), Elizabeth Goudie's (b. 1902) *Woman of Labrador* (1973), and narratives by Georgina Binnie-Clark (1871–1955) and Monica Storrs (1888–1967) provide a range of examples.

The experiences of the Strickland family in the bush around Peterborough and in the town of Belleville provide the clearest, most evocative account of this process of change. Samuel Strickland (1804–67) wrote a work called *Twenty-Seven Years in Canada West* (1853). More influential as writers were two of his six sisters: Susanna Moodie and Catharine Parr Traill (1802–99). (A third sister, Agnes Strickland, 1796–1874, who did not emigrate, made a literary reputation as the author of *Lives of the Queens of England*, 1840–8, which she wrote with a fourth sister, Eliza, 1794–1875; Eliza, in turn, as one of the editors for *The Lady's Magazine*, helped her younger sisters into print in the 1820s, before they emigrated, mostly with sentimental poems and moral children's tales. A friend of their father's edited another court and fashion magazine, *La Belle Assemblée*, which provided an outlet for Susanna's early Suffolk sketches.) Mrs Moodie's best-known settler narrative was *Roughing It in the Bush* (1852), based on her experiences of the 1830s when (with a sense of duty more than anticipation) she accompanied her husband, J.W.D. Moodie (1797–1869), himself a man of literary pretensions, to settle with half-pay on uncleared ground. *Life in the Clearings versus the Bush* (detailing their move into Belleville) appeared in 1853, also from Bentley's publishers in London, and she also published a number of novels, poems and sketches. Mrs Traill's thirty-odd works include *The Backwoods of Canada* (1836), *The Canadian Settler's Guide* (1854) and *Canadian Wild Flowers* (1868); the first of these is a series of letters describing bush life, the second a practical survival manual (initially entitled *The Female Emigrant's Guide, and Hints on Canadian Housekeeping*, it provides explanations of how to make soap, how to make tea from local plants, and other advice), and the third is a set of botanical descriptions, illustrated by Susanna's daughter, Agnes Fitzgibbon (1833–1913). Current estimates of the two writers emphasize Catharine's practicality, open-mindedness, ability to deal with the trials of bush life (she was more adaptive than her husband, Thomas Traill, 1793–1859), with whom she had emigrated in 1832). Moreover, these qualities are taken to distinguish her from Susanna, who is often described as stuffy, incompetent, resistant to change. Critics have contradictorily portrayed Mrs Moodie (observes Michael Peterman, b. 1942, in *Canadian Writers and Their Works*, 1983) as a one-woman garrison, a Methodist bluestocking, a heroic pioneer, a Crusoe ill-equipped for anything but middle-class society, and a schizophrenic torn between her life and her mind. While there is merit in the larger contrast (Catharine was certainly more of an amateur botanist, and a commercially successful guide-writer, Susanna more interested in the literary conventions of sensibility), Susanna adapted to Canada better than the prevailing image of her suggests.

The attraction Mrs Moodie and Mrs Traill have for contemporary readers lies in the attitudes of mind they bring to settlement, the politics of the adaptation they undergo, in part as reflected in style. Catharine is plainer, more seemingly objective, more idiomatic, more adept at recording dialect, hence more acceptable to twentieth-century taste; Susanna, infatuated with the literary sublime, tried for eloquence through adjectives, often avoiding the particularity that would root her descriptions in place, and distrustful of the sense of humour which she clearly possessed but which she only rarely voiced in her formal prose.

Behind Mrs Traill's writings lay her familiarity with works like St. John Crèvecoeur's (1735–1813) *Letters from an American Farmer* (1782) and William 'Tiger' Dunlop's (1792–1848) *Statistical Sketches of Upper Canada* (1832) – she appears to have drawn on both for specifics in shaping *Backwoods*, and on the earlier for her epistolary *The Young Emigrants; or, Pictures of Canada, Calculated to Amuse and Instruct the Minds of Youth* (1826). Behind such works, too, and more dominantly behind all Mrs Moodie's writings, lay four other kinds of books: the British sentimental romance then current (e.g., the works of Felicia Hemans, 1793–1835, and Sarah Trimmer, 1741–1810); the conduct literature then considered appropriate for children; Methodist doctrinal tracts espousing Enthusiasm (Mrs Moodie had been converted from Anglicanism in 1830, and found literary embodiments of Enthusiasm in writers who championed causes, such as Harriet Beecher Stowe, 1811–96, and Margaret Fuller, 1810–50); and the sketches of nature and Berkshire country persons then recently made popular by Mary Russell Mitford (1787–1855) in *Our Village* (1824–32).

Indeed, Mrs Moodie had written Miss Mitford directly, remarking that her brother Samuel, who had emigrated in 1825, 'gives me such superb descriptions of Canadian country that I often long to accept his invitation to join him, and to traverse the country with him' (*The Friendships of Mary Russell Mitford*, 1882). But this was a conventional remark, more indicative of her failure to grasp the empirical realities that her sister appreciated than of any real desire to travel to Canada in fact. Up close Canada was to seem less idyllic.

She and her sister both employed sentimental literary conventions in the process of recording Canada: Mrs Traill's *Canadian Crusoes* (1852), marketed to children, used the familiar ennobling trope of the child lost-and-found. In its 1852 version the book also built botanical description and local history into the story, emphasizing its base in 'real life'. But the Nelson revisions of 1882 – entitled *Lost in the Back-woods* – distorts the book by cutting the journal passages, truncating the text, and emphasizing the romance of conventional wilderness both in its preface and in its illustrations. (By the 1900s, Nelson editions of *Lost* were reproducing 'wilderness illustrations' indiscriminately from other Nelson books, portraying the Rockies, Western gunmen, peccaries, and the South Pacific as if they were all features of the Ontario backwoods. Mrs Traill, who by 1867 no longer owned the copyright, could not control the character of the text printed in her name.) Of the two sisters, however, Mrs Moodie was the more constrained by the *literary form* she admired, hence more divided from the colonial vernacular, hence more estranged by language from the place she made her home. It is for this predicament that she became a paradigm of the Canadian frontier mentality.

LETTERS AND EPISTOLARY FORM

Appreciating the context and character of these works requires familiarity with another literary device: the letter. Like the many forms of journal, the letter could be a medium of documentation (letters contained information, comment, gossip: examples range from Bishop Laval's, c. 1629–89, seventeenth-century politicking to Juliana Ewing's nineteenth-century domestic informalities) or a strategy of fiction. Moreover, as *Roughing It in the Bush* illustrates, whether a work is a random sequence of documentary observations or a coherent quasi-novel depends to some degree on the sense of form the reader brings to it. The late twentieth-century enthusiasm for 'open forms' (works which do not impose formal systems of closure on narrative but instead ask the reader to participate in interpreting a narrative's ability to establish meaning) has changed a number of critical judgments. Loosely-arranged texts have been found to possess formally discontinuous patterns, where in their own day they might well have been considered simply miscellanies.

A fascinating instance is offered by the work of the eighteenth-century Quebec writer Élisabeth Bégon (1696–1755), who secretly married the brother of the Intendant, travelled with him through much of the colony, and was widowed in 1748, at which point began the letter-writing for which she is now known. The correspondence (found in 1932, edited in 1972 by Nicole Deschamps, b. 1931), as *Lettres au cher fils*) was supposed to have been destroyed; it records not just a series of exact insights into Quebec society in the 1740s, but also (especially to the contemporary eye) the story of a tragic love affair, one doomed by distance and circumstance, ending in exile and death. The 'cher fils' of the title, the recipient of Mme Bégon's passionate longing, was her widowed son-in-law, Michel de Villebois de la Rouvillière, a man of about her own age. Over the course of the letters the affair develops – he is in France, she (a native Québécoise) in Montreal. In 1749 she packs up to leave, in order to join him in France – only to miss him, for by the time she arrives he has left for Louisiana, dying there in 1752. She herself dies three years later, still in exile. The letters tell nothing more than one half of a correspondence, but thus retold they become a narrative.

It is this transformation of letter into story that many eighteenth-century French and English writers drew on to construct the fledgling novel genre. The letters tell stories. Samuel Richardson's

(1689–1761) *Pamela* had appeared in 1740; an epistolary novel by Mme Jeanne Riccoboni (1713–92) appeared in 1759, to be translated the following year by Frances (Moore) Brooke (1724–89). In 1769 Mrs Brooke published her own *The History of Emily Montague*, the first novel written in Canada, an epistolary tale of politics and romance that combines a shrewd eye for life in the English garrison in Quebec in the 1760s with a conventional sense of what constituted culture and civilization. Satire interweaves with sentimental stereotypes.

Mrs Brooke's career ranged from journalism to light opera. The eldest of three daughters of a Lincolnshire clergyman, she used the pseudonym 'Mary Singleton, spinster' to edit a weekly periodical in England in 1755 and 1756, *The Old Maid*, contributing much of the material herself. Imitating the *Spectator* format, she included essays, letters, commentary on politics, religion and art; most significant is the feminist argument running through the journal, which asserted the rights of independence but at the same time conservatively acknowledged the claims of social order. These themes recurred through the rest of her work – a series of plays, novels, translations and libretti, among them the popular epistolary novel *The History of Julia Mandeville* (1763) – which won her a place in Samuel Johnson's (1709–84) literary circle and the close acquaintance of many stage writers. Towards the end of her career she was manager of the Haymarket Opera House. Her light pastoral operetta, *Rosina*, with music by William Shield (1748–1829), appeared first in 1783 and was revived to popular acclaim many times; one aria from it is still a staple item in coloratura repertoires. But it was as the wife of an Anglican clergyman that she visited Quebec between 1763 and 1769. The papers from Governor Murray's (1722–94) office indicate that she used her verbal talents there too – she was vainly angling to get her husband, the chaplain to the English garrison, named the first Anglican bishop of Quebec – but it is for *The History of Emily Montague* (1769) that she takes her place as Canada's first novelist.

Emily Montague concerns the fortunes of three sets of lovers. The central figures are Col. Ed Rivers, a rather pompous gentleman farmer who takes half pay and land in Canada because in England he cannot afford an estate of the size he thinks he deserves, and Emily Montague, the demure but penniless English ward of a family living in Quebec, who appears to have prospects of marrying only the 'civil but cold' Sir George Clayton, who condescends to have her. Ed and Emily fall in love, but Ed refuses either to marry Emily and keep her in the wilderness or to marry her and take her home to what he considers poverty in England. Hence Emily agrees to accept Sir George, and the plot is ripe for unravelling.

Meanwhile, Ed's sister Lucy in England has taken up with his rak-ish friend Jack Temple, against whom Ed has warned her, proving once more his psychological naïveté. And in Silleri, attached to the garrison in Quebec, Emily's friend Bell is coquettishly toying with various hearts (until she falls for Captain Fitzgerald), and amusingly discoursing on scenery and customs while her father reports home his Protestant advice on the political management of the new colony. The whole set of relationships is revealed through the letters the char-acters send one another, and is finally resolved back in England.

The plot is that of a conventional Arcadian romance. The book's interest lies elsewhere, in the force of a vocabulary that calls into question many of the attitudes that underlie such social and literary conventions, and in the implications such questioning has for the understanding of North America. From the beginning Emily is the conventional Arcadian heroine; but Ed, who longs for pastoral value, finds it initially not in Emily (the exemplar of English convention) but in Quebec. On arriving in Montreal he declares himself to be 'waited on at every stage by blooming country girls ... dressed like the shepherdesses of romance'. So inclined is he to see what he expects that he misses the reality. Even his vocabulary is convention-al – 'lively', 'tender': his epithets gloss over the harsher truths of political and natural wilderness. It is not Ed the putative hero but Bell the mock-coquette who has the real power to analyze human rela-tionships here. Bell's voice undermines the easy acceptance of plati-tudes; hence it is the voice by which Mrs Brooke turns her observa-tions of life in Quebec into an analysis of the conventions that restrain women's independence at large. The author examines the politics of social artifice; she uses literary artifice to political ends.

At one point Bell falls in love with the idea of Indian nobility ('Absolutely, Lucy, I will marry a savage, and turn squaw...') only to reject the prospect ('I declare off at once; I will not be a squaw; I admire their talking of the liberty of savages; in the most essential point they are slaves: the mothers marry their children without ever consulting their inclinations, and they are obliged to submit to this foolish tyranny'). She does so as easily as she falls in and out of love with the English soldiers. But on such occasions the flippant voice of the coquette carries a more serious message than do the ponderous epigrams of Ed or Bell's father. When on first sight Bell finds Chaudière Rapids 'irregular' and therefore disconcerting, and Mont-morenci more balanced and therefore more 'pleasing', she is impos-ing the implicitly moral judgments of eighteenth-century European landscape conventions upon the Canadian wilderness, but she learns, as the others do not, that the place, the cold, and the wilderness have their own charms *despite their rigour*. The English idea of charm and enchantment will not contain the New World; to pretend that the wilderness is an English garden *in ovo* is self-deluding. Bell never pretends except for a reason. Hence, at the end of the book, when Ed constructs a garden and Emily an artificial wilderness (Emily dressing up according to Ed's wish, as a French *paisanne*), Bell refuses to go. Bell has worn the mask of coquette, but she will not confuse it with reality. The novel comes to its close quoting from Voltaire's *Candide*: 'Il faut cultiver notre jardin' – a phrase that reverberates politically through the book (espousing the need both to recognize women's independence and to re-examine conventional attitudes toward the colonies). At the same time it reconfirms the book's structure of artifice.

A series of allusions runs through the book. The echoes of Rousseau's (1712–78) *Émile* (1762) are clear: should education make one more natural (the noble Indian) or more civilized (and if so, what is implied by *cultivation*)? The challenge to Pope's (1688–1744) Augustan acceptances ('Whatever is, is right') is even clearer. Bell's full name is Arabella Fermor, a name borrowed from the woman behind Pope's version of the empty coquette in 'The Rape of the Lock', and perhaps from Charlotte Lennox's (1720–1804) fiction. Bell is anything but empty: she is the deliberate coquette, wearing the theatrical mask only so that she may be more effectively political; she is the true 'farmer' her name implies, not the mock *paisanne* of Ed's garden. The cultivation she seeks has more to do with the opportunity to be effective than the invitation to be merely ornamental. It is Voltaire's world she lives in, not Arcadia; it comes complete with its own flaws and possibilities. That is what the novel recognizes. That the novel openly eschews any direct political purpose merely underscores its own indirect political strategy. The fact that the author couches her observations inside the context of conventional romance – it breaks at one point into a long sentimental aside, a moral disquisition on what happens to maidens who transgress society's rules – demonstrates Mrs Brooke's continuing conservatism despite her insights into the inadequacies of the status quo. She wrote commercially, appealing to current fashion even as she queried it. Perhaps because this fashion espoused conventional responses to Canada, the novel's politics long remained unrecognized. The Canadian setting was considered merely 'quaint' – an affectation of artifice, not an intrinsic element in an argument – and the novel was neither especially popular in England not had it any discernible direct influence on the subsequent course of writing in Canada. In its two main lines of development, however, lie two of the most obvious traits of early nineteenth-century Canadian literature: satire and sentimentalism. Thomas Chandler Haliburton (1796–1865) may be the chief exemplar of the satiric tradition, and Mrs Moodie of the sentimental. Both also represent a series of intrinsically conservative writers whose responses to landscape and society have their roots in the attitudes of the late eighteenth century.

SATIRE AND SPEECH

It was the satiric writers who most obviously drew on the epistolary tradition. Thomas McCulloch's *Letters of Mephibosheth Stepsure* offers one set of examples; Haliburton's *Sam Slick's Wise Saws and Modern Instances* (1853) and *The Letterbag of the Great Western* (1840) provide others. McCulloch's book claims to be the social observations of a naïve observer of current behaviour, Haliburton's to be a set of anecdotes by a worldly Yankee trader. All three books are witty, deriving from coherent visions of what the world should be like.

Maritime reformers, both writers depended on the existence of newspapers as the initial means of engaging their readers. After Sam Slick appeared in book form, however, Haliburton acquired international fame (his several books of Sam Slick stories went through a hundred printings in the nineteeth century alone, reached audiences all over Europe and America and influenced later American humourists like Artemus Ward, 1834–67, and Mark Twain, 1835–1910). A lawyer, judge, colonial historian, and later a Tory politician in England, Haliburton was Nova Scotia-born (in local speech, a 'Bluenose'). He was the son of a Loyalist family, who championed both the preservation of the empire and the reform of the colonial institutions in it. He urged religious tolerance towards Catholicism, the development of a common school system, the building of a railroad, and the rejection of the notion of Responsible Government, and he used his many satiric sketches – publishing the first of them in Joseph Howe's paper *The Novascotian* in the 1820s and 1830s – as weapons of social instruction and social ridicule.

McCulloch (1776–1843) was a Scottish-born Presbyterian minister who was sent out to a calling in Prince Edward Island in 1803, failed to reach it, subsequently accepted a church in Pictou and rapidly became involved with educational and theological disputes in Nova Scotia, opposing what he saw as the Anglican hegemony in education and political system. His cautionary tales of immigration, *Colonial Gleanings: William and Melville*, appeared in 1826, doctrinal uplift adhering to every page. The author of several theological works, McCulloch was the first president of Dalhousie University, the founder of *The Colonial Patriot*, a naturalist (whose work attracted Audubon's (1785–1851) attention in 1833), and a vigorous letter-writer to papers like *The Pictou Herald*.

Adept at handling dialect and understatement, McCulloch couched his Stepsure letters as innocent reflections on the events and characters of a fictional community, but they were anything but that. Appearing first (1821–3) as letters from 'Mephibosheth Stepsure' to the editor of *The Acadian Recorder*, they were collected in book form in 1862 and reissued in 1960 as *The Stepsure Letters*. Subsequent critics have hazarded guesses as to who the originals of Mr Stepsure's neighbours were – possibly some of the founding members of Pictou society. McCulloch was critical of many of them. His character Saunders Scantocreesh, joyless and punitive, invokes God's blessing on his own behaviour alone; Solomon Gosling has to pay an 'extended visit to the sheriff' when he neglects his farm, neglects his children's upbringing, and loses his money; other characters tell all by their names: Drone, Drab, Tipple, Trotabout. Stepsure, too, is an eponymous name: the only character ostensibly with moderation, slightly modified by the Old Testament allusion ('Mephibosheth') to lameness. His letters are designed so that they criticize the flawed behaviour of others while appearing only to describe it. Although Stepsure (not McCulloch) may seem to a modern reader something of a pious fraud, his didactic function was clear in the 1820s. The vignettes of town life served a political as well as a moral function. McCulloch was arguing through satiric fiction a case for reforming governmental and economic structures. Without the hard work that would develop an agricultural industry, he asserted, there would be no secure base for the young colony. The real barrier to success was social pretence.

Haliburton's wit is broader than McCulloch's, his handling of dialect more firmly in control, his use of the letter form less recurrent than his reliance on anecdote. But his writings are just as didactic, the episodes drawing frequently to a social moral, couched in epigrammatic form, and italicised, nowhere more clearly than in his sketches of Sam Slick:

An American citizen never steals, he only gains the advantage.

When reason fails to convince, there is nothing left but ridicule.

It's no use to make fences unless the land is cultivated.

Look to yourselves, and don't look to others.

Sometimes the epigram comes direct from the mouth of Sam, in which case it is less formal in delivery, if no less formal in its balanced structure (Haliburton valued order, and indeed, his wit depends on orderly contrasts):

... if a chap seems bent on cheatin' himself, I like to be neighbourly and help him to do it.

The Bluenoses ... expect too much from others, and do too leetle for themselves.

Brag is a good dog, but hold fast is a better one.

All these examples come from the three series of *The Clockmaker* (1836, 1838, 1840), which began as serial publications ('Recollections of Nova Scotia') in *The Novascotian* in 1835. Two further series were called *The Attaché* (1843–4), recounting Sam's observations as a member of the American legation in London. *The Old Judge* appeared in *Fraser's Magazine* in 1846–7, then in book form in 1849 (Sam appears in it only parenthetically). A further Sam Slick adventure in Nova Scotia, *Nature and Human Nature*, was published in 1855. In addition Haliburton wrote several works on colonial history, a set of letters to *The Times* in London denouncing Lord Durham's Report, and various comments on humour.

While it is on the Slick books and *The Old Judge* that his current reputation rests, these works cannot be so easily divorced from the historical commentaries. Haliburton wrote the humorous sketches to show how the colony could resolve its economic problems by attending to its own Bluenose (Nova Scotian) laziness; later works demanded changes in Colonial Office policy. Placing Sam in England in *The Attaché* was a way of criticizing the British as well as the Bluenoses. Later books still, *The Old Judge*, for example, attacked the weaknesses of the liberalized government after the Durham recommendations had been put into effect. Constantly, Haliburton was the critical social analyst, the radical Tory, which makes his literary reputation (especially outside the country) as a verbal wit rather than a social commentator all the more ironic. Artemus Ward purportedly called him the 'father of American humour'; some even have claimed that Slick is the original 'Uncle Sam'. Such observations acknowledge Haliburton's skill at caricature and dialect. But on Haliburton's own pages, these were not just comic turns; they were also weapons of ridiculing Yankee bumptiousness, Bluenose laziness, and British blindness to North American realities.

With emerging purpose, the sketches themselves change. In the earliest *Clockmaker* series, Sam is an itinerant clock pedlar, skilled at salesmanship and able to use 'soft sawdur' to gull the Bluenoses; the sketches link with each other because Sam has a travelling companion, a circuit judge to whom he tells his anecdotes and with whom he exchanges opinions and (as a later book puts it) 'brag for brag'. In the early works the judge is English-born; but as the politics of the books changes, Sam becomes less offensively egotistical, the reader is allowed to see something of a sensitive side to him, the judge turns into a Nova Scotian-born gentleman named Thomas Poker, Esq., and Sam and the Judge turn from mere accidental travelling companions into friends of long standing. Such a progress does not imply any particular growth in characterization – Haliburton's sketches do not boast such continuity – but it does indicate something of Haliburton's deliberate adaptation of literary form to his immediate political ends. He tempered his dislike for self-centred Yankee boastfulness with his admiration for Yankee ingenuity, energy and application; and he tempered his commitment to British imperial order with his commitment to a workable colonial policy. The mean between the two systems was an identifiable Canada as well. Haiburton's challenge was to translate this identification into politics and language.

Many of Haliburton's literary phrases are now so familiar as to seem proverbial. R. E. Watters (1912–79), in *The Sam Slick Anthology* (1969), attributes the following to him: 'upper crust', 'stick-in-the-mud', 'conniption fit', 'as quick as a wink', 'the early bird gets the worm', 'six of one and half a dozen of the other', 'an ounce of prevention is worth a pound of cure', 'as large as life and twice as natural', 'a nod is as good as a wink to a blind horse'. Such phraseology serves a political purpose. In *Nature and Human Nature* Sam attacks those Britishers who take one look at North America and dismiss it, writing 'as wise about it as if they'd see'd it all instead of overlookin' one mile from the deck.' In *The Attaché* Sam praises the sketch form because it is a way of painting 'natur' in detail and avoiding simply making 'bad copies' of British style. Sam's own speech becomes a political metaphor. He is not a colonial, an imitation; he is a Yankee individual: 'no two on us look alike or talk alike; but bein' free and enlightened citizens, we jist talk as we please.'

What about the accent of the Bluenose? The preface to *The Old Judge* finds it 'provincial, ... rapid, ... garnished with American phraseology, and much enlivened with dry humour', but so indiscriminate in its borrowings as to defy easy recognition. The Tory side of Haliburton prevents him from wholly identifying with what he hears around him; he admires the vigour of American vernacular and the power of received British formality, but feels he is granted neither vigour nor power by local speech. Hence the Nova Scotia narrators of his narratives are not distinguished by their voices; voice in that sense is given over to others. What *The Old Judge* nevertheless makes clear is that the Nova Scotia colony derives its coherence from the very 'diversity' that makes the accent puzzling to strangers.

The tales in *The Old Judge* are told by a variety of narrators; more functional is their variety and arrangement. There is an anecdote, a character sketch, a mutability tale, a legend, a romance, a transformation tale, but the whole work is a frame-story. The miscellany is diverse, containing the myths and legends of the various people in the colony, the various patterns of their literary inheritance. But the whole is framed so that it results in a common history, which is the author's preoccupation. He championed the possibility of a coherent society; in doing so he also happened to give literary substance to vernacular speech and the narrative sketch, forms of discourse which subsequent Canadian writing was increasingly to employ.

There was no immediate leap to adopt the vernacular; between the 1830s and the 1860s, the conflicting attractions of the old sentimentalism and the new romanticism urged writers in different rhetorical directions. Some writers aspired to an imported notion of high culture; others identified culture as the immediate experience of ordinary people. This distinction in some degree simply differentiates between urban culture and rural.

While lively folksong traditions had been brought from Europe in the sixteenth century, many new songs also developed in Quebec, Newfoundland, the Maritimes, and the West to adapt to new circumstances: 'En roulant ma boule', 'Les Raftsmen', 'Alouette', 'Vive la canadienne', 'A la claire fontaine', 'Old Grandma', 'Mary Ann'. Such songs were the staples of outport and camp; in them are to be found the vernacular rhythms and the ironic exaggerations of the new country as in the Newfoundland song, 'I's the B'y that Builds the Boat' (collected as late as 1951):

> Sods and rinds to cover yer flake
> Cake and tea for supper
> Codfish in the spring o' the year
> Fried in maggoty butter

> I don't want your maggoty fish,
> That's no good for winter;
> I could buy as good as that
> Down in Bonavista.

Writers such as Johnny Burke (1851–1930) and Arthur Scammell (1913–95), and the music halls of the 1880s and 1890s added to the store of Canadian folk tunes, and still later popular singers and song-writers – Buffy Sainte-Marie (b. 1941), Gordon Lightfoot (b. 1939), Robert Charlebois (b. 1945), Joni Mitchell (b. 1943), Gilles Vigneault (b. 1928), Édith Butler (b. 1942), Bryan Adams (b. 1959) – can be read as extensions of this same line of creativity. More acceptable at the time than the words of many authentic folksongs, however, were the discreet words and sentimentality of 'A Canadian Boat Song', which the Irish poet Thomas Moore (1779–1852) wrote after a visit to Canada in 1804: 'Faintly as tolls the evening chime, / Our voices keep tune and our oars keep time ... / Row, brothers, row, the stream runs fast, / The rapids are near and the daylight's past.' They are a far cry from the lyrics of 'Les Raftsmen': 'Des 'porc-and-beans ils ont mangé / Pour les estomacs restaurer/Bing sur la ring! / Bang sur la ring! / Laissez-passer les raftsmen, / Bing sur la ring! / Bing, Bang!'

POLITICS AND POETRY

In the cities of Upper and Lower Canada, as in the Maritimes, the sentimental tradition was the one that initially prevailed. A series of writers in Quebec was composing variations on pastoral themes, La Fontaine's (1621–95) fables, and eighteenth-century critical formulae: Joseph Quesnel (1746–1809), Denis-Benjamin Viger (1774–1861), Augustin-Norbert Morin (1803–65), Joseph Mermet (1775–c. 1828), Michel Bibaud (1782–1857). When Jules Fournier (1884–1918) prepared his *Anthologie des poètes canadiens* in 1920, the influential critic Olivar Asselin (1874–1937) dismissed the early poets not just for their sentimentality but also for being derivative. Even the great historian François-Xavier Garneau (1809–66) could write 'Le dernier Huron' (1840) in clichés: 'Triomph, destinée! enfin ton heure arrive, / O peuple, tu ne sera plus. ... / En vain le soir du haut de la montagne / J'appelle un nom, tout est silencieux.' ['The Last Huron': 'Triumph, Destiny! O people, your hour has finally come: you will exist no more. ... Every evening from the mountaintop I vainly call out a name, but all is silent.'] Heroism, nobility, loss; this little triumvirate stood behind many a conventional poem.

These literary preferences are instructive for other, more political reasons; they fed a growing sense of French Canadian nationalism in the early nineteenth century, one given secular support by Garneau's *Histoire du Canada* (1845–8), calling for the survival of a *canadien* consciousness. The satires and stories of Napoléon Aubin (1812–90) also fed political nationalism, as did the conscious attempt in Quebec to transcribe folk tales in written form. (An early version of the tale of Rose Latulipe, in which a devil disguised as a stranger seduces a village maid, is attributed to Philippe Aubert de Gaspé *père*, 1786–1871). Political romances were sometimes vitriolic; the several *Drames de l'Amérique du Nord* written by the French author Henri-Émile Chevalier (1828–79), after his residence in Montreal between 1853 and 1860, argued for revenge (seduction again being the main theme). In *Poignet d'acier* (1863), a deathbed utterance urges: "Vivez pour arracher le Canada à l'odieuse tyrannie anglaise!' ['Live to tear the odious English tyranny out of Canada!'] While various writers applauded the new political link in Canada – George-Étienne Cartier, for one, in 'O Canada! Mon pays! Mes amours!' (1835) – many others worked to preserve cultural independence in Quebec, a movement that came to one climax with the establishment of the Mouvement littéraire du Québec in 1860.

Though this movement lasted only about five years, it brought together some of the most creative and influential minds in Quebec City: Abbé Henri-Raymond Casgrain (1831–1904), the young writers Pamphile Le May and Louis Fréchette (1839–1908), the journalist Antoine Gérin-Lajoie, the Conservative newspaperman Joseph-Charles Taché (1820–94), the poet and educational administrator Pierre Chauveau (1820–90), professors from the newly-founded Laval University, and others – all in the back of the bookstore run by the poet Octave Crémazie (1827–79). The members of the group published many works, none more esteemed in their day than the poems of Crémazie himself, who was hailed as a national bard after publishing celebrations of Montcalm and the French presence in Quebec: 'Le vieux soldat canadien' (1855) and 'Le drapeau de Carillon' (1858) in particular. His delight in battle, his transformation of battle of all kinds into a motif of heroic resistance, appealed directly to the current taste for romance; it also reiterated the myths of Conquest, of a cultural battle lost in 1759. Subsequent to his trip to France in 1851, Crémazie located the source of Quebec's vitality in the history it shared with France; in his poems he turned from the realities of the present to celebrate an historical fancy, a notion of a French shelter in the pre-1759 past, to which Quebeckers might turn for joyful renewal. It was at the very least a poetic convention. Quebec culture had by this time been rooted locally for many generations, and for most Quebeckers – though not necessarily most intellectuals in Quebec – the political tie with France had long since been severed. The parallel with Haliburton is instructive: Haliburton's generation was one of the first to try to root its culture locally, and its difficulties in doing so stemmed in part from being unable to identify with what seemed either a raw local culture of a sophisticated imperial one.

Critics also stress the psychological implications of Crémazie's choices; in search of battle as a proving-ground, but at the same time in search of security, his poems argue a quest for a retrievable child-hood, a quest for mother-country which ultimately translates into a love affair with death and silence. Certainly after Crémazie exiled himself back to France in 1862 and changed his name to 'Jules Fontaine' – a questionable financial affair bankrupted the bookstore – he wrote no more poetry. To Casgrain he did write a number of let-ters, disenchanted with France and contemptuous of the intellectual apathy of his countrymen, but that was all. Shortly after his exile, the Mouvement littéraire du Québec fell apart: Albert Ferland died (1805–65); Taché and Gérin-Lajoie moved to Ottawa when the new national government in 1867 appointed them to federal posts; Chau-veau became the first premier of the new province of Quebec; and Fréchette, unhappy with the whole idea of Confederation, moved to Chicago to join his brother Achille (1847–1927). Both brothers in the course of time returned to Canada. Achille married Annie Howells (1844–1938), the sister of the American writer William Dean Howells (1837–1920), cementing a literary connection with the United States that was substantially to mark Canadian writing over the latter half of the nineteenth century. Louis was to become the more influential writer.

Among English-language poets, Peter Fisher (1782–1848) of New Brunswick wrote *The Lay of the Wilderness* (1833). J. Mackay (dates unknown) published *Quebec Hill* in 1797. Oliver Goldsmith (1794–1861), namesake and grand-nephew of the English author of *The Deserted Village*, wrote *The Rising Village* in 1825. Alexander MacLachlan (1818–96), best known in his own time for his Burnsian dialect verse, published *The Emigrant and other poems* in 1861. Thomas D'Arcy McGee (1825–68) celebrated his Irish connections in *Canadian Ballads* (1858). Other poets include Adam Kidd (1802–31), *The Huron Chief*, 1830), the Anglican lyricist (and later Irvingite, after he was expelled from the Anglican church) Adam Hood Burwell (1790–1849), and George Longmore (1793–1867, author of the humorous *The Chari-vari*, 1824, long attributed to Levi Adams, 1802–32). Charles Heavy-sege (1816–76), highly praised in his own day for his *Sonnets* (1856) and his closet dramas, *Saul* (1857) and *Jephthah's Daughter* (1865), val-ued literary diction of a sort indigestible to most modern readers. And Charles Sangster (1822–93) wrote a variety of patriotic songs ('Brock', for example, celebrating the War of 1812 hero), songs of nature ('Son-nets Written in the Orillia Woods'), and a long poetic contrast between two Canadian rivers, *The St. Lawrence and the Saguenay* (1856), which, like the Mackay work, draws on the eighteenth-century landscape poetry traditions of James Thomson (1700–48).

Sangster's long poem in Spenserian stanzas records a voyage from township into wilderness, using the local landscape as a metaphor of the artist's journey from convention towards creativity. Mackay's illustrates most clearly the character of the diction that was then thought to transform observations of nature into ennobling moral sentiments. Part of the 'Summer' section of his *Quebec Hill* reads:

> The stream, with lazy motion, pours along,
> While, in the sun-beam, gleams the finny throng;
> Its heaving banks with rip'ning increase clad,
> And, interspersed, the cottages are spread:
> Higher the flocks are skipping with their brood,
> How close behind appears th'entangled wood!
> The distant hills, with arbor richly clad,
> Afford the wild inhabitants a shade.

In such lines the poet makes every effort to avoid empirical detail; 'finny throng' instead of 'fish', "rip'ning increase' instead of particular crops, even 'entangled wood' (a term from the controlled British garden) rather than the more accurate and disorderly North American 'bush': the language attempted to read order where no order was, to control by diction what seemed chaotic to the empirical eye. By contrast, MacLachlan could rise to Blakean directness in his observation of urban chaos, which he lay at the door of churches that placed piety over action:

> We live in a rickety house,
>   In a dirty dismal street,
> Where the naked hide from day,
>   And thieves and drunkards meet.

In Goldsmith's poem these two impulses – towards the empirical directness of the vernacular and the generalizing artifice of the genteel – came together. Absorbed by his grand-uncle's accomplishment (the 'genius' that 'formed the glory of our name', as his own poem puts it), Goldsmith opens *The Rising Village* with a deliberate invocation to the memory of the earlier poet in order to give the new work, and the subject it describes (the building of a new community), the orderly context of tradition. The heroic couplets may even be a conscious archaism in 1825, an implicit appeal (by means of formal imitation) to the orderly patterns of the civilization to which the poet aspires. Everywhere the lines speak of 'charming' scenes, of events taking place 'by turns', of a neighbourhood growing 'By slow degrees', and of hierarchies of settlement, with the 'peasant's' 'low hamlet and the shepherd's cot' at the bottom. Even the trees fall down in orderly sequence; the 'sturdy woodman' chops them and 'See! from their heights the lofty pines descend, / And crackling, down their pond'rous lengths extend.' At other times the poem strains against its own conventions, rising to greater liveliness when it observes closely the characters of the new community – the ill-educated doctor, the incompetent schoolteacher – and catalogues the contents of a country store: nails and blankets, horses' collars, buttons and tumblers, fish-hooks, spoons and knives, shawls, flannel, woolcards, mill-saws and toys. The chaos, the wilderness – what Haliburton called the 'variety' – is what proves both functional and productive. But here it is contained within an imposed order. The poet accepts convention as the civilizing force in his society. Wilderness is implicitly considered dangerous, an equation made more apparent in the poem's parenthetical tale of Albert and Flora (a cautionary tale not unlike the one in Mrs Brooke's novel); here Albert abandons Flora when he emigrates to Canada, she goes mad, and the poem intones 'Come hither, wretch, and see what thou hast done'. This 'tale of real woe', as Goldsmith puts it, documents a wilderness of behaviour, which is what the poem ultimately argues against. Its sentimental character points to the true nature of virtue, which by extension is taken to reside in the acceptance of conservative structures of both literature and politics as well as in the observation of the codes of polite society. From this vantage point, liberty and virtue are possible only within the letter of the law; individualism (Albert's wilful emigration) is implicitly rebellious, for it challenges the orderly (therefore civilized) character of community.

ROMANTIC DOCUMENTARY

These literary trends, coupled with the politics of the 1830s and the generic character of the documentary narratives of travel and settlement, provide a fuller context for reading Susanna Moodie's *Roughing It in the Bush*. She was the reluctant pioneer – in love with the idea of nature but always suspicious of the actual wilderness – and the reluctant pioneer became in Ontario (as the hero-martyrs of history and folk myth did in Quebec) a kind of prototype for cultural memory. The heroic-martyr and heroic-pioneer versions of the past are both romantic; the degree to which they also shape different pasts has meant that the two memories have some repeatedly into conflict. The prefaces to various editions of *Roughing It in the Bush* reveal the difficulty of separating politics from style. The 'advertisement' to the third edition (1854) refers to the 'loyal lyrics' Susanna Moodie (using her maiden name, Strickland) wrote during the rebellion, songs which 'produced a great effect in rousing an enthusiastic feeling in favour of law and order'; the 'glowing narrative of personal incident and suffering', moreover, is full of 'delineations of fortitude' both 'interesting' and 'pathetic'. Enthusiasm and pathos are key motifs, attitudinal proofs as it were of Christian virtue, which extend by association into the shaping of law and political relationships. Mrs Moodie's own introduction to this edition roundly condemns the real estate speculators whose encouragements drew unwary middle-class settlers to Canada ('Oh, ye dealers in wild lands – ye speculators in the folly and credulity of your fellow man – what a mass of misery, and of misrepresentation ... have ye not to answer for!'); she also dismisses the desire to emigrate as a general 'infection', and contrasts the 'brave and honourable ... dupes' with the attitudes of servants, who arrive in Canada 'republican in spirit', meaning unwilling to tolerate any longer the disparities of class and custom with which they had been living.

In 1871, Mrs Moodie added another introductory essay to her work, called 'Canada: A Contrast', which reviews her motivations on coming to Canada in 1832 ('necessity, not choice') and recounts various changes that forty years' residence have seen. As for landscape, 'The rough has become smooth, the crooked has been made straight, the forests have been converted to fruitful fields'; in culture, 'We have no lack of native talent or books, or of intelligent readers to appreciate them'; most remarkably, in politics, the 'traitor and public enemy' William Lyon Mackenzie is transformed by her own words into a 'clever and high-spirited... injured man', whose weak blow 'laid the foundation of the excellent constitution that we now enjoy'. In all categories, the wild has been tamed by a change in perspective, most dramatically in the way the word 'We' by 1871 includes Susanna within that body of people called Canadians. *Roughing It in the Bush* has to be seen, then, not just as a document of its time, but as a changing document of changing times, bound by its rhetoric to the past, but struggling through its changing form to touch the future.

Formally, it is a miscellany, a gathering of essays, anecdotes, sketches of event and character, punctuated by occasional poems, some of them contributed by her husband. (Recent research suggests Mr Moodie may have had an even larger role in the book's composition.) The aim was to instruct, uplift, entertain and warn. The anecdotes criticized servants' insubordination and Yankee deviousness, praised courage, and consciously revealed her own lack of bush skills: she could not cook, she had no practice at bargaining, she had no preparation for the trials she would endure. It is easy from a late twentieth-century vantage point to patronize her (the interpretive apostrophes and her condescension to others invite it), but that would be to mistake the message for the messenger. Hers was a remarkable story of fortitude. While unlike many pioneers she managed to keep a servant, she nonetheless learned to cook, till, paddle, build, survive – and she bore, brought up, and lost children in a wilderness far from what she thought of as home.

Her episodic narrative tells initially of her arriving at Grosse Ile; 'it looks a perfect paradise at this distance', she tells the Captain, only to discover the rawer realities of the cholera depot on closer acquaintance. The passage offers a paradigm for the whole. The first glimpse is of what convention dictates: 'stupendous ... sublime view ... Titans of the earth, in all their rugged and awful beauty ... excess of beauty ... glorious ... so many striking objects blended into one mighty whole ... noblest features ... enchanting scene ... picturesque effect ... melancholy.' But such expectations limit one's preparedness for empirical details. Indeed she had difficulty finding vocabulary appropriate to specifics; she wrote to Richard Bentley (1794–1871) in an 1853 letter apologising for the 'want of individuality in my writings', but explained: 'A scene or picture strikes me as a whole, but I can never enter into details.'

In some respects her apology is true only for those circumstances for which she had an already shaped aesthetic system. For landscape, her education had taught her, there were conventions of vocabulary to use. Hence, 'Montreal from the river wears a pleasing aspect, but it lacks the grandeur, the stern sublimity of Quebec': the prose itself attempting to convey impressions but avoiding the very kinds of words that would establish appearance. Attitudes to diction extend also to her handing of dialect; she attempted from time to time to record the speech of Scots, Irish, French-Canadian and Yankee but did so stereotypically, using dialect not as Haliburton did, to individualize character and celebrate the energy of the vernacular, but to indicate how far removed these individuals are from the British speech she accepted as the normative standard of behaviour or civilized culture.

When it comes to the individuals she meets in the backwoods, however, she has no containing formulae of style, and they leap from the pages as dynamic sketches of character. The incorrigible Tom Wilson, a fellow-emigrant with a droller sense of humour than that of the Moodies themselves; Old Satan, the Yankee borrower; Betty Fye, who steals her apples; Brian, the still-hunter; Mr Malcolm, the taciturn and unwelcome visitor, with more transparent liking for her husband than for Mrs Moodie herself, which perhaps disingenuously puzzles her – these sketches transcend portraiture-by-type. So do the episodes that take account of a charivari and a logging-bee. But with the episode called 'The Walk to Drummer', an account of a charitable visit, she shifts back into the language of convention, drawing once more on the device of the cautionary digression to give sentimental (hence morally uplifting) dimension to her document of 'real life'.

The point is that Mrs Moodie chose her language. Contrasting the versions of these sketches as she published them first in the Montreal magazine *The Literary Garland* with the versions she prepared for her book published in London, Michael Peterman shows how the book form suppresses any raciness of subject or style which the originals employ, and excises details both surgical and matrimonial. At the same time it adds to the litany of euphemisms and biblical allusions and to the melancholy of the lost English connection. Many such stylistic embellishments can be tabulated:

Garland text (serial)	*Bentley text* (book)
trees	woods, groves
around	encircled
bite	masticate
Indian	the wild man
face	countenance
belly	stomach
a place called Dummer	a place situated in the forest-depths of this far western wilderness

The intention was to appeal to the cultivated literary taste of the England she remembered. But tastes were changing. Late nineteenth-century critics found her subsequent works dated, stereotypical, wanting in structure and interest. Even documents of real life were being read as fictions, and fiction was moving in new directions.

DOCUMENTARY ROMANCE

The colonies, moreover, were themselves altering. The changes which Mrs Moodie's 'Canada: A Contrast' refers to as aesthetic modifications (shaping the chaos of savage wilderness into systems of reputable regularity) had their statistical basis in the increased population of the Maritimes and the Canadas, and the development of towns and townships. Table 2 provides data concerning population growth in northern North America, though the figures were not initially collected according to uniform standards, and do not include data on the native peoples. The *Historical Atlas of Canada*, vol. I (1987)

Table 2   Population growth

	New France/ Lower Canada	Acadia	Prince Edward Island	Nova Scotia	New Brunswick	Upper Canada
1665	3,215					
1710		2,000				
1748			700			
1750		12,000				
1755			5,000			
1763				8,000		
1775	c. 70,000			17,000[a]		
1790				c. 40,000	c. 17,000[b]	10,000
1798			4,000			
1800	c. 150,000				c. 25,000	
1812						100,000[c]
1842						450,000
1850	c. 890,000		62,000	100,000	c. 200,000	950,000

[a] Over half from New England.
[b] 80% Loyalists.
[c] 80% US origin.

All Canada

1851	2,436,297		1961	18,238,247
1881	4,324,810		1971	21,568,311
1901	5,371,315		1981	24,343,180
1921	8,787,949		1991	28,120,100
1941	11,506,655		2001	30,007,094
1951	14,009,429[a]			

[a] Including Newfoundland from 1949 on.
Source: *The Canadian Encyclopedia* (to 1981) and Canada census figures.

reports, for example, that the Ontario Iroquois population – Huron, Petun and Neutral – grew from c. 2,000 in the fifteenth century to greater than 60,000 in the early seventeenth century. Although few Natives lived in the St Lawrence Valley during the same period the Algonquian speakers of the Maritimes numbered c. 12,000, the Beothuks c. 2,000, the Inuit of the Labrador Coast c. 2,000, and the West Coast Tsimshian tribes c. 11,000.

With the increased European population came newspapers and magazines – organs of communications which Mrs Beavan, in *Sketches and Tales ...* in 1845, called a shared social enterprise. With the growing sense of community came a desire to assert and explore the community's history. Built into this desire, however, was the regional character of the history itself (the 'story' of Upper Canada was different from that of Lower Canada, New Brunswick, or Nova Scotia); hence the impulse to document the shared cultural inheritance was coloured by the kind of story perceived in each region to evoke the local character. The stories in all the separate colonies were affected by similar aesthetic fashions: the romance of history, the morality of poverty and other problems, the role of Providence as the author of the future, the effect of sublimity on the soul (an effect experienced in Nature and believed to be re-enacted through elevated diction). But the particular incidents that each region's fiction turned to for uplift and entertainment were by the mid-nineteenth century already designing different psychological versions of the past.

The first English-language novel by a native-born writer was a melodramatic account of shipwreck and seigneurial Quebec entitled *St. Ursula's Convent* (1824), by Fredericton's Julia Catherine Beckwith (Hart) (1796–1867). Charlottetown-born Douglas Smith Huyghue's (1816–91) later *Argimou: A Legend of the Micmac* (1843) ostensibly concerns the expulsion of the Acadians in 1755; it also passionately protests the disappearance of the aboriginal culture. In Quebec, Napoléon Bourassa (1827–1916) serialized another novel about the Acadians in the periodical *La Revue Canadienne* (1865–6); called *Jacques et Marie*, it tells of heroism in the face of adversity and a foreign culture. The legends (*Forestiers et Voyageurs*, 1865) Abbé Henri-Raymond Casgrain and J. -C. Taché retold in the 1860s also tell of combat, heroism and martyrdom. Joseph Marmette (1843–95), Patrice Lacombe (1807–63) (*La terre paternelle*, 1846), and Pierre Chauveau (*Charles Guérin*, 1846) published romances of adventure and self-discovery, and the historical romances of the 1860s became testaments to the power of morality-in-action. The dramatist Pierre Petitclair (1813–60) wrote a comic warning against adopting English speech, *Une partie de campagne* (first performed in 1857). Meanwhile in Canada West, Abraham Holmes (c. 1821–1908), the son of a Methodist minister, was writing *Belinda; or, The Rivals: A Tale of Real Life*, published in Detroit in 1843. The story of a coquette's enticements, this novel is at once a jaunty satire of the fashionable romances of the time and a springboard (perhaps not altogether serious) for a conventional Wesleyan moral conclusion: the wild fashionable life, says the novel (after having recounted its scandals), leads to no good ends: therefore repent. The three separate regions – Maritimes, Quebec, Canada West (Ontario) – all bound by a comparable moral impulse, nonetheless produced three separate psychological sensibilities: those adumbrated by a literature of social protest, a literature embracing the heroism of loss, and a literature of fashion wearing a solemn mask.

In Montreal, Rosanna (Mullins) Leprohon (1829–79) became the voice of another element in the new society, that of the Irish Catholic. A presence in fashionable society in Montreal, and a friend of the assassinated politician D'Arcy McGee, Mrs Leprohon was the author of a number of sentimental poems and mannered romances, which she published in such journals as the *Literary Garland*, the Boston *Pilot*, the Montreal *Family Herald* and the *Canadian Illustrated News* from the 1840s through the 1880s. *Ida Beresford; or, The Child of Fashion* appeared in 1848, *The Manor House of de Villerai* in 1859–60, and her most famous novel, *Antoinette de Mirecourt; or, Secret Marrying and Secret Sorrowing*, in 1864. Mrs Moodie approved her work for its moral commitment ('let her keep truth and nature ever in view', she wrote in *The Victoria Magazine*), and the approval shows something of the reasons for which Mrs Leprohon's work was valued. *Antoinette* was a story set in the French regime; it tells of a young Canadienne who marries an English officer without parental consent, only to rue the day, discovering too late the wiles of men and fortune-hunters. The moral centre in the work derives from its Catholicism – the sinfulness of the unapproved cohabitation. The book was read widely in Quebec and early translated into French. The more widespread moral appeal, that which warmed Mrs Moodie, was to the preservation of social convention. The historical, 'French' setting, replete with hints of nobility, gave a sense of piquancy to the tale; the 'foreignness' of the setting to the Protestant anglophone reader also served to underscore existing stereotypes about the potential for degradation beyond the reach of British norms.

For their part, the francophone writers wove moral messages out of the reverse attitude. *Les anciens Canadiens* (1873), by Philippe Aubert de Gaspé (*père*) – his short-lived son and namesake (1814–41) had written the first French-language Canadian novel, *L'influence d'un livre* (1837) – told a story of a French (Canadian) noble and a Scots noble, whose friendship is disrupted when they find themselves on opposite sides in the Seven Years' War. Constructed anecdotally and interspersed with poems and songs, the book deliberately illustrates 'les moeurs des anciens Canadiens'; if things appear childish or irrelevant to a stranger, says the narrator, nothing is present that will not interest 'les vrais Canadiens'. The anglophone response to the book – largely through Charles G.D. Roberts' (1860–1943) 1890 translation *The Canadians of Old*, though there was also an 1864 translation by Georgiana Pennée (d. 1895) – was tied up in the image of happy togetherness (Roberts had written in his preface of the 'present day ... nationalism in Quebec' that is 'rather given to extravagant dreams', and used the book to champion the reconciliation between French culture and national unity). By retitling the 1905 reprint *Cameron of Lochiel*, Roberts even redirected the focus, as did a further, truncated version by T.G. Marquis (1864–1936), called *Seigneur d'Haberville* (1929). The conclusion to Aubert de Gaspé's book has to be appreciated more fully: the *Canadien* marries an *Anglaise*, saying 'nous vivons plus tranquilles sous la gouverne britannique que sous la domination française'.[We live more contentedly under the British government than under French domination.] But the *Canadien*'s sister refuses the Scot because of her patriotism, her adherence to French culture. She will not be seen to have been bought at any price. Sacrifice: that's the model.

Comparably, in Georges Boucher de Boucherville's (1815–98) serialized *Une de perdue, deux de trouvées* (1864–5), patriotism serves the cause of independence; a flamboyant, multiplotted tale, the novel begins in New Orleans (it was probably begun when the author was living there, exiled after the 1837 Rebellion); then it moves to Cuba, tells stories of slaves, sea battles and the acquisition of a fortune, then shifts to Quebec to put the fortune to the service of the Rebellion and to allow the hero to discover his long-lost family and live happily ever after. Antoine Gérin-Lajoie's *Jean Rivard le défricheur* (1862) is much more direct, more committed to a particular course of action; the title character, the eldest of twelve children, hesitates before choosing a career, but moves from success to success, eventually founding a town and acquiring political stature, only to give it up to devote himself to the land: 'l'image parfaite du bonheur et de la vertu'. [The perfect image of happiness and virtue.] It sounds a little like the conclusion to *Emily Montague*; but the land, here, is more a symbol of cultural self-possession. Devoted cultivation of the land, moreover, is a moral act, declaring a commitment to the psychology and politics of cultural sovereignty.

Behind all these novels lie the pressures of social expansion. Arable land was becoming scarce in Quebec by 1800, and by 1830 British immigrants were threatening to become the dominant cultural group: 45 per cent of the population of Quebec City and 61 percent of that of Montreal was anglophone by 1850; anglophones dominated business, hence came into conflict with the francophone bourgeoisie, which in turn helped reinforce the rule of the Catholic Church in the latter half of the nineteenth century as a way of reestablishing francophone cohesiveness. Fiction was also affected by the literary fashions of Europe and America. Sir Walter Scott (1771–1832) had published the first of the Waverley novels in 1814, establishing the vogue of historical fiction; Aubert de Gaspé translated Scott; James Fenimore Cooper (1789–1851) published *The Pioneers*, the first of the frontier Leatherstocking tales, in

1823, encouraging a taste for frontier romance. Dumas (1802–70) and Eugène Sue (1804–57) were publishing their sensational and adventurous narratives in the 1840s. Mrs Leprohon found both Sue and Balzac (1799–1850) to be 'pernicious', without the moral function of inspiration. Increasingly resistant to what was taken to be 'high life' fiction and its suggestion of imported and static urbanity, Canadian novelists were beginning to look for ways to express the distinctiveness of the new Canada, identifying it somehow with the wilderness.

In this respect Major John Richardson (1796–1852) became the dominant romance writer of the time. Of Loyalist and Native stock, a veteran of the war of 1812 and an habitué of various gaming houses in London and Paris, Richardson published a dozen novels, long poems and histories, largely melodramatic. Some of the tales drew on experience; some – as in *Wacousta* (1832) and its sequel *The Canadian Brothers* (1840; also published in 1851 as *Matilda Montgomerie*) – are perhaps better read as adventures in the dream-wilderness of one man's mind. There is a critical dispute involving *Wacousta* (one not helped by the fact that the nineteenth-century published text is corrupt): is it a novel about false wilderness or about true community? a novel about social choices or about a psychosexual imagination? The multiple plots of the narrative (much of the background revealed only in the revelatory final chapters) tell of the rivalry between two British soldiers for the same woman, a Scots Jacobite with an affinity for wild animals. De Haldimar treacherously wins her, managing at the same time to get his rival, Morton, court-martialled. The rival joins the French army, fights at the Battle of the Plains of Abraham, turns himself into 'Wacousta', an adviser to the Ottawa chief Pontiac, and vengefully plots De Haldimar's comeuppance. Meanwhile De Haldimar kills Morton's nephew-namesake (namesakes abound in the novel, producing some degree of narrative confusion, but for contemporary critics a feast of reflexivity), and Wacousta finally kills off several of the De Haldimars, leaving prophecies to be 'fulfilled' in the sequel. The novel reeks of terror, evil, sublime nature, chance circumstance and theatrical feeling; it is neither consistent in its moral stance nor divorced from the conventions of the sentimental tale; it is stylistically contrived. Where, then, is its appeal? The answer may lie in the psychological split that the novel represents: at once through the make-believe Indian Wacousta and the mock-gentleman De Haldimar. Order masking as wilderness, and wilderness masking as order: the novel provides a symbolic representation of the milieu of Abraham Holmes and Susanna Moodie – in other words of an emergent Ontario sensibility, one which years later reappeared in the work of Margaret Atwood (b. 1939) and Robertson Davies (1913–95).

A nation called 'Canada' was about to come into existence; what that meant for literature was less certain. 'When I was a youthful romance reader', observes a character in Catharine Parr Traill's 'Female Trials in the Bush' (a sketch she published in the *Anglo-American Magazine* in 1853), 'I should have fancied myself into heroine, and my old Irishman into a brigand; but in my intercourse with the lower class of Irish emigrants, I have learnt that there is little cause for fear in reality.' The main contrast of early-nineteenth-century Canadian writing is lodged in this single phrase: there is a shift towards comparison in the definition of what is real. Yet this anecdote-told-as-truth remains closeted in the artifice of speech and station. The landscape ('gloomy pines') conforms to conventional feeling; speech ('My heart thrilled with terror' at the sound of imagined wolves) conforms to conventional attitude; the faithful Newfoundland dog (named Nelson) even causes the female speaker to declare 'You have made a man of me', conforming to conventional role-modelling. Hence despite Mrs Traill's appeal to contrast and autobiographical *documentation* – or Richardson's appeal to *verifiable* historical event – their 'realities' remain fictitious.

By the mid 1860s there had come into existence a belief in a commonality that could be identified as the 'Canadian' character, but although this proved to be a functional political gesture, it too was at heart a fiction. Edward Hartley Dewart (1828–1908), writing the preface to this 1864 anthology *Selections from Canadian Poets,* observed the difficulties of nationalism even as he advanced a justification for it: 'A national literature is an essential element in the formation of national character. It is... the bond of national unity, ... the guide of national energy.' At the same time he asserted the 'imperfection' of much Canadian verse and declared 'Our colonial position ... is not favorable to the growth of an indigenous literature. Not only are our mental wants supplied by the brain of the Mother Country ... but the majority of persons of taste and education in Canada are emigrants from the Old Country, whose tenderest affections cling around the land they have left.' What he failed to acknowledge were the constraining biases of this Methodist anglophone Ontario perspective. 'Our French fellow-countrymen are much more firmly united than the English colonists', he said, 'though their literature is more French than Canadian, and their bond of union is more religious than literary or political.' On this point he was simply wrong. But his was a pervasive attitude, one that coloured the structure of politics for several generations, one that uncritically equated history with story, one that transformed the desire for a national historical tradition into the inventive telling of tales.

CHAPTER THREE

Tale-tellers: literature to 1922

ANGLO-PROTESTANT, ULTRAMONTANE, PRAIRIE

It is easiest to characterize the years between 1867 and the First World War as an age of expansion: Victorian, progressive, nationalist, Imperial. The age was also one of definition. The prevalent idea of nationalism declared a fundamental belief in cultural uniformity. In Canada, nationalist sentiment was anglocentric, male-dominated, and justified by appeals to God and National Law. In practice it not only shaped Canada territorially, it also shaped many of the regional and ethnic tensions which continue to challenge the language and structures of Canadian power. Much of Canadian history at this time is bound up with the events that defined the national from the (centralist) perspective of Ontario and Quebec; coincidentally these same events, in particular railway-building and the Riel Rebellion, invited future challenges to centralist ideas.

Literature also defined the character of the new society as it reflected upon it. In the latter part of the nineteenth century, writers were weaving romances out of history and the frontier, providing moral instruction, asserting the validity of the natural order. But the signal feature of such tale-telling was neither subject nor tone, but the expectation (realized in the formal conclusions to literary works) that an orderly sequence would lead to a definite resolution. By extension, rebellious challenges to orderly sequence (or to what was conceived as orderly sequence) would lead, it was argued, to unnatural results. These views, affecting literary *structure*, coloured interpretations and representations of contemporary politics, religion, historical personages, nature, law. By the 1910s, however, such definitive judgments came to seem ironic. At that point, critics found ambivalent conclusions to be more realistic than fixed ones; the social climate (and with it the literary vogue) was altering once again.

Building the railroad presupposed certain ideas about nationhood and imperial connection, attitudes to aboriginal peoples and immigrants, issues involving law, language, land use, moral obligation and economic control. Railways were perceived as signs of national unity, in that they linked far-flung settlements to each other, but they were also agents of centralization. The Grand Trunk and Great Western Railways had connected Windsor to Montreal and Quebec by 1860; by 1876, as one of the terms of Confederation, the Intercolonial Railway had joined Halifax to Quebec and Montreal, effectively defining Montreal as the national distribution centre. The so-called 'National Dream' of a Coast-to-Coast link, by means of the Canadian Pacific Railway, is usually portrayed as the offspring of the Tory 'National Policy' of Sir John A. Macdonald, from the 1860s into the 1890s; it underlay many of the policies of the Laurier years as well, following 1896. Macdonald's challenge was to establish the nation's territoriality; Laurier's (1841–1919) was to ensure its continuing survival. Both visions asserted independence; but the two charted different versions of railway policy and cultural sovereignty.

Canada was expanding politically and territorially. The Canadian government purchased Rupert's Land from the Hudson's Bay Company in 1869–70, fashioning Manitoba and the Northwest Territories (Districts of Mackenzie, Keewatin, Franklin) in 1870; Manitoba became a province that same year, British Columbia in 1871, Prince Edward Island in 1873. (In 1987, discussions were underway to divide the Northwest Territories into two 'self-governing' units: the Inuit nation 'Nunavut' to the east and north, the (Indian, non-native, and Inuvialuit) 'Denendeh' in the Mackenzie Valley, to the south and west.) After the railway had been completed and immigration had increased the number of settlers in the west, Alberta and Saskatchewan became provinces in 1905. Manitoba, Ontario, and Quebec expanded to their current northern borders in 1912. These facts hide numerous tensions. The reminiscences of John Sebastian Helmcken (1824–1920), for example, published in 1975, tell of the doubts about joining 'Canada' among the colonists of British Columbia. On the West Coast some people espoused independence, while others wanted to join California; indeed many were United States citizens who had arrived for the Cariboo gold rush of 1862. But British Columbia folksongs reveal suspicions about both Canadians and Americans. 'Annexation – 1846' opens: 'Yankee Doodle wants a state, / Oregon or Texas, / Sends some squatters in it straight / And quietly annexes. ... / Canada's a pleasant place, / So is California; / Yankee Doodle wants them all, / But first he cribs a corner. ...' As independence was not economically feasible, British Columbia opted for the Canadian link; Helmcken, who was Governor James Douglas's son-in-law and chief negotiator, asked for a railway as one of the terms, expecting a wagon road instead; but his terms were agreed to. Canada needed British Columbia to establish its authority over northern North America, to preserve Rupert's Land particularly against American settlement. (The USA had purchased Alaska from the Russians in 1867, and showed clear signs of moving into the prairies.) But British Columbia refused to be merely the periphery to a centralist expansionist vision of Central Canada, and threatened to secede when the railway was not completed on schedule, expressing a regional gesture that has been repeated since in the country (in Quebec and Alberta, for example) as a way of renegotiating the political contract of federalism. Whatever the national dream, the regions saw to it that the definition of nation did not stay fixed.

There is no denying the imaginative leap of faith required to plan the rail link, or the technological skill needed to build it; the 'sea of mountains' was more than simply a rhetorical flourish, and accomplishments like the spiral tunnel through the Rockies were remarkable engineering feats. That many of the railway labourers were Chinese, brought in because they worked cheaply, points, however, to growing economic and racial disparities in the society, and to unrest. That the completion date of the railway (1885) should have coincided with the hanging of the Métis leader Louis Riel, moreover, points to another set of tensions that underlay political expansion, tensions which were economic and cultural in origin, and social and narrative in expression. Simply put, as the railway was built westward through the prairies, it took settlers with it to farm lands that were once the hunting-grounds of several Aboriginal nations and of the half-French, half-Cree Métis. With the settlers (following the establishment of the North West Mounted Police in 1873) went the arm of the law to reinforce their claim to ownership. Modern Canadians have mythologized this period of settlement as one of peaceful, orderly expansion, often contrasting it with the Wild West stereotypes of the American frontier. Yet this placid contrast ignores the way in which settlement, however legally constituted, gave the Native peoples progressively less control over their natural hunting-grounds. When Louis Riel led protests against the settlers at Red River in 1869–70, and then again at Batoche in 1885 – reinforced by the resistance of the Cree chiefs Big Bear (c. 1825–88) at Frog Lake and Poundmaker (c. 1842–86) at Duck Lake – he was acting out (as his own poems show) a personal millenarian vision. He was also insisting upon the rights of the Métis, their desire for an independent political state, their resistance to the Canada-centred idea of nation which did not recognize

the validity of their own culture. What mattered more to the Macdonald regime was coast-to-coast territoriality, but it is hard with
hindsight not to feel that the failure of negotiations with the aboriginal peoples of the West had something to do with ethnic discrimination as well as with political aspiration. The contrast between the
Métis negotiations and those of the Oblate missionaries with the
Blackfoot in Alberta is striking. In Manitoba in the 1860s, attempts to
reconcile the Métis and Macdonald claims to territory failed; Riel's
two 'Rebellions' became violent, and Riel was subsequently hanged
for treason. In Alberta, history took a different course. Father Albert
Lacombe (1827–1916), who settled among the Cree in 1852, later
authoring a Cree grammar and dictionary, managed to negotiate a
treaty with Chief Crowfoot (c. 1830–90) in 1885 when Canadian Pacific Railway and Blackfoot land claims conflicted. Historians have not,
however, ignored the irony: Lacombe avoided bloodshed, but the
Blackfoot nevertheless lost their lands.

During his lifetime, Riel was always newsworthy. The *Canadian
Illustrated News*, which was established in 1869, owed much of its success to its reporting of the first Métis protest. After the massacre at
Frog Lake, survival journals jumped into print – by Theresa Gowan-
lock (*d.* 1899), William Bleasdell Cameron (1862–1951) and others –
justifying the government's actions. But with his public death in
1885, Riel promptly became a cultural symbol, serving purposes
beyond his own. In Parliament, Wilfrid Laurier eloquently used the
Riel events to champion the causes of French Canada; Elzéar Paquin
(1850–1947), in *Riel* (1886), presented history as a four-act tragedy.
Laurier was perhaps responding most to the kinds of prejudice that
tales of Riel were beginning to feed. For example, among the earliest
of Western Canadian fictions were the works of J. E. Collins
(1855–92), whose *The Story of Louis Riel* (1885) was a sensationalist
dime novel composed in seventeen days, with an eye more on market prejudice than on history. *Annette the Métis Spy* followed in 1887.
Such books used the Riel 'Rebellion' (as in 1837 this term implies an
unstated social norm) to feed the anti-French, anti-Catholic attitudes
then current in southern Ontario.

These attitudes also underlie the intellectual tensions of the time.
To some degree they influenced the formation of the anglo-Protestant
Canada First Movement in 1868, whose organisers included George
Denison (1839–1925), Henry Morgan (1819–93) and the Ontario poet
Charles Mair (1838–1927). Although these men did not always agree
on practical policy, certain principles united them. One was a belief
in the value of continental expansion to the Ontario economy. Early
in 1869 Mair was paymaster to a crew building a road between Port

Arthur (now Thunder Bay) and the Red River settlement, at which time he published letters in the *Globe* extolling the virtues of an economy in which the West served Ontario industry. Most pointedly, Mair's brief sojourn in the West resulted in the Manitoba writer Alexander Begg's (1839–97) dismissive novel *Dot It Down* (1871). The title figure is a caricature of a Mair-like newspaperman who misunderstands the Manitoba colony, whose Ontario perceptions – material, Protestant, at least implicitly anti-Métis – inhibit his understanding. In other words, the normative values of the Canada First Movement designed a Canada in which ethnic differences would be absorbed into an anglo-Protestant norm. But in different parts of the country these norms were simply not accepted. Even the Canada First Movement did not remain united. George Denison, who went on to champion Imperial Federation, and Goldwin Smith (1823–1910), who led a campaign for economic union with the USA, indicate the contrary directions subsequently taken. In their division, the two men (who sustained a bitter personal feud) demonstrated that the problem in agreeing on the character of the Canada they wanted lay in the character of the international affiliations they took for granted.

In part as an answer to the Canada First plans for an anglophile nation, ultramontane Catholicism came in Quebec to define an alternative, papally-influenced, national design. To the Protestant Ontario mind, the idea of papal supremacy was a rejection of Canadian political independence; but as became more clearly articulated by Henri Bourassa (Papineau's grandson, 1868–1952) and the *nationaliste* movement in the early twentieth century, Quebec politicians were not seeking Rome so much as a version of Canada that was independent of the idea of Great Britain. Instead of approaching each other, the anglo-Protestants and the ultramontane Catholics both sought ratification outside the country.

In some ways symptomatic of the failure of the two sides to bridge the gap between them is the story of the national anthem. In 1880, the French Canadian pianist Calixa Lavallée (1842–91), by then a resident of the USA and the author of a comic opera, *The Widow*, composed a song for a banquet in Quebec City; called 'O Canada', its words were by Adolphe-Basile Routhier (1839–1920). The tune was popular across the linguistic dividing-line, but while various English versions (*not* translations) appeared in subsequent years, official English words were not adopted until a parliamentary committee revised the R.S. Weir (1856–1926) version a full hundred years later. Long more popular in English Canada was a song full of imperial sentiment by Alexander Muir (1830–1906), a Scottish-born Toronto school principal, 'The Maple Leaf for Ever'; written in 1867, it proclaimed Wolfe as a 'dauntless hero'. Benjamin West's (1738–1820) painting 'The Death of General Wolfe' had years earlier drawn on a parallel iconography. Depicting the 'conqueror' of Quebec as a hero had little appeal in Quebec. In practice more communication took place between anglophone and francophone Canada in the late nineteenth century than these remarks suggest – both Quebec and Loyalist Ontario were founded on structures of loss – but the two versions of nationhood spilled over into literary *topoi*; Quebec tales of martyrdom and the *maudits Anglais* countered Ontario tales of quaint habitant, sophisticated Protestant and corrupt Catholic. Prejudices on both sides fed the tales; the mistake was to accept the *topoi* of tale-telling for historical fact.

The phrase 'both sides' hints here at the beginnings of the twentieth-century notion of Canada as a bicultural state. Political rhetoric was already recognizing the balance of power between Toronto and Montreal. Both cities doubled their population in the two decades before the First World War, and with this increase in numbers came a shift in their political significance. 'Central Canada' was industrializing; power was moving from the Maritimes westward, and Ontario was looking further west for raw materials, extending its own sphere of influence over the rest of the country. Economics invited expansion through the prairies; technology made it possible (not just in the transportation system but also through agricultural research); new strains of wheat helped increase prairie production from 8 million bushels in 1896 to 231 million in 1911. But political rhetoric which attempted in advance to define the character of the new region was inadequate to describe the changing reality. While many Western settlers were Canadian-born (Ontarians and Quebeckers seeking new frontiers), many others arrived from elsewhere. Hence despite its initial conservatism, the West was subsequently to challenge the idea of the nation as a *bicultural* structure, because neither the *anglo-Protestant* nor the *ultramontane* definitions adequately included the new population of the prairies (as they did not adequately account for the black, Asian and aboriginal groups already part of Canadian society).

In the early twentieth century, the federal government saw a need to increase the prairie population; CPR Immigration posters flamboyantly advertized the West, and Laurier's Minister of the Interior, Clifford Sifton (1861–1929), who had helped to devise makeshift solutions to the Manitoba Schools Question in 1896 and the Alaska Boundary dispute in 1903, brought in immigrants from Eastern Europe and the Ukraine. Sifton wanted 'peasant stock' to work the land; if he cast an eye on future generations at all, it would appear he presumed either in anglo-Protestant assimilation or in some continuation of an agricultural peasant sensibility. But these people were, among other things, often Catholic without also being French; they resisted the prevailing stereotype. Hence subsequent generations took command of language and culture in their own ways, disputing the existing generalizations about the Canadian character and turning western literature into a rhetoric of social reconstruction.

CURRENTS OF IDEAS

In the latter years of the nineteenth century, the shaping English-Canadian ideas of the time stemmed from a group of thinkers with roots in the Maritimes, whose careers took them into the corridors of central Canadian political influence. Their ideas are explained in Carl Berger's (b. 1939) *The Sense of Power* (1970), A.B. McKillop's (b.1946) *A Disciplined Intelligence* (1979), and Ramsay Cook's (b. 1931) *The Regenerators* (1985). George M. Grant (1835–92) was born in Nova Scotia, George Parkin (1846–1922) in New Brunswick, J.G. Bourinot (1837–1902) in Cape Breton, Andrew Macphail (1864–1938) in Prince Edward Island; associated with them was Colonel George Denison, of an Upper Canada Loyalist military family, whose members were involved in the Nile expedition in 1884–5 and later still in the Boer War. All espoused the Englishness of empire. *Stewart's Literary Quarterly Magazine* (Saint John, 1867–72) also fostered imperial ideas; and George Stewart (1848–1906), the editor, went on to become a charter member of the Royal Society of Canada when it formed in 1882. Denison was the friend of William Kirby (1817–1906), Rudyard Kipling and Alfred Milner (1854–1925); he connected the imperial ideal he admired with militarism, a sensibility Macphail went so far as to encourage, finding it a 'natural' attribute in the heart of every boy. Grant, influenced by Coleridge, Carlyle (1795–1881), and the Social Gospel Movement of Henry George (1839–97), was educated at Glasgow University, ordained in the Church of Scotland, and became principal of Queen's University in 1877; an enthusiast for the Imperial Federation League, he was the author of *Ocean to Ocean* (1873), a book which resulted from a trip he took with his friend, the engineer Sandford Fleming (1827–1915), to survey a possible railway route to the West. Fleming's scheme for Standard Time Zones was subsequently adopted worldwide. Grant's book argued that the discovery of the West proved the future of Canada, foreseeing at the time how Fleming's system, operating in Canada, would turn it into a polychronic society, constantly aware of the simultaneity of difference. Unlike some of the other Imperialist idealists of these years, Grant

opposed a narrow definition of rights and liberties; he opposed Cecil
Rhodes (1853–1902), opposed prohibition, and opposed those (for
example, the Trades and Labour Council) who would have kept Chinese workers out of Canada. Grant's view of the railway was that it
was a vehicle of trade; he saw trade with China as a key to Canada's
economic future, and indeed, the 'Empress' liners of the Canadian
Pacific steamship company were built in the 1890s to carry out a
rail–sea mail delivery contract between England, Halifax, Vancouver
and Hong Kong. One effect of this development was to establish Vancouver and Victoria as substantial seaports. Victoria in particular (as
is evidenced by the newspapers and other publications of the turn of
the century, including Martin Allerdale Grainger's, 1874–1941,
engaging fiction of the West Coast logging camps, Woodsmen of the
West, 1908), became at the time a remarkably cosmopolitan centre.

In some sense the central figure in the imperialist debates was not
Grant, however, but George Parkin. A teacher, deeply marked by his
Oxford education as well as influenced by the Anglican Bishop of
Fredericton John Medley (1804–92), whose beliefs also affected the
poets Charles G.D. Roberts and Bliss Carman (1861–1929), Parkin
called himself an 'Evangelist of Empire'. Agrarian and anti-urban, he
wrote a number of books on the geography and geopolitics of empire
and on the prospects of Canadian development; his Imperial Federation appeared in 1892, written as a direct response to Goldwin
Smith's 1891 declaration in favour of closer American ties, Canada and
the Canadian Question. (Matthew Arnold, 1822–88, attributed the acer-
bity of Smith, who had emigrated from Britain to Canada in 1871, to
his isolation from the centre of empire and culture; it is a summation
that expresses exactly the kind of attitude that the imperial thinkers
accepted and that many other writers were beginning to reject. In
Quebec, the journalist Arthur Buies, 1840–1901, was praising American democracy, and championing Garibaldi, 1807–82, in Italy – for
other reasons: to oppose the clerisy more than to oppose the British,
but the two attitudes were not unrelated. Later, Buies somewhat
changed his position, espousing the idea that Quebec might prove a
utopian sanctuary from corrupted Europe.)

Parkin's two daughters socially confirmed his own political cen-
trality; one married William Grant (1872–1935), the other Vincent
Massey (1887–1967), later the author of the Massey Report on Cana-
dian culture and the first Canadian-born Governor-General. Both
sons-in-law were involved in the imperial Round Table Movement.
Named headmaster of the influential Ontario private boys' school
Upper Canada College in 1895 (a position Grant later held, 1917–35),
Parkin acquired another kind of power through the curriculum he

espoused and the people he influenced. Stephen Leacock (1869–1944), who was for a short while a teacher at Upper Canada College, took his economic theories from his teacher Thorstein Veblen (1857–1929) at Chicago, but absorbed many of his political views from Parkin. When Leacock went on to teach at McGill University in Montreal, he became a close friend of Andrew Macphail (professor of medicine, minor novelist and editor of the political and literary journal *University Magazine*); and both he and Macphail were members of the Pen and Pencil Club, along with painters Maurice Cullen (1866–1934) and Robert Harris (1849–1919) and the poet John McCrae (1872–1918). The intellectual circles were close-knit, established especially through the social institutions. And the Upper Canada College curriculum marked anglo-Protestant high culture: Parkin stressed that education was to shape breeding, character development, the qualities of leadership and a proper accent.

On the issue of accent – championing *langue* over *parole* – Parkin was bucking the trend of Canadian speech and writing. While the vernacular would not become the dominant Canadian literary mode until the 1920s, there were already signs of its persistence as the natural pattern of speech. In 1832, Rebecca Radcliff (c. 1802–74) was writing to her family in Dublin of the 'dialect and mode of expression' of the farming classes; her remarks (collected in 1833 in *Authentic Letters from Upper Canada*) show her 'amused' at sentences that begin with 'Well', at phrases like 'pretty ugly', at the idea that anyone who does no manual work should be called 'lazy', and at simple solecisms like 'dreadful good'. By the later nineteenth century, not only had local speech patterns become acceptable (no longer to be dismissed as dialect or class marker), but there had also developed (both in English and in French) a number of distinctively Canadian vocabulary items and usages: for example, voyageur, habitant, *orignal*, muskeg, lacrosse, *arpent*, sault, oolichan, muskellonge, riding (meaning electoral district), coureur de bois, corduroy road, concession line, *bois-brûlé*, Red River cart, York boat, 'elected by acclamation' (meaning unopposed), kokanee, igloo, correction line, separate school, Reserve, saskatoons. In addition there were a number of regional usages. The *Dictionary of Newfoundland English* (1985) lists some 9,000 entries in use in that one province alone.

Speech was merely one side of the imperialist argument about culture. Canadian Victorian society was publicly, institutionally, conservative and yet fascinated by technology (Prince Albert even approved of science): how could these views be reconciled? In Ontario, nineteenth-century debates between religion and science influenced definitions of an appropriate and liberal education. During the 1840s, the Anglican bishop John Strachan (1778–1867) fought the Methodist leader Egerton Ryerson (1803–82) over the issue of institutionalizing the connection between church, state and school; Ryerson's views prevailed, and neither Anglicanism nor any other religious code became an established state belief. David Willson (1778–1866) championed Quaker non-conformism, and the Methodist circuit preacher John Carroll (1809–84) wrote historical and moral sketches, often in the manner of Thomas McCulloch. *Salvation! O The Joyful Sound!* (1967) samples Carroll's articles and six books from 1852–82.

Anglicanism markedly influenced late-nineteenth-century thought when it became affiliated with the idea of natural theology. As summarized in the teachings of William Paley (1743–1805), 'natural theology' taught that external nature shows a design, reasoned that there must be a designer, therefore asserted that nature was a reason to worship God. Moral philosophy did not exclude science, hence both were deemed necessary features of a university education. Beside Paley's views were the ideas of the Scots 'Common Sense' philosophers, which were taught by William Dawson (1820–99), professor of geology at McGill (author of *Fossil Men and Their Modern Representatives*, 1880), and Daniel Wilson (1816–92), professor of ethnology and literary criticism at University College, Toronto (author of *Prehistoric Man*, 1862, revised 1876). The adherents of 'Common Sense', accepting a distinction between mind and matter, between subject and object, could reconcile science with theology by identifying the human intelligence with the Divine Mind and allowing science to describe 'objectively' the empirical world. But the consequences would be conservative. The right reason of the mind, acting upon assembled empirical data, would 'naturally' lead away from excess and relativism. The political corollaries of such a stance involved rejecting urban industrialization and praising agrarian society, and rejecting American society because it was identified with instability and industrial unrest. (Related conservative literature consequently took a particular 'Red Tory' form. In his 1859 poem *The U.E.: a tale of Upper Canada*, an epic attempt to portray United Empire Loyalist Canada as an idyllic garden, William Kirby opposed *laissez-faire* doctrine – the Spencerian idea that a millionaire was economic proof of natural selection. Charles Mair's long 1886 poem *Tecumseh* attacks American behaviour as much as it celebrates its titular Indian hero.)

When Grant, Dawson and Wilson came to review Charles Darwin in 1859, they faced a problem: how did Darwinian theory fit in with natural theology? For Darwin argued that nature did not prove a designer, but simply demonstrated its own evolving designs. Wilson, espousing *empirical* observation, dismissed Darwin because Darwin was a *theorist*; although he himself would go on to proclaim in 1873 that Caliban was the 'missing link', he distinguished rhetoric from logic by seeing the one as the art of persuading the emotions and the other as the art of appealing to the mind. Dawson, researching the nature of 'mind' (psychology being still at this time a subdiscipline of philosophy), taught that reason and morality indicated the separation of humankind from animal species, from Creation. But William Dawson LeSueur (1840–1917), an Ottawa essayist of the 1870s and 1880s, argued that morality itself had evolved as a separate objective process. By the time of the Hegelian philosopher John Watson (1847–1939, writing between 1872 and 1890) and his student, a radical Methodist social gospeller and disciple of Grant named Salem Bland (1859–1950), there was a move away from 'Common Sense' dualism towards a dialectic of progress. At the same time, science moved out of moral philosophy and into the empirical laboratory; under the auspices of a government research program, Charles Saunders (1867–1937) developed new strains of wheat for the West, and J.B. Tyrell (1858–1957), who was also president of the Champlain Society and editor of various travel journals, led Geological Survey of Canada expeditions for seventeen years. The idea of progress hit Canadian thought in several ways.

For many, science offered explanations of the environment, and technology seemed to put control over the environment into human hands. Technology also entailed other kinds of power. T. Phillips Thompson (1843–1933), in *The Politics of Labor* (1887) and his essays in the *Labor Advocate* in the 1890s, attacked Spencerian social Darwinism as a capitalist exploitation of the working classes. But the Social Gospel movement was to adapt Darwinism as an indication that there was a godly, moral force behind social change. Many people in the movement went on to social activism: the Progressive Party formed in 1919; the United Church of Canada formed in 1925 (from Presbyterian, Methodist, and Congregationalist Assemblies).

To the exponents of imperialism, from the 1880s to the First World War, progress provided a way of reading history. History could be seen at once as the repository of heroic virtues (hence a justification for a closed system of social order) and as the record of the material and intellectual advancements made possible by Protestantism. Historians from John McMullen (1820–1907) in the 1850s to William Withrow (1839–1908) in the 1870s to J.G. Bourinot in 1900 all looked at Indians and considered them a people without art, and looked at the Roman Catholic *ancien régime* of Quebec and considered it a stag-

nant civilization. Withrow praised and popularized Francis Parkman's version of French Canada, and went on to justify British imperial expansion as the force of enlightenment that would bring
progress to North America. In some sense self-justifying, this attitude
also further intensified the tensions between Ontario and Quebec.
The reverse side of Withrow's argument is more apparent in G.M.
Grant's *French Canadian Life and Character* (1899), or the historical
writings of G.M. Wrong (1860–1948), which praised Quebec agrarian
conservatism. While the aristocratic Catholic establishment was
made to signify corruption, the agrarian habitant became a symbol of
natural goodness. Such attitudes both permeated and fortified the
romantic versions of past and present which characterized the anglophone writings of the time.

HISTORICAL TALES

In Quebec the romantic versions of the past appeared in historical
tales, both in poetry and in prose. Henri-Edmund Faucher de Saint-
Maurice (1844–97), himself a volunteer in the French expeditionary
force to Mexico and the recipient of the Legion d'honneur, wrote
some ten volumes of adventures and travel impressions, a mix of his
shorter tales appearing in *À la brunante* (1874). Pamphile Le May
wrote three adventure novels, stories, plays, and over ten volumes of
poetry. Laure Conan (Félicité Angers, 1878–1925), substantially
shaped by her Ursuline education and influenced by Garneau's history, spent much of her 50–year writing career composing saints'
lives and historical tales of Dollard des Ormeaux and the battle of
Sainte-Foy. Such works characteristically made romantic heroes out
of historical individuals whose lives could be read as examples of
how people could rise above their environment. Laure Conan
claimed godliness and the lineaments of the culture as the sustaining
forces in such people's lives; in English Canada, writers more often
saw such potential for self-mastery as a sign of the way science was
giving people control over the environment. Both were expressions
of wish-fulfilment, tuned to the prevailing market; uplifting sentiments were the order of the day in popular fiction, and the criterion
which most affected critical judgments. But counter-movements in
literary fashion were already at work, leading toward the conventions of social realism and verbal and political satire.

William Kirby's 1877 novel *The Golden Dog* gives evidence both of
the conventions of romantic fiction and of the conditions that made
social realism inevitable. In itself the novel is a costume gothic, a tale
set in Quebec in 1748, just as the French colony was about to fall. It is

a tale of crossed stars, bedevilled romance, a witch ('La Corriveau'), a poison plot and an underground passage; it is also a story of specific historical personages, of immoral (or at least amoral) ambition, and of a corrupt regime that self-destructs, fulfilling the enigmatic prophecy of the Golden Dog, carved in stone on a Quebec street:

Je suis un chien qui ronge l'os,
En rongeant je prends mon repos,
Un temps viendra qui n'est pas venu
Que je mordrai qui m'aura mordu.

In Kirby's English:

I am a dog that gnaws his bone,
I couch and gnaw it all alone –
A time will come, which is not yet,
When I'll bite him by whom I'm bit.

The enmities and power struggles that divide friends and families in Quebec have their parallels for Kirby in the court of Louis XV (1710–74) and Mme de Pompadour (1721–64). While there is some question as to who runs the colony, there is no question but that such power is evil. Such forces of good as there are rest among the common people: the bourgeois fight, but are defeated, the few survivors forced to retreat or flee; the habitants, wholly powerless, by contrast, furnish a kind of chorus to the main action. Observers, they comment without affecting the outcome of the plot. For Kirby they clearly asserted the stable social voice. But that is not where the interest of readers lay; readers were drawn to the melodrama, and subsequent editions have repeatedly abridged the book to remove all passages that seem to impede the main plotline.

It is difficult to comment securely, for the text has always been uncertain. Indeed, the publication history of *The Golden Dog* points to some of the kinds of social disparity that were subsequently to make romantic writing seem politically naïve. The novel was published with Lovell, Adam & Co. in the United States, the contract specifying that the work would be copyrighted on publication. When the firm failed in 1878, Kirby enquired about his rights, only to learn that copyright had been taken out on the Library rather than on the individual book, hence the plates fell to the firm's creditors; the more Kirby sought them, the higher the price for them rose, till a new firm (R. Worthington of New York) brought out an edition later that year, with the same typographical errors as had marred the original.

Kirby's appeal to Ottawa merely got the reply that he could only have copyright in Canada if a Canadian edition or a French translation appeared. Hence the first Canadian publication was Pamphile Le May's translation of the work in 1884, one which appealed to Quebec readers because it appeared to dramatize the moral tension between Good and Evil; the novel's implicit attacks on the evils of Catholic institutions went unremarked. Meanwhile, a possibly pirated version of the novel, by Walter Besant (1836–1901) and James Rice (1843–82), had appeared as a short story called 'Le Chien d'Or' in *The Graphic* and *Harper's Weekly* in 1878. When in 1896 Messrs Knight and Son of Boston proposed an Authorized Version to Kirby, this chronicle would seem to come to an end, except that Knight & Son defined 'authorized' as 'condensed' and when Kirby objected, they advised him that he had only moral right to the text, no legal right, and they would have someone else rewrite it if he would not. When Kirby and Knight agreed finally to a 'revision' of the text, Kirby went on to add even more historical material – but the publisher replied by heavily editing the work, and Kirby called the resulting text 'a poor mutilated thing'.

Behind this sequence of events lies the history of copyright. The Imperial Copyright Act of 1842 did three things: it forbade the reprint of British books in the colonies (attempting to cut back on the number of unauthorized periodical reprints); it permitted the import of American reprints (which were often pirated) on the payment of 12 ½ per cent duty; and it discriminated against Canadian publications in so far as no adequate account was taken of the separate rights of colonial authors *vis-à-vis* British and American. (A Canadian writer could not obtain British copyright if the British considered the Canadian production below their own standards.) After independence, Canada passed a Copyright Act in 1872 that formally legalized the reprint of British authors in Canada, but the Imperial Act still contravened it. An 1875 Act allowed American authors to get Canadian copyright by means of domicile. But the United States, feeding its own national industries, insisted that foreign books had to be remanufactured in the USA if reciprocal copyright were to be respected; hence Canadian publications were still open to pirating, and in effect the Canadian native book market was passing into American hands, a fact which the foremost editor of the time, G. Mercer Adam (1839–1912) protested. Adam edited the *Canadian Monthly and National Review* (1872–8) which became *Rose-Belford's Canadian Monthly* (1878–82); he contributed regularly to *The Week* (1883–96), and co-authored (with the poet Ethelwyn Wetherald, 1857–1940) a romance called *An Algonquin Maiden* (1887). Neither Canada nor the USA signed the Berne

International copyright convention (recognizing reciprocal copy-right) in 1886; both became signatories to the Universal Copyright after 1952. Yet ownership over Canadian distribution territory remains an area of contractual colonialism (Canada is sometimes considered separate, sometimes part of 'British and Commonwealth' territory, sometimes part of 'American'). The Canadian government issued its own Copyright Act in 1921, and introduced a new law, affecting newer media, in 1987. For Kirby in 1896, however, there was no further recourse.

To place the work of Sir Gilbert Parker (1862–1932) beside that of William Kirby is to realize how popular fiction was to intensify imperial sensibilities before it would turn to other subjects. Parker's own career is a study in advancement into British circles of power. From his Anglican boyhood in Ontario he went on to a journalism career in Australia in 1885 (becoming assistant editor of the Sydney *Morning Herald*), then left for England in 1889, becoming an MP in 1900 and a British propaganda officer for North America during the First World War. He acquired a knighthood (1902), a baronetcy (1915), and membership in the Privy Council (1916). His thirty-six romances sold internationally in the thousands, his works receiving an accolade of sorts when Scribner's published a twenty-three volume 'Imperial Edition' collected works (1912–23) in the same format they used for Dickens, Meredith (1828–1909), Kipling and James.

Kirby had always insisted on the device that truth was stranger than fiction; Parker's prefaces to the Scribner's edition, by contrast, justified his own departures from fact as the prerogative of fiction. Indeed, any connection between Parker's romances and historical event is more fanciful than contrived, for Parker wielded the conventions of 'French' dialect, theatrical melodrama, picturesque description and heroic imperialism to sway a readership more hungry for the propaganda of adventure than for the instruction of history. His was a *Boy's Own* world, prepared for adults. His first book, *Pierre and His People* (1892, first published in the New York *Independent* when Bliss Carman was assistant editor there), tells a series of tales of trickery and fortitude in the Métis 'North'. Such anecdotal exploits had their enthusiasts, but they told of a territory and experience of which Parker knew nothing; they were conventions, impure and simple. *The Battle of the Strong* (1898) depicted the Napoleonic Wars, *The Judgment House* (1913) portrayed South Africa, *The Weavers* (1907) and *Donovan Pasha* (1902) both looked at Anglo-Egyptian affairs; *When Valmond Came to Pontiac* (1895) takes a 'lost Napoleon' to Quebec, a setting repeated in *The Lane that Had No Turning* (1900). Probably his most popular romance, *The Seats of the Mighty* (1896), concerns an English spy who brings about the fall of Quebec in 1759. Kirby's version of history had sought moral reasons for decay and decline; in Parker's hands, the event turns into a justification for wedding British pluck with Gallic charm and producing the great Canadian nation.

In one of his prefaces Parker praises the French Canadian for being 'essentially a man of the home, of the soil, and of the stream; he has by nature instinctive philosophy'. The backhandedness of the compliment perhaps escaped him. It epitomizes, however, the agrarian bias of the imperialist sensibility. So do the many dialect verses of W.H. Drummond (1854–1907) – 'Leetle Bateese', 'The Wreck of the Julie Plante' – which lasted well into the twentieth century as a staple of English Canadian school anthologies. Of Drummond's several volumes, two stand out: *The Habitant and other French Canadian poems* (1897) and *Johnnie Courteau* (1901). They relied on the pathos and wit that derive from any comedy of national 'types'; all that saves the verse from condescension is its personality. Dr. Drummond himself was liked, hence even in Quebec his verse was defended as 'kindly' by Louis Fréchette. *La Patrie* allowed it the vitality of travesty. Other critics have acknowledged the step it takes towards vernacular poetry. None of these defences, however, erases the attitudinal context which gave such verse its dubious social nuance.

SENTIMENTALITY, SATIRE AND SOCIAL REFORM

A distant cousin of Wilfrid Laurier, Fréchette was early influenced by Crémazie and the folk stories of the Lévis shore. After he became more involved in anticlerical and republican journalism he exiled himself to Chicago where he remained as a lawyer for five years before returning to an independent Canada in 1871 and becoming an MP. He is the author of several volumes of poetry (including *Les Oiseaux de neige*, 1880, which contains a sonnet sequence on changing Canadian nature), two plays and four volumes of satires, reminiscence and folk tale.

His plays were unsuccessful. *Papineau* was first performed at l'Académie de Musique in 1880; a parallel English play of the time, John Hunter-Duvar's (1830–99) *De Roberval*, 1888, also followed formula, arguing in an historical framework that old world corruption destroyed new world possibility. More influential in theatre history is the development of local and travelling theatre companies (the chautauqua in the West, the taste for music hall, the Princess Opera House performances in Winnipeg in the 1880s, the performances by travelling groups at the Opera House in Vancouver after 1891). Montreal boasted several formal stages by the early years of the twentieth century: Le Théâtre Nationale (1900–16), The Théâtre des Nouveautés (1902–8). Fréchette and Beaugrand were involved in bringing Sarah Bernhardt (1844–1923) to perform in Montreal (she travelled to Canada seven times between 1880 and 1916, though she met with ecclesiastically-sanctioned anti-semitic demonstrations). Fréchette (at one time a freemason) even composed a poem of welcome which begins 'Salut, Sarah! Salut Charmante Dona Sol, / Lorsque ton pied mignon vient fouler notre sol.' [Greetings, Sarah, charming "Dona Sol," /When your dainty foot comes to tread on our ground.'] Bernhardt was admired more than the poem. When Louvigny de Montigny's (1876–1955) satiric play *Boules de Neige* appeared at Le Monument National in 1903, it met a delighted response from critics and audience alike: here at last was the popular language and the local scene given literary form on stage.

There were other French language poets at the time, variously Christian and patriotic (Benjamin Sulte, 1841–1923, and Adolphe-Basile Routhier), melodramatic and historical (William Chapman, 1850–1917), and lyric (Alfred Garneau, 1836–1904, an ancestor of the writers Saint-Denys Garneau, 1912–43, Simone Routier, b. 1900, Sylvain Garneau, 1930–53, and Anne Hébert, 1916–2000), but none rivalled Fréchette as a public figure. Accused of plagiarizing Hugo (1802–85) in his poems of historical heroes (Riel, Papineau, Joliet, and others in *La légende d'un peuple*, 1887) Fréchette was critic as much as entertainer, but sometimes his efforts fell short of his intentions. Hence his *Christmas in French Canada* (1899), which he translated into French as *La Noël au Canada* (1900), a set of sketches of habitant types and customs, was attempting to give new literary life to the *conte* form. Francophone readers, however, dismissed it as a minor work, and what anglophone readers liked was its presumed quaintness. Those who praised him thought he was realistically preserving tradition. They did not recognize the politics of a folk art.

By the turn of the century, a number of essayists were attempting (unsuccessfully) to reject anglophone stereotyping of Quebeckers as simple habitants – calling it an ahistorical pastoralism. For similar reasons, Quebec intellectuals dismissed the paintings of Cornelius Krieghoff (1815–72), which won enthusiastic respect in English Canada. Like Drummond's verse, Krieghoff's portrayals of habitant households, pre-technological farms and traditional customs like 'sugaring-off' (to manufacture maple syrup) all confirmed anglophone preconceptions.

In Quebec, there had been a series of literary folk tale tellers, from Aubert de Gaspé in the early century to Honoré Beaugrand

(1848–1906), whose *La chasse-galerie: légendes canadiennes* (1900) appeared in both French and English versions. (Beaugrand, who fought for the Emperor Maximilian in Mexico when he was seventeen, was the founder of the reform paper *La Patrie* in Montreal in 1879, and author of the pro-American novel *Jeanne-la-Fileuse*, 1878.) That his collection attempted to use the language of the tale as a vehicle of real life rather than of romance is apparent from the disclaimer Beaugrand wrote to the English version of the title story (which tells of a pact with the devil that lets some lumbermen fly their canoe to visit their sweethearts): 'It is hardly necessary to apologize for having used in the narrative expressions typical of the ruder life and character whose language and superstitions it is the intention of the writer to portray.' But that Beaugrand felt he had to write the disclaimer at all suggests that he recognized a disparity between French and English readers. To English eyes, the tales of an oral culture were simply a modern equivalent of the culturally picturesque. (The many black Canadian folktales of the nineteenth century were just ignored. Even more than Aboriginal myths, they were left for anthropologists to collect; *Folklore from Nova Scotia* (1931), ed. A.H. Fauset, 1899–1983, contains a sampling.) Hence while Catholic French Canada (and the Roman Catacombs of Catholic Europe, a feature of nineteenth-century Grand Tours) continued to fascinate the Protestant English mind, sentimental views of French Canadian life were the ones that continued to prevail, asserting the cultural centrality in Canada of anglo-Protestant (and Ontario) values.

Charles G.D. Roberts wrote several romances of Acadia that parallel the portraits of Quebec. His prolific brother Theodore (1877–1953) also wrote historical tales (both for adults and juveniles) set on Atlantic shores. Set in habitant Quebec were several books of romantic tales and sketches by such writers as Jean McIlwraith (1859–1938), William McLennan (1856–1904), Andrew Macphail, John Lesperance (1838–91; *The Bastonnais*, 1877), E.W. Thomson (1849–1924), Henry Cecil Walsh (dates unknown; *Bonhomme*, 1899), George Moore Fairchild (1854–1912; *A Ridiculous Courting*, 1900), Lily Dougall (1858–1923), Agnes Maule Machar (1837–1927), Francis William Grey (1860–1939; *The Curé of St. Philippe*, 1899), Susan Frances Harrison (1859–1935; *The Forest of Bourg-Marie*, 1898), Alice Jones (1853–1933), William Douw Lighthall (1857–1954) and James Edward LeRossignol (1866–1959). The series of writers from France who produced novels out of their Canadian experience only intensified the impression of French Canada as a cultural backwater.

Louis Hémon (1880–1913), especially, publishing *Maria Chapdelaine* in *Le Temps* in 1914 and then as a separate volume in 1916, produced the single most effective confirmation of anglo-Protestant presumptions about Quebec. Hémon's heroine is a rural woman of simple abiding faith, attached to the earth, untouched by technological progress; when the young man she loves does not return to her, she marries another, refusing escape in order to tend to the demands of home. For years the novel was accepted as a faithful account of Quebec life. Similar attitudes extended to the Maritimes and the West. The several novels written by French-born Maurice Constantin-Weyer (1881–1964) and Georges Bugnet (1879–1981) confirm the West as a land of wilderness; Constantin-Weyer's *Un homme se penche sur son passé* (1928) narrates turn-of-the-century adventures, and Bugnet's *La Forêt* (1935) tells of a battle between a French settler in Alberta and the forest itself, which finally wins when the colonist's child dies.

The careers of four other writers, all born within a year of each other, provide additional paradigms of the sentimentalizing of East and West. Separately, they tell of commitment and of manipulation, of struggles to match experience with the conventions of romance, or to free experience from them. Nellie McClung (1873–1951) was born to an Ontario Methodist family and grew up in Manitoba; she became a teacher, a writer, and an active member of the Women's Press Club, the WCTU, and the Women's Political Equality League. She fought vigorously for female suffrage, and was elected to the Alberta legislature in 1921. Arthur Stringer (1874–1950), with an Ontario background, farmed for some years in Ontario and Alberta, but ultimately followed a journalistic career, leaving permanently for the United States in 1921. Robert Service (1874–1958) grew up in Scotland, emigrated to Canada in 1896 when his bank sent him there, moved to Dawson in the Yukon Territory in 1903 on another bank move (capitalizing on northern development in the wake of the gold rush), left Canada for good in 1912, kept writing his many marketable volumes of prose and verse, and settled in Monte Carlo, where he died. And Lucy Maud Montgomery (1874–1942), born in Prince Edward Island, raised there by her grandparents and resident there again from 1898 to 1911, when she looked after her grandmother, took up writing for children after a brief career as a teacher. Marrying a minister in 1911, she moved to Ontario, continuing to write many books (which increasingly carried a sentimental moral message), and she maintained a spirited intellectual and emotional correspondence (since published) with Ephraim Weber (1870–1956), G.B. Macmillan (1880–1952) and others. A 1910 work was the first Canadian book published by the recently established firm of McClelland and Goodchild (later McClelland and Stewart).

L.M. Montgomery's most celebrated work remains her first, the classic children's novel *Anne of Green Gables* (1908). It tells of a red-headed orphan girl's many predicaments in a small island town, as she struggles for acceptance at home and at school. Ironic and engaging, the book trenchantly animated the bittersweet tribulations of adolescence, and in some degree espoused the cause of women's education. A romance, it is nevertheless openly aware of the restrictions of romantic formulae. It became a successful television film in 1986, and the Charlottetown Festival has annually staged a musical version of the story since 1965. Robert Service more obviously relied on a deliberate vernacular. In *Songs of a Sourdough* (1907), *The Spell of the Yukon* (1907), *Ballads of a Cheechako* (1909), *Rhymes of a Rolling Stone* (1912) and the many subsequent volumes, Service mastered the art of combining a gruff voice with a streak of sentiment, and possessed such skill with internal rhymes ('Now Sam McGee was from Tennessee, where the cotton blooms and blows') that his verses fairly invite memorization and party performance. 'The Cremation of Sam McGee' and 'The Shooting of Dan McGrew' are the two most famous of a whole series of narrative fantasies about northern life, whose wit serves both to ingratiate the poet with his readers and to sustain an illusion of crusty Western independent-mindedness.

Like Service, Stringer manipulated his market. Known for sentimental novels like *The Mud Lark* (1932) and his 'prairie trilogy' of 1915–21, Stringer may possibly be best remembered for the 'Perils of Pauline' serials he wrote for Hollywood films. There he found an apposite medium. *The Prairie Wife, The Prairie Mother*, and *The Prairie Child*, by contrast, pretend to a realism that exists only in conception (a fashionable New England woman moves with her gruff Scots-Canadian husband to the West, the marriage falls apart, she then devotes herself to independence and her son). Nellie McClung's novel *Sowing Seeds in Danny* (1908), which sold 100,000 copies, concerns a dynamic girl's education in self-worth, sketching the ground with which the author's non-fiction was more politically to engage. *In Times Like These* (1915) is a forceful feminist credo; and two volumes of Nellie McClung's autobiography, *Clearing in the West* (1936) and *The Stream Runs Fast* (1945), tell of her own encounters with life and politicians. As with *Sowing Seeds*, the effectiveness of the form derives from the author's handling of the tale. In her autobiography she tells anecdotes, achieving political comment by witty innuendo; in her novel she is sentimental, but an effective communicator, using sentimentality deliberately to educate an entire readership to the problem of being satisfied with the political status quo. At one extreme, then, the cult of sentimentality simply perpetuated stereotypes; at the other, when it coupled with didactic satire, it invited its own demise.

Technology continued to modify the culture. The telephone (which Alexander Graham Bell, 1847–1922, developed in Brantford, Ontario, and Nova Scotia in 1876) in effect collapsed distances and speeded up time. What with an increased economic base in the cities, by the 1890s, and a continuing increase in urbanization, Montreal and Toronto maintained their influence over cultural institutions. Newspapers and journals centred in the cities; theatres were built; organizations flourished. Church, press and service clubs were all agencies of contact. The suffragist Cora Hind (1861–1942), agricultural editor of the Winnipeg *Free Press*, became president of the Canadian Women's Press Club in 1904. The Toronto Women's Literary Club, founded in 1876 by Dr Emily Howard Stowe (1831–1903), was a centre for the suffrage reform movement, aided in the 1890s by the Women's Christian Temperance Union. Halifax in the 1870s and 1880s also became a centre for a book club, a Shakespeare Society, a suffrage movement, a school of design, and the Halifax Council of women – all founded by Anna Leonowens (1834–1915), best known for her earlier experiences as a governess in Siam, which became the basis for *The King and I*. In Montreal, the 'Groupe-des-six-éponges', a coterie devoted to symbolism, rhythm and rules of aesthetic perfection, renamed themselves 'L'École littéraire de Montréal' in 1895. Founding members included Jean Charbonneau (1875–1960) and Louvigny de Montigny; supported by Louis Fréchette, other poets and playwrights were attracted to the group, including at various times Paul de Martigny (1872–1951), Arthur de Bussières (1877–1913), Gonzalve Désaulniers (1863–1934), Albert Lozeau (1878–1924), Albert Ferland (1872–1943), and most notably, Charles Gill (1871–1918), Nerée Beauchemin (1850–1931), and Émile Nelligan. (The group, never cohesive, survived intermittently till about 1935, with several new writers of the 1920s attending later meetings.) Because many city groups – the imperial federationists, the Quebec symbolists – were agrarian in vision or rural in image, much of their writing did not attempt mimetically to represent the world in which most Canadians lived. Yet it was from urban writing, from works concerned with women's status in the society, from satiric writing, from philosophic challenges to the romantic ideal of progress, and from essays like those of Arthur Buies, critical of the clerical establishment, that the most forceful checks on literary sentimentalism derived.

Comic and satiric works included plays such as Nicholas Flood Davin's (1843–1901) political work *The Fair Grit* (1876); political cartoons such as. J.W. Bengough's (1851–1923) attacks on Macdonald in the *Globe*; jokes and witty, anti-pastoral essays such as those which Peter McArthur (1866–1924) wrote for *Grip* (a Toronto comic journal) in the 1880s, for *Punch* in the 1900s, and subsequently for the Toronto *Globe* and *Farmer's Almanac*; and novels. (The bathetic verses of the 'Great Cheese Poet', James McIntyre, 1827–1906, were gloriously, if unintentionally, comic and are recounted in W. A. Deacon, 1890–1977, *The Four Jameses*, 1927). One of the most striking examples of satiric fiction was Rodolphe Girard's *Marie Calumet* (1904). Girard (1879–1956), a reporter for *La Patrie* and *La Presse*, was forced to resign from the latter paper when his novel appeared and was denounced by the Archbishop of Montreal. Girard had dared to make clerics into figures of broad humour. Though he wrote a number of other works, and though he expurgated *Marie Calumet* substantially in 1946, it is the early version of this one novel that made his name. It tells of a priest's housekeeper, who inspires lusty responses from a number of lay people in the neighbourhood, but whose own naïve admiration for all things clerical makes her treat bodily priestly functions as holy enterprises, leading the text into an earthy, scatological humour. At a conservative extreme from this work is a polemical novel called *Pour la patrie* (1895) by the Kentucky-born Quebec City journalist Jules-Paul Tardivel (1851–1905). Envisioning the nature of federalism in 1945 – fifty years ahead – the novel portrays a government secretly run by masonic satanists, intent upon destroying French Canada's character; the plot is uncovered by an MP whose fervent devotion to true (that is, Catholic) faith brings about divine intervention. Highly influential because of its separatist politics, the novel counters the biases of anglo-Protestant imperialism with the prejudices (openly anti-Protestant, more covertly anti-semitic) of another kind of religious nationalism then current. It is also an example of futurist fantasy, a form quite common as the nineteenth century came to a close.

More complex in structure and implications, James De Mille's anti-Utopian novel *A Strange Manuscript found in a Copper Cylinder* (1888) combines an attack on an unadulterated view of progress with a satiric send-up of empty academic discussion. There is some uncertainty about the time of composition; the book may date from the 1860s. Certainly in 1869, De Mille (1833–80) published both the first of his many 'Brethren of the White Cross' boys' books, *The 'B.O.W.C.'*, and his comic account of the adventures of some crafty American tourists in Italy, *The Dodge Club*. Such works, along with his romances of Early Christianity, won him a wide readership. A classics and rhetoric professor at Dalhousie, De Mille used his linguistic knowledge to compose both credible dialogue in *Strange Manuscript* and an entire invented vocabulary for the people who inhabit his anti-Utopian territory. His novel tells of Adam More, who finds himself among the 'Kosekin' of Antarctica, a people who revere self-sacrifice, poverty, darkness and death. In due course the hero falls in love with a Kosekin woman, and after a variety of adventures the two are doomed (that is, 'chosen') to be sacrificed against the coming of the season of light. Ingenious arguments resolve this dilemma, but even more comic are the authorial asides made possible by the novel's form. It is cast as a frame story – a cruising party of gentlemen having conveniently discovered the strange manuscript at sea – and the gentlemen continuously interrupt the reading of the narrative to display their own learning. The sciences of geology and ethnology come into play (where are the volcanic islands to be found? What tribal customs can be adduced to the Kosekin?); so do philosophy, theology and linguistics: is the story of Adam More, they ask, a sensational novel, a scientific work, rot-and-rubbish or a satiric romance? They punctuate their own discussion with pseudo-learned allusions to German scholarship, comparative religions and Grimm's Law. Hence the author's focus shifts from the narrative itself to the processes of constructing narrative, and the equally problematic processes of interpretation.

Beside De Mille's work, most fiction of the 1890s pales, even though much of it also strives for tonal urbanity. Writers such as Grant Allen (1848–99), Robert Barr (1850–1912) and Albert Hickman (1875–1957; *Canadian Nights*, 1914) achieved popular success. Barr produced some thirty-five novels in all, almost half of them mysteries, though *The Measure of the Rule* (1907) provides an autobiographical account of the Toronto Normal School in the 1870s. A reporter for the Detroit *Free Press*, Barr moved to England in 1881, to help found *The Idler*, with Jerome K. Jerome (1859–1927). The attractions of the mystery showed in the stories of Allen as well. De Mille had managed to parody the conventions of Poe (1809–49) and Wilkie Collins (1824–89), but Allen used them more or less straightforwardly, causing Joseph Conrad (1857–1924) to dismiss him as simply another version of Hall Caine (1853–1931) or Marie Corelli (1855–1924). In *An African Millionaire* (1897), however, Allen produced an engaging story-sequence about a daredevil thief and incorrigible con-man, which plays with narrative point of view. Behind his popular fiction, too, lies Allen's interest – a not uncommon one in the 1890s – in the paranormal. Early in his career he wrote a number of works on Darwin, physiology and psychology, and on their connection with aesthetics.

A number of writers with American connections further added to the store of works both satirizing sentimentality and probing the character of urban life, among them Alice Jones, Basil King

(1859–1928), and Susan Frances Harrison. Harrison, a composer, who also used the pen-names Seranus and Gilbert King, produced a story collection called *Crowded Out and Other Sketches* in 1886. The title story attacks the colonial-mindedness of British publishers, who are willing to accept only wilderness versions of Canada; another story, 'The Gilded Hammock', is a comedy of manners satirizing the social pretensions of New York and New England. Norman Duncan (1871–1916) produced in *The Soul of the Street* (1900) a set of vignettes of a newspaperman's life in the Syrian quarter of New York, and another set of sketches of Newfoundland outport life in *The Way of the Sea* (1903), but in both cases, despite eloquent passages, the rhetoric tends to sentimentalize the life it purports to represent. More characteristic of Duncan's work is his didactic tribute to Wilfred Grenfell (1865–1940), *Doctor Luke of the Labrador* (1904), which is not far removed from the historical tale-telling of a previous generation. In contrast, the work of Edward William Thomson moves from rural stereotype to urban disenchantment. Thomson, who in his youth fought with the Union Army during the American Civil War, was a journalist for the *Globe* between 1878 and 1891, then a revising editor for the popular Boston *Youth's Companion* for ten years before returning to work for papers in Montreal and Ottawa. An able stylist with Irish and Scots dialect, and only somewhat less so with Canadian French, he produced in *Old Man Savarin and other stories* (1895) his most notable work. The change of title when he revised the book in 1917 – to *Old Man Savarin Stories: Tales of Canada and Canadians* – suggests he recognized the romance implicit in the literary form he was using. These were *tales*, sentimental character sketches, like the title story, and basically ethnic anecdotes, like the comic 'The Privilege of the Limits', which tells how a Scots farmer redefines the landscape in order to observe the letter of the law. In revising, however, Thomson shifted the tenor of his book; he dropped two stories from the early version and added five more, among them 'Miss Minnely's Management', a satiric 1910 story in which language itself becomes the subject of fiction.

'Miss Minnely', like a number of works of this time (S.F. Harrison's among them) was also pointing to the independence of urban women. Joanna Wood's (1867–1927) Ontario novels suggested that independence was less possible in small towns, and Laure Conan's most lasting novel, *Angéline de Montbrun* (1882), probes the expectations that limit a woman's options and shape her psychological character; after the title character loses her father and herself becomes disfigured in an accident, her lover refuses to marry her, and the novel closes with her meditations on her fate, seeking a solace in religion that she cannot find in society. But clearly there were changes underway in the status accorded women in Canada. Beside Wilfred Campbell's (1858–1918) heroic poetic (and convoluted) tragedies such as *Daulac* (1897), it would be easy to place Sarah Ann Curzon's (1833–98) play *Laura Second; or, the heroine of 1812* (1887) and let it stand as simply another example of romantic historical fustian. But *Laura Secord* was less an account of the past than a prescription for the future, a commitment to a cause, like Nellie McClung's work and the suffragist battle that Emily Stowe (the country's first woman doctor) fought for forty years. As Nellie McClung's anecdotes (and various histories: for example, Catherine Cleverdon's (1908–75) *The Woman Suffrage Movement in Canada*, 1950) reveal, the progress towards electoral rights was both slow and conservative. Among writers, many women resisted the label *aggressif* and were more concerned to give other women access to the printed page than to fight for the vote. In Quebec, Joséphine Marchand Dandurand (1862–1925), who edited *Le Coin du Feu* (1893–9), and Robertine Barry (1863–1910), who as 'Françoise' edited *Le Journal de Françoise* (1902–9), were among these. 'Françoise' published some of the writings of Adèle Bibaud (1857–1941) and herself published some vignettes of rural women's lives in the 1890s. Such was the force of orthodoxy, however, that even these mild incursions into social reality were attacked by J.-P. Tardivel in his newspaper *La Verité*.

Propertied women held the vote in Quebec between 1809 and 1849, but lost it when the legislature inserted the word 'male' into the Quebec Voting Act; as this happened, propertied women in the rest of Canada acquired municipal voting rights, but universal suffrage was a long way off. In 1916, Manitoba women were the first to win the right to vote and hold office in provincial elections; Saskatchewan and Alberta extended the right later that year, British Columbia and Ontario the year following, Nova Scotia in 1918, New Brunswick (with restrictions) in 1919, Prince Edward Island in 1922, and Newfoundland in 1925. Meanwhile the Wartime Elections Act of 1917 gave the vote to Caucasian women in the armed forces and women with male relatives in the armed forces (the scheme smacked of wartime propaganda, a fillip to volunteer service), but at the same time it removed the vote from all naturalized citizens. In 1918 all adult women acquired federal voting rights, and in 1919 the right to run for federal office. The right to run for provincial office in New Brunswick, however, was withheld until 1934, and provincial voting rights were withheld from women in Quebec until the campaigns of Thérèse Casgrain resulted in an act of enfranchisement in 1940. (In parallel developments – paternalism stemming from Empire – the

Inuit did not obtain the federal right to vote until 1950, or Natives on Reserve lands till 1960). It is against this background of social opportunity, political right and legal position *before* the law – legal status *within* the law was still to wait for a future occasion – that one reads the work of an acute social observer and polished stylist named Sara Jeannette Duncan (1861–1922).

Her writing was not directly concerned with female suffrage. Yet everywhere she addressed the subjects of independence and recognition. From her own actions to the actions of her characters, from her major themes to minor asides, none was without, in the broadest sense, political intent. In her 'Saunterings' columns for the *Globe*, for example, she managed to engineer her readers' reactions to events and characters. More specifically, an apparently casual moment in *The Imperialist* (1904) shows the intelligent Advena Murchison entering a political discussion with her brother and other men; she begins 'As Disraeli said', then breaks off with a question ('wasn't it Disraeli?'), knowing full well the answer. She hates 'the note of constraint in her voice', the reduction 'to falsetto' – 'and chose, since she must choose, the betrayal of silence'. Silence, as much as speech, becomes a political decision, and the novel as a whole concerns itself with political options. In her novels and sketches, the author repeatedly plants a women in foreign territory and watches her contend, or contrasts an independent-minded woman with a more conventional one. The results are sometimes melodramatic, more often ironic or seriocomic – language being wittily manipulated to reveal the limitations of social convention and to dramatize the various kinds of prison-house (conventional language itself being one) that constrain both women and men.

To a great degree these works all discover correlatives for events in the author's own career, though none is directly autobiographical. Born in Brantford (Canada West) in 1861, and a graduate of the Toronto Normal School, Sara Jeannette Duncan soon gave up teaching for journalism, accepting the opportunity afforded by the 1884 New Orleans Cotton Exposition to attend as a freelance journalist. She is reputed at that time to have established a number of literary liaisons, with Joaquim Miller (c. 1839–1913) and others. More securely documented is her friendship with William Dean Howells, whom she met when she was an editorial writer and book reviewer for the Washington *Post* in 1885–6, and who (along with E.M. Forster, 1879–1970, whom she met in India; Henry James, with whom she corresponded; and possibly Edith Wharton, 1862–1937) strongly affected her realist style. After her year with the *Post*, she became a columnist for the *Globe* and the *Montreal Star*, all the while publishing sketches and columns (as 'Garth Grafton') in the *Week*, until in 1888, with Lily Lewis, she set off on a round-the-Empire tour. Her travel articles (later edited and fictionalized as *A Social Departure: How Orthodocia and I Went Round the World by Ourselves*, 1890) animatedly exaggerate experiences, as in an episode farcically recounting a camel race to the Pyramids. India, familiarly, was the imaginative centre to the empire. (Such fascination persisted: in Toronto in 1909, Catharine Nina Merritt, 1859–1926, directed for the United Empire Loyalist Society a performance of her own play *A Masque of Empire*, in which Dora Mavor – later Dora Mavor Moore (1888–1979) – appeared resplendently as 'India'.) In Calcutta Sara Jeannette Duncan met Everard Cotes (1862–1944), a museum official, whom she married there in 1890; they lived in Calcutta, Simla and London until her death in 1922. Cotes went on to become the editor of the *Indian Daily News* (to which his wife contributed), and Sara Duncan (now sometimes writing as 'Mrs Everard Cotes') published nearly twenty books of fiction on Anglo-Indian and Anglo-American themes.

Although the words repeatedly touched on unconventional topics – interracial liaisons, for example – they also occasionally tripped into mannered drawing-room banalities or formulaic imperial adventures. Among the stories set in India, *The Simple Adventures of a Memsahib* (1893) stands out for its evocation of the difficulties an outsider encounters when confronting a closed system like that of the Anglo-Indian community. *His Honour, and a Lady* (1896) considers Indian politics; *Set in Authority* (1906, first published in the weekly edition of the London *Times*) intertwines a story of an English prisoner in an Indian court with a story of an English mother's search for her son; the stories in *The Pool in the Desert* (1903) portray the demands of motherhood and the difficult tensions between an artist and society. Recurrently, the author is more sympathetic to the Indian community than to the rigidity of the British social hierarchy; but while she may have written from the periphery of the ruling class, she wrote also from within it. Her works were ironies of protest, but not acts of rebellion.

A similar point could be made about the political stance of the Anglo-American novels. One group of works portrays English, American and Canadian women travelling abroad. In *An American Girl in London* (1891) Mamie Wick, a Chicago baking powder heiress, announces her national identity with brash authority wherever she goes (*A Voyage of Consolation*, 1898, takes her onto the Continent); it serves her well as a defence against money-hungry Englishmen, however aristocratic they are. The English coolly discover America in *Those Delightful Americans* (1902), or at least what they take to be America. In the witty *Cousin Cinderella* (1908) a Canadian girl *with her brother* discovers England, seeking recognition and national ratification at approximately the same time. Much is defined by speech. The Canadian recognizes speech all around her, identifiable because colourful; her own seems inconspicuous, therefore easy for others to ignore. It is not the vocabulary that counts here, but the ironic tone.

Two passages from *Set in Authority* (1906) illustrate her stylistic command. The opening bristles with political judgment even while it appears to use the arch mannerisms of an aloof observer:

It would be hard to contrive a friendly description of Lady Thame's drawing-room. ... In the end it would be necessary to deny oneself emotion, and make it a *catalogue raisonné*. ... [The surroundings] spoke for so small a part of her. Her drawing-room referred to Lady Thame in much the same proportion as it referred to Cavendish-square, outside, or as Cavendish-square referred to Lady Thame in much the same proportion as it referred to Great Britain, further outside. It was quite subordinate, and the conviction that it was negligible did much to help one stay in it.

Later the 'catalogue' comes into its own, when the narrator begins to describe a small town in India and the presence within it of the ladies of the Raj; then the ignorance of the ladies as they view the world outside becomes a further political judgment which the tonal shifts in the prose amply carry:

Out there the multitudinous mud huts are like an eruption of the baked and liver-coloured earth, low and featureless; but in the narrow ways of the crowded city by the river the houses jostle each other to express themselves. The upper storeys crane over the lower ones, and all resent their neighbours. They have indeed something to say with the ... dark stained arches, pointed and scalloped, ... their gods in effigy, their climbing, crumbling ochres and magentas. They have the stamp of the racial, the inevitable, the desperately in earnest which is the grim sign of cities. ... Never is there room for the ... chaffering and calling, ox-carts pushing, water-carriers trotting, vendors hawking, monkeys thieving. ... Pariahs dash out at bicycles, there are one or two haunting lepers, and cholera usually begins there; but it has a pictorial twist and a little white temple under an old banyan tree, which the ladies of the station always praise and generally sketch.

The rush of adjectives, verbs, participles: these dramatize a people in action. The balanced opposition of the concluding phrase, however, enacts a kind of closure that has an inferential parallel in the defined attitudes and limited connections that the ladies bring to their foreign environment.

The Imperialist (1904), Sara Jeannette Duncan's most overtly political work, depicts the Murchison family of Elgin, Ontario (a loosely disguised Brantford). Young Lorne, a disciple of imperialism, is to run for Parliament, much of the book spells out policy differences between Tory and Grit and the economic underpinnings of both, one wanting a US connection, the other espousing imperial preference tariffs. Lorne is as romantically as he is politically astute: in other words, naïve. To be elected, by this time, he needs to espouse a rough pragmatism, to be, as a foppish English immigrant later avers, 'as good an imperialist ... as is consistent with the claims of my adopted country'. The Englishman subsequently gets Lorne's ambitious, money-minded, intellectually empty girl. Meanwhile Lorne's sister Advena becomes betrothed to a minister who has his own rigid idealism to contend with. A second sister, Stella, offers shrewd cynical comments on the whole proceedings. The novelist was herself attracted to the cause of Imperial Federation, but the novel is acute about social change, not a *roman à thèse*. She observes a shift from the absolutes of nineteenth-century imperialist thought to the relative values of the twentieth; without being altogether happy about what these changes imply, she enacts them in her own style. The novel opens in absolutes (*Only, never*), closes in relatives (*though, not without, or perhaps*). The literary form becomes the embodiment of a set of ideas.

As a journalist, Sara Jeannette Duncan was equally acute. Several of her articles (edited by Thomas Tausky, 1943–2001, as *Selected Journalism*, 1978) show her forthright assessments of the literary and social scene. She championed Imperial Federation, attacked philistinism, urged an international copyright agreement, recognized what the cheap availability of American magazines implied ('Once Canadian minds are thoroughly impregnated with American matter, American methods, in their own work, will not be hard to trace', 1887) challenged fads, expressed her own enthusiasms, and warned against the overappreciation of literary works on simply national grounds, as when she wrote:

We are still an eminently unliterary people.

Another Canadian summer has waxed and waned; mysterious in our forests, idyllic in our gardens, ineffably gracious upon our mountains. ...

One would naturally suppose that climatic influences, influences which produce the bodily results to be found in the average Canadian, at least conduce toward giving him an active mind as well. Physically, Canadians compare with Americans to the great disadvantage of the latter; that they do not intellectually, alas! Is not the fault of the climate.

Let genius be declared amongst us, and the market may be relied upon to adjust to the marvellous circumstance.

(1886)

SOCIAL AND LITERARY RESISTANCE

Sara Jeannette Duncan's comments did not make her a literary panjandrum. The ruling attitude of the time espoused a particular moral cause, rigid in its interpretation of the factuality of historical models, absorbed in an idea of the universe as a clockwork unity, suspicious of art, and bombastic in judgment. Such an attitude is represented by J.G. Bourinot's 1893 pronouncements to the Royal Society of Canada:

I do not for one depreciate the influence of good fiction ...; it is inevitable that a busy people, and especially women ..., should always find that relief in this branch of literature which no other reading can give them; and if the novel has then become a necessity of the time ... I hope Canadians ... will study the better models, ... and not bring the Canadian fiction of the future to that low level to which the school of realism in France ... would degrade the ... story of every-day life. To my mind it goes without saying that a history written with that fidelity to original authorities, that picturesqueness of narration, that philosophic insight into the motives and plans of statesmen ... has ... a ... much more useful purpose ... than any work of fiction. (*Our Intellectual Strength and Weakness*)

The most immediate result of this critical context was the enshrinement of a set of conventions about nature. The world of nature represented a moral crucible in which to test manliness, strength, courage, heroic resources. It was also a world of science, apparently verifiable. At a time when it was deemed Canadian literature could do no better than to imitate the proved virtue of English literary models, nature was also a subject or setting that concurrently proved Canada's distinctiveness. Hence the nature story was thought quintessentially wholesome and Canadian. The equation won overwhelming popular approval, beside which the urbane satires of Sara Jeannette Duncan or E.W. Thomson were little competition. That they have lasted better testifies both to a taste for ironic artifice in the later twentieth century and to the way in which the nature writers, even while asserting their 'scientific' accuracy, managed to perpetuate the wilderness myth of Canada that underlay so many romantic tales.

Sentimentalism and religiosity combine most obviously in the work of poets such as Marjorie Pickthall (1883–1922), where Presbyterian didacticism is never far from a set of archaisms, inversions, and expletives ('lo!'), all used in the name of an aesthetics of beauty; landscape is always an arena for moral revelation, which sometimes discloses feminist commitments (as in her late play, *The Woodcarver's Wife*, 1922) and occasionally (as in 'Pere Lalemant' or 'Quiet') gives rise to striking concrete images: 'My boatmen sit apart / Wolf-eyed, wolf-sinewed, stiller than the trees.' To Pickthall could be added the names of the Anglican canon F.G. Scott (1861–1944, father of the 1920s satirist F.R. Scott, 1899–1985), the Salvation Army novelist Agnes Maule Machar ('Fidelis'), Lily Dougall, Wilfred Grenfell (the missionary doctor, whose stories were drawn from life), the preacher-poet Robert Norwood (1874–1932), and Marshall Saunders (1861–1947), whose *Beautiful Joe*, 1894, an animal tale, won an American Humane Society contest and went on to become a best-seller. Saunders wrote nearly thirty works altogether, but repeatedly her serious subjects (animal protection, child abuse, child labour) suffer from the weight of formulaic rhetoric. The introduction to William Douw Lighthall's 1889 anthology *Songs of the Great Dominion* furnishes more evidence of such rhetoric at work, making a set of admirable virtues serve a particular and narrow image of nationhood:

The poets whose songs fill this book are voices cheerful with the consciousness of young might, public wealth, and heroism. Through them ... you may catch something of great Niagara falling, of brown rivers rushing with foam, of the crack of the rifle in the haunts of the moose and caribou, the lament of vanishing races singing their death-song as they are swept on to the cataract of oblivion, the rural sounds of Arcadias just rescued from surrounding wildernesses by the axe. ... The tone of them is *courage*; – for to hunt, to fight, to hew out a farm, one must be a man! ... Canadians are ... the descendants of armies, officers and men, and every generation of them has stood up to battle. ...

Canada, Eldest Daughter of the Empire, is the Empire's completest type!

Lighthall subsequently nods to Canada's 'strength in lady singers' and to 'the French', in part for their 'quaintness' and for the 'charming old Chanson literature' in which 'mediaeval ballads . . . are embalmed'. Even in these charged asides, he gives voice to his main theme: the distinctiveness of the *Canadian landscape* and the preservation within it of the *imperial culture* to which 'every true Briton' aspires.

Such attitudes help explain the popular appeal of the many romances of Ralph Connor (the Rev. Charles William Gordon). A devotee of 'muscular Christianity' – which celebrated the virility of religious belief, requiring the strength of civilization to be tested

against hard pioneering circumstances, and which concurrently sublimated sexuality and idealized women – Connor serialized his works
in the Presbyterian magazine *The Westminster*. In book form his first
three novels – *Black Rock* (1898), set in British Columbia; *The Sky Pilot:
A Tale of the Foothills* (1899); and *The Man from Glengarry* (1901) –
together sold five million copies, and *Glengarry School Days* (1902)
another quarter million in its first edition alone. To readers, the geographical inaccuracies of a work like *Black Rock* were irrelevant; what
appealed were the detailed memories of growing up in Glengarry
County (Canada West) and the narrative triumph of virtue.

NATURE STORIES

Beside such works, the nature stories of C.G.D. Roberts, his younger
brother Theodore Goodridge Roberts, Ernest Thompson Seton
(1860–1946), Alan Sullivan (1868–1947) and Arthur Heming (1870–
1940) all seem like objective treatments of landscape and animal
behaviour, but that is simply a relative judgment, unsustained by
analysis. They, too, were tales for the popular market. The fascination
that the mock Indian writer/naturalist 'Grey Owl' was to work on
the public in subsequent decades (the English remittance man
Archibald Stansfield Belaney, 1888–1938, was the author of *Pilgrims of
the Wild* and *The Adventures of Sajo and Her Beaver People*, both 1935),
can be traced not only to the author's physiognomy and life-style but
also to the continued public willingness to accept picturesque versions of wilderness life and native people as empirical realities.

Seton, of all these writers, is least bound by the equation between
nature and Canadian distinctiveness. As his biographer Betty Keller
observes, in *Black Wolf* (1984), his compulsive admiration for Theodore
Roosevelt (1858–1919) ultimately took him permanently to the United
States. He settled in New Mexico and took out American citizenship in
1931, but his citizenship had earlier led to a dispute of some relevance
to his work. In 1906 Seton (born Ernest Thompson, he added the
'Seton' as a rebuff to his father, whom he blamed for having diluted an
'aristocratic' background) had published a children's work called *Two
Little Savages*, which tells of two boys who live 'as Indians' and learn to
deal with the wilderness; the work describes the credo that led Seton
also to found a boys' organization he called the Woodcraft Indians, and
which was ultimately replaced by Sir Robert Baden-Powell's
(1857–1941) Boy Scouts. When the Boy Scouts of America was founded in 1910, Seton became Chief Scout, but in 1915, when Seton charged
the organization with being militaristic, the organization replied by
expelling him because he was a foreign national.

Seton's other works, both scientific and fictional, showed him to be an accomplished naturalist, and his several books of animal sketches, beginning with *Wild Animals I Have Known* (1898) were popular successes. A better naturalist than Roberts, Seton was ultimately excluded from Roosevelt's attack on Roberts and others (cited in *Everybody's Magazine* in 1907) as 'nature-fakers'. But Seton nonetheless humanized nature by giving the animals names: Lobo, Bingo, Vixen, Foam, Krag, Johnny Bear. While they are not turned into pets, the wild animals are in this way rhetorically tamed, made accessible. Thus in his Darwinian, non-judgmental, value-free, survival-of-the-fittest world, there remain parallels with the human world which are not value-free. The stories carry a covert argument.

Roberts, like Seton, coupled his observations of animal behaviour with a desire to examine what he took to be its psychology. He declared there was 'truth' to be found in nature. Roberts argued that it was not instinct alone that dictated animal behaviour but something akin to reason. Such a belief laid a complex base for readers' identification with the natural subjects. These animals, hunters all, were also victims; to identify with the one side of nature demanded identification with the other as well. What in this way could be seen as a justification of Social Darwinism, Roberts took to argue the more familiar conventions of anglo-Protestant natural theology. The ostensibly realistic tales of animal behaviour thus turned into implicit demonstrations of the spiritual reality of nature, linking a behavioural code (political and human as well as 'natural' and animal) with a literary form.

The opening of 'The Prisoners of the Pitcher-Plant' (1907) demonstrates Roberts' stylistic skill at manipulating 'scientific' diction to familiar emotional ends:

At the edge of a rough piece of open, where the scrubby bushes which clothed the plain gave space a little to the weeds and harsh grasses, stood the clustering pitchers of a fine young sarracenia. These pitchers, which were its leaves, were of a light, cool green, vividly veined with crimson and shading into a bronzy red about the lip and throat. They were of all sizes, being at all stages of growth; and the largest, which had now, on the edge of summer, but barely attained maturity, were about six inches in length and an inch and a quarter in extreme diameter. Down in the very heart of the cluster, hardly to be discerned, was a tiny red-tipped bud, destined to shoot up, later in the season, into a sturdy flower-stalk.

The mathematics, the details of the description, the term 'sarracenia': these argue objectivity; but the metaphors (swept along by the documentary surface) constitute an anthropomorphic subtext. From cloth-ing to body to heart, from early growth to young maturity, 'sturdy' but 'little': the text invites fairly conventional sympathies for human child-hood and adds to them the idea of 'destiny'. Not only in his body of animal stories (almost twenty altogether, from *Earth's Enigmas* in 1896 to his most famous book *The Kindred of the Wild* in 1902, to *The Haunters of the Silences*, 1907, *The Feet of the Furtive*, 1912, *Hoof and Claw*, 1914) but also in his less effective human romances, Roberts asserted the possi-bility of *understanding* nature. In the novel *The Heart of the Ancient Wood* (1900), a girl named Miranda (the *Tempest* analogue being modified to give her Prospero's characteristics) identifies with nature, especially with a bear. When she gives up the animals for a human connection, it reads as something of a betrayal – for Roberts the wilderness is not barbarous and to be conquered, as in so many earlier romances; it is natural. Human identification with it is therefore also natural.

Because scientific surface of Nature came to have anglo-Protestant spiritual underpinnings, Roberts's stories did not justify Darwin so much as they legitimized in Canadian writing the very landscape of Canada, by connecting it to an inheritance of humane tradition. In his introduction to *Kindred of the Wild*, Roberts specified his intent:

The animal story ... helps us to return to nature, without requiring that we at the same time return to barbarism. It leads us back to the old kinship of earth, without asking us to relinquish ... the wisdom of the ages. ... The clear and candid life to which it reinitiates us ... has ever the richer gift of refreshment and renewal, the more humane the heart and spiritual the understanding which we bring to the intimacy of it.

The breaking of one literary stereotype did not mean the breaking of all. Still trying to affirm the 'wisdom of the ages', Roberts was to con-tinue to write until he died in 1943; but already by the 1920s his ver-sion of cultural inheritance was in dispute, and the writers of a new generation – F.R. Scott and Dorothy Livesay (1909–96) – were rebelling against him.

A related process characterizes changes in the form and subject of the visual arts in these decades. From William von Moll Berczy's (1744–1813) portraits of society of the 1800s to Paul Kane's portraits of Indians and Cornelius Krieghoff's drawings of habitant life in the 1840s, the subjects of art were local, but the techniques and colour sense European. When the Governor-General (the Marquis of Lorne, 1845–1914) and his wife Princess Louise (1848–1939) founded the Royal Canadian Academy in 1880, they hoped to encourage a native art, but the institutionalizing of taste reconfirmed for another generation certain idealizing conventions of landscape depiction. Late nineteenth-century painters included Paul Peel (1860–92), Homer Watson (1855–1936), Ozias Leduc (1864–1955). Charles Gill trained as a painter in Paris before becoming a Montreal art teacher, and his wife, Gaetane de Montreuil (pseud. for Georgine Bélanger, 1867–1951), became one of the foremost early female journalists in Canada. Lucius O'Brien (1832–99), following the post-Confederation interest in the regions of the country, and enabled to travel courtesy of a railway pass, painted massive landscapes of the Rockies, sometimes to advertise the railway, exaggerating the grandeur of the mountain scenery. Robert Harris, with photographic, draughtsmanlike care, executed the formal representation of *The Fathers of Confederation* in 1883. Only with the early impressionism of Maurice Cullen and J.W. Morrice (1865–1924) near the turn of the century did traditions of *colour* and *composition* begin to change.

In some sense more radical developments took place in photography. Louis Daguerre (1789–1851) and William Talbot (1800–77) had invented photographic processes in France and England as early as 1839, and some studios were already established in Canada by the 1840s. But it was the William Notman (1857–1913) studio of Montreal, established by the 1850s, which was the most pre-eminent in Canada for the latter half of the century. Important sociologically, in that Notman chronicled royal visits, bridge openings, the funeral of D'Arcy McGee, and other events, the studio was also one of the few in North America equipped with wind machines and other paraphernalia for producing composite and retouched photographs. The Canadian government contributed to this art when it funded photographers to accompany expeditions to the West; Humphrey Hime (1833–1903) produced engineering photographs for the 1858 Manitoba expedition, and Benjamin Baltzly (1835–83) accompanied the Geological Survey of Canada to the West in 1871. Though Baltzly was an artistic exception, many early photographers were more concerned with representing technology's impact on the environment than with making the photograph itself a medium of expression. Indeed, as newspapers began to print photographs, the public image of the process was that it recorded 'reality', that it was 'scientific' and 'objective'. (This notion accorded with Roberts's techniques in fiction, persisting even after George Eastman, 1854–1932, invented the small camera in America in 1880 and control over picture-taking passed literally into the ordinary person's hand.) Notman's studio compositions told otherwise: the photographer could arrange reality for the camera as much as the artist could arrange form in paint. When Edward S. Curtis (1868–1952) produced a 'documentary' motion picture film of the Kwakiutl Indians in 1913, it was all theatre, tradition re-enacted for the camera. Photographers in control over their apparently documentary technique could make it a medium of entertainment, full of atmospheric evocation yet also capable of subtle but persuasive emotional and political argument.

CONFEDERATION POETS

In the world of the Confederation Poets, the tensions between technological change and notions of ideal values found further expression. The most important Canadian poetic movement of the nineteenth century, the Confederation Group – so-called because its 'members' were all born in the 1860s – involved Sir Charles G.D. Roberts (1860–1943), his cousin Bliss Carman (1861–1929, a distant relation of Ralph Waldo Emerson, 1803–82), Archibald Lampman (1861–99), and Duncan Campbell Scott (1862–1947). They constitute a 'group' more for the purposes of literary classification than for any shared cause, though they were all shaded by the late-Victorian romanticism of Tennyson and the American Transcendentalists. To their number are sometimes added the names of Isabella Valancy Crawford (1850–87), Wilfred Campbell (1858–1918), and more rarely George Frederick Cameron (1854–85). Cameron was the least connected with the others and the most classically inclined; his few lyrics, collected posthumously by his brother as *Lyrics on Freedom, Love, and Death* (1887) reveal a skilled lyricist deeply troubled by the age in which he lived. An Arnoldian pessimism coloured the work of Lampman and others as well, though none of the writers was without joy. Their imagery and cadences spoke, however, more often of tension, in which the character of their closing century was out of kilter with the ideals that their culture had led them to perceive as the actuality of times past.

The paths of these writers variously crossed. Roberts and Carman came from Fredericton. Scott was an Ottawa Methodist minister's son, who joined the federal civil service in 1879 when his father asked the prime minister, Sir John A. Macdonald, to give him a job; he rose to become deputy superintendent of Indian affairs in 1923. Lampman was from Morpeth, Canada West, and like I.V. Crawford (Dublin-born, she had emigrated to Canada West when she was eight), he knew the Strickland sisters. Crawford's impoverished family moved house often, ending in Toronto. Lampman joined the Post Office branch in Ottawa in 1883, where he became a friend of Scott's and of E. W. Thomson's. He read Roberts's first book, *Orion* (1880) 'in a state of the wildest excitement', cheered by the fact that a countryman of his own generation displayed such lyric intensity, and he was thereby himself encouraged to write. Campbell was the son of an Anglican minister in Berlin, Canada West (a town which changed its name to Waterloo during the First World War), who went on to join the priesthood, only to give it up in 1891 and enter the Ottawa civil service. Carman became a journalist with such American papers as the *Atlantic Monthly* and the Boston *Transcript*; he lived out his life in New England, but he published his first poem in the *Week*, Goldwin Smith's Toronto paper, when Roberts was the editor. Roberts resigned from the *Week* in 1885, disagreeing with Smith's political views, then went on to become a Nova Scotia teacher and a professional writer in New York (1897–1907) and London (1907–25), before returning to Toronto. Lampman published verse in a variety of periodicals, including the Boston *Youth's Companion* when Thomson was an editor. Scott, Lampman and Campbell severally wrote a weekly column for the Toronto *Globe* in 1892–3. (Called 'At the Mermaid Inn', a selection of the columns was reprinted in 1979, sampling the poets' views on poetry, beauty, politics and religion. Lampman wrote on the sonnet; Campbell caused a stir when he classified Old Testament stories as forms of mythology; Scott wrote whimsically on the character of time and dreaming.) Scott edited a memorial edition of *The Poems of Archibald Lampman* (1900), altering a number of verses to bring them into line with his own sense of good taste. John Garvin's (1859–1935) inaccurate edition of I.V. Crawford's *Collected Poems* appeared in 1905, with an introduction by Ethelwyn Wetherald. *The Poetical Works of Wilfred Campbell* appeared in 1922. Duncan Campbell Scott's *Selected Poems*, with a memoir by a friend of his later years, the young critic E.K. Brown (1905–51), appeared in 1951. *The Poems of Sir Charles G.D. Roberts*, a critical edition prepared by Desmond Pacey (1917–75), was brought to publication by poet-critic Fred Cogswell (b. 1917) in 1985.

These comments suggest the kind of coalescence that was occurring in English–Canadian culture by 1900, and the beginnings of a sense of a tradition rooted in place as well as in time; they also point to the continuing link with Britain and the growing links with the United States: there were many family connections between New England and the Maritimes, and also between Quebec and New England as people moved off the land and (changing their names, for example *Leblanc* to *White*) entered the American mainstream. In many respects illustrative of late Romantic literary conventions outside the country – regular verse form, high ethical tone, pantheist sentiment, elevated diction – Confederation poetry also struggled with many Canadian dilemmas, especially those created by imperial conservatism, by the contrast between urban life and the values attached to rural poetic imagery, and by the disparities between literary land-scape conventions and empirical landscapes. These dilemmas showed in shifts of subject, in the handling of form, and in a variety of inconsistencies of stance. Though Scott was the most innovative stylist, Crawford most openly displays the poetic effort to find an appropriate form. Roberts wrote patriotic verses celebrating Canada, but Campbell more clearly reveals the tensions between imperial desire and colonial resentment. In the work of Roberts and Lamp-man, the pleasure the poets took in nature reveals itself in a detailed descriptive diction, which never quite succeeds in erasing their uneasy sense that beauty and harmony are illusions and dreams. Both writers ultimately resist identifying with nature – retreating to discretion when faced with adventure. (Even Lampman's late-dis-covered love poems to Katherine Waddell, 1865–1926, written while he was still married to Maud Playter, 1869–1910, burn with a careful flame; and Roberts's poems, like his animal stories, cast the persona in the observer/recorder's role.) Carman, by contrast – as his essays in *The Kinship of Nature* (1903) and other books declare – deliberately embraced adventure, using rhythm as an incantatory means to escape the constraints of logic and care; but the resulting verse, despite his energy and lyric ebullience, was sometimes less than melodious.

The scholarly study of Isabella Crawford's verse currently demands reference to her manuscripts in the Douglas Library at Queen's University; too few of the published texts can be relied on. One of her most sustained lyric passages, 'Said the Canoe' – 'My mas-ters twain made me a bed / Of pine-boughs resinous, and cedar' – may well be part of a longer narrative. Many of her other lyrics, from 'Love Among the Roses' to 'Baby's Dreams' and 'The Mother's Soul', adopt the sentimental convention of Victorian drawing-room melo-drama; dead mothers, fairy flowers, stags and thorns and hidden loves: the motifs in part reflect the historical high incidence of puer-peral fever and infant mortality, in part project a sublimated sexuali-ty. Heroic and dialect poems – involving Mavourneen, Gisli, Vashti and Caesar – are largely exercises in the manner of others, though one of the longer poems, 'Old Spookses Pass', is a comic narrative of a stampede in the Rockies, told in an assumed Western vernacular. The most substantial work, 'Malcolm's Katie', is also one of the most uneven. Repeatedly breaking into lyric songs and striking images, the poem is for the most part a blank verse narrative (with *Hiawatha* rhythm interruptions) telling of an Edenic love between Katie and Max, a love threatened by an evil villain named Alfred, who is finally overcome. By one reading, the story is all pathos, reminiscent of Goldsmith's 'Rising Village'. Other critics (following James Reaney, b. 1926) have endeavoured to read the poem for its mythic structure, to accept the open artifice of the drama and the dialogues as a simple vehicle for another concern. By such a reading the conflict – reiterated in the seasonal cycle:

> In this shrill moon the scouts of Winter ran
> From the ice-belted north, and whistling shafts
> Struck maple and struck sumach, and a blaze
> Ran swift from leaf to leaf, from bough to bough,
> Till round the forest flashed a belt of flame

– becomes a Jungian design. Summer and winter (light and dark, good and evil) must acknowledge their interdependence. In the narrative, Max and Katie ultimately name their child after the villain whom they survive.

The more theatrical Carman collaborated with the American poet Richard Hovey (1864–1900) in *Songs from Vagabondia* (1896), a volume with many sequels. It celebrated the free life, one that equated the open road with spiritual accomplishment, and rhythm with emotional insight. The title of a later volume, *The Pipes of Pan* (1906), hints at another expression of the *fin-de-siècle* style Carman carried flamboyantly into the new century. It was a style affected by one of the many semi-theosophical movements that were fashionable in the 1890s: 'Unitrinitarianism', a doctrine of nature, mind and spirit, to which he had been introduced by his companion, Mary Perry King (1861–1939), and by Hovey's wife Henrietta (1850–1918). With Mrs King, Carman wrote two dramas to express these notions: *Daughters of Dawn: a lyrical pageant or series of historical scenes for presentation with music and dancing* (1913) and *Earth Deities, and Other Rhythmic Masques* (1914). Sound ruled sense. More effective is the title work from *Low Tide on Grand Pré* (1893), which won immediate approval from James Russell Lowell (1819–91) when it was first published in the *Atlantic Monthly*. A poem of lost love, of grief at remembering the past and a life no longer retrievable except through grief, it rises through its images to heights of emotional intensity:

> Was it a year or lives ago
>   We took the grasses in our hands,
> And caught the summer flying low
>   Over the waving meadow lands,
>   And held it there between our hands?

Through its title, too, it hints at the Acadian Expulsion as a particular historical context for its archetypal conflict. It was an achievement Carman only approached again with the love lyrics of *Sappho* (1904).

He was the most popular of the Confederation Group in his own day – called Canada's 'poet laureate' by the press and anthologized in school texts for poems like 'The Ships of Yule'. As late as the 1920s, Carman (like his imitator, Wilson MacDonald, 1880–1967) crossed Canada on reading tours, appealing to audiences keen for notions of mystic understanding, intuition and sonority. Such aesthetic criteria were already being disputed by symbolists such as Nelligan, by poets such as Frank Prewett (1893–1962), who was on the fringes of London's Bloomsbury movement, and by the early modernists of the Eastern Townships (Frank Oliver Call, 1878–1956, Louise Morey Bowman, 1882–1944). That they nevertheless persisted suggests the conservative character of Canadian institutional fashion, the faddishness of theosophy and spiritualism, and also a continuing desire for security in the face of the kinds of change that were occurring in the material world. By 1905 the Curies, Einstein (1879–1955) and Max Planck (1858–1947) had introduced ideas of radioactivity, relativity and quantised energy that would alter peoples' understanding of the nature of matter. Nor was Canada uninvolved. The 1908 Nobel laureate, New Zealand-born Ernest Rutherford (1871–1937), developed his distinction between alpha and beta particles of radioactive decay while working as professor of Physics at McGill University, between 1898 and 1907. The very nature of science was changing; 'laws' were no longer laws: Newtonian determinations of the physical structure of reality could not explain the atom. The new physical world, still but dimly understood, was in constant motion, its truths relative, its nature unstable. Beside such ideas the world of the spirit could still be claimed to be eternal. The idea of Classical Verities, however, so appealing to literary tastemakers, came to seem like another romantic tale.

This tension between ideas of change and eternity surfaces repeatedly in Confederation poetry. Both Lampman and Roberts show signs of their Victorian education in the classics – like Carman, Roberts had been a pupil of George Parkin – and their poetic subjects, like their modes of technical experiment, hint at Tennyson (1809–92), Macaulay (1800–59) and Arnold. Classicism did not extend particularly to attitude. Lampman, from *Among the Millet* (1888) to *Lyrics of Earth* (1895) and *Alcyone* (1899), wrote of 'Xeonaphanes', 'Chione' and 'An Athenian Reverie' with the same attitude he took to Arabic and Icelandic subjects: here were conventional contexts for reflecting on romantic choices. Roberts's 'Memnon', 'Ariadne' and 'Marsyas' similarly evoke the poignancy of the emotional moment more than they attempt to portray through character any eternal forces of fate and circumstance. Hence these poets adopted the form of the monologue but without much of its drama; the poetry of their stance lay in the mollifluousness of line and the fact of observation in its own right.

In the Canadian environment, they sought contextual equivalents for these same stances; both found them in stories of Indians (Roberts versifying Malecite tales of Gluskap, and Lampman invoking Mani-tou), in the landscape (rivers were particularly attractive, but they inherently implied movement, change), and in the heroic version of Adam Daulac's (1635–60) doomed defence against the Iroquois at the Long Sault. Both tried their hands at nature sonnets, but portraying landscape was not an end in itself; it was a way of using the external world to probe what was conceived as a parallel condition inside the human breast. As Lampman wrote on 25 April 1889, to his friend Hamlin Garland (1860–1940), who had challenged his poetic tech-nique: 'My design ... in writing "Among the Timothy" was not ... to describe a landscape, but to describe the effect of a few hours spent among the summer fields on a mind in a ... despondent condition. The description of the landscape was really an accessory to my plan.' Such a distinction emphasizes (despite the parallel) the continuing separation between man and nature, and reinforces what for both poets would be the discomforting role of onlooker. Both felt ill at ease with the kinds of change they observed in society.

Lampman lived for a dream of peace and harmony, in his later years even taking up the ideas of Fabian socialism. 'In November' closes with a person 'alone / ... neither sad, nor shelterless, nor gray, / Wrapped round with thought, content to watch and dream.' But this dream proves transitory. 'The Land of Pallas' (a Tennysonian vision of the future) anticipates a time when 'the traps and engines of forgotten greed, / The tomes of codes and canons' will be aban-doned, kept only to remind the young and the restless of 'the world's grim record and the sombre lore', but when the poem's traveller-in-dream returns to the present, he is considered an anarch for preach-ing peace. An evocative sonnet called 'Winter Evening' reinforces this result, ending: 'Glittering and still shall come the awful night'. 'The City of the End of Things', an even grimmer vision of social desola-tion (which appeared first in the *Atlantic Monthly*), closes intoning that only 'the grim Idiot at the gate / Is deathless and eternal' in the technological future. The eternity bred of (social, moral) decay holds little attraction, and despite the mellow music of so many of Lamp-man's lines, the prevailing note he sounds is one of despair.

Roberts (who published twenty-one volumes of poetry during his lifetime) crossed the chasm to the world of the new technology more securely. His 1904 poem 'Monition' shows his awareness of mutability ('A faint wind, blowing from World's End, / Made strange the city street'), but Roberts was also able to derive pleasure from the urban landscape, as 'Brooklyn Bridge' and 'On the Elevated Railway at 110th Street' reveal. At the same time, he was immersed in the values of his age. He could write a stirring ode for the Shelley centenary ('Ave!' 1892), celebrate General Gordon (1833–85) at Khartoum, translate lyrics from Louis Fréchette. And he could eloquently adapt classical metrics to English, as he did with the elegiacs of one of his most sustained works, 'Tantramar Revisited' (1883), which opens: 'Summers and summers have come, and gone with the flight of the swallow: / Sunshine and thunder have been, storm, and winter, and frost. ...' The repetitions, the rhythm, the line length, all conspire to suggest the spatial distance associated with the subject – the tidal flats of the Tantramar Marshes – and the temporal distance implied by memory. Once stirred to 'rapture' by living in this place, however, the poet now experiences it as *scene* rather than *activity*, and he resolves finally to stay his steps, not revisit it in fact, but

> Muse and recall far off, rather remember than see, –
> Lest on too close sight I miss the darling illusion,
> Spy at their task even here the hands of chance and change.

In 'The Skater' (1901), too, the persona, speeding to the heart of the wilderness, turns away at a critical moment, resisting transformation; 'I turned and fled, like a soul pursued, / From the white, inviolate solitude.' Almost as though he were posing the same dilemma that the quantum theorists were trying simultaneously to resolve, Roberts was ratifying the outer world, but resisting the world of inner space which threatened its substantiality. That his poems should nonetheless claim to be expressions of the self has certain political as well as personal implications. A perspicacious observer of natural detail, Roberts adapted received forms to local occasions and local values, and renewed the life of the old forms by means of his accurate local diction. But he was no rebel. His poems give credence to the Canadian landscape as a setting for poetry by making it seem respectable, not by describing it in a distinctively new way. His resistance to the psychological implications of his images shows him to be a man of another age, for whom 'rather remember than see' was a sign of literary persuasion as much as a statement about a momentary choice.

If the poems of Duncan Campbell Scott appealed more to later twentieth-century readers, that is not because Scott was more revolutionary in belief (a conservative civil servant, he opposed 'irrationality' and approved the orderly extension of 'civilization' to 'primitive' peoples), but because he was more adventurous with form. He did not hide his lack of empathy with organized religion, or (even in his biography of Governor Simcoe) with the supercilious Britishness of certain elements in his culture. Fabianism attracted him. But so did the Romantic attitudes of the Pre-Raphaelite brotherhood, and such words as 'rhapsody', 'dream', and 'compline', which give his work its studied melancholy, testify to his sense of evanescent beauty. The musical allusions – reed-players, piano, lute, 'Fantasia', Adagio' – at once echo this sensibility (music being an aural process, a ringing of changes) and indicate one source of Scott's skill with lyric form. A musician himself, he relied on cadence as well as rhyme, but not on the incantatory effect of rhythm, as Carman did. Even when 'Powassan's Drum' does employ deliberate drum beats, Scott's purpose is more resistant than submissive, concerned to warn against the dangers of 'primitive' superstition. Through recurrent aural motif, often combining lines of unequal lengths (as in 'Night Hymns on Lake Nipigon'), and by breaking rhyme free from regular metric patterns, he made the phrasing of his poems serve his effects. A combination of free-flowing and occasional-rhymes, for example, marks the dramatic and cumulative tensions of 'At Gull Lake: August 1810' (a poem from his late collection *The Green Cloister*, 1935); comparably, a vernacular dramatic monologue called 'At the Cedars' (*The Magic House*, 1893) tells with spent breath of a Quebec raftsman's accident:

> The whole drive was jammed
> In that bend at the Cedars,
> The rapids were dammed
> With the logs tight rammed
> And crammed; you might know
> The Devil had clinched them below.

Scott's poems are aural works, asking to be heard. Conscious of change and loss, Scott himself sought in practice to find ways of linking an aesthetics of contemporary speech with the aesthetics of beauty to which his education and inclination had trained him.

The French-language poets of the turn of the century similarly looked to nature for equivalents to emotional experience, and in so doing extended the influence of the French poets Lamartine (1790–1869) and de Musset (1810–57) in Canada. Eager to avoid 'canadianismes' and 'anglicismes', they strove for artifice, contributing tangentially to a poetics of landscape in Quebec. Among them

were the writers of the École Littéraire de Montréal. Arthur de Bussières wrote sonnets. Nerée Beauchemin wrote descriptive lines on
the seasons, flowers and their emotional (joyous, melancholic) coun-
terparts. But the verse forms were conventional and the diction often
strained. Of more poetic and cultural significance is Émile Nelligan.

THE NELLIGAN SYMBOL

Émile Nelligan was born in Montreal in 1879, tracing his heritage
(like many in Quebec) to Irish as well as *québécois* roots. But he lived
for most of his life as the victim of a different kind of division; schizophrenic, he was incarcerated in the Retraite Saint-Benoît from 1899
to 1925 and l'hôpital Saint-Jean-de-Dieu from 1925 to his death in
1941. He wrote poetry for three years only, 1896–9, from the ages of
sixteen to nineteen (his hospital notebooks remain unpublished), and
he became one of the most striking influences on twentieth-century
Quebec culture. Partly this recognition of Nelligan as a cultural
emblem stems from the symbolic force of division and unfulfilled
desire; there is scarcely a commentary that does not refer more to
Nelligan's 'tragic destiny' than to his illness. A Nelligan figure
appears in novels by Réjean Ducharme (b. 1942) and Lazar Sarna (b.
1948); he is the subject of a ballet by Ann Ditchburn (b. 1949) and a
performance by Monique Leyrac (b. 1928). Music by Claude Léveil-
lée (b. 1948) and André Gagnon (b. 1932) alludes to Nelligan; plays
by Armand Laroche (b. 1949; *Nelligan blanc*, 1981), Michel Forgues (b.
1945; *Émile-Edwin Nelligan*, 1981) and Normand Chaurette (b. 1954;
Rêve d'une nuit d'hôpital, 1980) use the poet's madness as a way of dramatizing the dislocation of meaning. The Prix Émile Nelligan was
first given in 1979, and there was even a Montreal restaurant named
after his most famous sonnet, 'Le Vaisseau d'or'. Nelligan's literary
reputation, which steadily increased during the twentieth century,
has to do with the way he can be seen to have combined the Romantic and Parnassian movements in French poetry with the symbolist
work of Verlaine (1844–96) and Baudelaire (1821–67). He admired
Poe, Dante, Chopin. The brief association with the École Littéraire de
Montréal (to which his friend Arthur de Bussières introduced him)
gave him a place to read his work – he published his first poems in
Le Samedi under the pseudonyms Émile Kovar and Émile Lennigan –
and in 1903 his friend Louis Dantin (Eugène Seers, 1865–1945)
brought out a volume of his poetry; a critical edition of the *Poésies
complètes*, edited by Luc Lacourcière (1910–89), appeared in 1952. He
used conventional forms – nearly half of his 168 poems are sonnets
and rondels – but he played with language. His was a literary world;

his symbols and settings (from Spanish castles to Louisiana) derived from reading, memory and dreams.

Literature was, it appears in retrospect, an escape from reality; there was 'too much reality' in contemporary life and the Canadian winters, and therefore it was preferable to live in the world of dream. Unfortunately, the world of reality seemed to follow him there. His poems are haunted by a Catholicism that does not seem to comfort him, and by a melancholia that expresses itself in images of garden, chapel, ruins, wood and autumn evening. Even language proves claustrophobic. For example, a late poem, 'La romance du vin', struggles for joy, but the gaiety declares itself to be false: shouting 'Vive le vin et l'art! ... / J'ai le rêve de faire aussi des vers célèbres' ['Hurrah for Wine and Art!': 'I dream of also composing celebrated verse'], these lines also lament 'les musiques funèbres', 'Des vents d'automne' ['Funeral Music', 'Autumn winds']. Simply by naming these titles (of poems Nelligan had previously written), the new poem denies its own freedom. 'Clair de lune intellectuel' asserts the poet's predicament; 'Ma pensée est couleur de lunes d'or lointaines' ['Intellectual Moonlight': 'My thought is the colour of golden distant moons']. Everything is far away. Gardens belong to yesteryear; childhood has passed by; castles are for the traveller; 'Eden' is in Louisiana; the mother who might protect him would also enclose him; indeed, the whole world is a 'jardin clos', against which he protests, but about which he can do nothing, because the language that he sees as his medium of escape is the very medium that perpetuates constraint. The poet moves therefore not towards an exorcism of his personal demons and his nostalgia but towards a greater sense of entrapment, mortality and hallucination.

'Le vaisseau d'or' traces this progress within the compass of a single lyric. The first quatrain symbolically establishes a ship as a romantic conveyance for the artist's dreams; the images invite pleasurable associations – 'azur', 'amour' – echoing each other. In the second quatrain a different association takes over; the ship must sail on the sea, where the Siren sings, drawing sailors towards the Gulf. The sestet then comes aboard, discovering that the sailors are not romantic at all, but profane, named 'Dégoût, Haine et Névrose', quarrelling amongst themselves over the prospects of treasure. The closing tercet directs the symbol back to the poet and his split self:

Que reste-t-il de lui dans la tempête brève?
Qu'est devenu mon coeur, navire déserté?
Hélas! Il a sombré dans l'abîme du Rêve!

['Disgust, Hate, Neurosis': 'What remains of
him after the brief storm? What has become
of my heart, deserted ship? Alas! it has sunk
in the abyss of Dreams.']

In different circumstances, despite its verbal skills, such a poem might
fail to draw much attention, for in many ways it describes a conventionally romantic artistic stance: the suffering poet in conflict with the
material world and his own soul. What Nelligan represented to others,
however, was rather more: the power of the symbol and the potential
independence of language. Through Nelligan, poetry in Quebec
became a psychological art, not unaware of the political contexts of
writing, but not bound by mechanistic determinations of reality.

SKETCHES OF REALITY

The Confederation Poets were never so undermined by their personal dreams as Nelligan was, neither did they ever obviously enter the
world of language as he did, nor identify with words; they stayed on
the outside as though preserving control over them, ensuring that
words remained the agents of a pictorial purpose. For them, words
could engender feeling, create in the reader, by means of image and
musing, a sensibility that led on to understanding. Such understanding is a result rather than a part of the verbal process. Even Carman's
incantations and Scott's cadences relied on empirical associations. In
Nelligan words were artifice, and artifice real. In some ways the closest the Confederation writers ever came to this position was in their
prose, particularly in the sketches and stories of Duncan Campbell
Scott, which let verbal form enact psychological character. Partly for
this reason, Scott emerges as the chief short-fiction writer in Canada at
the turn of the century, the one writer who turned the genre into its
modern form. Ironically, his accomplishment was also long misrepre-
sented; the imperial bias intervened. Readers as late as the 1960s
responded conventionally to 'local colour'. Scott wrote 'about' French
Canada, 'therefore' portrayed the 'idyllic' character of village life and
folk custom. While not without its share of stylistic archaisms, his
mode was not the idyll, neither did he use the characteristic formulae
for sentimentalizing Quebec. In Scott's work, the church plays little
part in village life, but commerce does; the village and the frontier out-
post are never far from urban values. His vignettes are small dramas
of life on the boundary between love and psychological violence.

Scott was not the only short-fiction writer to address Quebec, Indian and frontier themes. But just as the conventional Quebec story
sentimentalized habitant life, so the conventional frontier story was a

romantic tale in form, even when claimed as true-life adventure. William Bleasdell Cameron, for example, the journalist who reported on Riel, even became editor of the New York magazine *Field and Stream* in 1898, publishing adventure stories derived from his own life. Most frontier stories were potboilers, such as Frederick Niven's (1878–1944) first novel *The Lost Cabin Mine* (1908), a testament to the appeal of 'Deadwood Dick' stereotypes. But Scott (after his initial forays into tale-telling, as in 'The Ducharmes of the Baskatonge', *Scribner's*, 1887) escaped these constraints. When he turned to the trading post, as in 'Labrie's Wife' (*The Witching of Elspie*, 1923), he focused on a factor's egotism, his failure to deal emotionally fairly with his co-workers, and his failure to appreciate either the signs or the dimensions of love. In the title story of *Elspie* and in 'The Pedler' (*In the Village of Viger*, 1896) Scott dealt with the presence of evil. In 'No. 68 Rue Alfred de Musset' he let a woman's cruel ambition speak for itself.

Thus while Roberts and Seton were developing the animal story, and Beaugrand was reanimating the folk tale, and Thomson was moving toward his trenchant ironies, Scott was experimenting with the effects of prose conventions. 'Labrie's Wife' turns the journal from a medium of objective documentation into a process of subjective revelation, the scope of which the narrator does not realize. 'The Witching of Elspie' and 'The Pedler' show how the folk tale gives the illusion of charming simplicity but encapsulates extraordinary acts of cultural violence. 'The Wooing of Monsieur Cuerrier' is a comic anecdote, its light touch allowing love to conquer petty jealousy in one swoop. 'Josephine Labrosse' is a sketch.

While the sketch form was generally considered a journalistic *feuilleton* or descriptive filler, it was the prose form that in Canada provided the main check on the excesses of the romantic tale. Through it, the documentary method that dealt most directly with Canadian subjects (the tale having been an imported scheme that perpetuated romantic stereotypes) entered Canadian short fiction. Plot was minimal; character existed in outline; story existed by implication. Fictional drama lay in perception. Such a form was to be distinguished from characteristic American short stories, full of plot and person, and also from the historical narratives characteristic of short fiction in Britain at the time. But it was not to be divorced from these other patterns, which still had their impact on Canadian writers.

Much as Haliburton's *The Old Judge* had done (or, in another context, Turgenev's (1818–83) *A Huntsman's Sketches* in 1852), Scott's *In the Village of Viger* brought together several prose forms into a single book. His short story sequence was unified neither by characters (though some recur) nor by plot, but by its expanding setting, and by the implications of the structural arrangement itself. The narratives comment on each other, most notably in the centre of the book, where the most sentimental fable, 'The Bobolink', is positioned adjacent to the most calculatedly ironic, 'No. 68. ...' Interpreting the charm of innocence in the one has to take into account the force of cold-hearted manipulation in the other; more broadly, the pastoral version of life has to take into account the violent underside of pastoral. That was what made Scott's sketches of rural Quebec so markedly unlike the local colour idylls of others. He was using the verbal structure of narrative sketch to prove what he took to be the realities of social co-existence; the structural cycles of *In the Village of Viger* argue a moral theme: that knowledge without feeling is sterile, callous. But given its setting and the attitudinal context in which it appeared, the book implies a political and psychosexual theme as well: that emotion without knowledge is self-destructive. With the popular success of the nature and animal stories, however, wilderness conventions were to remain for awhile the literary vogue, eclipsing Scott's nascent social modernism. And with the emergence of Stephen Leacock as a comic entertainer, the voice of the anglo-Protestant empire was to be heard from yet again.

Leacock was born in Hampshire in 1869 and moved to the Lake Simcoe area in 1876 when his father (who had already failed as a farmer in South Africa and Kansas) decided to try again there. Again the father failed, shortly abandoning his wife and eleven children, and heading out to the North West. Poverty was not at issue; Leacock's paternal grandfather sent an allowance, and in due course Leacock attended the prestigious Upper Canada College, the University of Toronto (taking a degree in modern languages), and the University of Chicago. He then took up his position as professor of political economy at McGill, and wrote what was to be his most profitable book, *Elements of Political Science* (1906). Fired with a belief that anglo-Protestant civilization represented the acme of progress, he toured the empire in 1907–8 to speak on behalf of the Imperial Federation Movement. He began also to make a name as a writer of funny sketches and as a comic lecturer. Typically, these sketches would appear in magazines (*Grip, Saturday Night*) then be collected in book form annually in time for Christmas sale. His first comic miscellany, *Literary Lapses*, appeared in 1910, and an average of one a year came out until he died in 1944, among them *Behind the Beyond* (1913), *Further Foolishness* (1916), *Frenzied Fiction* (1918), *My Discovery of England* (1922), and *My Remarkable Uncle* (1942). He left incomplete a fragment of autobiography which appeared in 1946 as *The Boy I Left Behind Me*.

Championing empire, Leacock did not at the same time champion colonial status. While the tone of his humour suggests a geniality towards life, his books expose pretence and provincialism wherever he saw it – in small town life, big city institutions, science, literature, education. The effect was double-edged, for Leacock was socially as well as economically conservative. Hence the humour constitutes a mode of resistance as well as a vehicle of simple entertainment. There is, moreover, a violent side to Leacock's genial humour which, though it would be easy to misrepresent, is also impossible to ignore. Some of it takes the form of mere slapstick, but there are other occasions where the author makes clear his opposition to such issues as higher education for women, which marks him already as a man out of phase with his time. His resistance to change shows up also in his parodies and swift burlesques. Often they took as their target the fads of polite society: melodramatic excesses, romances, theosophy; but often he used the stiletto on any theory of change, any scientific notion that seemed absurd by empirical logic, or a suggestion that educational practice might be improved. *Reductio ad absurdum* was one of his weapons; others included puns, deliberate anticlimaxes, artificial literalism. He appreciated style, and knew how to exaggerate stylistic foible. He relied on apparently naïve understatement. His was a comedy of voice, a wit made aural in his control over the artful pause, a humour that drew attention to, but did not mock, the inherent frailties of human ambition. It was a humour that celebrated the power of speech and the independence of art (he praised the artfulness of Dickens over the realism of Thackeray, which at the time was more highly regarded), but it nonetheless served socio-political ends.

All readers have their own favourite sketches (there are half a dozen books selecting the 'best' of Leacock); the following would be candidates for any new selection: 'We Have with Us Tonight', 'Gertrude the Governess' (in which Lord Ronald 'flung himself upon his horse and rode madly off in all directions'), 'Hannah of the Highlands', 'A, B, and C', 'My Financial Career' and 'The Retroactive Existence of Mr. Juggins'. The most sustained of his books were two early ones, *Sunshine Sketches of a Little Town* (1912) and *Arcadian Adventures with the Idle Rich* (1914). In both Leacock is the social scientist at work. The latter book exposes how urban bourgeois provincialism accepts the form of fads and institutions without ever appreciating the substance. The earlier book – which drew on his childhood observations of individuals in Orillia, Ontario, thus enraging a number of Orillia readers – is structurally more complex. Apparently it records a set of small town events (a bank mystery, a stock dividend, a club picnic, a new café, a churchman's resignation, a crooked election), but because it tells them by means of a naïve narratorial voice, it frames the whole as an act of the engaged reader's memory. The technique results in political criticism. Read individually, the episodes are parodic romances: the bank mystery proves to be a silly mistake on the part of an inept clerk, the club picnic disaster (when the lake ship sinks) proves to be a case of overheated imaginations (for the lake is only three feet deep and the damage can be repaired). To appreciate the naïve voice is to realize that there is an ironic dimension to the telling as well as to the tale; accepting the town's own exaggerated versions of itself (in the way that the townspeople accept as their own 'representative' the garish, manipulative, self-important saloon-keeper, an outsider named Smith) is to mistake where reality lies. To be then asked by the book's 'envoi' to identify with the town is Leacock's final authorial thrust; it appears to be a gentle recollection of the whimsy in everyone's life, but politically it is more judgmental. It dismisses the easy acceptance of provinciality, which Leacock locates in the cities as well as in the small towns to which the cities are connected. Culturally, moreover, it asserts the validity of a stringent set of normative values, at the very time the norms were beginning to change.

The social norm was rooted in race as well as in religion, a sign of which was the widespread resistance to Asian immigration. Chinese workers had been in British Columbia from the days of railway construction, and a number of Japanese fishermen came to settle on the Fraser River delta lands around Steveston, but there were legal, political and economic barriers put in the way of East Asian settlement – immigration of women was limited, for example. Such restrictions were rapidly extended to South Asian immigration when 5,000 Sikhs, Hindus and Muslims arrived in the four years between 1903 and 1907. In 1907 the Vancouver Khalsa Dhiwan Society was formed; so was the Asiatic Exclusion League, and people of Asian origin were disenfranchised.

In 1914, the *Komagata Maru* incident brought prejudices to a head. By Canadian law, the Canadian Pacific Steamship Company had been prohibited from taking South Asian immigrant passengers on its ships sailing from Hong Kong to Vancouver. When a Sikh leader organized a Japanese ship for them instead, it was prevented from docking in Vancouver and held offshore for two months, while legal battles were fought in the courts, health conditions on board declined, and animosities flared. The shipload of people finally returned across the Pacific after the Canadian navy intervened. But racial intolerance did not quickly fade. Literature in British Columbia through the 1920s was still filled with anti-Asian stereotypes; during the Second World War citizens of Japanese origin were summarily deprived of their land and removed to camps; Canadians of South Asian descent were not to get the right to vote until 1947.

During the First World War, Canadian literature turned again to Europe. Billy Bishop (1894–1956) became a flying ace, a war hero and another cultural icon. Passchendaele, Ypres and Vimy Ridge became familiar place names and rhetorical allusions with powerful cultural resonance – involving courage and loss, pride and resentment. In 1917 the issue of Conscription divided the country: Borden (1854–1937) and the Conservative Party passing the Act through Parliament, Laurier opposing it, anticipating that Liberal support for it would backfire, strengthening instead the appeal of Henri Bourassa's *nationalistes*. The split was largely on ethnic grounds, with Quebec opposing compulsory service in what was seen as an English war; politically, the effect was to establish the Liberal Party in Quebec for decades to come. Also in 1917 a Belgian relief ship and a French munitions ship collided in Halifax harbour, the resulting explosion destroying the city. A deadly flu swept through the civilian population a year later.

Many writers found themselves drawn into war service or various forms of propaganda. In 1918, when the war was over, many of the imperial values and standards had lost their public appeal. In 1919 the Winnipeg General Strike capped several years of labour unrest, trade union membership having almost tripled during the war, although employers, still suspicious of labour demands, scented in them some hint of the Soviet Revolution of 1917. J.S. Woodsworth (1874–1942), a Social Gospel minister, was elected to Parliament in 1921 for the Independent Labour Party, and the new Progressive Party, with 65 seats, became the Official Opposition.

There was a late bloom of Loyalist-imperial sentiment in the popular *Jalna* series of Mazo de la Roche (1879–1961); a massive romance begun in 1927, winning an *Atlantic* fiction prize, the series sold over eleven million copies, numbering sixteen volumes altogether, the last of them published in 1969. Eclipsing the entire series as a cultural icon, John McCrae's widely memorized rondeau of battle, 'In Flanders Fields', still marks Canada's November 11 Remembrance Day services. But in 1919 Sir Andrew Macphail closed down the *University Magazine* because it no longer seemed to have an audience. While Leacock kept writing, he increasingly seemed the captive of the past and his own reputation. Canadian society had changed. Cities were more industrialized. Women had the vote, and entered public life more – partly because some 60,000 men had been killed in the war, a generation removed from the nation. The structure of trade changed (the trans-Pacific liners, co-opted for the war effort, never returned after 1918 to their pre-war prominence: the cohesiveness of empire, which they had served, was no longer so apparent). Canada had gone to war automatically in 1914 when Britain had declared the empire to be at war; but signed the peace agreement as a separate nation. In 1922 Prime Minister Mackenzie King (William Lyon Mackenzie's grandson) refused to back the British involvement in the

Graeco–Turkish War. The nation was asserting its separateness. Canadian eyes were also turning more towards the United States.

Language and literature, too, were changing. Adjutor Rivard's (1868–1945) *Chez Nous* (1914) sounded one of the new notes; a book of sketches, it challenged linguistically the conventions of formal style and recognized 'regionalisms' as a medium of some literary sophistication, though thematically it also hung on to the traditions of the land. Georgina Sime's (1868–1958) *Sister Woman* (1919) sounded another. A collection of short stories, it sketched the impact of war on art and life, criticized men for the destructive ways in which they affected women, marriage and society, and lay bare the female realities of poverty, single parenthood, stillbirth and divorce. The whole is cast as a frame story, in which a woman tells a man that what women want is apparent from their experiences and that if the man listens properly, he will understand. The book indicates the way women have been made marginal beings in their own society; it is a feminist explanation of what matters. Such a position did not challenge empirical truths, but it did question normative values.

When Duncan Campbell Scott gave his presidential address to the Royal Society in 1922, surveying what had been happening to art, science and daily life, he was not altogether pleased. The 'poetry of our generation', he observed, 'is wayward and discomforting, full of experiment that seems to lead nowhither, bitter with the turbulence of an uncertain and ominous time.' He himself would seek refreshment in early days, 'when society appears to us to have been simpler, when there were seers who made clear the paths of life and adorned them with beauty.' As instructive as this phrase is for illuminating his own preferences, Scott was not sounding an epitaph for an era; he was recognizing that the simplicity of the past was an illusion. The real world is now: 'modernity is not a fad', he added, 'it is the feeling for actuality', and it seems distressing because

The desire of creative minds everywhere is to express the age in terms of the age.... Revolt is essential to progress, not necessarily the revolt of violence but always the revolt that questions the established past and puts it to the proof, that finds the old forms outworn and invents new forms for new patterns.

Despite his own preferences he therefore praised those who would use with skill the 'wilderness of natural accent.' The phrase flares with meaning. It takes the wilderness out of the empirical landscape and hands it over to speech. Idiom and place become one. What is seen as reality in society remains important; to literature it now also matters who is doing the seeing.

CHAPTER FOUR

Narrators: literature to 1959

NATIONAL ROMANCE AND THE LAND

The social forces that came into play in the years following the First World War were significantly to mark the next five decades. Essentially, social contexts became less British, more American. People began to think of their cultural identity in political terms, replacing the racial and religious definition of culture that had so governed the latter years of the nineteenth century. 'Canada' became a rallying cry: the nation independently joined the League of Nations, proclaimed its 'maturity' (the metaphor of the daughter-nation-growing-up was long-lived), and objected when Governor-General Byng (1862–1935) resisted Mackenzie King's government wishes, even though Byng was acting in strict accordance with received procedure. (The 'King–Byng' contretemps led to the Balfour Report in 1926, and indirectly to the Statute of Westminster in 1931, which brought the British Commonwealth into being, confirmed equality and independence among the 'members', saw an end to the idea of Imperial Federation, and began the slow dissolution of empire.)

Canada, nationally, also became a topical literary subject. Competing directly with the Philadelphia-based *Saturday Evening Post*, journals such as *Macleans* and the *Canadian Magazine* published light adventures, seeking a popular readership through local subjects. Canadian issues also featured in journals that competed more directly with *Atlantic* or *Harper's*: the critical review *Le Nigog* began in 1918 (committed to the avant garde, edited by Robert de Roquebrune, 1889–1978, and others), *Canadian Bookman* in 1919 (becoming the *Canadian Author & Bookman* in 1943), *Canadian Forum* and *Canadian Historical Review* in 1920, *Dalhousie Review* in 1921, *Canadian Mercury* (1928–9). The *University of Toronto Quarterly* (est. 1931) was to introduce its annual 'Letters in Canada' survey in 1937. Canadian literary histories and anthologies followed in their wake. Six literary surveys appeared in the 1920s: by Ray Palmer Baker (1883–1979), J.D. Logan (1869–1929) and D.G. French (1873–1945), Archibald MacMechan (1862–1933), Lionel Stevenson (1902–73), Lorne Pierce (1890–1961) and V.B. Rhodenizer (1886–1968); influential anglophone political histories by Donald Creighton (1902–79), A.R.M. Lower (b. 1889) and William Morton (1908–80) appeared respectively in 1944, 1946 and 1961. In Quebec, francophone literary histories by Camille Roy (1870–1943) and Guy Sylvestre (b. 1918) came out in 1934 and 1942, and political histories by Jean Bruchési (1901–79) in 1933, Marcel Trudel (b. 1917) in 1945, Guy Frégault (1918–77) in 1955, his *La guerre de la conquête* challenging the conventional heroic version of the past, and Michel Brunet (1917–85) in 1958. The Ryerson Press editor Lorne Pierce began a 'Makers of Canadian Literature' series in 1923; the Catholic secondary schools commissioned a series of Canadian literature manuals; and in 1936 the Governor-General's Literary Awards were established to honour significant accomplishments in poetry and prose. (Awards for French-language works did not begin until 1959, and a separate drama award was not instituted until 1981). *Chatelaine* began in 1928, a notably successful popular magazine designed for women. The nationalist Native Sons of Canada organization was founded in 1921 (though American service clubs – Rotary, Kiwanis – grew even faster); so was the enthusiastic Canadian Authors' Association, which went on to establish its own *Canadian Poetry Magazine* in 1936. It mattered greatly to this generation that Canadians should speak for themselves.

Hidden in this list of names and dates is the degree to which using their own voice meant speaking *of* themselves as well. (MacMechan's emphasis on Canadian history and setting, for example, confirmed a belief in the empirical basis of literature, effectively diminishing the quality of literary works that were set in imaginative circumstances, or set outside the country, by simply ignoring them; possibly this narrowing of focus to the Canadian scene also confirmed Canadians' sense of their separateness from both Europe and the war.) Hidden, too, is the degree of plain boosterism involved in the wave of national enthusiasm, fed by the popular magazines, the Authors' Association, and the influential *Globe* reviewer William Arthur Deacon. The *Forum*, more discursive in comment and more selective in its praise, resisted boosterism; young academics savaged it: Douglas Bush (1896–1983), the December 1926 issue of the *Forum* complained that the 'inflated rhetoric' of the politicians had become 'the language of literature, and one learns on all sides that Canada is taking its per-

manent seat in the literary league of nations'. The society was, broadly speaking, identifying place as its cultural subject. Younger writers,
responsive to the American Imagists and the European Modernists,
were in search of form (sometimes in the name of 'international standards' or 'universal truths'), but they still had to deal with the continuing popular taste for wilderness and land.

The 1920s was a decade of rapid social change. By altering civil
law to allow married women to maintain control over their own
salaries, Quebec caught up with the rest of Canada; and women
stayed in the industrial workforce after the war. Technological
changes also increased connections with the United States. Expanded automobile ownership reduced the effect of distance and (given
an increase in road-building programs) granted urban access to the
countryside. There was a passenger car for every 26 people in the
country in 1921; by 1931 the ratio had reduced to 1 for every 10 (by
1981 it was 1 for every 3). But while the cities continued to grow and
urban problems increased, few writers gave the cities their attention.
Social criticism was broadly equated with dangerous radicalism.
The founder of the Montreal PEN Club, Georgina Sime (Sir Daniel
Wilson's niece, and a relative of the English novelist Mrs Oliphant,
1828–97), wrote *Our Little Life* (1921), a novel of speech, class and
immigrant expectation in urban 'Regalia'. But it was largely ignored.
So were Douglas Durkin's (1884–1968) *The Magpie* (1923), concerning
the Winnipeg General Strike, and Charles Yale Harrison's
(1898–1954) *Generals Die in Bed* (1930), an attack on the bureaucracy
of war. As earlier, newspapers provided one outlet for social comment. Among them, *La Tribune* (est. 1910) specifically provided literary space for Eastern Townships women such as Éva Sénécal
(1905–88) and Françoise Gaudet (1902–86), women who were politically interested. Similarly, Jeanne Grisé (b. 1904) worked for *Canada-
Français*, Berthe Guertin (b. 1909) for *l'Action populaire*, Alice
Lemieux (1906–83) for *Page du foyer*. These writers used the
'women's pages' both for poetry and for social statement. In the
1930s, Medjé Vézina (1896–1981) and Adrienne Choquette (1915–73)
edited a Quebec government educational monthly; later still, radio
and television involved women in other forms of social journalism.
In separate fictions, moreover (Jovette-Alice Bernier's (1900–81) *La
chair décevante*, 1931; Éva Sénécal's *Mon Jacques*, 1933; Adrienne Maillet's (1885–1963) *L'oncle des jumeaux Pomponelle*, 1939), women
addressed 'real' subjects like adultery, bigamy and the fight for the
vote. The general resistance to 'city themes' was perhaps a refusal to
recognize social inequities in Canada, perhaps part of a continuing
rejection of women's newly visible role in literature and (urban)

politics. The city was in some sense figuratively theirs, just as received versions of 'Nature' were extensions of male myths of control. More to popular taste was the Georgian poetry of Blanche Lamontagne-Beauregard (1889–1958), Isabel Ecclestone Mackay (1875–1928) and Audrey Alexandra Brown (1904–98), and the James Oliver Curwood (1878–1927) stereotypes of a rough-and-romantic, unparticularized wilderness. It was a milieu in which Hémon, Bugnet, Roberts, Parker, Seton, Grey Owl and other 'nature writers' could still win attention.

Scores of writers produced lyrical tributes to place and youth ('youth', often, equating with 'place remembered'), or penned tender historical romances. Among the memoirists are Grace Campbell (1895–1963), Jessie L. Beattie (1896–1985), Frank Parker Day (1881–1950), Leslie Gordon Barnard (1890–1961) and 'Patrick Slater' (John Mitchell, 1882–1951), whose The Yellow Briar (1933) stands out both for its nineteenth-century detail and its avoidance of mawkishness. Only a few writers – Madge Macbeth (1878–1965), Fred Jacob (1882–1926), Robert Fontaine (1911–65) in The Happy Time (1945) – wrote popular satires or comedies. Although the plays of Merrill Denison (1893–1975) – especially 'Brothers in Arms' (collected in The Unheroic North, 1923) – satirize the exaggerations of local identity, it is as characteristic of the time that Denison also wrote romantic historical plays for radio (on Henry Hudson, Radisson and others) and corporate histories of the Molsons and Massey-Harris. The general stance taken towards the world – one that deemed social problems resolvable by individual choice and community will – carries on into later fictions, like those of Hubert Evans (1892–1986, the nature tales of Forest Friends, 1926; the literal portrait of Skeena Indian social difficulties, Mist on the River, 1954; or the semi-autobiographical account of a nineteenth-century Ontario childhood, O Time in Your Flight! 1979). Lyrical versions of a more distant history appeared in the escapist Oriental romances of Lily Adams Beck (d. 1931), the biblical romances of W. G. Hardy (1896–1979), the Elizabethan romances of Virna Sheard (1865?–1943).

The career of Frederick John Niven, the Chilean-born resident of British Columbia for whom a Scots literary prize is named, tells of the attraction of different generic choices: he lived by his journalism and his stereotypical 'Westerns', he attracted most Canadian attention for his autobiography (Coloured Spectacles, 1938) and his romances of Scots and Native history on the prairies (for example, The Flying Years, 1935), yet his most tightly-constructed and realistic works are the series of Kailyard novels, such as Justice of the Peace (1923) and Triumph (1934), for which he won little Canadian attention at all. Other romances of the Canadian past include Philip Child's (1898–1978) *Village of Souls* (1933) and Alan Sullivan's *Three Came to Ville Marie* (1941), all set during the French regime, which continued to haunt the English-Canadian imagination. Thomas Raddall (1903–94) later took up romance and historical forms in several novels and tales of the Maritimes, as did Grace Irwin (b. 1907) with her evangelical novels of the 1950s. In Acadia, romances of separation and identify characterise both prose and poetry: Thomas Gill's (1865–1941) *The Heart of Lunenburg* (1930), Antoine-J. Léger's (1880–1950) *Elle et lui* (1949). In Quebec, too, the historical novel attracted critical praise. Léo-Paul Desrosiers' (1896–1967) *Nord-Sud* (1931) and *Les engagés du Grand Portage* (1939, translated as *The Making of Nicholas Montour* in 1978), both won prizes; the first concerns the flight of young Quebeckers to the 1849 California Gold Rush, the second tells a tale of the fur trade. Desrosiers also published a biography of Marguerite Bourgeoys and a study of the Iroquois, and is best known by contemporary critics for his stream-of-consciousness study of the psychology of faith, *L'ampoule d'or* (1951). (Other historical works, such as the novels of Robert de Roquebrune published in the 1920s – *Les habits rouges,* 1923 – used history to explore the 'fugitive existence' of a society whose connection with the past had been broken. Alain Grandbois (1900–75), in his first book, *Né à Québec* (1933), used a 'biography' of the priest-explorer Louis Joliet to tell in three separate ways how history turns into story and legend.)

The stronger trend in Quebec writing involved an attraction to the land. (Much has been made of the fact that copyright at the turn of the century was registered in the Department of Agriculture, as though books and land were as one.) 'Littérature du terroir' which had developed in the 1890s and 1900s among poets like Ferland, de Bussières and Nerée Beauchemin, continued to draw adherents. Among prose works in this school are the stories of Adjutor Rivard (*Chez nos gens*, 1918), Lionel Groulx (1878–1967; *Les rapaillages*, 1916), Frère Marie-Victorin (1885–1944), best known as a taxonomist, responsible for developing much of Quebec's botanical vocabulary (*Récits laurentiens*, 1920), and Georges Bouchard (1888–1956; *Vieilles choses, vieilles gens*, 1920). The École littéraire de Montréal had published an anthology in 1909 called *Canada chanté: le Terroir* (with further collections in 1910 and 1925), which brought together some two dozen poets whose evocations of field, forest and stream were attempts to evoke the 'soul' of the people, including Lucien Rainier (1877–1956), Alphonse Désilets (1888–1956), Jules Tremblay (1879–1927), Louis Dantin and Jean Charbonneau. Gonzalve Desaulniers's *Les bois qui chantent* (1930), written when the author was 68, is a representative collection of poetic songs and legends, through which the voices of nature stimulate for the poet an appreciation of the divine.

There were reactions against this school. In prose the new 'realism' came early from Rodolphe Girard, and later from Albert Laberge (1871–1960), whose novel *La scouine* (1918, translated as *Bitter Bread* in 1977) was published in extracts in *Le Terroir*, *La Presse* and other papers from 1909 on, sometimes under the pseudonym Adrien Clamer. Condemned for immorality and anticlericalism, it was full of regionalisms and anglicisms, thus offending stylistic purists as well. It tells through disparate 'moral scenes' of the dissimulations of its title character, and of the sexual and social lives of various villagers. A 'chorus' reminds the reader all the while of the world of faith that frames the characters' lives, emphasising the disparities that daily undermine moral idealism. Laberge's 'norms', by contrast, are realistic, involving such things as lice and false teeth. From 1936 to 1954, several more Laberge volumes appeared, noting little difference in quality of life between town and country; in both the 'reality' was grim, a picture that by the 1930s writers had more generally come to expect.

In poetry, Jean-Aubert Loranger (1896–1942; *Poëmes*, 1920) experimented with haiku (Orientalism later touched the verse of Carol Coates, b. 1906, in the 1940s). Émile Coderre (who used the pseudonym Jean Narrache, 1893–1970) employed popular dialect in *Quand j'parl'tout seul* (1933); René Chopin (1885–1953) wrote prose poems as early as 1913; and in *Poèmes de cendre et d'or* (1922), Paul Morin (1889–1963) sought once again in Classical models for formal freedom from *terrien* romance. Greater change still was to come with the work of Alfred DesRochers (1901–78; *À l'ombre de l'Orford*, 1929, and other works), and Robert Choquette (b. 1905; *À travers les vents*, 1925; *Metropolitan Museum*, 1931; *Poésies nouvelles*, 1933; *Suite marine*, 1953). Both DesRochers and Choquette praised the immensity of the country (DesRochers's 'Hymne au vent du nord' may be his most cited work, one which seeks the symbolic meaning of space). Both, moreover, worked in binary patterns, with insights born of antithesis, seeking to combine a vision of the vast and untamable with a web of allusion to historical and Classical tale. DesRochers, strongly influenced by American writers like Jeffers (1887–1962) and Sandburg (1878–1967), contrasted the degeneracy of the day with the heroism of historical adventure in which imagination still allowed him to participate. *À l'ombre de l'Orford* primarily consists of several sonnet series, in which some of the most striking verses deal with closely observed rural events (animal slaughter, for example), the effect of the whole achieved through a synesthetic, incremental accumulation of sensory effects. Choquette's *Metropolitan Museum* employs a different technique; a single two-part poem, it records a visit to the New York art gallery, observing that the city (and not the habitant farm, by implication) is the contemporary centre of culture; an extended reflection follows, on the nature of 'centre' and on its significance as a symbol and an idea in modern Quebec.

The poem also underlines how much the visual arts affected these decades. Film was coming to be a familiar medium. The post-impressionist years were asking not only who sees, but also how they do so. In England, the Canadian-born writer and painter Wyndham Lewis was introducing 'vorticism' to the art world. Surrealism was taking hold in France, Expressionism in Germany. Although reality was still perceived as empirical, the perceiving itself also mattered, but perceiving varied subjectively. The Canadianism of the eye of the painter therefore also began to matter culturally. In this spirit the 'Group of Seven' was born in 1920, and Ernest Shipman (1871–1931) began producing film versions of Canadian novels like Ralph Connor's *The Man from Glengarry* and Alan Sullivan's 1920 novel about industrial expansion, *The Rapids*, in 1922. (There had been Canadian Pacific Railway immigration films as early as 1898, film versions of the *Long Sault* and *Evangeline* in 1913, and government films during the war. When the American company Famous Players acquired control over the Canadian film distribution market in 1923, this nascent Canadian film industry died. In parallel fashion, the McLaughlin Motor Car Company of Oshawa merged with General Motors in 1918 and disappeared.) Though the Canadian Government Motion Picture Bureau was set up also in 1923, film actors like Mary Pickford (1893–1979) went south, or like Raymond Massey (1896–1983, Vincent's brother) to London. The film image of the nation – as recorded in Pierre Berton's (b. 1920) *Hollywood's Canada* (1975) – passed into others' control, and came out as the familiar motifs of trapper, Mountie and snow. The reality of daily life again ran up against the image of reality, and sometimes the celluloid won.

PAINTERS AND THE MONTREAL GROUP

The extraordinary continuing appeal of the Group of Seven to Canadians owes much to the nationalist climate of the 1920s and its governing equation between nation and landscape. 'Canada', observed Arthur Lismer (1883–1969), was in 1920 'unwritten, unpainted, unsung.' Current art criticism now finds other painters finer craftsmen – David Milne (1882–1958), for example, who brought fauvist influences back to Canada when he returned from New York in 1929, or the earlier impressionist J.W. Morrice – but popular enthusiasm for the Group of Seven has become almost institutionalized. The Group claimed to portray Canada with an original and native eye. While it did attempt to represent the bold colours and shapes of Eastern Canada (the characteristic settings are those of Algonquin Park and the North Shore of Lake Superior), the claim for originality is exaggerated. The initial group included Franklin Carmichael (1890–1945), A.Y. Jackson (1882–1974), Franz Johnston (1888–1945), Arthur Lismer, Lawren Harris (1885–1970), J.E.H. MacDonald (1873–1932) and Frederick Varley (1881–1969). Tom Thomson (1877–1917), whose paintings 'The Jack Pine' and 'The West Wind' are possibly the most famous of this period, is frequently associated with the group – indeed painted with them, but died in 1917, before the Group was properly formed in 1920. (The events of Thomson's death, under mysterious circumstances on a painting trip, later became the basis for Roy McGregor's (b. 1948) 1980 novel *Shore Lines*.) Of disparate backgrounds, most (except Harris) were commercial illustrators. Jackson established his subsequent reputation as a painter of the Arctic; Harris, independently wealthy, of all the group headed most into abstraction, finding it a technique for rendering the rhythms of nature and achieving a theosophical transcendence of the world. Several were English-born (Lismer, for example, who also set up the South African art education program). Together they were influenced by the same forces that led contemporaneously to Edvard Munch's (1863–1944) expressionist painting in Norway. For all their claim to be a National School, too – they later expanded to include the Torontonian A.J. Casson (1898–1992), the Montrealer Edwin Holgate (1892–1977) and the Winnipegger L.L. Fitzgerald (1890–1956) – they were essentially a Toronto group. While, to begin with, their vigorous claims on national identity alienated the art establishment – Hector Charlesworth (1872–1945, later editor of *Saturday Night* and Chairman of the Canadian Radio Broadcasting Commission) had in 1916 dismissed one painting as a 'Drunkard's Stomach', and H.F. Gadsby (1869–1951) in 1913 called them the 'Hot Mush School' – nationalism began to cohere around them. By the 1920s (and long before their formal dissolution in 1933) they were favourable noticed and avidly collected.

Emily Carr, a West Coast painter, potter and writer who emerged at the same time, praised by Harris, was another with a revolutionary sense of vision. A native of Victoria, she was regarded as an eccentric, one who in her later years was known for keeping a pet monkey and pushing her painting equipment around the city in a baby carriage; more important than her idiosyncrasies was her resistance to conventional fashion. Trained in San Francisco, England and Paris (a student at one point of the New Zealand painter Frances Hodgkins, 1869–1947), she received her most influential training as a skilled observer among the Natives of British Columbia, especially in the years after 1912. Called 'Klee Wyck' ('laughing one') by the Nootka, she used the name as her pottery signature; it also became the title of a 1941 collection of prose sketches: 'D'Sonoqua', for example, tells effectively of feeling the presence of the Wild Woman of the Woods while on a painting expedition. Other prose works include *The Book of Small* (1942) and *The House of All Sorts* (1944), the latter about her childhood and her experiences as a landlady. Six collections of sketches and addresses were published posthumously. Her most powerful paintings strive not to represent life in miniature – the detail of trees, for example – but to evoke the energy and the large plastic shapes of the West Coast forest and the sky, to evoke a way of seeing that derives from place and that sustains the indigenous mythology. In a 1930 address to the Victoria Women's Canadian Club – published in 1972 as the title speech in *Fresh Seeing* – Emily Carr specified her equation between visual and cultural perspective. Asking if an ancient or a modern art will convey the strength, size and beauty of the West, she asserts that 'If we dressed her in the art dresses of the older countries she would burst them. So we will have to make her a dress of her own ... The spirit is different.' She goes on then to praise the 'oldest art of our West, the art of the Indians', as 'in spirit very modern, full of ... vitality', to champion her female and artistic independence, and to resist the squeezing and dwarfing that happen if the artist is more afraid of public opinion than of vision. Her sense at once of the nativeness and of the nativity of vision infused her own work with its characteristic energy; her passionate conviction subsequently made her the subject of a ballet, a musical and of literature, too: as in Herman Voaden's (1903–91) 1960 biographical play *Emily Carr*, in Dorothy Livesay's 'The Three Emily's' (1972), or Florence McNeil's (b. 1937) *Emily* (1975), where the will to be independent unites with the figure of the artist as a woman and the image of the wilderness as the creative matrix of art.

When, in 1925, Arthur J.M. Smith (1902–80) and Frank R. Scott founded a literary magazine at McGill University – *The McGill Fortnightly Review*, which lasted till 1927 – the two students were not only rebelling against the Victorian conservatism they identified with the literary establishment, they were also responding to the new wave of nationalism epitomized by the 1920s painters. At once they objected to the Authors' Association's boosterism and wanted to see truth more clearly, to invoke (as Smith put it in his 1926 poem 'The Lonely Land', subtitled 'Group of Seven' in its first appearance in the *Fortnightly*), through sound and syllable, through image and echo, a 'beauty / of dissonance, / this resonance / of stony strand.'

The universities had grown after the war (as they would again in 1946) – the student population at the University of Toronto had doubled to 21,869, and by 1939 reached 35,164 – and they became centres of cultural change as well as of cultural establishment. In the *Fortnightly*, Smith, influenced by his fresh acquaintance with Imagism and with the Georgian writings associated with Harold Monro's (1879–1932) London Bookshop, and Scott, just returned to Montreal from Oxford, produced a mature journal, one which attracted other young writers: Leon Edel (1907–98), who went on to become a US resident and the biographer of Henry James; Leo Kennedy (b. 1907), a Christian poet, influenced by T.S. Eliot (1888–1965) and Eliot's interest in the Metaphysicals; Lancelot Hogben (1895–1975), later the author of a book on mathematics; and Abraham Klein (1909–72), who never actually published in the journal because he refused to alter the single word 'soul' to meet the editors' demands. They came to be known as the Montreal Group.

While Scott became a lawyer and civil rights activist, based in Montreal, Smith became professor of English at Michigan State University, and later took out American citizenship. 'Eclecticism' was Smith's critical credo, a detached stance which prevents easy generalizations about his own poems – they do not argue a single political belief or 'metaphysical' position or any other consistent core of commitment, except in so far as they all strive for an 'objectivity' of formal independence. That is, Smith conceived each poem as a separate object. Yet the apparent influence of Eliot's 'objective correlative' meant that he was not free from ideology after all; he placed his faith in there being a connection between the empirical world and the world of ideas. What was modern about his work was his belief that language was the medium in which this connection might occur; his objection to Victorian Canadian poetry derived not only from his impatience with its open subjectivity but also from his belief that Victorian language (its desire for harmony, for mellifluous form) distorted the realities of art, land and people.

Although Smith published in a great many journals, from Marianne Moore's (1887–1972) *Dial* to *Poetry* (Chicago) and *Canadian Forum*, he published no separate volume until *News of the Phoenix* (1943); four volumes of new and selected poems followed between 1954 and 1978. He was also busy as an anthologist and at least until the 1950s was at the heart of controversy over the directions modern

Canadian writing was taking. *The Book of Canadian Poetry* (first edition 1943) and the bilingual *Oxford Book of Canadian Verse* (1960) became standard texts, though the earlier one aroused the ire of John Sutherland, whose own *Other Canadians* (1947) was a direct reply to Smith an a denunciation of Smith's artificial binary distinction of Canadian writers into 'native' and 'cosmopolitan' schools. Earlier still, Smith and Scott had established *The Canadian Mercury* as a successor to the McGill paper; it ran for six issues during 1928–9, and reaffirmed the young poets' objection to the 'decorum' and 'claptrap' of their elders, a stance reiterated in their anthology of satirical verse, *The Blasted Pine* (1957). Another anthology, *New Provinces* (1936), brought them, Klein and Kennedy together with two Toronto poets, Robert Finch (1900–95), whose own urbane lyric career was to last into the 1980s, and the Newfoundland-born academic Edwin John Pratt (1882–1964). Though by this time there was a handful of still other modern anglophone lyricists beginning to publish – among them Kenneth Leslie (1892–1974), L.A. MacKay (1901–82), Charles Bruce (1906–71), Alfred Bailey (1905–97), Floris Clark McLaren (1904–78), Anne Marriott (1913–97) and Dorothy Livesay – it was the poets of *New Provinces* who were the main force to shift critical attention away from romantic conventions to the exigencies of modern society and free form.

In the work of Frank Scott, the connection between literature and society was most evident. The sharpest satirist of the Montreal Group, Scott is possibly the most famous for 'The Canadian Authors Meet', a 1927 savaging of the Authors' Association: at a literary party 'the air is heavy with Canadian topics' and the Confederation Poets 'Are measured for their faith and philanthropics'; meanwhile these self-styled '*literati*' wonder 'shall we go round the mulberry bush, or shall / We gather at the river, or shall we / Appoint a Poet Laureate this fall, / Or shall we have another cup of tea.' The skilful transformation of allusion into innuendo, the arrangement of repetitions to function ironically, the zeugma: all work to dismiss the heady nationalism of William Arthur Deacon and the *Bookman*. Less remarked at the time was the too-easy refusal of tradition, and the specious chauvinism of another kind, the dismissal of 'Virgins of sixty who still write of passion'. Sometimes Scott's satire was less strident, as in 'Saturday Sundae', 'Yes and No', or wryly amused at the failure of bilingual signs ('DEEP APPLE PIE / TARTE AUX POMMES PROFONDES') in 'Bonne Entente'. But he wrote more often with critical sting. 'Brebeuf and His Brethren' asks which were the savages, the Indians who burned Jesuits or the Jesuits who burned heretics? 'The Canadian Social Register' attacks the implied entrenchment of a social hierarchy in an ostensibly classless sate. 'W.L.M.K.' attacks Mackenzie King's penchant for occupying the middle ground: he 'never let his on the one hand / Know what his on the other hand was doing.' The author of some eight volumes of poetry published between 1945 and 1981, and translator of Saint-Denys Garneau and Anne Hébert, Scott was also a political theorist, a law teacher (his students included future senators and senior civil servants, influencing Pierre Elliott Trudeau, 1919–2000), and an essayist (several prose writings are collected in *A New Endeavour*, 1986).

Besides the satiric verse, Scott published a number of Imagist poems (like the early 'Old Song', its echoic control over the durations of sound and silence reminiscent of Smith's 'Lonely Land'), but he moved rapidly into social verse in the 1930s. The 'sure wings' that carry the plane skywards 'Are the everlasting arms of science', says 'Trans Canada'; but Scott argued in *Canadian Forum* (1931) that the war had destroyed any belief in the old political order, theories of mythology had destroyed any conventional belief in the Deity, socialism and communism had cast doubt on the worth of the economic order, and Einstein was even querying the structure of the universe. In such a context, what credibility did any 'everlasting' institution have? Scott resisted a social structure that implied that order was fixed; for him, justice required social change. His legal and social career thus ties in with political development during the 1920s, 30s and 40s, and reveals the close connection that existed at the time between art and class.

B.K. Sandwell's (1876–1954) quip, on the occasion of Vincent Massey's becoming Governor-General in 1952, observed: 'Toronto has no social classes – / Only the Masseys and the masses.' There was a pungent accuracy about the distinction. The point is (as Jean Barman, b. 1939, demonstrated in her analysis of private schooling, *Growing Up British in British Columbia*, 1984), class in Canada came to be associated with mercantile wealth, and culture became established partly through corporate recognition. The Masseys provide a convenient illustration. The family financed two performance halls in Toronto: Massey Hall and Hart House (named after Hart Massey, 1823–96). Corporate investment in the Group of Seven (Lawren Harris was a member of the family affiliated with the Massey–Harris tractor company) helped to confirm the painters' value in the public mind. Further, when Marius Barbeau was trying in 1927 to get musicians such as Ernest Macmillan (1893–1973) and Claude Champagne (1891–1965) to compose music based on Canadian folksong, it was the Canadian Pacific Railway Company that provided a grant that enabled the Hart House String Quartet to perform Macmillan's work;

the publicity director for the CPR was John Murray Gibbon (1875–1952), a past president of the Canadian Authors' Association. The CPR and Massey–Harris were also involved in documentary film-making. And many writers had family connections with the industrial establishment. Later writers in the William Perkins Bull (1870–1948) family, for example (Bull was an Ontario corporate lawyer and local historian in the 1920s and 1930s), include T.H.B. Symons (b. 1929) and his brother Scott Symons (b. 1933). Timothy Findley's (1930–2002) grandfather, Thomas Findley (1870–1921), was at one time president of Massey–Harris. (Findley's character Robert Raymond Ross, in *The Wars*, draws the name 'Raymond' from the Massey connection). Alan Sullivan married into the Hees family. Still other establishment families invested in culture, from the Bronfmans and the Koerners (the latter family includes the painter John Korner, b. 1913) to the Killams (a family to which Margaret Atwood is connected). The Izaak Walton Killam (1885–1955) estate provided the seed money that set up the Canada Council. The poet Anne Wilkinson (1910–61) was an Osler, a family she wrote about in *Lions in the Way* (1956). The sociologist Paul Grayson (b. 1944), among others in the 1980s, examined many of the connections between cultural precedence and Canadian social power. But not all cultural expression was a sign of privilege; neither did all privilege have direct literary consequences. Much of Canadian life was being lived out at another level.

SOCIAL PROTEST AND SOCIAL CHANGE

Before the Depression hit in 1929, several pieces of social legislation had been passed in the Federal House: minimum wage laws, an old age pension. (Marketing controls like the establishment of the Bank of Canada and the Canadian Wheat Board would follow in the 1930s.) A brief attempt during the First World War to institute prohibition failed; one 1916 soldier's rhyme ridiculed:

Preachers over in Canada
Who rave about Kingdom Come
Ain't pleased with our ability
And want to stop our rum.

Water they say would be better
Water! Great Scott! Out here
We're up to our knees in water
Do they think we're standing in beer?

Many Canadians, indeed, made a substantial income contravening American prohibition laws (the Volstead Act) between 1919 and 1933. Primarily, Canadian social legislation was a response to the waves of social unrest that followed the First World War. Several factors led to change: the violence of the 1935 'Bloody Sunday' riots in Vancouver; a march on Ottawa by the unemployed; and the pressure exerted by the new Progressive Party (which later joined with the Conservatives) and the Social Gospel Movement under J.S. Woodsworth (which in 1932 was absorbed into the socialist political coalition called the Cooperative Commonwealth Federation or CCF, later the New Democratic Party). Frank Scott became involved with socialist causes during the Depression, when with the historian Frank Underhill, in 1932, he helped organise the League for Social Reconstruction; he also helped draft the founding 'Regina Manifesto' for the CCF, and was national chairman of the party during the 1940s.

At the same time Scott was instrumental in combatting some of the more restrictive legislation enacted in Quebec during these decades. The right-wing premier of Quebec, Maurice Duplessis (1890–1959), held power from 1936 to 1939 and again from 1944 until his death. Duplessis (popularly known as 'le chef') made his reputation as someone who controlled the clergy and broke the unions. His 'Padlock Act' in 1937 allowed the Quebec government to imprison for a year, without appeal, anyone who published or distributed 'communism or bolshevism', a notion that could be widely defined. Scott challenged the law, and the Supreme Court finally ruled it *ultra vires* in 1957. In the *Roncarelli* v. *Duplessis* case of 1958 Scott again defended civil rights. Duplessis had summarily removed the liquor licence of a Jehovah's Witness restaurateur, effectively closing down his business because of his religious denomination; the Supreme Court ruled in favour of Scott and Roncarelli. Further, Scott was associated with Thérèse Casgrain (1896–1981), the chief campaigner against Duplessis for female suffrage in Quebec. Mme Casgrain was a popular radio personality during the 1930s (for a program called 'Fémina'), president of the CCF during the 1950s, and later a federal senator. Also opposed to Duplessis were *Le Devoir* (the Montreal newspaper founded by Henri Bourassa in 1910), and the magazine *Cité Libre* (est. 1950), edited by Pierre Elliott Trudeau and Gérard Pelletier (b. 1919), which spoke out for democratic morality and rational humanism, and brought together writers as diverse as the social essayist Jean Le Moyne (1913–96); *Convergences*, 1961), the philosopher Pierre Vadeboncoeur (b. 1920) and the social activist Pierre Vallières (b. 1937). During the 1970s, some circles reclaimed Duplessis as a symbol of cultural independence from the 'English', and a scarcely disguised 'Frank Scot' would appear in the novels of Jacques Ferron (1921–85) as a sign of *anglais* interference in *québécois* culture.

Prior to this time, issues involving class, women, radio and religion had come together in other ways, shaping the institutions in which Scott and Mme Casgrain were involved. The 'Persons Case' was one of these. It began to develop in 1928 when the Supreme Court, in response to Emily Murphy ('Janey Canuck', 1868–1933), Nellie McClung and other Alberta petitioners, ruled that women could not hold office as Canadian senators. The BNA Act (establishing Canadian independence in 1867) had said 'persons' could be senators; women, the court ruled, were not persons in law. The following year, the British Privy Council, which was still a Canadian court of higher appeal, reversed the ruling.

Also in 1928, the Aird Commission Report recommended that the government establish a national broadcasting system. In tune with the time, the express aim was that of 'fostering a national spirit and interpreting national citizenship'. Given Sir John Aird's (1855–1938) background (he was president of the Bank of Commerce), public ownership seemed an unlikely recommendation, and industry opposition helped postpone any action on the report until 1932. But the commission had been established in the first place as a response to what was seen (especially by the established denominations) as a religious broadcast problem: the group that later became known as Jehovah's Witnesses was setting up private sectarian stations. Aird's recommendations offered a means of control; more directly, Aird wanted to avoid the broadcasting industry following the pattern already established by the film industry, that of simply falling into American hands and disappearing south of the border. Graham Spry's (1900–83) 1932 aphorism 'It's the state or the States' reiterated this fear. Co-founder with Alan Plaunt (1904–41) of the Canadian Radio League, Spry (a reporter and editorial writer for John Dafoe's, 1866–1944, Winnipeg *Free Press*, and another member of the League for Social Reconstruction) fought from 1929 on to have the Aird Report implemented. In 1932 the Broadcast Act espoused the principle of public ownership in some degree, and took over the broadcast system that the Canadian National Railway had by this time put in place; in 1936 the Canadian Broadcasting Corporation (CBC) was established (with a parallel Radio-Canada in French), a few weeks prior to the BBC in England. The system was a way of reaching across several time zones within Canada, of reaching out to other countries as well, and of guaranteeing to Canadians the right of public access to the airwaves. A CBC television service was established in 1952. Despite the 1983 recommendations of the Applebaum–Hébert

Commission, to the effect that the CBC be diminished in size and in some degree privatized, the system remains in place through the 1990s. All major cities have access to programming in both official languages, though English and French broadcasting (a response to both politics and economics) has increasingly been centralized respectively in Toronto and Montreal.

By the 1930s, despite the legislation that had been implemented, social problems still persisted. Voters reacted by electing entirely new parties into power: the right-wing Social Credit under William Aberhart (1878–1943) replacing the United Farmers in Alberta in 1935 (though Aberhart's attempts to put Major Douglas's (1879–1952) doctrinaire Social Credit economic theories into practice were ruled *ultra vires* by the Supreme Court of Canada); Duplessis's Union Nationale replacing the Liberals in Quebec in 1936; the Liberals replacing the Conservatives in Saskatchewan in 1934, to be in turn replaced by the CCF, the first socialist government in Canada, in 1944. Local pressures – a drought worsened the Depression on the prairies – emphasized regional disparities and the need for separate solutions in different places. The reaction of art and literature was to become even more political. Some writers and painters sought to alter the art of seeing by revolutionizing their medium: the painters Charles Comfort (1900–94) and Paraskeva Clark (1898–1986) turned to industrial subjects and portraits of the working classes; the playwright Herman Voaden explored the techniques of expressionism in several plays of the 1930s; and the painter Bertram Brooker (1888–1955) championed the theosophical significance of geometrical abstraction. As a writer, sometimes using pseudonyms (Huxley Herne, Richard Surrey), Brooker also produced a number of free-form poems (collected with some of his paintings and comments on art in *Sounds Assembling*, 1980), three books on advertising technique, a two-volume *History of the Arts in Canada* (1929 and 1936), which constitutes a small literary history of the two decades, and three novels, of which *Think of the Earth* (1936) tells of a worker who believes he must commit an evil act in order to save mankind.

Other writers turned openly to political movements: Dorothy Livesay to communism, Earle Birney to Trotskyist ideas – both of them responding warmly to the poetry of W.H. Auden (1907–73), espousing the Republican cause in the Spanish Civil War, and severing their Communist Party affiliations at the time of the Second World War. The Spanish Civil War also captured the imagination and the active involvement of a young doctor named Norman Bethune (1890–1939), who instituted the first mobile ambulance corps. Bethune went on to join Mao Tse-Tung's (1893–1976) forces in the

Great March, to become a hero of the Communist Revolution in China and another cultural icon in Canada, the subject of play and film. Ted Allan (1916–95) served with Bethune in Spain – the Canadian volunteers were known as the 'Mackenzie–Papineau Battalion'. Allan also published a 1939 novel of the Spanish Civil War called *This Time a Better Earth*, and in 1952 (revised 1971) wrote with Sydney Gordon (b. 1915) a biography of Bethune called *The Scalpel, The Sword*.

In Quebec, Rex Desmarchais (1908–74) was attracted to the right, his 1937 essays, *Tentatives*, calling for social change, and his 1942 novel, *La chesnaie*, espousing violent social upheaval in order that a dictatorial elite might establish Quebec as an independent Catholic nation. To a great degree, the work of the Catholic nationalist priest/historian Lionel Groulx lies behind this work – most particularly Groulx's 1922 novel *L'Appel de la Race* (translated 1986 as *The Iron Wedge*, adopting the book's working title). Published first under the pseudonym Alonié de Lestres (the name of one of Dollard des Ormeaux's companions), it was intended as a reply to government limitations imposed in 1912 on the amount of French that could be taught in francophone Ontario schools. It won quick (literary and theological) opposition from Camille Roy and others, but it was widely influential. Groulx himself defended the novel in print, using another pseudonym, Jacques Brassier. Full of stereotypical characters, the novel tells of a francophone champion in the House of Commons and of his vehemently confrontative anglophone wife, who ultimately splits the family. The novel ends up as a polemic against intercultural marriage. The eight psychological novels of the newspaperman Harry Bernard (1898–1979), and the meditative poetry and essays of 'François Hertel' (Rodolphe Dubé, 1905–86) also show the influence of Groulx. The 'call of the race' is most evident in Bernard's *La terre vivante* (1925) and *La ferme des pins* (1930), though in the latter it is an anglophone who fears assimilation when the francophones 'colonize' the Eastern Townships of Quebec and 'take back' the land. (Bernard's short stories, *La dame blanche*, 1927, use the more conventional forms of legend and history.)

Left-wing causes were by far the more dominant voice of the decade. The journals *Masses* and *New Frontier* emerged briefly in 1932 and 1936, the former being Stalinist in orientation and the latter, more moderate, publishing writers as different as Dorothy Livesay, Leo Kennedy and A.M. Klein. Chief among 1930s short story writers with proletarian sympathies were Klein (for trenchant social allegories), Sinclair Ross (1908–96, for narratives of domestic pressure, with

prairie settings, most published in *Queen's Quarterly*), Mary Quayle
Innis and Dyson Carter (b. 1910). (A representative sampling of 1930s
stories is Donna Phillips's (b. 1939) *Voices of Discord*, 1979. Irene
Baird's (1901–81) *Waste Heritage* (1939) portrays labour unrest in
Vancouver.)

Theatre, too, turned to the left, influenced indirectly by Herman
Voaden, and by a German *agit-prop* theatre company that had visited New York in 1931. *Masses* reported on several Canadian plays,
whose titles alone tell of their concerns: 'Deported', 'Solidarity, not
Charity', 'Eviction', 'Farmers' Fight', 'Theatre – Our Weapon',
'Relief'. The playwright Oscar Ryan (1904–88) talked of 'urgent
questions' and the need for plays to 'speak in direct terms'. Some
critics called it propaganda, but in the 1930s several performance
groups formed with these issues in mind. One was the New Theatre
in Winnipeg, responding in part to working circumstances among
Ukrainian-Canadians in the city. Associated with this theatre was
Laura Goodman Salverson (1890–1970), whose *The Viking Heart*
(1923) and *Confessions of an Immigrant's Daughter* (1939) portrayed
the exigencies of Icelandic settlement in Manitoba. Vancouver's
Progressive Arts Club was another new group; its staging of Clifford Odets' (1906–63) *Waiting for Lefty* ironically won praise from
the social establishment when it was taken to the Dominion Drama
Festival (an annual amateur competition begun in 1933) and nearly
won the Bessborough Trophy. In Montreal, plays by Len Peterson
(b. 1917) and Reuben Ship (1915–75) at the New Theatre Group ran
into opposition from Duplessis. In Toronto, the Theatre of Action
group attracted actors such as Lorne Greene (1915–87, later a Hollywood TV star), Louis Applebaum (1918–2002, later a composer
and royal commissioner), Johnny Wayne (1918–90) and Frank Shuster (1916–2002, later successful radio and TV comedians). Shuster's
cousin Joe Shuster (1914–92) was the artist who drew the *Superman*
comic strip, another response to Depression circumstances; Frank
Shuster's daughter Rosie Shuster (b. 1946) five decades later
acquired fame in New York as a comic scriptwriter for such shows
as *Saturday Night Live*. In 1933 Oscar Ryan and three others produced for the Theatre of Action a collaborative script called *Eight
Men Speak*, about the simultaneous arrest of eight communist leaders in Canada in 1931. Using mass chants, tableaux and other experimental forms, it showed the influence of expressionism. After one
performance, however, the police closed it down because of its politics. A substantial gap still separated official from reformative versions of social propriety and social need. The play appeared in print
in 1934.

REALISM

Characteristic themes of the time involved the life of factory workers, the plight of immigrants, the violent life of the city street. The 'American gangster' type became a convention. Though it would be invalid to claim that the new 'realism' was urban alone, 'realism' did come to be equated with 'ordinary' lives – that is, with the daily alternatives to the perceived cultural order. 'Realism' was less a particular form than a way of restructuring social norms by challenging the accuracy of those in place. Images of the working farm and the failing farm became counters to habitant pastoralism; urban settings became counters to nature. But sometimes they too could turn sentimental, as when in the 1940s and 1950s Hugh Garner wrote his many novels and stories of Toronto's Cabbagetown. Their gruff toughness was as much a convention as romantic deprivation had been in Hémon's *Maria Chapdelaine*.

The shift towards realism was apparent in subject as well as in setting. The francophone and anglophone versions of Canada barely took each other into account, let alone additional cultures and languages, but when Watson Kirkconnell (1895–1977) published his anthology *Canadian Overtones* in 1935, he was drawing attention to the ethnic diversity of Canadian writing. Kirkconnell translated into English poetry from six languages, among them Ukrainian and Icelandic – but his efforts still did little to change the general picture. (Another anthology, *Volvox*, edited by J.M. Yates, b. 1938, appeared in 1971; it was the 1970s before the idea of 'multiculturalism' began to come into its own.) While the poems Kirkconnell translated were fairly conventional lyrics, one of the writers deserves special mention. Stephan Stephansson (1853–1927), an Alberta farmer, had emigrated from Iceland as a child in 1889; his six volumes of poetry, called *Andvökur* (or *Wakeful Nights*), appeared between 1909 and 1938, with an extended selection of translations appearing in 1982. While conventional in his use of rhyme, Stephansson, widely proclaimed as one of the century's most important Icelandic-language writers, championed non-traditional causes: pacifism, the Bolshevik Revolution, the United Farmers Party – though a disillusionment with political parties rapidly set in. Through language and theme, he resisted the anglophone norms while at the same time committing himself to the local political culture. The 'realist' movement essentially worked at the ramifications of this distinction.

These changes in the way of seeing Canadian realities occupied fiction during the 1920s and 1930s. Martha Ostenso (1900–63), of Norwegian background, produced in 1925 a novel called *Wild Geese* (possibly co-authored with Douglas Durkin), in which the parallels between harsh land and harsh life show up in the person of the tyrannical character Caleb Gare. A fierce father, Gare tries to control the lives of 'his' wife and daughter; the novel focuses finally on the power of the daughter, Judith, to rebel. Sexual passion motivates change in the book; the need to possess and control resists it. A similar contrast shapes *Un homme et son péché* (1933), the most widely read of the fiction of Claude-Henri Grignon (1894–1976), a civil servant who established his name as a conservative journalist ('Valdombre'). While Grignon's short stories in *Le déserteur et autres récits de la terre* (1934) celebrate country values, *Un homme* dramatizes the economic pressures of the 1930s by depicting a submissive wife, whose cruel misogynist husband drives her to death. Robert Stead's (1880–1959) *Grain* (1926) portrays a prairie farmer named Gander Stake whose passionate attraction to mechanization thwarts any other kind of growth. An early Joyce Marshall (b. 1913) story, 'The Old Woman' (1952) later takes up this same theme, showing how a man's love for his machinery wins out over his love for his wife, limiting and confining him, while at the same time his wife discovers how her creative talents can carry her across apparent linguistic and cultural boundaries.

Yet the move toward realism was not constant. Stead's *The Homesteaders* (1916) was a less melodramatic account of prairie settlement than Wilfrid's Eggleston's (1901–86) later *The High Plains* (1938). And the works of the priest Félix-Antoine Savard (1896–1982) were less revolutionary than those of the journalist Jean-Charles Harvey (1891–1967). Savard's *Le barachois* (1959), for example, extends to Acadia the continuing francophone interest in folk idiom. Savard's highly-praised *Menaud, maître-draveur* (1937), another novel of Quebec nationalism, tells of a log-driver who is driven to madness by his suspicion that foreigners are depriving Quebeckers of their own land. A 1947 translation, *Boss of the River*, is based on the 1937 version; a 1976 translation, *Master of the River*, follows Savard's 1964 revision, one admired for building Quebec regionalisms into the classic structures of French fiction. But Harvey – especially with *Les demi-civilisés* (1934, revised 1962, translated as *Fear's Folly* in 1982) – won the opposition of Duplessis and Cardinal Villeneuve (1883–1947) because of his message. Harvey attacked the 'triple alliance' in Quebec (clergy, capitalists, civil politicians) for keeping ordinary people in fear and ignorance, serving the status quo. In his novel, his characters' sexual and intellectual affairs declare their freedom from passive servitude.

Opposing separatism because it threatened to perpetuate a narrowness of intellectual opportunity, Harvey declared the need for social change within a federalist state; at the same time, he criticized the way the English economic community had managed to control Quebec by framing a troika with politician and priest, a theme reiterated in Hugh MacLennan's (1907–90) *Two Solitudes*. Philippe Panneton (1895–1960, a doctor and later ambassador to Portugal, who published under the name 'Ringuet') also opposed narrow definitions of cultural possibility. His 1924 parody of Groulx was called 'Appel de la crasse'; a 1949 novel called *Le poids du jour* attacked a character who sacrifices affection for wealth and the illusion of power. But Ringuet's works resist easy political categorization, as his novel *Trente arpents* (1938; translated as *Thirty Acres* in 1940) illustrates. It balances a restrictive version of agrarian traditionalism against an equally restrictive version of progress. The central character, Euchariste Moisan, devoted to his land, finally must give it up when a lawsuit threatens to destroy him. His son persuades him to transfer the land to the next generation and to move away, ostensibly to visit another son who has emigrated to the United States, but in fact to live out his life in exile from both his land and his language. Change and progress do not coincide, but the dream of agrarian self-sufficiency is no longer a viable alternative. 'Reality' lies somewhere else – in the psychology of connection (with family, with land) – rather than in the politics of a particular cause.

It is against this context that the appeal of the writings of Frederick Philip Grove (1879–1948) becomes understandable. Written on the grand scale, in a style that some contemporary readers find epic and others turgid, Grove's novels concern the difficulty of locating values in a world riddled with change, where power comes from deceit, innocence invites manipulation, and the amorality of nature parallels the indifference of social institutions. Critics and friends – Kirkconnell, Barker Fairley (1887–1986), A.L. Phelps (1887–1970) – praised Grove for his naturalism; more recent critics have read the stories as fabricated perspectives on the truth. Grove courted recognition. But as his leading biographer Douglas Spettigue (b. 1930) revealed in *FPG* (1973), the life Grove claimed in his autobiography *In Search of Myself* (1946) was a tissue of disguises. 'Reality' lay in what people believed more than in 'fact'. Fabrication gave his characters power; it gave himself status.

His works followed the current fashion of addressing the sexual and moral dilemmas of ordinary workers; they also carried the air of sophistication that attached to Grove himself, who claimed to be of a noble Swedish family. But 'Grove' was really an assumed name, adopted by a German-born author named Felix Paul Greve (one of Grove's unpublished manuscripts bears the title 'Felix Powell's

Career'), the son of a Hamburg tram driver. A free spender, in 1903 Greve had been jailed in Germany for a year for fraud. Though by 1906, still in Germany, he had established a reputation with two novels, *Fanny Essler* (1905, a work reminiscent of Dreiser's *Sister Carrie* in its account of society's constraining impact on a woman's life) and *Mauremeister Ihles Haus* (1906), and with German translations from Wilde, Gide and other writers, Greve then faked a suicide, freed himself from his wife Else, and disappeared. German commentators accepted the death as fact. Six years later, in 1912, a writer named 'Grove' surfaced in Canada as a Manitoba teacher, married a Canadian, and began to write. Grove's first English book, *Over Prairie Trails* (1922), is an interconnected series of prose sketches, evoking several trips between two small Manitoba towns; as the weather changes, so does the character of the journeys, but their difficulty or ease depends less on the overt weather than on knowing how to contend with it. It is not an ideal given world, but an amoral one, dependent on perception. Hence the book at once establishes its authority as a book about nature, and hints at the presence of falsehoods and masks which the truly perceptive will be able to handle.

Grove, who ran unsuccessfully for political office (as a CCF candidate) after he settled in Simcoe, Ontario, in 1931, also published several volumes of descriptive essays, tales and criticism, together with a children's book, and several poems in both English and German. His *Letters* were edited in 1971. Yet his literary reputation depends primarily on the eight novels he published between 1925 and 1947: *Settlers of the Marsh* (1925), *A Search for America* (1927), *Our Daily Bread* (1928), *The Yoke of Life* (1930), *Fruits of the Earth* (1933), *Two Generations* (1939), *The Master of the Mill* (1944), and *Consider Her Ways* (1947). The last of these is an uncharacteristic allegorical fantasy, in which an ant colony examines the ways of humans. *Master of the Mill* tells a several-generation saga of an industrial Ontario family. Read initially for its social criticism, it has found later champions in critics absorbed by structural artifice: the recurrent naming patterns reiterate the motif of shifting identities and restricted power. The 'realistic' farm novels of the 1930s tell of pressure and failure, especially of a failure to transcend the limitations of selfhood. Len Sterner in *Yoke of Life* commits suicide when the world does not live up to his ideal expectations; Abe Spalding in *Fruits of the Earth*, like figures in Ostenso and Grignon, alienates wife and daughter as he pushes himself to power. The young Swedish immigrant Niels Lindstedt, in the earlier *Settlers of the Marsh*, is thwarted by his innocence; pressured by conscience to marry a woman to whom he has been sexually attracted, he realises too late she has been the town prostitute. The novel moves to more formulaic ends when his true sweetheart awaits him after he murders his wife and serves out a modified term in jail. In some ways the most absorbing of the fictions is *A Search for America*, a sprawling episodic journey through the continent of self, the adventures of an immigrant who in turn becomes waiter, encyclopaedia salesman, farm worker, labour organizer and teacher, who is offended by fraud and who passionately embraces Lincolnian egalitarianism. The novel hints repeatedly at autobiographical detail; it can also productively be read as a Jungian quest for self-knowledge that ends up mistaking ego for wisdom.

In the new fiction that followed the First World War, narrative strategies began to change. 'Objective' omniscient narrators were giving way to a perceiving 'I', who was generally untrustworthy but often received as though truth were unaffected by point of view. In the work of John Glassco (1909–81), Dorothy Livesay, Morley Callaghan (1903–90) and Raymond Knister (1900–32), this concern for the ramifications of first person experience began even more clearly to alter literary form. The differences between John Glassco and Dorothy Livesay also spell out the cultural distinction between the 1920s and the 1930s. As young writers, both were part of the general exodus to Paris, along with Callaghan, Leon Edel and Stanley Ryerson (b. 1911) (later a Marxist historian). But whereas Edel and Livesay were students at the Sorbonne in 1932, the former interested in literature and the latter in Marxist politics, Callaghan was a brief visitor in 1929 and Glassco a three-year expatriate from 1928 to 1931. Callaghan's visit – which reacquainted him with Ernest Hemingway (1899–1961), whom he had known when both worked for the Toronto *Star* in the early 1920s, and with Joyce (1882–1941) and Fitzgerald (1896–1940) – later became the subject of an engaging autobiography, *That Summer in Paris* (1963). Glassco, as his own autobiography *Memoirs of Montparnasse* (1970) avers, was a fashionable rebel against his privileged Montreal family, leading a dissolute life as an artful pornographer, surrealist, poet, translator and literary aficionado. He and Callaghan warily watched each other: Callaghan's unflattering portrait of a Glassco-like figure appeared in a story called 'Now that April's Here', and Glassco's arch portrait of Callaghan is one of many in the *Memoirs*. Glassco's skill at the stylish put-down is apparent from this glimpse of Gertrude Stein (1874–1947):

Gertrude Stein projected a remarkable power, possibly due to the atmosphere of adulation that surrounded her. A rhomboidal woman dressed in a floor-length gown apparently made of some kind of burlap, she gave the impression of absolute irrefragability; her ankles, almost concealed by the

hieratic folds of her dress, were like the pillars of a temple: it was impossible
to conceive of her lying down. Her fine close-cropped head was in the style
of the late Roman Empire, but unfortunately it merged into broad peasant
shoulders without the aesthetic assistance of a neck; her eyes were large and
much too piercing. I had a peculiar sense of mingled attraction and repulsion
towards her. She awakened in me a feeling of instinctive hostility coupled
with a grudging veneration, as if she were a pagan idol in whom I was
unable to believe.

The authority of latinate diction and balanced clauses does not hide
the youthful venom. Glassco's was a world of artifice, where fantasy
and the decadence of Aubrey Beardsley (1872–98) carried as much
meaning as daily routine; indeed, his later career saw him complet-
ing Beardsley's *Under the Hill* (1959), writing chiselled poetic lyrics
and satires, and sensitively translating Saint-Denys Garneau. But the
autobiography has also to be seen as fiction; while it tells a comic and
sometimes painful tale of growing up, it is also (as Thomas Tausky
has demonstrated, *Canadian Poetry*, 1983) a carefully arranged narrative, substantially altered in 1970 from its first form (fragments were
published in *This Quarter* in 1929) despite all its textual declarations
to the contrary.

For Dorothy Livesay, by contrast, art was not a tangent to politics
but a way of espousing it. The artist was an active participant in the
world, not simply the observer or hedonistic enjoyer of events. In her
poetry and prose the perceiving 'I' is a device for engaging the reader. From Glassco the reader can stand back, as though from a monologue, overheard; Livesay asks for dialogue – even for dialectic – and
so for the reader's presence and participation as well.

Right Hand Left Hand (1977) tells of her 1930s political education
through social work, Communist Party involvement and organisation, and literary apprenticeship. Early influenced by the Fabians and
the Imagists, she went on in the 1930s to absorb the political models
of Auden and Lorca (1898–1936). While her earliest volumes – *Green
Pitcher* (1928) and *Signpost* (1932) – show her already rebelling against
the Confederation School, the poems in them are personal more than
public lyrics. 'Lorca' (1939) or 'Day and Night' (1935) (the latter the
title of a 1944 volume) showed her political development. The monot-
onous assembly-line refrain in 'Day and Night' ('One step forward /
Two steps back / Shove the lever / Push it back') punctuates a series
of free form descants involving Negro spirituals and dreams of freedom from industrial routine. The radio play *Call My People Home*
(1950) again used the spiritual as an analogue, to protest the treatment
that had been accorded Japanese-Canadians during the Second World

War. (They had been moved to camps, their lands confiscated. This episode in Canadian history subsequently influenced several books: Muriel Kitagawa's (1912–74) 1940s essays opposing racism of all kinds, collected as *This Is My Own*, 1985; Takeo Ujo Nakano's memoir *Within the Barbed Wire Fence*, 1980; Shizuye Takashima's (b. 1928) book for children, *A Child in Prison Camp*, 1971; Ken Adachi's (1928–89) 1976 history *The Enemy that Never Was*; and Joy Kogawa's (b. 1935) poem 'What I Remember of the Evacuation' and novel *Obasan*, 1981.)

Dorothy Livesay founded the poetry magazine *CVII* in 1975. Her later poetry shows the influence of her experience as a teacher in Zambia between 1960 and 1963 ('The Colour of God's Face'), her academic studies in language (1963–5), and her interest in the politics of being female. As 'The Taming' declares her concern:

Be woman. I did not know
the measure of the words
until that night
when you denied me darkness,
even the right
to turn in my own light.

Do as I say, I hear you faintly
over me fainting:
be woman.

The Unquiet Bed (1967), *Plainsongs* (1969), *Ice Age* (1975), *The Woman I Am* (1977), and other books combine the personal with the political perspective. In them she adapts the formal innovations of 1960s poetic movements to declare the freedom of women from the implicitly political restrictions of male language and male social norms.

THE POLITICS OF LITERARY FORM

The politics of literary form is the issue that makes the work of Knister (about whom Livesay wrote memoirs in 1940 and 1987) and Callaghan so representative in the 1920s. Knister's short life (he died at 33 in a drowning accident) has tended both to eclipse and to romanticize his accomplishment. Of German extraction, he wrote frequently of the rural Ontario environment he knew, as in the interrelated 'Corncob Corners' sketches, or 'The First Day of Spring', which he left in manuscript. (Peter Stevens' (b. 1927) 1976 edition of Knister's work used the latter as the title story.) It was not setting, however, but the politics of setting and relationship that fascinated

Knister; his stories and novellas tell of ways in which sexuality and violence turn into assertions of power. Repeatedly, the lyric surfaces of life (childhood, the rural settings) are disrupted when a character recognizes the forces that underlie and manipulate the illusion of happiness or harmony. In this context, speech, too, becomes an agency of power, one which the artist-figures in Knister's stories always seek, recognizing sometimes only after the fact that such control over language also divides them from their past. The author of several formally experimental poems, and of four novels (two unpublished), including *White Narcissus* (1929) and a story about the last years of Keats's (1795–1821) life, *My Star Predominant* (1934), Knister was briefly on the editorial staff of the avant-garde Iowa City literary magazine *The Midland*, and published in *This Quarter* and *Saturday Night*.

He was also the editor of *Canadian Short Stories* (1928), a benchmark anthology, for which he wrote an introductory historical overview of the genre in Canada. Particularly impressive was his sympathy for the new writers (Callaghan, Thomas Murtha (1902–73), Will Ingersoll (1880–1969), Merrill Denison) whom he included along with those of the late nineteenth century (Parker, Thomson, Roberts, Scott). The review that B. K. Sandwell, editor of *Saturday Night*, wrote of the collection indicates, moreover, the magnitude of the literary change that the decade was witnessing. Sandwell liked best the older writers, whom he termed the 'four princes' of Canadian prose; sympathetic to the younger ones, he was nonetheless antipathetic to their 'lively interest in futility', which (however 'cleverly' they wrote) might not last as well as the artistic values of the 'good old days'. He was also puzzled by their method. Instead of using omniscient narrators and a formal received style, they wrote what he considered

dialect ... not merely when their characters are talking ... and ... thinking but when the author is thinking to himself. It is as if it were necessary for the author to impersonate an individual of the class with which he is dealing.

Such a technique later became known as 'free indirect discourse'. To Sandwell, it seemed like perverse subliterariness. To Knister and Callaghan (influenced by the American experiments of Sherwood Anderson, 1876–1941), it was a way of escaping the limits of elitist standards and plotted form. It was a way also of using local speech rhythm instead – not 'dialect', in their terms – as the structural basis for story-telling and the medium of social comment.

This excerpt from 'A Girl with Ambition' (*A Native Argosy*, 1929) illustrates Callaghan's method:

Mary hurried to the man that had been nice to her and demonstrated the dance she had practised all winter. He said she was a good kid and should do well offering her a try-out at thirty dollars a week. Even her stepmother was pleased because it was a respectable company that a girl didn't need to be ashamed of. Mary celebrated by going to a party with Wilfred and playing strip poker until four a.m. She was getting to like being with Wilfred.

Unornamented and tonally flat, the passage appears initially to be merely a report. Inside the statements (as explained in Victor Hoar's (b. 1933) *Morley Callaghan*, 1969) is a verbal series – *nice, good, well, pleased, respectable, celebrated* – which climaxes in *strip poker*. The contrast between the influential sequences, and the implicit contrasts inside the second sequence alone, carried Callaghan's message. He is not imposing a moral judgment, but rather exposing the way in which this society wears morality as a mask. It has to adapt to empirical realities if it wants to survive. The fact that the character Mary may be too calculated to be likeable is beside the point. In Callaghan's terms, she survives because she can accommodate herself to the ironic dimensions of modern urban life; the absolutes of conventional morality do not leave room for circumstances, and it is the shifting attitudes of circumstance that the short stories use narrative style to convey. *Morley Callaghan's Stories* (1959) collected such works as 'Ancient Lineage', 'Two Fishermen', 'Last Spring They Came Over', 'A Sick Call' and 'A Cap for Steve'. Several uncollected stories were gathered in 1985 as *The Lost and Found Stories of Morley Callaghan*, by his son, the writer (and editor of *Exile*) Barry Callaghan (b. 1937); among them is 'Loppy Phelan's Double Shoot', a psychologically perceptive narrative based on the exposé of Grey Owl.

Masks, frauds, pretence: these are the recurrent motifs of Callaghan's writing. A playwright, newspaper columnist, and radio and television personality, he had published a dozen novels by 1987. They have been read as Catholic narratives in which moral innocents come into conflict with the streetwise and the powerful. They have also been read as urban romances. In the novel, a tendency to melodrama becomes more apparent. Some readers find Callaghan at his most arresting in *Such Is My Beloved* (1934), *More Joy in Heaven* (1935), *The Loved and the Lost* (1951), and *A Time for Judas* (1983). In a series of moral questions, he probes the character of society, seeking reasons to explain why people hesitate to act when it appears they should and why they seem to act precipitately when it seems hesitation would be wiser. Is goodness merely foolishness, asks *Such Is My Beloved*. (The story concerns a priest whose earnest desire to help prostitutes brings his reputation and, say the authorities, the reputation of the Church, into question.) Is sainthood merely pride? (*The Loved and the Lost* tells of a woman who frequents a bar where black musicians play, and of the ambitious reporter who loves her, but who doubts her goodness at a critical moment when he ought to trust. His own irrational suspicions are what he ought to suspect, but it is they which debilitate him most.) Is goodness recognizable without the presence of evil? (*A Time for Judas*, cast in the familiar format of the 'discovered manuscript', purports to tell the real story of Judas Iscariot's betrayal of Christ: not for money, but because betrayal was necessary in order that Christ's goodness be finally recognized. Chosen to be the betrayer, Judas cannot refuse, but in order that he be effective in his greater role, neither can he explain and defend his action; hence he, too, wears a mask, earning the calumny of history when instead he deserves its forgiveness and recognition.)

Callaghan's analysis of social class is most apparent in *They Shall Inherit the Earth* (1935), yet he was not a social reformer like Klein and Livesay. He used literature not to change society but to represent it (lucidly, plainly, as though without the interference of 'art'), with the aim of evoking on the page the human centre and humane potential of even the most ordinary of people and actions. Clearly his practice was not 'artless', but it took some years for the character of his artifice to be recognized. He was adapting narrative voice to the attitude of the human dilemmas that interested him, and so was serving the development of the realist mode. Yet he was doing so by reanimating some of the oldest forms of narrative – parable, in particular, just as Klein was reactivating the social force of ironic allegory – in order to have stylistic form itself make a statement about human experience. Often the structural message ran counter or parallel to the declarations of the surface text, rather than in concert with them. Klein wrote with a scathing social irony, Callaghan with a morally earnest one. Both techniques were devices to engage the reader in separating the truths of artistic insight from the structures and solutions of literary and social convention.

LITERATURE AND WAR

As the 1930s wore on, and the nation again engaged in a European war, some of the same issues that had surfaced in the 1910s emerged once more: the role of women, the threat of conscription ('Not necessarily conscription', Mackenzie King said, 'but conscription if necessary', alienating Quebec), the role of industry, the extent of dependence on the USA, the nature of the link with Britain. The Canadian Labour Congress came into being during the war years, some unions separating from their US affiliates. But in other spheres there was more cooperation. The US and Canada together built the Alaska Highway as a military supply road; aerial surveys and mapping increased in the high Arctic. After the war, Canada joined NATO, NORAD, and worked with the United States in constructing the St Lawrence Seaway, and the DEW Line and other installations in a norther radar defence system. Separately, Canada would join SEATO and (until 1990) resist joining the Organisation of American States. Actively, Canada sought a world role, and world recognition.

The basis for certain forms of corporate expansion (forms which would oppose Keynesian theory by 1980 and approve Friedmanite monetarism instead) lay in the 1930s. Control over the newspaper industry provides an example. Ontario-born Max Aitken, Lord Beaverbrook (1879–1963), active in British politics even during the First World War, had acquired the London *Daily Express* and *Evening Standard* by 1930. Roy Thomson's newspaper chain began to grow in the 1930s, expanding during the early 1940s, and spreading after the war to England, where Thomson (1894–1976) acquired some measure of political influence. He became Baron Thomson of Fleet in 1963; a Toronto performance hall was subsequently named after him. By 1983, the Thomson Group controlled over 200 newspapers in Canada, the USA and the UK, including the London *Times* and the Toronto *Globe & Mail*, and also such corporations as the Hudson's Bay Company. In 1985, another Toronto industrialist, Conrad Black (b. 1944, later Lord Black of Cross Harbour, the author of an appreciative biography of Maurice Duplessis), acquired control over the London *Daily Telegraph*; by 1987 he had also purchased forty-five North American newspapers, including *Le Droit* (Ottawa), and *Saturday Night*.

Another biography, *A Man Called Intrepid* (1977) by William Stevenson (b. 1925), popularized the life of the Second World War Canadian intelligence expert (and model for James Bond) Sir William Stephenson (b. 1896), though the exploits are often more myth than fact. In the war, Canada lost several thousand lives – in Hong Kong and the Pacific as well as in Europe. Although national pride celebrated the Normandy Invasion and other theatres of battle, the landing at Dieppe in 1942 furnished one more metaphor of loss; it functions now in Canada the way a reference to Gallipoli functions in Australia. The allegation that 'colonial' Canadians were being used as cannon fodder in an unwinnable battle caused many people to feel betrayed. (As late as Margaret Laurence's (1926–87) *A Bird in the House*, 1970, the allusion to Dieppe stirs resentment.) From 1945 to the 1980s, the only other war Canada officially fought in was the United Nations war in Korea in the 1950s. In 1956, Canada once again refused to back Britain's military intervention in the Middle East. Prime Minister Lester Pearson (1897–1972) then proposed the idea of UN peacekeeping forces (for which he won the Nobel Peace Prize). This measure has subsequently constituted Canada's most prominent international military role.

Heather Robertson's (b. 1942) *A Terrible Beauty* (1977) collects examples of Canadian war paintings (by Charles Comfort and Carl Schaefer (1903–95, among others). Literary works affected by the Second World War include memoirs, historical commentaries and the many allusions to fascism and the Holocaust which continue to haunt Canadian writing after 2000. War stories include Hugh Garner's (1913–79) *Storm Below* (1944), Douglas Le Pan's (1914–98) *The Deserter* (1964), Jean-Jules Richard's (1911–75) *Neuf jours de haine* (1948), Philip Child's *Day of Wrath* (1945), Lionel Shapiro's (1908–58) *The Sixth of June* (1955), Earle Birney's *Turvey* (1949), Bertrand Vac's (b. 1914) *Deux ports ... une adresse* (1952), Norman Levine's (b. 1923) *The Angled Road* (1952), Colin McDougall's (1917–84) *Execution* (1958), and David Walker's (1911–92) *The Pillar* (1952). These range from Walker's formulaic work to Birney's satiric picaresque to McDougall's dour realism. As late as 1984, Douglas Lochhead (b. 1922) produced an eloquent memoir (in poem and journal) of personal war experience, called *The Panic Field*. Maria Jacobs's (b. 1930) memoir *Precautions Against Death* (1983), also a prose-poetry combination, tells of her childhood in Holland, and of the restrictions imposed on normal relationships when her mother hid a disparate group of Jews from Nazi discovery. The poets Y.Y. Segal (1896–1954) and Rachel Korn (1898–1982) are two of a number of Yiddish writers whose works, much concerned with exile and suffering, appeared during the 1920s, 30s and 40s. Klein translated some of this work; several translations appeared in Korn's *Generations* (1982), edited by Seymour Mayne (b. 1944). Georgina Sime's late novels (written in collaboration with Frank Nicholson, 1875–1962, one-time librarian of the University of Edinburgh) allude to the war, the underground and patterns of immigration. In *Les lilas fleurissent à Varsovie* (1981) and its sequel the lawyer Alice Parizeau (1930–90) took up another formal strategy, drawing on her own Polish background to tell a story of the concentration camps and the resistance movement.

Henry Kreisel (1922–91), born to Jewish parents, left his native Austria for England in 1938, was interned there when the war began, then sent to Canada where he was interned for another eighteen months, and where he began to learn English. In due course a professor of comparative literature in Edmonton, he published essays concerning his war experiences, together with several stories and two novels. *The Rich Man* (1948) concerns an Austrian immigrant who adopts a mask of wealth to impress his relatives when he revisits his native land, only to find himself powerless before their 1930s needs. *The Betrayal* (1964) tells of two Jews who confront each other in Edmonton, one having previously betrayed the other in Europe, as both struggled to survive. Like the latter work, several of Kreisel's short stories are morality tales. Collected in *The Almost Meeting and other stories* (1981), 'The Broken Globe' tells of a conflict between generations (figured in the globe of the title), which emphasizes two different expectations: one 'old-world' and mythic, the other 'new-world' and kinetic. Another story, 'The Travelling Nude', is a comic account of the difference between a sophisticated attitude towards art and a relentless prairie provincialism.

By the 1980s, Timothy Findley's works used the war setting as a frame against which to investigate the character of human violence, and Robert Harlow's (b. 1923) *Felice* (1985) proves what even after thirty years has not yet been learned from Auschwitz. To some degree writers had by this time shifted from personal engagement to generalization, seeking less to record the specifics of one war than to treat 'war' as a figurative attribute of human behaviour.

One of the striking concrete results of the Second World War, nevertheless, was the physical movement of whole populations. Refugees moved everywhere, and those who moved to Canada soon altered the country's character. Many who wrote fiction – Kreisel and the Hungarian-born John Marlyn (b. 1912, *Under the Ribs of Death*, 1957) being among the earliest – turned the immigrant character into a figure of contemporary exile and alienation. For the nation, the war altered yet another stereotype: Europe could no longer remain the image of culture and sophistication, against which a wilderness Canada was to be measured; it had become a place of violence, from which Canada was both exile and refuge. More intellectually debilitating for some was the realization that the anti-semitism uncovered in Europe was also endemic at home. Irving Abella's (b. 1940) history *None Is Too Many* (1983) observes how official government policy in the 1940s prevented Jewish refugees from reaching Canada. Anti-semitism surfaces as a subject also in novels by André Giroux (1916–77; *Au delà des visages*, 1948), Yves Thériault (*Aaron*, 1954), Gwethalyn Graham (1913–65; *Earth and High Heaven*, 1944), and in the poems and prose of A.M. Klein.

Ukrainian-born, Klein grew up in Montreal; trained in Talmudic tradition, he was committed in his own life to causes involving Zionism and social reform. Like Frank Scott, he practised law and became involved in socialist politics, running unsuccessfully for the CCF in the 1949 federal election; but law was never a fulfilling career, and ethnic pressures always marked his writing and his life. Several of his early poems in *Hath Not a Jew* ... (1940) and *Poems* (1944) reflect both his passionate commitment to his religious tradition and his awareness of the degree to which his tradition alienated him from the Canadian mainstream. Even tolerance was an attitude touched by difference, as is made clear by a cool line in an early sonnet: at a social gathering, 'Mr. and Mrs. Klein' are introduced as 'The Jews, you know', a phrase that encloses and distances, ostensibly embraces but actually holds apart.

Klein's witty poems of the 1920s and his psalms and prophetic poems of the 1930s and 1940s – 'The Soiree of Velvel Kleinburger', 'A Psalm Touching Genealogy', 'Psalm VI: A Psalm of Abraham, concerning that which he beheld upon the heavenly scarp' – range from social satire to political protest. As the Depression worsened and the war began , his writing protested more openly. In the editorials and allegories he wrote for *The Canadian Jewish Chronicle* in 1938 and 1939, he attacked the civil uninterest, the careful unawareness, that kept authorities from adequately addressing social problems. In 'Psalm VI', the Lord locks down at the 'unspeakable horde', the 'cattle cars: / Men ululating to a frozen land. / ... / Scholars, he saw, sniffing their bottled wars, / And doctors who had geniuses unmanned', and once more 'Summoned the angels of Sodom down to earth'. In *The Hitleriad* (1944), loosely based on Pope's *Dunciad* ('Heil heavenly muse'), Klein at once attacked Nazism and ridiculed Hitler, but it was not a subject that could sustain either wit or comedy; for all the brilliance of individual lines, and for all the justice of its social and moral passion, the poem as a whole remains the least successful of Klein's works. In subsequent poems – until, in the early 1950s, Klein entered the self-imposed silence from which he never emerged – he extrapolated more from Jewish experience to focus on the larger implications of alienation and exile in the modern world. He began, too, to reveal more clearly his debt to James Joyce and European modernism. Long influenced by his readings in Elizabethan and Metaphysical writers, in Joyce and in Hopkins (1844–89), Klein was a stylistic formalist, less inclined than Scott or Smith to follow the imagists or the minimalists, and more interested in the effects of textural density, polyphony, theme-and-variation. In the poems of *The Rocking Chair* (1948), in his novel *The Second Scroll* (1951), and in short stories such as 'The Bells of Sobor Spasitula') written about 1952 but not published until 1983, in *A.M. Klein: Short Stories*, one of the volumes in the Collected Works currently being edited by Zailig Pollock, b. 1948, M.W. Steinberg, b. 1918, and Usher Caplan, b. 1947), Klein made language his subject as well as his medium of expression. Language could orchestrate a dialectic of multiple identities; it could also constitute this dialectic, evoking in practice the politics and psychology of different points of view.

Language was also a temptation. Part of the argument of *The Rocking Chair* derives from the difference between poems that use language to symbolize social attitudes and poems that enact artistic and political choices in verbal phrasing. The whole volume looks at Quebec circumstances. 'Indian Reservation: Caughnawaga' describes the 'pious, prosperous ghosts' that modern Iroquois have become. The monologue 'Political Meeting' captures the rhetorical skills of Montreal mayor Camillien Houde (1889–1958), and demonstrates how charged words and emotional pacing – in this case geared to anti-*anglais* and anti-conscription sentiments – can turn a simple question into a racist innuendo. 'The Rocking Chair' employs metonymic and synaesthetic techniques to express the perceived passivity of Quebec culture; 'It is act / and symbol, symbol of this static folk / which moves in segments, and returns to base, – / a sunken pendulum: *invoke, revoke;* / loosed yon, leashed hither, motion on no space. / O, like some Anjou ballad, all refrain.' But in 'Portrait of the Author as Landscape', the poem asks what the poet wants to achieve by language in the first place: territory, power, fame, money? Mysticism, madness, message are all temptations. Fascinated by words, the poem says, the ambitious poet even wants to be words: 'to be talked about; / to be a verb; to be introduced as *The*'. Even to *be* is an attraction, muses the marginal narrator. But it is the 'status as zero' made into a 'rich garland' that is the real thing: the ability of the poet to 'seed illusions' but 'live alone' in 'anonymity' and shine 'like phosphorus. At the bottom of the sea'. Literature often seeks a deliberate connection with the world; the world often asks literature to name or reflect or even praise it. But none of these connections means anything to Klein if it is false to the writer's vision. The consequent temptation of solipsism, however, in later years undermined Klein's faith in his own art and in the power of art in general. Futility and despair characterize many of the writings he left in manuscript when he died in 1972.

'The Bells of Sobor Spasitula' asserts Klein's rejection of state control over art. Cast as a memory of Russia, a pulsing memory encouraged by waves of bell-sound, it tells of the brilliant artistry of a composer and of his resistance to the artistic direction of state authorities. In an ironic defiance of an edict to compose in a politically approved mode, he takes an old work, one full of passionate individualism, and retitles it according to the new approved rhetoric. Interpreted in the new way, it wins praise – until the irony is recognized. The persecution that follows sends art itself into exile, while the artist is sacrificed to political expediency. Exile and art are also entwined themes in *The Second Scroll*, which tells of a young Canadian's search for his uncle Melech ('King') Davidson in the years after the Second World War. Each time the nephew reaches the place where his uncle has been, the uncle has moved on, until the two have retraced the wandering steps of post-war Jewry to the newly founded state of Israel. Metamorphosed into the state, presumably, the uncle is finally 'found'. More arresting than this conclusion is the character of the prose. Written while Klein was composing a commentary on *Ulysses*, the novel everywhere shows Joyce's influence. It follows a structural paradigm (the Pentateuch) which it formally invokes as a frame of reference. It interweaves poetry with prose. It pushes at generic enclosure in order to free the achievement of the art from conventional cultural definitions. In form itself is meaning realized.

VOICE AND POINT OF VIEW

Klein had few contemporaries in Canada who insisted as passionately on the separation of art from state. The poet Gilles Héneault (1920–96), culminating in works like *Sémaphore* (1962), asserted that words did not imply social referents. A few other poetic modernists were breaking the stylistic conventions of realism. Ottawa-born Elizabeth Smart (1913–85), for example (who during the 1930s and 40s was living with the English poet George Barker, 1913–91), completed a novel/prose poem/meditation on pain and lost love, called *By Grand Central Station I Sat Down and Wept*, in 1941. But it had little Canadian audience (indeed, political pressure prevented it entering Canada) until it was reissued, revised, in 1966. Malcolm Lowry (1909–57) was living in Canada from 1939 to the early 1950s, but few Canadians acknowledged Lowry's work until the 1960s. Neither did they much notice Sheila Watson's (1909–98) *The Double Hook* (1959) or Howard O'Hagan's (1902–82) *Tay John* (1939), a mythic novel of a Métis 'Messiah', until 1970s taste rediscovered both books.

More applauded in his own day, the Nova Scotia writer Ernest Buckler (1908–84) published essays and stories during the 1940s. In 1952 his novel *The Mountain and the Valley* appeared, adapting the image of a patchwork quilt to the interrupted narrative (told through flashback) of the youth of David Canaan. For David, the thwarting of an artistic sensibility means ultimate death. Buckler's interest is as much in Canaan's limited society, in regional detail, as in the independence of literary form. As with his more openly descriptive book of memoir and sketch, *Ox Bells and Fireflies* (1968), Buckler turned an eloquent phrase, but he often also allowed eloquence to be its own justification.

The passionate explorations of the interior landscape, which characterize the poetry of Saint-Denys Garneau and Anne Hébert, come closer to the psychological aspect of Klein's accomplishment. The communications theories of Harold Adams Innis (1894–1952) – particularly *Empire and Communications* (1946, re-edited by Dave Godfrey in 1986) and *The Bias of Communication* (1951) – come closer to Klein's theory of form. Innis, an economist whose *The Fur Trade in Canada* (1930) has influenced many subsequent analyses of the role of business in Canadian culture, examined in his later works how particular systems of communication (mail, telephone, radio, train) imposed their own 'bias' or pattern of priorities on the messages they conveyed. Related to Innis's theories are those of Marshall McLuhan (1911–80), whose major works *The Mechanical Bride* (1951), *The Gutenberg Galaxy* (1962) and *Understanding Media* (1964) – the last of which popularized the phrase 'The medium is the message' – championed the power of representation, explored the kinds of cultural impact that different media could have, led in the direction of critical theories of semiotics, and profoundly marked post-modern writing during the 1960s and 1970s.

More characteristic of Klein's contemporaries in the 1940s and 1950s, however, were several writers whose experimentations with realism led primarily to variations in voice and point of view. While many of these works were exploring the limits of technique, they were more focused on an external subject: the agrarian conventions of society, which it was their prime aim to change. 'Identity' was both the end of a psychological quest and a current social desire, as the fiction of the time revealed. Hence novels such as Jean Simard's (b. 1916) *Félix* (1947) or Pierre Baillargeon's (1916–67) *La neige et le feu* (1948) caricature the clergy. Simard's *Mon fils pourtant heureux* (1956) speaks of accepting the limitations of reality. Robert Élie (1915–73, who with Jean Le Moyne, Robert Charbonneau, 1911–67, Paul Beaulieu, 1910–96, and Saint-Denys Garneau had in 1934 founded the magazine *La Relève*, which became *La Nouvelle Relève* in 1941) adapted the form of the private diary. In *La fin des songes* (1950), Élie tells of one man's suicide and another's efforts to fight the pressures of the society around him. Charbonneau, for his part, wrote a series of novels about the psychological quest for the personal self, beginning with *Ils posséderont la terre* (1941), a novel in which dreams of an intellectual order are effectively the only alternative offered to the restrictive empirical order of the clerical society. Charbonneau helped change the character of Quebec fiction more directly in 1940 when with Claude Hurtubise (1914–99) he founded the publishing house Les Éditions de l'Arbre, which reprinted banned books and published 'radical' young authors like Richard, Lemelin and Thériault. Such radicalism as they possessed existed primarily in their topics. Jean-Jules Richard wrote on such subjects as homosexuality. Roger Lemelin (1919–92), later the publisher of La Presse) wrote of clerical limitations and urban industrial unrest, as in Au pied de la pente douce (1944, translated as The Town Below in 1948). Yves Thériault, the part-Montagnais author, won a popular following for his numerous melodramas and allegories of violence and sexuality, and a readership in anglophone Canada mainly for his tale of Inuit confrontation called Agaguk (1958).

The Acadian New Brunswick writer Donat Coste (1912–57) raised the issue of racism in L'enfant noir (1950). Other novelists of the time included Selwyn Dewdney, Jean Filiatrault (1919–82), Pierre Gélinas (b. 1935), Patricia Blondal (1926–59), Louis Dantin, Ronald Hambleton (b. 1917), Clément Lockquell (1908–84), the Ottawa-born harpist Winifred Bambrick (1892–1969) and Eugène Cloutier (1921–75). Fred Bodsworth (b. 1918), in Last of the Curlews (1954), continued the tradition of nature fiction; English-born Roderick Haig-Brown (1908–76), in essay collections such as Fisherman's Fall (1964) and novels for children – for example, Starbuck Valley Winter (1946) and Saltwater Summer (1948) – portrayed nature as a moral backdrop to physical action. Bertrand Vac (Aimé Pelletier), in Louise Genest (1950), argued that the idea of wilderness is a weight around the socio-literary neck in Quebec, burdening those who carry it with the conventional attitudes of the past. It is the psychology, not so much the language, of literary convention that engages the author here.

In Le survenant (1945) and its sequel Marie-Didace (1946) – together translated in 1950 as The Outlander – Germaine Guèvremont (1893–1968) again employed the motif of the rural environment closed to the outsider; here she makes the outsider a figure of opportunity and openness, which the rural parish culture cannot bring itself to accept. Adele Wiseman (1928–92) examined in The Sacrifice (1956) the weight of convention in the lives of a family of Jewish immigrants to Winnipeg, a burden of belief in moral system that leads to violence when the immigrant's rhetoric of interpretation reads local life mistakenly.

While several of these authors had attempted to produce internal monologues of various kinds, the stance taken in their works largely involved the representation of a substantial central character against an empirically recognizable social background, and the realization of some parallel or opposition between the two. As Jacques Michon (b. 1945) observes in René Dionne's (b. 1929) *Le Québécois et sa littérature* (1984), such presumptions of referentiality governed the characteristic narrative technique: simple past tense, third-person historical or first-person autobiographical stance, the reservation of speech forms for dialogue, the acceptance of the existence of some neutral, universal reader. Often these works had as their aim the alteration of social norms, but in the matter of expression they illustrated the literary controls these norms still exerted. Few writers before 1960 went so far as Klein, Lowry, Elizabeth Smart or Callaghan did in the direction of multiple narrators, referential ambiguity, indirect discourse or sequential discontinuity.

Among several works which stand out even within the confines of conventional realism are those of Sinclair Ross, Gabrielle Roy (1909–83), Claire Martin (b. 1914), and Robert de Roquebrune. The latter two, who both wrote works of fiction, are more noted for their historical autobiographies. Martin's *Dans un gant de fer* (1965) and *La joue droite* (1966) – together translated in 1968 as *In an Iron Glove* – record a hateful childhood, for which the author claims to have 'forgiven all'. The fact that the first volume won a fiction award hints at the character of its narrative method. It tells of tyranny: the tyranny of a father most of all, and of the convent nuns. By implication the family tension criticizes the character of the state as well; the author sees the church and the state in the years between the wars as the structures which have perpetuated tyranny in the family by creating a system of laws which puts women down. Such themes recur in her novels, as in *Quand j'aurai payé ton visage* (1962). The autobiography, that is, reiterates the fictional formulae of Grignon and Ostenso in recounting a personal history; at once Martin's work validates and intensifies the concerns of those earlier novels, and also inherits their fictional frame of reference as its own milieu. Robert de Roquebrune's *Testament de mon enfance* (1951, translated 1964) is lighter in touch, more concerned with using prose form to trace the changes in childhood's perspectives. Though there were two further instalments to the autobiography, the first volume has attracted most attention, for the lucidity of the prose, for its internal narratives, and for the colour of its portraits of individual family members. In many ways *Testament de mon enfance* can also be read as a key to the light historical fiction Roquebrune published in the 1920s. *D'un océan à l'autre* (1924), for example, tells of cowboys, the Métis, the CPR and the West. The terms are conventional, but hidden in the book, as in his novels of the 1837 rebellion (*Les habits rouges*, 1923) and the *ancien régime* (*Les dames Le Marchand*, 1927) are glimpses of his family past, transformed into romance by an extended boyhood imagination.

Sinclair Ross's literary reputation rests on the short stories he published during the Depression and the war (for example, 'The Lamp at Noon', 1938; 'The Painted Door', 1939; 'One's a Heifer', 1944), and primarily on his first novel, *As For Me and My House* (1941), a diary-form revelation of the claustrophobia, resentment, suspicion and anger that bedevil a minister's wife in Saskatchewan in the 1930s. The best of Ross's stories were collected in *The Lamp at Noon* (1968); although the author published a second collection in 1982 (a retrospective, primarily) and three more novels, only the fourth novel *Sawbones Memorial* (1974) comes close to the strength of the first, and it does so largely because of its handling of point of view. It tells of a retirement party for a prairie doctor. Withholding direct authorial comment, Ross arranges dialogue, monologue, flashback and other breaks from sequential form to review fragmentarily the doctor's career. In both novels hypocrisy characterizes town life. In both cases, too, the rage that stems from being the victim of hypocrisy modulates slowly into an acceptance of the imperfections of humankind. At least, that is clear for *Sawbones Memorial*; greater uncertainty surrounds *As For Me and My House* because of the controlled ambivalence in the book's text. The diary form draws the reader into the perspective of the narrator (she is called 'Mrs. Bentley', the absence of a personal name anywhere in the book emphasizing how much her identity has become dependent on her husband's). But the figures and actions she records are sufficiently open to other interpretations that the reader is simultaneously invited to stand apart and weigh the evidence independently.

The way Ross embodies such ambivalence in formal technique – it extends to his imagery, which recurrently combines opposites: dust flows (like life), water parches (like faith) – has meant that there have been successive waves of critical reaction. Early readers responded to the social background of Ross's work, its representational accuracy, its authoritative account of domestic and historical pressure; another group of readers fastened on the main character, seeking especially a wholeness of personality, a genuineness of feeling, which could be seen to stand at the centre of a world that threatened to disintegrate. Later critics dispensed with notions of wholeness and accepted the idea that personalities are fragmentary and morally inconsistent. These critics looked in the text for the patterns of discourse that conducted a reader (through stories both declared and implied) towards suppositions and conclusions about the character of understanding. From the vantage point of the first group of readers, the third group is abstract, concerning itself with theories of communication. From the perspective of the third group, the first readers mistook the concreteness of the text for the concreteness of life.

As For Me and My House covers a year in the life of Mrs Bentley and her husband Philip, as they minister to Horizon, one of a series of Saskatchewan towns they have moved to during the 1930s drought. Nothing grows. No one has money. Nowhere is secure. The townspeople, to Mrs Bentley's recording eyes, follow an interminable repetitive pattern: she counts among them the self-important, the critical, the vulnerable, the cynical, the gossiping, the sly – and they fulfil her expectations. A would-be pianist, she herself is desperate for fulfilment, escape, and perhaps forgiveness for some unstated flaw. Her husband, a would-be artist, has lost his faith and equally wants a different future. But they can no longer communicate. When opportunity comes, it comes from a quarter they do not anticipate; they adopt an illegitimate child and prepare to leave town. At that point the townspeople become in Mrs Bentley's diary more warm and friendly than they have been all during their stay, which underlines how much the pressure has been self-imposed. By orchestrating the diary entries, Ross managed to turn Mrs Bentley's repetitive record of personal habits (the closing of doors), weather (wind, sun, dust), and conversation (their friend Paul's relentless fascination with etymology) into a rhetoric of despair. While readers may find Mrs Bentley a classically unreliable narrator as far as her judgments of character and motive are concerned (her own included), they have no reason to distrust the covert communication embodied in the narrative form. The form tells of *perceived* repetition, of a psychological sensibility that sees changes occur without effecting any difference, of a social experience wherein the future seems only to usher in the restrictive past.

The work of Gabrielle Roy is also open both to social and to psychological readings. Like Ross, the author was prairie-born (he in Saskatchewan, she in Manitoba); his banking career took him to Montreal, her teaching career and marriage took her to Quebec City, where she lived until her death in 1983. Both writers ranged between the prairies of their memory and the urban pressures of contemporary Quebec. Both wrote as outsiders and observers. Gabrielle Roy was, however, the more openly autobiographical, both in her prairie fiction and in her essays. *Ces enfants de ma vie* (1977, translated in 1979 as *Children of My Heart*) presents scenes from the lives of a teacher's 'children'. *Fragiles lumières de la terre* (1978) records her impressions of prairie immigrant groups (Doukhobor, Ukrainian, German) and comments also on her own fiction and the award of the Prix Fémina to *Bonheur d'occasion* in 1945. The linked stories of *Rue Deschambault* (1955) – translated in 1957 as *Street of Riches* – tell of a girl growing up in Saint-Boniface. The stories of *La route d'Altamont* (1966, translated in 1976) look at the same girl, at her connections with her mother and grandmother, at the way the matrilineal link shapes the way she sees the world. Told in the first person present, but telling of the imperfectly realized past, the latter work also reveals Gabrielle Roy's growing experimentation with tense patterns and narrative viewpoint.

Among her other books are two for children and several which range more widely in setting and intensity. For example, *La montagne secrète* (1961) and *La rivière sans repos* (1970, the title story translated as *Windflower*) portray life in the Arctic. The first treats the Arctic as a metaphoric landscape (an extension of the traditional Quebec 'pays d'en haut') in which artistic imagination can find a sort of freedom. The second uses it as a more referential setting for stories of contemporary conflict between white and Inuit ways of life. *La petite poule d'eau* (1950, translated as *Where Nests the Water Hen*) evokes in mellifluous prose the character of life in a remote northern Manitoba hamlet; *Cet été qui chantait* (1972, translated as *Enchanted Summer*) glimpses Charlevoix County in Quebec, but represents a break in technical method. *Un jardin au bout du monde* (1975, translated 1977 as *Garden in the Wind*) collects four stories that raise questions about multicultural settlements in the prairies. In 'Where Will You Go, Sam Lee Wong', a single Chinese shopkeeper settles among foreigners, alien among aliens, befriended by one who like the others fails entirely to understand him. Language separates, despite the will to connect. When the townspeople in a gesture of generosity, thinking Sam is about to leave, provide him with a parting gift, Sam discovers he must leave even though he had not intended to go. The circumstances of expectation have shaped at least some of the dimensions of his life. In another story, 'A Tramp at the Door', it is the circumstances of desire that shape people's lives. When a traveller arrives on some French-Canadian settlers' doorstep and claims to be distant kin from Quebec, he is asked in to eat, to tell recent tales of family, to convey messages, to stay. From the beginning, or soon after, the settlers know their visitor is a fraud; he relies on their isolation, and they are willing to live with the fiction for a while because they are eager to reaffirm any kind of connection with their language, and with Quebec, before they encourage the 'familiar' stranger to move on.

Gabrielle Roy is best known for two early books, *Bonheur d'occasion* (1945, translated as *The Tin Flute* in 1947 by Hannah Josephson, 1900–76, – a translation marred by certain inaccuracies – and in 1980 by Alan Brown, b. 1920) and *Alexandre Chenevert* (1955, translated as *The Cashier*, by Harry Binsse, 1905–71). In these works the literary motifs of the *roman du terroir* combine with the author's urban social realism. The novels work as grounds on which the appeal of the rural dream runs abruptly into the empirical truths of poverty, sexuality and routine. Characters in both books long for land and nature, but their brief enjoyment of it is less fulfilling than they might have hoped – 'solutions' to social problems lie elsewhere, in a series of compromises that reveal the inadequacies of existing situations.

The 'social realism' of these novels shows up in subject and setting: *Alexandre Chenevert* concerns a bank worker whose outer world thwarts the expression of his inner dreams; *Bonheur d'occasion* tells of the Lacasse ('box') family, of the St Henri district of Montreal, for whom the norms of life are poverty, illness, deceit and retreat. Entrapment is everywhere. The novels reiterate images of prison and cage. For the mater dolorosa Rose-Anna Lacasse, marriage and motherhood are constraints that she accepts, finally, with a stubborn grace, but not before the novel has protested the circumstances that make her lot so difficult. Her husband, Azarius, struggles to act nobly in her eyes, but repeatedly fails to live up to his own idea of heroism, never recognizing that she asks only for a human companion. For him, the Second World War seems a solution to the Depression – he joins up, to earn a regular paycheque – but to Rose-Anna it seems he is still running away. Their children, too, can solve their problems only by taking on other constraints; one chooses the nunnery, not out of faith but out of hunger for security; another dies; a third – Florentine, on whom so much of the novel focuses – longs for the flashy life she sees around her. She pursues a lover and becomes pregnant, but finally accepts as a husband a different young man whom she neither loves nor admires but who longs to be with her. (One of Robin Mathews's, b. 1931, stories in *Blood Ties*, 1984, brings Florentine's story 'up-to-date', using it to expose a conflict between a generation with bourgeois ambitions and the militant rebels of the generation that follows it. Michel Tremblay's, b. 1942, 'Chroniques du Plateau Mont-Royal' also allude to Roy's work, though finding it defeatist.) In *Bonheur d'occasion* Florentine's solution simply sets in motion another cycle of denial. What offends the author's eye most is that the church and the state either refuse to see the desperation around them or do not recognize their own role in perpetuating miseries in the lives of women and men, and do not choose to change.

Cage, cycle, see: these are useful words for understanding how Gabrielle Roy turns her observations of society into fictional texts with their own intrinsic formal patterns of argument. The circular structures of *Bonheur d'occasion* and *Alexandre Chenevert*, for example, carry quite separate messages. While the earlier novel separates the characters from the act of narration, it involves them in its pattern; the authorial narrator watches the characters, as though from a distance, but rather than imply objectivity, the distance reinforces the characters' inability to connect with others. They can only watch, only be the recipients of action; they can never initiate changes, or take part in consequential dialogue. Given as 'speech' only the language of the 'normative' institutions in their society, they are rendered silent, for such speech does not adequately embody the kinds of life they are forced to lead. They seek meaning elsewhere, and consequently lose meaning from their own lives, deny the possibility that their lives (as they are being lived) can have any significance – a circumstance that can be read as a political paradigm for the disenfranchised anywhere: Quebeckers, women, the poor. Alexandre Chenevert even dies believing that he has been a failure because his routine work has silenced him, disconnected him from others, separated his dream life from the world in which he has learned to believe 'success' lies. In this case, however, the novel draws attention to itself: whatever Alexandre may as a *character* think, the entire work of *fiction* becomes a separate instigator of social dialogue, a process that gives substance to the dream life that the fictional figure continues to live. In *La route d'Altamont*, moreover, the girl Christine, who is at once the past character and the present narrator, takes hold of her own history ('je crois'); speech allows her not to be locked into relationships but rather to be freed by them, making the art of reading an art of listening closely as well.

RADIO AND STAGE

The Canadian Broadcasting Corporation and Radio-Canada were instrumental in changing literary form. Radio developed during the 1940s and 1950s as a medium for art and information. Although anglophone Canadian radio actors long adopted a 'mid-Atlantic' speech norm – one represented by Lister Sinclair (b. 1921), for example, whose own plays won critical attention – radio broadcasting over the course of time validated documentary journalism and the literary possibilities of ordinary Canadian accents instead. Canadian narrators and Canadian speech sounds came to embody the separate political perspective of the culture. Robert Weaver (b. 1921) – who rapidly became identified with the Canadian short story (he founded *Tamarack Review* and edited several Oxford short story anthologies) joined the CBC in 1948 and developed a number of programs which encouraged attention to the arts: 'CBC Wednesday Night', 'Canadian Short Stories', 'Critically Speaking', 'Stories with John Drainie'. Through Weaver, various short story writers – Mordecai Richler (1931–2001), Alice Munro (b. 1931), Joyce Marshall – found their way to a listening audience. Actors such as John Drainie (1918–66) built their reputations as interpreters of Leacock and other masters of the Canadian voice.

Mavis Gallant (b. 1922), writing a radio review for the Montreal *Standard* in 1948, commented on the authorial lesson involved in listening: a story's faults, its lack of rhythm or its vagueness of characterization, show up immediately because the listener cannot reread. W.O. Mitchell (1914–98) emerged as a popular radio dramatist with his comic weekly 'Jake and the Kid' sketches (1949–57), Mary Grannan (1900–75) as a popular radio writer for children (especially for her character Maggie Muggins), and some years later Paul St Pierre (b. 1923), through the episodes of 'Cariboo Country', was again to demonstrate the success of the comic vernacular as a public art. (Ray Guy's (b. 1939) Newfoundland anecdotes, W. P. Kinsella's (b. 1935) controlled idiom in his Silas Ermineskin stories, Basil Johnston's tall tales of Moose Point Reserve: all these are later written forms of the anglophone vernacular, all – like the turn-of-the-century anecdotes of the Calgary *Eye-Opener* editor, Bob Edwards (1864–1922) – dependent on the reader being able to hear the ironic cadences of speech.) It was radio which established the frame of aural recognition. Mitchell's subsequent career as a novelist and television playwright (*Back to Beulah*, for example) led him to adapt the speaking voice to more serious themes. Best known for the anecdotal wit of his novels *The Kite* (1962) and *Who Has Seen the Wind* (1947), a gentle account of a young prairie boy's first acquaintance with drought, depression, death and the metaphysics that transforms people's attitude towards such realities, Mitchell turned in *How I Spent My Summer Holidays* (1981) to a solemn reflection on the origins of the power of evil.

To Radio-Canada, Yves Thériault was a frequent contributor; so were Robert Charbonneau, Claude-Henri Grignon, and Éloi de Grandmont (1921–70). Félix Leclerc (1914–88), the popular nationalist chansonnier, was a reader and announcer: his published works include collections of poems (*Andante*, 1944), fables (*Allegro*, 1944), stories (*Adagio*, 1943; *Le fou de l'île*, 1958, translated 1976 as *The Madman and the Island*). The first Radio-Canada serial in 1936 was Robert Choquette's *Le curé de village*. From 1937 to 1941, an even more popular series was that written by Gratien Gélinas (b. 1909), who had acted in Choquette's. This tragicomic series about the tribulations of a Chaplinesque character was called 'Fridolinons'; Gélinas then adapted these to the stage, in an annual revue called *Fridolinades*, which played from 1938 to 1946 (published 1980–1). Two of these sketches he later developed into his play about an illegitimate young soldier's problems with love, war and social custom, *Tit-Coq* (1950). Implicitly political, faithful to working-class speech, and quasi-allegorical, *Tit-Coq* is the play from which most contemporary Quebec drama can claim descent.

Another Radio-Canada success was Roger Lemelin, who won his greatest following with the television adaptations (beginning in 1952) of his 1948 novel *Les Plouffe*. Though the experimentations with joual which were to become familiar in Quebec literature during the 1960s and 1970s are related to Lemelin's skill at oral representation, they are both literarily and politically more revolutionary. While Lemelin was concerned with social change, he was a representational writer, therefore stylistically conservative.

On the stage, Canadian drama was given impetus by the formation of two acting companies in particular: Émile Legault's (1906–83) Les compagnons de Saint Laurent in Quebec City in 1937 (which influenced Leclerc, among others), and Dora Mavor Moore's New Play Society in Toronto, which produced forty-seven new Canadian plays between 1946 and 1956. Theatrical companies were active in various other parts of the country: Le cercle Molière in francophone Saint-Boniface, Manitoba (founded as early as 1925); Le théâtre du nouveau monde in Montreal (established 1951); the Montreal Repertory Theatre. The Stratford (Ontario) Shakespeare Festival began in 1953 and rapidly became the anglophone establishment theatre in the country (though Gélinas was one of several francophone actors associated with it). Francophone companies in the 1940s, by contrast, were offering performances of contemporary experimental dramatists: Sartre's (1905–80) *Huis clos* and Beckett's (1906–89) *En attendant Godot* – plays which heralded the composition of such *automatiste* Quebec plays as Claude Gauvreau's (1925–71) *Bien-Être* in 1947.

Plays and playwrights include Gwen Pharis Ringwood (1910–84, *Dark Harvest*, 1945; *Collected Plays*, 1982); Patricia Joudry (b. 1921, *Teach Me How to Cry*, 1955); the urban documenter Paul Toupin (b. 1918; *Brutus*, 1955); Marcel Dubé (b. 1930; *Zone*, 1955; *Le temps des lilas*, 1958; *Florence*, 1960); John Reeves (b. 1925; *A Beach of Strangers*, 1961); Belfast-born John Coulter (1888–1980; *The House in the Quiet Glen*, 1937; *Dierdre of the Sorrows*, 1944). Coulter was affiliated with the Abbey Theatre in Dublin, and worked for three years (1938–41) for CBS radio in New York before finally establishing his Canadian reputation with his later plays (notably *Riel*, 1962, revised 1975).

Robertson Davies, who edited the Peterborough *Examiner* from 1942 to 1963 (at which point he became Master of Massey College, University of Toronto), was also producing sketches, novels and plays in these years. The sketches include *The Diary of Samuel March-*

banks (1947) and *The Table Talk of Samuel Marchbanks* (1949), mannered opinion in the Thomas McCulloch tradition, reprinted from the *Examiner*. The plays include *At My Heart's Core* (1950), which dramatizes episodes in the lives of Susanna Moodie and Catharine Parr Traill during the 1837 rebellion, and *Hunting Stuart* (1955), an engaging comedy about snobbery, lineage and kingly behaviour. While there is a distinctive authorial voice in these works, Davies does not rely for his effects on any fidelity to Canadian speech norms. The radio playwrights were the more effective in this regard – among them Len Peterson, Fletcher Markle (1921–91), Esse W. Ljungh (1904–91), Earle Birney, George Robertson (b. 1922), Alan King (b. 1905), Gerald Noxon (b. 1910), Andrew Allan (1907–74) and Mavor Moore (b. 1919). The radio theatre scripts are now housed at Concordia University, and are being edited by Howard Fink (b. 1934).

Moore (Dora Mavor Moore's son) went on to become one of the most influential literary figures in modern Canada. Playwright, actor, director, *Globe* columnist, professor, translator: he influenced Canadian theatrical endeavour from coast to coast. Chief television producer for the CBC between 1950 and 1954, he was also the founder of the National Theatre School (1960), a bicultural enthusiast whose efforts led to francophone radio and stage performances in anglophone Toronto, and from 1979 to 1983 the outspoken head of the Canada Council. Among his own works are the annual *Spring Thaw* revues, which he produced from 1948 to 1966, and the English libretto for a bilingual opera, *Louis Riel* (1967), by Harry Somers (b. 1925).

Voice was not just an end in itself on radio; in many plays it also served social causes. Birney's *Trial of a City* (1952; reissued for the stage in 1966 under its original title, *The Damnation of Vancouver*) was a vocal tour-de-force, a many-voiced protest (involving styles from Middle English to contemporary Canadian) against unthinking urban development. The impact of the Cold War on 1950s literature (which incidentally explains why the Governor-General's prize for 1954 went to a romantic novel called *The Fall of a Titan*, attributed at the time to a Russian cipher clerk named Igor Gouzenko, 1919–82, who had defected to Canada) also shows up in radio drama: most notably in the international success of Reuben Ship's 1954 play *The Investigator*. It was a satire of McCarthyite tactics, involving the heavenly trial of an American senator. American audiences were startled at Ship's political audacity. Given the implications of McCarthyism in Canada – McCarthy had attempted at one point to indict Canadian citizens – Ship's wit was doubly pointed. He challenged the post-war political self-satisfaction of Canadians, and challenged Canadian literature to continue to reach for social reform.

PUBLIC AND PERSONAL POETRY

Various poets were involved with Radio-Canada (Alain Grandbois, for instance, and Anne Hébert, who was also briefly affiliated in the 1940s with the newly established government film bureau); but while radio, and the sound of the spoken word, undoubtedly had an impact on Anne Hébert and Saint-Denys Garneau – both of whom rejected received linguistic values and openly embraced the music of the vernacular – their connection with the medium was peripheral. These poets coupled their interest in patterns of sound with an interest in the visual rhythms of painting; their main books are coherent units, arrangements of impression and design. Anglophone poets of the same time were more interested in the effects of individual lyrics; their books were cumulations, miscellanies.

Anglophone poetry, on the whole, also tended to look outward at the political world, francophone poetry tended to look inward to the personal one. Francophone poetry tended to be the preserve of particular publishers (such as Éditions du Seuil, though Anne Hébert and Saint-Denys Garneau were both associated with the journal *La Relève*). Anglophone poets were first of all engaged with rival journals, especially two which began in Montreal in the early 1940s, *Preview* and *First Statement*. The former, largely because of the presence of English-born Patrick Anderson (1915–79), was interested in Freudian psychology, 'cosmopolitan' values, and Eliotian form (works by P.K. Page appeared here; so did the early poems of Miriam Waddington, b. 1917). *First Statement* was essentially the voice of Irving Layton (b. 1912), Louis Dudek (1918–2001) and Raymond Souster (b. 1921), espousing working-class points of view. The division between these two journals was not so sharp as their declared interests imply. Waddington's personal lyrics also keenly responded to social problems; Dudek's verse was rigorously modernist, committed to the artifice of verbal design and a universality of poetic intelligence. The two journals amalgamated in 1945 as *Northern Review*, under the editorship of John Sutherland (1919–56), whose own pronouncements on the literary scene Miriam Waddington edited in 1972 as *Essays, Controversies, and Poems*. Standing outside the quarrel was Alan Crawley's (1887–1975) West Coast journal *Contemporary Verse*, which printed works by Dorothy Livesay, Anne Marriott, Floris Clark McLaren, Earle Birney, and several others. From coast to coast new literary societies sprang up, from the Bliss Carman Poetry Society which Alfred Bailey organized in Fredericton in 1940 (and which sponsored the mimeographed *Fiddlehead* magazine from 1945 to 1952), to the several Vancouver clubs, involving, in the post-war years, Roy Daniells (1902–79), Ethel Wilson, the *Contemporary Verse* poets, and William McConnell (1917–2001), whose Klanak Press won praise for the art of its fine hand-printing.

Contacts between anglophone and francophone poets, however, tended to be minimal. F.R. Scott, John Glassco, A.J.M. Smith, Peter Miller (b. 1920), Gwladys Downes (b. 1915), Gael Turnbull (b. 1928), Fred Cogswell, R.A.D. Ford (1915–98, for some years Canada's ambassador to the Soviet Union), Ralph Gustafson (1909–95, whose lyric intensity and passion for music are apparent in his 1983 selected poems, *The Moment Is All*) – 'Partial Argument' (1977) celebrates

Poetry, the only act which separates
Truth from supposition . . .

Words in a poem come together
Implacably as an apple tastes;
A pond, a dog, three boys on skates;
Someone singing or a death.

– the philosopher Francis Sparshott (b. 1926), Louis Dudek, Eldon Grier (1917–2001): all these poets, making their own names as lyric writers, did translate some works from French to English. But (despite Alain Grandbois's work) translation in the reverse direction was rarer. Later, after journals such as Douglas Jones's *ellipse* (1970–) provided a place to publish translations, and after the Canada Council began to fund translators, the number of translations both into French and into English increased remarkably. In any event the francophone poets were read in English not for their entire books and their booklength visions of person and language but as the authors of brief lyrics. The translations altered the character of their accomplishment. In addition, the devotional impact that such writers as Simone Routier-Drouin and Rina Lasnier have in French – Routier's poems suffer anguish in the face of faith, and Lasnier also published plays based on the spiritual visions of Marguerite Bourgeoys and Catherine Tekakwitha (1656–80) – fails to reach most anglophone readers. Given Scott and Layton, Pratt and Birney, P.K. Page and Dorothy Livesay as their frame of reference, anglophones turn more readily to the political psychology of Garneau and Anne Hébert.

To list the names of another twenty poets who began to write between the 1930s and the 1950s is to emphasize the increasing depth and range of the literary culture: George Whalley (1915–90), Elizabeth Brewster (b. 1922), Bertram Warr (1917–43), Kay Smith (b. 1911), Dorothy Roberts (1907–93), Ronald Everson (1903–92), George

Johnston (b. 1913, famous as a wit and as a translator from Old Norse), Ronald Hambleton (who edited *Unit of Fire*, 1942), the diplomat Pierre Trottier (b. 1925), Ronald Després (b. 1935), Wilfrid Lemoine (b. 1927), Robin Skelton (1925–97), Alphonse Piché (1917–98), Roger Brien (1910–99), Sylvain Garneau, Malcolm Lowry, Anne Wilkinson, W.W.E. Ross (1894–1966, an experimenter with the visual arrangement of words, who influenced Raymond Souster), and George Woodcock, 1912–95. (Woodcock returned to his native Canada in 1948, a poet, critic, radio playwright, scriptwriter, travel writer, essayist, and social historian, after a long literary apprenticeship in England, where he had edited the libertarian journal *Now* and was affiliated with such figures as Herbert Read, 1893–1968, and George Orwell, 1903–50). All these writers won a readership and continue to attract critical attention. Several more – Al Purdy (1918–2000), Eli Mandel (1922–92), Phyllis Webb (b. 1927) among them – established their greater reputation in subsequent decades. A much smaller group of individual voices – notably Grandbois, S.-D. Garneau, Anne Hébert, P. K. Page, Souster, Dudek, and Layton – altered the directions that Canadian writing was taking.

Dudek, for example, who founded *Delta* magazine (1957–66), concentrated attention on the independent shapes of language and thought, and in his twenty books gave new vigour to the long poem (for example, *Europe*) and the epigram, probed the moral nature of modern man, disputed critical nationalism, and investigated the history of the role of print in relation to literature. Souster (whose *Collected Poems*, mostly urban imagist lyrics, implicitly judgmental, currently run to five volumes) established a taste for a poetry of laconic observation. Journals like *Contact* (1952–4) and *Combustion* (1957–60) extended Souster's influence, as did Contact Press (1952–67, which Souster formed with Dudek and Layton), ultimately leading toward 1960s poets such as George Bowering (b. 1935). Irving Layton announced the vitality of the physical world, the spirit of his Jewishness, the vigour of sexuality, the ethnic alternatives to both Anglo Saxon Protestantism and Catholic political conservatism. Saint-Denys Garneau swept aside the formalities of conventional verse, and explored the psychological depths of alienation. P.K. Page and Anne Hébert focused attention on the character of insight and the gender of power. Such concerns fed the new cultural nationalism; beside them, the sensibilities and rural imagery of a poet like Sylvain Garneau (however verbally accomplished his separate lyrics) seemed imitative and familiar, more concerned with traditional definitions of poetry than connected with the pressures of the current world, and the new wave of poetry simply swept them aside.

Alain Grandbois set the stage for such changes. Another Paris exile in the 1920s, he was an acquaintance of Hemingway and Cendrars (1887–1961); when he returned to Canada, he rapidly became involved in literary circles, bringing Eliot's influence to French poetry in Quebec. Many early poems saw limited distribution; the three volumes of poetry he published during his lifetime are *Les îles de la nuit* (1944), *Rivages de l'homme* (1948), and *L'étoile pourpre* (1957); a short story collection (*Avant le chaos*) appeared in 1945; several subsequent collections, up to 1980, brought previously unpublished poems into print. Repeatedly Grandbois observed the 'impending chaos' of world events; repeatedly 'désarroi' ['disorder'] threatened the narrating 'I' of his poems – yet consistently he refused to surrender to it. To take 'Demain seulement' as a representative example, he survives the successive metaphoric threats of solitude, envelopment, drowning, in order to assert 'Je vaincrai demain / La nuit et la pluie / Car la mort / N'est qu'une toute petite chose glacée / Qui n'a aucune sorte d'importance.' ['Tomorrow I will conquer / Night and rain / Because death / Is only a frozen little thing / Of no importance.'] Like several of the other poets of this time, Grandbois seems to have inherited clusters of images from Nelligan: death, tombs, falling (*tomber*). S.-D. Garneau and Anne Hébert add to these the images of hand, heart, bone and archipelago. Like Rina Lasnier, Grandbois achieved some of his effects by adapting the liturgical form of the litany; the ritual of repetition proves curative. Whereas Lasnier used rhyme, however, and Medjé Vézina experimented with image and monosyllable, Grandbois adopted the line as his poetic unit: each one measured, rhythmically end-stopped, the regularity of intonation affirming that control is still within reach.

Hector de Saint-Denys Garneau, by contrast, rejected all such apparent regularity, whether of rhyme, metre or line-length. Adopting free-form verse, he was rejecting the Classical models of traditional French poetry; juxtaposing unlike images and inventing unconventional metaphoric equivalences, his work was variously seen as refreshing, revolutionary, morbid and solipsistic. (The *Poésies complètes* appeared posthumously in 1949, edited by Robert Élie, and his *Journal* – a *journal intime* – in 1954, edited by Élie and Jean Le Moyne, the poet's close friends.) To find a familiar category for Garneau, some critics called him a mystic, and read his work as a map of the soul's progress, through the abyss of despair, towards enlightenment. He has been likened to Rimbaud (1854–91) and Hart Crane (1899–1932). More recent critics, drawing on the poet's letters to Jean Le Moyne, have emphasized the visual character of Garneau's work and his interest in painting. In some ways more comparable to his

main work (*Regards et jeux dans l'espace*, 1937) is Moussorgsky's (1839
–81) *Pictures at an Exposition*. 'Picture' in Garneau also translates into
sound. Repeatedly, Garneau sought a tonal equivalence for sensory
and mental impressions. *Regards et jeux* is a suite of poems full of
echoes, dependent on assonance as an associative technique and on
visual image as a motif of speech, an aural equivalent for an emotional state.

Heart and bone motifs recur through the book; so does the related
concept of centre-and-surroundings. What lives? asks the poet. What
covers and contains? What is it possible to make language do? 'Le
jeu' opens his collection with Metaphysical abruptness: saying, Don't
bother me, I'm busy – watching a child, it transpires, building toys
into an entire universe. The poem then goes on to examine what toys
the child makes of words: 'Il vous arrange les mots comme si c'étaient
de simples chansons / Et dans ses yeux on peut lire son espiègle
plaisir / À voir que sous les mots il déplace toutes chose / Et qu'il en
agit avec les montagnes / Comme s'il les possédait en propre.' He
arranges words for you as though they were simple songs, and in his
eyes you can read his mischievous delight to see that, through the
words, he displaces everything, and that he moves mountains as
though they were his own.] Later he adds: 'Tout le monde peut voir
une piastre de papier vert / Mais qui peut voir au travers / si ce n'est
un enfant'? [Everyone can see a dollar bill (green paper dollar), but
who except a child can see through one?] Only the child can be free
from the limitations of 'knowing' value in advance; only the child
mind, that is, commands creation. It is a romantic notion, which the
poet attempts to re-enact by separating himself from influence, but to
no avail. Like his letters, the book of poems plumbs the despair of
discovering absence within himself rather than possibility; preserving his isolation as a writer does not free him from influence so much
as it emphasizes the threats the active imagination contrives for itself.
As his lyric 'Cage d'oiseau' has it, he can reduce himself to a cage of
bone, but such solitude pressures him more than enlarges him. The
lines of the poem play with near-rhyme and pun ('cage d'oiseau' /
'cage d'os' [bird cage / bone cage]) only to end with death, the heart
bleeding and the soul pecked away.

'Accompagnement' concludes the book. The poet again punningly
announces his familiarity with joy, but it is still as a listener, at a distance: 'Je march à côté d'une joie / D'une joie qui n'est pas à moi que
je ne puis pas prendre / Je marche à côté de moi' ['Accompaniment':
I walk at the side of joy, a joy that is not mine (is not in step with me),
a joy of my own that I cannot claim; I walk beside myself in joy; I hear
in joy my step, which walks to the side of me.] – and so on. Joy is in

step with his shadow; it is apparently as much as he currently can hope for, the poem avers, though he longs to be one with the shadow and let his own steps fall away down a different street, shadows to a stranger. There is no resolution here, not even an indefinite 'tomorrow' to believe in.

Perhaps Garneau's dexterity with a simple language is to be seen as its own reward, but the fascination with death – as with Nelligan – has led critics to seek other dimensions to his work: sometimes Freudian, sometimes political. Is it the poet who is shadow to a stranger, or is it his culture, Quebec? Is he burdened by his personal psychology, or by the limitations of living 'contained by Canada'? Such distinctions describe trends in cultural criticism; they also help explain why Garneau, despite some verbal self-indulgence, was so readily claimed as the first 'modern' *québécois* poet. With the narratives of Gabrielle Roy, Garneau's poetry stands behind much recent writing. André Langevin's (b. 1927) novels about the temptations of despondency provide an example. His *Poussière sur la ville* (1953) is a lucid existential tragedy in which a doctor wars with himself, his unfaithful wife, the unfair choices in his job, a vengeful curé, and the bitter jests of God. *L'élan d'Amérique* (1972) uses a moose as a divisive symbol of androcentric sensibilities, the book as a whole denouncing the conservatism of Quebeckers. *Une chaîne dans le parc* (1974; translated as *Orphan Street*) balances fantasy against brutality, drawing on the author's own institutional childhood to attack the nuns and the system of upbringing that condemns children to a life of alienation. In such works, alienation is a condition of modern life. And orphanhood, taken up again in the novels of Gérard Bessette, is both a Freudian and a sociological theme.

When Garneau died suddenly in 1943 at the age of 31, his cousin Anne Hébert was deeply affected. The shift from her romantic first volume of poetry, *Les songes en équilibre* (1942), to the politically and psychologically forceful *Le tombeau des rois* (1953; reissued with new poems in 1960 as *Poèmes*) can perhaps be related to her response to Garneau's despair. Certainly her volume of short fiction, *Le torrent* (1950), further confirms the equation she drew between psychological and political denial. *Le tombeau des rois* signifies her commitment to creative change. In the early work all is dream and possibility, whereas subsequent works – including the plays and novels which extended her reputation in later decades – declare her will to control the shapes of speech. As with Garneau, the desire to strip self and language 'to the bone' – 'Je suis une fille maigre / Et j'ai de beaux os' [I am a thin girl and I have lovely bones] – declares a powerful resistance to the enclosures of other systems of utterance (figured also in images of tomb, château, room). Garneau had observed in 'Silence' that 'Toutes paroles me deviennent intérieures' [All speech becomes me inside], and that what he had to discover were the signs by which to link the interior and exterior worlds. Anne Hébert actively seeks to command 'parole'. The title poem, concluding Le tombeau des rois strongly declares her intent and accomplishment. A symbolic descent into the Egyptian tomb of kings, the poem describes both a psychological descent into self and a psychosexual attempt to deal with the (male) language of authority (the kings, the mask of gold, the ritual constraints of tradition). Turning finally back towards the light, the poet accepts her own speech as a medium of creation; by the time of 'Mystère de la parole' (1960), poetry can even celebrate the power of speaking.

Behind the psychosexual discoveries of Le tombeau des rois lies the work of Quebec women writers of the 1930s – Éva Sénécal, Jovette-Alice Bernier – but where they turned stories of pressure into melodrama, Anne Hébert turned the forms of melodrama into weapons of psychological revelation. Her several plays includes Les invités au procès (1952) and Le temps sauvage (1966). Her first novel, Les chambres de bois (1958), is now read mostly for its parallels with her poetry of the same period (the imagery, the theme of claustrophobia). Subsequent novels have established her as one of the most arresting contemporary storytellers, especially for the violent Kamouraska (1970; later made into a Claude Jutra film), and Les fous de Bassan (1982; translated as In the Shadow of the Wind). Two other books tell of witchcraft in Quebec City and vampirism in modern-day Paris; these two tell of murder. Kamouraska, based on an actual 1839 case in Quebec, recounts how Elisabeth d'Aulnières encourages her American lover, Dr Nelson, to kill her husband. He does so, then flees to the USA. She, arrested and released, marries someone else, living the mask of respectability – but when her second husband is on his deathbed, she relives the violent story from her past, realizing with chagrin how her choices have constricted her life with lies. Les fous de Bassan (the title phrase refers to gannets, though clearly it also hints at madness) tells a similarly violent tale, of the rape and murder of two girls in a Gaspé village. Like the voices of seabirds, the voices of six townspeople narrate separate versions of the night in 1936 when the girls disappeared, and come to ambivalent conclusions about the 'facts'. The rhythmic prose – controlled periodicity, controlled fragments – engages the reader in narrative decision; the romantic plots are not escapist in function, however much they are in form; they reiterate the schemes of enclosure (the social structures, the language of fictional convention) that victimize women. Like the narrating 'I' of 'Le tombeau des rois', the reader is invited into the darkness in order to recognize how much the dark is a human convention.

Patricia Kathleen Page was also interested (to use the title of the Robert Ornstein, b. 1942, book that marked her later writing) in 'the psychology of consciousness'. Her early works deal in psychoanalytic urban case portraits: the metaphysical romance she published under the pseudonym Judith Cape, *The Sun and the Moon* (1944), and poems such as 'Portrait of Marina', 'The Stenographers', 'Landlady', 'The Bands and the Beautiful Children' (from *The Metal and the Flower*, 1954). Later ones, as in *Cry Ararat!* (1967) or *Evening Dance of the Grey Flies* (1981), probe the character of metaphor and the sources of image.

P.K. Page's interest in visual as well as verbal art dates back to the early 1940s when she was a scriptwriter with the newly established National Film Board (NFB). John Grierson (1898–1972) was the first director of the Board (though he was forced to resign in 1945, in a post-war political witch-hunt), and it was he who shaped the NFB's dedication to cinematic excellence and – especially with Norman McLaren (1914–87), one of whose films in 1949 was set to the music of the Canadian jazz composer–pianist Oscar Peterson (b. 1925) – the art of animation. (Another NFB and CBC writer, Leslie McFarlane, 1903–77, achieved his greatest fame as a ghost-writer, from 1926 on, for the Edward Stratemyer, 1862–1930, syndicate; he was 'Franklin W. Dixon', author of the 'Hardy Boys' adventure stories.) Under the subsequent direction of Arthur Irwin (b. 1898, who also served as editor of *Maclean's*), Albert Trueman (b. 1902) and others, the Film Board went on to develop the skills of such film-makers as Claude Jutra (1930–86) in the 1950s and Gilles Carle (b. 1929) in the 1960s, and to support Canadian cultural enterprise. (In the 1970s, the NFB developed a series of biographical films, on such writers as Lowry, Birney, Margaret Laurence and Jack Hodgins.) P.K. Page married Arthur Irwin in 1950, and later moved to Australia and Brazil when Irwin was appointed Canadian High Commissioner and Ambassador. As the excerpts from her journal (1987) indicate, she learned to paint in Brazil – as a painter, she uses the name P.K. Irwin – and several of her pen-and-ink works illustrate *Cry Ararat!* and *The Glass Air* (1985). The experience of Australia led to several of her finest poems. To contrast one of them ('Cook's Mountains') with an early work like 'The Landlady' or 'Photos of a Salt Mine' is to observe the character of the change in her work.

'The Landlady', for all its compelling irony, is told from without. The landlady is nosy, a case study in the desperate need to control others' lives by observing the details of their privacy – or else a case study in projection, of a tenant's neurosis. 'Photos of a Salt Mine' opens similarly removed: 'How innocent their lives look, / how like a child's / dream of caves of winter.' The simile of innocence proves false; at the end of the poem, it is pointedly 'not innocence but guilt' to be seen in the mine, yet it is another simile that structures how the observer sees: 'Like Dante's vision of the nether hell / men struggle with the bright cold fires of salt.' In her later work, P.K. Page was to develop the implications of the oxymoron rather than the simile, and to begin to question the identifying enclosures of metaphor. 'Cook's Mountains' tells of Captain Cook perceiving the mountains of Queensland for the first time:

By naming them he made them.
They were there
Before he came
But they were not the same.
It was his gaze
that glazed each one.
He saw
the Glass House Mountains in his glass.
They shone.

Given this identify, they 'altered to become / the sum of shape and name'. In addition, however, they reflect Cook, 'his tongue / silvered with paradox and metaphor'. Reality (the landscape) takes on the imagination of the viewer, with all his biases and preconceptions. What the poem does not say is as important as what it declares – the force of oxymoron is to hint at suspended alternatives. What it hints at is the validity of the aboriginal identity that existed before Cook, and the constraint of living with the Adamic codes of male determinations of reality. What alternatives, the poem covertly asks, are there for women? – while simultaneously acknowledging the power and beauty of the reality Cook has named into existence.

Garneau's efforts to renew poetry showed in his handling of line and syllable, Anne Hébert's in her psychology of image and *parole*, P.K. Page's in her figures of speech; Irving Layton's contribution to the process of change has to do with the openness of passion in the public world. Layton (born Israel Lazarovitch in Romania in 1912) emigrated to Canada at the age of one, and grew up in Montreal. Like Mordecai Richler, he attended Baron Byng High School, and he has always felt an affinity with the Montreal Jewish cultural and literary community (from Klein to Leonard Cohen, b. 1934, and Seymour Mayne). Mayne (also a poet, and later the editor for Ottawa's Mosaic Press/Valley Editions) edited *Engagement*, Layton's prose writings, in 1972, and Layton himself is the author and editor of some forty other volumes, including a 1985 autobiography, an anthology of love poetry, and several prize-winning poem collections. Among his titles are *The Black Huntsman* (1951), *The Long Pea-shooter* (1954), *The Cold Green Element* (1955), *The Bull Calf and Other Poems* (1956), *A Red Carpet for the Sun* (1959), *Balls for a One-Armed Juggler* (1963), *Periods of the Moon* (1967), *For My Brother Jesus* (1976) and *The Gucci Bag* (1984). A passionate lyricist, Layton excels at expressing the immediacy of rage and joy; these emotions well up from all experience – they are not reserved for meditation; they spring up out of daily life, which is physical as well as emotional and intellectual. Words refuse no experience, therefore, and experience refuses no words.

Layton's poems consequently range from the tenderest of lyrics ('Keine Lazarovitch', 'Mrs. Fornheim, Refugee', 'Song for Naomi', 'Samantha Clara Layton') to the comic, the bawdy, the lusty ('Berry Picking'), the political ('Fornalutx'), and the taunting. Several contrive deliberately to contravene anglo-Protestant norms of propriety. These immediately earned Layton a name for being 'egotistical' and 'offensive' – which missed the point. As with the angry poems of *For My Brother Jesus*, where Layton attacks the values of the 'Xian' world, many readers misconstrued the words, which reconfirmed Layton's reasons for writing as he did. That is, Layton was not attacking the 'Christian' world, as readers supposed, but attacking what he called 'Xian', a world that had lost its true 'Christian' values (as embodied in Jesus) and has substituted for them a set of rigid hierarchical codes that inhibit love and the freedom of expression. 'Xians' in Layton's work are afraid of themselves, afraid of their bodies most of all, and afraid of language. The poems that celebrate the humanness of passion and passionate expression constitute the positive side to this same observation. The humanness of passion, moreover, is nothing if not also personal. Hence the celebratory 'I' in so many of Layton's poems is sometimes the man behind the poet, sometimes a mask, sometimes a Dionysian poet-figure, sometimes an invention to celebrate the nature of self. The violence of a poem like 'Whom I Write For' is not designed 'to improve your soul; / or to make you feel better, or more humane; / Nor do I write to give you any new emotions' – that's for 'the fraternity of lying poets' – but rather to confront individuals with themselves, pain and the responsibility for pain. Being alive means ego, selfhood, pain and the responsibility for pain. Not knowing these things means a person is living only an automatic life; knowing them means more suffering, but also more capacity to love.

If system is the agent of death, then language is the agent of fertility in Layton's poetry. 'Sun-Bathers' observes the will of 'Europe' to accept the 'subtle drug' of 'defeat'; 'Boys Bathing' declares the power of invention: the 'history' of a thing seen being 'what my eye made for it'. The eye makes image: simile, metaphor, strikingly apt in so many lines, as in 'Maxie' ('All summer the months grovel / and bound at his heels like spaniels') or 'Butterfly on Rock' ('There is no death in all the land, / I heard my voice cry; / And brought my hand down on the butterfly / And felt the rock move beneath my hand'). Blakean in cast, 'The Improved Binoculars' spells out the poet's vision of the demonic impulses of human beings, determined to imprison themselves in hurt. A 1956 poem, 'Colony to Nation' (adopting the title of a 1946 book by the historian A.R.M. Lower), specifies that Canadians are complicit in this stupidity: 'A dull people, without charm / or ideas, /settling into the clean empty look / of a Mountie or dairy farmer / as into a legacy / One can ignore them / (the silences, the vast distances help) / And suppose them / at the bottom / of one of the meaner lakes. . . .' The ramifications of these lines take Layton at once into social and literary commentary (the images and phrasing echo Smith, Scott, Klein, and parody the public fascination with the Group of Seven) and into reflections on the character of poetry itself. Silence may be the breeding-ground of speech, but speech is the necessary child of invention; poems like 'The Birth of Tragedy', 'The Cold Green Element', 'The Fertile Muck', 'Whatever Else, Poetry Is Freedom', 'For Mao Tse-Tung' and 'The Gucci Bag' all show through image and declaration what poetry can do, provided it stays free of schools.

'Prologue to the Long Pea-Shooter' (*The Darkening Fire*, 1954) makes clear how Layton in the 1950s was aware that conventionality could tame all poetic revolutions (his own included) into establishment taste. Only semi-jocularly, he lampooned his contemporaries in tetrameter couplets (the form working against conformity) in order to keep himself apart:

> But if you have the gifts of Reaney
> You may help your verse by being zany,
> Or write as bleakly in a pinch
> As Livesay, Smith, and Robert Finch. ...
>
> But the soundest, most successful plan
> Is to compose like Douglas Le Pan:
> Appear, though men and nations reeled,
> A Lampman on a battlefield;
> Express in words vacuous and quaint
> The cultured Englishman's complaint
> That decency is never sovereign,

That reason ought to, but doesn't govern
That maids have holes, and men must find them
(Alas, that Nature WILL so blind them!)
In short, here's the sum of this advice:
Say nothing, but modulate the voice.

For Layton, the new nationalism that had started to grow in the 1920s was simply the old nationalism of Lampman in a new set of masks. He wanted to shake it up anew – as, in another medium, did the influential theatre critic Nathan Cohen (1923–71). The Communist 'worker poet' Joe Wallace (1890–1975) suggested even more radical social changes. But by the 1950s, and in different ways, the young rebels had themselves become established. Canada was declaring itself a 'Middle Power', material 'realism' was the order of the day, and Canadians were sitting back despite the Cold War to enjoy their suburban prosperity.

NATIONAL PRESUMPTIONS

By 1959, several new social welfare programs were in place (Unemployment Insurance in 1940, Family Allowance in 1945); a distinctive medicare system followed in the 1960s. The birth rate rose in the postwar years; immigration was increasing (Hungarian and Czech refugees arrived in 1956 and 1968). In 1947 Canadian citizenship became formally recognized in law. Such national growth had specific literary consequences as well as more general social ones. In popular rhetoric, Canada was the 'mosaic' as opposed to the American 'melting pot'. That it was nevertheless full of hierarchies of ethnicity and power – a 'Vertical Mosaic', to use the title of John Porter's (1921–79) 1965 sociological analysis – spells out the reality. Elizabeth Loosley's (b. 1911) *Crestwood Heights* (1956) probed the sociology of suburbia. Pierre Berton, Phillips Thompson's grandson, became managing editor of *Maclean's* in 1952 and was shortly to embark on his successful career as a media star and a popular interpreter of Canadian culture (with books on the Klondike, the war of 1812, Vimy, the Dionne quintuplets, the 'National Dream' of building the CPR); his children's fantasy, *The Secret World of Og*, appeared in 1961.

In 1949, the government requested Vincent Massey to investigate education, the mass media, the nature of cultural affairs, and in 1951 Massey brought down his report on National Development in the Arts, Letters and Sciences. The immediate impact on the culture was striking. The National Library was established in 1953. In 1957 the Canada Council came into being, empowered to fund composition, performance, publication and research in the arts. (It was subdivided in 1978, the Canada Council keeping responsibility for composition and performance, and the new Social Sciences and Humanities Research Council acquiring responsibility for research; there was a separate parallel Science Council as well.) Internal policy of the Council was to be kept free from political interference, and peer review was to be the measure of judgment. The council's inestimable support helped to bring about the extraordinary increase in literary activity that was to mark the next twenty-five years. Various long-range projects got underway – the *Literary History of Canada* (first edition 1965), the *Dictionary of Canadian Biography* (the *Dictionnaire des oeuvres littéraires du Québec* followed in 1978, with a subvention from the Quebec Ministry of Cultural Affairs). With this wave of interest and the availability of texts (McClelland & Stewart's New Canadian Library paperback reprint series began in 1957), Canadian literature broadly entered the schools.

There were anthologies available: Guy Sylvestre's *Anthologie de la poésie canadienne française* had appeared in 1942 and Carl Klinck (1908–90) and R.E. Watters' *Canadian Anthology* in 1956. Marie Tremaine's (b. 1902) bibliography of Canadian imprints was published in 1952 (the Bibliographical Society of Canada had been formed in 1946). Critical journals such as *Canadian Literature* and *Liberté* began in 1959, respectively in Vancouver and Montreal; the first was edited until 1977 by George Woodcock at the University of British Columbia, the latter by Jean-Guy Pilon (b. 1930) and Michel van Schendel (b. 1929), with the support of writers Jacques Godbout (b. 1933), Gilles Hénault and Fernand Ouellette (b. 1930). At the university level, the University of Manitoba had accepted postgraduate theses on English-Canadian writing as early as 1903, and Queen's University in Kingston and McGill in Montreal with some regularity since the 1920s; those on French-Canadian literature were accepted first at the Universities of Paris and Bordeaux in the 1930s. But there had been only sporadic teaching of Canadian literature – a course in American and Canadian literature (McGill, 1912), in the history of Canadian literature (J.D. Logan at Acadia, 1915), in poetry (University of Manitoba, 1919). The first survey course in Canadian literature appears to be that given by Carlyle King (b. 1907) at the University of Saskatchewan in 1946. During the 1950s, such courses multiplied, but it was the late 1970s before Canadian writing acquired extensive recognition abroad and greater prestige at home.

The academic attention given to anglophone writing even in the 1950s, however, produced a literary canon, thus giving precedence to certain tastes, genres, subjects and styles: the Protestant hierarchy of

taste and culture, and the now conventional definition of Canada in
Group of Seven terms – to which Layton objected. The novel was considered superior to the short story, poetry superior to both; epic was
deemed a greater accomplishment than lyric; and the tenets of 'realism' (however romantic in execution) were more readily approved
than those of discontinuous narrative. 'Documentary' maintained its
appeal, and though Yousuf Karsh's (1908–2002) photographs provided tangible images of Great Canadians, the natural landscape (rather
than people) was still accepted as the distinguishing national characteristic. Poems like 'Canoe Trip' and 'A Country Without a Mythology', from *The Wounded Prince* (1948), the first collection by the civil
servant Douglas Le Pan (later Undersecretary of State for External
Affairs), satisfied these criteria. Stately, if not epic, the poems celebrate the many opportunities of discovery in virgin territory; they
reiterate the Protestant observations of Bruce Hutchison's (1901–92)
The Unknown Country (1942) and several score of earlier writers. But
they celebrate passion more as an idea than as an action. And impas-
sivity was one mask Layton refused to wear. Fulfilling the general
critical expectations of literature even more than Le Pan was the
work of E.J. Pratt and Hugh MacLennan. Gabrielle Roy, read as a documentary social realist rather than as structural innovator, came to
epitomize for most anglophone readers the quintessential character
of francophone writing – though in Quebec a writer such as André
Langevin or Saint-Denys Garneau was undoubtedly more in the
mainstream. But Pratt and MacLennan came to represent 'Canada' as
a 'whole'; hence for younger writers they came to represent everything that was conventional and to be rejected: the cast of mind, the
handling of language, national themes, all.

As David Pitt's (b. 1921) 1984 biography demonstrates, Edwin John
Pratt was deeply marked by his Methodist youth in Newfoundland.
The fact that he gave up the ministry, ultimately rejecting the system
of centralized authority to which it deferred, appears to have haunted him. His poems repeatedly set duty against guilt, with individualism winning out: 'No! by the Rood', declares the 'little genus homo'
to the mechanistic, totalitarian authority figure 'the great Panjandrum' at the end of 'The Truant': 'We will not join your ballet' – a conclusion as political (when it was published in 1943) as it was psychological. Such defiance is not without cost. Throughout Pratt's work
there is a fascination with giantism, power, the male romances of
speed and size: the imagination lived what the daily world denied, or
what the daily world covertly admired. The two became one.

Pratt seems to have stepped out of his generation in some respects.
A contemporary of Hémon and Nelligan, he did not publish his first

book of poetry (*Rachel*, 1917) until he was thirty-five. *Rachel* and *New-foundland Verse* (1923) show more kinship with Roberts than with Smith, more affinity with a late Victorian progressive version of science than with the uncertainty principles of Werner Heisenberg (1901–76) and Max Born (1882–1970) in the 1920s. The tendency to archaism that colours these works disappears from later lyrics such as 'Sea-Gulls', 'From Stone to Steel' and 'The Prize Cat', all dating from the 1930s: the last is an especially acute political adaptation of lyric form, written in response to the Italian invasion of Abyssinia. By 1923, with *The Witches' Brew*, Pratt gave vent to his comic talents and to the Newfoundland tall tale tradition. A mock epic about the effects of alcohol on fish, the poem constitutes a lapsed Methodist's reaction to Canada's brief wartime flirtation with prohibition. Biographically, it came to be associated with the poet's bonhomie at University of Toronto dinners. Technically, the poem shows Pratt experimenting with diction, marrying the vernacular with specialized terminology and the rhythms of speech with rhyme and octosyllabic regularity. Various features of epic form (the catalogue, the extended simile, the narrative convention of beginning *in medias res*) would subsequently become his trademark. But his long poems are less epics than dramatic romances, making myth out of historical contexts and designing fantasies about magnitude.

From *Titans* (1926) to *The Titanic* (1935), *Brébeuf and His Brethren* (1940), and *Towards the Last Spike* (1952), Pratt tried to represent the human-sized heroism that would combat whatever problems men perceived as huge or impassable. History and myth provided images of such confrontation. He wrote of whales and krakens ('The Cachalot', 1926), dinosaurs ('The Great Feud', 1926), ships (*The Roosevelt and the Antinoe*, 1930), the Jesuit missions (*Brébeuf* draws extensively on Parkman's version of New France, reiterating the heroic version of history), and the building of the Canadian Pacific Railway. Susan Gingell's (b. 1951) *E.J. Pratt: on his life and poetry* (1983), the first volume in an edition of the poet's collected work, amply reveals the character of the research Pratt undertook before writing. Poems about the Second World War ('Dunkirk', 1941, or *Behind the Log*, 1947, an account of Canada's North Atlantic corvette navy) were perhaps too close to the subject to escape the whiff of propaganda. The poet was most effective with such works as *The Titanic* and *Towards the Last Spike*, where history was more distanced, where nature warred with machine, where the stubbornness of man wills him on to accomplishment and the pride of man interferes.

The way *Towards the Last Spike* simultaneously celebrates and subverts the heroic suggests the ironic, post-lapsarian sensibilities of

English Canadian life; the way it uses metaphoric speech to articulate nationhood equates social identity with a particular cast of mind. When the poem was published, it appealed because it brought together the whole set of conventions that underlay the nationalism of the time. Concerned with the Canadian Pacific Railway, it turned history into narrative, transformed an economic enterprise into a visionary act of nation-building, depicted nature (the Canadian Shield, animated as a giant reptile roused from sleep by the puny engineers) not as an enemy but as a force with which human knowledge could deal. It cast Sir John A. Macdonald as a flawed hero, celebrated the power of metaphor over the mundane truths of cost-accounting, placed its faith in the future (echoing Laurier's misquoted phrase, to the effect that the '20th Century would belong to Canada'), and asserted a centralist version of Canadian history. In an allegorical moment, for example, British Columbia is cast as a winsome if knowing lady, courted by a 'sinuous' Latin lover California as well as by dour Macdonald; British Columbia chooses Canada because it seems the more likely way to preserve the Britishness of heritage. Yet in the strategies of the poem, Pratt emphasizes Canada's expectation, not British Columbia's: Canada extends itself outward to acquire a western extremity. The poem presumes that the value system of the centre will constitute the value system of the whole. ('Where are the coolies in your poem, Ned?' asks F.R. Scott's 'All the Spikes But the Last'.) Inherent in the one territorial notion is another, which implies that the language of men is the language of all, to which women (like the 'lady B. C.') naturally defer. It seems fair to say that such attitudes recorded the status quo. It is also a clearly anglophone, clearly European version of nation, and it was shortly to be challenged.

Behind Ontario nationalism lay in some measure the writings of the conservative historian Donald Creighton, whose own biography of Macdonald (volume I; *The Young Politician*) appeared in the same year as Pratt's poem. Creighton launched his centralist version of Canadian history in *Dominion of the North* (1944). In this study he espoused what has come to be known as the 'Laurentian thesis', an economic history of metropolis and hinterland; by the terms of this study, Montreal was the metropolis (or 'centre') of Canada as long as it controlled the fur trade. But when Toronto established itself further upstream, it cut the hinterland off from Montreal, usurping its role and becoming the new national metropolis. It is a theory which fastens on the tensions between anglophone and francophone Canada (or more specifically between the power brokers of Toronto and Montreal) as the distinguishing feature of Canadian society, and it has since influenced writers such as Margaret Atwood and Ronald Sutherland (b. 1933) as well as Pratt. Opposed to Creighton, the Manitoba historian W.L. Morton countered his arguments in such books as *The Canadian Identity* (1961), but for the writers of the 1950s Creighton offered the more persuasive paradigms. On none was this influence more direct than on Hugh MacLennan, especially in his 1945 novel *Two Solitudes*, which seemed to epitomize the prevailing cultural sensibility.

MacLennan had already published his allegorical *Barometer Rising* (1941), clearly charged by contemporary violence, which dramatizes Canada's social coming-of-age during the First World War. Allegory appealed to MacLennan. Perhaps a sign of his education in Classics (he was a Rhodes scholar, and took his doctorate at Princeton), certainly an indication of the didactic bias of his fiction, the technique was yet another indication of the desire of writers during these decades to devise indirect methods of narration. Direct language repeatedly proves a mask or a lie in such fiction; the kernel of truth exists at some remove, implied by the literary form especially when the surface language seems placed and familiar. Hence *Barometer Rising* reads on the surface like a conventional romance: a woman, separated from the man she loves, must cope alone until love, common sense and unnatural disaster bring them together again. But the allegory leads the narrative into politics. The younger generation (the ship-designer Penny, the soldier Neil and their infant daughter) represent Canada in the present and future; Penny's anglophile father Colonel Wain represents the imperial/colonial past (standing in Neil's way, for Colonel Wain has attempted to court-martial Neil in order to cover up his own egregious wartime judgment); and the conflict between them comes to a head, freeing Penny and Neil from the past, when in 1917 the Halifax Explosion occurs (itself representing the First World War). It is then that the talents of the new generation are found to be most effective for dealing with the new world. MacLennan, a doctor's son, recalled the explosion from his own boyhood; the chapter describing it here constitutes one of the most sustained examples of heightened descriptive narrative in Canadian prose, rivalled by a section in MacLennan's 1959 novel *The Watch that Ends the Night*, describing Jerome Martell's boyhood *rite de passage* flight from a violent logging camp. In both books Odyssean parallels are strong, the romantic quest recurrently structuring the way the male characters grow to manhood. In both cases, too – in contrast to Callaghan's stories, which repeatedly assert the enlivening possibility of cross-generation connections – the conflict with fathers (or the absence of fathers, as with Langevin's orphans) underlines the Freudian potential of the search for self-knowledge.

A representative sampling of MacLennan's several books of essays appears in *The Other Side of Hugh MacLennan* (1978), edited by his biographer Elspeth Cameron (b. 1943). By turns descriptive and expository, the essays – 'On Living in a Cold Country' or 'The Street Car Conductor' – demonstrate MacLennan's meditative and comic strategies of composition. Other works design allegories of American-Canadian relations, and of Calvinist responsibility. *Return of the Sphinx* (1967) – almost parallel in structure to Gratien Gélinas's 1967 play *Hier les enfants dansaient* (translated by Mavor Moore) – attributes the violence of Quebec separatism to the Freudian rebellion against paternal authority and Mother Church. *Voices in Time* (1980), set in a post-nuclear holocaust future, constitutes a fragmentary but documentary history of the present. At once a cautionary tale and a forceful analysis of the sources of fascism in Canada in the 1970s and 1980s, it also criticizes the naïveté of any generation that treats history as a fiction to be misremembered, forgotten or ignored. *The Watch that Ends the Night* (1959) is in part a love story, a sensitive tribute following the death of MacLennan's first wife (the American writer Dorothy Duncan, 1903–57); in part, too, it contrasts the character and careers of two men, the earnest pedagogue George Stewart and his flamboyant – and less 'reliable' – acquaintance Dr Jerome Martell. Stewart tells the story: his is the 'Canadian' voice; Martell's enthusiasms for Spain, China and moral causes show the book to be echoing, if not precisely based upon, the life of Norman Bethune.

By the time MacLennan wrote this work he had been living in Montreal about fifteen years; after leaving Lower Canada College, where he had been teaching Latin and history, he lectured in English at McGill University, retiring in 1979 to North Hatley, Quebec, a village where other writers – Ralph Gustafson, Douglas Jones (b. 1929), Frank Scott – also lived. *Two Solitudes*, like the later novels, draws upon this Montreal perspective, and upon the Laurentian Thesis that makes divided Montreal (English/French) the epitome of the Canadian identity. The title 'two solitudes' (though drawn from lines by Rilke, 1875–1926, to refer to love) even gave a name to the motif.

Two Solitudes divides into two generational sections, the first recording how Athanase Tallard, the seigneur/politician, loses his position in the village of St Marc-des-Érables when he sells land to *les Anglais*, collaborates with the Montreal tycoons, remarries (this time to an Irish Catholic), and is excommunicated when he opposes the Church. The Church, condemning Athanase for his pride, is riddled with ambition. The whole novel proceeds by parallels. Tallard's two sons, by two marriages, continue the tensions through the next generation. The first, Marius (child of the saintly Adèle), is sexually puritanical, politically ambitious, a tool in the hands of the Church and the fledgling separatist movement; the second, Paul (child of Kathleen), is an athlete and writer, a man of cool judgment and declared social conscience, who ends up marrying Heather Methuen, the equally independent daughter of the *anglais* plutocracy. As political allegory (the future rests in a 'marriage' between equals) this novel is little advance on Mrs Humphrey Ward's (1851–1920) Edwardian romance *Canadian Born*, though the fact that it ends in 1939 does deny a happily-ever-after close. Initially praised for 'representing' Canada, *Two Solitudes* has since been attacked for what it leaves out: the working class, Native peoples, other ethnic groups, regional politics. At the heart of such a reaction is a documentary desire that even romantic narratives should reflect the empirical world. Once critics began to query the value system implicit in conventional 1950s fiction, they challenged both the social reality and the structures of language and the strategies of narrative.

SOURCES OF CHANGE

Simple burlesque was one of the first ways of disputing the status quo. The Manitoba chemist Paul Hiebert (1892–1987), in two lampoons of verse form and biographical method – *Sarah Binks* (1947) and *Willows Revisited* (1967) – challenged the vagaries that went by the name of criticism. And a popular 1950s revue called *My Fur Lady* (about a romance between the Governor-General and an 'Eskimo princess', which preserves Canadian sovereignty during an international crisis) satirized the reigning arts elite. Such burlesques were not reformative; they were simply amused reactions to the quirks of established 'national' behaviour.

   The works of several other writers could also be read as detached amusements – Ethel Wilson (1888–1980), Earle Birney, Gérard Bessette, even Mordecai Richler. Though all four were calling for thoughtful engagements with art and society, to read them only as amusing writers removed the sting from what they actually said. Selective reading turned Alberta-born Birney, for example, into a nature poet with an ironic eye for national foible (which carefully avoided dealing with the anarchic tendencies of his technique). It turned Ethel Wilson into a writer of mannered comedies about privileged lives and determined women (which ignores the covert violence of her work). Bessette became an 'academic' novelist; Richler was classified as a critic-in-exile and tolerated for his outsider's idiosyncratic view of ethnic diversity. But it was the sting in their works that interested subsequent readers.

Birney, whose poetic career spans five decades, repeatedly sought order, concerned himself with his role as 'makir' (for many years he was a professor of Old and Middle English, an influence which shows up most overtly in the alliterative metrics of his effective Cabbagetown war poem 'Anglosaxon Street'). In life he followed a succession of careers: in politics, the army, journalism (from 1946 to 1948 he edited *Canadian Poetry Magazine*, but his efforts to free it from tepid conventions met with resistance), and academia (he instituted the first formalized creative writing program in Canada, at the University of British Columbia in the early 1960s). His fiction satirized the military bureaucracy and probed the failure of McCarthyite ambitions and North American communism. In poetry he early followed Auden and Frost (1874–1963) as models ('Vancouver Lights', 'The Road to Nijmegen'), later turned to dramatic narrative ('David', 1942), and the freer forms of *Ice cod bell or stone* (1962). Later still he turned to contrapuntal meditations like *November Walk Near False Creek Mouth* (1964), employed unfamiliar forms like the sestina in a series of remarkable poems based on his travels in the 1960s and 1970s ('Six-Sided Square: Actopan', 'The Bear on the Delhi Road', 'A Walk in Kyoto'), and experimented – in a half-dozen works that appeared after 1969 – with concrete and sound poems. In the early 1980s, aged 80 himself, he was travelling with a sound performance group called Nexus. Birney has also written several plays, fragments of autobiography, and an irrepressible account of poetry-writing, *The Cow Jumped Over the Moon* (1972).

While he was early praised for the nature imagery and the force of the narrative in 'David', it was Birney's continuing willingness to reshape literary form that gave him his later reputation. Early commentary could accept with relaxed amusement his social critique ('Canada: Case History: 1945' – 'This is the case of a high-school land / dead-set in adolescence'; or 'Can.Lit.': 'we hacked in railway ties / what Emily etched in bone / ... / no Whitman wanted / it's only by our lack of ghosts we're haunted'). Such critiques, after all, did not fundamentally dispute the idea of progress. But fewer were happy with the 1973 revision of 'Case History' which found 'senescence' where 'adolescence' had been. Neither did they at once perceive the significance of being 'haunted' by absence: of being given a freedom from the organization of verbal precedent. Perhaps because it was possible to read 'Billboards Build Freedom of Choice' as a raucous send-up of an American truckdriver ('yegotta choose fella yegotta / choose between/ AMERICAN and UN—'), fewer readers recognized

that it was the binary structure in the rhetoric that Birney was exposing as shallow, or that the restrictiveness of the 'American' binary
form could operate in Canada too. Openness, as he demonstrated in
'Alaska Passage' (which moves visually, from the enclosures of 'Alas'
and 'age' to the freedom of 'pass'), was an attitude of mind, one that
could be evoked by the empirical arrangement of words and letters
on the page. Disrupting verbal form, therefore, became a commentary on the resistant rigidities of the very attitudes that were often
taken to express the social norms.

So it was with Ethel Wilson. South African-born, orphaned when
young, she was brought up in Vancouver by her mother's mercantile family, the Malkins, who had achieved some social prestige in
the city. Much of her work displays her insider's knowledge of social
fashion: the boarding school of *Hetty Dorval* (1947), the partying and
the bridge clubs of 'The Window' (in *Mrs. Golightly and Other Stories*,
1961), the social connections and the family history that inform *The
Innocent Traveller* (1949). The delight Mrs Wilson shows in the naïve
enthusiasms of the maiden aunt Topaz in *The Innocent Traveller* is,
however, countered by the realization that such innocence is only
possible for those who (like fortunate children) live protected by
others. Ordinary people face intrusion, invasion – the military
metaphor is deliberate in a story like 'We Have to Sit Opposite', a
tragicomedy about the onset of the Second World War. Invasion,
moreover, like any violence, is irrational; women are the most vulnerable to it, and it can even well up from within oneself. Hence
'Hurry, hurry!' tells fragmentarily of a murder, realized inferentially
from a narrative which appears to be offering careful advice under
genteel circumstances; 'The Window' suggests the threat of personal violence by superimposing the image of an intruder outside a
plate glass window on the reflected image of the householder within; *Swamp Angel* (1954), arguably Mrs Wilson's most sustained novel,
tells of a woman who walks out on her destructively shallow husband and establishes herself in a fishing camp in the interior of the
province, only to find that she even there as to deal with the past and
the unexpected. While these works could be praised for their celebration of equanimity, Mrs Wilson recognized that equanimity often
comes at a cost and is always temporary. Hence the beauty of the
style – the calm pacing, the leisureliness – is often deceptive. It contains formal surprises ('Ten twenty fifty brown birds flew past the
window and then a few stragglers, out of sight' or 'Suddenly Rose
surprised her grandmother and aunts by growing up and getting
married'). In such sentences, narrative is not the issue; form is. The
form conveys a way of seeing, one which is often (because it often

has to be, for survival's sake) at odds with the conventions of empirical record.

Ethel Wilson probed the interactions between society and the internal lives of women. Gérard Bessette examined the repressed lives of Quebec men. Mordecai Richler exposed the social and sexual ambitions of Montreal's privileged insiders (Anglo Saxon Westmount) and ethnic outsiders (the St Urbain Street Jews, the Catholic labourers, the poor). The interests of these writers begin in their observations of society. (Richler's first critical success, his 1959 novel *The Apprenticeship of Duddy Kravitz*, is in many respects a rejection of the MacLennan/Creighton anglo-Protestant version of Canadian nationhood, recognizing not so much a world made up of academic trends and patters as one made up of cheats, frauds, dupes, money and bawdiness. In his essays, moreover – as in *Home Sweet Home*, 1984 – Richler openly attacks Canadian smugness.) But it is the handling of language that distinguishes their perspectives from that of conventional social realism.

Both Bessette and Richler were trenchant satirists, Bessette especially in *Le libraire* (1960, translated as *Not for Every Eye*), attacking Duplessis's censorship laws, and Richler most popularly with *The Incomparable Atuk* (1963; published in the USA as *Stick Your Neck Out*), about faddish nationalism, and *Cocksure* (1968), about the theatricality of sexual fetishes. (Film and the stage have a continuing attraction for Richler. He spent some years in England in the 1950s and 1960s as a screenplay writer – for example, *Life at the Top*, 1965 – and in the 1980s adapted *Duddy Kravitz* into a musical comedy called *Duddy*, and turned *Joshua Then and Now*, 1980, into a film.) Both writers broached heretofore taboo topics; Richler was more jocular in doing so, and in particular broke verbal taboos as he recorded the animated lives of ghetto-dwellers in quest of stardom.

A reader needs to accept his straight-talking language as reality, but not as the only reality. Sometimes it is a sign of the characters' verbal poverty and moral superficiality; sometimes it is a mask to keep the enemies of tenderness at bay. Richler's imaginative children's story, *Jacob Two-Two and the Hooded Fang*, 1975, reveals how gentle he can be with people who matter to him, and how fierce with absurdity.) The ambivalence keeps the reader sympathetic to characters that other novels might have cast as villains; Richler makes them picaresque anti-heroes, true to life. For Duddy Kravitz, or for Jake Hersh in *St. Urbain's Horseman* (1971), or for Joshua Shapiro in the later novel, success is everything. The problem is, all of them define it in advance, and none of them knows how to recognize it when it happens. Duddy cheats his way to the success he thinks he wants, only to find that he's offended the one person he wants most to impress; Jake, already a successful author, is afraid of trusting the judgments of critics and readers, hence consorts with failures in order to prove something to himself, only to discover that they start to control him in a way he had not anticipated. Joshua thinks success exists in Protestant values and a Westmount connection, but only comes to some equilibrium when – the first of all Richler's 'heroes' to do so – he reconciles himself with his own imperfect father. Despite all the verbal finesse and the comedy of set scenes, such characters, and the fictions in which they appear, still refer back to the world.

For Bessette, by contrast, the ratification of self takes the form of interior monologue. An anthologist, poet and critic (especially of Nelligan and Roy) as well as novelist, Bessette avers in *Mes romans et moi* (1979) that he has been influenced by his readings in Freud and Charles Mauron (1899–1966), by his working-class roots, by the lectures of Lionel Groulx, and by his extended residence outside Quebec. *La bagarre* (1958; translated as *The Brawl*) is his most 'realistic' account of social failure. But from *Les pédagogues* (1961), through *L'incubation* (1965), *Le cycle* (1971), *Les anthropoïdes* (1977), and *Le semestre* (1979), Bessette moved from reflecting on the ways society is falling apart to finding structures that incorporate the reflective process. Especially in *Les anthropoïdes*, he seeks out the moment in imagination when primitive consciousness begins to think in the terms we call 'history'. As he experiments with technique – using present participles to avoid pronouns, coining neologisms, abandoning conventional punctuation, substituting multiple sets of parentheses to divide the associations of the unconscious from the sensory perceptions of the conscious and also from the hallucinatory figures of the preconscious – he probes further the character of language. In so doing he examines the character of the thought that brings language into existence and that is in turn constituted by words. His fiction moves from a documentary mode to a psychological one, in the process questioning normative judgments about social reality by showing how language is not simply a medium of social record but also a substantive reality.

An even sharper break from the techniques of representational realism derived once more from the visual arts. In 1948, primarily in reaction against the climate of fear they found in Quebec under Duplessis, the painters Jean-Paul Riopelle (1923–2002) and Paul-Émile Borduas (1905–60), together with the poet-playwright Claude Gauvreau, issued 400 copies of a mimeographed manifesto called *Refus Global*. It was to become a kind of bible for artistic and social reformers. A collection of essays (translated in Ramsay Cook's 1969 history

French-Canadian Nationalism), together with three short Gauvreau plays (Gauvreau, who committed suicide in 1971, was 'discovered' the year after that, for his play *Les oranges sont vertes*), the manifesto attacked the triumvirate of church, state and business. Further, it denounced the contemporary emptiness of Western culture, and proposed that a 'refus global' or collective refusal to endorse the culture's utilitarian demands was the only prospect for fulfilling change. True art, they said, is unpredictable, spontaneous, anarchic and therefore liberating. True art was therefore not representational, in that it rejected the current forms of received reality. In language, this shift in direction meant that conventional word order, vocabulary, syntax and sound systems would all be disrupted. In stance, it meant that the poses of libertine prophet and polemicist would draw attention to alternative realities. If 'being' implied conscious possession of a valid identify, then for Quebeckers 'non-being' was their true norm. Conventional grammar (like conventional politics) controlled thought; hence free association was a technique for artistically and unpredictably ordering the unfettered imagination.

Only by embracing the surreal (or, as with Gauvreau, the devices he called 'automatiste') could people genuinely get in touch with themselves. Variously called Marxist and Freudian, the movement dramatically reiterated that art, even in its most non-representational forms, is intrinsically linked with social attitude. The movement was also to divide *québécois* poetry from that in the rest of the country particularly strongly. Although there were a few anglophone poets – Wilfred Watson (1911–98), for example – interested at the same time in 'radical absurdity', 1950s surrealism in Quebec embodied a political anger that would not emerge to any degree in anglophone poetry until the early 1980s.

Besides Gauvreau's plays – *Bien-être* (1947), *L'asile de la pureté* (1953), and several others (the *Oeuvres créatrices complètes* appeared in 1971) – the poetry of Paul-Marie Lapointe (b. 1929) demonstrated the early influence of the new wave of surrealism, though Lapointe's *Le vierge incendié* (1948), which Gauvreau helped bring into print, probably owes more to the French writers Paul Eluard (1895–1952) and André Breton (1896–1966) than to *Refus Global*. Gauvreau's work stands at one edge of 'anti-language' (an exemplary line: 'Glyxodène marcatipoliss wiss wiss diomm nouc nouc nugala pwouf pwouf zigala mneur mneur mneur'). Descriptive lyric poetry did not immediately die: Gemma Tremblay (1925–74) published during the 1960s. Nor were Lapointe's poems at first so removed from ordinary discourse. But for their commitment to revolt, their disconcerting mix of religious and profane images, and their apparent freedom of syntax, they in turn excited young poets of the 1970s – Raoul Duguay (b. 1939), Claude Péloquin (b. 1942), and the writers of *La Barre du Jour* – when they were collected and published in 1971 as *Le réel absolu*. They include such words as a 1960 poem called 'Arbres', in which a catalogue of names constitutes an act of – social? verbal? erotic? – pleasure. Gilles Hénault's *Théâtre en plein air* (1946) and *Voyage au pays de mémoire* (1959), and Roland Giguère's (b. 1929) *L'âge de la parole* (1965) contributed to this same process of socio-linguistic deconstruction. Illustrator and designer, Giguère founded Éditions Erta in Montreal in 1949. Lapointe's subsequent work – *Écritures* (1979), for example – took him even further in the direction of revolutionary artifice; here words lose referential character entirely. They resist 'meaning' in order to 'be', purely: to be material things, the materiality of print and paper constituting its own *raison d'être*.

By contrast, the work of Gaston Miron (1928–96), the other poet of the 1950s on whom *Refus Global* had a significant effect – and who in turn influenced subsequent poets like Jacques Brault, Paul Chamberland (b. 1939), Gatien Lapointe (b. 1933), Michel Garneau (b. 1933), Pierre Morency (b. 1942) and Juan Garcia (b. 1945) – related more directly to a material society. Upset by the character of the French language during the 1940s and 1950s, when it appeared that it was becoming increasingly anglicized, Miron sought not to revivify it through *automatisme*, or to follow Pierre Trottier into the structures of 'universal' myth or emulate the *joualisme* of Gérald Godin (1938–94), but rather to extend the work of Grandbois and Anne Hébert. He tried to resist the controls of the past by embracing present social causes (the CCF, and then separatism after 1962) and the techniques of literary fragmentation.

A publisher, Miron founded the influential Éditions l'Hexagone in 1953, along with the poet Olivier Marchand (b. 1928, with whom he collaborated in Hexagone's first book of poetry, *Deux sangs*, 1953), and the filmmaker Gilles Carle. He also published Paul-Marie Lapointe, Jean-Guy Pilon, Roland Giguère, Gilles Hénault and Fernand Ouellette, thus providing a home for the voices of literary engagement. Hexagone also organized a poets' group – known as 'La Rencontre des Écrivains' among other names – which brought together Brault, Yves Préfontaine (b. 1937), Ouellette and others for readings and political discussion. It was through Hexagone that Casablanca-born Juan Garcia (later praised for his lyrics on the torments of the body and the infinity of love) met and was influenced by Miron, Brault and Gilbert Langevin.

But for many years Miron resisted collecting his own work into book form, suspicious of being absorbed into the literary establishment he was trying to challenge. The prize-winning *L'homme rapaillé* (man 'gathered together', like bits of straw from a hayfield) appeared in 1970. (It was translated in part, with other poems, as *The Agonized Life* in 1980, and reprinted in a bilingual edition in 1984 as *Embers and Earth*.) *Contrepointes* followed in 1975. What Miron rejected were the forces that would turn him (representative Quebec man) into 'l'homme du cheap way, l'homme du cheap work / le damned Canuck' [the man of the 'cheap way', the man for 'cheap work', the 'damn Canuck']. What he wanted to praise was Quebec: 'Compagnon des Amériques / mon Québec ma terre amère ma terre amande / ma patrie d'haleine dans la touffe des vents' [Companion of the Americas / my Quebec, my bitter land my almond land / my country of breath in the wisp of the winds]. The challenge is to find his own eyes in the embers, his heart in 'les champs de tourmente' [the fields of torment], and a tongue, a language, in the 'hives of nighttime'. Overcome at last by shadow and silence, the poet discovers sudden, occasional rays of light, 'la profuse lumière des sillages d'hirondelles' [the light, the wake, of swallow-flight]. These signs of hope separate his writing attitudinally as well as technically from the despondency and madness to which Gauvreau's dramas descend. The hope exists because Miron ultimately resists the idea of meaninglessness. Hence out of non-being emerges something new.

In his 1965 essay 'Un long chemin', translated in *Embers and Earth*, Miron further explained his poet's progress. From a colonial condition, he observed, any writer must write both to overcome himself and also to 'write *against* nature'; for himself, colonized in Quebec, the challenge was to find an authentic speech. If silence was his first choice, in the face of 'semantic perversion' and the absence of anything more natural, then to turn *parole* into poetry became his next. He would do so through neologism and precise ecological terminology, as well as by speech rhythm. The aim was to upset the status quo:

speech and language are the whole of a man's presence in the world, and if this presence is altered through its implement, if it is mutilated, then no compromise is possible. We can no longer account for reality. Here man is denaturalized, severed from his rightful ecological ties, and culture, that's to say alienated from his culture; he finds himself in a colonial situation that dehumanizes him. The state of language reflects all social problems.

Anyone, moreover, who is conscious of the deprivations that colonialism has invoked – 'linguistic duality, ... socio-economic inferiority, ... political dependency ... (a situation to which the alienated colonized man reacts by clinging to the land, by aping the colonizers, or by withdrawing into himself)' – is already on the way towards 'renewal'.

Those who have been completely assimilated reject these statements ...; either unknowingly or with conviction, they have adopted the image that the Other has of them: their specificity has been abolished by the other culture.

Plurality was not a *québécois* idéal; unity was. 'Nationhood' was about to be redefined. With the Quiet Revolution underway in 1960 – Jean Lesage (1912–80) winning the 1962 Quebec election with the slogan 'Maîtres chez nous' [Masters in our own house] – Quebec writers and politicians (they were often both) were drawing further away from Canada even as the anglophone version of Canada was shifting towards a norm of biculturalism. In the 1960s and 1970s, 'separatism' became a more potent force than ever, and 'colonialism' a watchword for women, Native people, ethnic minorities and regional territories as well as for Quebeckers. Writers began to seek structures of expression that would rephrase and so reinterpret their culture, free it from the definitions of 'Other', so to speak, and hence encode a new authenticity of self.

CHAPTER FIVE

Encoders: literature to 1985

LANGUAGE, LITERATURE, THE STATE AND THE ACADEMIES

One of Hugh MacLennan's ironic memoirs in *Scotchman's Return* (1960) – 'Boy Meets Girl in Winnipeg, and Who Cares?' – trenchantly reflected on the link between popular image and marketable taste. Canadian settings, especially in the United States, MacLennan observed, simply did not sell. Yet by 1985, Canadian Studies academic programs were active not only in the United States but also throughout Europe, the Commonwealth and East Asia. To trace the source of this interest back to the Massey Report and the tangible support the Canada Council gave to writers makes sense, though it oversimplifies the process. From 1960 to 1985, many new agencies of support for writing, research and publication came into existence (the Ontario Arts Council, for one), in part as a response to the cultural nationalism surrounding Canada's centennial year. Other developments also intensified writers' public profiles: creative writing and writer-in-residence programs (though many contemporary writers received training outside Canada: for example, Godfrey, Harlow, Blaise, Mukherjee, Kinsella, Valgardson, b. 1939, and Kroetsch all studied at the Iowa Writers' Workshop); organized readings (such as Greg Gatenby's, b. 1950, International Festival of Authors in Toronto); the activities of newly founded organizations (the League of Canadian Poets, the Union des Écrivains Québécois, the Writer's Union); the establishment of Canadian literature courses in schools. Bookstores began to stock Canadian books; people read them. Art became at once more academic and more popular. The Canadian feature film industry also re-emerged, and film-makers such as Gilles Carle, Claude Jutra, Paul Almond (b. 1931), Michel Brault (b. 1928),

Don Shebib (b. 1938), Norman Jewison (b. 1926), Sandy Wilson (b. 1947), Denys Arcand (b. 1940) and Anne-Claire Poirier (b. 1932) began to attract critical praise and popular attention. Several Royal Commission and other institutional reports also influenced public opinion. T.H.B. Symons' *To Know Ourselves* (1975) was one of these; commissioned by the Association of Universities and Colleges in Canada, it ultimately had the effect of doubling the number of under-graduate Canadian literature courses taught in the country, and of encouraging the Department of External Affairs to embark on a delib-erate policy of raising Canada's cultural profile abroad.

Another report, Thomas Berger's (b. 1933) *Northern Frontier, North-ern Homeland* (1977), primarily had economic and sociological impact, redesigning federal policy towards Native land claims and cultural independence. But it also affected language, bringing such terms as *Inuit* (replacing *Eskimo*) into public parlance, and giving impetus to the official use of the word *aboriginal* to replace *Indian* – all this at a time when the word *Québécois* was replacing the words *Canadien* (in French) and *French-Canadian* (in English). Ethnic and social minorities were rejecting the verbal terms that excluded them from power. Women, too, objected to the socio-political attitudes of the status quo, and to the language which contained them; the 1970 report on *The Status of Women in Canada*, chaired by Florence Bird (1908–98), began slowly to influence legislation, publication, education and social pol-icy. Relatedly, the regions of the country also objected to the controls of the self-proclaimed 'centre'. In ferment, often noisily, the society gave rise to many new social structures and a lively art. But the speed of change and the geometric increase in the number of writers and other artists confound a brief literary history. During the twenty-five years from 1960 to 1985 some four hundred new serious writers appeared (the post-war baby boom came to its maturity). To survey these years is to be more selective than ever, and to chart patterns and strategies of composition more than the details of personal careers.

Ethnicity, region, gender: these three issues stood behind many a resistance movement. All fastened on language as a means of redefin-ing the parameters of power and the character of available history. They marked the literature of the quarter century between 1960 and 1985; they encouraged the rapid development of the social sciences; they shaped the force and direction of political movements. Native rights protests became more intense in the 1980s, when the claim to aboriginal 'nationhood' became persuasive.

The more familiar claim to 'nationhood' during these years was heard in Quebec, which offers a ready paradigm for the tensions of the time. Quebec's francophone population was 41 per cent rural in

1941, but only 6 per cent rural in 1971. *Les raquetteurs* (1958), an influential anti-Duplessis film by Michel Brault and Gilles Carle, emphasized the force of membership in a 'national community'. Some Quebeckers interpreted nation as 'Canada', others as 'Quebec'. Following Duplessis's death, Jean Lesage's Quiet Revolution set several changes in motion. Educational and economic structures were both reformed. Far-reaching changes also derived from the province's cultural policy. Lesage declared French the official language of the provincial government, and embarked on 'national' acts – for instance, negotiating foreign cultural and educational agreements – incurring the opposition of the federal government. Tensions spread.

While the reformers of the *Cité Libre* years (Jean Marchand, b. 1918, Gérard Pelletier, Pierre-Elliott Trudeau) moved into federal politics in 1965 and at once into ministerial position, others were seeking more abrupt and definitive transfers of power. The Front de Libération du Québec (or FLQ) adopted terrorist tactics to encourage the separation of Quebec from Canada, attacking randomly many physical symbols of the 'English' or 'federal' presence in Quebec – tactics which were given moral support when General Charles de Gaulle (1890–1970), on a state visit to Canada, uttered the separatist slogan 'Vive le Québec libre' to a massed crowd. But the tactics turned sour in 1970 (in the 'October Crisis') when they led to the kidnapping of the British diplomat James (Jasper) Cross (b.1921) and the murder of the Quebec cabinet minister Pierre Laporte (1921–1970). Trudeau, prime minister since 1968, invoked the War Measures Act, resolving one crisis only to set others (involving civil rights) in motion. Writers, most of whom were committed to the ideal of individual liberty, fastened on these events as partisan subjects – as did Brian Moore (1921–99) with *The Revolution Script* (1971), Al Purdy with 'The Peaceable Kingdom', and Yves Beauchemin (b. 1941) with *L'enfirouapé* (1974) – but seldom convincingly. (Moore, an Ulster immigrant who took out Canadian citizenship before leaving for California and a screenwriting career, wrote over twelve novels; his reputation is based on those which couple fantasy with Catholic morality, such as *The Great Victorian Collection*, 1975, or *Black Robe*, 1985 – the latter, influenced by Parkman, concerns the Jesuit missionaries to New France and the tensions between their sexuality and their aspirations to martyrdom.) Robin Spry (b. 1939) produced National Film Board documentaries on the October Crisis. The political tensions between Quebec and federal Canada also informed Jacques Poulin's (b. 1938) novel *Mon cheval pour un royaume* (1967), Jacques Godbout's *Le couteau sur la table* (1965), Claude Jasmin's (b. 1930) *Ethel et le terroriste* (1964), Robert Gurik's (b. 1932) plays *Hamlet, prince du Québec* (1968) and *Les tas de neige* (1971), and

Françoise Loranger's (1913–95) plays about language disputes (*Médium saignant*, 1970) and hockey (*Le chemin du roy*, 1971). Generally, in anglophone Canada, political events fell to hands of popular writers such as Arthur Hailey (b. 1920), James Clavell (1924–94), John Ralston Saul (b. 1947), or Anthony Hyde (b. 1946), though occasionally (with David Helwig, b. 1938, Hugh MacLennan, or David Lewis Stein, b. 1937) serious stories about the politics of generation conflict were only one filter away from analyses of Canadian governmental tensions. In francophone writing, by contrast, politics was both subject and methodology.

The essayists took up the cause of reform. The essay is a central literary genre in modern Quebec – more so than in English Canada, though there continued to be effective anglophone naturalists (Farley Mowat, b. 1921, Andy Russell, b. 1915), memoirists (Harry Bruce, b. 1934, Kildare Dobbs, b. 1923, Silver Donald Cameron, b. 1937, Fredelle Bruser Maynard, 1922–90), social ironists (Laurence Peter, 1919–90, of the 'Peter Principle', Erika Ritter, b. 1948, Mordecai Richler), and political commentators (George Woodcock, Frank Underhill, Mel Watkins, b. 1932, Eugene Forsey, 1904–91, George Grant, 1918–88, and the journalist-essayists of *Saturday Night*, *Canadian Forum*, *Canadian Dimension*, and *This Magazine*). From Buies, Bourassa, Asselin and Groulx, however, to Jean Le Moyne (for some time a speechwriter for Trudeau and later a senator), Jacques Grand'maison (b. 1931), Pierre Trottier, André Laurendeau (1912–68), Pierre Vadeboncoeur, Solange Chaput-Rolland (1919–2001), Jean Ethier-Blais (1925–95), Fernand Ouellette, Jacques Brault and Fernand Dumont (1927–93), Quebec essayists have been at the heart of intellectual dispute and cultural reform. In 1960, Jean-Paul Desbiens (b. 1927) declared the need for educational changes when he published *Les impertinences du Frère Untel*. Whereas these essays, like those of Grignon and others before him, called for higher *standards* of speech and intellectual challenge, other intellectuals were championing the rights of ordinary working-class people, as a way of emphasizing how far-reaching cultural change now had to be. *Joual* (the term a corruption of the word 'cheval'), a Montreal dialect, thus became the verbal medium of much new literary work of the 1960s and also a political comment in its own right. The broken forms of joual implicitly attacked the intellectual authorities in Quebec, whose fidelity to past standards of speech was made to equate with political deference to English Canada.

Foremost in this political and verbal rebellion were the Montreal writers who formed the Parti Pris movement (1963–8): André Major (b. 1942, poet playwright, novelist, best known for his violent trilogy

Histoires des déserteurs: L'épouvantail, 1974, *L'épidémie*, 1975, and *Les rescapés*, 1976, the first two volumes translated as *The Scarecrow of Saint-Emmanuel* and *Inspector Therrien*); the poet Paul Chamberland (whose *L'afficheur hurle*, 1964, expresses his early Marxist or Fanonian rebellion, but whose later poetry turns in hermetic and sexual directions); the film-maker Pierre Maheu (1939–79); the film critic Jean-Marc Piotte, b. 1940; and the critic André Brochu, b. 1942 (who in 1968 helped found the journal that became *Voix et Images*). As a journal, *Parti Pris* espoused a 'free, secular, and separatist' society in Quebec; it allied itself with Marxist thought, Sartrean existentialism, and the whole process of decolonization that during these years was bringing independence to former British and French colonies worldwide. *Parti Pris* declared the need for a revolution to bring about an independent and socialist state in Quebec, and it rejected the term 'French Canada' from the outset, insisting instead on 'québécité'. It published works in *joual*. As a publishing house, moreover (organized by the poet Gérald Godin, later the Minister for Cultural Communities and Immigration in René Lévesque's government), Parti Pris published some twenty works, two of the most significant being Jacques Renaud's (b. 1943) novella *Le cassé* (1964) and Pierre Vallières essay collection *Nègres blancs d'Amérique* (1968). Renaud's joual story tells of a down-and-outer, both 'broken' and 'flat broke' as the title has it, whose violent life epitomizes the level of cultural deprivation to which Quebec has stooped. Vallières's account of Quebec (translated as *White Niggers of America*) borrows the vocabulary of imperialism and then-current American civil rights protests to make its point: Quebec is Canada's colony, the argument runs, the Quebeckers are second-class citizens. 'Speak White', a poem by the radio writer Michèle Lalonde (b. 1937), a board member of *Liberté*, adopts the same rhetoric to characterize the anglophone's attitude to Québécois; 'speakwhiter' (that is, to speak white) even became a joual verb for Chamberland. The most effective literary use of joual occurs in the plays of Michel Tremblay; it was also one of the most far-reaching, for like the fact of joual itself – the vernacular used as an agent of political reform (some Acadian writers used their vernacular, *'chiac'*, for similar ends) – Tremblay began to have an impact outside Quebec as well as within. One of the most lucid English accounts of joual is Malcolm Reid's (b. 1941) *The Shouting Signpainters* (1972), its title a translation of the title of Chamberland's 1964 poem. Joual shortly began to peter out as a forceful literary tactic in Quebec, however, its decline hastened when Marie-Claire Blais (b. 1939) parodied the technique in *Un joualonais, sa joualonie* (1974). Renaud abandoned it. By 1985 Yves Beauchemin would declare 'joualisme' to be infantile, a literary dead end. The Parti Pris movement, moreover, dispersed when social reform appeared in practice to be on the way, especially in 1968 when René Lévesque (1922–1987), who in 1962 had been minister of natural resources in Lesage's Liberal government, accepted the leadership of the avowedly separatist Parti Québécois. Eight years later, Lévesque took the new party to power.

The careers of the journalist Lévesque and the lawyer Trudeau offer striking parallels. Both were Jesuit-educated. Both became party leaders in 1968; both resigned (in 1985 and 1984 respectively) only to see their parties defeated in the next election. Both were articulate ardent nationalist centralists – symbols throughout Canada of Quebec's new presence – though their sense of nation and centre differed markedly. Between them there existed an acute public polarity, which affected social politics in Canada for fifteen years. The legislative records of the two politicians reveal the impact both had upon the structure and character of the society at large. Lévesque's concern for language, and for the basis of *québécois* culture and independence in language, declared itself in Bill 101, which made French the sole official language of business, state and law court in Quebec (a law later challenged in the Supreme Court of Canada); Trudeau's concern for language emerged in the Official Languages Act of 1969, which made Canada legally bilingual. The disparity between the two positions was significant; neither was it made easier by pockets of political resistance to the French language throughout the country. Yet within three years the federal government was responding to other social pressures (regional and ethnic ones) and setting a new rhetoric in motion; in 1972 a minister of state was responsible for an official policy of 'multiculturalism', which also had reverberations within Quebec. For many Quebeckers, *Québécois* was a culturally restrictive term, not an altogether franchising one. New francophone writers emerged whose roots were not narrowly *Québécois* at all; the critic Max Dorsinville (b. 1943) drew on a Haitian background, the dramatist Marco Micone (b. 1945) on an Italian one, the novelists Alice Parizeau and Negovan Rajic (b. 1923) on Polish and Yugoslav roots, and Naim Kattan (b. 1928) on the world of an Iraqi Jew. (Essayist, novelist, short story writer, playwright, Kattan headed the cultural affairs division of the Canada Council – his works include *Le réel et le théâtral*, 1970; *Adieu Babylone*, 1975; and *Dans le désert*, 1974.) In 1980, Lévesque put a referendum on 'Sovereignty-Association' before the people of Quebec, who voted 60 per cent in favour of remaining in Canada. Trudeau, in the meantime, was working towards 'repatriating' the Constitution, and in 1982 the Constitution Act was proclaimed, removing the last remnant of British government authority over Canadian law. But the new Act was not without problems. Whereas, in the last days of negotiation, the equal rights of women were included in the Act, and so established in law, clauses that might deal with native rights were ultimately left for later discussion. Quebec, moreover, did not sign the agreement, leaving many social tensions unresolved.

The fabric of the society was altering, partly by the changes in the authority and shape of its institutions, partly by the ongoing shifts in ethnic character. New immigration legislation in the 1970s opened the borders to larger numbers of Asian immigrants, whose impact on Canadian writing was beginning to manifest itself by the mid 1980s, in journals such as *The Toronto South Asian Review* and in the work of individual writers – Saros Cowasjee (b. 1931), Rohinton Mistry (b. 1952), and others. Table 3 indicates changes in patterns of Canadian ethnic derivation, though the table needs to be read cautiously. Based on census statistics, it demonstrates the biases that historically have defined heritage and national culture: 'Jewish' was used as a term of ethnic classification rather than simply a religious affiliation; 'Indian and Inuit' is classed as one cultural group rather than as a plural set of 'nations'; 'American' was never used as a term of ethnic heritage (if it had been, the numbers would shape a radically different pattern: from the Loyalists to the numerous people who left the USA for Canada in the 1960s and 1970s, as a political gesture against the Vietnam War, Americans have been influential and often invisible immigrants). Most fundamentally, 'Canadian' is still not accepted as an 'ethnic' classification, even for families who have been in the country for generations. The 1981 census was, however, the first to allow respondents to declare their maternal as well as their paternal heritage, which provides a limited opportunity to reveal more than one ethnic background. Early data are incomplete, and the 1871 data refer to only the four original provinces.

Table 3 does not indicate the impact of the uneven regional distribution of ethnic *groups*: the impact of a South European concentration in Toronto, for example, or a Haitian concentration in Montreal. Compounding the fact of ethnicity in society, therefore, is the overlap with region, class and gender, sometimes reinforcing such issues as urban poverty and discrimination, sometimes pointing towards the generation conflicts that derive from the contrast between old and new world expectations of behaviour. Central to any of these experiences is the sense of alienation from the structures of power that constitute the social norm. In Quebec, Vadeboncoeur (in *La dernière heure et la première*, 1970) had argued that such marginality can be an advantage, that Quebec's historical lack of influence was a legitimate

Table 3 Ethnic origins, 1871-1981 (percentages of population)

	1871	1881	1901	1911	1921	1931	1941	1951	1961	1971	1981
African											.18
Asiatic		.10	.44	.60	.75	.81	.64	.52	.67	1.30	
British	60.55	58.93	57.04	55.49	55.41	51.86	49.68	47.89	43.85	44.60	40.16
British and French											1.78
British and other											3.57
Caribbean											.33
Chinese											1.20
Dutch	.85	.70	.63	.78	1.34	1.44	1.85	1.89	2.36	2.00	1.69
European and other											.96
French	31.07	30.03	30.71	28.61	27.91	28.22	30.27	30.83	30.38	28.70	26.73
German	5.82	5.88	5.78	5.60	3.35	4.56	4.04	4.43	5.75	6.10	4.74
Greek											.62
Indian and Inuit	.66	2.51	2.38	1.46	1.29	1.24	1.09	1.18	1.21	1.40	1.71
Indo-Pakistani											.81
Italian	.03	.04	.20	.64	.76	.95	.98	1.09	2.47	3.40	3.10
Jewish		.02	.30	1.06	1.44	1.51	1.48	1.30	.95	1.40	1.06
Latin American											.15
Philippine											.30
Polish			.12	.47	.61	1.40	1.45	1.57	1.77	1.50	1.05
Portuguese											.78
Russian	.02	.03	.37	.61	1.14	.85	.73	.65	.65	.30	.20
Scandinavian	.05	.12	.58	1.56	1.90	2.20	2.12	2.02	2.12	1.80	1.17
Ukrainian			.10	1.05	1.21	2.17	2.65	2.82	2.59	2.70	2.19
Other East Asian											.40
Other European	.11	.13	.44	1.35	2.44	2.51	2.45	2.47	3.90	3.90	2.88
W. Asian / N. African											2.64
Others not stated	.84	1.51	.91	.72	.45	.28	.56	1.34	1.33	1.00	.50

basis for building something authentic for itself. Women writers reiterated this notion in terms involving gender: to rid the language of its masculine biases was only a preliminary step, they argued, to the uttering of an authentically female voice. Literary coteries, moreover, sprang up in various places to sound the suppressed voices of region. In a more general way, the idea of marginality stood behind Canada's national reaction to the United States, too, especially in the 1960s and early 1970s: the USA represented technology, power, economic control – but Canada constituted a legitimate alternative.

The 1967 national centennial was therefore both a celebration and a symbol. Cultural nationalism, buttressed by economic nationalism – Canadians' desire, for example, to regain control of the publication and book distribution industries from American companies – inspired many a literary and pedagogical commitment in these years. It was part of the cultural ferment. But such nationalism, in the wake of economic depression, became a diluted if not a spent force by 1985; for a subsequent generation, the illusory objectivity of 'international standards' and the conservative politics of material success became substitute ideals.

There thus emerged in the 1960s a debate between those who saw technology as the future and those who saw it as the loss of the past. Marshall McLuhan exemplifies the first attitude, George Grant (the grandson of George Parkin and George Monro Grant) the second. Both influenced literature. McLuhan's writings on the medium of message and the 'global village' (the post-national character of technological communication) further disrupted conventional notions of syntax and elegance. Grant's *Lament for a Nation* (1965) and *Technology and Empire* (1969) argued that systems of technological communication were quintessentially American, not post-national at all. Grant's arguments thus fed the cultural nationalism of the 1970s, marking writers as diverse as Margaret Atwood (in both her novel *Surfacing*, 1972, and her thematic guide to Canadian literature, *Survival*, 1972), Dennis Lee (b. 1939, in critical articles like 'Cadence, Country, Silence', published in *Open Letter*, and in the poems of *Civil Elegies*, revised in 1972), Dave Godfrey (b. 1938, in political action within the publishing industry). The 'Red Tory' essays of Charles Taylor (b. 1931) and the novels of Scott Symons also show Grant's influence. Lee's *Civil Elegies* reads in part:

Many were born in Canada, and living unlived lives they died
of course but died truncated, stunted, never at
home in native space and not yet
citizens of a human body of kind. And it is Canada
that specialized in this deprivation.

Yet Grant (brother-in-law to both the diplomat George Ignatieff, 1913–89, and the liberal educator Geoffrey Andrew, 1906–87) was Ontario-centred, his analysis of Canada limited by the terms of his conservative version of history. By the 1980s, he was championing the 'structures of loss' by which he characterized the Loyalist heritage, and also attacking notions of progress and individuality, which his philosophical essays – continued in *Technology and Justice* (1986) – confused with technology (defined as the falling away from man's God-given original nature), with America, and with various issues (affecting women's rights, for example) that argued for changes in the presumptive values of existing social structures.

To reduce the question of technology to a simple dualistic acceptance or rejection was misleading. The swift changes in the technology of communication and transportation systems, which characterized the quarter-century following 1960, had had several consequences. American media had begun more effectively than ever to penetrate the Canadian market, significantly shaping taste and values. Yet Canadian artists had also begun to reach the world, jet travel increasing their own range of experience and their opportunities to meet writers in other societies. Satellite communication (the Anik series in particular) and computer production techniques resolved some of Canada's problems with distance; they also affected the course of publishing and the very shape of literature. Some of the 1980s poems of Marco Fraticelli (b. 1945), for example, were physically shaped like computer program flow-charts; Frank Davey's 1980s critical journal *Swift Current* was accessible only by computer screen; library catalogues and many bibliographies went 'on-line', enabling swifter access and easier update; and publishing systems adopted computer print designs, as is apparent in the aesthetically appealing works produced by Coach House Press.

In retrospect the technological changes of the early 1960s seem less dramatic, but they, too, served the processes of social change that affected cultural policy and publication. To take one example: when the mimeographed little magazine *Tish* began in Vancouver in 1961, it was received primarily as the voice of a coterie – George Bowering, Frank Davey (b. 1940), Fred Wah (b. 1939), David Dawson (b. 1942), Lionel Kearns (b. 1937) and to a much lesser degree Daphne (Buckle) Marlatt (b. 1942). All had been influenced by critic Warren Tallman (1921–94) at the University of British Columbia. The 1963 Vancouver Poetry Conference held there, involving the American Black Mountain poets (Robert Creeley, b. 1926, Robert Duncan, 1919–88, Denise Levertov, 1923–97), further influenced *Tish*'s direction (and won the opposition of several critical nationalists who saw the American

influence as inimical to native Canadian verse). The magazine proclaimed Black Mountain poetics ('No ideas but in things') and the
poets sought systems of notation that would allow the poetics of
speech rhythm to matter more than the social respectability of
appearing in print.

The relation between these and various Eastern poets, such as
Dudek and Souster, became clearer later, as did the connection with
Margaret Avison (b. 1918), also influenced by Black Mountain poetics. Avison's *Winter Sun* (1960) relies on networks of images and on
the multiple meanings that derive from aural ambiguities – they
resist 'fix', as in 'Tennis', and oppose terror, as in several translations
from East European writers. The world observed in 'A Sad Song'
shapes an aural meditation:

> The young catalpa
> tree on Robert Street
> sickens. Storms
> break branches, strip
> the crisping leaves, soak
> the fake-brick wall-front. ...
> June is now sealed, silent.
> Form without springing makes of it
> a wrong season.

As the title poem of *The Dumbfounding* (1966) indicates, succour
derives ultimately from an intense personal Christianity:

> Winning one, you again
> all ways would begin
> life: to make new
> flesh, to empower
> the weak in nature ...
>
> lead through the garden to
> trash, rubble, hill,
> where, the outcast's outcast, you
> sound dark's uttermost, strangely light-brimming, until
> time be full.

The overlap with the *Tish* poets was more in aesthetic intention than
in subject. For both, the world was Heraclitean, a challenge to speech
as much as to social custom. Bowering and Davey continued to
challenge convention in critical presumption and literary form

(Bowering's journal *Imago*, for example, founded in Calgary in 1964, was dedicated to redefining the long poem at a time when length was identified with narrative and narrative poetry was presumed to be dead). What *Tish* further emphasized was that significant literary change did not have to originate in the now traditional centres of Eastern Canada.

In the publishing industry at large, the rapid shifts from a mimeograph to a photo-offset technology underscored this change. It freed up the printed page to concrete poems (such as bp Nichol's 'Blues', a

punning print design responding to the blues-singer's phrase 'love, oh love, oh careless love'). Among other visual patterns were the *naïf* satires of Bill Bissett (b. 1939), the typographical designs of Lucien Francoeur (b. 1948), the 'found poems' of John Robert Colombo, and the visual play of Joe Rosenblatt's (b. 1933) *Bumblebee Dithyramb* (1972) and *Dr. Anaconda's Solar Fan Club* (1978). Technological change also encouraged the development of a score of new publishing houses and journals in different regions of the country, emphasizing cultural vitality, variety and sheer numbers of production all at once: Oberon Press in Ottawa, Breakwater in St. John's, Square Deal and Ragweed in Charlottetown, Hurtig and NeWest in Edmonton, Alive Press in Guelph, Talonbooks and Douglas & McIntyre in Vancouver, Oolichan in Lantzville, Sono Nis in Mission City and Victoria, Turnstone in Winnipeg, Thistledown in Saskatoon. Even in the traditional publication centres, Toronto and Montreal, small presses emerged to provide alternatives to the publishing policies of the established presses: Anansi, New Press, Véhicule, VLB Éditeurs, Coach House, Playwrights Canada. Often particular writers were involved, as Ken Norris (b. 1951) was associated with Véhicule, Bill Bissett with blewointment, Lesley Choyce (b. 1951) with Pottersfield Press, Margaret Atwood and Dennis Lee with Anansi, Gilles Vigneault with Éditions de l'Arc, Gary Geddes (b. 1940) with Quadrant. bp Nichol (1944–88) edited for Coach House, and Douglas Gibson (b. 1943) was an influential editor for Munro, Hodgins, and other Macmillan writers (who followed Gibson when he moved to McClelland & Stewart in 1985). Jay Macpherson (b. 1931) ran Emblem Books. Robin Skelton, Stephen Scobie (b. 1943) and Constance Rooke (b. 1942) were all associated with *Malahat Review*; Bill Schermbrucker (b.1938), Ann Rosenberg (b. 1940) and Pierre Coupey (b. 1942) with *Capilano Review*; Sheila Watson with *White Pelican*; the surrealist poet Denis Vanier (b. 1949) with *Hobo-Québec*. Writers were idiosyncratically involved with 'underground' magazines as well: bp Nichol and David Aylward (b. 1942) edited *Ganglia* from 1963 on; and one issue of Andrew Suknaski's (b. 1942) magazine *Elfin Post* was apparently 'released' by being floated down the North Saskatchewan River in Al Purdy's empty cigar containers. When Dave Godfrey and Ellen Godfrey (b. 1942) moved Press Porcépic from Erin, Ontario, to Victoria, British Columbia, the implied and practical politics of this decision became the subject of a meditation at the heart of Dave Godfrey's *Dark Must Yield* (1978). The continuing impact of technological development shows strikingly in the ongoing history of this press, whose offshoot company Softwords subsequently became an innovator in computer software development and marketing.

Government arts support further encouraged developments in publication; grants in aid of research led to several new critical magazines coming into existence: *Journal of Canadian Studies*, *Essays in Canadian Writing*, *La Barre du Jour*, *Les Herbes Rouges*, *Studies in Canadian Literature*, *Canadian Poetry*, *Canadian Children's Literature*. Journals such as *Ariel* and *WLWE* stressed the Commonwealth dimensions of Canadian writing. Adrien Thério (b. 1925, b. Thériault), who had helped found *Livres et auteurs québécois* in 1961, was instrumental in establishing *Lettres québécoises* in 1976. *Les Herbes Rouges* (established in 1968), together with journals such as *Cul Q*, *Chroniques* and *Hobo-Québec*, attracted numerous influential francophone writers, from Chamberland and Francoeur to Claude Beausoleil (b. 1948), Normand de Bellefeuille (b. 1949), Madeleine Gagnon (b. 1938), Philippe Haeck (b. 1946), André Roy (b. 1944), Yolande Villemaire (b. 1949), France Théoret (b. 1942) and François Charron (b. 1952). They were more concerned with changing society than with reaffirming it. Pierre Nepveu (b. 1946) was typical of his generation in turning poetry from the land to the city, from the romance of space and forest to the anxiety of artifice and speed. The volatility of the culture showed up even more in popular magazines (*Mainmise*), alternative publications (*This Magazine, Stratégies, The Ontario Indian*), and journals that focused on women's studies (*Room of One's Own, La Nouvelle Barre du Jour, Atlantis*).

Cultural volatility and the availability of support funds also facilitated the writing and production of Canadian drama. Offering alternatives to familiar repertoires, regional theatres encouraged local playwrights and developed audiences. Many new theatres opened: Neptune (Halifax, 1963), Arts Club (Vancouver, 1963), Citadel (Edmonton, 1965), Globe (Regina, 1966). The Charlottetown Festival began in 1965, the Shaw Festival in Niagara-on-the-Lake in 1962; the Lennoxville Festival ran from 1972 to 1982. The playwright Chris Heide (b. 1951) was active in Nova Scotia with *The Coady Co-op Show* in 1978. Two Newfoundland troupes, Codco (1973–6) and the Mummers Troupe (1972–82), satirized society, as did various radio and television performers, from Nancy White (b. 1945) to 'Dr. Bundolo'. The opening of theatre schools in Quebec encouraged several new companies. John Juliani's (b. 1940) Savage God troupe opened in the 1980s in Montreal. In Vancouver, Tahmanous began in 1971, Green Thumb Players for Children in 1975 (drawing on the plays of Dennis Foon, b. 1951), and the annual International Theatre Festival for young people in 1978. Toronto's Young People's Theatre produced John Lazarus (b. 1947) and Joa Lazarus's (b. 1949) realistic play about adolescent awakening, *Dreaming and Duelling*, in 1981. Four other Toronto companies encouraged theatrical innovation: Factory Theatre Lab (1970) – whose founder, Ken Gass (b. 1945), learned his craft at John Herbert's (1926–2001) Garret Theatre, which closed in 1971 – Bill Glassco's (b. 1935) Tarragon (1971), Toronto Free Theatre (1972), and Paul Thompson's (b. 1940) Theatre Passe Muraille (1971). Thompson became head of the National Theatre School in 1987. Passe Muraille's collective creations (*The Farm Show*, or Rick Salutin's (b. 1942) *1837: The Farmer's Revolt*, 1976), brought new energy and personality to the stage spectacle. Le Théâtre Experimental des Femmes (established 1979), was one of several feminist development in performance and publishing in Montreal, Marie-Claire Blais being one of the writers involved in collective theatrical presentations.

The degree of government and academic involvement in literature in these years emphasizes how broadly political cultural affairs had become. What individual plays and publications emphasize, moreover, are the several ways in which authors coded – devised a verbal strategy for conveying – their political feelings, their concern for the contexts of history and language, and their practice and theory of criticism. Some of these systems of coding constitute the subject and the shaping structure of the rest of this chapter. They stress the numerous interconnections between generic and verbal decisions, critical theory, and a shifting literary practice.

CODES OF MYTH

In the face of such apparently sudden, and to many seemingly radical, changes in the character of Canadian life, it is not surprising that a number of writers and critics sought still to find order at the heart of speech and social custom. Nowhere was this quest for coherence clearer than in the criticism of Northrop Frye (1912–1991), a University of Toronto professor, specializing in Shakespeare and Blake, who produced the annual *University of Toronto Quarterly* surveys of Canadian poetry during the 1950s, and whose later career was turned to an elucidation of the mythological and verbal structures of the Bible (*The Great Code*, 1982). Frye's *Anatomy of Criticism* (1957) – isolating the cycles of rhetorical strategy he identified with literary genre: tragedy, comedy, irony, romance – substantially influenced a generation of writers. His essays on Canadian culture, in *The Bush Garden* (1971) and elsewhere – drawing on Jung (1875–1961), Frazer (1854–1941) and his own training in theology – lodged Canadian criticism for some years in a belief in the 'disorder' of 'wilderness'. An influential phrase was his suggestion (perhaps most applicable to the literature of Ontario) that Canadian writing expressed a 'garrison mentality'. Psychological in import, this analysis derived from Christian metaphor and from Frye's belief that literature is not about life but about other literature: that is, it recodes the cultural heritage by re-enacting the patterns of previous writings. Implicitly, this version of cultural expression was linear because cyclical; it accepted European culture as the ideological frame of reference for interpreting Canada, and anticipated 'mythic' patterns of recurrence. It drew attention to the significance of form, but it attributed value most to those works which corroborated Jungian patterns of archetype, at the end of which was a belief in wholeness, harmony, balance (an ideal of perfectibility, an image of the mandala). Such criticism directly influenced the poetry and commentaries of Douglas Jones (for example, *Butterfly on Rock*, 1970); *Under the Thunder the Flowers Light Up the Earth*, 1977), the fiction and poetry of Gwendolyn MacEwen (1941–87; for example, *Noman*, 1972), the criticism and poems of Jay Macpherson (especially *The Boatman*, 1957, whose title poem uses Noah's Ark as a metaphor for the artistic process of shaping meaning and the psychological process of reshaping 'all the world' into a unified personal vision), and the poems, plays, critical essays and publishing enterprises (for example, the magazine *Alphabet*, 1960–70) of James Reaney.

Jay Macpherson's later poem-cycle (*Welcoming Disaster*, 1974) adapts archetypal patterns of quest to a concern for the ideological constraints which silence women's voices in literature. With a teddy-bear as Tammuz, her guide, the persona recounts the failure of expression:

> While we loved those who never read our poems,
> Answered our letters, said the simple things we
> Waited so long for, and were too polite to
>   See we were crying,
>
> Irony fed us.

Then she descends, in order to recognize the constraints of belonging to others' worlds:

> Where I laid my murdered brother,
> Where I laid my angry mother,
> Where I laid my luckless sister,
>   In that cellar
> They lie, they lie, they lie. ...
>
> There I lie, to them committed.

The 'changeling' bear,

> Of death and hell the key,
> [Is] gone to mend the primal wrong,
> That rift in Being, Me.

But independence from others is elusive, especially when part of the past self has been suppressed, allowed to die. 'Something in both of us', adds the 'Epilogue', 'never got born'; such recognition does not equate with change, nor does irony disappear:

> too late to hack it out,
> or to unlearn
> needed, familiar pain.
> Come, little thorn.

Hence the crying continues – not without words so much as without a ready body of listeners attuned to what they really say. (Just as

Macpherson was a student of Frye, so was Margaret Atwood a student of Macpherson, her early work in particular showing the influence of Macpherson's theories of the history of romance. Marian Engel 1933–85, by contrast, was a student of Hugh MacLennan, her novels marked more strongly by the conventions of social realism.) Less directly influenced by Frye but nonetheless involved in Jungian patterning were the francophone writers Pierre Châtillon (b. 1939), Yvon Rivard (b. 1945), Jacques Garneau, (b. 1939), and Normand Rousseau (b. 1939), and the anglophone novelists Malcolm Lowry and Robertson Davies.

When Davies, in his Salterton trilogy of the 1950s (*Tempest-Tost*, 1951; *Leaven of Malice*, 1954; *A Mixture of Frailties*, 1958), adopted a satiric voice, drawing on Shakespeare's (1564–1616) *The Tempest* as an analogue to expose the foibles of small-town Peterborough, Ontario, he re-enacted Leacock's conservative position, but in so doing – by means of his narrative stance – removed himself from events. The author-narrative was the observer, apart from the action. While the articulate and sometimes recondite voice does not radically change from any one Davies novel to any other, a difference in stance separates the Salterton trilogy from the Deptford trilogy of the 1970s (*Fifth Business*, 1970; *The Manticore*, 1972; and *World of Wonders*, 1975) and the first two novels (*The Rebel Angels*, 1981; *What's Bred in the Bone*, 1985) of the Francis Cornish trilogy of the 1980s. The Cornish trilogy is more connected with historical persons, the Deptford trilogy more engaged with the culture as Davies himself conceives of it. In particular, the three separate Deptford novels describe a Jungian analysis of the tensions between a public Protestant guilt and a private passion for magic and mystery which Davies sees as characteristic of Canadian life. The 'real' identity ('self' in Jung's terms) hides behind masks of its own invention, subconsciously identifying archetypal figures (wise old man, anima, magus, shadow) through the encounters of daily life. With the 'self' suppressed, life will prove trying, until therapy of some sort (actual, in the psychiatrist's office, or vicarious, through art) can reconcile all. The story tells of the ramifications of an apparently inconsequential event (the throwing of a snowball) in the intertwined lives of an entire town; the second volume extrapolates from the particular wilderness of local landscape and behaviour to the archetypes of wilderness (and of national resistance to the wilderness) which are embodied in European religion, art and literature. The third volume concerns itself with illusion. The quest which structures the narrative ultimately works both psychologically and historically, though it also functions as a deliberate, self-conscious literary device, a playful strategy of suspense, which undercuts the tone of the entire enterprise.

For Lowry, too, the European equation between Canada and wilderness lies behind the mythological and psychological structures of his fiction, but in Lowry's case there is little authorial distance involved. Lowry's alcoholic life became his fiction; he wrote his experiences, guilts, griefs and aspirations out into an ongoing cycle of novels he referred to in his letters as 'The Voyage that Never Ends'. Always it changed, because each new experience had to be built into what had gone before (an early novel, *Ultramarine*, 1933, written under the influence of American writer Conrad Aiken, 1889–1973, was rewritten to fit in with the events of later fictions). Lowry was pursued by the past – through guilt and memory (he rejected his Merseyside, mercantile, Methodist, Cambridge background, but constantly relived it) and also in the way he hung on to systems of explanation. He appeared desperate for a final explanatory systematic order, but at the same time resisted stasis. In his later years he seemed to be working towards a fictional form which would allow him the flexibility of cinematic technique. The successive drafts of *Under the Volcano* (1947), however, which he composed in Mexico and in Dollarton, British Columbia, show him experimenting with myths of narrative closure. To Classical structures (Ixion, Sisyphus) he added literary and philosophical ones (Joycean, Neoplatonist, Mexican Catholic), on top of which he embroidered a system of cabbalistic allusion which he learned in North Vancouver from a writer named Charles Stansfield-Jones (1886–1950).

No one system alone explains the book, a narrative of the alcoholic decline of a British consul in Mexico during the 1930s, and of the powers of memory that reanimate him. It is a work in which texture is all, and which (cyclically constructed) turns in on itself, endlessly repeating its tragedy of ego. In the larger scheme, the book was to have been read as a novel 'written' by a fictional novelist who was created in turn by Lowry's fictional novelist-character Sigbjørn Wilderness. Later books in the sequence – *Dark as the Grave Wherein My Friend is Laid* (1968) and *October Ferry to Gabriola* (1970), published posthumously, and 'La Mordida', still in manuscript – were ostensibly to have turned towards triumph, Wilderness embracing the harmonious possibilities of wild Canada (and himself) rather than foundering in the hellish south. But the design remains uncertain, the books (as published) being edited versions of manuscripts which were still in flux at the time of the author's death. The versions of the character Wilderness apparent in the stories collected as *Hear Us O Lord From Heaven Thy Dwelling-Place* (1961) suggest some of the directions Lowry was following. Lowry expressed his pastoral aspirations in 'The Forest Path to the Spring', his comic talents in 'Elephant and

Colosseum' and 'Strange Comfort Afforded by the Profession', and the pressures of disengagement in the textual disruptions of 'Through the Panama'. Technically diverse, the stories unite formally, reiterating journey motifs until the single book can be read as a prototype for the entire 'voyage' cycle: a quest for self that life and art together contrive to deny to the fretful soul.

For James Reaney, the connection between person and place is at once more direct and less febrile. Married to the poet Colleen Thibaudeau (b. 1925), Reaney has long lived in Western Ontario, and has repeatedly adapted the archetypal patterns apparent in Frye's literary taxonomy to the persons and places of local history and culture. Some of Reaney's poems and essays declare the formative influence of popular culture (cartooning to folk tales) on people's imaginations, and celebrate the environment by using regional speech to name local flora and fauna. At another level the local stories take on the structure of the past, but grow into themselves by means of such structures: *A Suit of Nettles* (1958) adopts the form of Spenser's (1552–99) *The Shepheardes Calendar*; the 1972 play *The Easter Egg* adapts Christian ritual to domestic circumstances; a children's play employs the epic catalogue, using the simple incantation of the numbers of parents, grandparents and other ancestors each child has, to assert how history and cultural inheritance become individualized in every life. Constantly crossing generic borders, Reaney has collaborated at different times with the painter Jack Chambers (1931–78) and the musician John Beckwith (b. 1927), emphasizing the interconnections between speech, sight and sound. Most recently he has focused on local literary and historical events. He transformed John Richardson's novel into a 1979 play called *Wacousta!* A nineteenth-century academic dispute turned in *The Dismissal* (1979) into a symbolic comment on contemporary academic practice. Most successfully, his trilogy *The Donnellys* (1976–7) turns the events of a famous 1880 Ontario murder case into a theatrical myth about the shapes of heroism in conventional times. Reaney's impulse thus is not to repeat history but to reinterpret it, celebrating not the Europeanness of archetype but the archetypal fascination of one's own history and experience, and the power of myth to reconstruct it in terms that carry contemporary meaning.

CODES OF HISTORY

For many other writers it mattered more to record the passing present than to retrieve the past, though there was some distinction to be made between writers who reconstructed or replayed the moment of

experience or revelation only, and writers who portrayed the
sequence of events that led up to or followed on from a moment of
revelation or crisis. These generalizations apply more to books than
to authors, for (as with Richard Wright, b. 1937, or Robert Harlow) an
author could well use fiction to mirror society in one novel (Harlow's
Paul Nolan, 1983; Wright's *In the Middle of a Life*, 1973) and to refer to
the reflexive powers of language in another (Harlow's *Scann*, 1972;
Wright's *Farthing's Fortunes*, 1976). Nonetheless, a continuing interest
in social realism directed many writers to refer to the empirical world
about them, to use the conventions of representation to create in the
reader a sense of observing real life. Crisis was central to such works.
While a resolution was not always possible (even an acceptable
explanation for crises was often uncertain), clear motivations lay
behind individuals' behaviour. Individuality and observation (rather
than literary types) were the watchwords of critical judgement; value
lay in the authenticity of empirical detail.

Much popular writing followed these conventions: Sheila Burnford (b. 1918; *The Incredible Journey*, 1961), Jean Little (b. 1932), Janet
Lunn (b. 1928), Brian Doyle (b. 1930), Kevin Major (b. 1949), all writing for children; John Peter (b. 1921), Ronald Sutherland, Harold Horwood, Ian McLachlan (b. 1938), Helen Levi (b. 1929), L. R. Wright
(1939–2001), Stephen Vizinczey (b. 1933), Janette Turner Hospital (b.
1942), writing for adults. All took social issues (the French-English
conflict, immigration, the tense borders between men and women)
and sought a set of representative events by which to express them (a
family dispute, a generational recurrence, a residence abroad. Much
writing about women's independence in contemporary society – or
their break out of a closed society – followed such patterns, as the
work of such writers as Carol Shields (b. 1935), Constance Beresford-
Howe (b. 1922), Doris Anderson (b. 1921), Monique Bosco (b. 1927)
and Joan Barfoot (b. 1946) shows. Marian Engel's *No Clouds of Glory*
(1968) and Rachel Wyatt's (b. 1929) *The Rosedale Hoax* (1977) are both
more satiric in tone, their wit serving to separate the process of
story-telling from simple mimetic record. In her novel *Bear* (1976),
which told of a woman's recovery of her passionate self, Marian
Engel used the realistic format sardonically, to overturn C.G.D.
Roberts' *Heart of the Ancient Wood* version of women and wilderness,
and so to combat the conventional attitudes which still governed
readers' taste. Male satirists – Mordecai Richler, Guy Vanderhaeghe
(b. 1951), David McFadden (b. 1940; *A Trip Around Lake Erie*, 1980),
among others – provide another distancing perspective. But by and
large, male realists represented social structure and sex roles less by

portraying men in direct conflict with society than by adapting the conventions of adventure to the record of intercultural contact.

Hence there arose in the 1970s a new enthusiasm for indigenous subjects; books by Howard O'Hagan and Hubert Evans were rediscovered, and new books involving Aboriginal and Inuit characters appeared from Alan Fry (b. 1931), James Houston, Yves Thériault, Wayland Drew (b. 1932), Peter Such (b. 1939), Rudy Wiebe (b. 1934), W.P. Kinsella, Thomas York (1940–88), James Polk (b. 1939), Philip Kreiner (b. 1950; *People Like Us in a Place Like This*, 1984), and Matt Cohen (1942–99). Fry's *How a People Die* (1970) criticizes the many European encroachments on the indigenous culture of northern British Columbia; George Ryga's (1932–87) play *The Ecstasy of Rita Joe* (1970) exposes the way the existing system fails the urban Indian. Such's less representative *Riverrun* (1970, later revised) – like Thériault's *Ashini* in some respects: a lyrical lament, told associatively, from an indigenous viewpoint – records the last days of the Beothuk culture. Michael Cook's (1933–94) play *Colour the Flesh the Colour of Dust* (1972) deals with the same subject. Drew's *The Wabeno Feast* (1973) counterpoints two stories: one detailing contemporary urban disorder, the other telling of an early explorer's wilderness discovery of the 'Wabeno' or destructive power recorded in indigenous legend. From one vantage point these works are sympathetic reappraisals of cultural values, attempts to come to terms with 'real' (as opposed to 'official') Canadian culture from American or British. From another they redefine they redefine the character of manliness, or more generally of selfhood. John Newlove's (b. 1938) poem 'The Pride' (*Black Night Window*, 1968) probes the past, discovers that the land was not empty before European arrival but was alive both with person and with myth – Cree, Tsimshian, Haida, Kwakiutl. The poet asserts 'we stand alone, / we are no longer lonely / but have roots, / and the rooted words / recur in the mind, mirror, so that / we dwell on nothing else, in nothing else.' The poem then discounts the attitude that identifies Aboriginal peoples only as romantic subjects, and in the words of a declarative imagination concludes that they 'still ride the soil / in us'; that 'we become them / in our desires'; that 'they / become our true forebears... / and in this land we / are their people, come / back to life again.'

The crossover between a politics of culture and a politics of person recurs in other forms as well. In the poetry and prose of several female writers – Linda Rogers (b. 1944), in *Queens of the Next Hot Star* (1981), Anne Cameron in *Dreamspeaker* (1978), Susan Musgrave (b. 1951) in the violent *The Charcoal Burners* (1980), Ann York (b. 1945) in

In This House There Are No Lizards (1980), Margaret Laurence, Byrna Barclay (b. 1940), Beatrice Culleton, Maria Campbell (b. 1940), or Jovette Marchessault – Native themes served as an empirical subject and also as a metaphor for an alienation as much sexual as cultural. These connections between culture, person and language further appear as a theme in the stories of Beth Harvor (b. 1936), Hélène Holden (b. 1935), Margaret Gibson Gilboord (b. 1948), Oonah McFee (b. 1922), Jack Ludwig (b. 1922), Diane Giguère (b. 1937, Jean-Charles Harvey's granddaughter, author of *Le temps des jeux*, 1961), W.D. Valgardson (b. 1939), David Helwig, Kent Thompson (b. 1936), David Williams (b. 1945), C.J. Newman (b. 1935), Shirley Faessler (b. 1921), George McWhirter (b. 1939) Terrence Heath (b. 1936), Keath Fraser (1944) and several other writers.

David Adams Richards (b. 1950), in the dour works set in the rural Miramichi – among them *Blood Ties* (1976) and *Lives of Short Duration* (1981) – portrays a world where individuals are powerless to escape the numbing effect of the community in which they live, an angry world where the lack of opportunity and the lack of language confirm each other, and where empty oaths express alike frustration and despair. John Metcalf (b. 1938, who was active in the 1970s organizing the Montreal Story Tellers, a performance group which involved himself, Clark Blaise, Ray Fraser, b. 1941, Ray Smith, b. 1941, and Hugh Hood (1928–2000) was more satiric. Metcalf's carefully composed works – among them *The Lady Who Sold Furniture* (1970), *General Ludd* (1980), several effective short story anthologies, and a brittle indictment of the Canadian literary scene called *Kicking Against the Pricks* (1982) – variously depict individuals thwarted by community thoughtlessness and individuals bucking against community mores. The comic results are seldom without hollow implications: a terrible loneliness accompanies both a raucous and a passive individuality. The connection between society and self shows up in another way when Juan Butler's (1942–81) *The Garbageman* (1972) uses a garbage metaphor and violent language in order to shock readers into recognizing the repellent character of contemporary society. Gilbert LaRocque's (1943–84) *Le nombril* (1970) does likewise, though his later *Les Masques* (1980) follows more sympathetically the associative fantasies of a man whose child has just drowned. Jane Rule (b. 1931), in more modulated terms – a 1986 collection of essays on such subjects as lesbian love, literary nationalism, and freedom of speech is called *A Hot-Eyed Moderate* (1986) – balances the needs of individuals against the public pressures of the worlds in which they live. Sometimes directly addressing lesbian themes – as in the novel *Desert of the Heart* (1964; adapted as the film *Desert Heart* in 1986) or in a critical book called *Lesbian Images* – Jane Rule's work is more characteristically represented by her 1980 novel *Contact with the World*, a book which quietly (but with subtle variation in narrative voices) examines the kinds of life that artists choose, the reasons that bring them to this pass, and the simple virtues of recognition and respect that make the choices honourable.

For all these writers it was not the fact of individuality or language alone which was crucial, but also the existence of social surroundings against which individuality and language were to be measured. 'History' was a matter of engagement, both physical and moral. Such attitudes permeated poetry and drama as well. Dramatists who applied realist techniques to current social issues include Bryan Wade (b. 1950), Tom Walmsley (b. 1948), André Simard (b. 1949), Jacqueline Barrette (b. 1947), Jeanne-Mance Delisle (b. 1941), Claude Jasmin, Marcel Dubé, Marie Laberge (b. 1951), and Larry Fineberg (b. 1945). In addition to those writers who fastened on French-English tensions, Ann Henry (b. 1914) drew on the Winnipeg Strike for her social commentary *Lulu Street* (1972); John Murrell (b. 1945), in *Waiting for the Parade* (1980), looked back to the lives of women on the home front during the Second World War; in both cases the historical context referred to social tensions and inequities in the present. John Herbert's *Fortune and Men's Eyes* (1967) directly addressed the fact of homosexuality in Canadian prisons and more allusively the metaphoric implications of rape; and Herschel Hardin's (b. 1936) *Esker Mike and His Wife Agiluk* (1969) criticized the inefficacy of white management systems among the Inuit, his play moving resolutely towards violence as it closes. David Fennario's (b. 1947) *Balconville* (1980), employing both official languages, portrayed francophone and anglophone neighbours on Montreal's street balconies; their sometimes comic quarrels with each other reveal the poverty that engenders their uncertain reliance on each other. Françoise Loranger exposes three generations of family tension in *Une maison ... un jour* (1965), and Jean-Claude Germain (b. 1939) more scathingly satirizes the inequities of family life in *Digui-di, Diguidi, Ha! Ha! Ha!* (1972). Often dramatists approached a social problem by means of a representative single figure, sometimes historical (as in Sheldon Rosen's (b. 1943) *Ned and Jack*, 1978; Thomas McDonough's (b. 1924) *Charbonneau et le chef*, 1968; Robert Gurik's *Lénine*, 1975; or Carol Bolt's (1941–2000) play about the anarchist Emma Goldman (1869–1940) *Red Emma*, 1974). Sometimes they were autobiographical, as in David Freeman's (b. 1947) *Creeps* (1972), an emotionally wrenching account of paralysis of various kinds, set in a 'sheltered workshop' for victims of cerebral palsy. *Creeps* exposes both the will to rebel against inadequate authorities and the many dimensions of powerlessness. David French's (b. 1939) Newfoundland plays – beginning with *Leaving Home* (1972) – record the generation conflict that divides members of a single family (and exposes its source in poverty and changing sex role definitions). Somewhat less representationally, though still referring to the empirical world, Beverley Simons' (b. 1938) *Crabdance* (1969) depicts the traumas of being middle-aged and female. For Gilles Derome (b. 1928) in *Qui est Dupressin?* (1972) and Timothy Findley in *Can You See Me Yet?* (1977), the mental hospital was an apt setting for contemporary discussions of social values. But by such means as setting, song and speech – in the plays of Normand Chaurette, or most obviously in the non-linear sequences of Yves Sauvageau's (1946–70) *Wouf! Wouf!* (1970), in which the characters add the phrase 'wouf wouf' to whatever they say – playwrights moved gradually away from realism, choosing instead to adopt absurdist techniques to evoke the absurdity of the world or the instability of meaning.

In poetry, lyric statement was one of the most dominant forms of the 1970s; it was referential in ways similar to those of historical realism in fiction or drama; social themes and authenticity of detail were paramount, vocabulary and rhythm drew on vernacular speech, the presence of a recording 'I' as observer or participant in political and social issues reinforced the immediacy of the literary work. To list the names of several effective anglophone poets in this mode, articulate shapers of image and line, is simply to hint at the numbers of people and publications involved: Marilyn Bowering, Dale Zieroth (b. 1946), Erin Mouré (b. 1955), Susan Glickman (b. 1953), Crispin Elsted (b. 1947), Paulette Jiles (b. 1943), Robert Gibbs (b. 1930), Peter Trower (b. 1938), George Amabile (b. 1936), Lorna (Uher) Crozier (b. 1948), Neile Graham (b. 1958), Marc Plourde (b. 1951), David Solway (b. 1941), Pier Giorgio di Cicco (b. 1949), Marya Fiamengo (b. 1926), Lloyd Abbey (b. 1943), Derk Wynand (b. 1944), George Fetherling (b. 1949), Pat Lowther (1935–75), Roo Borson (b. 1952), Brian Fawcett (b. 1944), M. Travis Lane (b. 1934), Heather Spears (b. 1934), Len Gasparini (b. 1941), Cyril Dabydeen (b. 1945), Sharon Thesen (b. 1946), Eugene McNamara (b. 1930), Gerry Shikatani (b. 1950), Artie Gold (b. 1947), Rhea Tregeboy (b. 1953), Kevin Roberts (b. 1940), Charles Lillard (1944–97), Pasquale Verdicchio (b. 1954), Mike Doyle (b. 1930), Sid Marty (b. 1944), Andrew Wreggitt (b. 1955), Peter Stevens, John Steffler (b. 1947), Richard Stevenson (b. 1952), Dennis Gruending (b. 1948). Mary di Michele (b. 1949) is one of several writers who have explored the divided allegiances of the Italian-Canadian immigrant. Jeni Couzyn (b. 1942) is one whose allusions to the political tensions of her native South Africa and to the personal tensions of liberty and choice have expressed themselves through the ancient oral poetic forms of charm, curse and blessing. Reshard Gool (1931–89) is another whose South African background shows itself in theme and motif. Patrick Lane (b. 1939), interpreting the poet's role as witness to human folly, pain and alienation, effectively used his observations of South American life (*Poems New and Selected*, 1979) as a base for a critique of the self-preoccupations of contemporary Canadians. In *Old Mother* (1982), Lane probed the violent recurrences of human history. Gruending, too, and Eli Mandel, Earle Birney and George Ryga, found South American travel a stimulus to political comment, and Chile also figures politically in poems by Tom Wayman (b. 1945) and Andrew Suknaski. Joy Kogawa in *A Choice of Dreams* (1974) grieved for the experience of the Nisei and Sansei in Canada during the Second World War. Glen Sorestad (b. 1937) turned prairie characters and small events into observed dramas of human tension. So widespread was the vernacular observer's stance in poetry that a 1983 David Donnell (b. 1939) poem satirically classified it as 'the Canadian Prairies View of Literature' (*Settlements*); the poem opens: 'First of all it has to be anecdotal; ideas don't exist.' That the mode offered more diverse opportunities than the satire suggests is self-evident; ideas abounded (inside Donnell's vernacular poem as well as elsewhere). The laconic stance denied neither intelligence nor passion.

Behind the vernacular verse of all these writers stands that of Al Purdy (metaphorically in some cases, literally in others: Purdy edited the second (1976) edition of Suknaski's *Wood Mountain Poems*; he edited Milton Acorn's (1923–85) finest volumes into their published form – for example, *I've Tasted My Blood*, 1983 – and with Acorn, Purdy edited the journal *Monument*, 1960–2). Purdy's nearly thirty volumes of poetry (from 1944 on) – *Being Alive* (1979) offers a twenty-year selection – display his fascination with observed detail and his rhythmic skill with laconic idiom. The opening of 'The Cariboo Horses' (1965) uses the loping rhythms of the western ranch rider to set the observer's imagination going:

> At 100 Mile House the cowboys ride in rolling
> stagey cigarettes with one hand reining
> half-time bronco rebels on a morning grey as stone
> – so much like riding dangerous women
>   with whiskey coloured eyes –

but imagination (whether it takes the mind into Western clichés or mythologies of history) can never utterly escape the present. The observer's several associative forays, all stemming from the stimulus word 'horses', return him finally to empirical fact, and the poem closes in sensory, measurable detail:

arriving here at chilly noon
in the gasoline smell of the
dust and waiting 15 minutes
at the grocer's

As with the West, so with the Arctic (*North of Summer*, 1967), the poet's home base of Ameliasburgh, Ontario (*In Search of Owen Roblin*, 1974), and places as distant as the Galapagos Islands and the Soviet Union (*Piling Blood*, 1984); each in turn, Purdy took the regional experiences of his society and observations of an ordinary intelligent working-class traveller, made them his own, and turned them and himself into a representative voice of the multiple identity that is modern Canada. The voice celebrated a personal past and a range of futures. Yet it was also an implicitly political voice, with which many contemporary writers, conscious more of the divisions inherent in immigration and ethnic diversity than of any social 'ideal' that they might represent – 'multiculturalism,' for instance – could not identify. Robert Bringhurst, for example, resisted the most obvious boundaries of Canadian nationalism to claim a personal literary tradition, in his case involving the USA, Japanese philosophy and West Coast Native mythology. (bp Nichol and Jacques Brault, too, were influenced by Japan, Gary Geddes and Ken Mitchell by their personal experience of China, David Day – as in the 'Ravenwood' sequence in *The Animals Within*, 1984 – by West Coast shamanism, and writers such as Juan Garcia and David McFadden by their more traditional conceptions of the poet as spiritual moralist.) In a specifically social context, Rienzi Crusz (b. 1925) distinguishes between the 'idiom of the sun' available to him in his native Sri Lanka, and the speech available 'Here in this white land', where 'I can only spit frozen-eyed, and gently demur'. Raymond Filip (b. 1950) is more explicit still; punningly, in a 1978 poem, he writes: 'I am the language that is lost. / The name that is changed… / I am the Canadian Mosaic: a melting pot on ice. / I am always the next generation… / You were Commonwealth, / I am common loss.'

Hence there emerged among writers concerned to declare the experience of a particular ethnic group a series of semi-documentary works that in fiction most characteristically took the form of the *Bildungsroman* or novel-of-growing-up. One typical premise results in integration and success. A more common one involves a child of immigrant parents who adapts to the new land more readily than the parents do but who never seems quite to belong; the impulse to reject old values (or the desire to retain them) recurrently stands between the individual and the majority. Rudy Wiebe's earliest novel *Peace Shall Destroy Many* (1962) applies the latter premise to the Mennonite community, with some finesse; the novel uses the tensions of adolescent choice as a means to assess the values of traditional pacifism and to question the way authorities even within a community founded on Christian values can usurp their position. In other works (and in addition to the several concerned with Jewish religious alienation), Marika Robert (emig. 1952) traced the plight of the Hungarian refugee, Jan Drabek (b. 1935) that of the Czech, Lorris Elliot (b. 1931) and Austin Clarke (b. 1934) that of the West Indian in urban Canada; Illia Kiriak (1888–1955), Maara Haas (b. 1920), Yar Slavutych (b. 1918) and Myrna Kostash (b. 1944) wrote of Ukrainians. In all cases their works resisted the label 'immigrant', probing instead the representative life of workers, mothers, and other individuals whose 'immigrant status' in the New World tended to block other estimations of their quality, character, social role, or options for the future. Several works written for children – especially those by Barbara Smucker (b. 1915) and Dennis Foon, and the easy-readers published by James Lorimer and Kids Can Press – also fastened on this motif. One of Foon's plays, *New Canadian Kid* (1981), dramatizes linguistic alienation by having the immigrant child on a new school playground speak English, while the 'anglophone' children speak gobbledygook.

Harold Sonny Ladoo (1945–73) looked back with anger to Trinidad (where he was later murdered), Samuel Selvon (1923–94) with more irony. Neil Bissoondath (b. 1955, V.S. Naipaul's, b. 1932, nephew) sophisticatedly examined the intellectual implications of the motifs of changing places and exchanging cultures, in a short story collection called *Digging Up the Mountains* (1985). Bharati Mukherjee (b. 1942), in the stories of *Darkness* (1985), angrily attacked the forms of racism that continue to stalk North American society. Marilú Mallet (b. 1945) drew on her Chilean background in *Les compagnons de l'horloge-pointeuse* (1985) to castigate Canadians' political naïveté. Writers with East European origins often wrote semi-autobiographically about political innocence and political choice – in poetry (Wacław Iwaniuk, b. 1915, George Faludy, b. 1910), prose (George Jonas, b. 1935, Marion Andre Czerniecki, b. 1921), and fiction Josef Škvorecký, b. 1924, especially in the bleakly comic novel *Dvorak in Love*, 1986).

The *Bildungsroman* patterns appear in fiction by Leonard Cohen, Noël Audet (b. 1938), Jean-Paul Filion (b. 1927), Keith Maillard (b. 1942), Ann Copeland (b. 1932), and in Jacques Poulin's *Jimmy Trilogy* (translated 1979). In poetry, Joe Rosenblatt's *Escape from the Glue Factory* (1985) combined initiation patterns with the theme of escaping the Holocaust. The related 'initiation stories' of Alistair MacLeod (b. 1936) – especially 'The Boat' in *The Lost Salt Gift of Blood* (1976) – or the sequence of Davey Bryant stories by David Watmough (b. 1926) demonstrate how the revelations and pressures of memory and change could structure short fiction as well. Further, in novels by Réjean Ducharme (*L'avalée des avalés*, 1966) or Marie-Claire Blais (*La belle bête*, 1959; *Une saison dans la vie d'Emmanuel*, 1965; *Les manuscrits de Pauline Archange*, 1968) the form became a statement about psychological rebellion. But especially with writers for whom English or French was not the speech of home, the *Bildungsroman* also served a second function, as Frank Paci's (b. 1948) novels about Italian generations in Canada – *Black Madonna* (1982), for instance – illustrate. Here the desire to belong to the mainstream is in essence a desire for language; the *Bildungsroman* fades into the *Künstlerroman*, as the characters (and through them, the writer) try to find the forms of word that will communicate with the larger community around them without surrendering the values that inhere in the language and culture of the ethnic minority to which they also belong. For Joy Kogawa, in *Obasan* (1981), similarly, the narrator's desire for knowledge leads her through several cultural barriers (both Canadian and Japanese) into the heart of a mystery: what explains her mother's disappearance? what explains the Canadian government's treatment of Japanese-Canadians during the war? The barriers are often attitudinal: when she has grown past the silences of bitterness and the ironies of rejection, Kogawa's character is ready to try to understand the implications of Nagasaki. Here once again the historical event is both translated into personal experience and translated by it, turning silence into speech.

For several prominent writers of the time, the historicity of heritage was a motif that shaped still larger canvases, in which the autonomy of historical events and the subjectivity of the individual record of history are related but separate measures of the reality of experience. Among those writers are Hugh Hood, Mavis Gallant, Margaret Laurence, Michel Tremblay, Jacques Ferron (who recast history as fable), and Alice Munro. At the heart of Hood's fiction lies the distinction he draws in his 1984 essay 'The End of Emma' between 'psychological fiction' and fiction that is of necessity autobiography: 'the historian of fine consciences is in truth the historian of no conscience but his own'. Knowing this, he writes not out of his own motives (which 'are mysterious to me'), but out of his architectonic response to the sensory world ('I can see you'). The move in the visual arts toward 'super-realism' – involving the West Coast naturalists Robert Bateman (b. 1930) and J. Fenwick Lansdowne (b. 1937), Ontario painters Jack Chambers and Ken Danby (b. 1940) and several Maritimers: Alex Colville (b. 1920), Christopher Pratt (b. 1935), Mary Pratt (b. 1935) – offers a development roughly parallel.

Tonally and thematically, Hood's work varies, from the ironic and satiric to the tender and almost sentimental, from the subjects of urban crime and suburban rituals to those of spiritual grace and social movements. But neither of these distinguishes Hood's stories so much as does his control over sentence shape and sentence rhythm. The structures of observation are personal, but translated into the cadences of fiction. Hood's Catholicism, for example, imparts a particular moral cast to his stories; it also shapes the triune structures and the dualist tensions that occur in them. The language of fiction is thus an arrangement, a deliberate design provided to focus the reader's attention on a specific code of conduct; it is, as Hood's 1972 essay 'Sober Coloring: The Ontology of Super-Realism' specifies, a 'scaffolding for the imagination'.

Hood's interest in athletics, film and other expressions of popular culture shows up in several of his early novels and non-fiction accounts of hockey figures. He established his main reputation, however, with a 1967 book, *Around the Mountain*, a collection of Montreal sketches, unified by the formal way it traces an annual cycle. The sketch (adapted from Leacock and the nineteenth-century practitioners) allows Hood to use an impressionistic, kinetic technique to come to terms with his ongoing experience of the urban collectivity he calls his culture. His prose, stylistically shifting from sketch to sketch, engages the reader with the process of looking; implicitly this is a moral as well as a sensory act (a position Hood shares with Callaghan). The author looks at language as a method to an end: his purpose (however resistant to fixed conclusions) remains a portrait of the behaviour of an empirical society. In subsequent story collections – *Flying a Red Kite* (1962), *The Fruit Man, the Meat Man & the Manager* (1971) – he recurrently meditates on the dual personalities many people enjoy; in *Dark Glasses* (1976), *None Genuine Without This Signature* (1980), and *August Nights* (1985), he looks at their ritual engagements with games, holidays and relationships. Repetition (like simultaneity) is both subject and method, the technique directing the reader to appreciate what life is like. Life continues; life changes. Hood's characters are afraid and alive, each because of the other, each in succession to the other, each in spite of the other, each with the other in the same breath of apprehension.

The fascination with the moral character of memory (hence the moral, if selective character of history) surfaces also in Hood's ongoing *magnum opus*, a cycle of twelve novels under the collective title *The New Age*. The first volume, *The Swing in the Garden*, appeared in 1975; others followed: *A New Athens* (1977), *Reservoir Ravine* (1979: a book that alludes to the 1919 Winnipeg Strike), *Black and White Keys* (1982), *The Scenic Art* (1984), *The Motor Boys in Ottawa* (1986). Sequentially, they trace (primarily through the narrative sensibilities of a character named Matthew Goderich) the interrelated history of one man, one family, and one modern society (from 1880 to 2000), using Hood's own experience of southern Ontario as the representative model. (An Ontario native, Hood later taught English at the Université of Montréal.) Proustian in concept if not precisely in structure, the sequence engages Matthew with the events and moral decisions of his time. *Black and White Keys* eloquently alternates between Canada and Europe during the Second World War, probing the moral antinomies and political juxtapositions that governed the way people chose to act in those years. *The Scenic Art* takes a theatre metaphor to examine the masks of public and private behaviour, focusing on the nascent Stratford Festival in the 1950s. Subsequent volumes involved other narrators and (nearing the millennium) a science-fiction forecast of history yet to come.

Memory, history, fantasy and reality come together in the work of Mavis Gallant and Margaret Laurence as well; and for all three writers – a sign, perhaps, despite their varied backgrounds, of the effect of coming-of-age in wartime – the Second World War focuses their moral concern with social conduct. Gallant began her career in the 1940s, working for the National Film Board and as a reviewer and caption-writer with the Montreal *Standard*. The newspaper experience is taken up in the faintly autobiographical Linnet Muir stories collected in *Home Truths* (1981). A Montrealer by birth, Mavis Gallant has since 1950 lived in Europe, mainly in Paris, the setting of much of her work, and has published her several score of short stories (many of them still uncollected) primarily in *The New Yorker*. The author of a play and two novels (*Green Water, Green Sky*, 1959, and *A Fairly Good Time*, 1970), she has also written a number of broadly political observations on such events as the 1968 Paris student rebellions, collected with other essays in *Paris Notebooks* (1986). Her introduction to *The Affair of Gabrielle Russier* (1971) documents some ways in which French law limits the social freedoms it extends to women. The politics of the power of choice, as well as the liberty of opportunity, are recurrent themes. They take their most stylistically concentrated forms in her novellas and short stories, especially in *My Heart is Broken* (1964; entitled *An Unmarried Man's Summer* in England), *The*

Pegnitz Junction (1973), and *From the Fifteenth District* (1979). A 1973 selection of her work called *The End of the World and other stories* was edited by Robert Weaver, one of her earliest enthusiasts.

While her stories repeatedly recount the lives of expatriates and exiles, they do so not simply as a mimetic representation of contemporary experience; exile is more fundamentally an attitude of mind: 'I might have been a person', says a character to her mother in *Green Water, Green Sky*, 'but you made me a foreigner.' This phrase functions at once to displace the 'blame' for life being what it is, and to specify that reality derives as much from the act of naming ('you made me a   ') as from the 'truth' of events as they empirically occur. Hence language is a process of history-making, a process of reconstruction, as often as not at war with memory – one or the other having often to be suppressed in the circumstances of which the stories tell. Canada appears repeatedly as a place of exile, Mavis Gallant articulating for another generation a perennial theme in Canadian writing; it is not so much that the country houses exiles, though that is part of the 'exile syndrome', but that Canada is a society in which foreignness and familiarity are one. 'Foreign territory' (to reverse Margaret Atwood's phrase from *Surfacing*) is 'home ground'. Mavis Gallant extends this sensibility to her analysis of post-war Europe. *The Pegnitz Junction*, for example – the title deriving from a railway junction where travellers are stranded between home and away – collects several stories about post-war Germany and about the kinds of alienation that people can suffer in their own (unfamiliar) familiar surroundings. Refugees, travellers, war veterans and others: all find themselves in a new divided Germany they do not recognize, suffering and resisting the memories of older Germanys, reshaping their history into something they can equably accommodate. *From the Fifteenth District* takes up related motifs. 'The Latehomecomer' reiterates directly the tensions of the *Pegnitz* stories: a German prisoner-of-war in France, released late because of a bureaucratic mix-up, returns home to find his mother remarried and his society changed, more concerned with the economics of survival than with the morality of memory or the persistent politics of behaviour. The ex-soldier's mother dreams of her other child returning home also, so that the family will again be as one; the young man himself knows that everything has altered, and dreams of a time just a few hours earlier, when he still had expectations of reunion. In 'The Modern Wife', comparably, a young woman named Netta Asher grows up an English expatriate in France, her father expecting her to carry on his line in family and conduct. Marriage and the war alter circumstances, however. The 'civilization' inherited from the past, though it may continue to structure externals, seems to lose its practical relevance to daily actions. The main point is that after the war (which has utterly changed her), Netta finds she can no longer communicate with her husband, who has spent the war in America, protected from what she has had to live through. But rather than confront his invalid version of 'what-it-was-like', she surrenders to it, her accurate but inarticulate memory being no match for his facile terms of reconstruction. In 'From the Fifteenth District', moreover, Mavis Gallant wittily pierces the sham 'realities' that custom and language erect. A fantasy in form, the story 'documents' three occasions on which ghosts are haunted by living memory: a dead major complains that the church is turning him into a tourist spectacle, a dead mother complains that neither the doctor's nor the social worker's self-serving report of her demise is accurate, a dead wife complains that her husband is turning her into an angel, which she is not. ('Nowhere in any written testimony will you find a scrap of proof that angels are "good". Some are merely messengers; others have a paramilitary function. All are stupid.') Throughout, the author is concerned to represent sympathetically the predicaments of ordinary life and yet also to *tell stories*; her style directs attention implicitly at the identities language creates and at the political force of the modal connections that language draws. What kind of discrimination does a term like 'likeness' draw, her stories ask; what is meant by 'there', 'now', or 'before'? Thus the conscious style deliberately subverts the documentary illusions of historical narrative, and questions all simple explanations of cause-and-effect.

The stylistic structures of Margaret Laurence seem somewhat simpler, though once again the writer turns from an historical pattern into an analysis of personal heritage and possibility. She focuses on the force of the spoken vernacular (in the context of inherited, 'written' norms), and uses her familiarity with the voice and culture of the West to challenge the political hegemony of the society at large. In her later years a resident of Lakefield, Ontario, and an articulate advocate for anti-nuclear causes, Margaret Laurence began writing as a child in her birthplace, Neepawa, Manitoba. She contributed to school and college magazines, having invented the name 'Manawaka' (a fictional version of Neepawa) as early as 1939; but her mature writing career began in Somaliland and Ghana, where she lived with her engineer husband between 1950 and 1957. She translated Somali tales in *A Tree for Poverty* (1954), a book which showed her early concern for women's rights in a male-dominated culture. In four other works concerned with Africa – a novel, *This Side Jordan* (1960); a short story collection, *The Tomorrow-tamer* (1963); a travel journal, *The Prophet's*

Camel Bell (1963; published in the USA the following year as *New Wind in a Dry Land*); and a critical tribute to Chinua Achebe (b. 1930) and other Nigerian writers, *Long Drums and Cannons* (1968) – she worked out her understanding of the connections between politics and speech. Africa enlightened her political thinking (her travel book reveals her indebtedness to O. Mannoni, 1899–1989); it also taught her how speech, in an oral culture, shapes reality, and how ancestors are traditionally deemed to be an enlivening presence among the living, rather than a dead past from which the present must flee. The stories of *The Tomorrow-tamer* evoke this distinction, often by stylistically contrasting the forms of spoken and written language. Yet the stories also confront the predicaments of a modern Africa for which old traditions no longer function, and of modern Africans for whom alienation is more familiar than continuity. Only superficially 'about' Africa, these stories probe more closely the 'otherness' of the Anglo-European observers. This political sense of 'difference' (expressed in terms of region and of gender), together with an appreciation of the enlivening voices of the ancestral past, brought Laurence to write the set of novels and stories that came to be called the Manawaka Cycle. In them, Laurence took what she learned from Africa back home.

The 'Manawaka' books (so-called because they centre on Manitoba, though the settings range from the West Coast to Ontario and Scotland) comprise four novels and a book of stories. *The Stone Angel* (1961) tells of the stubbornness, marriage and death of the 93-year-old narrator Hagar Shipley; *A Jest of God* (1966; published in England in 1969 as *Now I Lay Me Down*, and filmed in 1968 as *Rachel, Rachel*) tells of a spinster schoolteacher, whose brief affair and bout with disease bring her closer to independence; *The Fire-Dwellers* (1969), stylistically the most adventurous of the group, concerns the middle-class and middle-aged traumas of Rachel's suburban Vancouver sister; *A Bird in the House* (1970) is a linked series of episodic stories, cast as the memories that free Vanessa MacLeod from the constraints of family history, Depression and wartime; and *The Diviners* (1974) reconciles Morag Gunn with her memories of her lower-class adoptive parents, her chauvinist ex-husband, her passionate Métis lover, and her grown child Pique. From Hagar to Pique, Margaret Laurence tells of three generations of women whose lives evoke the history of Western Canada and whose determined reach for independence repeatedly modifies the norms of social judgment. Largely conventional in form – in that, despite the apparent breaks in narrative, the narratives themselves follow a progressive linear development – Laurence's fiction is complex in its handling of the details of voice and allusion. The opening of 'The Sound of the Singing' illustrates the careful

balance between formal phrasing and vernacular image that coin-
cides with the narrator's twin sense of history – as inheritance and as
process:

That house in Manawaka is the one which, more than any other, I carry with
me. Known to the rest of the town as 'the old Connor place' and to the family as the Brick House, it was plain as the winter turnips in its root cellar,
sparsely windowed as some crusader's embattled fortress in a heathen
wilderness, its rooms in perpetual gloom except in the brief height of summer. Many other brick structures had existed in Manawaka for as much as
half a century, but at the time when my grandfather built his house, part
dwelling place and part massive monument, it had been the first of its kind.

In the larger scene, Margaret Laurence's fiction was instrumental
in freeing English-Canadian prose from its unthinking male biases; it
also provided by means of its Western perspective an alternative paradigm of social change to that which involves French-English (Que-
bec-Ontario) tensions, which up to this point had been taken as the
quintessential Canadian dilemma. For Margaret Laurence, national
social adjustments involve gender, class and other subtleties of discrimination; story by story, the Manawaka series traces the processes
of change that reconcile first the Scots with the English and Irish, then
the British with the Ukrainians, then the Europeans with the Asians
and finally (most ironically, most resistantly) with the indigenous
Métis. The West, by this view, becomes the cradle of multiculturalism. But it does so while remaining a bed of passionate personal tur-
moil, which persistent biases continue to enflame. Margaret Laurence's work thus represents society, even while formalizing a
dialogue between speech and social value.

Michel Tremblay's continuing novel sequence, the 'Chroniques du
Plateau Mont-Royal' (including *La grosse femme d'à côté est enceinte*,
1978; *Thérèse et Pierrette à l'école des saints-anges*, 1980; and *Des nouvelles d'Edouard*, 1984), performs something of the same function
using one Montreal neighbourhood as its representative locale. Song-
writer, translator, the author of five filmscripts, two musical comedies, six novels and a striking collection of contemporary fables,
Tremblay is best known for his eighteen joual plays. Here speech and
setting combine to chart a vernacular paradigm of Quebec's historical sense of alienation within Canada. Realist in method, sociological
in intent, the plays are also indirect, their technique being to explore
Quebec's attitudinal condition by means of correlative dramatic conflicts. The world of the plays is incestuous, homosexual, transvestite:
the men appear weak, the women stronger but shriller; sex and reli-

gion pull them in contrary ways but both derive from the same will towards absolutes. The social problem is the willingness to wear the mask of an identity not one's own (Quebec in Canada, hence transvestitism). Theatre is metaphor. Articulating the politics of local speech becomes a process of exorcism.

Tremblay's main play cycle began in 1968 with *Les belles-soeurs*, continued with *La duchesse de Langeais* (1970), *À toi pour toujours, ta Marie-Lou* (1973), *Hosanna* (1973), *Bonjour là, bonjour* (1974), *Sainte Carmen de la Main* (1976), and closed with *Damnée Manon, sacrée Sandra* (1980). The Main (or St Lawrence Main) is a street in Montreal noted for its seedy nightlife, the metaphor of the 'main' (like that of 'snow') also taking on drug-culture inferences during the 1970s – most pronouncedly in novels by Richler, Hubert Aquin, Marie-Claire Blais, Trevanian (b. 1925) and Leonard Cohen. 'Sainte Carmen', a make-believe country-and-western singer seeking success on this scene, is inevitably trapped by her inappropriate mask, but like many other Tremblay figures is only destroyed when she attempts to find a voice of her own. Carmen's story reveals traps of other forms of imitation, too, as in *À toi*, where she and her zealously religious sister Manon reach back to their long-dead parents. *Bonjour* specifies more directly the character of psychological incest, the desire for a parent transferred unproductively to a sibling. Carmen at least wants out; Manon wants only to perpetuate her mother's self-sacrificing role. (Dubé's play *Au retour des oies blanches*, 1972, first performed in 1969, also uses incest as a motif by which to probe the character of social/family behaviour.) *Hosanna* suggests some possibility of affirmation, in that the transvestite character throws off his Cleopatra costume at the end of the play and admits to his own identity. But in *Damnée Manon* it is the vitiating desire for certainty that takes over once again; Manon, totally absorbed with her version of Christ, parallels the transvestite Sandra, totally absorbed in his sexual desire for his own 'godlike' lover. Despite the wit of these plays, the social prognosis is scarcely positive, except in so far as the use of joual declared the playwright's own resistance to the linguistic (hence attitudinal) enclosures of received convention.

Many writers using realist conventions were thus trying to counter the attitudes that realism customarily relied upon. 'Orality' was one such method, disputing the written character of historicity. Disrupting the narrative sequence was another, as in Tremblay's *En pièces détachées* (1970) or Keith Maillard's fictional trilogy about growing up American in the 1960s. Fracturing form was a way of exposing a false notion of psychological 'wholeness' or cultural 'unity'.

Fracture was even more readily apparent in short fiction, especially in the linked-but-broken series of stories that in Canada by the 1960s had become a familiar pattern. Malcolm Lowry spelled out the theory behind the form when in 1940 he wrote to the Irish writer James Stern that he thought it possible 'to compose a satisfactory work of art by the simple process of writing a series of good short stories, complete in themselves, ... interrelated, correlated, ... but full of effects and dissonances that are impossible in a short story.' It was what he later claimed to his editor Albert Erskine that *Hear Us O Lord* was turning into: 'a sort of novel of an odd aeolian kind'. Lowry thought at the time that the same set of characters would be necessary for unity, though his own book relies more on shifts of identity and formal pattern than on continuity of character. Other writers realized that it was the issue of change which made the broken series credible. In Alden Nowlan's *Various Persons Named Kevin O'Brien* (1973), for example, a set of short stories revealing the separate identity a character enjoys at different stages in his life finally connects into a loose autobiography of a man with a complex rather than a singular personality. George Elliott's (b. 1923) *The Kissing Man* (1962) follows the fabular title figure through the lives of several Ontario townspeople, focusing not so much on individuals as on the ambivalent effects of the touch of a shadow. Other writers (Dave Godfrey; Louise Maheux-Forcier, b. 1929) turned the technique to openly political and metatextual ends. One of the most adept practitioners was Alice Munro, who transformed her native Wingham, Ontario, into the fictional town of Jubilee, let it live its own life, and with a poet's eye for evocative detail crafted a set of literary 'rooms' (Munro's metaphor) in which reality might happen.

Coincidentally, Alice Munro's work also provides one gauge of changes in critical estimations of 'reality' over twenty years. When her first story collection, *Dance of the Happy Shades*, appeared in 1968 (a time when short stories were mooted as a dying art), it came complete with an introduction by Hugh Garner, lending his own name to the book and recommending it for its authenticity of observed detail. Garner was then highly regarded as a realist writer. 'Real Life' was the book's original, discarded title, and photographic accuracy of 'observation' remained a critical watchword applied to Munro for some time. Wingham residents (like those of Leacock's Orillia) even objected to being depicted in fiction – despite Munro's own assertions that her stories were fictions, and her open admiration for the 'super-realism' of Colville's paintings. By the time of *The Moons of Jupiter* (1982) and *The Progress of Love* (1986), reviewers were trying to find a different, more applicable vocabulary of praise: Munro's stories were 'poems', 'meditations', 'truths' – their reality inhering not in observed persons or events but in the 'processes' of discovery that they took narrator and reader through. The author turned from writing stories involving 'epiphanies' or revealed meaning to stories that recorded the continuing adjustments of sensibility. The later stories were open-ended, without conventional conclusions (the early ones had almost all turned on negation and paradox). Simple conclusions no longer made sense. Such techniques as the oxymoron revealed the author's multiple, simultaneous perceptions of single events, her recognition that events and memories, experience and fictional reconstruction, never precisely coincide. What the mind understands, how the mind makes connections: these more diffuse and less 'knowable' realizations became the substance of the later fiction. The two-part story 'Chaddeleys and Flemings' (the first is titled 'Connection') illustrates a version of the later process of narrative construction. The narrator reflects in one story on matrilineal, in the other on patrilineal connections – less discovering how different the two branches of heritage are (something she knew already) than finding a stylistic equivalent for the kinds of isolation and of sensibility (or connection) which each set of links engenders.

Style is thus at least as much of a focus here as in the 'town' of Jubilee and the empirical referent it might or might not have. And style performs a reconstructive, often broadly political act. An episodic novel, *Lives of Girls and Women* (1971) – which many have read as a linked story series – fractures the linear structure of the *Bildungsroman* in order to trace the unequal opportunities and the power struggles of growing up female. With *Something I've Been Meaning to Tell You* (1974) and *Who Do You Think You Are?* (1978) – the latter called *The Beggar Maid* in editions outside Canada – Alice Munro pursued the psychosexual ambiguities of language and social relationships. She also continued to experiment with the patterns of the discontinuous series; the stories of the 1974 volume interconnect by means of the rhetorical structures they employ, those of the later work by means of recurrent characters, Flo and Rose.

In all her experiments with discontinuity, however, Munro has held back from the techniques of post-modernism. The appeal of the empirical world remains strong. Yet for many other writers, especially in the 1970s and 1980s, systems of language became a more accurate measure of truth than systems of social continuity, historical recurrence or referentiality. Ray Smith wrote in John Metcalf's anthology *The Narrative Voice* (1972) that one of his stories was about italics and the semi-colon, but that it resisted being reduced to a single theme. Thematic analyses of literature came under attack. The very character of the physical world, on which presumptions about empirical themes depended, was in dispute. In devising a fractured speech, for example, Christopher Dewdney (b. 1951, his poems selected in *Predators of the Adoration*, 1983), was seeking equivalents for science, not just breaking arbitrarily with convention. Contemporary theories of entropy and quantum physics had remodelled reality; both the new universe, and ways of interpreting it, were indeterminate.

CODES OF FIGURE AND PERSON

Codes of historical process and historical 'figure' often operate within the same work. Matt Cohen's *The Disinherited* (1974) and *The Sweet Second Summer of Kitty Malone* (1979), for example, are torn between a desire to trace the linear roots of Loyalism in Ontario and an interest in reconstructing representative individual lives; so with *The Spanish Doctor* (1984), which uses fourteenth-century Spain as a base for analyzing the tensions between Catholic and Jew that (inferentially) reappear as twentieth-century anti-semitism. The numerous literary reconstructions of historical figures – or events: 1759, 1837, Vimy, Dieppe – have as their primary aim not the romance or pageantry of history but what might be considered the iconic character of a particular historical dilemma, iconic at least as far as the present is concerned. Such works thus do not interest themselves in what historians have received as 'fact' so much as they seek to reinterpret or reclaim the past from one particular interpretation of it, with an eye on some present tension. Hence current attitudes towards Indians, landscape, Jews, women, America, self or nationhood are reconstructed in terms of received definitions of such words as 'savagery', 'wilderness', 'property' or 'rebel'. If, for example, 'savagery' existed as much in the acts of the Inquisition as in Native tribal rituals, then the distinction between civilization and barbarism is less easy than history books said. If 'wilderness' was not by linguistic implication 'savage', then living with it is not so difficult. And if William Lyon Mackenzie, in Rick Salutin's play *1837*, was not a rebel but a civil reformer, a moderate democrat, driven to protest by official ineptitude, then the cause for which he stood (still, according to Salutin, suppressed) was not disloyal but just.

Numerous examples of such figurative restructuring emerged in the literature of the 1970s: from poems by Dennis Cooley (b. 1944), Jon Whyte (1941–92), Frank Davey (*The Clallam*, 1974), Stephen Scobie, and Gwendolyn MacEwen (in her T.E. Lawrence poems) to the several works referring to Nelligan or Duplessis. Other examples include Andreas Schroeder's (b. 1946) *Dustship Glory* (1986), a novel about the Finnish Saskatchewan immigrant/dreamer/boatbuilder Tom Sukanen; Pierre Gravel's (b. 1956) 1986 novel of the 1837 exiles in Australia, *La fin de l'histoire*; and Heather Robertson's popular *Willie* (1983), a fictional portrait of Mackenzie King. Linda Griffiths (b. 1953) wrote a one-woman play about the Trudeaus, *Maggie and Pierre* (1980), Michael Ondaatje (b. 1943) a novel about the jazz musician Buddy Bolden (1868–1931) in *Coming Through Slaughter* (1976), passionately running theme-and-variation on the meanings of 'making' and 'breaking': jazz subject, jazz motif, the terrible continuum of art and personality. George Hulme (b. 1932) based a play on Hitler, Michael Mercer (b. 1943) on Lowry and Aiken, Jean-Louis Roux (b. 1923) on Riel, Wilfred Watson on Gramsci (1891–1937), Tom Cone (b. 1948) on Picasso (1881– 1973). Jean-Claude Germain's play *Un pays dont la devise est je m'oublie* (1976) – the title repudiating Quebec's claim to its provincial motto, 'je me souviens' – draws on the figures of Quebec's popular culture (Louis Cyr, 1863–1912; Maurice Richard, 1921–2000; the voyageur, the curé) to satirize the current state of society. In John Gray's (b. 1946) play about the First World War flying ace, *Billy Bishop Goes to War* (1981), a solo performer plays all the roles, to a running piano accompaniment. Breathlessly, *Billy Bishop* re-enacts the pilot's rise to fame and glory. It also taps the nascent nationalist attitudes in Canada that sought out a hero, placed Billy in this role, then found him the more compelling when it turned out he was in some measure flawed. George Woodcock, writing of Riel's lieutenant in his biography *Gabriel Dumont* (1975), goes so far as to claim that it is the failure (for example, Riel) rather than the success (for example, Dumont, 1837–1906) who perennially appeals to Canadians – perhaps because such a person more readily than the American hero-type represents their own experience, that of living in an imperfect world.

Riel appears in other guises in these years – in Carol Bolt's play *Gabe* (1973), Rudy Wiebe's novel *The Scorched-Wood People* (1972), and in a poem by John Newlove. Newlove also wrote 'Samuel Hearne in Wintertime', raising yet another figure from the past in order to probe the (contemporary) moral ambivalence of an historical figure's choices and actions:

… Samuel Hearne,
I have almost begun to talk

as if you wanted to be
gallant, as if you went
through that land for a book –

as if you were not SAM, wanting
to know, to do a job.

One of the poetic tetralogies of Don Gutteridge (b. 1937) reaches to these
same two figures and three more: *Riel* (1968), *Coppermine* (1973, on
Hearne), *Borderlands* (1975, on John Jewitt and Chief Maquinna), and
Tecumseh (1976). Michel Garneau's play *Emilie ne sera plus jamais cueillie
par l'anémone* (1981) establishes what Emily Dickinson's (1830–86) life
would have been in Quebec and perhaps implies what Quebec would
have with a Dickinson. Leonard Cohen, in *Beautiful Losers* (1966), co-
opts St Catherine Tekakwitha into a stylistic *tour-de-force* about the need
for anonymity in any quest for true identity; it was a message particularly attractive in the late 1960s, not unrelated to the appeal of the more
conservative nationalist philosophy of George Grant. Jovette Marchessault's 1981 play *Le saga des poules mouillées* brings four female writers
together (Conan, Guèvrement, Roy and Hébert) in order to 'read' Quebec's creative history from a feminist perspective. Sharon Pollock (b.
1936) turned to the United States for a figure of moral ambivalence,
retracing the story of the Lizzie Borden (1860–1927) murders in *Blood
Relations* (1981); her earlier plays – *Walsh* (1974) and *The Komagata Maru
Incident* (1978) – had looked back to Canadian history, to incidents variously involving Sitting Bull (*c.* 1834–90) and the immigration of East
Indians, in order to castigate Canadian racism and provoke reform in
current social policy. One play by Regina writer Ken Mitchell, *The Medicine Line* (1976), also drew a portrait of the RCMP Major, James Walsh
(1843–1905); while other plays – *Davin* (1976) and *Gone the Burning Sun*,
written in the 1980s – respectively portray such nonconformist individ-
ualists as the Victorian politician-author Nicholas Flood Davin and the
political physician Norman Bethune. Roland Lepage (b. 1928), in *La
complainte des hivers rouges* (1974) returns again to the 1837 Rebellion for
the figures through whom to complain of the 'Canadian' presence in
Quebec. Gary Geddes, in his quietly eloquent, prize-winning poetic
sequence *The Terracotta Army* (1984), went back to the third century BC,
to the days of the first emperor of China, Ch'in Shi Huang Di (*c.* 259–210
BC) – who had had an army some eight thousand strong carved in pottery and buried with him (the figures were accidentally unearthed in
1974). Animating several of the figures, Geddes's poems reflect on the
character of power, arguing that neither poets nor ministers of war are
free from the desire to control the shape of history: both attempt to
design the future's images of the past by controlling who may read and
who may hear. Figures from history thus turn severally into occasions
for examining the political possibilities – and temptations – of language.

When Margaret Laurence's character Morag Gunn in *The Diviners* talks to Catharine Parr Traill, a related process is at work; Mrs Traill is reanimated as the voice of practicality in the narrator's ear, but it is the narrator's *version* of the past which turns Mrs Traill into a personal icon. So with Mrs Moodie in Margaret Atwood's serial poem *The Journals of Susanna Moodie* (1970), in which the reader glimpses not the historical person who emerges from her own letters but an icon of cultural schizophrenia, a symbol of what it is to be female and Canadian in 1970. Margaret Atwood's Moodie, torn between desires, is a pioneer who still lives, a contemporary Everywoman who rides the Toronto transit system and speaks (inferentially at least) of culture and feminism. She is crafted to demonstrate how custom in this case has created a social position for women by denying them a place in speech. 'Disembarking at Quebec' establishes her alienation:

> Is it my clothes, my way of walking,
> the things I carry in my hand
> ...
> or is it my own lack
> of conviction which makes
> these vistas of desolation,
> long hills, the swamps, the barren sand, the glare
> of sun on the bone-white
> driftlogs, omens of winter,
> the moon alien in day-
> time a thin refusal
>
> The others leap, shout
>   Freedom!
>
> The moving water will not show me
> my reflection.
> ...
> I am a word
> in a foreign language.

Subsequent lyrics at once echo and alter this predicament –

> Whether the wilderness is
> real or not
> depends on who lives there.
>   ('Further Arrivals')

in this area where my damaged
knowing of the language means
prediction is forever impossible
('First Neighbours')

– until she becomes aware of the instructive power of both her 'voices' (of 'manners' and of 'knowledge'): voices that 'took turns using my eyes'. The long poem (as the papers of the 'Long-Liners' conference printed in *Open Letter*, 1985, indicate) was emerging with new vigour in the 1970s, sometimes for narrative but more often for meditative purposes. The very discontinuity of so many serial poems challenged the rhetorical illusion of order that linear continuity projected. (*Arché/Elegies* was the punning title of a 1983 volume by the critical theorist E.D. Blodgett, b. 1935). The literary concern for historical figure thus often constituted a challenge to the normative reading of history itself.

A distinction must therefore be made between the historical impulse of a writer such as Robertson Davies and that of writers like Rudy Wiebe and George Bowering. *What's Bred in the Bone*, the second volume of Davies' Cornish trilogy, as Robert Fulford (b. 1932) persuasively argued in a *Saturday Night* editorial, is a *roman-à-clef* which turns on the reader's recognition of the real historical Canadian base for an apparent tale of mystery and romance: in this instance the lives of the National Art Gallery director Alan Jarvis (1915–73) and the art patron Douglas Duncan (1902–68). Like so many Ontario fictions, Davies's work relies on a covert narrative referentiality. (However misleadingly, the genre of the mystery implies a hidden *solution*.) Wiebe's work, which repeatedly tells of historical *movement*, concerns itself more with distinguishing the kinds of history that different modes of narrative reconstruct. In *The Blue Mountains of China* (1970), for example, Wiebe recounts the history and heritage of the Mennonite peoples, tracing their path from Germany and Russia variously to China, Paraguay and Canada. But the novel develops by interleaving passages of documentary, family chronicle, oral history (much of this vocabulary in Low German), and testament – each form of discourse shaping the reader-listener's perception of experience in a different way.

Bowering's *Burning Water* (1980) emphasizes the personality of history even more openly, taking the saga of discovery in which Captains Vancouver and Quadra explore the North Pacific Coast, embroidering it with invention, asserting the power of language over the shaping of reality and the involvement of the author-artificer in this process. Hence George Vancouver overlaps with George the Third,

George the Sixth, and George Bowering; as the 'prologue' to *Burning Water* puts it:

we Georges all felt the same sun, yes. We all live in the same world's sea. We cannot tell a story that leaves us outside, and when I say we, I include you. But in order to include you, I feel that I cannot spend these pages saying *I* to a second person. Therefore let us say *he*, and stand together looking at them. We are making a story, after all, as we have always been, standing and speaking together to make up a history, a real historical fiction.

When Margaret Atwood calls one of her books of political verse *True Stories* (1981), she stresses the same principle of artifice: truth and memory are not the same, but not intrinsically exclusive either. Sometimes the substantiality of the truth depends on the authenticity of the person remembering: even the self becomes a figure re-collected from the past. Hence numerous works turned to use the strategy of autobiography, and so to examine the character of the narrative 'I'.

Once again a distinction is necessary. Some autobiographies, like Irving Layton's *Waiting for the Messiah* (1985), are conscious literary creations. And some literary works are transparent adaptations of personal experience, as in the case of Lowry. Sometimes this transformation appears in recurrent motifs, as in the way Margaret Laurence's reiterated references to adoption or absent parents might be said to grow out of her childhood loss of her own mother and father. Audrey Thomas's (b. 1935) *Songs My Mother Taught Me* (her first novel, though not published till 1973) clearly draws on the writer's Binghamton, New York, background. Clark Blaise's *Resident Alien* (1986) mediates between autobiographical essay and the autobiographical form of first-person fiction. Many poets, moreover, – Roy Kiyooka (1936–94) and Bill Bissett among them – frankly recall moments from childhood or recount their subjective response to things seen. In other cases, the 'I' is a deliberate persona or fictive device. The 'Realities' section of Dave Godfrey's *Dark Must Yield* is among other things a way of focusing the alternative lenses of 'tale' and 'myth'. The 'Wayman' of Tom Wayman's left-wing poems is sometimes a pose; the 'Garber' of Lawrence Garber's (b. 1937) bawdy *Garber's Tales from the Quarter* (1969) is a vehicle to satirize the cultural passion for identity. Milton Acorn's poetry effectively uses personal experience as a casebook example for Marxist analysis of the class struggle; Nichol's life-in-poetry is the basis for his serial *The Martyrology*, a poem as the book-of-life. The 'I' of Norman Levine's openly autobiographical stories (as in *I Don't Want to Know Anyone Too Well*, 1972) is also a strategy for exploring the limits of first-person perspective. The 'Wah' of Fred Wah's *Breathin' My Name with a Sigh* is a reflexive pun, a tribute to the power of breath to name, utter meaning, be poetry. ('So. So. So.', writes Phyllis Webb in 'Sunday Water' (1984), 'Ah – to have a name like Wah / when the deep purple falls.') In the strategy of autobiography, the forms of subjectivity and documentary coalesce, sometimes to intensify a sensibility, sometimes to challenge a contextual authority.

In *Wife* (1976), for example, Bengali-born Bharati Mukherjee provided a realistic account of the pressures facing an Indian woman in a male-dominated American society. But the story is fiction. With her husband, American-born Clark Blaise, she also wrote a dual autobiography, *Days and Nights in Calcutta* (1977, later extended), an account of a year they spent together in India, she to revisit a world she had left, he to meet a world he had married into. But the autobiography, too, is a form of fiction. The modal contrast between the two halves of the book stresses the difference in perspective the two writers took to the experience: he sees richness, strangeness, narrative anecdote, event; she (speaking the language, though she is in exile from it) hears gossip, pain, privilege, pressure. The same episodes carry different resonances, and the echoes between the two halves keep shifting the social and literary contexts which give the episodes their implications. Blaise, moreover, in short story collections such as *A North American Education* (1973) and *Tribal Justice* (1974) or in a novel (for example, *Lusts*, 1983), effectively manipulates first-person strategies so as to probe the emotional displacements of adolescence, change, exile and marriage breakdown. In 'Eyes', the deliberate distance of second-person technique isolates the character and reader even more, the very phrasing stressing the loss of identifiability, privacy, security, in a world open to dislocation and the chaos of public scrutiny.

Lyric, genre-crossing 'journals' all extend the range of the autobiographical method. Examples include works by Daphne Marlatt (in a novel called *Zócalo*, 1977, the voyage poems of *How Hug a Stone*, 1983, or the Penang journal printed in *Capilano Review*), Michael Ondaatje (*Running in the Family*, 1981, a 'gesture' in anecdotal and autobiographical form summoning the experience of growing up in Sri Lanka), Nicole Brossard (b. 1943) ('Journal Intime', 1983) and Eli Mandel. With Mandel (after early experiments with mythology) and Daphne Marlatt, in particular, the world is phenomenological, an extension of consciousness. Perception is a structure. Poetry and critical appreciation come essentially to be one.

A York University (Toronto) professor, Mandel never disconnected himself from his Jewish Saskatchewan background; his fascination with doppelgangers and his insistence that language is place, a region

of understanding, alike derive from his own past. *Crusoe* (1973) casts
him as survivor; *Stony Plain* (1973) and *Life Sentence* (1981) – the latter
interweaving poems with excerpts from a travel diary – reveal by
their punning titles his mordant delight in meditative ironies. His
desire is to find in image and cadence, pared to minimal gestures,
those verbal expressions of self that evoke the mind's arrangements of
reality. Each poem, he writes, 'speaks to another poem': mind and
world are resonant with echoes. Repeatedly he revises his poems, yet
all versions (including new ones) co-exist in the mind's ear: hence in
his two volumes of selected poems he does not consistently choose the
'later' version – he sometimes reverts to an earlier form, sometimes
probes a different verbal possibility, allowing 'self' to range across the
received boundaries of genre, place and time. Two 1977 works reveal
the kinds of crossover that link experience (mind, senses, self, journal)
with poetry and criticism. *Another Time* is a collection of essays on
such subjects as the character of literary regionalism (his essay 'Writing West' overlaps deliberately with the titles and themes of W.H.
New's (b. 1938) 1972 critical book *Articulating West* and Robert
Kroetsch's 'Out West' trilogy). *Out of Place* is a serial book of poems,
counterpointed by Ann Mandel's (b. 1941) photographs. Together,
these two works record a return journey into regional sensibility; the
poet goes 'home' to Saskatchewan's Souris Valley, in search of 'doors
of perception', 'signs', 'petroglyphs' and 'metaphors', but he finds
'lost places', 'ghosts' and 'badlands' instead. Speech and understanding refuse to coincide neatly. In 'The Double', Mandel writes:

indian names are secret
poetry is the naming of secret names
among these are:

  god
  spirit
  alphabets

  names in stone
  doubled names
  the psalms
  hoodoos
  animals
  eyes
  jewels
the place of no shadows called badlands
the place of shadows called badlands
you begin to see the difficulties.

For Daphne Marlatt, too, language is an extension of person, though her relation to place progressively differs from Mandel's. Her attempt to achieve speech reveals a sense of alienation from the norms of the world around her (in her early years a resident of Malaysia and Australia, she records in her journal how as a young immigrant she long attempted to disappear into Canadian society): it also reflects her subsequent determination to restructure sound and syntax so that expression and location will coincide, will come from within. *Leaf/leafs* (1969) is written in single word lines, single syllables, the minimalism stressing the momentariness of percep-tion, revelation, the brief touch that joins experience to under-standing. *Steveston* (1974) rhythmically depicts the river and tidal flow of its setting (a fishing port, where Japanese-Canadians lived before being expelled during the Second World War); a verbal struc-ture that evokes cyclic change, the poem also transforms history, makes it female, the body of speech shaped by the body of self. *Net Work* (a 1980 volume of selected poetry and prose) describes by its precise title the poet's attempt to resist the linearity of metaphor and to write by metonymic, associational patterns instead. Such patterns, further, resist the linearity of patriarchal connection; her alternative structures of communication (concentric, multiple) describe a process of re-vision, one which reflects on the relation between autobio-graphical paradigms, geographical metaphors and the question of social authority. Simply put, Daphne Marlatt and many other female writers reject the 'explorer' metaphor that establishes man-in-place, man-with-the-power-to-chart-and-name. For them, place flows dif-ferently (though the contrast in attitude does not correspond absolutely with gender: Matt Cohen has a character in *Wooden Hunters* reject the male intellectualism of map-making, and one of Dave Godfrey's personae in *Dark Must Yield* muses, 'When you say place I think movement'). Daphne Marlatt and others ask what the 'I' actually stands for. If it implies authenticity, they ask, who has the right to speak? who has language available to them? who is privi-leged by existing linguistic conventions? (who is not made margin-al?) The notion of 'immigrant', for example, presumes a norm to which an immigrant can never quite belong, for the identity 'immi-grant' keeps such a person out. So the conventional centrality of 'man' makes 'woman' marginal. By extension, a unitary authoritari-an perspective in literature – the 'I' that names the world – imposes prescriptive definitions on the nature of reality. As the poems written between Daphne Marlatt and Betsy Warland (b. 1946) specify (Betsy Warland's *Open Is Broken*, 1984, tried to 'untie the tongue', to find the etymologies of 'de-sire', to express the female idiom of 'scentext', or sensory syntax), there are validating ways of rewriting the certainties of territorial metaphor. Absence is one (silence being an articulate expression). Multiplying identities is another: the network created by verbal fracture ('open is broken') opens new avenues of associative connection. Through such processes, moreover, the codes of person connect with the codes of gender.

CODES OF GENDER

It could well be argued that language and literary forms that have historically been accepted as 'standards' have largely been male-coded all along, a circumstance that has repeatedly fostered much feminist rejection of literary conventions. In the 1960s, such resistance received further stimulus from the United States and France. While many anglophone Canadian women writers responded to the social criticism of American feminists (Kate Millett, b. 1934), and others), the literary theory of French critics (Hélène Cixous, b. 1937, for example) was to influence francophone writers first (Nicole Brossard, France Théoret, Jovette Marchessault) and anglophone writers such as Daphne Marlatt through them. But neither male-coding nor feminism takes a single literary form. Hence Margaret Atwood, Margaret Laurence, Audrey Thomas and the cartoonist Lynn Johnston (b. 1947; *For Better or For Worse*) can all be read as feminist writers, though all four, to the degree that they repeatedly concern themselves with the roles and the language of motherhood, cross the boundary line that one of the narrower definitions of feminist independence draws. (The penultimate words of Laurence's *The Stone Angel* – 'There. There.' – at once indicate place and employ the conventional words of maternal comforting.) Similarly, it is possible to read the works of both Robert Kroetsch and Scott Symons as open declarations of what it means to be male, though the two stances differ markedly, and though codes of gender must also be distinguished from the plain subject of sexuality. Kroetsch's bawdy and ironic work (as in *The Studhorse Man*, 1969, and *Alibi*, 1983), or his idea of an 'erotics of space', which he explores in his essay collection *Labyrinths of Voice* (1981), celebrates the predicaments and passions of heterosexual desire. Symons' *Combat Journal for Place d'Armes* (1967) and *Helmet of Flesh* (1986) equally passionately celebrate the discovery of male self through revelations of the male body – in part in order to oppose what the author sees as the female domination of Canadian writing, the bland liberalism of Canadian politics, and the debilitating loss of Tory traditions in both English and French Canada.

Poets such as Jean-Guy Pilon, Michel Beaulieu (1941–86) and

Fernand Ouellette continued to praise Quebec through images of the female body, whereas André Roy's *Monsieur Désir* (1981) concerns homosexual fantasies, and Timothy Findley's work probes the maleness of fascism. Gérard Bessette's fiction and criticism provide one conventional interpretive frame for such works: a Freudian psychoanalytic analysis of the construction of character and the interpretation of social behaviour. But the presumptions of this perspective came into dispute. Nicole Brossard, among others, rejected both the 'patriarchal' version of Ideal Woman and its concomitant, the conventional image of the country *as* a woman.

While heterosexuality is the primary subject of writers such as Audrey Thomas and Robert Kroetsch, lesbian experience – and the political implications of female relationships both in particular and in general – is the central concern of a number of others. For them Freud is either mistaken or irrelevant. Mary Meigs (1917–2002), for example, wrote autobiographically in *The Medusa Head* (1983) about her connection with Marie-Claire Blais; Jane Rule and Betsy Warland, respectively in prose and poetry, concern themselves more generally with the character, the body and the language of relationship itself. In *Triptyche lesbien* (1980), Jovette Marchessault, the Native *Québécoise* painter and playwright, attacked the codes of a male-dominated society by envisioning a 'lesbian' society (that is, one not so much without men as without the maleness of domination). For Jovette Marchessault, *woman* and *lesbian* are terms that alike declare alienation, whereas neither applies to being a victim. To be a woman is to be active creator. the stories of *Triptyche lesbien* trace the source of creative power through a generational cycle of women: part lecture, part fairytale, part prophecy. Power lies in the female control over choice.

Two formal features of this work – its discontinuous structure and its concern for the artistry of *crafts* – extend an appreciation of the gender codes in contemporary art. For example, Joyce Wieland (1931–98), in 'Reason Over Passion', produced a quilt design that implicitly did two things: satirize arid (male) intellectualism, by making a bedcover diminish the importance of emotional and physical connection, and elevate the artistic status of those whose art – quiltmaking, tapestry, design, needlework – was customarily denigrated as 'female' or 'folk' activity. Evelyn Roth's (b. 1936) knit designs and mixed media art works served a similar purpose, as did the so-called 'primitivism' of the paintings by Elisabeth Hopkins (1894-1991), a distant relative of Gerard Manley Hopkins). By contrast, William Kurelek's (1927–77) paintings, though to some degree similar in primitivist technique, served much more restrictive Christian fundamentalist ends. Adele Wiseman's tribute to her mother and her mother's doll-making artistry, *Old Woman at Play* (1978), gathers more than autobiographical force by being read in this (matrilineal, creative) context. The Canadian showing of the American artist Judy Chicago's (b. 1939) influential work 'The Dinner Party' during the 1970s – emphasizing vulvular shapes and needlework artistry – further reiterated the political message being conveyed here: women's art is a political art, explicitly rejecting what French theorists call 'phallogocentrism', and declaring that an alternative aesthetics, founded in the female body, can create other modes of authentic exchange.

These lines of connection touch issues that are social, sexual, formal and verbal. The more conventional systems of gender encoding are substantially referential in character, though they often invert conventional prototypes of 'femininity' in the process, or challenge the male codes of the standard 'ritual-of-passage' story. The more complex denials of convention involve various kinds of formal discontinuity, ultimately fastening self-reflexively on the language of connection itself. In the first (loose) category might be classed fiction by Monique Proulx (b. 1952), Hélène Ouvrard (b. 1938), Sharon Butala (b. 1940), Edna Alford (b. 1947), Janice Kulyk Keefer (b. 1953), Suzanne Jacob (b. 1943), Pol Pelletier (b. 1947), Louise Cotnoir (b. 1948), Monique Bosco (*La femme de Loth*, 1970), Gabrielle Poulin (b. 1929), Helen Weinzweig (b. 1915), Aritha Van Herk (b. 1954), Joyce Marshall, Sandra Birdsell (b. 1942), Katherine Govier (b. 1948), Anne Hébert and Madeleine Ouellette-Michalska (b. 1934; *La femme de sable*, 1979). In the second category might appear such writers as Audrey Thomas, Madeleine Gagnon (*Lueur*, 1979), Smaro Kamboureli (b. 1955), France Théoret (*Une voix pour Odile*, 1978), Ann Rosenberg (*The Bee Book*, 1981), Suzanne Paradis (b. 1936), Désirée Szucsany (b. 1955), Sharon Riis (b. 1947; *The True Story of Ida Johnson*, 1976), Frances Duncan (b. 1942), Yolande Villemaire (*La vie en prose*, 1980), Louky Bersianik (b. 1930), Gloria Sawai (b. 1932) and Nicole Brossard. A similar distinction affects poetry and drama, though Nicole Brossard, Madeleine Gagnon, Yolande Villemaire and Louky Bersianik would all resist the very generic system of classification implied by this sentence. The plays of Marie Laberge, Betty Lambert (1933–1983), Anne Cameron (as Cam Hubert), and Margaret Hollingsworth (b. 1940), whose *Alli Alli Oh* (1977) tells of a woman's retreat into madness, as she reacts to a world with which she cannot connect, keep the empirical world constantly in view. So do the poems of Linda Rogers, Dionne Brand (b. 1953) , Judith Fitzgerald (b. 1952), Sharon Thesen, Roo Borson, Anne Szumigalski (1926–99) and Suniti Namjoshi (b. 1941). Judith Copithorne (b. 1939), Cathy Ford (b. 1952) and Eva Tihanyi (b. 1956) focus more evidently on language itself, on the character of syntax and semantics. For Trinidad-born Claire Harris (b. 1937), in *Fables from the Women's Quarters* (1984), dialect and broken speech enact forms of sexual and political alienation. For bilingual Lola Lemire Tostevin (fl. 1980s), access to both French and English (as in *Color of Her Speech*, 1982) turns poetry into a process of 'unspeaking' –

> '*tu déparles*'
> my mother says
>
> *je déparle*
>
>   yes
>
> I unspeak
> . . . .
> baby lulled
> by a lie
> byaliebyaliebyaliebyaliebyalie

– an active working out of the ways identity can be split by the contrarieties possessed in language.

While writing sometimes became an erotic act for male as well as female writers (as in the poetry of Philippe Haeck and a number of younger Quebec poets, political in part to the degree that their work declares the sexuality of speech), it was erotic for many women because they regarded language as a *body* rather than a *landscape*. The difference shows up in various literary treatments of Africa. In Jacques Godbout's *L'aquarium*, Africa is only implied, an indeterminate, contained, tropical landscape by which to watch the world in microcosm. Hugh Hood's *You Can't Get There from Here* (1972) uses Africa as a fanciful setting for an industrial satire. In Jacques Ferron's *Le Saint-Élias* (1972) Africa provides a political parallel for a Quebec historical event. In Gérard Bessette's *Les anthropoïdes* (1977) it constitutes an archetypal setting for a psychological speculation about ancestral origins. In Dave Godfrey's *The New Ancestors* (1970) – more locally specific to Ghana and Mali (Godfrey taught with CUSO [Canadian University Service Overseas] in West Africa in the early 1960s, an experience recorded in his *Man Deserves Man*, 1968) – Africa is the political ground for a study of the workings of power. But for Dorothy Livesay, Audrey Thomas and Margaret Laurence, Africa is sexual; it constitutes a tacit revelation of the 'otherness' in female experience for which the ordinary words of North America do not suffice.

Audrey Thomas spent two years in Kumasi, Ghana, between 1964 and 1966. From her first published story, 'If One Green Bottle' (*Ten Green Bottles*, 1967), through two novels (*Mrs. Blood*, 1970, and *Blown Figures*, 1974), to stories in *Ladies & Escorts* (1977), Africa has shaped an alternative structure of mind. It is a place of possibility, but for her recurrent central character also a place of miscarriage, the experience out of which separateness and separation both develop. While later works – 'Natural History', in *Real Mothers* (1981), *Intertidal Life* (1984) or *Goodbye, Harold, Good Luck* (1986) – tell of cyclical recurrence and lives renewed by tide and time, the stories frequently pause over moments of sexual hesitation. A boy in Greece recoils from the sexuality he dimly begins to feel within himself (and unconsciously to recognize in the symbols of the world outside); a woman in Mexico sharply reflects on a failure of male commitment, which has resulted in an abortion and in her travelling alone. Such divisions find expression also in the formal structures of the novels. *Mrs. Blood* records the central character's split sensibility; 'Mrs. Blood' is her sensual person, capable of imagining but not controlling her life, while the otherself called 'Mrs. Thing' is the female 'object' whom others manipulate and manage. In *Blown Figures* (as in a number of Daphne Marlatt's and Phyllis Webb's poems), space on the page itself emphasizes the fragmentariness of insight, the durations of silence, which together interrupt and sustain the character's enquiries into the validity of her own feelings.

Phyllis Webb, who with Gael Turnbull and Eli Mandel first published poems in a 1954 anthology *Trio*, had early been concerned with the paired duality of 'making' and 'breaking', as is illustrated in the lyrics of *Even Your Right Eye* (1956) and *The Sea Is Also a Garden* (1962). This intellectual understanding took feminist form in the minimalist *Naked Poems* (1965), the aesthetics of speech and silence often arranging single words – 'Oh?' adrift in a page of space – so that they resonate with existential doubt and sexual questioning. 'Field notes' for Webb are the fragments of understanding that still remain to be interpreted. With *Wilson's Bowl* (1980) – a volume which responds to two suicides (those of the anthropologist Wilson Duff, 1925–76, and the poet's friend Lilo Berliner, d. 1977) – Phyllis Webb turned to a greater range of subjects. These include the anarchist prince Kropotkin (1842–1921), the painter Vasarely (1908–97), and the dreams of possibility, as in these closing stanzas from 'The Days of the Unicorns':

It was only yesterday, or seems
like only yesterday when we could
touch and turn and they came
perfectly real into our fictions.

But they moved on with the courtly sun
grazing peacefully beyond the story
horns lowering and lifting and
lowering

I know this is scarcely credible now
as we cabin ourselves in cold
and the motions of panic
and our cells destroy each other
performing music and extinction
and the great dreams pass on
to the common good.

As her prose works in *Talking* (1982) show, the poet has long been concerned with the intellectual implications of syllable and line. Experimenting with the long English line in her Kropotkin poems, she turned subsequently (influenced by John Thompson, 1938–76, Michael Ondaatje, and Adrienne Rich, b. 1929) to rediscover the Persian love lyric form called the ghazal. In *Sunday Water: Thirteen Anti-ghazals* (1982), she breaks past the male strictures embodied in the ghazal, seeking a way to make the body of the text dance to the mind's own rhythm. 'Leaning', a poem in *Water and Light: Ghazals and Anti-Ghazals* (1984), influenced Timothy Findley's writing of *Not Wanted on the Voyage*.

Various forms of division thus focus on the alienation embodied in language. Space (as in Webb), narrative duality (as in Thomas), triptych (as in Marchessault or the novels and plays of Louise Maheux-Forcier), verbal game (as when the stories of Maheux-Forcier's *En toutes lettres*, 1980, titularly follow alphabetical sequence): all call attention to processes of linguistic rearrangement which enact or imply the need for social and attitudinal change. As with Daphne Marlatt, 'writing' becomes 'righting'. These writers seek to *touch* rather than to *explore*; they resist the controlling imperial implications of the related images of mapping / exploration / penetration. The neologistic systems of hyphenation, parenthesis and fracture that recur in the vocabulary of feminist criticism – 'de-sire', 're-vision', 'herstory', 'lo(u)nging', 'gyn/ecology' or (in French) *'misandrie'* – further emphasize the sexual restrictions built into conventional terminology. They do so in part by revealing the overlap between the semiotic condition of language and the interpretive process of reading. Especially in the work of Nicole Brossard, these critical and creative principles come together in metatextual narrative.

Editor of *Les stratégies du réel / The story so far* (1979) and involved in shaping the feminist orientation of *La nouvelle barre du jour*, Nicole Brossard has always pushed at syntactic and semantic conventions. Her texts (the boundary between poetry and fiction becoming progressively diffuse), show the continuing influence of the French *nouveau roman* and of writers such as Paul-Marie Lapointe. They turn more directly to feminist theory with the poems in *Mécanique jongleuse, suivie de masculin grammaticale* (1974, translated as *Daydream Mechanics*) and the prose of *Un livre* (1970), *Sold-out* (1973, translated as *Turn of a Pang*), and *French Kiss* (1974, translated 1986). In particular, the gender assumptions of French draw her attention. If three hundred women and one cat or one truck are in a street (say the placards in Bersianik's *L'Euguélionne*, paraded before the Académie française), the women will disappear into the male French plural (*ils*) or male adjectival suffixes, implying female irrelevance – or at least a subservience to the cat and the inanimate truck in the grammatical hierarchy. To combat such notions (and their social ramifications) Nicole Brossard eschews conventional patterns. She deliberately employs paradoxical puns (Barbara Godard, b. 1941, translator of *L'amèr ou le Chapitre effrité*, 1977, translates *de fait* simultaneously as 'defeat' and 'de facto' in one place, and elsewhere on the same page as both 'actually' and 'acted upon'). Brossard also disrupts the gender agreements of French grammar. As Barbara Godard notes, she removes the silent 'e' at the end of words, 'as in *laboratoir*, to mark the absence of the feminine in the activities carried out there'. Or it disappears from *mère* (as in the title of *L'amèr*) 'to underline the process of articulating this silence, of moving toward a neutral grammar, which occurs in the text'. Translated, *L'amèr* becomes *These Our Mothers Or: The Disintegrating Chapter*, implying 'The Sour Mothers' as well. The book testifies to the sexuality of speech and reading – to the labial, lingual and creative acts of language and chapter-making (breaking). It is also a claim upon a female (matrilineal / lesbian) presence in the connections between generations, hence a way of resisting the critical 'erasure' of women in the systems of language. *Picture Theory* (1982) develops these principles in both fictive and critical terms – Gertrude Stein and Ludwig Wittgenstein (1889–1951) providing a frame of reference within which language serves to 'create' or 'depict' characters and also to resist (a photographic pun) the definition implied by words like *portray*. The hologram offers a comparison: what precisely is present? what reality exists in the image? how functional (or how purely inventive) is the angle of perception? Metatextual, the book tells of its own composition, and of the difficulties inherent in theorizing a justification for a system of literary portrayal. 'Images' of women (objects, fictional conventions) have to be replaced by the 'voices' of the real if the lives of women in history are to be set free. While Nicole Brossard thus moved in theoretical directions, other writers, such as Louky Bersianik (Lucile Durand), were attacking the status quo through the forms of the fantastic, using the conventions of the 'unreal' to envision alternatives to present verbal discourse and social structure.

CODES OF FANTASY AND FOLKLORE

Fantasy, an element in Canadian writing from the early days of the tale-tellers and map-makers, often appeared as documentary. Nineteenth-century animal stories, like the maps of beasts and dragons, posed as empirical truth. But from the 1960s on, a taste has grown for the unreal or truer-than-real: sometimes as an escape from speech, change, nuclear threat, and social conflict, sometimes as a way of dealing with these issues and of probing the implications of solutions to them. Children's literature was a barometer of such change. It began to play with possibility, both in theme and in language, whether in the verses of Dennis Lee (*Alligator Pie*, 1974) and Robert Heidbreder (b. 1947), the plays of Dennis Foon, television programming (*Mr. Dressup, Chez Hélène, Fraggle Rock*), or fiction. Lee, Carol Bolt and Tim Wynne-Jones (b. 1948) all wrote scripts and lyrics for *Fraggle Rock*. Among the most widely-read fiction writers were Christie Harris (1907–2002), praised especially for her 'Mouse Woman' stories, blending European fairytale motifs with West Coast Indian 'narnauk' figures), Antonine Maillet (b. 1929; *Christophe Cartier de la noisette dit Nounours*, 1981), Suzanne Martel (b. 1924), Monica Hughes (1925–2003), Claude Aubry (b. 1914) and Marie-Louise Gay (b. 1952). Readers also rediscovered the works of Catherine Anthony Clark (1892–1977), whose *The Golden Pine Cone* (1950) traced a magical adventure into a child's inner world, where Indian legends give the characters the moral ability to deal with chaos and return to society.

Overt moralizing is not a necessary attribute of fantastic writing, but it is a recurrent one, inviting readers to see it sometimes as the inverse side of domestic realism rather than as a negation of it. A similar generalization touches science fiction writing as well. Again from the 1960s on, Canadian practice in this genre began to be recognized as a serious enterprise. Practitioners included Phyllis Gotlieb, William Gibson (b. 1948), Stephen Franklin (b. 1922), Guy Gavriel Kay (b. 1954), Robert Zend (1929–85), Candas Jane Dorsey (b. 1952) and Spider Robinson (b. 1948). Judith Merril (1923–97), introducing her anthology of Canadian sf, *Tesseracts* (1985), comments that science fiction is both a world of literature based on the premises *what if* and *if this goes on*, and a way of thinking usefully about the possibility that there might be no future at all (an indication of why, in an age of nuclear threat, fantasy literature should be so popular among young adult readers). Merril's statement codifies the social-moral dimensions of the genre, especially those that meditate on survival or lead towards speculative fantasy. The other face of sf involves science – especially the 'uncertainty principles' and 'Feynman digramming' to which contemporary research in quantum theory and supermolecular physics was giving rise. The work of the two sons of the novelist Selwyn Dewdney is illustrative here. Christopher Dewdney recurrently devised poetic structures to deal with the paradoxes of existence and physical motion (the intellectual tensions between fixity and pulsar movement, the reversibility of time, the instantaneousness of experience). A.K. Dewdney (b. 1941), who succeeded Martin Gardner (b. 1914) as the mathematical puzzle-writer for *Scientific American*, wrote in *The Planiverse* (1984) a seriocomic enquiry into the nature of a two-dimensional universe, one revealed through the character Yendred, met (or 'interfaced') on a computer screen. Ranging from meditation to moral adventure to didactic fable to verbal and numerical game, such works display the variety of sensibilities brought to the unknown.

Yet the visions of the unknown are usually lodged empirically in the dimensions of the known, which is the point of J. Michael Yates's story 'The Sinking of the Northwest Passage' (*The Abstract Beast*, 1971). Born with no 'Northwest Passage' to discover, the characters here live out their lives with their absences inside them: the Commodore goes down with his ship, sinking through the pavement of his driveway, while his wife sinks parenthetically in her domestic tasks – and readers are invited to look at their own lives for metaphoric parallels. The approximate visual counterpart of such stories lies in the work of the Saskatchewan painter Ivan Eyre (b. 1935), whose precise photographic draughtsmanship (often involving icons of the popular culture) reveals dreams and psychological tensions the eye can only guess at, or whose use of distancing and framing techniques throws an apparently pastoral landscape into question.

Sean Virgo (b. 1940; *White Lies*, 1981), Andreas Schroeder (*The Late Man*, 1972), Virgil Burnett (b. 1928; *Towers at the Edge of a World*, 1980), Pegeen Brennan (b. 1928; *Zarkeen*, 1982), Jacques Benoît (b. 1941; *Jos Carbone*, 1967; *Les princes*, 1973), Susan Kerslake (b. 1943; *Penumbra* 1984), Jovette Marchessault (*Comme une enfant de la terre*, 1975), Stephen Guppy (b. 1951; *Another Sad Day at the Edge of Empire*, 1985),

Brian Fawcett (*The Secret Journal of Alexander Mackenzie*, 1985), Michel Tremblay (*Contes pour buveurs attardés*, 1966), Susan Swan (b. 1944; *The Biggest Modern Woman in the World*, 1983), Martin Myers (b. 1927; *The Assignment*, 1971), Matt Cohen (*Columbus and the Fat Lady*, 1972), Charles Soucy (b. 1934, *Un dieu chasseur*, 1976), Wilfrid Lemoine, Michael Bullock (b. 1918), Gaétan Brulotte (b. 1945), François Barcelo (b. 1941), André Carpentier (b. 1947), Gilles Archambault (b. 1933), Jean-Yves Soucy (b. 1945), André Langevin, Anne Bernard (b. 1922) and others similarly construct fantasy with the empirical world in mind. Burnett's work roughly recounts a history of the world in the shifting prose forms of literary convention; as magical motifs disappear, to be replaced by the laconic idiom of everyday, so does each character's (and by implication the world's) ability to dream a way out of its own predicaments. Graeme Gibson's *Perpetual Motion* (1982) dips into nineteenth-century Ontario history to challenge the (obsessive, pioneer) male fantasies of a dynastic future; for Gibson (b. 1934), as for Blais and Butler, fantasy turns into nightmare. Jacques Godbout's eye in *Les têtes á Papineau* (1981) is directly on contemporary politics, Swan's and Brennan's on the rights of women. Denise Boucher's (b. 1935) 1978 play *Les fées ont soif*, deconstructing the image of woman idealized in the Virgin Mary, attacks what politics and religious system have done to women's roles within society. Paul Quarrington's (b. 1953) *Home Game* (1983) – like other baseball stories, by George Bowering and W. P. Kinsella, for example – uses the techniques of fantastic exaggeration in order to amuse, as well as to reflect seriously on the power of dreams.

But fantasy more often works to reformative ends. Louky Bersianik's *L'Euguélionne* (1976) is a case in point. The first of several books (*Pique-nique sur l'Acropole* and *Maternative* followed in 1979 and 1980), *L'Euguélionne* is a futurist story cast basically in present-day Quebec. The qualification is necessary because the novel suggests that the title figure (ironically, the 'bearer of good news', a woman from another planet looking for a better world) is recognized wherever she lands on earth. She is 'read' in whatever terms the local recognition allows – identified in Acadia as 'La Sagouine' (Antoine Maillet's imaginative rebellious cleaning-woman, from her 1971 play of the same name), while Quebeckers recognize her as 'Pauline Archange' (from Marie-Claire Blais), 'Eva-Maria' (using the terms of religion, the folk-witch 'La Corriveau' (who derives from history and shows up as an ominous character in novels by Kirby and Aubert de Gaspé, or the indigenous 'Manikoutai'. Louky Bersianik's point is manifold: she is concerned both with the specificity of women's experience and with the seeming universality of men's attempts to control and diminish women. She is concerned also with the kinds of identity that conventions allow, with the power that inheres in language, and with the control that a male language exerts upon both the men and the women who accept and use it. The novel – cast as a tryptych, containing several hundred numbered sections – tells of the Euguélionne's history on and escape from 'The Planet of the Legislators', and of her attempts to find a 'positive planet' (she herself is figured as a photographic negative) she might call home. Earth, it transpires, will not do, for despite its claims to sophistication, it only disguises its discriminations; its history and language tell the real story; the language of religion, patrilineal genealogy, Freudian psychology, children's literature, philosophical criticism: each is analyzed in turn and found presumptive. She takes the language apart; she speaks in puns, denying unitary authority to words; she speaks in the French present historic tense, emphasizing process rather than unchangeable 'fact'. Perceived to be dangerous (the Euguélionne is a teacher, therefore suspect to the planet's authorities), she is condemned by earth's own legislators. But nothing destroys her, not even her eventual departure. From her teachings, earth's women have learned at least that they are not 'absences', but rather 'holes' into alternative perceptions of being, bodies capable of life and of a positive realization of self.

Parallel to the renewed interest in fantasy was the revival of attention to folklore, both in direct forms (collections of songs, myths, legends, oral histories, such as those of Joan Finnigan, b. 1925, Edith Fowke, 1913–96 and Carol Carpenter, b. 1944) and by indirect adaptations of folkloric forms, especially in fiction and drama. (To a lesser degree the interest showed up in poetry, too, especially in that of Kristjana Gunnars, b. 1948, whose *One-Eyed Moon Maps*, 1980, *Settlement Poems*, 1980, and *Wake-Pick Poems*, 1981, adapt the forms and figures of Icelandic myth.) Academies, such as Memorial University in St John's, established departments of folklore studies. Among anglophone writers there was a rediscovery of people who could be claimed as 'antecedents' for such a movement: Howard O'Hagan for *Tay John*, Sheila Watson for *The Double Hook*. Norval Morriseau published Ojibwa legends, and Basil Johnston his contemporary anecdotes using traditional tale-telling forms. Bernard Epps's (b. 1936) *Pilgarlic the Death* (1967), moreover, joyfully celebrating the dilemmas of being alive, peopled the Eastern Townships with the character-types of folk legend (Dougal the School, Milly-from-the-Hill, the preacher named Hell Fire) and so perceived how European folk tradition continues to show up in Canadian life. Among francophone writers, entertaining folk forms have much longer been used for political declarations of cultural survival. While there were some (Philippe Haeck, for example, whose poems were translated in 1983 as *The Clarity of Voices*) who condemned the persistent 'folklorizing' of culture as a reactionary resistance to philosophy, a passive acceptance of political inertia, a refusal to recognize the need for substantive social revolution, many more writers were to adapt the characteristic *contes* – especially those of the Gaspé and Beauce regions – to contemporary idiom and purpose.

The delayed impact of Sheila Watson's *The Double Hook* (1959) derived largely from its unembellished, elliptical, cinematic style. Readers initially sought *story*, looking in vain for the familiar closed structure of a plotted tale. While the novel is full of melodramatic incidents (matricide, a blinding, flight), the focus is not on narrative sequence, or on character as 'realistically' conceived. The characters here are figures in a dream-landscape, less perceived than perceiving, each action caught in process, recorded in participial fragments ('His hand half-raised. His voice in the rafters, James walking away. The old lady falling.') and in thin-sections of dialogue. Action takes place in the fragments; events occur in the spaces between. Hence the reader is engaged in mentally assembling the sequences, associatively participating in the action. In effect the author was recasting the novel form as a process of revelation. She reduced the narrator's role in story-telling, controlling the language so that the very shapes of prose would tell a particular set of violent circumstances and at the same time imply the larger shapes of 'mystery' that give recurrent pattern to human behaviour. But as with folk tale, the effect here turns on a paradox: human circumstances prove anarchic, and recurrent pattern remains uncertain. Behind the characters, therefore, moves yet another voice: not one involving a godly authority, implying absolutes of judgment and models of heroic behaviour, but that of Coyote, the trickster, whose world is uncertain and human-sized. Through him, human choice can be seen to be simultaneously consequential and inconclusive; the folk tale form in modernist dress takes the abstractions of desire and fear and roots them in self-conscious artifice.

This process of adapting folk tale, however, need not deny contextual references to history or society. Michael Cook drew repeatedly on Newfoundland legend and idiom for plays about the social pressures of the fishing outports, as in *The Head, Guts and Sound Bone Dance* (1974) and *Quiller* (1975). Like Cook, Guy Dufresne (1915–93) dipped back into history as well as legend, most effectively with a series of *téléromans*. Louis Caron (b. 1942), in *Bonhomme Sept-heures* (1978), adapted legends of the bogeyman (the title is a fearsome

French aural 'equivalent' for the English 'bone-setter') to tell of the persistence of childhood (including childhood fears) in adult life, and the inevitability of death. Dave Godfrey, in his story collections *Death Goes Better with Coca-Cola* (1967) and *Dark Must Yield* (1978) – most notably in 'The Hard-Headed Collector' and 'A New Year's Morning on Bloor Street' – overlapped allusions to European, Asian, Judaeo-Christian, American and indigenous mythologies in order to emphasize the plurality of contemporary Canadian culture. Re-enacting everything from the *I Ching* to Arthurian tale and the 'shaking tent' ritual of the Ojibway, Godfrey is not thereby rewriting myth; rather he is calling attention to the processes of change, and at the same time criticizing the exclusive impulses in modern society that would force Canadians to choose their ancestors singly, therefore inaccurately. Whereas Pierre Châtillon in *Le Fou* (1975) relied on the closed systems of myth, telling a tale in which the figures of Quebec legend (Rose Latulipe, La Corriveau) become the archetypes of the unconscious, other writers used the *conte* form as a medium of social protest, as does Madeleine Ferron (b. 1922), in *La fin des loups-garous* and *Coeur de sucre* (both 1966). Her story 'Be Fruitful and Multiply', translated in 1974 by Sheila Watson, tells a seemingly placid tale of a woman's life from early marriage through many births to old age. Old, however, she can no longer distinguish place or tell the generations apart. The tonal placidity (all on the surface) serves to establish a volatile irony; implicitly the story protests this illusion, using the tale-telling conventions to undermine the social norms to which they refer, and to condemn the way the 'narrative rules' of marriage and religion have emptied the woman of meaning rather than given her fulfillment.

Using the oral forms of folk narrative thus became for several contemporary writers a means of claiming a world of difference, a more valid world lodged variously in gender, region, politics and a separate cultural history. For Antonine Maillet, who won the Prix Goncourt for *Pélagie-la-charrette*, 'difference' stems from the separate history of Acadia. (Other contemporary Acadian writers include storytellers Jacques Savoie, b. 1951, and Claude LeBouthillier, b. 1946, and poets Raymond Leblanc, b. 1945, Ronald Després, b. 1935, Calixte Duguay, b. 1939, Herménégilde Chiasson, b. 1946, and Ulysse Landry, b. 1950. By the 1980s there had also been established a small body of *franco-ontarien* literature – with the poet Patrice Desbiens, b. 1948, novelist Hélène Brodeur, b. 1923, comic playwright Robert Marinier, b. 1954, for example – and *franco-manitobain* literature with Gilles Valais, b. 1929, and others.) Roch Carrier's (b. 1937) plays (*La céleste bicyclette*, 1980), novels, stories and children's tales (many published in the

journal *Vidéo-Presse*) extend the Quebec tradition of playful grotes-
querie, sometimes sentimentalizing the past, but like Antonine Maillet's work looking to shared cultural experience for the validation of
the present. For Jack Hodgins (b. 1938), growing up on northern Vancouver Island, 'difference' lay in cultural separation from all the rest
of Canada, anglophone and francophone traditions alike, making
them simply one of several influences (along with Faulkner and the
'magic realism' of modern Latin American writers) that shaped his
literary creations.

Hence for Hodgins, Carrier and Antonine Maillet, though in dissimilar parts of the country, a seriocomic imagination reclaimed history for the present. As Margaret Laurence had made clear in *A Bird
in the House*, the point of such an enterprise was to seek truth, distinguishing it both from memory and from the structures of convention.
Yet as Jack Hodgins was to underline in *The Invention of the World*
(1977), reclamation has its own dangers. Distinguishing false 'invention' from true 'creation', his novel exposes the numerous ways in
which quests for truth – autobiography, history, interview, rumour –
invite their own misconstructions of reality. The anthropologist Franz
Boas once explained trickster myths by suggesting that people
explain things as a result of change in their own lives. Hodgins's
novel takes up this premise, using the relationships among contemporary characters to frame a narrative tale about the mythic birth of
one Donal Keneally, who has led a faithful (or trusting, or at least
willing) band of Irish villagers off to found the Revelations Colony of
Truth in western Canada. The mythic birth is all fanciful exaggeration; the tale exposes the illogicality of blindly ascribing causes to
observed events: if Keneally was great, runs one argument, then his
birth *must have been* spectacular. This provides a good story, but
proves untrue. Even 'facts' are illusory, for when they enter the novel
they only confirm the characters in their mistaken belief that they are
rationally in control. The contemporary character Maggie Kyle distinguishes finally between these forms of untruth and the enlivening
and intrinsically moral power of imagination; in Maggie's life all
forms of storytelling then come together in an epic, comic, wedding-
day climax – which reiterates folk motif and makes a literary commitment to the forces of love and renewal.

Among Hodgins's other works – a novel, *The Resurrection of Joseph
Bourne* (1980), and two structured volumes of short stories, *Spit
Delaney's Island* (1976) and the more anecdotal *The Barclay Family Theatre* (1981) – similarly turn the absurdities of human behaviour into
parodic romances of the human spirit. Characters and events that at
first seem the designs of inventive extravagance – a tidal wave that

brings ashore a Peruvian ship and a magical beauty, an overweight salesman for Eden Realty who gets stranded on a cliffside and has to be rescued by sea – prove to be simple extensions of the ordinary. Roch Carrier, too – the author of more than a dozen volumes – has shown himself adept at allegorical fantasy (*Jolis deuils*, 1964), gothic fable (*La dame qui avait des chaînes aux chevilles*, 1981), comic incident and personal memoir (*Les enfants du bonhomme dans la lune*, 1979, translated as *The Hockey Sweater and other stories*), Rabelaisian social satire (*Le jardin des délices*, 1975), and parabolic history (*Il n'y a pas de pays sans grand-père*, 1979, and the trilogy that begins with *La guerre, yes sir!*, 1968).

The trilogy – the subsequent volumes are *Floralie, où es-tu?* (1969) and *Il est par là, le soleil* (1970), the last translated as *Is It the Sun, Philibert?* – tells of the shifts in the quality of Quebec village life as old traditions start to break down during the *anglais* Second World War (*La guerre*) and the throes of urbanization (*Il est par là*); *Floralie* looks back to earlier days, to the wedding night of the parents of the central figure in *La guerre* and to the series of separations and nightmare adventures that disrupts their life together. As with Carrier's other works, each novel is constructed with a traditional village custom in view. The exaggerated figures of folk legend are present in plenty: the cast of *Le deux-millième étage* (1973, translated as *They Won't Demolish Me!*) includes a health-enthusiast, a balladeer, a kind-hearted prostitute, a crotchety landlord, twin wrestlers, and an extra-large mother of thirteen (fat women abound in Canadian fiction, appearing in works by Hodgins, Margaret Laurence, Leon Rooke and many others). Yet these figures (except in so far as they ultimately hold the absurd at bay, keeping it on the laughable side of alienation) are as Felliniesque as they are ingratiating. They are paradigms and types of a demonic inversion of the ostensibly orderly traditional world. Carrier's novels do not dream ritual back into existence so much as they burlesque traditions that have been ill-advisedly deemed permanent. At his gentlest, as in the nineteen semi-autobiographical sketches of *Les enfants*, there appears less to be viciousness in society than there is mere foible. 'The Hockey Sweater' (which since its first publication has appeared in an illustrated children's version and as an animated film) tells of a boy's youthful trial on the hockey rink, when his mother orders a sweater from the T. Eaton Co. catalogue and the company substitutes the sweater of the *anglais* Toronto team for the desired colours of the Montreal *Canadiens*. 'What Language Do Bears Speak?' tells equally comically but more pointedly of a travelling *anglais* circus. When the circus bear escapes to the woods, the villagers retrieve it, but when the circus performer's wrestling match with the bear turns violent, the villagers allow it to proceed: not because they are cruel, but because they cannot speak English and so (the narrator says ingenuously) they consider the performer's shouts – to the effect that the bear is the wrong one, a wild beast they have retrieved from the forest – to be either English noises or else appropriate noises in 'bear'. Anecdote at this point turns into fable, and Carrier's story becomes an indirect critique of cultures that assume too much about each other's understanding.

With Antonine Maillet, the central issue is once again marginality, an issue which sometimes takes the form of historical narrative and sometimes probes displacements in the lives of women. Plays such as *La Sagouine* (1971) and *Evangeline deusse* (1977) – and a novel called *Mariaagélas* (1973) – at once assert the earthy independence of several Acadian women and expose the kinds of demand that others have placed upon them: they sell services, body, liquor – but they ultimately resist selling self and soul. The author (like the singer Edith Butler a student at one time of Luc Lacourcière) is an authority on Rabelaisian elements in Acadian folk literature. Repeatedly the Rabelaisian earthiness in her own works expresses the will of her characters to separate self from the 'proper' speech of authority figures. The women are all individuals, but the authority figures are always typed, as in the spiritual high seas bootlegging escapades of *Crache à Pic* (1984; translated as *The Devil Is Loose!*) or the fictional adventures of *Don l'Orignal* (1972). Individuality lies in being faithful to the truths to which custom and folk motif have given shape.

With *Pélagie-la-charrette* (1979) and its sequel *Cents ans dans les bois* (1981), Antonine Maillet animates folkloric characters by the roles they have played in Acadian history. Pélagie, for example, besides being an individual in her own right, is also the 'cart', the force around whom the expelled Acadians slowly gather and the means by which they return from Louisiana to their common homeland. She is also the centre around whom tales are told, till Acadia re-establishes itself in (and by means of) its own never-ending story. At once critique and celebration, these novels reinvest folk motif with meaning. For Carrier, and occasionally for Hodgins, parody is a necessary agent in the reconstruction of a moral mythology; for Maillet, by contrast, irony and indirection do not necessitate an inversion of form.

PARODIC CODES

The characteristic feature of contemporary parodic codes, as Linda Hutcheon (b. 1947) observes in *A Theory of Parody* (1985), is neither wit nor the impulse to deride (both of which may be absent) but the implied repetition of a second literary text. This text can be a specific work or a more general form for which examples are familiar (such as romance, detective story or melodrama). The shape of the new work is in some sense governed by the shape of the other, or the familiar old shape (with all its normative implications) is somehow reinterpreted by the character of the new (or 'intertextual') reference to it. Wit is a frequent attribute of such literary play, and the playful (often self-referential) quality of such works sometimes goes by the name the Russian critic Mikhail Bakhtin (1895–1975) gave it: 'carnavalesque'. The carnival emphasizes the vitality of the 'unofficial' culture, the masks and spaces in people's lives rather than any easy correspondence between names and things, words and events. Yet neither wit nor comic tone nor playful verbal texture denies the possibility that parodic works might at the same time perform a serious function. Some of the most formally parodic contemporary plays, poems and fictions are also among the most reformative in purpose.

There are also several whose primary purpose is to entertain. Among such works are the essays of Erika Ritter and Eric Nicol (b. 1919); the plays of Bernard Slade (b. 1930; for example, *Same Time, Next Year*, 1975) and the ebullient children's novels of Gordon Korman (b. 1963), who started to publish when he was himself a teenager. The stories and novels of David Arnason (b. 1940), David Knight (b. 1926), Jean Basile (b. 1932), John Mills (b. 1930), Stan Dragland (b. 1942) and Morley Torgov (b. 1928) also probe society satirically. While there is a judgmental edge to their comic works, readers are engaged initially by the handling of phrase and tone, appreciating the wit of both conception and execution, the incongruity that – by exaggerating 'real subjects' to laughable dimensions – draws attention to the liveable absurdities in modern society. The humour derives from readers' ability simultaneously to distinguish two or more codes of representation: one that exists in the text, one that makes a divergent 'text' out of normative experience. For example, the opening of Arnason's 'Girl and Wolf' (*The Circus Performers' Bar*, 1984) works both as an iterative fairytale, deceptively simple, and as a subversive judgment of daily life:

It is morning. The possibilities for the wolf are open and endless. The paths through the forest run in every direction. The pale green new leaves on the trees are welcome after a hard winter. The breeze is gentle and ruffles his fur. The wolf is hungry, he is always hungry. That is what it is to be a wolf. The wolf is sleek and limber. As he runs, he admires his own grace.

The red-haired girl is going to see her grandmother. The weather is the same for her, same morning, same breeze, same new green leaves. The girl is tall and well made. She has already forgotten all her mother's cautions. She is ready to talk to strangers, she is eager for strangers and adventures. A girl's life is surrounded by cautions, she is circumscribed by rules. Only a forest offers freedom.

The paths through the forest run in all directions. They meet and intersect. They double back on themselves, intertwine. There are a thousand nodes, a thousand crossings. At any one of these crossings the girl might encounter the wolf. There are so many crossings that it is inevitable that at one of them wolf and girl will meet.

The same principle underlies many passages in the works of writers such as Ducharme, Kroetsch, Hodgins, Margaret Atwood, Alice Munro, Mitchell, Metcalf, Basil Johnston and Beauchemin.

Some of the poems of Gérald Godin and the prose of Andrée Maillet are satiric in effect; and in the novels of Robertson Davies and Leo Simpson (b. 1934), wit is an essential (and deliberately misleading) element in an authorial game of indirection. Art becomes play for different reasons: sometimes joyfully (celebrating with the reader), sometimes aloofly (elevating authorial intellect above the reader), sometimes as a formal act, whereby the text works not against the activities of an implied social backdrop but against the verbal structures (hence implied expectations) that society conventionally uses. Michel Garneau's play *Les voyagements* (1977) takes the conventional image of the 'journey' to represent human progress from birth to death, but the author alters the effect of the image by having his four characters perform their roles while riding stationary exercise bicycles.

Parallels exist in the visual arts. Painters such as Greg Curnoe (1936–92), Evelyn Roth and Jack Shadbolt (1909–98) have made witty use of colour, texture, materials and form; others – Jack Bush (1909–77), Guido Molinari (b. 1933) – have painted 'pure' blocks of abstract colour to challenge the principles and expectations of formal design; Michael Snow (b. 1929) has used kinetic modes of creation (moving sculpture, collage, videotape, hologram) to celebrate art-as-process and to challenge such notions as 'universality'. In Martin Vaughn-James's (b. 1943) *The Cage* (1975), a sequence of drawings turns into a 'visual-novel' or narrative of signs rather than words. In bp Nichol's 'Captain Poetry' sequence, poetry even turns into comic strip (and vice versa).

As it is with sight, so with sound. Murray Schafer's (b. 1933) music challenges conventional harmonies, venues for performance and instrumentation, and his several essays reflect both on his musical intentions and on the current status of music in Canada. The 'performance poetry' of a group like the Four Horsemen (bp Nichol, Steve McCaffery, b. 1947, Rafael Barreto-Rivera, b. 1944, Paul Dutton, b. 1943), which formed in 1970 – or the sound poetry of Doug Barbour, the songs of Gilbert Langevin (b. 1939), and the mantric chanting of Bill Bissett – stresses the significance that can be conjured out of sounds and simple syllables, complexly framed or arranged. At the same time, as is clear in the poems of Péloquin and Duguay, sound and syllable could also be made to challenge the authority of language entirely, to deny the conventions of 'meaning'. Hence the amusing face of parodic formulation exists on a continuum with revolutionary deconstruction; one position asks readers to recognize the foolishness of the society of which they are a part, the other asserts the absurdity of recognizing society at all.

Part way between these extremes, the prose of Jacques Ferron – which amounted to more than thirty volumes – mediated between a desire for Quebec's political independence and a jocular suspicion of the efficacy of politics. The brother of Madeleine Ferron, he (like her) drew extensively on the folk forms of Quebec writing, especially the Gaspé *conte*. In his *Contes du pays incertain* (1962), *Contes anglais et autres*, and *Contes inédits* (1968), he used ironic fable and allegory to champion political causes. In doing so, he also criticized the 'two-solitudes' version of Canada (making MacLennan and F. R. Scott the butt of his ridicule of English-Canadian cultural designs) and the passivity of many Quebec writers, who preferred anguish and alienation to an active cultural engagement. Himself a doctor, Ferron repeatedly turns a medical figure into a cultural 'healer' in his fiction. But as a more direct action, Ferron founded the absurdist Rhinoceros Party, entering the federal political scene. Rhinoceros candidates vowed not to serve if elected, devised intentionally silly solutions to significant problems, satirized real political bungling – and won a remarkable degree of public support, outpolling candidates for some traditional parties in several ridings.

The political reverberations of Ferron's games with absurdity are most evident in one of the 1962 stories, 'Mélie et le boeuf': here the favourite calf of a typical literary *québécois* mother grows up into an English bull, which promptly tramples through the rural traditions of the entire countryside. Similar kinds of foreshortened narrative characterized Ferron's longer tales as well. In *Cotnoir* (1962), *La charrette* (1968), *Le salut de l'Irlande* (1970), and *La chaise du maréchal ferrant* (1972), Ferron played with deliberate anachronism, much as George Bowering did in *Burning Water*, though Bowering's purpose was to reconstruct self and literary method, Ferron's to reconstruct attitudes towards society. In so doing, he encouraged a reassessment of the workings (and relevance) of history by combating its received definitions of sequence and person. Hence Ferron himself, together with his conservative father (whom Ferron rejected), Duplessis and Mackenzie King (whom Ferron casts as villains), the 1837 Patriotes (appearing in his 1958 play *Les grands soleils* as well as in his longest novel *Le ciel de Québec*, 1969), the FLQ, 'Frank Scot', and various devils and figures of magical folklore all walk in and out of his tales, oblivious to time.

As they enter each other's presence they alter the character of the identity Quebec can claim. In *Le ciel de Québec*, for example, with a canvas of scores of fictionalized historical figures, Duplessis becomes Prometheus, Saint-Denys Garneau becomes Orpheus, Camille Roy holds mass, and Borduas, Riel, Gauvreau and Garibaldi all appear against a background that joins *conte* with Greek myth and *Alice in Wonderland*. The sequential world is overturned. Ray Ellenwood (b. 1939), who translated the book in 1985 as *The Penniless Redeemer* (basing his work on Ferron's 1979 revision, published by Victor-Lévy Beaulieu, b. 1945) quotes Philippe Haeck's enthusiasm for the novel – 'our great and only novel of initiation ... our Bible' – praising its ability to join polemic with aesthetic fidelity. In particular Ferron's polemic attacked the Jansenist version of Quebec, a version perpetuated by both English-Canadian expectation and *québécois* surrender to personal angst. Hence *anglais* writers like Glassco and Drummond (and their versions of Quebec) come in for parodic attack; even more so does Saint-Denys Garneau, whose poetry of anguish, according to the novel, became a limited cult in the 1930s (and was mistakenly claimed to be universal) at precisely the time Quebeckers should have been engaging actively in local politics. Parody thus celebrates the self rather than perpetuates self-abnegation. Catholicism, Ferron argues, is larger than Jansenism (an issue on which he agrees with the poet Pierre Morency); and social engagement can both substitute for and provide a solution to the limitations of the Jansenist mind-body dualism.

Like Ferron, Audrey Thomas also drew on *Alice in Wonderland* as an inferential text against which to measure the events of her own fiction; for her, Alice (and at other times Shakespeare's Miranda, as in *Prospero on the Island*, 1971) are paradigms for a feminist reconstruction of role-playing. Other writers drew on a range of different literary patterns: whether as functional allusions (as when Michel Garneau adapts *The Tempest* and *Macbeth*, or Alden Nowlan and Walter Learning, b. 1939, turn *Frankenstein* into a play); as a structural paradigm (as when Dubé makes *Au retour des oies blanches*, 1969, follow the pattern of *Oedipus the King*, or Ken Mitchell bases his 1976 rock opera *Cruel Tears* on *Othello*); as a formal authority (as when poets as different as Cécile Cloutier, b. 1930, Daryl Hine, b. 1936, Richard Outram, b. 1930, Robin Skelton, Francis Sparshott or Peter Van Toorn, b. 1944, write *haiku* or emulate Classical poetic models); or as the base for an oblique comment on contemporary literature and society. Louky Bersianik's *Pique-nique sur l'Acropole* is to be seen as a critical comment on the limitations of 'recorded history'; it depicts a woman's picnic on the Acropolis at the time of Plato's *Symposium* (but pointedly neglected by it), and examines the articulate lives that, taken together, trace an independent history of women. Gurik's *Hamlet, prince du Québec* re-enacts Shakespeare in modern political masks; Dave Godfrey's *Death Goes Better with Coca-Cola* inverts a popular commercial slogan in its title, to make a point about the ownership and marketing of culture; in many instances Gertrude Stein stands behind the poems of bp Nichol and George Bowering, as does French critical theory behind those of Alexandre Amprimoz (b. 1948). Bowering's *The Kerrisdale Elegies* (1984), however, recasts Rilke's *The Duino Elegies* in suburban Vancouver, reflecting on the resonance of language, rejecting despair, and finally finding occasion to celebrate life and age – the echoes of the original poem in this case shaping not a comic but a meditative counterpoint. Leo Simpson's *The Peacock Papers* (1973) owes its tone and style to Thomas Love Peacock (1785–1866); Chris Scott's (b. 1945) *Bartleby* (1971) plays with the style of various other authors (Melville, 1819–91, and Fielding, 1701–54, among them) in order to take authority over identity away from the author and give it back to words. Scott's characters are a mélange from other people's books (not unlike some of Leacock's reinventions of Dickensian characters). Whereas Leacock's figures offered a spirited defence of Dickens's ability to create character, however, Scott's collected characters (speaking here in their several original styles) become annoyed with their new 'author's' attempts to control them, therefore hide chapters from him, assert their own independence from authorship, and play other metatextual games. Victor-Lévy Beaulieu's several novels, plays and television serials also draw on Melville, and on several other literary models: Lowry, Kerouac, Hugo – and in *Don Quichotte de la démanche* (1974), Joyce and Cervantes (1547–1616). An influential publisher, first with Jacques Hébert's (b. 1923) Éditions du Jour and then with his own firm, VLB Éditeurs (which he established with Jean-Claude Germain, Michel Garneau, Gilbert LaRocque and others), Beaulieu has cast his own fiction in a multivolume cycle called 'La vraie saga des

Beauchemin'. Repeatedly, too, he interrupts this sequence (itself punctuated by the erotic imaginations and punning sensibilities of contemporary urban culture) with extended essays on authorial creativity. *Monsieur Melville* (1978) runs to three volumes. The point is to emphasize not the linearity of creation but the reintegrative processes of imagination; in the author's mind, all of creation takes place at once – hence the punning technique, the concern for simultaneous meanings. Creation takes place, moreover, in several contexts, involving both society and other writers' fabricated worlds.

Parodic forms are attempts to achieve self-expression without resorting either to actual violence or to the familiar techniques of social representation; they occur most frequently within a frame of reference involving received language and tradition but are themselves gestures against passive surrender to such traditions. The mockery that exists in the distance between subject and language, or between the new text and the model with which it obliquely connects, establishes the voice of the present as an independent one, however marked it is by place, past, class and gender. Yet not all efforts that were parodic by impulse could sustain the distance they established between self and society. For some writers – Yves Préfontaine, Michel van Schendel – political commitment resulted more in a poetry of impassioned direct statement than in a poetry of metonymic implication. For others – André Roy (influenced by cinematic technique), Alexis Lefrançois (b. 1943, fond of phonetic spellings), François Charron (responding still to Borduas) – language itself was incapable of 'distance' until it was fractured, distorted, taken out of its linear mould. For the poet Roland Giguère, imagination was a subversive act, the surreal its most potent expression. Fragmentation became a theme in its own right, the body of order replacing a poetry of infinite space. Charron's *Peinture automatiste* preceded by *Qui parle dans la théorie* (1979) conducts a textual conversation with *Refus Global* in order at once to claim the artistic or imaginative freedom of *automatisme* and to recognize the inevitability of there being historical analogues for any new work, and hence a historicity of context and implication.

In some sense this dilemma was the one that confronted, energized, and confounded Hubert Aquin. A committed worker on behalf of Quebec independence, Aquin published only a few novels during his short lifetime: *Prochain épisode* (1965), *Trou de mémoire* 1968, translated as *Blackout*), *L'antiphonaire* (1969), *Point de fuite* (1971, which punningly refers to 'un canadien errant', reiterating the 1837 political resistance theme), and *Neige noire* (1974, translated as *Hamlet's Twin*). He was working on another, called *Obombre*, in later years. He

quarrelled publicly with many established Quebec figures, from
Roger Lemelin of *La Presse* (whom he saw as a perpetuator of Quebec's colonial status), to René Lévesque (whose Parti Québécois he
considered a dilution of the will to achieve independence by revolution). He quit the board of *Liberté* and refused the Governor General's
Award when it was awarded him in 1969. He called himself a terrorist, and he was arrested in 1964 for terrorist activity (he wrote his first
novel while incarcerated). His novels take the form of parodic detective stories – in which the reader participates in working out cause,
means and figures responsible for action – ultimately implicating
both reader and writer in revolutionary activity. But in his personal
life, parodic distance was impossible. He identified with Quebec, and
others identified him with a revolutionary free future; when he committed suicide in 1977, a wave of public empathy transformed him
(as years earlier it had transformed Nelligan) into another symbol of
cultural sacrifice. This last public act, like his political activities and
his novels themselves, was a defiance of the paralysis he perceived to
be Quebec's historical inheritance; yet it was also a negation. The
paradox seemed to suggest to him the possibility of transformation:
out of destruction would come the new order.

The novels – influenced by Robbe-Grillet (b. 1922) and Nabokov
(1899–1977), often employing mirror techniques – tell of characters
whose lives make similar points about Quebec's cultural crisis. The
lead characters of *Trou de mémoire* and *L'antiphonaire* commit suicide;
the denial of life – blasphemous and violent by conventional terms –
is made the symbolic equivalent of a moment of cultural rebirth.
Recurrently two styles interweave: one mimicking the constrained
voices of the present, another lyrically anticipating the revolutionary
future. The violence that exists in the detective-novel form, moreover,
has for Aquin a further counterpart in Quebec history, expressed
most obviously in *Trou de mémoire*, where rape is associated with the
1759 'Conquest' of Quebec and with imperialism in colonial cultures
generally. In turn, this historical consciousness both invites and justi-
fies for him the new violence he espoused. *Prochain épisode* is ostensibly a tale of a separatist who writes a novel to escape from his present constrained circumstances and to recapture his revolutionary
idealism. In the story-within-a-story, the fictional hero is also a separatist, also constrained – physically, by being resident abroad in
Switzerland, and attitudinally, by being a hesitant artist rather than
an active fighter – who discovers that his establishment antagonist
(one H. de Heutz) is also his double or brother. Paradigms of a fractured Quebec, the 'brothers' mirror those parts of the society that severally embrace and reject 'English Canada.' The cinematic novel

Neige noire, however, echoing *Hamlet* (itself unfolding through internally framed plays), ultimately proves a treatise in despair. Formally it tries to be a revolutionary act in its own right, engaging the reader, but (like *Hamlet*) its message is one about hesitation and delay, about the inertia of an inherited history that never quite allows a fresh start. The delay necessitates acts of greater magnitude and violence as signs of a break with the past, action and reaction repeatedly doubling in an infinite regress from effective change.

While parodic form thus led Aquin into psychological entanglements with political stasis, the technique he used – one which he shared with numerous other 'post-modernist' writers of the 1970s – called for reconsideration of the language in literary use in Canada and of its philosophical presumptions. Representational techniques (and assumptions) were anathema. Language was its own territory, self-referential, the field on which imagination played. At one extreme, language was pure game, and for many readers objectionable because it appeared to spurn any of the familiar bases of literary form: narrative pattern, moral, social import, logic. But the 'pure' extreme was rare: most post-modernist works were exercises in rearrangement. For this very reason, they drew (parodically) on the most easily accepted (and therefore the least questioned) forms of popular culture: adventure novels, thrillers, detective and horror stories, B-movies, comic strips, romances. In the popcult forms, such genres perpetuate myths of region (the 'Western'), gender roles (dark macho hero, fainting submissive heroine), ethnicity and politics (the spy novel), values (those of the status quo). One form of rearrangement was to shape language so that violence and discrimination (rather than language by itself, oaths of bodily function or blasphemy) came to be seen as the true pornography of the times. Another was to adopt the popcult form as a mock model, as in several volumes of stories by Leon Rooke (including the fabular *Cry Evil*, 1980) or in George Bowering's fictional excursion through the artifice of the Canadian novel, *A Short Sad Book* (1977), or in Bowering's parody of the Western, *Caprice* (1987), or in Allan Stratton's (b. 1951) play *Nurse Jane Goes to Hawaii* (1981), or in poems by Bowering, Ondaatje, Margaret Atwood, Dennis Cooley and others. Here the texts shift arbitrarily from one convention to another, so that language comes to celebrate (often comically) the freedom of the imagination from the strictures of social and literary routine, if not always from the terrors and trials of human relationships.

Pierre Turgeon (b. 1947) and Jean-Marie Poupart (b. 1946) both wrote novels based on detective stories and murder mysteries. The novels of Robertson Davies can be read in a similar light, as ghost stories or detective thrillers, burnished by a high style; but their greater popularity with a general readership than the more determined post-modernists enjoy (Robert Kroetsch, for example) suggests that Davies's novels argue less with the status quo. Characteristically, the popcult format throws an historical subject or literary prototype into (bizarre, refreshing, instructive) relief. For example, Chris Scott's *Antichthon* (1982) uses the spy novel format to consider the implications of the Inquisition's control over the public utterances of Giordano Bruno (c. 1548–1600); to question the received forms of historical fiction in turn questions the validity of official history. Yves Beauchemin's *Le Matou* (1981, translated as *The Alley Cat*) joins the suspense novel to the sentimental romance; inhabiting his pages with the figures of *contes* in modern dress (devil-outsider, wayward child, magical transformer, devoted lover), Beauchemin sardonically tells a moralistic picaresque tale about the ambition of a foolish young man and the events that bring him traumatically to ordinary maturity. The playwrights Hrant Alianak (b. 1950) and Jean Barbeau (b. 1945) variously adapted received traditions to popular experience; Alianak turned *Titus Andronicus* into a western, and Barbeau's 1972 *Manon Lastcall* mixed a 'high' culture into the romantic life of an urban waitress. Leon Rooke's novel *Shakespeare's Dog* (1983) played with history by using a dog as narrator (a dog equipped with Elizabethan vocabulary and syntax) to document the Stratford life of the soon-to-be-great London playwright. Antonine Maillet's works at once acknowledge and reject Longfellow's popular, familiar, but inauthentic 'Evangeline' version of history.

Michael Ondaatje, in his discontinuous poetic narrative *The Collected Works of Billy the Kid* (1970), collapsed the divisions between history and legend in order to probe the boundary worlds between sanity and insanity, between self and other, between reason and imagination, between an outlaw dream of America and the fantastic reality of American violence. Ondaatje collapsed genre distinctions as well, invited genres to enter into a kind of dialogue with each other; like his contemporary David Young (b. 1946), author of the mock-confessional autobiography *Incognito* (1982), he introduced photographs into his text, pushing at the barrier that divides *watch* from *see*, *artist-observer* from *reader-voyeur*. (In turn, Ondaatje's poem became another literary stimulus – it was dramatized at Stratford, and Ondaatje's friend bp Nichol, about whom Ondaatje had made a film, promptly wrote a comic version of 'Billy'.) Another poem, 'White Dwarfs', recounts the tantalizing temptations of uncertainty, whether to live in combat, popular thriller, space exploration, or poetry:

This is for people who disappear
for those who descend into the code
and make their room a fridge for Superman
…
this is for those people
that hover and hover
and die in the ether peripheries

There is my fear
of no words   of
falling without words
over and over   of
mouthing the silence
Why do I love most
among my heroes those
who sail to that perfect edge
where there is no social fuel

George Walker's (b. 1947) plays – like *Zastrozzi* (1977), *Beyond Mozambique* (1978), or *Criminals in Love* (1985) – drew on cinematic stereotypes to pierce the ennui of contemporary existential thought; witty dialogues and absurd juxtapositions comically expose the extent of middle-class despair. Timothy Findley variously took the war novel, the chronicle of political intrigue, the love story involving the Duke and Duchess of Windsor, and the story of Noah's Ark and turned them all into contemporary fables about the sources of violence and separation. In many cases, the pop treatment of serious subjects appeared flippant to readers, but for the writers this methodology offered a way of freeing various subjects from the unthinking vacuity of cliché. These works all ask to be read purposefully. Réjean Ducharme attacked verbal convention in a critically more elaborate way, by writing his novel *La fille de Christophe Colomb* (1969) as a mock epic entirely in ridiculous verse. Such a work asks finally what 'meaning' means, or if it can mean anything at all. If it cannot, then what can 'civilization' mean, or 'history' or 'tradition' or 'culture'? The short stories of Raymond Fraser and the plays of René-Daniel Dubois (b. 1955) similarly resist 'interpretation'. By contrast, the works of Margaret Atwood and Audrey Thomas deliberately invite interpretation, partly by taking familiar stories – the tale of Bluebeard in Atwood's *Bluebeard's Egg* (1983), the fairytale of Rapunzel in Thomas's *Ladies & Escorts* (1977) – and overturning their conventional implications. Convention is a frame, etymology a game of revelation that takes apart fixed limits of meaning. *Pain*, for Audrey

Thomas, is a bilingual pun – most amusing, most devastating, she comments, when it is to be 'baked fresh daily'. She sees the 'other' in 'mother', the 'over' in 'lover'. Words tell stories. Framing the familiar, such stories then become narratives about the unstated and implied.

With the work of Robert Kroetsch, Timothy Findley and Margaret Atwood, literature (in several genres) repeatedly turned into meditations on the power of words to create alternatives and the power of people to resist them. Like many Canadian writers before them (Roberts, Klein, Hébert, Roy), they have written in various modes. All three are novelists and essayists, Kroetsch and Atwood critics and poets, Findley and Atwood short story writers, Findley a dramatist and (sometimes with William Whitehead, b. 1931) a TV scriptwriter, Atwood a librettist, children's writer, anthologist, social activist (with Amnesty International), painter, and cartoonist (for *This Magazine*). In some sense (as with Nicole Brossard) the use of various genres is an attempt to collapse old distinctions, an impulse which shows up also in the character of particular works. Kroetsch concerns himself with clarifying the authenticity of a region's voice (that of the prairies), Margaret Atwood with the differing perspectives of women, Findley with modifying social attitudes, particularly those involving confrontation. There are other differences. Findley and Margaret Atwood, both with family connections to the Ontario Establishment, adopt and quarrel with the language of small-town Loyalist authority; Kroetsch, the Albertan, locates in his version of Canada an apposite ground for the discontinuous structures of post-modernism. All three, however, rely on literary structures involving parallels and correspondences rather than systems of identification; the result is a series of works in which dualism of various kinds seems to predominate, but in practice such divisions prove misleading. In Margaret Atwood's *Surfacing* (1972), for example, a nationalist character identifies crude hunters as 'American', until she finds out that they are Canadians in name; the author is making a cultural point about unexpected overlap, about a need to recognize the 'Americanness' in Canada. The central character must purge herself of various kinds of such linguistic classification, all of them interfering with her authentic self-expression. In Findley, divisions often come together in a single image, as when (at the end of the flood story in *Not Wanted on the Voyage*, 1984), rain works at once as a hint of hope for a humane future and a despairing reminder of the extent of human viciousness and suffering. In Kroetsch's work, even more than that of the others, two separate narrative lines or two forms of poetic structure interweave, often apparently arbitrarily, emphasizing discontinuity rather than sequence. But the discontinuities work with their own associative logic, requiring the reader to participate in the process of assembling meaning. Language is itself a process, not a body of fixed terms. Hence language-in-creative-action requires the reader to shake free from the limits of conventional association and follow the texts wherever they lead.

For Kroetsch, the problem has never been what story to tell, but always how to tell it: how to use language in order that the reader will not mistakenly hear an old story, rooted elsewhere, instead. In his poem *Seed Catalogue* (1977) – part of a longer continuing sequence, collected in interim form as *Field Notes* (1981) – he asks this question in a set of cumulative variants: how do you grow a garden, a gardener, a lover, a poet, a shared past, a prairie town? The answer to the last question lies in the form the language takes – in an image of history (temporary town, momentarily on the landscape, a cycle repeated many times) that is as kinesthetic as it is visual, occupying rhythm and tempo:

> the gopher was the model.
> Stand up straight:
> telephone poles
> grain elevators
> church steeples.
> Vanish, suddenly: the
> gopher was the model.

Kroetsch's early novels show him moving gradually away from an externally rooted literary past towards one in which the old identities are fragmented and reconstructed. His experience editing the postmodernist journal *Boundary 2*, during his fourteen-year stint teaching in Binghamton, New York, urged him critically in this direction.

Later novels – *Gone Indian* (1973), *Badlands* (1975), *Alibi* (1983) – drew on myths from several sources (Cree, Norse, Greek, Latin American) not for their psychological pattern (as Davies, for example, would employ them) but for their implications about the role of narrative in society. By the time of *The Studhorse Man* (1969) – the second volume of his 'Out West' trilogy, which *Gone Indian* concluded – he had written a parodic version of the *Odyssey*, in which the title character's ironic quest for a brood mare for his stallion Poseidon re-enacts in local terms Odysseus's many adventures. Anti-heroic, Hazard Lepage's escapades are bawdy, comic and metatextual more than mythic and romantic: it is, in other words, impossible to 'read' the West in the old mythic terms, which are not universal. Poseidon (whose nicknames Posse, Poesy, and Pussy spell out the fields that Hazard ventures into) may be an agent of fate (*mare/mer*: the punning recurrently invites the reader to make misleading identifications) but he is no god. The narrative point of view – the tale is recounted by Hazard's mad cousin Demeter Proudfoot, from his bathtub – constantly undermines the heroic parallels. It is, in fact, Demeter's crazy vision that attempts to order Hazard's life by means of the *Odyssey*. If there is rebirth here, it is finally out of myth into reality. The local forms of narrative, Kroetsch observes about Alberta in his later *The 'Crow' Journals* (1980), a documentary companion to his ebullient, Marquezian *What the Crow Said*, 1978), are anecdotal. The anecdotal tall tale, moreover, is a form that exaggerates and fantasizes, and invites deconstruction. So, for Kroetsch, is academic criticism: speech is play. Literature, therefore, is an ongoing set of 'field notes' – the characters in *Badlands* even have a specific set of geological field notes to decipher (one modelled in turn on an historical set) – or verbal gestures of where the author has been. They ask to be put together, but they resist being put together in one way only, calling attention instead to the ways in which the power of imaginative recreation lies within the reader's mind, and underscoring the need in any society to shape the received past anew and read the fragmented present through terms appropriate to it.

In Timothy Findley's fiction, reading the past (and the present through the past) results in other kinds of textual structure. *The Wars* (1977) – Findley's third novel – adopts a contrast between photographic technique and narrative history. As in Rudy Wiebe's story 'Where Is the Voice Coming From?' it is art more than the journal entry or the snapshot which has the power to make others 'see'. But 'seeing' (as in Clark Blaise's 'Eyes') engages viewers in complicity with what they perceive. In this First World War story of a young man's commitment to life (figured in his devotion to animals), readers are made witnesses to the way family pride, social status, sexual assault, moral passivity and political inertia all destroy him. What is it, Findley asks, that separates people from each other – separates them from 'nature' – induces them to violence? A question that haunts his earlier fiction, it is one that centrally occupies the three novels that were immediately to follow *The Wars*. *Famous Last Words* (1981) tells of the rise of fascism in the 1930s and its possession of European civilization. *The Telling of Lies* (1986) probes the meaning of 'complicity'. *Not Wanted on the Voyage* (1984) elaborates the narrative of the Flood, casting God as an ageing magician, Lucifer as a female wilderness angel of natural imagination, Mr Noyes as a social pretender in love more with dynastic power than with people, and Mrs

Noyes as the protector of affection and animals, whose desperate efforts are not enough to save the fairies, the dragons and the gentle unicorns from manic destruction.

Once again, speech is both medium and subject, the means by which history is conveyed and the architect of the kinds of values people choose (or are allowed) to remember. Power over speech controls the shape of the past; power over the past controls the mind of the present and the kind of future that the present can conceive. Findley's fictions concern fascist impulses in the North American present, therefore, as much as they recreate versions of a European inheritance. They ask about the absences in history, the fictions that societies create in the name of culture and the greater desire for power. *Famous Last Words* emphasizes this paradox by giving the history of fascism to a fictional character (Ezra Pound's, 1885–1972, Hugh Selwyn Mauberley, who has written it out on hotel walls, to be found and read, and ill understood, at the end of the Second World War), and by making historical figures (the Windsors, von Ribbentrop, 1893–1946, Sir Harry Oakes, 1874–1943) the subjects of fictional narrative. Who does a society regard as its elite, Findley asks – and concurrently, what values do they share with the people at large? In the name of purification (of the language, the culture, the tribe), what evils do they perpetuate as truth?

For Margaret Atwood, this question recurs in terms involving society and gender. In an early volume of poetry, *The Circle Game* (1966), she examined the ways by which (in Rosemary Sullivan's, b. 1947, phrase) people 'invent convenient versions' of themselves, using stereotypes and conventions of language and 'belief' to exclude from their consideration whatever is uncertain, unknown, or threatening. 'Journey to the Interior' muses:

> A compass is useless; also
> trying to take directions
> from the movements of the sun,
> which are erratic;
> and words here are as pointless
> as calling in a vacant
> wilderness.
>   Whatever I do I must
> keep my head. I know
> it is easier for me to lose my way
> forever here, than in other landscapes

Later poems consider this impulse as an aspect of colonialism – the colonizers' refusal to recognize the virtues in a society different from their own. In *Power Politics* (1973) and *You Are Happy* (1974) – as in her novels *The Edible Woman* (1969) and *Life Before Man* (1979) and her critical book *Survival* (1972) – she considers women's lives as submissive territories colonized by men, though the aphoristic wit and ironic edge to her language recognize other possibilities, and play with images of role-reversal.

> Next time we commit
> love, we ought to
> choose in advance what to kill.

In *True Stories* (1981), some of the short stories in *Bluebeard's Egg*, and the novel *Bodily Harm* (1981) – variously echoing works by V.S. Naipaul, Joan Didion (b. 1934), and Derek Walcott (b. 1930) – the two motifs of gender and politics overlap. Portraits of women as victims and tourists intersect with reflections on the imperial role Canada plays in the Caribbean, blithely unaware of the extent of its own ignorance about 'truth' and violence. *Bodily Harm* extends a further theme, evident earlier in novels like *Life Before Man* (1979, set in the halls of the Royal Ontario Museum) and *Lady Oracle* (1976, concerning the domestic relationships that bedevil the life of a Costume Romance writer): language. The author, by framing the narrative codes of conventional romance in *Lady Oracle*, for example, asks how romance language has been used to control versions of the norms of social reality (such as heterosexuality; domesticity; power; the male rituals of sport, game and hunt; the aesthetic that evaluates the romance itself). Such language denies women positions of effective social equality. Like the 'historical' work that depicts oral cultures and draws on oral techniques – thus calling itself into question, challenging the system that equates written history with civilization and so gives it precedence – these fictions use the technique of literary structure to challenge the frames of enclosure and the aesthetic of 'wholeness'.

Repeatedly, Margaret Atwood's work illustrates the degree to which her own language derives from Loyalist Ontario. While *Lady Oracle* shows her talent for pastiche (her subjects being always elliptically grounded in small-town behaviour), her comments are not always so overt. *Bodily Harm*, though set in the Caribbean, linguistically declares that its main concern is the restraint imposed on political articulateness by the 'circle game' of the small-town Loyalist inheritance *in Canada*. The (ironic) inherited language is, therefore, both an inhibition and the chief available means by which to free oneself from inhibition. The imagination that will not extend to other possibilities – for reasons of fear or reasons of purity (perhaps the same) – is doomed to atrophy; further, by so refusing (by appearing to distance 'wilderness') such a mind opens its society to the greater violence of rigid order. The prose poems of *Murder in the Dark* (1985) adapt the speech of thrillers to address the character of language directly: the nature of the 'true story', the writer suggests, is designed to entice readers out of the circle, make them question their familiar ease with cliché and their presumptions about the safety of the world.

But reconstructing has its own dangers, as *The Handmaid's Tale* (1985) makes clear. Set in twenty-first century America (by this time a theocracy called the Republic of Gilead), this dystopian novel speculates about present-day trends: the verbal controls that commercial advertising exerts over roles and expectations, the legal controls that society claims over women's lives and bodies, the active will to assert power, the passive wish for anonymity that leads many people to surrender authority to institutions, the existence of economic structures more powerful than legislative ones, the resurgence of influential fundamentalist groups that imposed preconceived boundaries around the design of truth. These, too, are circle games in the Atwood lexicon. Nothing that happens in the novel is without some basis in current practice in the 1980s. What happens, however, involves a wilful reorganization of society to deny women any rights at all. They lose identities (there are few choices). If they are fertile, they can become 'handmaids' or official child-bearers for the largely infertile elite, in which case they are named only by their relation to the one they service: 'Offred', for example, 'Ofwarren', 'Ofglen'. Or they can become nuclear waste cleaners, with limited expectations of a lifespan; or temporary 'illicit' mistresses with no status and no expectations of the future; or 'Aunts' or 'Wives'.

The roles of Aunts and Wives – members of the corporate structure, therefore part of the problem for other women – shows how a 'nice' language can be made to reshape truth for political purposes: a language can be corrupted, and can corrupt, and people will not complain. 'Angels', 'Eyes', 'Guardians': these persons no longer watch over, they now spy out. They purge society of resistant elements, they manipulate judgment (the wives, not incidentally, all bear names derived from household products currently advertised on television), they rely for their own position on sanctioned violence and fear. 'Alternative codes' (and here Atwood is questioning the rigidity of certain brands of revolutionary rhetoric as well as that of the status quo) all run the danger of reconstructing society and leaving freedom, individuality, choice and imagination – leaving people, in other words – out of account. The problem is that, even though words hypothesize truths, people recurrently react to them morally, preferring to read them not as a dialectical arrangement but as an absolute fix on reality. The novel not only raises this issue, it also enacts it formally. Ostensibly the diary notes of 'Offred', a rebel-handmaid, the whole narrative is thrown into uncertainty by a final frame: one in which twenty-first-century historians gather (in the Arctic) to 'reconstruct' or interpret the past. Art and history are themselves framing systems, the frame itself a code. By framing the central narrative as a *mise en scène*, the author calls attention to absences, that which is not said, or not yet said, as well as to the controls that the frame exerts over perspective. By fracturing the frame, however, she at the same time resists current systems of enclosure and categorization.

EPILOGUE

The categories and frames in this chapter therefore also come into question. They constitute not systems of definition (or a pattern of 'progress') so much as a network of connections amongst forms and themes, between writers, their society and the language they use. In Canadian literature the language is plural, the network of associations (both within the country and beyond its political boundaries) complex. Few writers can adequately be contained by a single classification. Few write completely in isolation or anonymity. Most write with a particular context in view, which critical generalizations sometimes cloud.

In the two decades following 1960, while many writers continued to reach beyond national borders for parallels, personal interest and measurements of difference, more and more writers in both official languages were responding directly to traditions inside their own country. The mythmakers, journalists and storytellers who preceded them became consciously part of the context within which they wrote. To acknowledge a tradition, however, is not to be bound by it. Contemporary writers reinterpreted their literary inheritance in their own terms, for their own time. They shaped the words of speech and history into the malleable forms of a contemporary art. Further changes will follow.

The tendency towards fracture, discontinuity, uncertainty and disorder that characterizes so much writing of the 1970s and 1980s is therefore not fixed. Its purpose is clear: to challenge the status quo, an aim not yet necessarily realized. But the renewed literary interest in distant historical subjects already perhaps signals a shift in direction. Other indications of change are both political and verbal. They include the upsurge of indigenous writing, the influence of multiculturalism, the innovative experiments with drama and the long poem, the revival of a formal literary language and conventional poetic patterns, the retreat from the vernacular, the engagement with sophisticated literary theory, and the persistence of several codes of ethical and aesthetic belief. Because 'definitions' of inheritance and culture remain in flux, change will likely take several simultaneous forms.

CHAPTER SIX

Reconstructors: literature into the twenty-first century

DEMOGRAPHY, POLITICS, TECHNOLOGY

After 1984, conventional versions of Canadian nationhood went through another sequence of adjustments, partly political in origin, partly technological, partly demographic, but all far-reaching in their implications. To begin with, the demographics of the baby-boom generation (those people who in the latter decades of the twentieth century reached the ages of thirty, forty, and fifty, and were planning for retirement at least as early as 2010) affected everything from fashion and income distribution to social policies governing health care, education, and other systems of community support. The so-called echo boom (the children born to boomers in their thirties and forties, rather than in their twenties, as had been conventional for an earlier generation), together with other statistical factors, affected the social dynamic but were often not taken adequately into account by the architects of social planning.

For example, the birth rate in Quebec, in the wake of legislative changes introduced after the Quiet Revolution (divorce became a less cumbersome procedure; the advertising and sale of birth control measures were made legal), plummeted to the lowest in the country, an effect that the Catholic Church deplored and that the provincial government tried to counter through tax measures and immigration. Immigration continued to be a solution to population decline. With changes in federal immigration policy late in the century, more (and larger) families were moving to Canada from Asia and Latin America. There were consequences for the teaching of English and French as 'second languages'; given the demand for language fluency and cultural integration, these programs were inconsistently funded. In some urban schools, up to 95 per cent of students spoke neither

English nor French as their mother tongue at home, and by 2002, something in the order of a third of Canada's entire population had been born outside the country. In Quebec, where the criterion of language effectively governed local immigration policy, the numbers of French speakers from Haiti, Vietnam, and West and North Africa increased, altering some long-held (if historically inexact) assumptions about ethnic and cultural uniformity in the province.

Demographics and technology interconnected when the 'computer revolution' of the 1980s and 1990s profoundly altered both domestic and industrial behaviour. By the end of the century, all of the following had become commonplace: e-mail communication, electronic publishing and graphic design, cellphone miniaturization, on-line banking and shopping, redefinitions of the traditional workplace, and a 'bubble' in tech stock sales. The 'Y2K' fear of computer meltdown diverted millions of dollars from the service economy into programming repair (early programming had not adequately planned for the year 2000, when the century number changed from 19 to 20: the fear was that automatic year-end financial conversions would not take place because the pre-set programs would crash and mass industrial confusion would follow; in fact, the transition took place smoothly). Douglas Coupland (b. 1961) gave a name to the generation that first learned from childhood the intricacies of computer technology, especially in his first book, *Generation X* (1991).

The term referred to people born between 1958 and 1968 (in the wake of the baby boom or yuppie generation). Coupland portrayed them as both economically engaged and emotionally insecure, and he designed for them a language of sound bites instead of extended substance, witty in order to stave off desperation. This group and its language gave rise to a fashion for urban chic, as in the writings of Russell Smith (b. 1963) and Zsuzsi Gartner (b. 1960). It was perhaps inevitable that the much smaller generation that followed 'X' should come to be known as 'Generation Y'; this group, however, faced unemployment and other restrictions on opportunity. By 2001, as the international economy was teetering into recession, many Canadians were espousing religious fundamentalism, unfettered individualism, and closer political links with the USA as solutions to the fear they felt about the future and as expressions of the dissatisfactions they were experiencing in their own lives. Frustration leads, as sociologists have often demonstrated, to sudden shifts in direction and action. They are not always productive. Hence many other people were seeking more practical solutions and more constructive measures to secure social equity.

These contrary directions were signalled in a variety of political decisions, social acts, economic policy changes, changes in literary fashions, and often abrupt shifts in popular taste. One such marker of social attitude was the election of Brian Mulroney's Progressive Conservative government federally in 1984, with consequences affecting social policy and American relations. Others include the international success of Canadian musical and theatrical figures, both popular and classical (Céline Dion, The Barenaked Ladies, Ashley MacIsaac, Sarah McLachlan, Shania Twain, The Tragically Hip, Alanis Morissette, Ben Heppner, Richard Margison, Diana Krall, and Mike Myers, among numerous others). Increased international attention also turned to Canadian writers. But 'globalism' created problems as well. On one particular front, the so-called 'fish wars' with France and Spain in the 1990s, and with the USA in 1997, when an Alaska ferry was embargoed in Prince Rupert, B.C., occurred because of disputes over the survival of the Atlantic cod and Pacific salmon stocks; while these 'wars' were earnest if ineffective responses to the problem of overfishing in both the Atlantic and Pacific Oceans (and frustration at the apparent reluctance of government bodies to secure solutions), they were treated by some commentators as comic footnotes to the main action. Writers of fiction and social analysis (as in books by Lisa Appignanesi [b. Elsbieta Borenstejn, 1946] and Nora Kelly, b. 1945) dealt much more seriously with the Montreal Massacre, a criminal act that took place in December 1989, when a gunman named Marc Lepine burst into a Université de Montréal engineering classroom and killed fourteen women, ostensibly to demonstrate his hatred of 'feminists.' (Lepine, born Gamil Gharbi to an Algerian father, was objecting to Western social values in general, but the political aspect of his crime was minimized in the media.) The murdered women became symbols of one of the forms that violence has taken within Canadian society. Ethnicity, sexuality, poverty, and their relation to civil rights provided other examples; literature dealt with them all.

The Mulroney years (1984–93) adapted government to a privatized business/profit model, which seemed to have roots more in the now-debunked American 'monetarist' theories of Milton Friedman than in the long-standing Canadian paradigm of the mixed economy. The increased influence of conservative social policy in Alberta and Ontario also shaped federal policies in these years, as when these two provinces alone elected the Tory majority that returned the Mulroney-led government to power in 1988, thus enabling the signing of the so-called Free Trade Agreement with the USA. Misnamed, in that the treaty's function was not to enable freer trade across the border but rather to make Canadian trade practice subject to US trade law, this trade agreement was ambiguous in its clauses governing, for example, water resources and cultural policy. Simply put, it made them vulnerable to external control. Signed in January 1988, the Agreement came into effect a year later, and reconfigured as NAFTA, the North American Free Trade Agreement, it was extended on 12 August 1992 to include Mexico. Initially popular (and continuing so among some business operations), it subsequently became the target of much abuse when it became clear that many Canadian businesses would close in consequence, and jobs move south. (The failure of the softwood lumber treaty led to the loss of some 5000 jobs in this industry in British Columbia alone.) In 1993 Mulroney was briefly replaced as prime minister by Kim Campbell (whom Frank Davey, in a 1993 biography, likened to Anne of Green Gables), but despite commitments to the contrary, the Free Trade Agreement was not repealed when the Liberal Party under Jean Chrétien was elected to power on 25 October 1993 and all but two Tories lost their seats. Indeed, the Liberals also did not repeal the much-hated 7 per cent GST (a tax on all goods and services, including books and writing), which the Tory government had introduced. (Approved in the House, the bill was defeated in Senate, and passed only when Prime Minister Mulroney used an archaic legislative manoeuvre to permit him to name eight party-positive senators to tip the vote.) Over the course of the 1980s and early 1990s, ties with the United States in business and politics grew; and conservative policies (under various banners, including 'Liberal,' 'Conservative,' and 'Reform') began to affect provincial politics in British Columbia, Quebec, and Atlantic Canada as well. The bankruptcy of several bookstores and publishing and distribution companies (such as General Publishing in 2002) and the prairie drought and stock market crash that occurred in the same year led many commentators to liken the time to the 1930s. Poverty continued to plague northern and urban districts; wealth concentrated in fewer and fewer hands; and war talk increased. Even as Canada remained one of the most fortunate nations, by United Nations evaluations of living standards, social inequities continued to confound those who sought to deal effectively with job creation, health care, housing, education, violence, and other social challenges.

Reconsidering former policies (whether by legislative intent or because a judicial decision required a change) came to characterize many other aspects of the Mulroney and Chrétien years: the 1988 act that compensated Japanese Canadians for the seizure of assets and dislocation of families during the Second World War; or the removal of abortion from the Criminal Code in 1998; or the 1996 Human Rights Act, which prohibited discrimination on the basis of sexual preference. Militarily, too, Canada began to engage more actively with opposition both at home and abroad, though not always with glory. Some responses to United Nations requests (the familiar 'peacekeeping' role that Canada adopted from the Pearson years on) proved to be fiascos, as in Somalia in 1993 and Rwanda in 1994, although the reasons for the failure of these UN missions have yet to be adequately disclosed. Other patrols, as in Bosnia in 1992 and Haiti in 1992–93, were deemed at least moderately successful; still others, under pressure from Republican policy in the United States, led to more active roles. Participation in the so-called operations in George Bush's Gulf War in 1990 was approved by Parliament only after the fact, in December of that year. An active military engagement in George W. Bush's 'War on Terrorism' followed in 2002 in Afghanistan. It came in the wake of the 11 September 2001 attack on the World Trade Center in New York and other targets, during which some 2,800 people were killed, some half of whom (including 24 Canadians) were citizens of seventy countries other than the USA.

Domestic military and police actions were directed primarily against First Nations resistance groups: for example, the armed disputes in 1991 involving municipal encroachment into Mohawk reserves in Oka and Kahnawake, Quebec, or a later dispute over lobster catches in the Maritimes, the 2000 fisheries dispute with the Mi'kmaq, or various roadblocks in British Columbia. The signing of Nunavut into reality in 1999 and of the land treaty with the Nisga'a in British Columbia in 2001 revealed the success of alternative approaches to the resolution of long-standing disagreements; but in 2002 even the treaty-making processes were coming under attack from conservative forces.

There had been some efforts during the Mulroney years to reconsider existing relations between a federal Canada and the two groups that felt most alienated within the country, Quebec (under Premiers Robert Bourassa and Jacques Parizeau) and the First Nations. These efforts in fact preoccupied political discourse in the country (and much literary expression) at least from 1987 to 1998, or perhaps 2000 (when Pierre Elliott Trudeau's death brought the country into a renewed wave of empathy, and when younger generations were beginning to look towards the future instead of the past). In the face of separatist dissent in Quebec – Parizeau called the existing arrangement of Confederation 'dysfunctional' as late as 1994 – Mulroney declared that it was the intention of his government to 'bring Quebec into the Constitution.' This rhetoric was misleading, in that Quebec was in fact covered by the Constitution already, although not a signatory to it at the time of its enactment. Moreover, by one of Premier Bourassa's decisions, Quebec had made use of the Constitution's 'notwithstanding clause' in order to refuse the Supreme Court the right to strike down the civil ramifications of the French-language laws that Quebec had passed in 1988; the action thus tacitly acknowledged in practice the federal law's relevance to Quebec statutes. Mulroney's two main enterprises in constitutional change came to be known as the Meech Lake Accord of 1987 and the Charlottetown Accord of 1991. Both were ultimately defeated, results that were read for political advantage by all parties in dispute. The reasons for defeat, however, were more complex than the political rhetoric of the time might suggest.

Part of the problem with both accords was that the public had been insufficiently involved in their planning and so felt at once suspicious and excluded. Both proposals were negotiated among leaders of federal and provincial governments and would have introduced policies that would have been next to impossible ever to alter. The more the public learned about all the implications, the more dissatisfied they became. Meech (agreed to by the prime minister and the premiers on 30 April 1987 at Meech Lake, Quebec, with a final draft prepared on 3 June) agreed that Quebec would sign the 1982 constitutional document *if* Quebec were recognized as a 'distinct society,' granted the right to pass French-language protection laws, and given greater power over immigration into the province. All provincial governments were required to ratify the agreement by 1990. No direct public input was required. When a newly elected Newfoundland government suspended its support by 1990, and when a single Native vote in the Manitoba legislature defeated the measure there, Meech was dead and a Quebec separation movement gathered momentum. National resistance, however, expressed not so much an arrogant dismissal of Quebec (as separatist arguments averred) as – at least in part – an insistence that the new constitutional proposal was failing to acknowledge the place of the First Nations in Confederation. Yet another cultural voice, that is, was calling for a revisioning of the state.

The Charlottetown Accord devised a different strategy, one that would combine a set of constitutional proposals (Quebec's demand) with a reformed Senate (Alberta's demand) and a declaration of Native rights. What became clear when people read the document – as they did, in remarkable numbers, prior to voting it down on 26 October 1992 – is that the fine wording effectively granted the Quebec *provincial* government a veto right over all federal legislation, that an elected Senate still left power with custom rather than opening it to popular change, and that the wording of the Native rights clauses still did not grant power to Native *women*. Because of the various flaws in conception, people rejected the proposal on several grounds (except in Ottawa and Toronto, where the vote went in favour). The defeat was nonetheless read by separatist forces in Quebec as a rejection of Quebec, leading Jacques Parizeau to call for a provincial referendum in 1995 on the establishment of a separate Quebec state. The result was a near-even split: 49.4 per cent yes, 50.5 per cent no. Some read this as 'defeat'; others saw the outcome as a positive reaffirmation of the possibilities still inherent in the idea of the Canadian nation. Some writers, including John MacLachlan Gray (b. 1946), affirmed that neither Charlottetown nor Meech was sufficiently principled or eloquent to serve as a constitution and publicly wrote an alternative version, which ended up affirming the decent values of 'this ancient, northern land.' Resident in Montreal, Mordecai Richler took another tack. He wrote an historical account of the separatist movement, *Oh Canada! Oh Quebec! Requiem for a Divided Country* (1992). While it was carefully documented, it nevertheless won him fiercely negative reviews (his opponents said that because he was not fluent in French, he was not sufficiently conversant with francophone cultural sensibilities); these reviews in turn informed his later satiric novel *Barney's Version* (1997). By setting up the ironically named 'Prix Parizeau,' moreover, and the Impure Wool Society to recognize the vitality of anglophone culture within Quebec, Richler was also openly criticizing the *pure laine* exclusiveness of separatist rhetoric.

The wording of Parizeau's referendum was ambiguous, but in retrospect it was clear that the premier himself intended to declare unilateral independence had the 'yes' vote reached more than 50 per cent; his political star faded somewhat, however, when he openly blamed the Northern Cree and the allophones of Montreal for 'defeating' the *pure laine* Québécois. Power passed almost at once to the effective orator Lucien Bouchard and to Parizeau's then lieutenant (and later premier) Bernard Landry, who kept the idea of another 'sovereignty' referendum alive; in September 2002 Landry promised that, if re-elected, he would hold yet another referendum, and that 'sovereignty' would come within a thousand days (at the time, his Parti Québécois was running third in electoral polls). But when it became clear that linguistic survival was not in doubt within Canada and that, with the new century, a new generation of citizens in Quebec held different social priorities, questions of economic success and social mobility began to take precedence over political independence in most people's lives.

This partial shift in sensibility ('partial' because 35–40 per cent of Quebec's population remained in some measure sympathetic to cultural separation) became apparent during the 1990s in francophone literature and popular lyrics. While the songs of Daniel Boucher (b. 1971) carried on the nationalist flame from writers such as Félix Leclerc and Gilles Vigneault, those of Richard Desjardins (b. 1948) were more committed to ecological causes and saw the nationalist position as a betrayal of them. The group called Les Colocs positioned themselves somewhere between these two, Quebec nationalist but in a world context, affirming some version of *métissage*, or dual identity; when the group's leader, Dédé Fortin (1962–2000), committed suicide, his action resonated throughout the younger generation.

The tone of what came to be called 'post-referendum' literature is hinted at by such titles as *La vie provisoire* (1995; tr. as *A Provisional Life*, 1997) by André Major, *Les maladresses du cœur* (1998) by Gilles Archambault, or *Presque rien* (1996) by Francine d'Amour (b. 1948). Moodiness prevailed (perhaps especially in the books published by Boréal). Major, Archambault, d'Amour, Pierre Nepveu (b. 1946), and Yvon Rivard (as in *Le milieu du jour*, 1995) all speak of a crisis of identity during a time of transition. In *Des mondes peu habités* (1992; tr. as *Still Lives*, 1997), by the teacher and critical theorist Nepveu, a character named Jérôme takes a photograph each day to measure the passing of time, and as others look on, he does turbulent battle with himself and his demons. In *Agonie* (1984), by the much celebrated poet Jacques Brault, an ostensible commentary on a poem by Giuseppe Ungaretti turns into a poetic fiction on identity and death. Marie-Claire Blais's *Soifs* (1995; tr. as *These Festive Nights*, 1997), set on the Caribbean shores of Mexico, examines a crisis in politics and person, asking how one can be committed to any cause when the world is hung powerless between values. For her part, the novelist and journalist Lise Bissonnette (b. 1945), who became the *présidente-directrice-générale* of a major library project, the Grande Bibliothèque du Québec, in 1998, identified political crisis with dehumanization. But in her several works of fiction she not only explored this attitude, she called for reaffirmation instead. In *Marie suivait l'été* (1992; tr. as *Following the Summer*, 1993), *Choses crues* (1995; tr. as *Affairs of Art*, 1996), and *Quittes et doubles* (1997; tr. as *Cruelties*, 1998), all praised for their precision of language, her vulnerable characters must also be tough; the marginalized must find a voice; survival is paramount. These writers together set up the motifs that the generation to follow would pursue.

In the years following the 1980s, writers constructed a kind of dialectic between a desire for political separation (the intellectual goal of many earlier writers) and a recognition of the reality that life goes on. More and more often, however, writers began to investigate how Quebeckers might engage with whatever a *pure laine* mindset had previously defined as 'other': a particular conception of 'Canada,' for instance, or allophone and Native cultures within Quebec, or 'America,' conceived of continentally and embracing Mexico and the United States. These works appeared in the wake of Jacques Poulin's *Volkswagen Blues* (1984; tr. 1988), where a male character crosses the USA in search of what he is not, and Nicole Brossard's postmodern and fragmentary *Le désert mauve* (1987; tr. 1990), where a female teenager drives across the Arizona desert in a white Meteor, under the illusion that she is getting away from her mother and her mother's lesbian relationship. The later encounters with America ('encounters,' not exactly 'engagements' with it), whether in travel writing or in fiction, include works by François Barcelo, Monique LaRue (b. 1948), and Jacques Godbout. Godbout's *Une histoire américaine* (1986) provides one example of this connection, *Le temps des Galarneau* (1993; tr. as *The Golden Galarneaus*, 1995) another; the latter book most obviously turns away from the author's earlier *Les têtes à Papineau*, where the satire depicts the political culture of Quebec through a two-headed creature who has inherited all the least creative characteristics of its parents. *Le temps des Galarneau* replaces political divisiveness with family affection, though satire is never far away; as Quebec becomes more multicultural, the book suggests, the only place to start anew might be in space, a conclusion that could perhaps be read as a more conservative, less radical break than was intended. Barcelo's trilogy begins with *Nulle part* in 1989, follows with *Ailleurs en Arizona* in 1991, and finishes with *Pas tout à fait en Californie* (1992); the satire here suggests that the author is fascinated by all that is represented by 'America' (Texas oil, Arizona desert, Hollywood) but not blind to its limitations; the ironies in the titles take the itinerant central character Benjamin Tardif (i.e., 'last born and last to arrive') from nowhere to elsewhere to not quite there, and at the end he resolves to return to Quebec and write about it. The irony is more complicated still, for Tardif also works as a translator of advertising – in other words as one who actively introduces American culture into the Quebec milieu. LaRue, finally, in *Copies conformes* (1989; tr. as *True Copies*, 1996), tells polyphonically of characters who search the Silicon Valley for Dashiell Hammett and the Maltese Falcon. What LaRue discovers here is the Americanness of Quebec; the 'copy' is more 'American,' as it were, than the 'original.' In such an environment, France is cast as the new Other, and the fortress sensibility that has marked the past falls away.

CHANGING PERCEPTIONS

In the two decades after 1984, George Orwell's vision of a global bureaucracy seemed to become a tangible phenomenon. As technological systems integrated worldwide, the idea of personal privacy seemed less and less important to many people and the reality more and more elusive. As corporate ownership and international trade practices fell into fewer and fewer hands, the economic and narrative control over the media ('story' taking precedence over 'fact' as the dominant metaphor in media practice) began to govern access to information and to skew how information was to be read. Many people complained of 'information overload' and sought simplification in fixed systems of belief and social absolutes. Hard data thus turned soft, becoming the servant of advertising, whether obviously commercial or (through political discourse) indirectly so.

In this context, many literary scholars turned to theory as a literary discourse in its own right, as in Linda Hutcheon's *A Theory of Parody* (1985) and *The Poetics of Postmodernism* (1988), Jean Marcel's *Pensées, passions et prose* (1992), Fernand Dumont's *Genèse de la société québécoise* (1993), Sneja Gunew's *Framing Marginality* (1994), Tillottama Rajan and Michael J. O'Driscoll's *After Poststructuralism* (2002), or Lori Saint-Martin's *Le nom de la mère* (1999). Alternatively, they used theory as a medium through which to explain the nature of 'literature' in some finite way, and thus to ascertain the subjectivity of 'judgment' and the parameters of 'meaning.' With alternative methodologies affecting both reading and writing, critics began to focus more closely on the social issues associated with postcolonialism (class, race, gender, ethnicity; i.e., marginality and 'otherness') and to take up the challenges of interdisciplinarity. Some academic examples of interdisciplinarity include (a) Canadian Studies programs: literature in economic, historical, geographical, and political contexts; (b) Women's Studies programs: literature in gendered context; (c) Cultural Studies programs: literature in the context of 'popular' taste and iconography. Some critics therefore came to read literature as one kind of discursive practice among many. But the appeal of the text did not utterly die away. Indeed, announcements of the 'death of the author' were premature, and by century's end, many (especially younger) writers were turning away from postmodern narrative and formal indeterminacies and back towards story and conventional form (rhyme, stanza, etc.), even as they challenged the conventions that textual order had for a previous generation implied. Critical theorists, however, focused not on specific textual explication but on such subjects as the meaning of taste and subjectivity, the abstract function of metaphor and metonymy, the psycholinguistics of genre, the politics of spatiality, and the social construction of gender.

This process of critical reimagining led to reassessments of some individual writers and texts but more particularly to rereadings of the contexts within and through which writers and texts might be read. One strategy was to reread the past through the changed values of the present. A writer-critic such as George Elliott Clarke, for example, drawing on his 'Africadian' roots in Nova Scotia, focused on the racism that permeated the writings of Thomas Chandler Haliburton, among others, and consequently called for such writers not to be so readily accepted in the Canadian canon. Moral message (however defined) thus once again surfaced as a primary criterion for artistic evaluation. Adherents to the notion of globalism suggested that the idea of nationalism in literature was obsolete, and they pointed to the power of international media as their evidence and the recurrent use of non-Canadian settings in contemporary writing; such arguments swelled even as new prizes were being inaugurated to celebrate Canadian books: the Giller Prize ($25,000; est. 1994 by Jack Rabinovitch, in honour of his late wife, the literary journalist Doris Giller) for the 'best book' in the year's fiction, or the biennial Charles Taylor Prize for Literary Non-fiction ($25,000, est. 2000 by Noreen Taylor in memory of her late husband). Despite the enthusiasm for ridding criticism of any reference to nationality, such prizes rapidly became marks of serious literary accomplishment, and 'Canadian' nominations to (and winners of) such international awards as the Orange, Man Booker, Kiriyama, Impac, and Pulitzer Prizes were highlighted yearly in the popular and critical press.

Other critics sought to historicize a previous critical judgment, a practice that led to the recuperation of numerous nineteenth- and twentieth-century women writers (as is apparent in Carole Gerson and Gwendolyn Davies' 1994 anthology *Canadian Poetry: From the Beginnings through the First World War*), as well as of popular writers from the past such as Pauline Johnson, Nellie McClung, Jean McIlwraith (1858–1938, reclaimed especially for her editorial influence}, and Constance Lindsay Skinner (1877–1939). Reconstructed, too, were those writers whose reputations had been damaged by previous judgment and critical rivalry, such as Eudore Évanturel (1859–1919), one-time secretary to the historian Francis Parkman, and Marcel Dugas (1883–1947). The latter's work reappeared under the title *Poèmes en prose* (1998). While Dugas's work had been sidelined for its anticlericalism and his personal friendship with Albert Laberge, Évanturel had been effectively silenced when a powerful reviewer (who was politically opposed to his patron, Joseph Marmette) dismissed him simply by association. In the 1990s Évanturel's lyrics in *Premières poésies* (1878) were regarded as the most promising modernist poems of his day, while Dugas's work was celebrated for its symbolist departure from convention.

Some reputations had, of course, never been affected by the public knowledge of personal behaviour; even the fraud charges against Octave Crémazie and Frederick Philip Grove (as F. P. Greve) did not affect estimations of their work. A substantial body of 'prison writing' also emerged in the later twentieth century, and while some books were read for titillation, most reviewers tried to separate estimations of a writer's actions from those of his or her literary practice. What came to be more critically discussed were the reasons for previous evaluations, particularly the power of censorship (as in the Guibord Affair, which began in 1869, when a man named Joseph Guibord was refused burial in consecrated ground because he had refused to resign from the intellectually liberal Institut Canadien; after legal appeals to the Privy Council in London overturned Bishop Ignace Bourget's decision in 1875, Guibord was reburied, but Bourget then deconsecrated the plot). Pierre Hébert's *Censure et littérature au Québec: Le livre crucifié, 1625–1919* (1997) importantly analyzes the Roman Catholic Church's role, historically, in restricting access to books and controlling their content and reputation. A more recent civil case involving Little Sisters Book & Art Emporium in Vancouver (which specializes in gay and lesbian books) began with hearings before the Supreme Court in 1994; a judicial decision came in January 1996 (although the case continued with appeals in 1998 and 2000). With the Civil Liberties Association in support, the bookstore charged that Canada Customs was discriminating against a gay bookstore on indefensible grounds, in that it was permitting certain texts that dealt with homosexuality to be imported by other stores but restricting Little Sisters' ability to import the same books. The case hinged in part on definitions of 'obscenity.' A 1985 law affirmed that 'undue exploitation of sex' should be deemed 'obscene' in Canada, but the 1996 judges' decision observed, first, that the Customs office's application of this definition was 'non-systematic' and, second, that *proof* of obscenity (the burden falling now on the Customs office rather than on the importer) would be required before books could be stopped at the border. In 2002, competing definitions of obscenity continued to confound easy determinations of 'proof,' meaning that the law governing border control remained inconclusive. Meanwhile, however, social tolerances in Canada were beginning to widen.

In the 1990s, while private behaviour was generally deemed irrelevant to a book's aesthetic quality, there did emerge a body of theory that read into and through private behaviour for a writer's strategies of literary construction. Hence autobiography – or various forms of what came to be called 'life writing' (autobiography, journal, letter) –

came into its own as a literary genre. Women's lives were reread against a feminist ideology and for alternative techniques of expression; one consequence of this critical concern was the validation of such forms as the diary (long dismissed as a 'non-literary' genre). At the same time, because the categories of literary history also came under scrutiny, any claim upon an 'essentialist' relation between an author or subject and a represented real-life group was open to instant critique. Hence terms such as 'women writers,' 'Native writers,' 'gay writers,' 'ethnic writers,' 'Black writers,' or even 'Canadian writers' were read as restrictive or excluding categories as often as they were treated as categories describing some authorial attribute or feature of residence. Outside Canada, however, more and more readers and critics were looking closely at Canadian books for aesthetic pleasure and for insights into the characteristics of Canadian culture. No critical position offered a consistent model for the time.

Even as a politics of capitalist globalization moved to encourage a commonality of popular taste, that is, many people began to oppose it. Such 'underground' magazines as *Geist* (est. 1990) and *Adbusters* (est. 1989) represent critical faces of this protest; *No Logo* (2000) by Naomi Klein (b. 1970) even became a best-seller. The visual arts also addressed the relation between corporate advertising and economic disparities, whether through the urban photographs of Roy Arden (b. 1957) or the photo-realist paintings of Chris Woods (b. 1970), who represents human figures, ironically, against a backdrop of what he calls 'McTopia': mall culture, pop ads, and disposable products. Many of the people who opposed the market monopolies represented by such globalization, however – and its seeming obliteration of independence, difference, and choice – nevertheless espoused globalism: that is, the act of recognizing their own community within a larger set of communities or within a principle of ecology and interconnectedness. Yet even while these developments were taking place, literary and psychological theory was disputing the integration of the individual personality. Not only did the 'wholeness' of any person came into question, but so did the idea of 'entirety' itself; hence so did the degree to which any text could claim to be 'representative' (of a writer, a group, a culture 'at large'). A paradigm thus emerged: inside a text, an individual could represent the 'position' of a group or place or especially a margin, but no *group category* could be taken to represent (or even necessarily include) any given individual. A literary position could invite recognition of a group (especially a marginalized group), but any critical 'recognition' of the group could also be read as discriminatory, in that it might appear to exempt the group from the 'mainstream.' A logical conundrum inevitably followed.

The ability to speak from the inside tended to be accepted as author-itative or authentic, but speaking from outside a category was con-sidered presumptuous and co-optive. Yet from this perspective, the category 'mainstream' (the 'canon': whatever was or had been con-ventionally called 'Canadian literature') was accepted as though it were a given (however much it remained undefined), at the same time as categories of 'otherness' were redefined as the only legitimate position to hold. Claiming legitimacy – identifying the 'subject posi-tion' of the critic/speaker – came to mean as much as or more than verbal facility, though what was meant by 'verbal facility' itself became yet another subject of critical dispute. Who speaks, and for whom? critics asked. The identity of criticism as a 'field' of power, of competitive marginalities, was never more clear.

CONTINUITIES

Many writers who had established their reputations prior to 1985 continued, of course, to write and publish after this date. Others moved away from Canada into other milieux (Clark Blaise and Bharati Mukherjee to California, Paulette Jiles to Texas, Janette Turn-er Hospital to Washington, DC, Dany Laferrière to Miami, Florida), and while their works continued to be read and even published in Canada, the attention given to them began to lessen (Blaise being the exception; his collected stories and his 2001 biography of Sir Sand-ford Fleming, *Time Lord*, won him renewed attention). Laferrière's reputation and Mukherjee's began to grow in the United States; both authors repeatedly emphasized their desire to be read as writers rather than as immigrants. The continuing reputations of writers who had died before 1985, such as Margaret Laurence, Sheila Watson, Ger-maine Guèvremont, and Malcolm Lowry, was confirmed by a num-ber of publishing enterprises that kept their names before the reading public. Among such works are Sherrill Grace's two-volume edition of Lowry's *Collected Letters* (1995–96), Kathleen Scherf's edition of his *Collected Poetry* (1992), Laurence's autobiography *Dance on the Earth* (1989, left unpublished at her death and edited into print by her daughter Jocelyn), and the appearance of Watson's first novel, *Deep Hollow Creek* (1992), a personal tale of a Cariboo teacher written in the 1950s, years before *The Double Hook* had made the author famous. Major French-language publishing enterprises also took up the chal-lenge of re-editing the past, and the primary works of such writers as Octave Crémazie and Alain Grandbois appeared in critical editions. Odette Condemine's selection of Crémazie appeared in 1989; four volumes of Grandbois's work appeared between 1990 and 1996, under the editorship of Jean-Cléo Godin, Chantal Bouchard and Nicole Deschamps, Marielle Saint-Amour, and Jo-Ann Stanton. The latter books appeared in the Québec Pléiade series from the Bibliothèque du Nouveau Monde, which published critical editions of works by Honoré Beaugrand, Paul-Emile Borduas, Arthur Buies, Henriette Dessaulles, Alfred DesRochers, Marcel Dugas, Louis Fréchette, Claude-Henri Grignon, and Albert Laberge in the same series.

The latter decades of the twentieth century were also a time when the final works of such writers as bp Nichol, Robertson Davies, Mordecai Richler, George Woodcock, Matt Cohen, Anne Hébert, Jacques Ferron, Al Purdy, and Gérald Godin appeared. Nichol, his life cut short, left his long poem *The Martyrology* uncompleted; Woodcock's massive output was capped by his volumes of autobiography, especially *Beyond the Blue Mountains* (1987), and the personal poems of *The Cherry Tree on Cherry Street* (1994). Purdy's death marked the end of an extraordinary career in a kind of poetry (and perhaps a kind of national vision) that many imitated and few equalled, where the rhythms of speech and the vernacular lexicon embodied a wide-ranging and sophisticated intelligence. *Beyond Remembering* (2000), edited by Purdy and Sam Solecki, collects his poems. Anne Hébert returned from France (where she had long written about Quebec) to Canada, and in her last works (*Est-ce que je te dérange?*, 1998, and *Un habit de lumière*, 1999, both translated by Sheila Fischman) turned (as she had in 1981 with *Héloïse*) to France, portraying elegiacally how characters from elsewhere lived their days in Paris. Davies' final novels – among them *The Cunning Man* (1994) – captured more attention abroad than at home, and though publishers' efforts to keep the Davies name alive resulted in several volumes of letters, talks, and short notes, readers on the whole returned to *Fifth Business* as the capstone of his career. With Cohen and Richler, a different picture emerged. Cohen's last works – *Elizabeth and After* (1999), for example – were at last bringing him the attention he warranted, demonstrating the sensitivity to character that earlier novels had promised; his posthumous autobiography (*Typing: A Life in 26 Keys*, 2000; edited by his wife, the children's publisher Patsy Aldana) pungently conveys his views on the publishing industry. Only posthumously was it revealed that Cohen had also written the children's books that appeared under the pseudonym Teddy Jam.

Richler, too, was moving from strength to strength – by turns caustic and gentle in his essay collections and commentaries on sport, insightful and open in his political commentary, and wittily urbane in his social satires. With *St. Urbain's Horseman* in 1971 and *Joshua Then and Now* in 1980, Richler had signalled his return from Europe to Canada, pursuing the implications of moral ambiguity and aesthetic ignorance among those in his own generation who actively sought power. However his characters try to lead 'ordinary' lives, they always run afoul of those who use slur and petty vengeance to give themselves popular eminence and political advantage. Such slurs categorize Joshua in the latter novel as a criminal suspect and a sexual 'deviant,' with no basis in fact for either the accuracy or the morality of the accusation. Joshua at least closes with a reconciliation between a son and his father, and like all of Richler's work, this book is studded with comic scenes. With *Solomon Gursky Was Here* (1989), set in the North rather than directly in Montreal, Richler turned in a slightly different direction, adapting Trickster narratives from First Nations culture (especially those of Raven) to tell the title character's story: he is a mischief-maker born into a family of bootleggers who have later risen to social power. Some readers claimed the Gursky family to be a thinly veiled portrait of the Bronfmans, an identification the author disputed. More of a fantasy than was true of earlier books – except perhaps for *The Incomparable Atuk*, Richler's first venture into Arctic territory – this novel again criticizes the Canadian penchant to mythologize itself as a northern utopia. In *Barney's Version* (1997), widely considered the author's finest and most personal novel (told in the first-person, with an engaging set of comic 'editorial' footnotes by the narrator's son), the title character, Barney Panofsky, writes an unrepentant *apologia pro vita sua*, in which he explains what really happened to the man whom he was suspected of doing away with. The 'truth' of this version is not the novel's point; its success derives from its witty impatience with (and condemnation of) the hypocrisy, the pettiness, and the ethnic divisiveness of the society in which he lived.

For other writers, these decades were more a time of consolidation. Mavis Gallant's international reputation as an artist in the short story form continued to grow, as did Alice Munro's, and both produced volumes of collected stories in the late 1990s. Though both writers were remarkably active, Munro remained the more productive of the two; four new collections of stories (and one volume of selected stories) appeared between 1990 (*Friend of My Youth*) and 2001 (*Hateship, Friendship, Courtship, Loveship, Marriage*). The latter was the first book to be labelled that it was printed on ecologically acceptable paper, i.e. (at the author's insistence) not made from old-growth forest. Widespread international praise followed the publication of each volume. *Hateship* draws its title from a children's choosing rhyme. These and the stories of *Open Secrets* (1994) and *The Love of a Good Woman*

(1998) demonstrated Munro's increasing skill with complex structures; embedded stories reveal why 'secrets' are often 'open' –
because no one can ever know all about other people or explain their
motivations or behaviour. Stories open into other stories, 'Menesete-
ung' providing an apposite example, where the boxes shaped by
research and recognition demonstrate that no one can fully explain
why people behave as they do. Experience, simply, is ambiguous. In
Love, moreover, the women on whom the stories focus behave in
ways that others judge moralistically, but Munro's characters do not
regret. Having come to terms with their actions, at the time or in later
life, they placidly move on. The stories' careful style invites the reader not into understanding, particularly, but into awareness, a state
that permits, finally, recognition.

With Timothy Findley, Jane Rule, Richard Wright, Ray Smith,
Austin Clarke, Gilles Archambault, Réjean Ducharme, Jacques
Poulin, Roch Carrier, Victor-Lévy Beaulieu, and Robert Kroetsch, too,
new works reconfirmed as much as they advanced established reputations: Findley with *Pilgrim* (1999), for example, a Jungian journey
through time, Clarke with his eloquent reflection on what power
does to people, *The Polished Hoe* (2002), and Rule with *Memory Board*
(1987), a quietly desolating story about Alzheimer's disease, examined close relationships and loss. Robert Kroetsch, with *The Man from
the Creeks* (1998), turned back to Robert Service for his narrative,
fleshing out the psychology of how and why readers construct
iconography out of story. Richard Wright's epistolary *Clara Callan*
(2001) pits 1930s radio soap opera against the religious rivalries of
Ontario and the real-life traumas of Ontario women; Smith's *The Man
Who Loved Jane Austen* (1999) reanimates Austen's characters in Montreal, to reveal the harrowing influence of status, wealth, and family
– the manipulative power of Establishment politics; Poulin's *Le vieux
chagrin* (1989; tr. as *Mr. Blue*, 1993) turns to the sentimental; and
Ducharme, with *Gros Mots* (1999) and other novels, turns at last away
from childhood stories so as to address more directly how politics
permeates modern Quebec.

Still other writers in mid-career produced their most accomplished
works to date. Among them (in addition to Archambault and Poulin)
were D.A. Richards, Carol Shields, Jack Hodgins, Audrey Thomas,
and Guy Vanderhaeghe. Richards, for example, with his second
prizewinning trilogy – *Nights below Station Street* (1988), *Evening Snow
Will Bring Such Peace* (1990), *For Those Who Hunt the Wounded Down*
(1993) – focuses on the nature of memory, emphasizing its unreliabil-
ity. Shifting points of view make clear that people's willingness to
turn real figures and real events into heroes and demons always

falsifies them. Subsequent fictions (he wrote personal accounts of hockey and fishing as well) also pursued this theme, most effectively in *The Bay of Love and Sorrows* (1998), where the story asks the reader to re-examine the accuracy of a judicial decision, and where the recursive style repeatedly emphasizes the power of reconsideration. Here, as in the trilogy – telling stories about storytelling – Richards demonstrates how narrative happens in context, not in isolation, once again foregrounding the more-than-local characters he draws from the Miramichi.

Hodgins, along with an effective guide to the practice of writing, *A Passion for Narrative* (1994; 2nd ed. 2001), and an Australian travel narrative, wrote several novels that extended his range. In the contemporary politics of *The Honorary Patron* (1987) and in *Innocent Cities* (1990), a critique of the 'Victorian' empire (drawing on all the meanings of this adjective), Hodgins exercised his social conscience, claiming artistic freedom from the conventions of fashion. This narrative inquiry *into* both storytelling and history – the tense relation between the personal and the communal – came to the fore more effectively with the trilogy begun with *The Macken Charm* (1995), about a young man's discovery that he can make his own opportunities, and continued with *Broken Ground* (1998). The latter novel, praised as Hodgins's finest to date, probes the explosion of values (and language) that followed the First World War, in the minds of many different characters: those whose lives were disrupted by it, those who sought physically to escape involvement, those whose memories clouded and displaced the reality, and those in a subsequent generation who seek to reconstruct the past and so reinterpret its relevance to themselves. Unsurprisingly, both world wars continued to engage the imagination of contemporary writers, many of whom were children while the Second World War came to a close. Sometimes this writing served as an act of homage and memory (as in some biographies and most post-Shoah Jewish writing); sometimes it encoded past acts of conflict as a way of coming to terms with political or personal strife in the present, when violent acts were happening in local neighbourhoods as well as 'elsewhere' and when they were being replayed nightly on the television news. Among the many works besides Hodgins's that capture the pressures of life in a wartime setting, *The Lost Garden* (2002) by Helen Humphreys (b. 1961) stands out for its elegant simplicity, the way it tells of isolation and responsibility imposed upon the young, and the way it characterizes everyone's past as a process of haunting.

Carol Shields, whose stories and novels had circulated since 1977, leapt to public attention with *Swann* (1987), *The Stone Diaries* (1993;

winner of the Pulitzer Prize), and *Larry's Party* (1987; adapted as musical theatre in 1997 by Richard Ouzounian). The first of these is a comic 'mystery' in which a writer's life is claimed by a diverse set of competitive critics. The other two also adapt the biographical mode, and in 2001 Shields wrote an appreciative life of Jane Austen. *The Stone Diaries* traces the life of Daisy Goodwill; complete with photographs that appear to fix reality, the novel makes it finally clear that no one ever knows another person. For its part, *Larry's Party* attempts with mixed success to explain the uncertainties and preoccupations of a middle-aged man. None of these books, however, matches the skill of *Unless* (2002), in which a young woman goes silent, her parents try to explain and understand this behaviour, and the language of connection – conjunctions, adverbs, prepositions: the unnoticed small words in ordinary discourse – becomes the structure on which rests (in the face of insecurity) the possibility of continuing to believe in goodness.

Audrey Thomas, too, won mixed reviews – praise for her short stories, selected in *The Path of Totality* (2001), but uneven reactions to her novels, all of which probe the dark corners of family history: her own (Corbett) family in *Graven Images* (1993), a young Canadian man's search for his African roots in *Coming Down from Wa* (1995), and a young Orkney woman's masquerade as a man in the Hudson's Bay Company fur trade, *Isobel Gunn* (1999). The last of these is based (as is *The Ballad of Isabel Gunn,* 1987, Stephen Scobie's poem about the same figure) on a real-life event. Thomas adapts it to her recurrent motif, that of the 'lost child.' In the fiction (as in life), Isobel was dismissed from the HBC when her pregnancy made her gender unmistakeable. The novel, however, hypothesizes, then probes, the reasons for her acts, and asks what happened to the baby. The novel's focus therefore falls on the responsibilities of the person who narrates Isobel's life. As with Thomas's earlier work, the book does not use language simply as a system of communication; it animates writing as an active, ongoing medium of locating knowledge.

While, like Richler, Thomas, and Shields, Guy Vanderhaeghe also dealt with parent-child tensions – as in the father-son stories of *Things as They Are?* (1992, with its significant punctuation mark) – this author's larger themes involve the choices people make when they confront history. Do they accept conventional wisdom or query it? – a question asked in his plays as well and in the historically sensitive fictional inquiry into the real life of the Métis scout Jerry Potts (who helped negotiate the Blackfoot Treaty), *The Last Crossing* (2002). But nowhere does Vanderhaeghe more successfully achieve a kind of mythic version of how history attends the present, or more clearly show his characters pursuing quests, when they make their choices, than in the twin narratives of *The Englishman's Boy* (1996). One story in this novel tells of the events that lead to the Cypress Hills Massacre in southern Saskatchewan in 1873, the other tells a 1920s Hollywood story in which a young Canadian writer tried to land a screenwriting job. Given the chance to 'succeed,' however, by writing western clichés or else to interview a man who might possibly have been at Cypress Hills and to tell the 'real' story, he opts for the latter, returning home into fidelity rather than accepting glitz and commercial restraint. In the interconnection between the two quests, the narratives overlap.

In poetry and drama, too, several established figures continued to attract attention, among them the playwrights Judith Thompson (b. 1954), Sharon Pollock, George Walker, Michel Tremblay, John Murrell (and others associated with Tarragon Theatre in Toronto), and Jovette Marchessault; the poets Robert Bringhurst, Patrick Lane, George McWhirter, Christopher Dewdney, Jan Zwicky (b. 1955), Don McKay (b. 1942), Lorna Crozier, Robin Blaser (b. 1925), Jacques Brault, Claude Beausoleil, Pierre Morency, and Fernand Ouellette. Thompson continued to work in radio and television as well as to write for the stage; *Lion in the Streets* (1992) began as a radio play, but (as adapted for the stage) it uses fragmented scenes to tell of a murdered Portuguese girl's cry against the tyranny of violence. Her other works include *Sled* (1997) and *Perfect Pie* (2000); the latter, about the traumas of girls growing up, was adapted to film in 2002. Beausoleil, too, worked across conventional forms, his fiction being adapted to performance in 1994; another volume of poems, *Le chant de voyageur*, appeared in 1998. Morency continued to work with Hexagone publishers; among the twenty books he had published by 1996 was *Les paroles qui marchent dans la nuit* (1994). Bringhurst in 1996 revised his elegant analysis of print form in *The Elements of Typographical Style*, but in the 1990s he turned even more to his studies of classical Haida poetry; his introductory survey and commentary *A Story as Sharp as a Knife* (1999) was followed by translations of the nineteenth-century poets Ghandl (Walter McGregor, c. 1851–c. 1920) and Skaay (John Sky, c. 1847–c. 1910). Barry Callaghan's translation of Ouellette's selected poetry appeared as *Wells of Light* (1989). Lane's lyrical *Winter* (1991) was followed by such books as *Too Spare, Too Fierce* (1995), where the poems touch on the maturity that can follow despair. Lane's partner, Crozier, published several image-based volumes, including a series devoted to Sinclair Ross's character Mrs Bentley; while McWhirter's several books (fiction as well as poetry) included *The Listening* (1991), set in Ireland, *Incubus* (1995), set in Mexico, *A*

Staircase for All Souls (1995), which engages with nature on the British Columbia coast, and *The Book of Contradictions* (2002), with its eloquent adaptation from the Greek classics, 'Ovid in Saskatchewan.' Dewdney (involved in film and other media as well as poetry) turned away from his rigorously anti-lyrical mode, and though more personal in such collections as *Demon Pond* (1994), he remained committed to the need for poetry to engage with science; in the essays of *Last Flesh* (1998), he pursues his interest in cybernetics. On the whole, however, the 1980s and 1990s belonged to Margaret Atwood and Michael Ondaatje, both for their poetry and for their fiction.

Ondaatje's interest in the arts and his talent for mixing and crossing genres – poetry, film, fiction – had been well established by the time he came to write his next major works: the novels *In the Skin of a Lion* (1987), *The English Patient* (1992; which won the Booker Prize and, in its film adaptation, a 1997 Academy Award as well), and *Anil's Ghost* (2000). By this time his personal life had also changed; he and the photographer Kim Ondaatje (b. 1943) had divorced, and with his marriage to the novelist Linda Spalding (b. 1943), Michael Ondaatje also became the stepfather of the editor and screenwriter Esta Spalding (b. 1966; herself the author of the poems in *Lost August*, 1999). Like *Anil's Ghost*, Ondaatje's erotically charged poetry collection *Handwriting* (1998) returned to his native Sri Lanka, the novel to reveal how the touch of the past affects the lives of the present and future. While *Anil's Ghost* uses the metaphor of forensic anthropology to expose the politics of civil war, the two earlier novels fasten respectively on Toronto's urban history and on the indeterminability of 'fact' in narrative histories of the Second World War. *In the Skin of a Lion*, cast as a kind of mural in which the reader must assemble the continuity of narrative, fastens on the language of received history and the Macedonian narratives (spoken or unspoken, lived or dreamed) that have nevertheless helped to give shape to the 'book' that is the city itself. In *The English Patient*, too, narratives of individuals – the Indian sapper Kip, an expert in explosives; the Canadian nurse Hana; the thief Caravaggio, who appears in *Lion* as well – become the filters through which readers, like the characters, reconstruct the life of the 'English' patient, a wounded man who is dying in their care in a half-razed Italian villa. That the patient's 'real' narrative should differ quite markedly from what they initially assume (and that his life's 'language' therefore should differ from how they 'decipher' it) asks the reader to engage as much with the process of historical interpretation and narrative reconstruction as with the over-tale of love, spying, loss, and war itself. The poetics of 'layering' – interweaving images, narratives, even abrupt shifts in perspective

– thus reconstructs history not as a set of determinable events, each with fixed consequences, but as enigmatic planes of value, moving imperturbably across each other, while individuals stretch and flay themselves to choose among them, in narratives of complication and desire.

Where Ondaatje repeatedly seeks to elucidate private trauma, Margaret Atwood characteristically uses fiction (and criticism) to dramatize public issues and the implications of fashionable trends. The poems of *Morning in the Burned House* (1995) do deal with more intense experiences, and Atwood's comment that writing poetry requires more time and greater durations of silence suggests why this may be so. *Negotiating with the Dead* (2002), essays on the writer's craft, provides another glimpse of the author's compositional strategies. The stories and novels that extended her international reputation through the later twentieth century – and won her the Booker Prize for *The Blind Assassin* (2000), about authority and aging – are less revelations of covert character, however, than constructions of competing social tendencies. The short narratives of *Good Bones* (1992), for example, sardonically recast social stereotypes and literary models, using the bare and, by this time, didactic bones of fable and fairy tale. Like the genre-breaking writings (neither stories nor poems) collected in *Murder in the Dark* (1983), they seek to expose the violent underside of childhood and spring.

In *Cat's Eye* (1988) Atwood looks at the relation between siblings and between girl friends, and follows the different directions their lives take. In *The Robber Bride* (1993) the lives of adult female friends are disrupted when the return of an amoral figure from their past causes them to revisit their childhood dependencies and frailties. In the Giller Prize–winning *Alias Grace* (1996), moreover, the historical character Grace Marks (whom Susanna Moodie once referred to) is reanimated when a doctor reviews the contrary evidence that convicted her of murder. Behind all these books lies the dystopian *The Handmaid's Tale* (1985), the resonant politics of feminism and its limits (the women in Atwood's novels are notoriously cruel to one another), and of nationalism and its limits (when Grace Marks is freed, she immediately chases off to the United States). New in the later books is the author's fascination with science as history, that is, with science as a changing system of explaining phenomena, behaviour, and interconnection: string theory in *Cat's Eye*, phrenology in *Alias Grace*. In these works, empirical forces complicate received systems of economic, sectarian, and political authority, and yet piercing even them is the gothic chaos of personality, the tips of wilderness that rake through people's carefully constructed illusions of security.

RETHINKING SOCIETY

The contrast between the paintings of Charles Pachter (who illustrat-ed the first edition of Atwood's *The Circle Game* in 1964 and the 1980 edition of *The Journals of Susanna Moodie*, among other works, and who collaborated with Dennis Lee as well) and those of Jin-me Yoon suggest some ways in which the visual arts in the 1990s represented changing attitudes and social experience in Canada. Pachter's satiric paintings place moose images in incongruous places – dropping over the edges of a cliff, standing atop the CN Tower in Toronto, reimag-ined as a state replacement for the Queen's horse. Certainly, the sar-donic literalism of a painting such as *Queen and Bay*, which takes Toronto street names and represents them as an intersection between the monarch and a parodic Group of Seven Georgian Bay scene, uses irony to undercut a too-easy equation between artistic and political convention and cultural identity. Pachter's collaboration with Atwood suggests that Atwood's short story 'Death by Landscape' can be read in this same context, asking to what degree people can be absorbed into a mindset, adopt unthinkingly a particular way of see-ing, and come to identify themselves by means of a conventional rep-resentation of land.

Jin-me Yoon's 'Souvenirs of the Self' (a 1991 postcard series) approaches in a different way this need for a change in social per-ception. The series depicts the standard iconography of Canadian identity – photographs of Lake Louise in the Rockies and other tourist spots – and into each 'landscape' Yoon introduces a photo-graph of her own Korean face. The effect of the photographs is to assert that the 'visible minority' can no longer be identified *apart from* the 'Canadian' norm: that is, made politically *in*visible by some genteel form of socially sanctioned racism. Instead, marginality must be perceived both within and against the received convention, in the process deconstructing whatever had been accepted as the norm. The irony of the titles the artist applies to each image (post-card descriptions, which are written in both 'official' languages but also in Chinese, Korean, and Japanese script) extends in words the social comment that the pictures convey. For instance, the image of Lake Louise is glossed this way: 'Feast your eyes on the picturesque beauty named to honour Princess Louise Caroline Alberta, daughter of Queen Victoria. She discovers the lake on a sunny day; before that she did not exist.' Yoon's other projects – among them, 'The Group of 67,' a series of photographs of sixty-seven recent Korean immi-grants taken (from both the front and the back) against the backdrop of Lawren Harris and Emily Carr paintings – reiterate this claim upon *presence* in the community and in the iconography of social identity.

Members of some 'communities' within the state adopted other strategies in order to be heard: vocally affirmative, sometimes confrontative, occasionally competitive about who most needed recognition. Such communities were by no means parallel: terms such as 'Asian,' 'Black,' 'gay,' 'Latin American,' 'Italo-Montréalais,' 'worker,' and 'Native' (sometimes in combination) described separate versions of marginality. In French, vocal Acadian and Franco-Ontarian communities also attracted attention, differentiating themselves both from the anglophone cultures near them and from the Québécois domination of the image that francophones have long held within Canada. What writers themselves seemed generally to seek was a balance between the need to represent their own experience within one such community and the desire that they and their work not be categorized in a way that excluded them from engaging with life outside that community. In other words, they asked readers and critics to recognize that a book about, say, a gay Asian man in urban Toronto could as well be an inquiry into the nature of love, justice, and neighbourhood in general, and not confined to being a commentary on a particular ethnicity, region, or sexual preference. The categories in use in this critical discussion, therefore, have to be read as a form of descriptive shorthand rather than as a restrictive enclosure.

For it is clear that in the decades following 1980, a significant number of writers emerged who claimed East and South Asian, Afro-Caribbean, Latin American, East European, and First Nations heritage. Some of these writers specifically disputed ethnicity as a category (Neil Bissoondath, b. 1955, declared his wish to be read as a writer or as a Canadian writer, but not as a Caribbean-Canadian writer inside a subcategory with a hyphen). Others wrote directly about what it means to be Native or Jewish or Japanese, taking their ethnicity or their religion as their primary subject. Examples would include Lawrence Hill (b. 1957), Cecil Foster (b. 1954), Roy Miki (b. 1942), and numerous others – perhaps most acerbically (and comically) Dany Laferrière in his mordantly titled *Comment faire l'amour avec un Nègre sans se fatiguer* (1985). Exile, moreover, was a primary motif for a large number of Quebec writers, including Mona Latif-Ghattas (b. 1946), Émile Ollivier (1940–2002), Gérard Étienne (b. 1936), Ying Chen, Naïm Kattan, Wajdi Mouawad (b. 1968), Sergio Kokis (b. 1944), and Marco Micone (b. 1945). All write in French; all, by drawing respectively on their Egyptian, Haitian, Chinese, Jewish Iraqi, Christian Lebanese, Brazilian, and Italian cultural inheritance, reveal the multiculturalism of modern Quebec. Critics referred to 'l'écriture migrante.' Kattan's *La fortune du passager* (1989) continued his reconstruction of the route his characters take into exile, though here 'exile' acquires a more positive identity than it had in earlier books. Étienne's *La pacotille* (1991) was more willing than Ollivier's *Mère-solitude* (1994) to criticize superficiality (pacotille = gimcrackery) in the mindset of the émigré as well as in the culture to which the immigrants have come. Latif-Ghattas's *Double conte de l'exil* (1990) stresses the two sides of its subject, while in her later *Les lunes de miel* (1996), the marriage between a French Canadian man and an immigrant woman does not work. *Métissage* – mixing – proved in these writers' minds to be difficult to make real within Quebec. Mouawad, the playwright-director of Théâtre de Quat'sous in Montreal, focused on the littoral, the boundary line; his plays (with a nod to Jean-Paul Sartre) look back to his Lebanese roots, but with rootlessness in mind: emblematically in one, a man takes the corpse of the father he has never known across a wartorn landscape. 'Home' is difficult to affirm. Committed to social reform, Micone's plays seek reconciliation; the three generations of characters who struggle to speak with one another in *Déjà l'agonie* (1988; tr. as *Beyond the Ruins*, 1995), for example – unable either to go back to the life they left or to leave it behind – seek some way of devising in the present an equitable society to share. Montreal-born Antonio d'Alfonso (b. 1953), in *In Italics* (1996), comments on Micone and other Italian Canadian writers, reflecting on the consequences of living according to a different script. Kokis's *Le pavillon des miroirs* (1994; tr. as *Funhouse*, 1999), no less attuned to social disparities, focuses openly on the self more than on the state, and his central character comes to recognize himself in what he calls his 'deformities.'

Some writers used the experience of a particular heritage to focus more generally on how memory invokes history or how language constructs any quest for truth. Examples would include books by Michael David Kwan (1934–2001) or the several autobiographical travel narratives that searched out family histories (especially women's histories) in China or India or Hungary or Ukraine, such as those by Denise Chong (b. 1952), Wayson Choy (b. 1939), Anita Rau Badami (b. 1961), Anna Porter, Lisa Appignanesi, or Janice Kulyk Keefer (b. 1952). At the same time, still other writers were probing local Canadian histories for their family connection with place, and in this context lies a way of reading the remarkable flowering of contemporary writing from francophone Ontario, Acadia, Cape Breton, and Newfoundland.

The work of Antonine Maillet provides a prototype for this development; the quest for the Acadian past, the Cajun migrations home, and the spirit of exile as a powerful force in contemporary Acadian culture were the recurrent subjects of Maillet's stories and plays in the 1970s and 1980s. Other writers of the 1970s worked in a related tradition, using the Acadian vernacular to dispute the conservative and pastoral conventions epitomized by Longfellow's *Evangeline*; among them were Raymond Leblanc, Herménégilde Chiasson, who worked in film as well, and the folksinger Édith Butler (b. 1942). While Maillet's interest in linguistics, folk culture, and Bakhtinian carnival reshaped how Acadian writing might be imagined, another influence came from what might be called contemporary folk sources, namely popular music. The Acadian rock groups 1755 and Beausoleil-Broussard were particularly influential into the 1980s; Jacques Savoie (b. 1951), the founder and lyricist of the latter group, also produced in *Les portes tournantes* (1984) and *Le cirque bleu* (1995) novels that move in yet another direction, confronting reality through dream. By the 1990s, Zacharie Richard (b. 1950) had become one of the most popular musicians and lyricists, for his CD of Cajun zydeco, *Cap Enragé* (1998). While Claude Lebouthillier (b. 1946) would continue to write historical Acadian fictions through this decade, the new generation of writers was represented more by the autobiographical but fictional plays of France Daigle (b. 1953), whose *1953: chronique d'une naissance annoncée* (1995) turns personal history into social emblem.

Newfoundland and Cape Breton writers and performers similarly revamped how to imagine their personal place and region. The novels of Wayne Johnston (b. 1958) and John Steffler – encounters between history and invention – along with the elliptical short stories of Lisa Moore (b. 1964), the poems of Carmelita McGrath (b. 1960), and the comic and musical performances of CODCO and Great Big Sea, provide a quick sampling of modern Newfoundland cultural expression, while the novels and stories of Alistair MacLeod and Lynn Coady (b. 1970) and to some degree Raymond Smith, together with the music of the many Celtic rock groups that Nova Scotia produced, sample 1990s developments in Cape Breton. Yet another cultural revival took place in francophone Ontario, where the difference from the anglophone surrounds was further complicated by the insistent claim that the difference from francophone Quebec had also to be proclaimed and preserved. There is, of course, a long history of writers born outside Quebec who have been swept into generalizations about 'Quebec literature,' from Lionel Groulx, Alfred Garneau, and Gabrielle Roy to Gérard Bessette, Cécile Cloutier, and Marie-Claire Blais. But the emergence of a declaredly Franco-Ontarian literature came with the founding of Théâtre du Nouvel-Ontario and the publisher Prise de Parole in Sudbury in the 1970s. *Lavalléville* (1975), a musical comedy by André Paiement (1950–78), gave another face to this expression of identity. So did the poetry, drama, and prose of Patrice Desbiens, Daniel Poliquin (b. 1953), Jean-Marc Dalpé (b. 1957), Michel Dallaire (b. 1957), and Michel Ouellette (b. 1961). Poliquin's Ottawa-based work in translation and his polemical novel *Visions de Jude* (the publisher's title, 1990, which the author changed to *La côte de Sable* in 2000) expressed his affiliation with Jack Kerouac. Related to Quebec writers' rediscovery of 'America,' Poliquin's work has also called upon Quebec writers to re-examine prevailing definitions of *la littérature québécoise*. Published in Quebec (as is Poliquin's work), Dallaire's *Terrains vagues* (1992) also constructs a fiction about alienation, though Dallaire represents it here through a Franco-Ontarian who travels to Paris. Staying within Northern Ontario, Dalpé's 1982 play *Hawkesbury Blues* focuses on the closing down of a factory town. And Ouellette's play *French Town* (1994) depicts the impact of economic alienation on another Northern Ontario town, the alienation compounded by the setting: the francophone community lives on the fringes of an anglophone community that spends its working life cutting the timber which feeds a New York paper company. Twice removed from power, the francophone community has to find alternative ways of celebrating its capacity to persevere.

LITERATURE AND ABORIGINALITY

Gathering even more widespread attention from the 1990s on were those writings that dealt with Aboriginal cultures, including the many works of poetry, drama, oratory, and fiction that First Nations writers themselves composed. Several earlier writers were rediscovered. Included among these were George Copway (Kahgegagahbowh; Ojibwa, 1818–69), whose autobiography first appeared in 1847 and was reissued as *Recollections of Forest Life*, 1850); Mourning Dove (Christine Quintasket; Colville, 1888–1936), whose *A Salishan Autobiography* was reprinted in 1990; Harry Robinson (Okanagan, 1900–90), whose stories of nature and its relation to traditional life (edited by the ethnographer Wendy Wickwire as *Write It on Your Heart*, 1989) influenced many contemporary Aboriginal writers because of how they adapt oral storytelling methods to written form; and Pauline Johnson (Tekahionwake; Mohawk, 1861–1913). Johnson's collected works were reissued in 2002, edited by Carole Gerson and Veronica Strong-Boag, who also wrote a new biography, and more than one writer in the 1990s – the Métis poet Joan Crate (Taylor) (b. 1953), for example, in her lyric sequence *Pale as Real Ladies*, 1989)

– emphasized how the Mohawk poet used her Native heritage as a strategy of gender identity and survival. The 1990s also saw more extensive literary and anthropological responses to oral cultures, such as Robert Bringhurst's translations of the epic Haida myth tales of Skaay and Ghandl. While the stories and songs of such nineteenth-century mythtellers and shamans as Lizette K'atchodi (Northern Athapaskan, c. 1800–c. 1880) and Kâ-kîsikâw-pîhtokêw (Coming Day; Cree, c. 1850–1935) had been translated early on (by Émile Petitot, Leonard Bloomfield, and others), sensitive and accurate new editions remain to be prepared. Several ethnographic works, however, have addressed how First Nations cultures traditionally functioned; among these are Julia Cruikshank's *The Social Life of Stories* (1998), Robin Ridington's *Little Bit Know Something* (1990), and Hugh Brody's *Maps and Dreams* (1981).

Another dimension of this recuperation of Aboriginal voices within Canadian culture is represented by the new forms of fiction that (with greater sensitivity and more faithful inquiry into fact than had conventionally been the case) acknowledged the Native presence in North American history – Guy Vanderhaeghe's fictions, for example, which dramatize the interactions among the Cree, the Blood, the Blackfoot, and assorted Europeans in the cross-border territories of the West. Still another approach was taken by several writers – Jovette Marchessault, Warren Cariou (b. 1966) – whose writings inquired into their own family history, discovering Native or Métis connections that had long been suppressed or forgotten. And yet a third aspect of this topic emerges from the politics of such representation and recuperation. In the work of Robert Lalonde (b. 1947), for example – especially *Sept lacs plus au nord* (1992) – the politics of White-Native conflict informs the personal politics of the narrative; written after the crisis in Oka (where Lalonde was born, though he himself is not Native), the book does not refer directly to the Oka incident but assumes it as a political context. So too with *Cowboy* (1992) by Louis Hamelin (b. 1959), which posits a parallel between poor Natives and poor French Canadians, presenting again the case concerning cultural marginality. Stylistically, Hamelin won praise for the way he combined a popular with a sophisticated lexicon. More generally, Lalonde and Hamelin demonstrate one of the recurrent strategies of post-referendum writing in Quebec, in that, by acknowledging the presence of Cree and Maliseet voices, they are again resisting the narrowest of definitions of local culture and engaging with a wider world. The more visible the presence of Aboriginal peoples, moreover, the more willing were readers to look for Native writers. The major support for the emergence of new Native voices, however, came not from the fictional strategies of non-Native writers but from a variety of Native organizations themselves. These include the Enow'kin Centre, a Native literary arts training centre in Penticton, BC, run by Jeannette Armstrong and Greg Young-Ing (b. 1961), which publishes a literary annual called *Gatherings*; the Saskatchewan Indian Federated College in Regina; the Native Earth Performing Arts Company (est. Toronto, 1984); and the Committee to Re-establish the Trickster, a Toronto cultural organization. Affiliated with the last two groups are the playwright Tomson Highway and the poet Daniel David Moses.

Simply to list a few contemporary Native, Inuit, and Métis writers is not only to suggest the number of active writers but also to insist on the range of cultures that the number represents: poets Kateri Akiwenzie-Damm (Chippewa, b. 1965), Annharte (Anishinabe, b. 1942), Beth Brant (Mohawk, b. 1941), Beth Cuthand (Cree, b. 1949), Marilyn Dumont (Métis, b. 1955), Connie Fife (b. 1969), Louise Halfe (Sky Dancer; Cree, b. 1953), Wayne Keon (Ojibwa, b. 1946), Rita Joe (Mi'kmaq, b. 1932), Daniel David Moses (Delaware, b. 1952), Armand Garnet Ruffo (Ojibwa, b. 1955), and Gregory Scofield (Métis, b. 1966); fiction writers Jovette Marchessault (b. 1938), Robert Arthur Alexie (Gwich'in, b. 1956), Jeannette Armstrong (Okanagan, b. 1948), Bernard Assiniwi (Algo-Cree, 1935–2000), Thomas King (Cherokee, b. 1943), Lee Maracle (Métis, b. 1950), Beatrice Culleton Mosioner (Métis, b. 1949), Eden Robinson (Haisla/Heilstuk, b. 1968), Ruby Slipperjack (Farrell) (Ojibwa, b. 1952), Richard Van Camp (Dogrib, b. 1971), and Jordan Wheeler (Cree, b. 1964); dramatists Marie Humber Clements (Métis, b. 1962), Tomson Highway (Cree, b. 1951), Monique Mojica (Kuna-Rappahannock, b. 1954), Ian Ross (Métis, b. 1960), and Drew Hayden Taylor (Ojibwa, b. 1962); autobiographers Maria Campbell (Métis, b. 1940), Lee Maracle, Agnes Nanogak (Inuit, b. 1925), and Jane Willis (Cree, b. 1940); and storytellers, artists, and essayists Alootook Ipellie (Inuit, b. 1951), Lenore Keeshig-Tobias (Anishinabe, b. 1950), Basil Johnston (Ojibwa, b. 1929), Bill Reid (Haida, 1920–98), and Shirley Sterling (Salish, b. 1948).

These writers' works recurrently foreground racism and ways to control racism, particular historical incidents and their consequences, and the plight of reserve poverty and urban isolation. But such topics were by no means confined to First Nations, Inuit, and Métis writers; nor are the writers restricted by these topics. The *Bildungsroman* (Van Camp), autobiographical narrative (Campbell, Highway, Willis), oral chant (Keon), polemic (Keeshig-Tobias), linguistic fracture and pun (Annharte), traditional tale (Johnston, Reid), myth (Highway), satiric comedy (King), cartoon (Ipellie) – forms ranged widely. So did themes: gay experience (Scofield, Highway), lesbian feminism (Brant, Fife), the welfare system (Taylor), cultural extinction (Assiniwi, in *La saga des Béothuks*, 1996), nature (Moses, Halfe), irrational violence (Eden Robinson), AIDS (Wheeler, Highway), and residential-school and sexual and cultural abuse (Mosioner, Highway, Alexie, Willis, Sterling). One important characteristic of the works that tried to refuse the condition of being 'peripheral' to opportunity and power involved the regeneration of the language that writers had available to them. In *Monkey Beach* (2000) Eden Robinson not only uses Haisla words but recuperates the traditional didactic role of the tale-teller to explain how terms sound and what the sound means. Ipellie, in *Arctic Dreams and Nightmares* (1994), combines drawings with Inuit myth. Lee Maracle, in *Ravensong* (1993), sings Raven's story again; King lets Coyote loose; Mojica, in her play *Princess Pocahontas and the Blue Spots* (1989), juxtaposes European and Native images until the biases of power come clear. Tomson Highway animates Ojibwa mythical figures in his plays. Zacharias Kunuk's (b. 1957) Cannes Prize–winning film *Atanarjuak (The Fast Runner*, 2001; written by Paul Apak Anqilirq in Inuktitut; English subtitles) adaps Inuit myths of inheritance and power to a study of rivalry, growth, and retribution in a contemporary family; the filmscript, in a dual language text edited by Gillian Robinson, appeared in print in 2002. And a poem such as Akiwenzie-Damm's 'I lose track of the land' parodies the English linguistic conventions that have marginalized Native peoples – terms such as 'garrison,' 'bloodline,' 'scalping.' By so doing, the author reclaims the culture that has been 'lost track' of: a culture based in dance, tale, and song, one that lived in the light of stars rather than in urban glare, in the land rather than in pavement drains and wasting away.

The school narrative was a particularly recurrent motif, signalling not just the power of memory but also the psychological need for recuperation of self-esteem among a generation of dislocated people, a reaffirmation of their connection with community. The residential school system, like many an institutional model, began with good intentions but little sensitivity to the persons and culture involved. In schools for Natives and non-Natives alike (as several high-profile legal cases in the 1990s made clear, particularly that involving the now-defunct Christian Brothers school for boys in St. John's) authorities also paid insufficient attention to the specific emotional, linguistic, and often sexual abuses practised by some of the people charged with running the schools. The history of these schools is thus contextually relevant to a reading of contemporary literary texts.

While boarding schools had been established by Récollet and Jesuit priests and by Ursuline nuns in New France in the seventeenth century, they and later systems of custodial integration (many initially established with Native cooperation) proved short-lived. The modern version of the Canadian boarding school began in 1803, when several 'industrial schools' were set up off reserves in the West, funded by the federal government and run by Christian missionary groups (60 per cent of them Roman Catholic); these were designed to provide basic English literacy, training in a trade, and cultural assimilation. The number of these schools increased markedly through to the 1960s and extended across the country. When their characteristically harsh disciplinary practices became known, however, along with their active efforts to silence Native languages, their general refusal to recognize the value of cultural differences, and in some instances their scandalous improprieties, they were then mostly phased out. At least six schools were still operating in the 1990s. The responses of Native writers to this experience – even though, in some cases, the writers openly delighted in having learned English or French – was almost uniformly negative. Rita Joe's 'Hated Structure' in *Eskasoni* (1998) speaks of the 'misery' of the school she attended. In an interview in 1989, Tomson Highway spoke of the 'dark landscape' of assimilationism. Jane Willis's autobiographical *Geniesh* (1973), Beatrice Culleton Mosioner's novel *In Search of April Raintree* (1983), Shirley Sterling's children's novel *My Name Is Seepeetza* (1992), Highway's *The Kiss of the Fur Queen* (1998), and Robert Arthur Alexie's *Porcupines and China Dolls* (2002) all emphasize how manipulative, disruptive, and even destructive the residential schools were, and how difficult the subsequent lives of the deracinated children. Effectively, Alexie explains, the schools, by removing the children from their parents and elders, robbed the children of appropriate models of parenting, thus having an impact on the next generation as well.

The two most widely recognized Native writers of the time were Tomson Highway and Thomas King. Highway, trained as a concert pianist, turned to acting, writing, and directing in the early 1980s, in some instances collaborating with his brother René (1954–90), a choreographer and dancer, whose death from AIDS lay behind the novel *Kiss of the Fur Queen*. Tomson Highway's plays combine verbal wit with passionate politics, fantasy, myth, and physical theatre, especially music and dance. *The Rez Sisters* (1986) tells of seven women on a Manitoulin Island reserve who hope to win enough at bingo to satisfy their deepest fantasies. In a presentation alternately naturalistic and surreal (critics have likened Highway to Michel Tremblay in this regard), the women lead lives at once traumatic (struck by cancer, alcoholism, star-crossed love) and uplifting.

Throughout the play they are touched – even when they don't know it – by the presence of the sexually ambivalent trickster Nanabush. *Dry Lips Oughta Move to Kapuskasing* (1989) was written to echo *The Rez Sisters*, focusing on several male characters. Like the earlier play, it also adapts Cree/Ojibwa myth and language into the text. A dream play – its action manufactured in the mind of Zachary Jeremiah Keechigeesik, the dreamer – it too tracks through sexual satire, disease, social distress, and nightmare before it retrieves a moment of fulfillment. As with his fiction, Highway's plays recognize negation, but finally they refuse it, paying tribute instead to the power and possibility of healing.

The work of Thomas King (who was born in California of Cherokee, Greek, and German descent) is lighter in tone but no less serious in social comment. A university professor of Native Studies and Creative Writing at the University of Guelph, King is the author of critical studies of Native writing, an editor of anthologies, and a master storyteller. His short narratives and novels, together with his mock mystery, *Dreadful Water Shows Up* (2002) – written under the pseudonym Hartley Goodweather – and the satiric deadpan drama series called *The Dead Dog Café*, which he wrote for CBC radio, all won enthusiastic devotees. The stories of *One good story, that one* (1993) exemplify King's talent for combining the playful voice with a pungent social point. In 'Borders,' for example, a Blackfoot woman gets temporarily stranded on the US-Canada border because she refuses to claim either of the majority identities as her own; in 'A Seat in the Garden' the conventional epithets that distinguish White from Native get cleverly reversed; in 'Totem' the power of the totem proves to outlast the power of museums and their curators; and in several of the other stories, Coyote the trickster (changing gender, colour, and shape more or less at will) enters narrative to unhinge it, to twist the unexpected into life so that the status quo might never be sustained.

King's novels also satirically undermine existing social hierarchies. *Medicine River* (1989) tells of an outsider – a Toronto photographer and would-be onlooker – who has to come to terms with himself and his connections with a prairie community; *Green Grass, Running Water* (1993) is a set of interlocking narratives in which various characters (who live their working-class or professional lives away from their Blossom, Alberta, reserve) get caught up in a series of creation narratives; and in *Truth and Bright Water* (1999) the denizens of two border towns have to deal both with the conning artists of the Americanized present and with their own continuing contact with tradition. The creation narratives in *One good story* – the master narratives that shape the mythologies of received behaviour – are primarily Biblical and Trickster tales; in *Green Grass* they are literary and include the Noah story in Genesis, *Robinson Crusoe, Moby Dick,* Natty Bumppo (*The Deerslayer*), and the Lone Ranger, all of which are Western narratives of contact and conquest, with power lodged in might, mask, technology, and language. The humour of *Green Grass* undercuts the efficacy of all of these. Through an elaborately clever set of allusions to Native history in North America – largely unmentioned in mainstream histories and built here into phrases and names – the novel returns power to those who would use it humanely and creatively, with respect for both people and the past.

LAUGHTER AND SOCIAL CRITICISM

The serio-comic title story in King's *One good story, that one* supposes that the reader is listening in on the creation tale that an 'Indian' man is telling to a couple of white male anthropologists, who have arrived on the scene with camera and white teeth. The white men laugh a lot, without apparently understanding why. They ask for a story. The tale-teller starts off suggesting stories about recent real life: a story about 'Jimmy runs the store near Two Bridges' or a determinedly funny story about 'Billy Frank and the dead-river pig.' His friend Napiao (a Blackfoot creator's name) interrupts him to say that the white men want an 'old' story – 'maybe how the world was put together. Good Indian story like that ... Those ones have tape recorders, he says.' What follows is a mimic version of the first book of Genesis, one that Coyote the trickster seems to have perpetrated on humankind. But when the smiling white men nod, 'Make happy noises,' and leave, the story closes with the narrator 'clean[ing] up all the coyote tracks on the floor.' Who, the reader wants to know, is the trickster, and who has been tricked? The teller tells the listeners the story they want to hear, but the listeners' presence in the teller's world has already modified it. Identifying who the trickster is, therefore – teller, character, or listener – is perhaps less important than realizing that everyone (reader included) is susceptible to the tricks that Coyote plays in the world. Everyone might even be the agent of the trickster's foolery. Laughter is consequently a medium of recognition and reconciliation for human beings, a sign of their engagement with and refusal to be subdued by the frailties of being alive and open to history.

In the wake of '9-11' (2001), many media commentators affirmed that irony was now impossible and laughter a sign of disrespect. They were proved wrong by time and human nature, which soon

sought laughter as a palliative, as a way of coping with pain and perhaps fear, and then as an agent of ridicule and a medium of political
comment. Politics, of course, has long been irony's purview, and
political humour has functioned in at least two ways, to reaffirm and
to condemn. While in some instances, therefore, irony has been a
medium of condescension (dismissing whatever persons or practices
an authority-in-place deems irrelevant or inconsequential), it has also
functioned as a medium of political reform (refusing the validity of
the authority-in-place and affirming the worth of the previously marginalized). In Canada (itself marked by the WTC bombings – lives
lost, transportation disrupted, foreign and defence policies altered)
irony perhaps momentarily faltered in 2001, but TV sketch comedy
and parody (*Juste pour rire, 22 Minutes, Point Blank*) soon returned
laughter to the airwaves with renewed vigour.

In literature, too, irony (both sardonic and comedic) functioned as
the voice of protest against marginalization and as a claim upon significance. Hence many writers who espoused a particular 'politics of
the margin' used humour as a strategy of making the position engaging. Some, such as Moyez Vassanji (b. 1950) in the tragicomic scenes
of *No New Land* (1991) and *Uhuru Street* (1992), or Rohinton Mistry (b.
1952) in *Tales from Firozsha Baag* (1987), or Dany Laferrière in *Comment
faire l'amour avec un Nègre ...*, took up the politics of ethnicity through
humour, whether discussing Muslim, Parsi, or Caribbean Black culture. For Vassanji's Tanzanian characters, whether in Toronto or
urban East Africa, the comedy of people's behaviour heightens the
tensions they feel at meeting discrimination, but at the same time the
power of perspective (which is one of the benefits of humour) sustains them. For Laferrière, in his later *Cette grenade dans la main du
jeune Nègre est elle une arme ou un fruit?* (1993) and *Pays sans chapeau*
(1996; tr. as *Down among the Dead Men*, 1997), humour masks despair,
for light-hearted humour is scarcely possible in a Haiti governed by
threat, violence, and the Tonton Macoute. Laferrière emphasizes that
the will of people to survive still sustains them; and their need to be
recognized informs how he will use fiction to voice a serious social
protest. Identity politics in Quebec followed a related path. The
ironies of writers such as Jacques Ferron or Jacques Godbout (especially in *Les têtes à Papineau*, 1981) criticized the status quo, ridiculing
presumptuousness and celebrating alternative social possibilities.
While later writers such as Paule Noyart and Monique Proulx might
bewail what they construe to be a loss of cultural solidarity, they also
acknowledge the irony that follows from it: less collectivity brings
about cultural crisis but permits a different kind of cultural richness.
François Barcelo is more satiric in his novels, Louise Desjardins (b.

1943), in *La Love* (1993), more polemical, using the English-language term ironically in her title so as to demonstrate stylistically how she sees social change to be happening. Gaétan Soucy (b. 1958), by contrast, as in *La petite fille qui aimait trop les allumettes* (1998, tr. 2000), is openly critical of the traditional world of social and religious paternalism and of those who would romanticize its passing. The ironies here emphasize the power of change, rather than the power of loss.

Ironies of gender and sexuality express the politics of still other social margins, as in feminist and gay writing. Feminist irony, that is, while often earnestly activist, also sometimes invited engagement through laughter, as with Susan Haley (b. 1949) in *Getting Married in Buffalo Jump* (1987) or various works by Aritha Van Herk, such as *No Fixed Address* (1986). Strongly marked by her political commitment to women's rights and her aesthetic commitment to genre blur, Van Herk's fictions, histories, and critical writings celebrate the vitality of both the body and the imagination. In a different vein, the bawdy romps of the characters in the inventive fictions of Terry Griggs (b. 1951), such as *Rogue's Wedding* (2002), adapt the ironic strategies of the picaresque; here Griggs laughs at the restrictiveness of sexual and social conventions, from marriage customs in small-town Ontario to the petty ambitions of revenge. The arch ironies of Eric McCormack's (b. 1938) fantasies in *First Blast of the Trumpet against the Monstrous Regiment of Women* (1997), the title drawn from the writings of John Knox, may well be tangentially related to these versions of gender politics. Gay writing, too, insisted on the leaven of comedy, as throughout Michel Tremblay's plays and fictions – for example, his 1998 play about his loving but resistant relationship with his mother, *Encore une fois, si vous permettez* (tr. 1998 as *For the Pleasure of Seeing Her Again*). The unlikely combination of comedy and murder that characterizes the gay mysteries of Edward O. Phillips (b. 1931) gives sexual irony a quite different aspect: more mordant, less relaxed in its acceptance of the alternatives it addresses. But these marginalities are not necessary to irony. Sometimes, as in the satiric objectification of Larry in Carol Shields's *Larry's Party* or the funny-sad subjectivity of the stories of Mark Anthony Jarman (b. 1955) – for example, the hockey player's 'herky-jerky picaresque' in *Salvage King, Ya!* (1997) – even being white, male, and heterosexual could be seen as an identity open to laughter. And it often was.

Other writers took world and national politics as their subject and again found laughter to be a way of reading public events through the lens of the comedy of life. Josef Škvorecký's (b. 1924) Czech dissidents in his early novels and the comic characters in *The End of Lieutenant Boruvka* (1989), say, provide examples of how black comedy functions as a form of political resistance, an intellectual survival tactic in politically restricted time. Irony combines with social exposé. More gently, Ven Begamudré's (b. 1956) allegorical adaptations of Czech folk-tale conventions in *Laterna magika* (1997) sympathetically shape tales of love and greed into comments on the human condition across national borders. And focusing on Canada, John MacLachlan Gray's eloquent essays (*Lost in North America*, 1994), along with his exuberant theatre (e.g., *Don Messer's Jubilee*, 1987), celebrate the nation through its habit of irony as well as its civic strengths. The irony functions as a voice of affirmation in the face of powers that speak more loudly but with only apparently more force.

Inevitably, language became the subject – even the target – of humour as well as its method, as when George Bowering's *Caprice* (1987) or *Shoot!* (1994) skewers not just the form of the gunslinger Western but also the stereotypes and verbal clichés that conventionally identify hero and villain, Indian and Woman, vernacular speech and Western regional preoccupation. Nonsense verse also found practitioners, as in the bathroom humour of the popular children's books by Robert Munsch (b. 1945) or the verbal wit of such collections of children's verse as *Eenie Meenie Manitoba* (1996) by Robert Heidbreder, *Llamas in the Laundry* (2002) by William New, or the many books of Dennis Lee (*Bubblegum Delicious* appeared in 2000). Sometimes, genre fiction entertained through wit, as in the delightful mysteries by C. C. Benison (Douglas Whiteway, b. 1951); set in British royal palaces, they combine the sleuthing talents of Jane Bee, a Canadian housemaid (daughter of an RCMP officer) who bears a distinct resemblance to Anne of Green Gables, with those of the Queen. Popular song lyrics, too, sometimes played wittily with literature, as when the folk-rock Moxy Fruvous single 'My Baby Loves a Bunch of Authors' (subsequently released on *Live Noise*, 1998) rhymes 'who needs a shave/ He's' with 'Robertson Davies.' Sometimes, in other words, laughter has little directly to do with the state and nearly everything to do with the enjoyment of idiosyncrasy, incongruity, the play of the unexpected, and the playfulness of sound. But in any utterance, ideology is never far away. And humour may well be as culture-marked as it is personality-bound.

FROM LAUGHTER TO VIOLENCE

Clearly, not all writers wanted in their writing to endorse the state or engage with its possibilities, and especially towards the end of the twentieth century, a number of essays, stories, poems, and journalistic articles appeared that took sardonic delight in the very superficiality of fad and fashion. If such works commented on the state at all, it was only by implication. They tended more to engage with popular culture than to criticize it. Douglas Coupland's work (for all its later claim on spiritual illumination) perhaps exemplifies the popularity of such urban chic, though its creative insight into the national culture is evident nevertheless in *Souvenir of Canada* (2001). Equally characteristic are the writings of Russell Smith, Zsuzsi Gartner, Hal Niedzviecki (b. 1971), and Barbara Gowdy (b. 1950). Niedzviecki's *We Want Some Too* (2000) champions the value of alternative subcultures. Gartner's *All the Anxious Girls on Earth* (1999), however, reveals the pathos underlying contemporary mores; Smith's *Young Men* (1999) hints at the angst beneath alternative lifestyle choices; and Gowdy's send-up of politically correct social preoccupations in *Mister Sandman* (1995), while as painful as it is comic, suggests an impatience with the superficiality of conventional ideas as well. Her parable of African elephant behaviour, *The White Bone* (1998), more openly espouses the value of family and caring, though it closes in disruption, intrusion, and destruction. Family stories in this decade – *A Good House* (1999) by Bonnie Burnard (b. 1945), for example, along with Gowdy's work – characteristically, in fact, represent 'happiness' cautiously, refusing to treat it as an absolute, either to be experienced or to be desired; instead, happiness is ordinary and interrupted by the equally ordinary 'violence' of pain, death, disease, hurt, anger, envy, and betrayal.

In the 1990s, works appeared that expressed a darker vision of these same subjects: sexuality, children's lives, religion, politics, science, the world. Three of the most effective science essayists of the time, for example – David Suzuki (b. 1936) and Wade Davis (b. 1953), both television personalities as well, and Marq de Villiers (b. 1940) – all warned of ecological disaster. Davis's *The Clouded Leopard* (1998) told of species loss; de Villiers's *Water* (1999) told of drought, pollution, political competition, and other direct or indirect agents of starvation for many citizens of the planet. David Adams Richards's explorations of a fictional underclass in the Miramichi, in other words, had plenty of corroboration in sociological detail, and disenchantment was dramatized in multiple ways. The cyberpunk actions of the characters of William Gibson (b. 1948), as in *Mona Lisa Overdrive* (1988) and *The Difference Engine* (1991), forecasts a technological future both violent and uncontrolled. The stories of Derek McCormack (b. 1969), as in *Dark Rides* (1996), tell of junkies, violence, and sexual plunder, less as a sign of commodification than as the facts that constitute some people's daily lives. These titles, moreover, were by no means the only signs of a younger generation's encounters

with drugs, aimlessness, escapism, and random cruelty, as the stories
of Nancy Lee (b. 1979) in *Dead Girls* (2002) suggest, or those of Camil-
la Gibb (b. 1968). The tales that the twin sisters Claire Dé and Anne
Dandurand (b. 1953) separately wrote also reveal the preoccupations
of their generation: the 'real' world, that is, and the predictability
only that the same empty 'realities' that exist in the present will continue into the future. As with many others of this time, the intent of
their writing seemed to be to shock the middle-class reader. In the
work of Michael Turner (b. 1962) – especially in *The Pornographer's
Poem* (1999), where a (judicial? religious?) inquiry is cast as a porn-
film loop in which the reader becomes the voyeur – the shock is
extreme, both because of the subject and because of the method. The
author's central target is the loss of values in the suburbs – in other
words, the pornography of middle-class support of (even investment
in) the porn industry, and therefore of the middle class's hypocrisy,
its apparent willing sacrifice of the young to models of profit and
greed even while it criticizes the existence of the skin trade. 'Pornography' is represented as a sexual industry here; in many (especially
feminist) works, by contrast, pornography was redefined as violence
itself, however much it might be tolerated in society at large. 'Realism' came to denote the life of an underclass, and 'realistic' in this
context implied alternative politics, activist protest, and desperate
resignation. On rare occasions the term 'realism' was celebratory, as
in the 'work poetry' of Tom Wayman. More often, it condemned the
iniquitousness of a social and economic system that fostered
inequities and seemingly approved of them.

Sexuality was clearly represented as one site of such violence,
whether as an actual social phenomenon or as a literary subject: the
bullying tactics of gay bashing, open attacks on women, or less overt
but also destructive acts of sexual discrimination. The gay and lesbian poems of John Barton (b. 1957) and Ian Iqbal Rashid (b. 1965),
the plays of Tremblay and Bouchard, the stories of Andy Quan (b.
1969), Shyam Selvadurai (b. 1965), and Evelyn Lau (b. 1971), both fictional and personal: all provide ample evidence of attack and insecurity. Nor is child life always depicted as rosy, as Turner's work and
the many books on residential schools make obvious. By fetishizing
the body, Turner's novel further argues, so-called respectable society
robs the young of the joy of sexuality, instructs them in aimlessness
and despair, and victimizes them. Pornography, the novel paradoxically argues, is at once the articulation of whatever a society finds
anathema and the tease that invites the susceptible into other people's destructive orbit, where money and power are all.

In all these worlds, though Quan and others affirm the possibility of their characters coming personally to terms with their sexuality, the very idea of 'progress' is suspect. Whatever individuals might aspire to, the world around them does not facilitate it: families do not necessarily cohere, social legislation does not readily open to change; communities and religions and organizations continue to discriminate on suspect grounds. Such publications had consequences, but they did not always change minds. In fact, while the frank sexual vocabulary and occasional scatology of several of these works attracted some readers, it dismayed others and confirmed still others in their taste for more conventional topics and strategies, narrative closure among them. Whether to satisfy this desire for conventional simplicity or merely as a coincidental enterprise, a number of publishers during the 1990s began successfully to print and market 'escape literature' – pop poetry, 'true' tales of the strange and peculiar, romances, mysteries, and other genre fiction. Here too, however, linguistic and social frankness was not unknown. Harlequin romances at the end of the twentieth century nudged their way closer and closer to explicit descriptions of sexual intercourse. The Saskatchewan mysteries of Gail Bowen (b. 1942) dealt with racism in Regina as well as with fictional crime. The Yorkshire mysteries of Peter Robinson (b. 1950), as in *Aftermath* (2001), dealt with the trauma of crime's consequences as well as with detection and solution. In literature, that is, the condition of living came to seem more tenuous than secure. And other media reiterated such trauma. The films of David Cronenberg – *Crash* (1996), for example – collapsed sex with violence, while John Greyson's 1995 adaptation of Michel-Marc Bouchard's 1987 play *Les feluettes* (*Lilies*) collapsed violence with sex and religion. In such a milieu, laughter (unless it is merely cruel) dissipates.

RECUPERATIVE PARADIGMS OF IDENTITY: ETHNICITY & SEXUALITY

Given such a perceived mix of social conditions – peacefulness along with covert danger, happiness along with psychological trauma, wealth along with poverty, disease along with health, inconsistencies of legal practice and attitudes to gender and age, and multiple differences in language, communal assumptions, and systems and degrees of belief – it is not surprising that a culture of victimization should take hold. Canada in the 1990s, in short, was in many respects like numerous other late-twentieth-century societies. But it nevertheless proved more stable than many others, and despite a reputation in some quarters for blandness (its penchant for irony and strength of social vision occasionally go unrecognized even at home), it provided opportunities for personal expression in which most Canadians continued to take pride. Within this environment, several voices took up opportunities to assert difference; they called for general social reform, sought a personal place within the state power structure, declaimed against racism, demonstrated the inequities of cultural history, asserted their own worth, occasionally claimed the 'margin' as the only respectable social position from which to speak, sometimes declared the virtue of remaining apart from and sometimes affirmed the value of engagement with whatever they identified as the 'mainstream,' and repeatedly examined the ambiguity of competing codes of identity. Some of these voices won a wide audience, a few the attention of only a coterie. Generalizations mislead. But on the whole, the writings that addressed these issues were lively. Their recurrent effect, moreover, was to declare *presence*: being in the world, being in Canada, being 'X.' Not just being 'Generation X,' though that was the focus for Coupland and others, but being in – finding 'being' through – their self-proclaimed category, one that provided the grounds for speaking, that permitted these speakers to claim validity for their own experience of life.

These 'categories' (which rapidly became academic specializations as well) include everything from religion and ethnicity to colour and sexual preference, from gender and age and 'class' or status to region and the experience of a particular disease or physical condition. Christian, Jewish, Ukrainian, Italian, Black, Asian, gay, lesbian, female, male, worker, urban, Maritime, Northern – these and other adjectives became active markers of identity. Perhaps inevitably, some claims upon the validity of the margin became competitive – as though whoever was most disenfranchised was most worthy, as though degrees of discrimination could be adequately or constructively tallied. At other times, too, works were written plainly as therapy, and in such cases, regardless of how personally important their observations might be, the resulting literature seldom transcended the page. Some writers, however, made of their chosen category not so much a place of refuge as a place of resonance. In these instances, the category labels may articulate a position of origin, but they do not restrict or contain the literary experience or the insight into human behaviour. Non-Christians, for example, can read and appreciate the work of Margaret Avison, whose avowedly Christian *No Time* appeared in 1989; non-Jews can read Anne Michaels (b. 1958), whose poems (*Miner's Pond*, 1991) and post-Shoah novel *Fugitive Pieces* (1996) won international attention, or the work of Abraham Klein (whose poems, fiction, essays, notebooks, and editorials were edited into six volumes between 1983 and 2000, under the general direction of Zailig Pollock). So can informed 'outsiders' read First Nations texts with appreciation, read gendered texts with sensitivity, and (with a will to understand) also read texts that declaratively associate themselves with a particular ethnicity. Briefly to focus here on gay writing and on four such ethnically constructed cultural groupings – South Asian, East Asian, Latin American, and Black (each further divisible) – is not to exhaust critical possibilities. Indeed, the range of ethnicities that contemporary Canadian writing represents includes Arabic, American, German, Greek, Hungarian, Icelandic, Irish, Italian, Norse, Polish, Russian, Scottish, Turkish, and a host of other identities as well. The Polish-language poetry of Bogdan Czaykowski (b. 1932), such as *Okanaganskie sady* (1998), is only one example of the literary work that Canadian writers have published in languages other than the two 'official' ones. In a different genre, the popular film *My Big Fat Greek Wedding* (2002), directed by John Corbett (b. 1961) and written by Winnipeg-born Nia Vardalos (b. 1962), comically renders the tribulations of one of the daughters in a Greek immigrant family in the months leading up to her marriage to a man from outside the ethnic community. The number of critics of 'multiculturalism,' moreover – Smaro Kamboureli, Winfried Siemerling, Neil Bissoondath, Cecil Foster, Joseph Pivato, Sneja Gunew, and Antonio d'Alfonso, for instance – testifies to both the range of this subject and its complexity.

A brief statistical digression at this point might prove useful. Census data regarding population in Canada (from the surveys of 1997 and 2001) reveal the following:

- DISTRIBUTION: of the total population (30,007,094 in 2001, up 4 per cent in five years) approximately 78 per cent is urban, with 32 per cent of the population living in the three largest metropolitan areas (Toronto, Montreal, Vancouver); this percentage of city dwellers represents a rise of 8 per cent since 1971; the absolute number of rural residents has remained approximately the same since 1891 (between 4 and 6 million), with urban dwellers outnumbering them since 1921.
- AGE: the average age of Canadians is growing higher, the median age being 37.6 in 2001 (the group aged between 0 and 14 years accounted for approximately 20 per cent of the population in 2001, compared with nearly 30 per cent in 1971).
- IMMIGRATION POLICY CHANGES: while 69 per cent of immigrants between 1961 and 1971 came from Europe, 6 per cent from the USA, 7 per cent from the Caribbean and Latin America, 3 per cent from Africa, and 14 per cent from Asia, the distribution subsequently

changed: between 1981 and 1991, 25 per cent of immigrants came from Europe, 4 per cent from the USA, 16 per cent from the Caribbean and Latin America, 6 per cent from Africa, and 48 per cent from Asia.

- ETHNICITY: in 1991 approximately 28 per cent of Canadians declared they had multiple ethnic origins; of those Canadians who declared a single ethnic origin, approximately 22 per cent declared their inherited ethnicity to be French, 15 per cent English, 3 per cent each German, Scottish, Irish, and Italian, and 2 per cent Chinese; perhaps of more significance, approximately 3 per cent declared their 'ethnicity' to be 'Canadian' (see also Tables 3 and 4).

- RELIGION: 71 per cent of Canadians claimed to be Christian (45 per cent Roman Catholic and 36 per cent Protestant, of whom one-third were members of the United Church of Canada); approximately 1 per cent of Canadians were Muslims, and 1 per cent Jews, while just under 1 per cent each adhered to Buddhism, Hinduism, or the Sikh religion; approximately 13 per cent of Canadians claimed no religious affiliation; these figures represent a statistically large percentage increase in the number of those espousing Asian religions during the last decade of the twentieth century, though the absolute numbers remain small.

- LABOUR FORCE: approximately 3 per cent of the population was employed in cultural industries (including publishing and printing, film and theatre, photography and distribution, broadcasting and bookselling, museums, archives, and library services); census data also supply statistics on declared reading habits, book sales, television preferences, periodical subscriptions, and related information.

An ambiguity of terms is at once apparent. 'Asian,' for instance, includes East Asian, South Asian, Central Asian, and Arabic, but not Russian; religious affiliations ('Muslim,' 'Christian,' 'Jewish') do not uniformly overlap with conventional determinations of 'ethnicity,' but 'ethnicity' in ordinary speech can refer inconsistently to colour, nationality, citizenship, and/or religion, making both the term and whatever the term refers to hard to interpret. Nevertheless, in Canada in the 1990s the categories 'South Asian,' 'East Asian,' 'Latin American,' and 'Black' were all in use.

South Asian refers to a range of people of Indian, Pakistani, Bangladeshi, or Sri Lankan background – Muslim, Hindu, Sikh, Buddhist, Parsi, Christian – from East Africa, Fiji, and the Caribbean as well as from the Indian subcontinent. Among noteworthy contemporary writers in Canada who have cultural links with South Asia are

Table 4 Ethnic origins, 1991–2001 (percentages of population)

	1991	2001
AFRICAN	.09	.6
AMERICAN	.7	.8
ARAB AND NORTH AFRICAN	.6	1.1
ASIAN: West (primarily Armenian and Iranian) and East (excluding Chinese and Philippine)	1.60	2.0
AUSTRALIAN/NEW ZEALAND	.1	.1
BLACK	.83	.2
BRITISH	28.13	.5
British and French	3.97	
British and other	9.32	
English	23.9	20.2
Scottish	14.7	14.0
Welsh	1.2	1.2
CANADIAN	2.83	23.0
Canadian and other	.21	16.0
Acadian	–	.2
Québécois	–	.3
CARIBBEAN	.34	1.6
CHINESE	2.17	3.7
DUTCH	1.32	3.1
FIRST NATIONS	1.35	3.4
FRENCH	22.77	15.8
GERMAN	3.37	9.3
GREEK	.50	.7
INUIT	.11	.2
IRISH	13.2	12.9
MÉTIS	.27	1.0
'MULTIPLE' ETHNICITY	28.87	38.0
British and Canadian	.43	
French and other	1.57	
INDO-PAKISTANI	1.50	3.3
ITALIAN	2.77	4.3
JEWISH	.91	1.2
LATIN AMERICAN (primarily Chile and El Salvador)	.32	.58
PACIFIC ISLANDS	.03	
PHILIPPINE	.58	1.1
POLISH	2.7	2.8
PORTUGUESE	.90	1.2
RUSSIAN AND OTHER EUROPEAN	3.60	5.85
SCANDINAVIAN	.64	3.5
SPANISH	.30	.7
UKRAINIAN	1.35	3.6
OTHERS AND NOT STATED	3.00	.06

Figures from Canadian census data.

The numbers total greater than 100 per cent because census respondents described themselves by more than one category; the categories are not mutually exclusive. Of more interest, therefore, than the exactness of numbers are the categories themselves, which differ markedly from those that appear in Table 3; the ways in which Canadians described their ethnicity reflected, in some cases, a desire for greater specificity and, in others, the accuracy of declaring a multiple heritage. Of particular interest is the number of Canadians who declare 'Canadian' as an ethnicity.

Ven Begamudré, Uma Parameswaran (b. 1938), Michael Ondaatje, Rienzi Crusz (b. 1925), Nazneen Sadiq (b. 1944), Cyril Dabydeen, Bharati Mukherjee, Shyam Selvadurai, Rohinton Mistry, Suniti Namjoshi (b. 1941), Hiro (McIlwraith) Boga (b. 1949), Shani Mootoo (b. 1957), M. G. Vassanji, and Neil Bissoondath. While a critical literature about diasporic writing could apply to all, these writers' particular experiences of emigration and exile spell out radically different experiences of home. For Selvadurai, Namjoshi, and Mootoo, questions of sexuality are as important as those of authenticity; for Boga, in *Shahnaz* (2000), emphasis falls on opportunities for women's education. Bissoondath challenges the 'divisiveness' of the idea of multiculturalism, as does Mukherjee, who through works such as *Jasmine* (1989) went on to position herself within the social contexts of American iconography. Begamudré and Ondaatje sought wider frames of reference than South Asia alone, while Parameswaran, Crusz, Vassanji (the creative force behind TSAR publications and the *Toronto Review of Contemporary Writing Abroad*), and Dabydeen returned repeatedly to the binaries that divide Canada from, respectively, their native India, Sri Lanka, Kenya, and Guyana. The divisions are not clear-cut. In some of his stories, for example, Dabydeen (born in Guyana) records how in India he discovers the degree to which he has become Canadian. But cultural binaries do nonetheless have a continuing force; they are also the inheritance of a second-generation writer such as Danielle Lagah (b. 1977), whose poems evocatively confront the limits and possibilities of language-in-place (her own Canada) and the inconstant temptations of the unknown (her father's India).

The Indian subcontinent also features, of course, in many books by non-Asian Canadian writers, whether they were born in India, as Rona Murray was, or travelled there, as did such writers as Frank Davey, Janette Turner Hospital, Andrew Wainwright (b. 1946), and Keath Fraser. Among francophone travel writers, three of the most accomplished also take India as their subject: Louis Gauthier (b. 1944) pursuing a quest for Nepal in *Le pont de Londres* (1988), Yvon Rivard (b. 1945) seeking a guru in *Les silences du Corbeau* (1986), and Yolande Villemaire (b. 1949) inquiring into Indian mythologies in *Le dieu dansant* (1995).

Of all 'South Asian Canadian' writings, those of Rohinton Mistry won the most widespread attention, garnering national and international awards (Commonwealth Prize in 1991 and 1995, Booker short list in 1991, Giller Prize in 1995, Kiriyama Prize in 2002); *A Fine Balance* then became an 'Oprah Pick of the Month' (celebrated on Oprah Winfrey's popular television program), and the author's sales soared.

Mistry came to attention twelve years after he had emigrated from India, when *Tales from Firozsha Baag* (1987) was shortlisted for a Governor General's Award. A collection of linked tales set in a Bombay *baag* (or apartment complex), it records the sour-sweet lives of the largely Parsi families who live there. (The Parsi, or Zoroastrian community, once centred in ancient Persia, moved in large numbers to Bombay to avoid discrimination and conversion when Persia turned to Islam; by the end of the twentieth century, only about 70,000 Parsis remained in Bombay, while some 30,000 had emigrated, many relocating in Toronto.) Mistry's book also reveals the mixed options that open to several boys and two girls in the younger generation who grow up in the baag. One young man commits himself to social reform, another to thievery; one tries to emigrate to Canada but cannot adapt, another proves unsuccessful in breaking at all away from his mother; one emigrates to New York and pretends to turn his back on all things Indian, while the central character (Kersi Boyce, who also moves abroad) – and perhaps Kersi is the internal 'author' of the stories told here – commits himself to maintaining links with the past at the same time as he actively learns to adapt to his new life in Toronto. With recurrent humour and with the sudden pathos of revelation, these stories highlight what it means to be a storyteller, in tune with the narratives of continuity and at the same time acutely aware of the unpredictable and artfully ambiguous processes of social change.

These issues recur in the novels that Mistry subsequently published – *Such a Long Journey* (1991), *A Fine Balance*, and *Family Matters* (2002) – as did his primary focus on India, its social traumas, and the 'bonheur d'occasion' for which individuals strive. Gustad Noble and his wife, Dilnavaz, in *Such a Long Journey* slowly move from the exclusiveness that they initially believe their cultural status gives them to an acceptance of the cultural hybridity of India (and, by extension, Canada). While *Family Matters* also seeks to close in happiness, *A Fine Balance* more effectively narrates the difficult lives of two Hindu tailors who have apprenticed to a Muslim and who now board with a Parsi widow. Various cross-cultural (and cross-linguistic) negotiations take place as the tailors and widow try to live outside politics and the restrictiveness of religious rule. (Mistry makes liberal use of Gujerati and Hindi terms both to emphasize the particularity of detail – dress, food, ritual, vernacular epithet, social role – and to dramatize in speech the exile's experience: the alienation that accompanies unfamiliarity.) The tailors Darji and Omprakesh cannot plan for fate, however, and when Indira Gandhi's 1975 'Emergency' politics sweeps them violently, randomly out of place, the novel challenges character and reader alike to make sense of loss, and in the face of despair to try to find out how still to affirm self-worth.

East Asian writers – those Canadians who claim a Chinese, Japanese, Korean, Philippine, Vietnamese, Singaporean, or Malaysian connection – include the Eurasian sisters Winifred Reeve ('Onoto Watanna,' 1875–1954) and Edith Eaton ('Sui Sin Far,' 1865–1914), along with more recent poets Goh Poh Seng (b. 1936), Lakshmi Gill (b. 1943), Fred Wah, Thuong Vuong-Riddick (b. 1940), Andy Quan, Jim Wong-Chu (b. 1949), and Rita Wong (b. 1968); fiction writers Joy Kogawa (b. 1935), SKY (Sharon Kwan Yin) Lee (b. 1952), Ying Chen (b. 1961), Evelyn Lau (b. 1971), Hiromi Goto (b. 1966), Madeleine Thien (b. 1974), and Rui Umezawa (b. 1959); writers of autobiography and other prose forms Adrienne (Poy) Clarkson (b. 1939), a CBC television broadcaster and academic, who was named governor general of Canada in 1999, Wayson Choy, Denise Chong, Roy Miki, and Michael David Kwan; and children's writer Paul Yee (b. 1956). These writers attracted attention for different reasons. Roy Miki's political work to ensure redress for Japanese Canadians (who had had property seized and been summarily relocated during the Second World War) carried over into the politics of his literary criticism, which affirmed the bilateralism of the 'hyphenated' experience and the need to validate difference, rather than pretend that racial integration had erased it. Yee's *Breakaway* (1994), aimed at child readers, carries a similar message. Kogawa and Goto also addressed the Japanese relocation issue, Goto in *Chorus of Mushrooms* (1994) and Kogawa especially in *Obasan* (1981), where a brother tries to live invisibly in white society while his sister seeks to find out about and come to appreciate the lives of the generations before her. Umezawa, in *The Truth about Death and Dying* (2002), like Kogawa (and Dennis Bock, b. 1964, in *The Ash Garden*, 2001), takes up in fiction the personal consequences of the 1945 bombings of Hiroshima and Nagasaki. Kogawa's later works turn passionately, if less persuasively, to questions of abuse, religion, and spiritual service.

For other writers, 'difference' was narrated in sexual or generational terms. Gill, Choy, and Quan explored homosexuality as well as race. Lau retold, in *Runaway* (1989) and other works, of her teenage years as a prostitute. Thien's subject in *Simple Recipes* (2001) was the fractured family, the subject also of such Chinese Canadian films as Mina Shum's *Double Happiness* (1994, starring Sandra Oh) and Ying Chen's novel *L'ingratitude* (1995), which traces the insufferability of a mother's involvement in her child's life. Choy, in *Jade Peony* (1995) and his autobiography *Paper Shadows* (1999), also sought to resolve the ambiguities of his family history, an inquiry that similarly influenced Lee's novel *Disappearing Moon Café* (1990) and the autobiographical narratives of Chong (*The Concubine's Children*, 1994) and Kwan (*Things that Must Not Be Forgotten*, 2001). Kwan's tale of his Chinese father's apparent collaboration with the Japanese in the early 1940s, and Chong's and Lee's of the women whose lives were silenced by the exclusionary practices of Canadian immigration policy in the earlier twentieth century, reveal the force of history in the lives of the generation that inherits it and the emotional as well as intellectual power of the need to know what happened.

Fred Wah's writings – established initially with the *Tish* Group in 1961 – came more and more to be associated with electronic technological innovation (with Frank Davey, editing *The Swift Current Anthology*, 1986), with appreciations of postmodern art (with Roy Miki, editing *Beyond the Orchard*, 1997, on bp Nichol's *The Martyrology*), and with questions of ethnicity and social ethics (with Miki, editing *Colour. An Issue*, a 1993 issue of *West Coast Line*). Wah's own creative work, notably his several poetry volumes (including *Music at the Heart of Thinking*, 1987, and *Alley Alley Home Free*, 1992) and the fictions of *Diamond Grill* (1996), celebrate language in the act of movement, meaning in the process of changing. In other words, drawing on his own mixed heritage, he challenges conceptions of identity that assume it to be uniform. The result is a language equivalent to jazz, the body's plurality 'breathing thinking' through sounds and signs.

Latin America: Unlike Wah and Kogawa, writers in Canada with Latin American connections tend to be recent arrivals, not the sons and daughters of generations of previous immigrants. Among them must be counted writers who had established reputations in their own countries before emigrating to Canada (some as political exiles) and who continue to write in Spanish: Chileans Gonzalo Millàn (b. 1947) and Leandro Urbina (b. 1949), Salvadoran Alfonso Quijada Urías (b. 1940), Argentinian Pablo Urbanyi (b. 1939). Writing in French and Portuguese, the Brazilian novelist Sergio Kokis relocated to Quebec, as did Marilú Mallet (b. 1945). Kokis, in particular, attracted critical attention in Canada for *L'art du maquillage* (1997; tr. as *The Art of Deception*, 2002), *Le pavillon des miroirs* (1995; tr. as *Funhouse*, 1999), and *Saltimbanques* (1999). Recurrently, he deals with the differences between the real and the facsimile. *Funhouse* opens mirrors into personal identity, for example, and *The Art of Deception* into the art trade: does a skilled young painter, the novel asks, who has the ability to see past surfaces into another dimension, lose his claim to artistic integrity when he begins to paint forgeries for a criminal ring? Implicitly, Kokis's writing asks about the parameters of cultural identity as well: what is real when a person is displaced, or when a person acquires allegiances to more than one place? This is the central question that Guillermo Verdecchia (b. 1962) asks in another way, especially in his play *Fronteras americanas* (1993). Dramatically, Verdecchia explores the bilateral sense of home that variously illuminates and desolates the life of an immigrant (perhaps especially one for whom Canada's official languages are both 'foreign'); what the central character ultimately discovers is that he lives 'on' the border he knows, rather than on one side or another.

Among other Latin American Canadian writers, Argentinian-born Alberto Manguel (b. 1948) became an important anthologist in Canada, as well as a gay rights commentator, broadcaster, and historian of reading. Chileans Jorge Etcheverry (b. 1945) and Carmen Rodríguez (b. 1948) established new reputations in English to go with their continuing work in Spanish. At the same time as this movement north was taking place, moreover, many Canadian-born writers, from Gary Geddes to Lake Sagaris (b. 1956), or writers such as Northern Ireland–born George McWhirter, made Latin America their home for at least brief periods and the subject of much of their own work. So did the English-born travel writer Ronald Wright (b. 1948), in works that highlighted the plight of the Native peoples in modern times, *Time among the Maya* (1989) and *Stolen Continents* (1991). Andrew Pyper (b. 1968) set one of his adventure novels, *The Trade Mission* (2002), in the Amazon jungle, drawing on some of his own observations of rainforest cultures. And finally, the ethnoanthropologist and conservationist Wade Davis won renown for his dramatic and articulate investigations into toxic and narcotic practices in various world communities, including those of the Amazon and the Caribbean.

Africa and the Caribbean: Black history in Canada – as recorded in Cecil Foster's *A Place Called Heaven* (1996) and Robin Winks's *The Blacks in Canada* (rev. 1997) and in such anthologies as *Other Voices* (1985), edited by Lorris Elliott (b. 1931), and *Bluesprint* (2001), edited by the poet and short story writer Wayde Compton (b. 1972) – began as early as 1783, with Loyalist emigration from the newly independent USA., primarily to Nova Scotia. This move lay behind the beginnings of Africville, the Black Nova Scotian community about which Maxine Tynes (b. 1949) writes. Many of the African Canadians who were moved in this manner were slaves at the time, some not freed until Britain's emancipation legislation in 1833. Others were displaced from Jamaica to Canada in 1796 as a 'solution' to slave revolts in the Caribbean, though some of these people were sent on directly from Nova Scotia to Sierra Leone, newly established in 1808 as a 'free' nation for 'returned' slaves (though with little planning or sensitivity to cultural differences or the culture in place). As a result of a further contretemps between the British North American colonies and the USA in 1812–14, more Black refugees arrived north, followed by up to 75,000 persons by 1861 (the numbers were exaggerated at the time to make political points) on the 'underground railroad to Heaven' in the years leading up to the American Civil War. A utopian society called the Negro Colony of Dawn was established in Canada West (Ontario) in 1842. And the governor of Vancouver Island, James Douglas (himself part Guyanese), in 1858 invited a group of skilled, free, literate Black men and women to emigrate north from California to what is now British Columbia, with guarantees of voting rights and the opportunity to own land. Reactions to these groups all differed, and the responses of writers who trace their history to the separate groups – George Elliott Clarke in Nova Scotia and Wayde Compton in British Columbia, for example – differed accordingly. Clarke's work, as in *Beatrice Chancy: A Passional* (1999), which adapts operatic techniques to poetry, is sharply critical of racism. Compton's *49th Parallel Psalm* (1997) is another poetic tour de force, combining the strategies of the blues, lament, rock and roll, and other musical forms to tell of the disparity between Governor Douglas's promise and the reality of discrimination and exclusion that became the lot of many a subsequent generation.

As Foster and others make clear, the social experience of those who emigrated in the later twentieth century, especially from the Caribbean and Africa directly, differed substantially from those who traced their cultural history in place. In Canada this later wave of arrivals impacted upon Canadian life in a myriad ways, ranging from the popular (the annual Caribana festival in Toronto) to the institutional (the visibility of Black local politicians and ministers of the Crown). African-born Black writers include Archie Crail (b. 1948), Jane Tapsubei Creider (b. 1948), Miguna Miguna (b. 1962), Paul Tiyambe Zeleza (b. 1955), and Nega Mezlekia (b. 1958), whose visually evocative, prizewinning autobiography *Notes from the Hyena's Belly*, about Ethiopian civil war and family disruption, caused a critical stir about the relation between author and editor when it appeared in 2000. Their various works reflect on such issues as political corruption in Zimbabwe, social injustice in Kenya, adolescence and ambition in Ethiopia, and racism in Canada. White African writers who relocated in Canada, largely from South Africa, Kenya, and

Zimbabwe, include fiction and poem writers William Schermbrucker (b. 1938) and Jeni Couzyn (b. 1942), the poet-critic Méira Cook (b. 1965), and the prose writer Ernst Havemann (b. 1918), who later moved to New Zealand. Couzyn's *Selections* appeared in 2000.

More directly influential on other Canadian writers were those who traced their immediate origins to the Caribbean (Jamaica, Barbados, Trinidad, Antigua, and other islands, as well as Guyana and Belize). These writers recorded life histories – Austin Clarke in his critique of the imperial curriculum in Barbadian schools, *Growing Up Stupid under the Union Jack* (1980) and his later *Pigtails 'n Breadfruit: Rituals of Slave Food: A Barbadian Memoir* (1999); Dionne Brand in her exploration of racism and gender inequities, *Another Place, Not Here* (1996). Clarke also powerfully portrayed the relation between culture and the individual life through his depiction of a character named Miss Mary-Mathilda in *The Polished Hoe* (2002), which interconnects a contemporary confession with a social history of Black-White relations in Barbados. In *Land to Light On* (1997), (Marlene) Nourbese Philip (b. 1947) articulated her vision of alternatives to racist criticism. Claire Harris (b. 1937) championed the freedom of women from the constraints of society in long poems such as *Fables from the Women's Quarters* (1984) and *Drawing Down a Daughter* (1994). Philip (in *Looking for Livingstone*, 1991) and Harris (in *Travelling to Find a Remedy*, 1986) also looked to Africa for roots and spiritually sustaining mythologies. Writers in Quebec from the francophone Caribbean, primarily Haiti and Martinique (Étienne, Ollivier, Laferrière), pursued the politics that linked *négritude* with language. Still other writers with Anglo-Caribbean Jamaican connections include the poets and story writers Olive Senior (b. 1941) and Lorna Goodison (b. 1947) and the performance poet and publisher Pamela Mordecai (b. 1942). Of special interest are the techniques of orality that such writing brought to the observation of the Caribbean-Canadian connection: Harris's linguistic skills demonstrate her academic training in the field of linguistics as well as her ear for the vernacular. And various techniques of Caribbean 'performance art' – prophecy, 'cuss-cuss' or name-calling, and especially dub – guide the composition of the poetry of Lillian Allen (b. 1951) and several others.

Clearly, the category *'gay/lesbian'* is of a different order from those that define identity by means of ethnicity, class, or region; it is singled out here not to presume exact parallels with ethnic or other categories but to record the fact that many writers of the late twentieth and early twenty-first centuries took the fact of their being gay or lesbian to be the central generating element within their identity and hence the central subject of their writing. The sexuality of the writer, as distinct from the sexuality of a subject, therefore became a focus of interest for some commentators, even a matter of critical substance (as in studies of eroticized same-sex relationships in books that ranged from John Richardson's *Wacousta* to George Bowering's *Burning Water*). For others, it remained as inconsequential an attribute of identity as eye colour or fashion preference, but for those for whom it deeply mattered, the open declaration of sexual choice was a political as well as a personal decision. Critics responded by reinterpreting a play such as Tremblay's *Hosanna* (which had been read as a political allegory about Quebec 'in drag,' needing to find its own clothes) as a 'coming out' narrative about a homosexual man openly claiming his personal identity. To challenge legal codes and social practices that discriminated against homosexuality became a way of reconsidering social norms and recuperating self-esteem. It also produced a sense of community, a recognition on the part of such writers that they were not alone. Hence the *berdache* or *bote* figure from Native cultures (the sexually ambivalent seer and healer) began to appear in some texts (generally as a person whom Europeans could not initially appreciate), and numerous writers from the distant and more recent past were read against their declared or presumed sexuality, among them F. O. Call (1878–1956), Sinclair Ross, John Glassco, John Herbert, Timothy Findley, Scott Symons, David Watmough, Daryl Hine, and Jane Rule. To their number, many contemporary names could be added. The numbers, however, say little, except that the substantial portion of the Canadian population that is homosexual (about 10 per cent, across all ethnic lines) has likely varied little over time.

While adult homosexual relationships remained covert in Canada as long as they were deemed illegal, changes in legislation in the late 1960s, 'taking the state out of the nation's bedrooms,' largely removed the social and moral stigma that had been attached to them. Various forms of discrimination remained, however, in the law (survival benefits, book imports), as well as in immature and criminal behaviour (schoolyard slurs, gang violence, etc.) and in some religious tenets. Many people in subsequent decades consciously challenged these discriminations; the increasing gay and lesbian visibility within the culture (parades, advertising, open declarations of personal sexual preference) pronounced an activist refusal of denigration. The consequent claim upon on an alternative norm of life choice (removing it from the judgmental category 'abnormal') contextualized many a gay or lesbian literary text. Self-styled 'queer theory' thus challenged 'heteronormativity.' As with other studies of the margin, that which was identified as the 'marginal territory' was at once set apart from the mainstream *and* used to frame it, in this instance emphasizing the degree to which normative practices are intrinsically social constructions.

Among contemporary writers whose works have lent themselves to gay and lesbian criticism and theory are the playwrights Tomson Highway (in his fictional tribute to his brother as well as in his plays), Sky Gilbert (b. 1952, one-time director of Toronto's Buddies in Bad Times Theatre), René-Daniel Dubois (b. 1955; *Being at Home with Claude*, 1986), Michel-Marc Bouchard, Brad Fraser (b. 1959; *Poor Super Man*, 1995), Makeda Silvera (b. 1955), Ann-Marie MacDonald (b. 1959), and Michel Tremblay. To this list can be added the poets Ian Iqbal Rashid, Daphne Marlatt, Shani Mootoo, Connie Fife, Betsy Warland (b. 1946), André Roy (b. 1944), Dionne Brand, and John Barton and the fiction writers Shyam Selvadurai, Wayson Choy, Dennis Denisoff (b. 1961), Patrick Roscoe (b. 1962), Nicole Brossard, SKY Lee, Larissa Lai (b.1967), Anne-Marie Alonzo (b. 1951), Yolande Villemaire, and Stan Persky (b. 1941). But such a list is far from complete, and it is primarily useful as a generalization about criticism's preoccupations with identity politics in the 1990s. Sexuality might be a marker of identity, but the particulars of sexual liaison in gay and lesbian writings, as in heterosexual writings, can be treated with sensitivity or with titillation in mind. Literary texts can be fresh and original or stale and repetitive. As with any subject, a simple *topic* can come to seem routine, whether the topic is a cliché of character, a claim about ethnic difference, an account of a physical condition, or the athletics of intercourse; hence the writings of these authors, like those of others, tend most to transcend their immediate topic where (with Findley, for example, or Michael Turner in *The Pornographer's Poem*, or Michel-Marc Bouchard in *Les feluettes*, 1985) they reveal the larger moralities of community and violence, where they commit themselves to political action, where they examine the sometimes isolating consequences of choice, or where they argue a theory of relationship between language, love, and the body (as in the writings of Brossard). Marlatt's *Ana Historic* (1988) expresses this relationship as a process of discovery. Literary successes were to be found also in poetry (the sheer lyricism of the poems of Rashid, Marlatt, Barton, and Mootoo is a reward in itself) and in popular literature (the mysteries of Eve Zaremba, b. 1930, feature a lesbian detective named Helen Keremos). Filmmakers, too, turned to narratives of gay identity and isolation, as in *Lilies* or Thom Fitzgerald's *The Hanging Garden* (1997), and the homoerotic paintings of Attila Richard Lukacs (b. 1962) won international renown.

MacDonald's play *Goodnight Desdemona (Good Morning Juliet)*

(1990) investigates what differing roles women play on stage and in life, while her popular novel *Fall on Your Knees* (1996), a multi-generational narrative set in Cape Breton, uses the motif of incest to expose the violence of assumption, particularly that which makes an underclass out of being female. It is less the overt topic of sexuality in such works that distinguishes them, therefore, than their challenge to previous notions of social norm – hence their implicit invitation to critics and readers to re-examine their own subjectivity and to seek to understand from alternative perspectives the norms of desire. Such psychoanalytic techniques as projection and dislocation recur as strategies to enable this understanding; the often gothic settings (as in the theatre of Fraser and Bouchard or the fictions of Findley and Anne-Marie MacDonald, which deal with Protestant and Catholic restraints as well as with sexual and social excess) further destabilize conventions by revealing the psychological undercurrents of the placidly real.

LIVING IN PRINT AND PERFORMANCE

In that so many of the works that highlight questions of ethnicity and sexuality focus on the lives of individuals in society, it seems inevitable that these thematic categories should overlap both with each other and with the various forms of 'life writing' that became *de rigueur* in the later twentieth century: biography, autobiography, diary, journal, letters, papers, and postcards home. 'Being X' affirmed not just a recuperative refusal of discrimination (albeit sometimes cast as a validating claim upon victimization) but a place in the larger society as well. Implicit in the examination of minority experience were comments on whatever was assumed to be a majority understanding of norm (stereotypically, this phrase meant straight, white, middle-aged, Ontario, male). Being 'X' (the category of margin) thus generally functioned as both an asterisk to and a frame for the inferential narrative of being 'Canadian.' As this 'norm' itself deconstructed, social patterns (and publishers' priorities) also changed, and the patterns that appeared in literary texts changed along with them. The category of race (as measured by skin pigmentation) came under attack; critics and sociologists analyzed various codes of masculinity; working men and women turned at least temporarily away from the socialist left to the fundamentalist right. Meanwhile, 'grey power' advocates actively asserted their opposition to changes in social policy (an outspoken group called 'The Raging Grannies' became the darling of the media at protests across the country). Old assumptions about the uniformity of social behaviour and its relation to race, gender, class, status, and age, in other words, abruptly died, and with them died the conventional notion of a uniform personality, the consistent and whole individual that had long lain at the assumed 'centre' of realist writing. In their place came such forms as the theatre of revelation, the serial poem, and a variety of prose experiments in hypothesis and recall.

Of the scores of new plays written and performed in the 1990s, many – examples include works by Monique Mojica, Guillermo Verdecchia, Michel Tremblay, Djanet Sears (b. 1959; *Harlem Duet*, 1997), Judith Thompson, Robert Lepage, Sally Clark (b. 1953; *Moo*, prod. 1984, pub. 1989), Drew Hayden Taylor, Daniel David Moses – functioned as insights into the conflict of being gay, Native, female, Black, Hispanic; that is, they posed the question 'What is it like to live life with this identity in modern times?' The answer repeatedly resisted easy closure. The several plays that Michel-Marc Bouchard wrote during the 1990s, for example, repeatedly flirt with comedy, but the seriousness of the issues they address ask their audiences to think about social trauma as well. Frequently Bouchard highlights parent-child relations as a model of politics and empire, not just as a personal phenomenon. In *Les muses orphelines* (1989; tr. 1995), set during the Quiet Revolution, a mother returns on resurrection day; in *Voyage du couronnement* (1995; tr. 1999) a mafia boss goes to the coronation of Queen Elizabeth II. *Les grandes chaleurs* (1993; tr. as *Heat Wave*, 1995) asks its characters to live again after a patriarch dies, but in *Le chemin des passes-dangereuses* (1998; tr. 2000) sons get together fifteen years after the death of their father and rediscover their ambivalence towards him. Inasmuch as ambivalence is as often an internal quarrel as it is an externally directed attitude, playwrights often adopted the monodrama as a form in which to wrestle with it, as in *The Soldier Dreams* (1997) by Daniel MacIvor (b. 1962), or *The Dragonfly of Chicoutimi* (1995), by Larry Tremblay (b. 1948), or *The Occupation of Heather Rose* (1987) by Wendy Lill (b. 1950). In Tremblay's play a francophone gives up his French, only to disappear into the mainstream; in Lill's a white woman on a northern reserve cannot ever exorcise those characters she has 'occupied' and who now inhabit her – the ambiguity of inheritance and experience is social as well as personal. Other plays by Lill (who was elected to Parliament in 1997 and became the NDP critic for culture and communications) further demonstrate this fusion: *Sisters* (1989) deals with white nuns who run a residential school and who try to come to terms with what, despite their good intentions, must be considered its failure; and Lill's *The Glace Bay Miners' Museum* (1996), based on Sheldon Currie's short story, itself became the basis for the screenplay of Mort Ransen's 1995 film *Margaret's Museum*; imbued with a sense of the grotesque, it traces the impact of a Nova Scotia mine disaster on the mind of a female survivor and the community in which she survives. What might be called 'Maritime Gothic' characterized many a Canadian film of the 1990s – other examples include *The Hanging Garden* (1997) and Stephen Reynolds's 1998 film adaptation of Wayne Johnston's *The Divine Ryans*. Such films might suggest that Canadian filmgoers hanker for Grand Guignol, but the style perhaps owes more to the fact that in the 1990s the Canadian Film Development Board (est. 1967) appeared more willing to fund 'serious drama' than comedy, at which (paradoxically) many Canadian writers excelled.

Still other playwrights focused more on personal and family politics (as with Sharon Pollock's *Doc* in 1984) or on political issues in the society at large, as in Sally Clark's reconsiderations of the history of women or Kevin Kerr's 2002 play *Unity* (1918) and as in the many works by Quebec dramatists Daniel Danis (b. 1962), Jean-Marc Dalpé (b. 1957), Michèle Magny (b. 1944), Patrick Leroux (b. 1971), Yvan Bienvenue (b. 1962), Claude Poissant (b. 1955), Dominic Champagne (b. 1963), Jean-François Caron (b. 1961), Anne Legault (b. 1958), Wajdi Mouawad (*Littoral*, 1999), and Normand Chaurette (b. 1954). Through a hybrid combination of forms, *The History of the Village of the Small Huts* (1994), by Michael Hollingsworth (b. 1950), re-examines Canadian history by representing Native, francophone, and anglophone versions of it in sequence and in juxtaposition. Production – staging – was often a particular challenge, for reasons both of time and of space. Jean-Pierre Ronfard's (b. 1929) *Vie et mort du roi Boiteux* (1981–82) required several hours to perform. John Krizanc (b. 1956), who in *Tamara* (prod. 1981, pub. 1989) takes the history of Italian fascism as his theme, requires the audience to track the cast through an entire house, ostensibly the home of the patriot Gabriele d'Annunzio. Krizanc followed this play with a slapstick but serious examination of communism and censorship in his prizewinning *Prague* (1987).

Generally more comic in effect were the many successful new experiments in improvisational sketch, circus, mime (Axis Mime Theatre), television satire, children's theatre, and clowning, as in the work of Richard Pochinko (1946–89). Pochinko, who taught at the National Arts Centre and later set up the Theatre Resource Centre in Toronto and Les Foufounes Électriques in Montreal, directly influenced writers such as Highway and the practice of acting and clowning in contemporary performance. Fringe theatre, too, which expanded from Edmonton to venues in Toronto, Winnipeg, Vancouver, and other centres, often served as the first opportunity for new comedy troupes to try out their material. More characteristically, writers of stage drama developed a kind of tonal uneasiness to convey particular psychological effects: black comedy and tragicomedy used humour so as to be able to admit to whatever the characters found difficult to accept. The Shakespeare character in Findley's *Elizabeth Rex* (2000), for example, dreams creativity into existence, only to find it fleeting; Highway's trickster gods offer some degree of understanding of the world but do not relieve it of pain; the son in Michel Tremblay's *For the Pleasure of Seeing Her Again* has to find a way to come to terms with the mother's death. Comedy and death combine in *Vigil* (1996) by Morris Panych (b. 1952) as well. And even in the performance of Panych's adaptation of Nikolai Gogol's *The Overcoat* (where the Axis Mime theatre company acrobatically told the story, played to the music of Dmitri Shostakovich, but with no spoken dialogue), the narrative-in-action combines humour with pathos. In some instances, however, a touch of humour is not enough, and only despair remains, as is characteristic in the work of Brad Fraser, or Robert Lepage's (b. 1955) *Le polygraphe* (1985; film version, 1996), about AIDS, or the metatheatre of Normand Chaurette, whose *Provincetown Playhouse* (1981), for example, presents the mind of a prison inmate in an insane asylum, who relives a moment from the past when, as an actor on stage, he has accidentally killed a child.

Such plays are seldom obviously autobiographical. They tell lives by projecting life, by dramatizing on stage or screen the traumas and the occasional celebrations of relationship and self-revelation that punctuate everyone's experience. The life stories that emerge as serial long poems, by contrast, tend to derive more obviously from the writer's personal or professional perception of what it means 'to be.' By the 1990s the long poem had moved a remarkable distance from Pratt's romances, Gutteridge's historical reconstructions, and the nineteenth-century sagas of settlement and sentiment – though perhaps they resonated more closely (however indirectly) with the sonic flow of Saint-Denys Garneau's *Regards et jeux dans l'espace* (1937). More directly, the new long poems responded to the American work of Jack Spicer and the life-poem model of bp Nichol's *The Martyrology*. Sharon Thesen's (b. 1946) *The New Long Poem Anthology* (1991; 2nd ed., 2001) was one of several collections to build on anthologies edited earlier by George Bowering and Michael Ondaatje. Smaro Kamboureli's critical analysis of the new form, *On the Edge of Genre* (1991), gave it substance in theory as well.

Long poems nevertheless enact different dances with language and life, the only constant perhaps being duration: the way they accumulate meaning over space and time, generally through a set of formal and perspectival variations, as in Robin Blaser's life work *The Holy Forest* (1993) or Robert Kroetsch's enigmatically titled *Completed Field Notes* (1989). Lola Lemire Tostevin's *Gyno-Text* (1986) concerns language as a body and the body as writing: in other words (as critical theory renamed it), *écriture feminine*. George Bowering's *Kerrisdale Elegies* (1984) draws on the German poet Rainer Maria Rilke's *Duino Elegies* for its form, while the suburban Vancouver setting of which it partly makes use inscribes a quite different environment for meditation. In *Urban Snow* (1992) and *His Life* (2000), by contrast – as in the prose of *A Magpie Life: Growing a Writer* (2001) – Bowering (in 2002 named Canada's first poet laureate) structures his anecdotal engagements with words, persons, and place as open memoirs. As with memoir, so with history: Bowering's book-length histories of British Columbia, Canada, and the prime ministers approach conventional historical topics with anecdotal liveliness and a fascination with the unusual details of ordinary experience (Aritha Van Herk's history of Alberta supplies a comparable example).

Other poets designed book-length poems in numerous different ways, from the linearity of some memoirs to the diary-form fragments of Anne Carson or the interrupted triptych of William New's *Stone/Rain* (2001). *The Fells of Brightness* by Jon Whyte (1945–92) – only two of a proposed five volumes were completed (1983, 1985) – gathered attention some years after publication, for the way the poem combined visual and aural techniques with records of geology and Native and settlement history; the entire project would have composed a massive portrait (or 'experience') of the Rocky Mountains. Still further examples of the range of the long poem form include Erin Mouré's *WSW* (1989), Nourbese Philip's *She Tries Her Tongue, Her Silence Softly Breaks* (1989), George Elliott Clarke's *Whylah Falls* (1990), Dionne Brand's *No Language Is Neutral* (1998), and works by Wah, Dennis Cooley (b. 1944), Claire Harris, Colleen Thibaudeau (b. 1925), Madeleine Gagnon (b. 1938), and Steve McCaffery (b. 1947). Many long poems drew on the line-breaking patterns of jazz, and as with other publications, the record of individual lives recurrently focused on race and gender.

Performance poetry expresses yet another way of lifting poetry from the page, emphasizing its dramatic character and its direct engagement with an audience through the power of sound itself. Although dub, together with rap, hip hop, and other rhythmic forms, was one of several manifestations of the popularity of the form in the 1990s, performance poetry was by no means all directly related to African or Caribbean oral forms. The compositions of the Four Horsemen (Paul Dutton with bp Nichol, Steve McCaffery, and Rafael

Barreto-Rivera, b. 1944), along with competitive 'poetry slam' events (improvisational composition), exemplify other faces of this phenomenon. Related, too, is the world of sound poetry, with its roots in the theatricality of Dadaism, nonsense verse, and chant. It was given new impetus as an 'intermedia' form with the advent of new technologies in the 1960s (tape, re-recording) and the work of bill bissett, Claude Gauvreau, and bp Nichol. Established poets such as Claude Beausoleil (*Extase et déchirure*, 1987), Pierre Morency, and Fernand Ouellette (*Les heures*, 1987) also worked in visual and aural forms. From the work of these earlier writers, through that of Sean o huigin (b. 1942), David UU (i.e., David W. Harris, 1948–94), and the Four Horsemen, it was a short stop to such performance groups as Re:Sounding (Doug Barbour and Steven Scobie) and Owen Sound (primarily Michael Dean, b. 1947, Steven Ross Smith, b. 1945, and Richard Truhlar, b. 1950), with a crossover into popular culture in Acadian folk-rock. Also related is the work of individual sound poets Raoul Duguay and Penn Kemp (Penny Chalmers, b. 1944), whose performances of sliding syllables, crafting meaning out of pure utterance, began to appear as audiocassettes as well as in printed form. While a dozen or more composers of sound poetry emerged in the 1980s and 1990s, Lillian Allen's dub, Christian Bök's (b. 1966) tonal achievements in alphabetic arrangement, as in *Eunoia* (2001), bill bissett's continuing voice, and the sonic politics of the L=A=N=G=U=A=G=E poets associated with the Kootenay School of Writing in Vancouver – among them Lisa Robertson (b. 1961) and Jeff Derksen (b. 1958) – were among the most prominent forms of composition.

Not all noteworthy poets practised in longer forms, of course, or experimented with sound poetry or dub. Rather more conventional lyric forms attracted the attention of many. Among these writers were Bronwen Wallace (1945–89), whose life was cut short by cancer, and such other poets as Rashid, Halfe, Yves Boisvert (b. 1950), Jean-Paul Daoust (b. 1946, *Les cendres bleus*, 1999), Gérard Étienne (b. 1936), Lorna Crozier (b. 1948), Eva Tihanyi (b. 1956), and Tim Lilburn (b. 1950), whose lines returned to nature, and Trinidad-born Lucy Ng (b. 1966), whose lyrics reflected on her family and personal life. British Columbia poets George McWhirter, Patrick Lane, Ron Smith (b. 1943), and Marilyn Bowering (b. 1949) all continued to publish arresting poetry, and in Atlantic Canada the generation of Travis Lane (b. 1934) was meeting that of Carmelita McGrath (b. 1960). Contemporary francophone lyric writers include Carle Coppens (b. 1972), Marlène Belley (b. 1963), Carole David (b. 1954), Michael Delisle (b. 1959), Guy Ducharme (b. 1959), Yves Gosselin (b. 1959), France Mongeau (b.

1961), Jacques Ouellet (b. 1947), Elise Turcotte (b. 1957), and Robert Yergeau (b. 1956). *Poésie intime,* that which distills the intensity of private emotion, whether the emotion is communicated through image or couched in a poetry of statement, continued to dominate expression. Among many accomplished younger anglophone poets, Stephanie Bolster (b. 1969) published *White Stone* (1997), a series of lyrics based on the original Alice of *Alice in Wonderland,* which approximates the serial long poem, and in other works demonstrated her skill with metaphor. Michael Crummey's (b. 1965) poems in *Hard Light* (1998), which deal with his Newfoundland family, demonstrate his skill with voice; Anne Michaels's *The Weight of Oranges* (1986) shows her skill in crafting effective imagery. Newer directions were represented by the work of Lynn Crosbie (b. 1963) and Ken Babstock (b. 1970). Babstock, with *Mean* (1999) and *Days into Flatspin* (2001), reveals a remarkable ability with the vernacular, giving lyric power to apparently minimalist observations. Crosbie, with her selected poems *Queen Rat* (1998) and novels drawn from media narratives (*Dorothy L'Amour,* 1999, tells a fictionalized version of the life of the murdered *Playboy* centerfold Dorothy Stratten), combines a lyric sensibility with sensational representations of criminality and sexual brutality. The contrast highlights the cruelty of violence (especially that directed towards women); the intent is to shock.

In many respects, Anne Carson (b. 1950), a classics scholar who teaches in Montreal and San Francisco (and who adapts classical metrics to modern English), emerged as the chief inheritor of Nichol's serial poem practice. Bursting onto the literary scene in the 1990s with a major American literary prize and the enthusiastic backing of Ondaatje (though facing the ongoing criticism of the poet David Solway, b. 1941), Carson often combined logical scholarly commentary with a desire for metaphysical illumination; she produced half a dozen books of non-linear poetry and prose between *Eros the Bittersweet* (1986) and *The Beauty of the Husband* (2000). Characteristically opposing the mordant with a taste for spirituality (thus satisfying two of the most earnest needs among twenty-first-century critics), Carson's works, as in *Short Talks* (1992) and *Glass, Irony, and God* (1995), punctuate precise anecdotes and observations with disjuncture. Hence gaps in communication are as informative as statements, nowhere more clearly than in the work that many readers found to be her most impressive, *Autobiography of Red: A Novel in Verse* (1998). Based on one of the tales of Herakles and declaratively more narrative than her other works, the poem tells the life story of the red monster Geryon, whose 'monstrosity' exists only in the eye of the 'normative' beholder. Exploring the logic (or illogic) of human categories

of understanding, it comments along the way on childhood, sexuality, and other arenas of physical power and social manipulation.

Other poets presented life as a system of thought. Christopher
Dewdney, for example, uses language to embody the way that science and nature integrate meaning with process. Jan Zwicky presents
poetry as a medium of philosophy. (The novels of Nancy Huston, b.
1953, informed by her readings in literary theory, might be read
through a related lens.) Don McKay (b. 1942) transforms words into
an agency of feeling; he reads nature as emotion-in-action and emotion as nature-in-relationship. Zwicky, an academic at the University
of Victoria, where she teaches philosophy, assembled in her book-
length *Lyrical Philosophy* (1992) fragments of utterance, arguing
against linearity as the only acceptable structure of thinking. In
Wittgenstein Elegies (1986), moreover, she uses the lyric fragment to
convey not only her philosopher-subject's ideas but also the interrupted stages of his life. *Songs for Relinquishing the Earth* (1998) – like
much of her work, elegiac – demonstrates how exact metaphor con-
denses and articulates complex ideas. At once meditative and observant, this poetry moves simultaneously through abstract theory and
the physical world. Zwicky's partner, Don McKay, a long-time editor
with *Fiddlehead* and Brick Books and silent mentor of many poets,
won early attention with *Long Sault* (1975; rpt in Ondaatje's anthology of long poems) and with *Birding, or Desire* (1983), which turns the
world of the amateur ornithologist into a meditation on why people
dream of satisfaction. Other works, which variously experiment with
collage, quest narrative, wordplay, and music, explore more fully the
difference between process and possession, notably in the metaphorically rich, Governor General's Award–winning volumes *Night Field*
(1991) and *Another Gravity* (2000). McKay's essays in *Vis à Vis* (2001),
particularly 'Baler Twine,' eloquently meditate on how poetry happens, in the observation of nature and on the page. 'By "wilderness,"'
he writes, 'I want to mean not just a set of endangered species, but the
capacity of all things to elude the mind's appropriations.' Moreover,
'poetic attention is based on a recognition and a valuing of the other's
wilderness; it leads to a work which is not a *vestige* of the other, but a
translation of it.' 'Read,' he advises others; 'There is imaginative work
to be done.' Mark Cochrane (b. 1965), himself a fine poet of the
rhythms of desire (in *Change Room*, 2000), praises McKay for the wonder he discovers in the wilderness of both things and people; such
discoveries emphasize his effort to *meet*, his refusal to *claim*.

This contrast informs much writing that is more overtly biographical or autobiographical: to what degree does a written 'life,' that is,
contain or constrain an identity, and to what degree is it only an

approximation, a tissue of metaphors and lies? Theories of life writing distinguished among the *forms* of expression but deconstructed the idea of totality, foregrounding methods of reading metaphor over assumptions about inclusive detail. It was the ambiguity of identity more than an expectation of finality that captivated life writers and drove their books. Several biographies of Canadian writers appeared during the 1990s and 2000s – among them, studies of Milton Acorn, Leonard Cohen, Earle Birney, Gwendolyn MacEwen, Roy Daniells, Margaret Laurence, the Strickland sisters, Gabrielle Roy, François-Xavier Garneau, Jacques Ferron, Émile Nelligan, Alice Munro, George Woodcock – and scores more that reconstructed persons who had made their names in politics and popular culture. Figures such as Emily Carr, moreover, continued to attract attention, in both poetry and prose. Susan Crean's (b. 1945) *The Laughing One* (2001), subtitled a 'journey to Emily Carr,' stresses that process was a feature of Carr's life and art, and therefore that any representation of the life and art has to undergo a process of reading text, place, and painting. As strategies of representation more readily embraced the principle of uncertainty, moreover – and drew from data across disciplinary methodologies (using plates and soundtracks along with a family tree, say) – biographies began to resist mere chronology. Clark Blaise's *Time Lord* (2001) combines a history of time measurement with a study of Sandford Fleming's design for standard time zones; within the study, too, is a narrative of writing this book – hence the author and his journey towards his subject become an integral part of the biographical narrative. Perhaps no biography more than François Ricard's *Gabrielle Roy: une vie* (1996) succeeded in conveying the many sides of a distinctive personality, contextualizing Roy's literary life within a reading of sibling rivalry, marriage, place, and place-in-history.

Declared autobiographies proved even more experimental, with George Bowering's 'magpie' anecdotes exemplifying what could be done with narrative form. *Fishing with John* (1988) by Edith Iglauer (b. 1917) is both a memoir of life with her fisherman husband and a tribute to love. Mary Meigs (1917–2002) wrote a companionate account of her life with Marie-Claire Blais, in *Lily Briscoe* (1981) and its sequels, and another book on her own role in a film about aging, *In the Company of Strangers* (1991). Rachel Manley (b. 1947), in *Drumblair* (1996), recalled her Jamaican childhood and the lives of her distinguished political forebears. Autobiography overlapped with narrative in various ways, with Rudy Wiebe's collaboration with Yvonne Johnson (Cree; b. 1961) being an obvious example; their *Stolen Life* (1999) tells a story of how social systems failed and then jailed Johnson. Fiction was one of the genres recurrently used to stress the importance of the relation between memory and the Holocaust, too, as Anne Michaels's and Dennis Bock's novels attest. Autobiography further overlapped with travel writing, as in the Thai adventures recorded in *Touch the Dragon* (1992) by Karen Connolly (b. 1969); and biography overlapped (poetically) with cultural studies in *Mothertalk* (1997), the tribute to his mother that Roy Kiyooka (1926–94) began and that his former partner Daphne Marlatt completed.

Two further works received particularly warm attention: *The Danger Tree* (2001) by David Macfarlane (b. 1952) and *Baltimore's Mansion* (1999) by Wayne Johnston (b. 1958). Both are family biographies – collective accounts within which the author (or narrating historian) positions himself, or perhaps 'discovers' himself, especially in relation to his father. Macfarlane's book looks back to the First World War and to the impact of that family narrative (of expectation, participation, and consequence) on subsequent generations. Told with warmth and lyrical compassion, it looks towards death and yet celebrates life. Like Macfarlane's, Johnston's book is eloquent with disagreement and affection. It focuses on Newfoundland's entry into Confederation in 1949 and on the family divide: the father was opposed to Joey Smallwood's dream of nationhood, while the son grows into a connection with Canada. In their separateness they come together, the book a testament to pride and connection, place and appreciation.

Ontario and Newfoundland come alive as characters in these books, showing that life can also be lived as place. 'Regional' writing – that which recorded place, the politics of being there, and the ecology of living there – demonstrated such a sensibility. In works by Noël Audet (b. 1938; *L'ombre de l'épervier*, 1988), the Gaspé setting establishes a sense of distance and the past. The popular *Les filles de Caleb* (1987–88) by Arlette Cousture (b. 1948) is set in La Mauricie. The Abitibi region of Quebec functions as both setting and metaphor ('outskirts') in *L'écrivain public* (1996) by Pierre Yergeau (b. 1957) and some of Lise Bissonnette's work, as does the Saguenay in *L'hiver de pluie* (1990) by Lise Tremblay (b.1957), which in this particular book is used to contrast with California. Other books take up different locales: urban Montreal, Toronto, Vancouver, or Winnipeg, together with rural areas, small towns, and the North, all being familiar Canadian settings. To them must be added foreign locales from Bombay to Paris, Japan to Trinidad. Rudy Wiebe's *Playing Dead* (1989) and John Moss's (b. 1940) *Enduring Dreams* (1994) both contemplate the implications of Arctic lands; the tundra appears to give meaning here to each itinerant author-observer-recorder. In the works of Marie Clements and Arthur Alexie, the North is populated, not represented as place only, but Yukon and Northwest Territories spaces continue to resonate beyond mere 'settings.' Still other examples multiply: the British Columbia Interior in the work of Harold Rhenisch (b. 1958), or Germany during the years between the wars, reconstructed in some of Rhenisch's poems; the West Coast in the work of Charles Lillard (1944–97), whether he was writing on history or on Chinook jargon; the *Lake of the Prairies* family history that 'locates' Warren Cariou; the travel dialogues of Wade Davis; and a series of nature essays and warm tales of childhood that depend deeply on their evocation of place, as in the Manitoba stories of Sandra Birdsell (b. 1942), the ecological essays of Sharon Butala (b. 1940; *Coyote's Morning Cry*, 1995), the journalism and commentary of Stephen Hume (b. 1947; *Off the Map*, 2001) and Wayne Grady (b. 1948; *Chasing the Chinook*, 1998), or the nature essays collected by Seán Virgo (b. 1940) in *The Eye in the Thicket* (2002). Place is not mere background in these works, but integral to the lives being led in relation to it; the complex workings of place constitute both an empirical reality and a metaphor for human-natural interconnection. To understand the connection is to see the individuals' relevance to ecological design.

'Nature,' long an obsession in Canadian writing, continues in these writings to attract the observer's eye, but as Don McKay's poems reveal – or those of Derk Wynand (b. 1944) in *Dead Man's Float* (2002) and Adam Dickinson (b. 1974) in *Cartography and Walking* (2002), for example – earlier writers' preoccupation with region as landscape and place as 'setting' turns in contemporary writing into a fascination with environmental ecology. Dickinson's close observations of animals-in-place and of place-in-relationship (as in 'Lake Filling In with Land') implicitly ask readers to participate in nature as a process of life, rather than assume it as a simple backdrop to activity. Tim Lilburn's remarkable collection of essays on 'poetry and the practice of philosophy,' *Thinking & Singing* (2002) – essays by Robert Bringhurst, Dennis Lee, Don McKay, Jan Zwicky, and himself – reflects even more directly on how poetry (as a form of knowing) and nature (as another form of knowing, an instruction from the world to the world) interconnect. In critical writing, the new field of 'ecocriticism' also attracted practitioners, most notably Pamela Banting (b. 1955) for her 1998 anthology *Fresh Tracks* and Laurie Ricou (b. 1944) in *The Arbutus/Madrone Files* (2002); the intent of such work was to further readers' appreciation of the ecological context within which imaginations function, books are written, and cultures live or die.

By extension, the metaphor of place can also function as a frame within which families or nations behave, as in Bonnie Burnard's *A Good House* or a score of other family sagas. *Il y aura toujours des printemps en Amérique* (1987), a best-seller by Louis-Martin Tard (1921–98), for example, traces fourteen generations of a family, for whom survival constitutes success, a recurrent claim upon the place they live in, and the spring they live for. A variety of other works are constructed more to focus on the individual within the community or family, but the individual as a fragmented being rather than a representative entirety. *Self* (1996) by Yann Martel (b. 1963) deconstructs the idea that identity is uniform. *Childhood* (1998) by André Alexis (b. 1957), *Heroine* (1987) by Gail Scott (b. 1946), *Amnesia* (1998) by Douglas Cooper (b. 1960), *City of Forgetting* (1997) by Robert Majzels (b. 1950) – in each of these books, place is a literary construct for another literary construct to live in; life, lived as fiction, is rendered as fiction. Martel's central character, something of a *feu follet*, shifts gender as readily as clothes; Cooper's amnesiac acquires identity by losing it; Majzels's Clytemnestra walks off the page into a disintegrating Montreal. These works also indirectly ask what morality, culture, and custom 'mean' when fiction – that is, artifice – starts to take the place of living.

In some ways, the stories of Alice Munro can be read in this context also, not because they delight in metatextuality but because their careful artfulness draws attention to the indeterminability of 'character.' Yet any Munro character comes clearly to life on the page; 'arranged unreality' casts insights into real lives and their unknowability, the paradox being part of the point. The short story is also a genre in which this flash of insight repeatedly takes place and recurrently focuses on individuals, and it was, for numerous writers of the 1990s, again a preferred form. While the decade witnessed a number of English-language works that were written in Munro's shadow, numerous younger writers demonstrated their technical skills and imaginative reach and their ability to extend the genre. To single out only a few, the following collections of stories warrant close attention: *Flight Path of the Emperor* (1992) by Steven Heighton (b. 1961), *Marine Life* (1992) by Linda Svendsen (b. 1954), *Visible Light* (1993) by Carol Windley (b. 1947), *Bad Imaginings* (1993) by Caroline Adderson (b. 1963), *The Exalted Company of Roadside Martyrs* (1998) by Warren Cariou, *Open* (2002) by Lisa Moore, *Dead Girls* (2002) by Nancy Lee, *Red Plaid Skirt* (2002) by Diane Schoemperlen (b. 1954), *Pool-hopping and other Stories* by Anne Fleming (b. 1964), *Mount Appetite* (2002) by Bill Gaston (b. 1953), *When X Equals Marylou* (2002) by Tamas Dobozy (b. 1969), and *Olympia* (1998) by Dennis Bock. Adderson's and Gaston's range of techniques, for instance, or Cariou's play with the novella, or Heighton's ironic engagement with cultural difference and Fleming's with gender and identity, Moore's minimalist revelations, Schoemperlen's ellipses, Lee's expressive exposés of the reality of the grotesque, or Dobozy's rampant imagination – these capsule comments describe narratives of considerable literary power.

RECONSTRUCTING HISTORY

Postmodern techniques in the 1970s and 1980s emphasized the power of the storyteller to disrupt illusions of reality, highlight the artifice of narrative instead, and generally play with speech formulae and conventional expectations. Hence Bowering's 'George' in *Burning Water* was at once author, narrator, British king, and ostensible historical subject, the explorer George Vancouver, who in 'real history' touched the West Coast of Canada in the 1790s. *Burning Water*, however, permits Vancouver to touch base ahistorically with a Spanish captain, Juan Francisco de la Bodega y Quadra (1744–94), and Bowering thereby constructs an erotics of composition, using linguistic play in the service of invention. Susan Swan's (b. 1945) *The Biggest Modern Woman of the World* (1983) writes back into the real world the conventional story of Anna Swan (1846–88), the 'giantess' exhibited in P. T. Barnum's circus, using postmodern techniques to tell an allegory of how the 'norms' of imperial history construct colonial identities, exhibiting and boxing them up at the same time. Robert Kroetsch's emblematically named Hazard Lepage in *The Studhorse Man* re-enacts parodically the archetypal wanderings of Odysseus, exposing his preoccupations as he goes, the bawdy authorial wit playing across the surface of prairie stereotype and literary imitation.

Such works continued to attract attention for their deconstruction of maudlin romance and conventional 'epic' national history. But some subsequent writers also began to ask if history were not more substantial than 'mere' narrative and to use postmodern techniques of interruption and fragmentation not as a refusal of history's 'reality' but as part of a process of rereading or reconstructing the reality. Themes of gender, ethnicity, race, class, and region returned in this context as well. These social issues were housed in the new form of historical fiction – or 'historiographic metafiction,' as it came to be called – that is, historical narrative aware of its own constructedness but calling at the same time for social reformulations. They were dramatized in story and reconfigured as models for present social change and/or understanding. For the most part 'postcolonial' in effect, these new historical fictions sought to elucidate and attach value to the perspectives (the points of difference) that normalizing (i.e., 'imperial') versions of behaviour and state had chosen to erase or ignore. Or they sought to explain the ambivalence of choice in any age of competing contradictions. In some sense, that is, the new historical fictions (aware of the paradox implicit in what they were doing) were investigating the unpredictability of the past.

Many of the works that this chapter has already mentioned can consequently be read from this historiographic perspective as well: (1) the lives of individuals, especially if conceived as types, representatives of a time; the quests for mothers or lost children, as in Denise Chong's or Audrey Thomas's work or Madeleine Ferron's *Adrienne, une saga familiale* (1992), where retrieving intention in the past might give acceptable meaning to the present; (2) the mysterious moments in life that call for re-examination, as in Richards's work; (3) the reconstructions of uncertainty, as in Atwood's *Alias Grace*, or of iconographic moments, as with Vanderhaeghe's drama of the Cypress Hills Massacre or the broken ground of Hodgins's world war veterans; and (4) the communal retellings of the Shoah, the Holocaust, where the Hebrew 'we' keeps ancestors alive for a subsequent generation but (as in Anne Michaels's work or Robert Majzels's comic and postmodern *Hellman's Scrapbook*, 1992, in which growing up in Montreal interweaves with the fragmented narratives that are told to a psychiatrist) makes those who do not personally remember the past responsible for retrieving it as well. Some writers inventively filled in missing chapters in the lives of real-life people whose careers became iconic in their own time, such as the avian artist John Jacques Audubon in *Creation* (2002) by Katherine Govier (b. 1948) or the rival Arctic explorers Frederick Cook and Robert Peary in Wayne Johnston's *The Navigator of New York* (2002). Here Audubon's mysterious origins serve up the possibility of a human passion that might parallel the painter's quest for fame; and Cook's deliberate fabrications – lying about reaching the North Pole first, lying about climbing Mount McKinley first, and being celebrated and then disgraced – enfold a young (fictional) Newfoundlander named Devlin Stead in a disappointed quest for glory and a successful exploration of New York, where at last he retrieves his personal history.

Canadian settings and historical moments supplied the background to numerous examples of this form. When Margaret Sweatman (b. 1953) in *Fox* (1991) uses the Winnipeg General Strike of 1919 as the central event of her fiction, neither the city nor the date nor the particularity of the strike needs to be re-established as 'history.' Instead, the fictions dramatize the economics of power and the conditions of social distrust that flashed into 'class' violence at that moment in Canada and that continue to burn – continue, if not precisely in European class terms, at least in rivalries over status and opportunity. The historical moment acquires power as an iconographic moment because readers in the present can recognize this continuity of tension. So with the perennial fascination with Louis Riel or the 1837 Rebellions or Susanna Moodie or Emily Carr: the figures and times *embody* social paradoxes that ask to be rethought or sets of attitudes that ask to be recontextualized. It is not the history in and of itself that needs redressing, but the degree to which the present accepts it as a given. In Gail Scott's words (in *Spare Parts plus Two*, 2002, citing the US composer Ernest Bloch): 'It is the artist's task … to bring now-time into line or focus with like historical moments when thought's not emptied out, a turning point. When time has lost its thickness. Talent may be only knowing how to grasp a vector when our lives flow along it.' Hence Sweatman's second novel, *When Alice Lay Down with Peter* (2001), focuses on two 'ordinary' people who live through Riel's rebellious times; the conflicts and the executions take place again on these pages, but by asking what they had to do with daily lives rather than with history's textbook arcs, Sweatman moves the historical novel away from both re-enactment and romance. What is 'ordinary' except another face of 'significance'? But what is meant by 'significant' no longer necessarily implies the high life and legislative acts of an elite or dominant group; rather, it comes to refer to whatever makes meaning in any person's world.

Wayne Johnston's fictional glimpse of Joey Smallwood in *The Colony of Unrequited Dreams* (1998) provides a related example; invented fictional characters here (with whom a 'real' Smallwood connects) modify historical 'truth' but suggest ways to understand *how* past motivations affect the present. Michael Crummey (b. 1965) in *River Thieves* (2001) and John Steffler (b. 1947) in *The Afterlife of George Cartwright* (1992) both reconsider the Beothuk past of Newfoundland, to revisit the conditions under which the Beothuk disappeared. For both writers, easy condemnations and easy romances are alike unsatisfactory strategies to follow. Instead, their characters (set in the past) are contemporary; they act with ambition and seethe with doubt. In Steffler's work the historical Cartwright has a consequential life after death. And who precisely the 'thieves' are of Crummey's title is likewise ambiguous in the text, referring at once to those who came later and to those who were there before. Narratives of contact, these books illuminate what it means to 'know' – what it means to know another, what it means to know oneself, and what it means never to know enough to act wisely. Other contexts produced comparable books. Fred Stenson (b. 1951) in *The Trade* (2000) and Audrey Thomas in *Iso-*

bel Gunn revisited the Hudson's Bay Company for narratives; Guy Vanderhaeghe, with the story of the guide Jerry Potts in *The Last Crossing,* also looked again at the narrative of western expansion. Some books dealt more conventionally with the past, as in Arlette Cousture's romances of the *filles du roi* or *Marie Laflamme* (1991) by Christine Brouillet (b. 1958). Inventively, in *Icefields* (1995), however, Thomas Wharton (b. 1963) responded to the history of the European 'discovery' of the Rocky Mountain glaciers near Jasper in a more intellectually adventurous way. More than simply re-recording the event, Wharton chose to revisit the conventional narrative of 'discovery' as well as the act. His characters include a man of science who seeks angels, a British xenophobe who seeks renown, a female adventurer who seeks facts, a commercial zealot who seeks ownership, and a cast of ethnic minorities whose familiarity with place and the techniques of survival grant them substance in a contradictory world of frozen preconceptions. But ice moves, and so do the icefields. In due course, even the fictions that underpin belief, in this book, give rise to generation. Paradoxes, the novel suggests, are what permit a society to grow. It grows family by family as well, as much francophone historiographic fiction demonstrated. The best-selling *Le roman de Julie Papineau* (1998) by Micheline Lachance (b. 1944), the biographer of Cardinal Paul-Émile Léger, brought the author's research skills to bear on a life (told as fiction) of Louis-Joseph Papineau's more radical sister. The Franco-Ontarian Daniel Poliquin in *L'homme de paille* (1998) looks back to a time prior to 1759 when the American Midwest was French but not New France; his character wanders through this *pays d'en haut* and then fights for France in the wars with Britain. Injured, he regains his memory in due course, but by then he is living in 'another country,' and the alienation he feels resonates through to the present time. Louis-Martin Tard (1921–98) brought a child's perspective to the years 1764–84 (the two decades after France surrendered New France to Britain); in *Le bon Dieu s'appelle Henri* (1993), a little girl thinks the inscription INRI on a cross is God's name, though in this work, it is less easy to explain where God is assumed to stand in people's daily political life. In *Adrienne, une saga familiale* (1993), by contrast, the politics are clearer; here Madeleine Ferron writes a kind of tribute to her writer-brother Jacques, who had died eight years earlier. A story about her own family's history, it domesticates the political argument that Jacques Ferron had written so often into allegory, demonstrating that the state saga which he wrote can be recast as a family saga, its memories proving as political, as long-standing, and as warm.

Other writers let their fictional or fictionalized characters be clutched or shadowed by major world events, as when David Gurr (b. 1936) casts Hitler's Third Reich as the Wagnerian Ring Cycle in *The Ring Master* (1987), each 'act' in the novel intensifying the reader's perception of 'heroism' as ego glorified by insecurity. Dennis Bock's *The Ash Garden* (2001) turns North America into the middle-ground stage where the Holocaust dramas of Europe and the Hiroshima dramas of Japan meet and (despite love, the intellect, and good intentions) drift into paralysis. Jane Urquhart (b. 1949) introduces female and gay characters into her narrative of war and recuperation at the Vimy Memorial, *The Stone Carvers* (2001), thus extending through fiction the parameters of heroism and social admissibility. *Ostend* (1994) by François Gravel (b. 1951) looks back to the 1960s, to a time of Mao and Che, Jimi Hendrix and JFK, when the narrator was young and remembers being interesting; writing now as a suburban anarchist in modern Quebec, his narrator lives what he thinks is a less exciting life in a more orderly, more predictable world. Still other venues for 'historical memories' include the Polish America of Keith Maillard's (b. 1942) West Virginia cycle of novels, as in the fundamentally comic *The Clarinet Polka* (2002), Sandra Birdsell's and Nancy Richler's (b. 1957) Eastern Europe (in *The Russländer*, 2001, and *Your Mouth Is Lovely*, 2002, respectively), and Paulette Jiles's Missouri during the Civil War in *Enemy Women* (2002). In these works, history both acts upon the characters and is acted upon by them; the reader begins to see how much a 'received history' is open to interpretation *as narrative* – in other words, as a *formulation* of time, place, and value, rather than as an unassailable truth.

One further way to read this re-rendering of historical assumptions is provided by a series of books written by women, each addressing how gender theory can reinterpret ways to read time. Marlatt's *Ana Historic*, for example, takes a woman (Annie) into the history of the city of Vancouver, looking for data on a real person (Mrs Richards) who seems to have been written out of history; the backwards glance is 'anahistoric.' But as the Greek prefix *ana-* means both 'backward' and 'upward,' time is moving in two directions simultaneously; hence Annie's inquiries into the past lead her ultimately towards her mother (Ina) and a future with her lesbian lover – named 'Zoe' – the progress towards personal fulfillment rendered alphabetically as well as through the psychology of character development. The motif of going-back-to-go-forward is not new, of course, but it is given an edge in women's writing because this writing calls for women to move out of the arc that men's history has designed and the language through which men's history demarcates priorities and values. What is called for (by France Théoret in *Entre raison et déraison*, 1987, and by Nicole Brossard and others) is an *écriture feminine* – a language of the (woman's) body – something different from what has up to this point existed.

Seeking an alternative means of communicating, or expressing, this sensibility does not mean that only one alternative exists, and a few writers rendered their desire for independence in fairly traditional forms. Yolande Villemaire's *Vava* (1989), for example, follows a linear narrative, during which a teenaged girl (the title figure) in May 1968, the time of student revolutions, discovers sex and nationalism in Quebec. A *Bildungsroman*, the novel takes Vava through to a version of maturity; working for Bell Canada, however, she comes to realize that 'English' is also part of her identity, a conclusion that marks the book's departure from pastoral québécois convention. Technically more experimental in trying to express women's experience are works by Esther Croft (b. 1945), Suzanne Jacob (b. 1943), France Théoret, Élise Turcotte (b. 1957), and Anne-Marie Alonzo. The thirteen stories in Croft's *Au commencement était le froid* (1993), for example, posit that the world (i.e., the sum of relations between people) is cold; through a set of thematic variations, the characters go back to the past to try to discover the warmth they are now missing. The title allusion to the Gospel according to St John, however, suggests an absence of speech, of the 'word,' in the world that these women are trying to convey. Suzanne Jacob's series of works, by rendering a series of portraits of unacceptable mothers – from *La passion selon Galatée* (1987) through *Maude* (1988) to *Plages du main* (1989) and *L'obéissance* (1991) – instructs the reader to resist passivity. The mother in the first book is synonymous with cruelty; in the second she violates the intimate relation she could have had with her daughter; the third constructs her as beautiful but destructive at the same time, and therefore as a figure who must be distanced; the fourth depicts infanticide.

In this context, it is possible to reread the several works by Denise Chong, SKY Lee, Hiro Boga, and others that go in search of absent or lost mothers (and also perhaps the books by Audrey Thomas and Claire Harris that talk to missing children), but to see that while so many francophone works (Jacob, Blais, Anne Hébert in *Le torrent*, 1950) represent the mother as monster – as a collaborator, perhaps, in male domination – these works of the 1990s seek sustenance from the missing generation. In other works, too, the mother has gone missing – or at least her voice has gone missing from history – and writers in these instances seek to use their skills as writers to give the mother a chance to speak and the mother's voice a chance to be heard. So with France Théoret in *L'homme qui peignait Staline* (1988), where the central character is a writer; and so with Élise Turcotte in *Le bruit des choses vivantes* (1991; tr. as *The Sound of Living Things*, 1993), where the relation between a little girl and her creative mother is not confrontative and where both characters are permitted a voice. Significantly, perhaps, no father is present here, possibly suggesting why the relationship is presented as idyllic. Certainly, *La mémoria* (1996) by Louise Dupré (b. 1949) mourns the impossibility of relationships with men but uses the metaphor of translation to speak of creation rather than loss; and in Brossard's *Le désert mauve*, men are equated with violence, Los Alamos, Robert Oppenheimer, and those who 'kill' others. Brossard takes this principle into literary theory and practice – translation and interpretation are also in this context taken to be acts of control, 'death' – but with Hébert's *Le premier jardin* and Madeleine Ferron's *Adrienne*, the focus falls once again on the real world with which fiction connects. Hébert's novel returns to the first settlers in Quebec, finding her own family names among them, locating an Eden of sorts in the world that the *filles du roi* created, and Ferron celebrates her own mother's history, and her ability to engender dialogue between women and men.

THE PLAY OF STORYTELLING

There remain several other enterprises during the 1990s to comment upon, from children's writing to fantasy, from conservative appeals to tradition to the sheer delights of language at play. For only in some instances did writers write as if their rededication to the historically verifiable world should be taken as 'truth,' whether newly perceived or newly revealed. Far more often – as the many authorial afterwords make clear – writers' fascination lay in character and language. What might happen, they asked, if a character entered the world of the past? What might happen if a character entered a world of language, a world where changes in the manner of expression actually altered time, place, and identity?

Children's writing and speculative fiction provide clear examples not just of playful rhyme and fanciful pretence but also of historical imaginings and moral advice for people who live in an uncertain age. But while generalizations are misleading, it is possible to point to certain recurrent trends in both fields. Almost all the most widely read writers of the time (Atwood, Munro, William Gibson, W. P. Kinsella, and Michel Tremblay among them) tried their hand at speculative forms, probing social possibilities through allegory or dystopia, hypotheses about the supernatural or exaggerations of reality, thrillers of the years to come or predictions of disaster. The 1989 transformation of the *Tesseracts* series of anthologies into an annual and the founding of the journal *On Spec* in 1996 provided lively venues for Canadian SF writings. The works of writers who take SF as their primary form, moreover – including Sean Stewart (b. 1965;

Nobody's Son, 1993), Dave Duncan (b. 1933; *Hero*, 1991), Guy Gavriel Kay (*Tigana*, 1990), Candas Jane Dorsey (b. 1952; *Machine Sex*, 1988), Robert Charles Wilson (b. 1953; *The Harvest*, 1992), Robert Sawyer (b. 1960; *Golden Fleece*, 1990), Élisabeth Vonarburg (b. 1947; *Chroniques du pays des mères*, 1992), Yves Meynard (b. 1964; *The Book of Knights*, 1998), Spider Robinson (b. 1948; *Callahan's Legacy*, 1996), and Charles de Lint (b. 1951; *Trader*, 1997) – mostly deal in fantasy or 'alternate worlds.' Kay tends towards the psychological, exploring how identity can be taken over; Duncan and Sawyer pursue the consequences of fabricated identities and human flaws; Stewart and Meynard ask what follows conventional closure in people's lives. 'What if' is the motivating question throughout: what if something had happened or hadn't, will happen or won't, might happen or might not? The form provides a freedom from the constraints of real-world concerns and at the same time a freedom (without escaping the real world) to consider where alternative trajectories and hypothetical solutions might have led or might lead.

For their part, children's writers had earlier tried their hand at fantasy, as in such works as *The Root Cellar* (1981), a time-travel adventure by Janet Lunn, the Isis Trilogy (1980–81) by Monica Hughes, and *De zéro à minuit* (1981) by Marie-Louise Gay. While this impulse continued to some degree in the stories of Sarah Ellis (b. 1952; *The Back of Beyond*, 1996), even Ellis turned more often, in the later years of the twentieth century, to narratives about family crises (adoption, crib death, puberty, sibling rivalry). More common in the 1990s were books that featured historical romance, picture-book wit, self-help advice, or adolescent realism, with Hughes proving adept at all these forms; her *The Story Box* (1998) deals with storytelling itself. During the 1990s, moreover, the publication of books for children increased dramatically, until by 1999 it was estimated that one in three French-language books published in Quebec annually was written for child readers. Among writers who looked back to the past, a frequent narrative strategy was to install a child figure in a real historical time and grant the child power to affect history, the moral message for the child reader being abundantly clear. Such works tended to be plot-driven and didactic – not only with self-empowerment in mind but also with a commitment that Canadian history be made exciting to younger readers. They were not always captivating simply because of this intention, but among those books that critics found more effective are *Out of the Dark* (1995) by Welwyn Wilton Katz (b. 1948), about the Beothuk and the Vikings; *Ghost Train* (1996) by Paul Yee, about Chinese railway labourers; and *The War Guests Trilogy* (1989–93, 1999) by Kit Pearson (b. 1947), about British children resettled in Canada during the early 1940s. Marie-Louise Gay continued to play with language, both in illustration and in comic drama for children. Sue Ann Alderson (b. 1940), Diana Wieler (b. 1961), and Kevin Major all addressed children's or adolescents' personal conflicts. Major's work with Craig Kielburger (b. 1982) to protest worldwide child labour resulted in *Free the Children* (1998); Wieler's work ranges from *Bad Boy* (1989), about a boy coming to terms with homosexuality, to the Ran-Van trilogy (1993–97), which combines fantasy with real-life hardships in a tale about computer games and warrior adventurers. Alderson's work, which highlights children's capacity to help deal with problems in the real world, is lighter in tone than these, though Major, too, in other works, is adept at humour, and even if lighter, Alderson is serious. The best of the children's writers demonstrate, in fact, a broad ability to cross and combine genres, though each of them tends to specialize in reaching a particular age of reader.

Children's writers thus participated in the same literary inquiries that writers for adults pursued in the 1990s – sexuality, ethnicity, technology, class divisiveness and gendered opportunities, personal self-esteem, and historical reconstruction – often using humour as a way of diffusing trauma and experimenting with cross-genre and cross-media forms of communication. Fantasy, when it occurred, was not an escape from daily reality but a way of coping with it, and humour not generally a flippant gesture but a serious commitment to the world of language, to the fact of irony in Canadian speech, and to the social resonances that tonality conveys. 'How we speak,' that is, constitutes one of the implied meanings of 'what we say.'

And yet some writers were impatient with the present to such a degree that they sought reconnection with a European past as their route back to an idea of culture, and no survey of the late twentieth century can ignore this return to conservatism. The stylistic densities of Swiss-born Paul Zumthor (1915–95), a medieval specialist, and Montrealers Jean Marcel (Jean-Marcel Paquette, b. 1941) and Rober Racine (b. 1956) express these writers' commitment to scholarly detail; research into the past not only supplies them with their plots but also grants them a venue sympathetic to their systems of value. In Marcel's works, with their consciously archaic titles – *Hypathie, ou, La fin des dieux* (1989), *Jérôme, ou, De la traduction* (1990), *Sidoine, ou, La dernière fête* (1993) – the past becomes an embodiment of culture; our own time is seen as anti-culture, barbaric, a poor translation. With their focus on pre-Christian philosophers, Christian saints, and the imminent invasion of barbarians into Europe, therefore, the novels imagine the past as a preferable place for the life of the mind. Racine, in *Le mal de Vienne* (1992), also defines 'art' and 'literature' as European accomplishments.

These novelists write out of a European intellectual tradition and in order to reintegrate with it. With a somewhat different focus, Zumthor, in *Les contrebandiers* (1989) and *La traversée* (1991), writes about nomads whose narratives extend European values: Columbus in the first, frontiersmen in the second. But Europe remains central. Such writings implicitly suggest that past European accomplishments constitute the aesthetic pinnacle of civilization and that the closest that contemporary writers and readers can come to art is to immerse themselves in scholarship and imitation.

This dense intellectual fiction was by no means the only face of the return to formalism, however. Indeed, the appeal of received form in most writers' hands (whether the retrieval of narrative line or the revitalization of metric convention) did not return to the past; nor in the narrowest sense did it parody past forms. For the 'return' was not exact: it came within the context of what had been learned from postmodern conventions about disruption and fragmentation. The new 'formalism,' in some sense, was therefore in continuous dialogue with anti-formulaic practice: resistant to enclosure at the same time as it employed older narrative and verse forms (plot, sonnet, rhyme) – at best reanimating them. Anne Carson writing a 'novel-in-verse,' Ken Babstock integrating the vernacular with the formal, Tomson Highway building larger-than-life dance into mundane reality, Robert Lepage and Michael Ondaatje working with theatrical illusion and cinematic forms, Daphne Marlatt seeking the language of phenomenology, and a great many writers involved in Web page design and serial composition on computer-based networks – examples everywhere testify to writers' desire to use conventions in order to reimagine their potential.

The elegant sentences of Michael Redhill (b. 1966) in *Martin Sloane* (2001) offer one face of innovation; in this novel, about a woman's obsession with a man who has abruptly disappeared from her life, the narrative coolly traces her pursuit of him. That the ending should be other than she desires *and* other than the reader might suspect gives the book its remarkably compelling power; the crafted formality of the prose contributes directly to this effect by consciously distancing answers from the questions the narrator asks. A second example is provided by the novel that many consider Jacques Poulin's masterpiece, *Le vieux chagrin* (1989; tr. as *Mr. Blue*, 1993). About a cat – the figure named by the English-language title – the work gains further substance from the way the metaphor functions to talk about language itself: words, says Poulin, are independent, like cats. The pacing of Ray Smith's prose, the eloquent imagery in McKay's poetry and Highway's plays, the clarity of Wade Davis's essays, the lyricism that distinguishes the fiction of Christiane Frenette (b. 1954) and Helen Humphreys – these further examples simply record, across genres, a remarkable range of accomplishment. Frenette's brilliant *La terre ferme* (1997; tr. as *Terra Firma*, 1999) traces the impact on an entire town – the shaping of memory itself there – when youngsters are drowned in the St Lawrence River and seemingly lost to the future. Humphreys's *The Lost Garden* (2002) also deals with memory, returning to the Second World War in England for its setting; here a narrator, suffering the loss of her lover in the war and of her idol Virginia Woolf to suicide, is haunted by both. The garden she is asked to tend, while the war continues, is marauded by foxes and only obliquely given shape, but it is where she manages over time the compromises that let her persist. So, perhaps, with Carol Shields's *Unless* (2002), which after (or *while*) its narrator copes with literary composition and personal loss, commits itself to goodness: it is a choice, not an accident of circumstance or station. Nor, matter-of-factly, is it ever equated with permanent bliss.

Authors' stylistic choices are not accidental; they are integral to the particular work, the literary achievement, whether their choice is to use formal diction or the vernacular, employ received syntax or break away from it, depend primarily on image or more on a relation between sense and sound, structure their way towards unity and closure or give precedence to fragmentation and uncertainty. That language – the *play* of language, its joys and its elasticity – should be one of the subjects addressed by still other works is therefore unsurprising. That such works – especially *Stanley Park* (2001) by Timothy Taylor (b. 1963) and *Salamander* (2001) by Thomas Wharton, among many examples – should become numerous as the twenty-first century began perhaps hints at a retreat from the confrontations of real life: literature as escape or as desperate entertainment in difficult times. More positively, it more likely suggests the willingness of a new generation of writers to find delight in discovery all over again. For these works do not, finally, retreat from reality. Taylor deals with economic disparities, social power, murder, manipulation, shallowness, industrial greed, and personal hope in an uproarious and sad tale of a young chef's reconnection with his imperfect father and his ongoing quest for the perfect meal. And for his part, Wharton takes the reader on a journey across centuries into the power of the imagination; when an amazing invention permits his characters to enter books – literally to enter books, to become one with print – and when gothic plots, libraries, and clockwork castles all have the power to entrap these characters or free them, then the colonial history of Quebec (the ostensible frame of the narrative) comes alive in a brand new way. Wharton celebrates here the 'ocean of story,' the place where the imaginations of writers and readers can still connect, in part by refusing convention, in part by putting it to work to feed the future.

One of the most widely read essayists of these years, John Ralston Saul (b. 1947), wrote about philosophy and society in Canada at the end of the twentieth century, addressing these same issues of inheritance and the state, memory and class, insight and ethnicity, place and the past, in books that ranged from *Voltaire's Bastards* (1992), on the 'dictatorship' of reason in the West, to *On Equilibrium* (2001). Speaking as a writer, independent of literary faction (although his position as spouse of Canada's governor general, Adrienne Clarkson, is not irrelevant to his readership), he vigorously opposed what he called the mythology of victimization. 'The professional victim,' he writes in *Reflections of a Siamese Twin* (1997), 'is a professional innocent. As the one to whom things are done, the victim has no responsibility.' This 'comfortable position of passivity,' moreover, is 'the classic description of a colonial mind-set,' and it is both easy to fall into and dangerous to embrace. Avoiding this trap is one of the challenges he sees that Canadians need directly to face: to resist believing selective interpretations of the past, to cautiously accept the country's place in the Americas, to resist the reductive arguments of 'self-indulgent' politicians who espouse either centralization or decentralization as absolute solutions to problems of poverty, racism, language, or health, to appreciate the country's multiple inheritances and multiple differences as sources of strength, and to seek solutions within a 'context of reconciliation and reform.' 'The Inuit quality of *isuma*,' he goes on, 'summarizes that essential context ... It [means an] intelligence that consists of the knowledge of our responsibilities towards our society. It is a characteristic which grows with time. If you choose to look, you can find it at the core of events through the long line of the Canadian experience. It is an intelligence, the Inuit say, which grows because it is nurtured.' Occasionally Saul talks about literature in this book. But while his conclusions do not focus directly on literary texts, he might well have been summarizing the trends of writing in the 1990s. Writers in all genres, sometimes writing across genres, called repeatedly upon readers to reconsider what they believed about Canada. Despite the unhappy, even devastating experiences they sometimes wrote about, moreover, they for the most part placed faith still in the power of choice and the possibility of communication. They affirmed the possibilities of language, in short, in a place still livable and still to be lived.

Chronological table

Abbreviations: (A) = anthology, (D) = drama, (P) = prose, (V) = verse

Date	Author and Title	Event
BC		
13000		Niagara Falls forms as glaciers retreat
11000		Earliest records of the Bluefish Cave people (Yukon)
10000		Receding of the last ice sheet
9000		Earliest records of the Fluted Point people (Ontario)
7000		Earliest records of human habitation on the West Coast of Canada Nomadic 'Archaic Boreal' Indian culture moves into Arctic mainland
3000		Aboriginal habitation in the Maritimes
0800		Dorset culture develops around Hudson Strait
AD		
0300		Village tradition established on prairies
0499		Chinese Buddhist monk Hui Shen reputed to have sailed to Fu-Sang (possibly America)

Date	Author and Title	Event
0500		Beans, corn and squash cultivated in Eastern Woodlands
0875		Irish monks land on Magdalen Islands
0995		Leif Erikson sets out on expedition to Vinland
1000		Viking settlement at L'Anse aux Meadows, Nfld – possibly Leif Erikson's Vinland Thule culture replaces Dorset Culture in Arctic
1390		Mohawk, Oneida, Cayuga, Onondaga and Seneca establish the Iroquois confederacy (Tuscarora joins in 1722)
1400		West Coast tribes establish trading network
1431		Joan of Arc is burned at Rouen
1497		John Cabot discovers the Grand Banks
1504		Est. of St John's as English fisheries base in Newfoundland
1513		Balboa crosses Panama to the Pacific
1516		More: *Utopia*
1517		Beginnings of Protestant Reformation
1519		Cortez conquers Mexico
1526		Founding of the Moghul Empire
1532		Machiavelli: *The Prince* Rabelais: *Pantagruel*
1534		Est. of Jesuit order Jacques Cartier explores St Lawrence River

Date	Author and Title	Event
1537		Est. of Ursuline order
1541		John Calvin introduces Reformation into Geneva
1544		English translation of the Bible
1556		Ramusio's Italian translation of Cartier's journal
1564		D. of Michelangelo
1569		Mercator's map of the world
1570		Luke Foxe explores Hudson's Bay
1572		Luis de Camoens: *The Lusiad*
1576		Martin Frobisher searches for the Northwest Passage
1579		Spenser: *The Shepheardes Calendar*
1580		John Florio's English translation of Cartier's journal Montaigne: *Essays*
1583		Sir Humphrey Gilbert claims Newfoundland for England
1588		Marlowe: *Doctor Faustus*
1589		Hakluyt: *The Principall Navigations*
1600		Giordano Bruno burned as a heretic in Rome
1601		Shakespeare: *Hamlet*
1604		Founding of Port Royal
1605		Cervantes: *Don Quixote*
1606		Champlain founds L'Ordre du Bon Temps (Order of Good Cheer) First theatrical performance in North America: *Le théâtre de Neptune* by Marc Lescarbot
1607		Jamestown settlement in Virginia

Date	Author and Title	Event
1608		Champlain founds Quebec
1609	Marc Lescarbot (c. 1570–1642): *Les muses de la Nouvelle France* (D.V)	
1610		Henry Hudson explores Hudson' Bay in search of Northwest Passage
1611		King James version of the Bible
1613	Samuel de Champlain (c. 1570–1635): *Voyages* (P; vols II & III follow in 1619 and 1632)	
1615		Franciscans arrive in New France; Récollets set up missions
1616		William Baffin maps Ellesmere Island and Baffin Bay
1619		Jens Munk leads Danish expedition to find Northwest Passage
1620		Plymouth Colony in Massachusetts
1625		Jesuits arrive in New France
1627		Richelieu organises Company of 100 Associates to colonize New France
1628	Robert Hayman (1575–1629): *Quodlibets* (P)	
1632	Annual Jesuit *Relations* begin; continue to 1673	Galileo confirms Copernican theory, is forced to recant by the Inquisition
1633		Olivier Le Jeune (a black slave) is baptised in Quebec
1635		Est. of *Académie française*
1636		Founding of Harvard College
1639		Ursulines (nursing & teaching order) and Augustines arrive in New France
1640		*Bay Psalm Book* (first book printed in America)

Date	Author and Title	Event
1641		Jeanne Mance and Gov. De Maisonneuve arrive in New France
1642		de Maisonneuve founds Ville-Marie (later Montreal)
1644		End of the Ming Dynasty, beginning of the Manchu (to 1912)
1649		D. of Fr. Jean de Brébeuf (b. 1593) and Fr. Gabriel Lalemant (b. 1610), both canonised in 1930
1650		D. of Descartes
1653		Marguerite Bourgeoys opens hospital and school and Quebec Completion of the Taj Mahal
1654		Radisson and Groseilliers depart on their first exploratory journey to the west
1659		Radisson & Groseilliers explore St Lawrence headwaters Laval becomes first Bishop
1660		Adam Dollard des Ormeaux and Battle of the Long Sault Royal Society founded (London)
1663		New France comes under direct royal rule
1665		Jean Talon becomes Intendant (to 1672)
1667		Milton: *Paradise Lost*
1668		La Fontaine: *Fables* (to 1694)
1669		D. of Rembrandt
1670		Molière: *Le bourgeois gentilhomme* Founding of Hudson's Bay Company
1672		Marquette & Jolliet explore Mississippi Basin

Date	Author and Title	Event
1677		Racine: *Phèdre*
1678		Bunyan: *Pilgrim's Progress*
1680		D. of Catherine Tekakwitha (beatified 1980)
1681	Marie de l'Incarnation (1599–1672): *Lettres de la vénérable mère ...* (P)	
1682		La Salle reaches mouth of Mississippi
1683	Fr. Louis Hennepin (1627–c. 1705): *Description de la Louisiane* (P)	Brébeuf calls the Algonquin game of baggataway 'lacrosse'
1685		Birth of Handel (d. 1759), Bach (d. 1750), Scarlatti (d. 1757)
1687		Newton: *Principia Mathematica*
1690		Henry Kelsey reaches Saskatchewan River System
1692		Witchcraft burnings in Salem, Mass.
1697		Perrault: *Contes de ma mère l'Oye*
1698	Hennepin: *A New Discovery of a Vast County in America* (P)	
1713		Peace of Utrecht (end of War of the Spanish Succession
1714		Pope: *The Rape of the Lock*
1719		Defoe: *Robinson Crusoe*
1721		Bach composes *Brandenburg Concertos*
1726		Swift: *Gulliver's Travels*
1730		Substantial roadway system established in the colonies by this time
1735		Hogarth: 'The Rake's Progress'

Date	Author and Title	Event
1736	John Gyles: *Memoirs of Odd Adventures ...* (P)	
1737		First iron foundry opens in Canada (Trois-Rivières)
1740		Samuel Richardson: *Pamela*
1741		Death of Vivaldi (b. 1678)
1742		First performance of Handel's *Messiah*
1748		François Bigot becomes Intendant (to 1759) Peter Kalm's travels through America
1749		Cornwallis founds Halifax
1752		Est. of first printing press in Nova Scotia and the Halifax *Gazette* England adopts Gregorian calendar
1754		Anthony Henday explores the prairies
1757		Edmund Burke: *Philosophical Enquiry into the Origin of Our Ideas of the Sublime and Beautiful*
1758		Fall of Louisburg Nova Scotia gets legislative assembly
		Cook maps the St Lawrence basin Battle of the Plains of Abraham; death of Generals Montcalm and Wolfe Voltaire: *Candide*
1762		Rousseau: *Le contrat social*
1763		Treaty of Paris (New France ceded to England at end of Seven Years' War Cook maps the Newfoundland coast (to 1767)
1764		First printing press in Quebec; first bilingual newspaper in Canada: *La Gazette de Québec*

Date	Author and Title	Event
1768		Royal Academy of Art founded (London) Royal Society commissions Cook to chart the South Pacific, observe the Transit of Venus; Cook introduces lime juice to sailors' diet to prevent scurvy (lime juice was made part of the standard British Navy diet in 1795)
1769	Frances Brooke (1723–89): *The History of Emily Montague* (P)	Nova Scotia and Prince Edward Island become separate colonies
1771		Benjamin West: 'The Death of Wolfe' (painting) Goldsmith: *The Deserted Village*
1771		Samuel Hearne reaches the mouth of the Coppermine River
1772		John Harrison perfects chronometer
1774		Quebec Act (protects Roman Catholic religious freedom and French civil law in Canada) Perez Hernandez reaches Nootka Sound
1776		Smith: *The Wealth of Nations* American Declaration of Independence (war with England lasts from 1775 to 1783)
1777		Sheridan: *The School for Scandal*
1778		James Cook explores the Pacific Coast Peter Pond trades into Athabasca region
1779		Captain Cook dies in Hawaii (Sandwich Islands)
1780	Jonathan Odell (1737–1818): *The American Times* (V)	
1782	Henry Alline (1748–84): *Hymns and Spiritual Songs* (V; vol. II appeared in 1786)	Crèvecoeur: *Letters from an American Farmer*

Date	Author and Title	Event
1783	Brooke: *Rosina* (opera)	Mass immigration of United Empire Loyalists to Maritime colonies and Upper Canada North West Company founded
1784		First Russian settlements on West Coast of North America New Brunswick becomes a colony
1785	Jacob Bailey (1731–1808): 'The Adventures of Jack Ramble, the Methodist Preacher' (V)	Watt invents steam engine
1787		American and Nova Scotia blacks resettled in Sierra Leone
1788	Roger Viets (1738–1811): *Annapolis Royal* (V)	Chief Maquinna and Captain John Meares reach agreement to turn Nootka Sound into a foreign trading centre
1789	Thomas Cary (1751–1823): *Abram's Plains* (V)	Alexander Mackenzie follows the Mackenzie River to the Arctic Ocean French Revolution
1790	Joseph Quesnel (1746–1809): *Colas et Colinette* (D)	Nootka Sound Convention signed in Madrid
1791	Peter Fidler (1769–1822): 'Hudson's Bay Journal' (ed. J.B. Tyrell, 1934), in *Journals of Samuel Hearne and Philip Turnor* (P)	Constitutional Act (creates Upper Canada and Lower Canada, each with its own Assembly) Haitian Rebellion (Toussaint L'Ouverture) Elizabeth Simcoe (d. 1850) begins her diary of Upper Canada life (1792–6); pub. as *Mrs. Simcoe's Diary*, ed. Mary Quayle Innis, 1965)
1792		Captain Vancouver and Captain Galiano chart Pacific Coast
1793		Upper Canada Parliament abolishes the practice of bringing slaves into the colony Est. of Fort York as town of York (incorporated as city of Toronto in 1834) Alexander Mackenzie reaches Pacific Coast by land

Date	Author and Title	Event
1795	Samuel Hearne (1745–92): *Journey from Prince of Wales's Fort in Hudson's Bay to the Northern Ocean* (P)	Founding of Orange Order D. of Robert Burns (b. 1759) David Thompson explores the Columbia River
1797	J. Mackay: *Quebec Hill* (V)	
1798	George Vancouver (1757–98): *Voyage of Discovery ...* (P)	Wordsworth & Coleridge: *Lyrical Ballads*
1799		Discovery of the Rosetta Stone
1801	Alexander Mackenzie (1763–1820): *Voyages ... through the Continent of North America* (P)	
1802		Lamarck coins the word 'biology' Dionisio Alcalá Galiano: *Relación del Viage Hecho por las Galetas Sutil y Mexicana*
1803		Chief Maquinna takes John Jewitt captive
1804		Napoleonic Code comes into effect as basis for law in France and in Quebec Lewis and Clark expedition to Oregon (to 1806) Thomas Moore: 'Canadian Boat Song'
1806		Mutiny on the *Bounty*
1807		Webster: *Dictionary*
1808		Simon Fraser reaches the mouth of the Fraser River
1809	Alexander Henry (1739–1824): *Travels and Adventures in Canada and and the Indian Territories* (P)	John Molson builds the *Accommodation,* Canada's first steamship D. of Haydn (b. 1732)
1811		John McIntosh, in Upper Canada, discovers McIntosh apple David Thompson explores Columbia River Founding of Fort Astoria by party financed by John Jacob Astor

Date	Author and Title	Event
1812		First of Grimm's fairytales published
		Selkirk settlement
		War of 1812 (ends in 1815)
		Battle of Queenston Heights
		(Tecumseh and General Brock)
1813		Battle at Beaver Dams (Laura Secord); Battle of Châteauguay
		Austen: *Pride and Prejudice*
1814		Battle of Lundy's Lane
		Scott: *Waverley*
1815	John Jewitt: *A Narrative of the Adventure and Sufferings of John R. Jewitt ...* (P)	Whale oil streetlamps installed in Montreal
		Battle of Waterloo (end of Napoleonic Wars, 1796–1815)
1817		Est. of *Blackwood's Magazine*
		Keats: *Poems*
		M. Shelley: *Frankenstein*
1818		Est. of Dalhousie University
1820		Colony of Cape Breton joins Nova Scotia
1821	Thomas McCulloch (1776–1843): publishes 'letters' of 'Mephibosheth Stepsure' in the *Acadian Recorder* (to 1823; pub. in book form in 1862)	Founding of McGill University
		Merger between Hudson's Bay and North West Companies
		Opening of the Santa Fe Trail
1823	John Franklin (1786–1847): *Journey to the Polar Sea* (P)	Cooper: *The Pioneers*
1824	Julia Catherine Beckwith Hart (1796–1867): *St. Ursula's Convent* (P)	Est. of *The Novascotian* (to 1926)
	George Longmore: *The Charivari* (V)	Est. of *Colonial Advocate*
		Completion of Lachine Canal
		M.R. Mitford: *Our Village*
1825	Oliver Goldsmith (1794–1861): *The Rising Village* (V; rev. 1834)	Stephenson's steam railroad opens in England
1826	Catharine Parr Traill (1802–99): *The Young Emigrants* (P)	Est. of *Acadian Magazine* (to 1828)
		Cooper: *Last of the Mohicans*
1827		Est. of *Colonial Patriot* in Pictou
		Est. of first Mechanics' Institute in Canada (St John's)
		Second Franklin expedition to the Arctic Coast

Date	Author and Title	Event
1828	Joseph Howe (1804–73): 'Western Rambles' and 'Eastern Rambles' pub. in *The Novascotian* (P)	
1829	John Richardson (1796–1852): *Ecarté* (P)	Est. of Methodist Book Room in Toronto (became Ryerson Press in 1919, after first editor, Egerton Ryerson, 1802–82) Death of Shawnadithit, last of the Beothuks
1830	Adam Kidd (1802–31): *The Huron Chief* (V) Michel Bibaud (1782–1857): *Epîtres, satires, chansons, épigrammes ...* (V)	Orange Lodge est. in Ontario Josiah Henson (ostensibly the original for Harriet Beecher Stowe's 'Uncle Tom') escapes to Upper Canada Daniel Massey develops the threshing machine Stendhal: *Le rouge et le noir*
1831	William Fitz Hawley (1804?–55): *The Unknown* (P)	Charles Darwin embarks on the *Beagle* voyage John Galt: *Bogle Corbet*
1832	William 'Tiger' Dunlop: *Statistical Sketches of Upper Canada* (P) Richardson: *Wacousta*	D. of poet Levi Adams (b. 1802) Cholera epidemic (followed by others in 1834, 1849, 1854)
1833		The *Royal William* (Samuel Cunard a major shareholder) becomes first ship to cross Atlantic entirely by steam
1835		Sam Slick sketches appear as 'Recollections of Nova Scotia' in *The Novascotian* Balzac: *Le père Goriot* Publication of Andersen's fairytales
1836	Anon., *The Awful Disclosures of Maria Monk* (P) Thomas Chandler Haliburton (1796–1865): *The Clockmaker* (first series; the second and third series appeared in 1838 and 1840 (P) Traill: *The Backwoods of Canada* (P)	Dickens: *The Pickwick Papers* (to 1837)

Date	Author and Title	Event
1837	Philippe-Ignace-François Aubert de Gaspé (Aubert de Gaspé fils, 1814–1841): *L'influence d'un livre* (P) Pierre Petitclair (1813–60): *Griphon* (D)	Rebellions in Upper Canada (led by William Lyon Mackenzie against the Family Compact) and in Lower Canada (led by Louis Joseph Papineau against the Château Clique) 'Shiner's Wars' (to 1845) Victoria becomes Queen (to 1901) Sarah Josepha Hale becomes editor of *Godey's Lady's Book* Agassiz coins term 'Ice Age' Froebel opens first 'kindergarten'
1838	Anna Jameson (1794–1860): *Winter Studies and Summer Rambles in Canada* (P)	John Lovell est. *The Literary Garland* (to 1851) Charles Fenerty makes first usable newsprint from wood fibre, in Nova Scotia British Parliament abolishes slavery Samuel Morse develops Morse Code
1839		Durham Report John Strachan (1778–1867) becomes first Anglican bishop of Toronto First bicycle developed
1840	Eliza Lanesford Cushing (1794–1886): *The Fatal Ring* (D) Richardson: *The Canadian Brothers* (P; an expurgated version appeared as *Matilda Montgomerie*, 1851)	Act of Union joins Upper and Lower Canada, renames them Canada West and Canada East Rev. James Evans devises Cree syllabics Poe: *Tales of the Grotesque and Arabesque*
1841	Standish O'Grady (c. 1793–1841): *The Emigrant* (V)	Est. of Queen's University City of Halifax incorporated
1842	Antoine Gérin-Lajoie (1824–82): 'Un Canadien errant'	Jesuit Order re-established in Canada (after dissolution in 1763) Kit Carson serves as frontier guide on Fremont Expedition (Oregon Trail) Browning: *Dramatic Lyrics* Stowe: *Uncle Tom's Cabin*
1843	Haliburton: *The Attaché* (first series; the second series appeared in 1844) (P) Abraham Holmes: *Belinda* (P)	King's College (Toronto) opens Kierkegard: *Either-Or*

Date	Author and Title	Event
1844		First edn of Toronto *Globe* (1872 becomes *Globe & Mail*) New Brunswick passes Indian Reserve Act '54–40 or Fight' (James Polk's presidential election slogan) Dumas: *Le comte de Monte-Cristo* Captain Marryat: *The Settlers in Canada*
1845	François-Xavier Garneau (1809–66): *Histoire du Canada* (P; 3 vols, to 1848)	Potato blight in Ireland, and famine, leading to emigration Manifest Destiny Paul Kane begins his sketches among the Indians Codification of the rules of baseball
1846	Pierre Chauveau (1820–90): *Charles Guérin* (P)	Oregon treaty 49th Parallel established as international boundary from the Great Lakes to the Pacific Patenting of the sewing machine
1847	Charles E. Beardsley: *The Victims of Tyranny* (P) Douglas Smith Huyghue (1816–91): *Argimou* (P)	D. of the Franklin expedition in the Arctic Est. of *The Snow Drop*, for children (to 1853) Mrs Moodie est. *The Victoria Magazine* (to 1848) Mormons settle in Utah Longfellow: *Evangeline* Thackeray: *Vanity Fair* Turgenev: *A Huntsman's Sketches*
1848	James Huston: *Le Répertoire national* (A; 4 vols, to 1850)	Second Baldwin–LaFontaine ministry (to 1851) brings about 'Responsible Government' Formation of Re-Raphaelite brotherhood Marx and Engels publish *Communist Manifesto*
1849	John Swete Cummins (1811–?): *Altham: A Tale of the Sea* (P) Haliburton: *The Old Judge* (P)	Crown colony of Vancouver Island established Fraser gold rush D. of poet Adam Hood Burwell (b. 1790) Dickens: *David Copperfield*

Date	Author and Title	Event
1850	Richardson: *the Monk Knight of St. John* (P)	Hawthorne: *The Scarlet Letter* Est. of *Harper's Magazine*
1851		Est. of the New York *Times* Melville: *Moby Dick* Baudelaire: *Les fleurs du mal* Parkman begins his history of North America (to 1892)
1852	Susanna Moodie (1803–85): *Roughing It in the Bush* (P) Traill: *Canadian Crusoes* (P)	Founding of Université Laval Verdi: *La Traviata* Roget's original *Thesaurus* published
1853	Haliburton: *Sam Slick's Wise Saws and Modern Instances* (P) Moodie: *Life in the Clearings Versus the Bush* (P); *Flora Lyndsay* (P); *Mark Hurdlestone* (P)	
1854	Octave Crémazie (1827 –79): *Premiers poèmes* (V) Traill: *The Female Emigrant's Guide* (P)	Abolition of seigneurial system Crimean War (ends 1856) Thoreau: *Walden*
1855	Haliburton: *Nature and Human Nature* (P) Moodie: *Geoffrey Moncton* (P)	Refinement of oil into kerosene Cities of Ottawa and Charlottetown incorporated Bulfinch: *The Age of the Fable* Samuel Colt uses mass production methods to stockpile revolvers and rifles David Livingstone reaches Victoria Falls on the Zambezi First train crosses Niagara Falls suspension bridge Whitman: *Leaves of Grass*
1856	Charles Sangster (1822–93): *The St. Lawrence and the Saguenay and other poems* (V)	William Notman sets up photo studio in Montreal Mendel experiments with genetic hybridization
1857	Charles Heavysege 1816–76): *Saul* (D)	Palliser expedition, recorded in journal of Henry Youle Hind Ottawa chosen as the national capital D. of Alfred de Musset Flaubert: *Madame Bovary*

Date	Author and Title	Event
1858	R.M. Ballantyne (1825–94): *Ungava* (P) Robert Traill Spence Lowell (1816–91): *New Priest in Conception Bay* (P) Thomas D'Arcy McGee (1825–68): *Canadian Ballads and occasional verses* (D)	Crown colony of British Columbia established Completion of transatlantic telegraph cable (New York–Newfoundland–Ireland)
1859	Paul Kane (1810–71): *Wanderings of An Artist Among the Indians of North America* (P) William Kirby (1817–1906): *The U.E.* (V) Rosanna Leprohon (1817–79): 'The Manor House of De Villerai' (P; serialised in *The Family Herald* to 1860)	Blondin walks over Niagara Falls on a tightrope Gounod: *Faust* Darwin: *On the Origin of Species* Tennyson: *Idylls of the King* Eliot: *Adam Bede* Mill: *On Liberty*
1860	Sangster: *Hesperus and other poems and lyrics* (V)	Abbé Casgrain helps found Le Mouvement littéraire de Québec, breaking away to found *Le foyer canadien* (1863–6) Graeme Mercer Adam (1839–1912) takes over printing company in Toronto Cornelius Krieghoff: 'Merrymaking' (painting)
1861	Abbé Casgrain (1831–1904): *Légendes canadiennes* (P) Alexander McLachlan (1818–96): *The Emigrant* (V) Mary Anne Sadlier (1820–1903): *Elinor Preston* (P) Joseph-Charles Taché (1820–94): *Trois légendes de mon pays* (P)	Grand Trunk Railway completed American Civil War (ends in 1865) Ignaz Semmelweis declares the need for antiseptic medical practice during childbirth (his findings are ignored, until Joseph Lister makes them acceptable during the 1880s)
1862	Antoine-Gérin-Lajoie: *Jean Rivard* (P) Daniel Wilson (1816–92): *Prehistoric Man* (P)	Acting debut of Sarah Bernhardt Hugo: *Les misérables*
1863	Philippe-Joseph Aubert de Gaspé (1786–1871): *Les Anciens Canadiens* (P; tr. 1864 by G. Pennée as *The Canadians of Old*; 1890 by C.G.D. Roberts as *Canadians of Old*, rereleased 1905 as *Cameron of Lochiel*; condensed by T.G. Marquis 1929 as *Seigneur d'Haberville*) Taché: *Forestiers et voyageurs* (P)	

Date	Author and Title	Event
1864	Georges Boucher de Boucherville (1814–94): *Une de perdue, deux de trouvées* (P) Arthur Buies (1840–1901): *Lettres sur le Canada* (P) Edward Hartley Dewart (1828–1903): *Selections from Canadian Poets* (A) Leprohon: *Antoinette de Mirecourt* (P)	Charlottetown Conference Est. of Ingersoll cheese factory Pasteur develops pasteurisation Verne: *Voyage au centre de la terre*
1865	Napoléon Bourassa (1827–1916): *Jacques et Marie* (P) Heavysege: *Jephthah's Daughter* (D)	May Agnes Fleming (1840–80) begins to sell serial stories to newspapers in Boston, New York, and Philadelphia Lewis Carroll: *Alice's Adventures in Wonderland* Tolstoy: *War and Peace* (to 1872)
1866		Fenian raids on Canada, from the USA Organization of the Ku Klux Klan SPCA founded Nobel develops dynamite Parnassian Movement in French poetry begins
1867		Confederation; Canada becomes independent (British North America Act unites Ontario, Quebec, Nova Scotia, and New Brunswick as the Dominion of Canada) Sir John A. Macdonald becomes prime minister George Stewart (1848–1906) founds *Stewart's Literary Quarterly Magazine* (to 1872) Juliana Horatia Ewing sends letters home from Fredericton (to 1869); pub. 1983 as *Canada Home*, ed. M.H. & T.E. Blom) Dr Emily Howard Stowe becomes first woman to set up medical practice in Canada First paperback book (Goethe's *Faust*) goes on sale in Germany Russia sells Alaska to USA Emperor Maximilian executed in Mexico Ibsen: *Peer Gynt*

Date	Author and Title	Event
1868	Charles Mair (1838–1927): *Dreamland and other poems* (V) Traill: *Canadian Wild Flowers* (P) Arthur Buies est. *La Lanterne*	'Canada First' Movement founded Assassination of D'Arcy McGee
1869	James De Mille (1833–80): *The Dodge Club; or, Italy in MDCCCLIX* (P); *The 'B.O.W.C.'* (P) Joseph Stansbury (c. 1742–1809): *the Loyal Verses ...* (V)	Development of rotary snowplow Hudson's Bay Company sells Rupert's Land to Canada Character of 'Johnny Canuck' makes first appearance, in Montreal magazine *Grinchuckle* Suez Canal opens Guibord Affair
1870	*Oeuvres de Champlain* (P)	First Riel (Red River) Rebellion Northwest Territories established Manitoba enters Confederation Battle of Sedan (Franco-Prussian War, 1870–71) Italy becomes a united kingdom
1871	Alexander Begg (1839–97): *'Dot It Down'* (P)	British Columbia enters Confederation Est. of Willis & Co. piano manufacturers in Montreal Bismarck becomes Chancellor of a united Germany First P.T. Barnum circus opens (in Brooklyn)
1872	William Francis Butler (1838–1910): *The Great Lone Land* (P)	Wild Bill Hickok stars in first Wild West Show, in Niagara Falls Samuel Butler, *Erewhon*
1873	George Monro Grant (1835–1902): *Ocean to Ocean* (P)	Prince Edward Island enters Confederation Est. of *Grip* (to 1894) by cartoonist J.W. Bengough (1851–1923) Pacific Scandal North West Mounted Police formed Bizet: *Carmen* Verne: *Le tour du monde en quatre-vingts jours*
1874	Alexander McLachlan (1818–96): *The Emigrant and other poems* (V) Howe: *Poems and Essays*	Mennonites immigrate to prairies First exhibition of Impressionist painters in Paris (Cézanne, Degas, Monet, Pissarro, and Renoir) Moussorgsky: *Pictures at an Exposition*

Date	Author and Title	Event
		Wagner completes *Ring* cycle, begun in 1848; first Bayreuth production is in 1876
1875		Icelanders immigrate to Manitoba Development of modern game of ice hockey, in Montreal, the rules written by J.G.A. Creighton Guibord Affair continues Mount Allison University is first in Canada to award degrees to women Madame Blavatsky founds Theosophical Society
1876		Alexander Graham Bell invents telephone Dr Emily Howard Stowe founds Toronto Women's Literary Club D. of balladist Pierre Falcon (b. 1783) Est. of Université de Montréal and Royal Military College City of St Catharine's incorporated Kropotkin becomes leading exponent of anarchism
1877	Kirby: *The Golden Dog* (P)	Blackfoot nation signs treaty with Canadian government Edison invents phonograph Emile Berliner invents disc recording, establishes Montreal studio
1878	Honoré Beaugrand (1848–1906): *Jeanne-la-fileuse* (P)	Est. of *Rose-Belford's Canadian Monthly* (to 1882) Karl Benz develops first internal combustion engine automobile Gilbert & Sullivan's *H.M.S. Pinafore* opens
1879	Louis Fréchette (1839–1908): *Les oiseaux de neige* (V)	Beaugrand founds *La patrie* First written version of 'Alouette' Dostoevsky: *The Brothers Karamazov* Ibsen: *A Doll's House* Edison invents light bulb
1880	John William Dawson (1820–99): *Fossil Men and Their Modern Representatives* (P) L. Fréchette: *Papineau* (D)	Sarah Bernhardt performs in Montreal (returns six times before 1916) Zola: *Nana* Calixa Lavallée composes 'O Canada'

Date	Author and Title	Event
	Sir Charles G.D. Roberts (1860–1943): *Orion, and other poems* (V) William Henry Withrow (1839–1908): *Neville Trueman, the Pioneer Preacher* (P)	National Gallery of Canada founded 'Donnelly Murders' in Ontario Sherriff Pat Garrett captures Billy the Kid
1881		Chinese workers brought to Canada to build CPR tracks
1882	Crémazie: *Oeuvres complètes* (V) Withrow: *Valeria, the Martyr of the Catacombs* (P)	Royal Society of Canada founded Est. of free library system in Ontario Pile o' Bones est. as the town of Regina (incorporated as a city 1903) D. of Jesse James
1883	Horatio Hale (1817–96): *The Iroquois Book of Rites* (P) Moses Harvey (1820–1901): *Newfoundland* (P)	Est. of *The Week* (to 1896) Regina made capital of North West Territories
1884	Laure Conan (pseud. Marie-Louise-Félicité Angers, 1845–1924): *Angéline de Montbrun* (P) Isabella Valancy Crawford (1850–87): *Old Spookses' Pass, Malcolm's Katie, and Other Poems* (V)	First Eaton's Catalogue distributed Imperial Federation League formed Canadian Nile Expedition Legal prohibition of potlatch ceremony Opening of Toronto Public Library Standard Time Zone system adopted (designed by Sir Sandford Fleming in 1879) Twain: *Huckleberry Finn*
1885	Félix-Gabriel Marchand (1832–1900): *Les faux brillants* (D)	Second Riel Rebellion (Batoche) Louis Riel executed Completion of Canadian Pacific Railway Incorporation of city of Calgary Sara Jeannette Duncan becomes correspondent for the Washington *Post* Poet and dramatist Nicholas Flood Davin (1840–1901) reports on Riel Rebellion Howells: *The Rise of Silas Lapham* Vaccination for smallpox becomes mandatory
1886	J.E. Collins: *Annette the Métis Spy* (P) Susie Frances Harrison (1859–1935): *Crowded Out and Other Sketches* (P)	City of Vancouver incorporated Toronto Conservatory of Music opens

Date	Author and Title	Event
	Mair: *Tecumseh* (D) Roberts: *In Divers Tones* (V)	Est. of Canadian Trades and Labour Congress Robert Harris: 'A Meeting of the School Trustees' (painting) American Federation of Labour established Hardy: *The Mayor of Casterbridge* Stevenson: *Doctor Jekyll and Mr. Hyde* James: *The Bostonians*
1887	G.M. Adam & Ethelwyn Wetherald (1857–1940): *An Algonquin Maiden* (V) George Frederick Cameron (1854–85): *Lyrics on Freedom, Love and Death* (V) Sarah Anne Curzon (1833–98): *Laura Secord* (D) Fréchette: *La légende d'un peuple* (V) Archibald Lampman (1861–99): *Among the Millet* (V) T. Phillips Thompson (1843–1933): *The Politics of Labor* (P)	International Copyright Convention signed (but not by USA) Cargo shipping via CPR connects the Orient with London Conan Doyle: *A Study in Scarlet*
1888	Buies: *Anglicismes et canadianismes* (P) De Mille: *A Strange Manuscript Found in a Copper Cylinder* (P) John Hunter-Duvar (1821–99): *De Roberval* (D)	D. of Big Bear
1889	William Douw Lighthall (1857–1954): *Songs of the Great Dominion* (A)	
1890	Sara Jeannette Duncan (1861–1922): *A Social Departure* (P) James MacDonald Oxley (1855–1907): *Up Among the Ice Floes* (P)	John J. McLaughlin registers 'Canada Dry' as a trademark
1891	S.J. Duncan: *An American Girl in London* (P) Goldwin Smith (1823–1910): *Canada and the Canadian Question* (P)	*Empress of India* arrives in port of Vancouver D. of Rimbaud
1892	Agnes Maule Machar (1837–1927): *Roland Graeme, Knight* (P) George Parkin (1846–1922): *Imperial Federation* (P)	'At the Mermaid Inn' column appeared in the Toronto *Globe* (to 1893) Stanley Cup donated Fort Edmonton est. as a town (incorporated as the city of Edmonton 1904) Lizzie Borden axe murders

Date	Author and Title	Event
1893	Bliss Carman (1861–1929): *Low Tide on Grand Pré* (V) T.G. Marquis (1864–1936): *Stories from Canadian History* (P) Roberts: *Songs of the Common Day* (V) Duncan Campbell Scott (1862–1947): *The Magic House and other poems* (V) Egerton Ryerson Young (1840–1909): *Stories from Indian Wigwams and Northern Campfires* (P)	Est. of *the Canadian Magazine* (to 1939) Est. of *Queen's Quarterly* James Naismith devises game of basketball in Almonte, Ontario Death of Tchaikovsky (b. 1840)
1894	Joanna E. Wood (1867–1927): *The Untempered Wind* (P) Marshall Saunders (1861–1947): *Beautiful Joe* (P)	Dreyfus Affair begins to unfold in France Est. of *The Yellow Book* (to 1897)
1895	Carman, with Richard Hovey: *Songs from Vagabondia* (V) Lily Dougall (1858–1923): *The Madonna of a Day* (P) Jules-Paul Tardivel (1851–1905): *Pour la patrie* (P) Edward William Thomson (1849–1924): *Old Man Savarin and other stories* (P; rev. in 1917 as *Old Man Savarin Stories: Tales of Canada and Canadians* Withrow: *Barbara Heck, A Tale of Early Methodism in America* (A)	Est. of École littéraire de Montréal (to c. 1930) Est. of *The University of Toronto Quarterly* Trial of Oscar Wilde Marconi develops 'wireless' Roentgen develops X-ray
1896	S.J. Duncan: *His Honour, and a Lady* (P) Gilbert Parker (1862–1932): *The Seats of the Mighty* (P) Roberts: *Earth's Enigmas* (P) D.C. Scott: *In the Village of Viger* (P) John Watson (1847–1939): *Christianity and Idealism* (P)	Sir Wilfrid Laurier becomes prime minister Klondike gold rush begins in the Yukon Est. of *Maclean's Magazine* Manitoba Schools Question Binet develops IQ test Jewett: *Country of the Pointed Firs*
1897	Grant Allen (1848–99): *An African Millionaire* (P) Nérée Beauchemin (1850–1931): *Les floraisons matutinales* (V) William Henry Drummond (1854–1907): *The Habitant and other French-Canadian poems* (V)	Adelaide Hoodless founds the first Women's Institute D. of Cree leader Almighty Voice (b. 1874) Discovery of the electron
1898	Wilfred Campbell (1858–1918): *The Dreaded Voyage* (V)	Doukhobors immigrate to prairies Yukon becomes a separate territory; gold rush

Date	Author and Title	Event
	Harrison (as 'Seranus'): *The Forest of Bourg-Marie* (P)	Spanish-American War
		Marie and Pierre Curie discover
	Ernest Thompson Seton (1860–1946):	radium
	Wild Animals I Have Known (P)	Shaw: *Plays Pleasant and Unpleasant*
		Wells: *The War of the Worlds*
1899	Fréchette: *Christmas in French Canada* (P)	Empire Day (24 May, Victoria Day holiday) first celebrated
	Francis Grey (1860–1939):	Boer War (ends 1902)
	The Curé of St. Philippe (P)	Dewey: *The School and Society*
	Pamphile Lemay (1837–1918):	Sibelius: 'Finlandia'
	Contes vrais (P)	Thorstein Veblen: *The Theory of the*
	William McLennan (1860–1904) and	*Leisure Class*
	& Jean McIlwraith: *The Span o' Life* (P)	
1900	Beaugrand: *La chasse-galérie* (P)	Founding of *Académie Goncourt*
	Norman Duncan (1871–1916):	Max Planck develops quantum
	The Soul of the Street (P)	theory
	Roberts: *The Heart of the Ancient Wood* (P)	Freud: *The Interpretation of Dreams*
		Boxer Rebellion in China
	D.C. Scott, ed.: *The Poems of Archibald Lampman* (V)	Baum: *The Wonderful Wizard of Oz*
		Conrad: *Lord Jim*
		Dreiser: *Sister Carrie*
1901	Richard Maurice Bucke (1837–1902): *Cosmic Consciousness* (P)	Johnny Burke (1851–1930) publishes first songbook
	Ralph Connor (pseud., Charles Gordon; 1860–1937): *The Man from Glengarry* (P)	Est. of University of Toronto Press
		Est. of *University Magazine* (McGill, to 1920)
		Carnegie Library system developed
		Australia becomes independent
1902	S.J. Duncan: *Those Delightful Americans* (P)	
	Connor: *Glengarry School Days* (P)	
	Roberts: *The Kindred of the Wild* (P)	
1903	Carman: *The Kinship of Nature* (P)	Seton promotes 'League of
	Louvigny de Montigny (1876–1955):	Woodcraft Indians'
	Les boules de neige performed	Sir Charles Saunders appointed
	(D; published 1935)	Dominion cerealist, develops
	Norman Duncan: *The Way of the Sea* (P)	Marquis wheat in 1904, which
		becomes commercially available
	Émile Nelligan (1879–1941):	in 1908
	Émile Nelligan et son oeuvre (V)	Est. of Canadian Associated Press
	Seton: *Two Little Savages* (P)	(first Canadian wireservice)
		Alaska boundary settlement
		South Asian immigration begins
		Wright Brothers fly plane at Kitty Hawk

Date	Author and Title	Event
1904	S.J. Duncan: *The Imperialist* (P) Rodolphe Girard (1879–1956): *Marie Calumet* (P) Lemay: *Les Gouttelettes* (V)	Cora Hind (1861–1942) becomes president of Canadian Women's Press Club Tommy Ryan devises game of 5-pin bowling, in Toronto Beginnings of German Expressionist movement Barrie: *Peter Pan* Synge: *Riders to the Sea* Chekhov: *The Cherry Orchard* London: *The Call of the Wild*
1905	Frederick Philip Grove (as 'Felix Paul Greve'; 1879–1948): *Fanny Essler* (P)	Alberta and Saskatchewan enter Confederation Canadian National Atlas published Einstein publishes first theory of relativity
1906	S.J. Duncan: *Set in Authority* (P) Wilfred Grenfell (1865–1940): *Off the Rocks* (P) Grove (as 'Greve'): *Mauremeister Ihles Haus* (P) Stephen Leacock (1869–1944): *Elements of Political Science* (P)	Est. of McClelland & Stewart Ltd book publishers Reginald Fessenden develops radio technology, makes first public broadcast of music and voice
1907	Robert Service (1874–1959): *Songs of a Sourdough; The Spell of the Yukon* (V) Robert Barr (1850–1912): *The Measure of the Rule* (P) Albert Lozeau (1878–1924): *L'âme solitaire* (V)	Andrew MacPhail becomes editor of *Univerity Magazine* First daily newspaper comic strip begins Ziegfeld Follies opens in New York Robert Baden-Powell founds Boy Scout movement in UK New Zealand becomes independent Maria Montessori develops educational methodology
1908	W. Campbell: *Poetical Tragedies* (D) S.J. Duncan: *Cousin Cinderella* (P) Martin Allerdale Grainger (1874– 1941): *Woodsmen of the West* (P) William Dawson LeSueur (1840–1917): *Mackenzie* (P; not published till 1979) Lucy Maud Montgomery (1874–1942): *Anne of Green Gables* (P) Nellie McClung (1873–1951): *Sowing Seeds in Danny* (P)	G.S. Brett (1879–1944) becomes philosopher at Trinity College, Toronto Canadian government takes possession of Arctic islands Est. of University of British Columbia as a branch of McGill (became independent 1915) McLaughlin Carriage Co. produces General Motors Cars in Oshawa Assembly line production of Model T Fords Piltdown Man Hoax

Date	Author and Title	Event
1909	Service: *Ballads of a Cheechako* (V) Stephan Stephansson (1853–1927): *Andvökur* (V, five subsequent vols appeared to 1938)	Felix Paul Greve's faked suicide Robert E. Peary and others reach North Pole Maeterlinck: *The Blue Bird*
1910	Leacock: *Literary Lapses* (P)	Henri Bourassa founds Montreal daily newspaper *Le Devoir* Ukrainians immigrate to prairies Mrs Humphrey Ward: *Canadian Born*
1911	Pauline Johnson ('Tekahionwake', 1861–1913): *Legends of Vancouver* (P) Leacock: *Nonsense Novels* (P)	Roald Amundson and others reach South Pole Sun Yat-Sen becomes first president of Chinese republic Igor Stravinsky: 'The Rite of Spring' Discovery of the atomic nucleus
1912	Hector Demers (1878–1921): *Les voix champêtres* (V) Pauline Johnson: *Flint and Feather* (V) Leacock: *Sunshine Sketches of a Little Town* (P) Camille Roy (1870–1943): *Propos canadiens* (P)	Emily Carr paints among the Kwakiutl Boundaries of Ontario, Quebec and Manitoba extended north to their present limit Sinking of the *Titanic* Mann: *Death in Venice*
1913	René Chopin (1885–1953): *Le coeur en exil* (V) Theodore Goodridge Roberts (1877–1953): *The Toll of the Tides* (P; also pub. as *The Harbor Master*)	Marius Barbeau (1883–1969) meets American anthropologist Franz Boas, and begins collecting Quebec and indigenous folk tales Vilhjalmur Stefansson leads Canadian Arctic Expedition(to 1918) First Canadian 4-H Club organized in Manitoba Est. of *Le Droit*, Ottawa Est. of Ligue des droits du français (becomes Ligue d'Action français in 1921) Carl Jung rejects Freudian psychological theory and advances his own Suffragette demonstrations in London and elsewhere Lawrence: *Sons and Lovers* Proust: *À la recherche du temps perdu* (to 1928)
1914	Albert Hickman (1877–1957): *Canadian Nights* (P)	*Komagata Maru* incident Serial publication of Louis Hémon: *Maria Chapdelaine* in *Le Temps* (Paris)

Date	Author and Title	Event
	Leacock: *Arcadian Adventures with the Idle Rich* (P) Adjutor Rivard (1868–1945): *Chez nous* (P)	First World War (ends 1918) Panama Canal completed
1915	A.S. Bourinot (1893–1969): *Laurentian Lyrics* (V) Peter McArthur (1866–1924): *In Pastures Green* (P) McClung: *In Times Like These* (P) Arthur Stringer (1874–1950): *Prairie Wife* (P)	Battle of Ypres (poison gas attacks) Buchan: *The Thirty-Nine Steps*
1916	Leacock: *Further Foolishness* (P) Robert Norwood (1874–1932): *The Witch of Endor* (D) Marjorie Pickthall (1883–1922): *The Lamp of Poor Souls* (V) David Thompson (1770–1857): *David Thompson's Narrative* (P)	Manitoba women win right to vote Emily Murphy ('Janey Canuck', 1863–1933) becomes first female magistrate in British Empire Easter Rebellion in Dublin Beginnings of Dadaism Tom Thomson: 'The Jack Pine' (painting)
1917		Est. of *Action française* Conscription crisis Halifax explosion Women in soldiers' families get the right to vote Est. of National Hockey League D. of Tom Thomson Russian Revolution
1918	Albert Laberge (1877–1960): *La scouine* (P; tr. as *Bitter Bread*) Wilson MacDonald (1880–1967): *Song of the prairie* (V) Y.Y. Segal (1896–1954): *Vun Mein Velt* (V)	Est. of *Le nignog* All women get right to vote federally; most provinces extended provincial franchise to women by 1925 (Quebec in 1940) Influenza epidemic D. of Claude Debussy (b. 1862) Cather: *My Antonia*
1919	John McCrae (1872–1918): *In Flanders Fields and other poems* (V) Jessie Georgina Sime (1868–1958): *Sister Woman* (P)	Est. of *The Canadian Bookman* (becomes *The Canadian Author and Bookman* in 1943) Canada becomes separate signatory to the League of Nations Women get right to stand for political office Winnipeg General Strike First aerial survey of Canada

Date	Author and Title	Event
		Gandhi organises civil disobedience in India Anderson: *Winesburg, Ohio*
1920	Frank Oliver Call (1878–1956): *Acanthus & Wild Grape* (V) Jean-Aubert Loranger (1896–1942): *Poèmes* (V) Frère Marie-Victorin (b. Conrad Kirouac, 1885–1944): *Récits laurentiens* (P) Alan Sullivan (1868–1947): *The Rapids* (P) Ray Palmer Baker: *A History of English Canadian Literature to the Confederation*	Est. of *Canadian Forum* First 'Group of Seven' exhibition Arnold Schoenberg develops music for 12-tone scale
1921	Edward Sapir (1884–1939): *Language* (P)	Est. of Canadian Authors Association Agnes Macphail becomes first female Member of Parliament Mackenzie King becomes prime minister (to 1948, with two interruptions) Est. of *Dalhousie Review* Est. of Native Sons of Canada Progressive Party becomes official Opposition in federal House Launching of schooner *Bluenose* Wittgenstein: *Tractatus*
1922	Lionel Groulx (using pseud. 'Alonié de Lestres'; 1878–1967): *L'appel de la race* (P; tr. as *The Iron Wedge*, 1986) Grove: *Over Prairie Trails* (P) Leacock: *My Discovery of England* (P) Paul Morin (1889–1963): *Poèmes de cendre et d'or* (V) Pickthall: *The Woodcarver's Wife and later poems* (D, V)	William Arthur Deacon (1890–1977) becomes literary editor of *Saturday Night* (to 1928) Lorne Pierce (1890–1961) editor of Ryerson Press (to 1960) Discovery and opening of tomb of King Tutankhamen Banting and Best, in Toronto, discover insulin (Banting and MacLeod win Nobel Prize for medicine, 1923) Galsworthy: *The Forsyte Saga* Joyce: *Ulysses* Mansfield: *The Garden-Party and Other Stories* T.S. Eliot: *The Waste Land*

Date	Author and Title	Event
1923	Lily Adams Beck, using pseud. E. Barrington (d. 1931): *The Chaste Diana* (P) Douglas Durkin (1884–1968): *The Magpie* (P) Tom MacInnes (1867–1951): *Roundabout Rhymes* (V) Montgomery: *Emily of New Moon* (P) Frederick John Niven (1878–1944): *Justice of the Peace* (P) D.C. Scott: *The Witching of Elspie* (P) E.J. Pratt (1882–1964): *Newfoundland Verse* (V) Robert Laroque de Roquebrune (1889–1978): *Les habits rouges* (P) Laura Goodman Salverson (1890–1970): *The Viking Heart* (P; rev. 1947)	Lorne Pierce and Ryerson Press launch 'Makers of Canada' series
1924	Georges Bugnet (1879–1981): *Nipsya* (P) Archibald MacMechan: *Headwaters of Canadian Literature* (P)	Amalgamation of Methodists, Congregationalists and Presbyterians into the United Church of Canada Sir William Stephenson develops wirephoto process Beginnings of Surrealist movement George Gershwin: 'Rhapsody in Blue' Forster: *A Passage to India* Hemingway: *In Our Time* Breton: *Surrealist Manifesto*
1925	Harold Bernard (1898–1979): *La terre vivante* (P) Hector Charlesworth: *Candid Chronicles* (P) Robert Choquette (b. 1905): *À travers les vents* (V) Grove: *Settlers of the Marsh* (P) Diamond Jenness & Helen Roberts: *Songs of the Copper Eskimo* (A) Lampman: *Lyrics of Earth* (V) Leacock: *Winnowed Wisdom* (P) J.-A. Loranger: *Le village* (P) Martha Ortenso (1900–63):, with Douglas Durkin (1884–1968): *Wild Geese* (P) Pratt: *The Witches' Brew* (V) Salverson: *When Sparrows Fall* (P)	Est. of *McGill Fortnightly Review* (to 1927) Est. of Le cercle Moliére in Saint-Boniface 'Bible Bill' Aberhart begins his weekly radio broadcasts in Alberta Scientific aerial photography of Canada begins (intensifies during Second World War, when Arctic charting becomes necessary) Scopes 'Monkey Trial' Charlie Chaplin film *The Gold Rush* Kafka: *The Trial* Fitzgerald: *The Great Gatsby* Est. of *The New Yorker* Gide: *Les faux-monnayeurs*

Date	Author and Title	Event
1926	Maurice Constantin-Weyer (1881–1961): *La bourrasque* (P) Pratt: *Titans* (V) T.G. Roberts: *The Lost Shipmate* (V) D.C. Scott: *The Poems of Duncan Campbell Scott* (V) Robert J.C. Stead (1880–1959): *Grain* (P) Lionel Stevenson: *Appraisals of Canadian Literature* (P)	'King-Byng Affair'; Balfour Report Bombardier develops snowmobile in Quebec
1927	Deacon: *The Four Jameses* (P) Mazo de la Roche (1879–1961): *Jalna* (P) Grove: *A Search for America* (P) Basil King (1859–1928): *The Spreading Dawn* (P)	Canada sends first ambassador to Washington Labrador–Quebec boundary settlement Lindbergh's non-stop flight across the Atlantic Premiere of the first talking motion picture Werner Heisenberg proposes 'uncertainty principle'
1928	Morley Callaghan (1903–90): *Strange Fugitive* (P) Constantin-Weyer: *Un homme se penche sur son passé* (P) Frank Parker Day (1881–1950): *Rockbound* (P) Grove: *Our Daily Bread* (P) Raymond Knister (1899–1932): *Canadian Short Stories* (A) Dorothy Livesay (1909–96): *Green Pitcher* (V) B.K. Sandwell (1876–1954): *The Privacity Agent and other modest proposals* (P)	Aird Commission Report on broadcasting Est. of *Chatelaine* Helen Creighton begins to collect Nova Scotia folk songs (to 1942) Fleming discovers penicillin
1929	M. Callaghan: *A Native Argosy* (P) Alfred DesRochers (1901–78): *A l'ombre de l'Orford* (V) Raymond Knister: *White Narcissus* (P) Seton: *Krag, the Kootenay Ram and Other Stories* (P)	'Persons' case (privy council rules, on appeal, that women are 'persons') Est. of minimum wage law and old age pension First frozen fish becomes commercially available in Maritimes Wall Street financial collapse Faulkner: *The Sound and the Fury* Woolf: *A Room of One's Own*
1930	Bernard: *Le ferme des pins* (P) Gonzalve Desaulniers (1863–1934): *Les bois qui chantent* (V)	Cairine Wilson becomes first female senator Toronto doctors develop Pablum

Date	Author and Title	Event
	Thomas Gill (pseud. 'Sabattis', 1865–1950): *The Heart of Lunenburg* (P; his translation called *L'étoile de Lunenburg*) Harold Adams Innis (1894–1952): *The Fur Trade in Canada* (P) Charles Yale Harrison (1898–1954): *Generals Die in Bed* (P)	Crane: *The Bridge* Eluard & Breton: *L'immaculé*
1931	Jovette-Alice Bernier (1900–81): *La chair décevante* (P) R. Choquette: *Metropolitan Museum* (V) Léo-Paul Desrosiers (1896–1967): *Nord-Sud* (P) Wetherald: *Lyrics and Sonnets* (V)	Est. of *University of Toronto Quarterly* Statute of Westminster creates British Commonwealth Cather: *Shadows on the Rock*
1932	Merrill Denison (1893–1975): *The Unheroic North* (D) Malcolm Lowry (1909–57): *Ultramarine* (P) Pratt: *Many Moods* (V); *The Fable of the Goats and Other Poems* (V) Stringer: *The Mud Lark* (P)	Establishment of Canadian Radio Broadcasting Commission Est. of *Masses* (to 1934) Founding of Co-operative Commonwealth Federation (CCF, later NDP or New Democratic Party) Founding of League for Social Reconstruction Game of table hockey is patented Discovery of neutron
1933	Philip Child (1898–1978): *Village of Souls* (P) Chopin: *Dominantes* (V) R. Choquette: *Poésies nouvelles* (V) Alain Grandbois (1900–75): *Né à Québec* (P) Claude-Henri Grignon (1894–1976): *Un homme et son péché* (P) Grove: *Fruits of the Earth* (P) Leo Kennedy (b. 1907): *The Shrouding* (V) Oscar Ryan and the Theatre of Action Collective: *Eight Men Speak* (D) Éva Sénécal (b. 1905): *Mon Jacques* (P) Patrick Slater (pseud. John Mitchell, 1880–1951): *The Yellow Briar* (P)	First Dominion Drama Festival Est. of Banff School of Fine Arts Joe Shuster and Jerry Siegal develop *Superman* comic strip
1934	Jean-Charles Harvey (1891–1967): *Les demi-civilisés* (P; tr. as *Fear's Folly*)	Olivar Asselin founds *L'Ordre* Saint-Denys Garneau founds *La Relève*

Date	Author and Title	Event
	Niven: *Triumph* (P) Simone Routier-Drouin: *Tentations* (V) Frederick George Scott (1861–1944): *Collected Poems* (V) Medjé Vézina (1896–1981): *Chaque heure a son visage* (V)	Roy Thomson (later Lord Thomson of Fleet) buys *Timmins Press*, beginning a newspaper empire that would later include the London *Times* Gideon Sundback is legally established as the inventor and patent-owner of the modern zipper
1935	Archibald Stansfield Belaney, using pseud. Grey Owl (1888–1938): *The Adventures of Sajo and Her Beaver People* (P); *Pilgrims of the Wild* (P) Bugnet: *La forêt* (P) M. Callaghan: *They Shall Inherit the Earth* (P) Jean Charbonneau (1875–1960): *L'école littéraire de Montréal* (P) Watson Kirkconnell (1895–1977): *Canadian Overtones* (A) Marie-Victorin: *Flore laurentienne* (P) Niven: *The Flying Years* (P) Pratt: *The Titanic* (V) Francis Sherman (1871–1926): *The Complete Poems ...* (V)	Aberhart leads Social Credit to power in Alberta 'Bloody Sunday' riots in Vancouver MGM film *Rose Marie* codifies pop film version of Canada Game of Monopoly first marketed in USA Arthur Waley translation of Lady Murasaki: *The Tale of Genji*
1936	Bertram Brooker (1888–1955): *Think of the Earth* (P) M. Callaghan: *Now That April's Here* (P) W.E. Collin: *The White Savannahs* (P) Louis Dantin (pseud., Eugène Seers, 1865–1945): *Contes de noël* (P) McClung: *Clearing in the West* (p) Jean Narrache (pseud., Émile Coderre, 1893–1970): *Quand j'parl'tout seul* (V) C.G.D. Roberts: *Selected Poems* (V) A.J.M. Smith & F.R. Scott: *New Provinces* (A) Herman Voaden (1903–91): *Murder Pattern* (D; pub. 1980)	Maurice Duplessis founds Union Nationale party (holds power in Quebec, with short interruption, until 1959) Est. of Canadian Broadcasting Corporation and Radio-Canada Est. of *Canadian Poetry Magazine* Est. of *Sir Ernest MacMillan Fine Arts Clubs* William Arthur Deacon becomes literary editor of the *Globe and Mail* (to 1960) Spanish Civil War (ends 1939) D. of Lorca (b. 1898) Patent for nylon issued Prokofiev: 'Peter and the Wolf' Cocteau: *La machine infernale*
1937	M. Callaghan: *More Joy in Heaven* (P) John Coulter (1888–1980): *The House in the Quiet Glen* (D)	Governor-General's Awards initi- ated (for books published in 1936); the first prizes for French-language works were awarded in 1959

Date	Author and Title	Event
	D.G. Creighton (1902–79): *The Commercial Empire of the St. Lawrence* (P) Hector de Saint-Denys Garneau (1912–43): *Regards et Jeux dans l'espace* (V) Floris Clark McLaren: *Frozen Fire* (V) Félix-Antoine Savard (1896–1982): *Menaud, maître-draveur* (P; tr. as *Boss of the River*, 1947, and as *Master of the River*, 1976)	Gratien Gélinas begins radio sketches 'Fridolinons' (to 1941) Trans-Canada Airlines founded (later Air Canada) Émile Legault founds Les Compagnons de Saint-Laurent Duplessis imposes Padlock Law (rescinded 1957) D. of Brother André (beatified 1982)
1938	Desrosiers: *Les engagés du Grand Portage* (P) Kenneth Leslie (1892–1974): *By Stubborn Stars* (V) Niven: *Coloured Spectacles* (P) Ringuet (pseud. Philippe Panneton; 1895–1960): *Trente arpents* (P; tr. as *Thirty Acres*)	Gélinas begins annual revue *Fridolinages* (to 1946, with one further further review in 1956) A.M. Klein becomes editor of *The Canadian Jewish Chronicle* Founding of Winnipeg Ballet (becomes Royal Winnipeg Ballet in 1953) Disney animated cartoon *Snow White* Brecht: *The Good Woman of Setzuan* Sartre: *La nausée*
1939	Irene Baird (1901–81): *Waste Heritage* (P) Child: *Village of Souls* (P) Franklin Davy McDowell: *The Champlain Road* (P) Sir Andrew Macphail (1864–1938): *The Master's Wife* (P) Anne Marriott (1913–97): *The Wind Our Enemy* (V) Howard O'Hagan (1902–82): *Tay John* (P) Salverson: *Confessions of an Immigrant's Daughter* (P)	Canadian Harold Foster develops *Prince Valiant* comic strip Est. of National Film Board Canada enters Second World War (ends 1945) Rilke: *Duino Elegies*
1940	A.M. Klein (1909–72): *Hath Not A Jew ...* (V) Antoine-J. Léger (1880–1950): *Elle et lui* (P) Pratt: *Brébeuf and His Brethren* (V)	Claude Hurtubise and Robert Charbonneau found Les Éditions de l'Arbre Canadian William Stephenson becomes British intelligence agent 'Intrepid' Est. of unemployment insurance in Canada Rowell-Sirois Report on federal-provincial economic relations Pound: *Cantos*

Date	Author and Title	Event
1941	Emily Carr (1871–1945): *Klee Wyck* (P) Robert Charbonneau (1911–67): *Ils posséderont la terre* (P) Hugh MacLennan (1907–90): *Barometer Rising* (P) Sinclair Ross (b. 1908): *As For Me and My House* (P) Sullivan: *Three Came to Ville Marie* (P)	Alan Crawley founds *Contemporary Verse* (to 1952) Kenneth Millar (1915–83) emigrates to USA and a career as the mystery writer 'Ross Macdonald' Est. of Service du cinématographie à Québec (becomes Office du film du Québec in 1961)
1942	Earle Birney (1904–95): *David* (V) Carr: *The Book of Small* (P) Ronald Hambleton: *Unit of Five* (A) Anne Hébert (1916–2000): *Les Songes en équilibre* (V) A. Laberge: *La fin du voyage* (P) Leacock: *My Remarkable Uncle* (P) Guy Sylvestre: *Anthologie de la poésie québécoise* (A)	Conscription plebiscite (Quebec opposes by 72%; other provinces approve by 80%) Dieppe raid Est. of *First Statement* and *Preview* Internment of Japanese-Canadians Est. of Bloc Populaire to oppose conscription First atomic chain reaction
1943	E.K. Brown (1905–51): *On Canadian Poetry* (P) Bruce Hutchison (1901–92): *The Unknown Country* (P) Lampman: *At the Long Sault and other new poems* (V) Félix Leclerc (1914–88): *Adagio* (P) A.J.M. Smith (1902–80): *News of the Phoenix and other poems* (V); *A Book of Canadian Poetry* (A; rev. 1948, 1957) A.E. van Vogt (1912–2000): *The Weapon Makers* (P)	D. of critic Camille Roy (b. 1870) First Rodgers and Hammerstein musical
1944	Carr: *The House of All Sorts* (P) Hugh Garner (1913–79): *Storm Below* (P) Gwethalyn Graham (1913–65): *Earth and High Heaven* (P) Grandbois: *Les îles de la nuit* (V) A.M. Klein: *Poems* (V); *The Hitleriad* (V) F. Leclerc: *Allegro* (P) Roger Lemelin (1919–92): *Au pied de la pente douce* (P; tr. as *The Town Below*) Livesay: *Day and Night* (V) P.K. Page (using pseud. 'Judith Cape'; b. 1916): *The Sun and the Moon* (P) Yves Thériault (1915–83): *Contes pour un homme seul* (P)	Beginning of the CBC 'Stage' series (to 1955), involving playwrights Andrew Allan (1907–74), Fletcher Markle, Len Peterson, Joseph Schull, Lister Sinclair, Gerald Nozon, Reuben Ship and others RCMP vessel *St. Roch* completes first two-way Arctic crossing First CCF government elected (in Saskatchewan) Normandy landing (June 6) Borges: *Ficciones*

Date	Author and Title	Event
1945	Will R. Bird (1891–1984): *Here Stays Good Yorkshire* (P) Birney: *Now Is Time* (V) Child: *Day of Wrath* (P) Robert Fontaine (1911–65): *The Happy Time* (P) Grandbois: *Avant le chaos* (P) Germaine Guèvremont (1893–1968): *Le survenant* (P) MacLennan: *Two Solitudes* (P) de Montigny: *Au pays de Québec* (P) Gabrielle Roy (1909–83): *Bonheur d'occasion* (P), wins Prix Fémina, tr. as *The Tin Flute* F.R. Scott (1899–1985): *Overture* (V) Elizabeth Smart (1914–86): *By Grand Central Station I Sat Down and Wept* (P) Miriam Waddington (b. 1917): *Green World* (V)	Est. of family allowance First edn of Dr Spock's *baby and Child Care* Aaron Copland: 'Appalachian Spring' Atomic bombs dropped on Hiroshima and Nagasaki
1946	Winifred Bambrick (1892–1969): *Continental Revue* (P) Grove: *In Search of Myself* (P) Roderick Haig-Brown (1908–76): *Starbuck Valley Winter* (P) Gilles Hénault (1920–96): *Théâtre en plein air* (V) Innis: *Empire and Communications* (P) Leacock: *The Boy I Left Behind Me* (P) A.R.M. Lower: *Colony to Nation* (P) Joyce Marshall (b. 1913): *Presently Tomorrow* (P) Christine van der Mark (1917–69): *In Due Season* (P) Robert Finch (1900–95): *Poems* (V)	Est. of Les cahiers de la file indienne Luc Lacourcière begins publishing studies in comparative folklore John Morgan Gray (1907–78) becomes president of Macmillan of Canada Dora Mavor Moore founds New Play Society Robertson Davies becomes editor of Peterborough *Examiner* (to 1963)
1947	Robertson Davies (1913–95): *The Diary of Samuel Marchbanks* (P) Claude Gauvreau (1925–71): *Bien-Être* (D) Grove: *Consider Her Ways* (P) Guèvremont: *Marie-didace* (P) Paul Hiebert (1892–1987): *Sarah Binks* (P) Livesay: *Poems for People* (V) Lowry: *Under the Volcano* (P) Edward McCourt (1907–72): *Music at the Close* (P) W.O. Mitchell: *Who Has Seen the Wind* (P) Pratt: *Behind the Log* (V) D.C. Scott: *The Circle of Affection* (P, V)	Canadian Citizenship established Oil discoveries in Alberta Test flights break the sound barrier India and Pakistan become independent

Date	Author and Title	Event
	Jean Simard (b. 1916): *Félix* (P) Raymond Souster (b. 1921): *Go to Sleep World* (V) John Sutherland: *Other Canadians* (A) Ethel Wilson (1888–1980): *Hetty Dorval* (P)	
1948	Pierre Baillargeon (1916–67): *La neige et le feu* (P) Paul-Emile Borduas: *Refus Global* (P; tr. 1986, ed. Ray Ellenwood) Birney: *Strait of Anian* (V) Eddy Boudreau (1914–54): *La vie en croix* (V) Jean Bruchési (b. 1901): *Canada* (P) Roy Daniells (1902–79): *Deeper into the Forest* (V) Gélinas: *Tit-Coq* (D) Grandbois: *Rivages de l'homme* (V) A.M. Klein: *The Rocking Chair and Other Poems* (V) Henry Kreisel (1922–91): *The Rich Man* (P) Paul-Marie Lapointe (b. 1929): *Le vierge incendié* (V) Lemelin: *Les Plouffe* (P) Douglas Le Pan (1914–98): *The Wounded Prince* (V) Françoise Loranger (1913–95): *Mathieu* (P) Jean-Jules Richard (1911–75): *Neuf jours de haine* (P) Lister Sinclair: *A Pay on Words and Other Radio Plays* (D)	North Magnetic pole located James Houston sets up Inuit co-operatives, encouraging development development of Inuit art Gerhard Herzberg joins National Research Council (wins Nobel Prize for physics, 1971) F.R. (Budge) Crawley: *The Loon's Necklace* (film) State of Israel established by United Nations Assassination of Gandhi Kinsey report
1949	Birney: *Turvey* (P) Coulter: *Riel* (D; printed 1962; rev. 1975) Napoléon-P. Landry (1884–1956): *Poèmes de mon pays* (V) Len Peterson (b. 1917): *Chipmunk* (P) James Reaney (b. 1926): *The Red Heart* (V) Saint-Denys Garneau: *Poésies complètes* (V) Wilson: *The Innocent Traveller* (P)	Newfoundland enters Confederation Mao Tse-Tung comes to power in China (Norman Bethune is involved as a doctor on the 'Long March') Simone de Beauvoir: *Le deuxième sexe* Orwell: *Nineteen Eighty-Four* Miller: *Death of a Salesman*
1950	Catherine Anthony Clark (1882–1977: *The Golden Pine Cone* (P) Donat Coste (1912–57): *L'enfant noir* (P) Davies: *At My Heart's Core* (D)	Est. of *Cité libre* (to 1966) Horace Gold (b. 1914) founds *Galaxy* magazine The Beaver bush plane developed Korean War (ends 1952)

Date	Author and Title	Event

Robert Élie (1915–73): *La fin des songes*
(P)
Anne Hébert: *Le torrent* (P)
Livesay: *Call My People Home* (D)
Thomas Raddall (1903–94): *The Nymph
and the Lamp* (P)
G. Roy: *La petite poule d'eau* (P)
Bertrand Vac (pseud., Aimé Pelletier,
b. 1914): *Louis Genest* (P)

1951

Charles Bruce (1906–71): *The
Mulgrave Road* (V)
M. Callaghan: *The Loved and the
Lost* (P)
Dantin: *Les enfances de Fanny* (P)
Davies: *Tempest-Tost* (P)
Rodolphe Dubé (pseud. 'François
Hertel'; 1905–85): *Mes naufrages* (V)
Sylvain Garneau (1930–53): *Objets
trouvés* (V)
Innis: *The Bias of Communication* (P)
A.M. Klein: *The Second Scroll* (P)
André Langevin (b. 1927): *Evadé de la
nuit* (P)
Irving Layton (b. 1912): *The Black Hunts-
man* (V)
MacLennan: *Each Man's Son* (P)
Roquebrunne: *Testament de mon enfance*
(P)
Kay Smith (b. 1911): *Footnote to the Lord's
Prayer* (V)
Roger Viaú (1906–86): *Au milieu,
la montagne* (P)
Anne Wilkinson (1910–61): *Counterpoint
to Sleep* (V)

Founding of National Ballet
of Canada
Potlatch ceremony allowed again
by law
Est. of Canadian Folk Music Society

1952

Ted Allan (b. 1916): *The Scalpel,
The Sword* (P; rev. 1971)
Birney: *Trial of a City* (D; also pub.
as *The Damnation of Vancouver*)
Ernest Buckler (1908–84): *The
Mountain and the Valley* (P)
Layton, Dudek and Souster:
Cerberus (V)
Lemelin: *Pierre le magnifique* (P; tr.
as *In Quest of Splendour*)
Norman Levine (b. 1923): *The
Angled Road* (P)
Nelligan: *Poésies complètes, 1896–
1899* (V; comp. Luc Lacourcière)

Canadian television begins
Vincent Massey becomes first
Canadian-born Governor-General
Fred Cogswell (b. 1917) becomes
editor of *Fiddlehead* and founds
Fiddlehead Books
Raymond Souster founds *Contact*
(to 1954)
Norman McLaren: *Neighbors* (film)
Barbara Pentland: *The Lake* (opera;
lyrics by Dorothy Livesay)
Est. of *Quarry*
Lester Pearson becomes President
of the UN General Assembly

Date	Author and Title	Event
	Aimé Pelletier: *Deux portes ... une adresse* (P) Pratt: *Towards the Last Spike* (V) Thériault: *Le samaritain* (D; pub. 1958) Paul Toupin (b. 1918): *Brutus* (D; pub. 1955) Wilson: *The Equations of Love* (P) George Woodcock (1912–95): *Ravens and Prophets* (P)	Universal Copyright Act Fanon: *Peau noire, masques blancs* Beckett: *Waiting for Godot*
1953	R. Choquette: *Suite marine* (V) Anne Hébert: *Le tombeau des rois* (V) Hénault: *Totems* (V) A. Langevin: *Poussière sur la ville* (P) Layton: *Love the Conqueror Worm* (V) Le Pan: *The Net and the Sword* (V) Gaston Miron (1928–96): and Olivier Marchand: *Deux sangs* (V)	Miron helps found Éditions de l'Hexagone Est. of National Library of Canada Est. of *CIV/n* (to 1955) John Beckwith: *The Night-Blooming Cereus* (opera; lyrics by James Reaney) Est. of Stratford Festival Edmund Hilary and Tenzing Norkay conquer Mt Everest
1954	Fred Bosworth (b. 1918): *The Last of the Curlews* (P) Bruce: *The Channel Shore* (P) Davies: *Leaven of Malice* (P) Hubert Evans (1892–1986): *Mist on the River* (P) Saint-Denys Garneau: *Journal* (P) Igor Gouzenko (1919–82): *The Fall of a Titan* (P) Layton: *The Long Pea-shooter* (V) Page: *The Metal and the Flower* (V) Malcolm Ross: *Our Sense of Identity* (D) Reuben Ship: *The Investigator* (D) Thériault: *Aaron* (P) Wilson: *Swamp Angel* (P)	Alex Colville: 'Horse and Train' (painting) Jonas Salk develops polio vaccine
1955	Birney: *Down the Long Table* (P) Thomas B. Costain (1885–1965): *The Tontine* (P) Davies: *Hunting Stuart* (D) Marcel Dubé (b. 1930): *Zone* (D) Louis Dudek (1918–2001): *Europe* (V) James Houston (b. 1921): *Canadian Eskimo Art* (P) Patricia Joudry: *Teach Me How to Cry* (D) Carl Klinck & R.E. Watters: *Canadian Anthology* (A; rev. 1966, 1974) Layton: *The Cold Green Element* (V) Brian Moore (1921–99): *The Lonely Passion of Judith Hearne* (P)	Pierre Teilhard de Chardin: *Le phénomène humain*

Date	Author and Title	Event
	Mordecai Richler (1931–2001): *Son of a Smaller Hero* (P) G. Roy: *Alexandre Chenevert* (P; tr. as *The Cashier*); *Rue Deschambault* (P) Sandwell: *The Diversions of Duchesstown* (P) Wilfred Watson (1911–98): *Friday's Child* (V) Wilkinson: *The Hangman Ties the Holly* (V)	
1956	Leonard Cohen (b. 1934): *Let Us Compare Mythologies* (V) Mavis Gallant (b. 1922): *The Other Paris* (P) Layton: *The Bull Calf and other poems* (V); *The Improved Binoculars* (V) Elizabeth Loosley: *Crestwood Heights* (P) J. Simard: *Mon fils pourtant heureux* (P) Lister Sinclair (b. 1921): *The Blood Is Strong* (D) Wilkinson: *Lions in the Way* (P) Adele Wiseman (1928–92): *The Sacrifice* (P)	Est. of *The Tamarack Review* (to 1982) L.B. Pearson devises UN Peace Force system (wins Nobel Peace Prize 1957) Hungarian Revolution Elvis Presley & rock-and-roll Civil rights protests begin in USA
1957	Patrick Anderson (1915–79): *Search Me* (P) Northrop Frye (1912–91): *Anatomy of Criticism* (P) Grandbois: *L'étoile pourpre* (V) D.G. Jones (b. 1929): *Frost on the Sun* (V) Jay Macpherson (b. 1931): *The Boatman* (V) John Marlyn (b. 1912): *Under the Ribs of Death* (P) Richler: *A Choice of Enemies* (P) Dorothy Roberts: *Dazzle* (V) F.R. Scott & A.J.M. Smith: *The Blasted Pine* (A) Pierre Trottier (b. 1925): *Poèmes de Russie* (V)	Est. of Canada Council Louis Dudek founds *Delta* (to 1966) Ellen Fairclough becomes first female federal cabinet minister USSR launches space satellite 'Sputnik'
1958	Gérard Bessette (b. 1920): *La bagarre* (P) Ronald Després (b. 1935): *Silences à nourrir de sauf* (V) Dudek: *En Mexico* (V)	Est. of New Canadian Library reprint series Richard and Mary Bonnycastle buy Harlequin Books of Winnipeg, and transform it into an international Romance publisher

Date	Author and Title	Event
	R.G. Everson (1903–92): *A Lattice for Momos* (V)	Michel Brault & Gilles Carle: *Les raquetteurs* (film)
	Ralph Gustafson: *The Penguin Book of Canadian Verse* (A; rev. 1967)	F.R. Scott wins the *Roncarelli v. Duplessis* case
	Anne Hébert: *Les chambres de bois* (V)	
	F. Leclerc: *Je fou de l'île* (P)	
	Levine: *Canada Made Me* (P)	
	Colin McDougall (1917–84): *Execution* (P)	
	Desmond Pacey (1917–75): *The Picnic and other stories* (P)	
	Pratt: *Collected Poems* (V)	
	Thériault: *Agaguk* (P)	
	Michel Van Schendel (b. 1929): *Poèmes de l'Amérique étrangère* (V)	
1959	John Buell (b. 1927): *The Pyx* (P)	Opening of Saint Lawrence Seaway
	Marie-Claire Blais (b. 1939): *La belle bête* (P; tr. as *Mad Shadows*)	Founding of *Canadian Literature*
	M. Callaghan: *Morley Callaghan's Stories* (P)	Founding of *Liberté*
	Edmund Carpenter: *Anerca* (A)	D. of Maurice Duplessis (b. 1890)
	George Grant (1918–88): *Philosophy in the Mass Age* (P)	Fidel Castro takes over in Cuba
	Hénault: *Voyage au pays de mémoire* (V)	Unexpurgated version of Lawrence's *Lady Chatterley's Lover* published in USA
	Michèle Lalonde (b. 1937): *Geôles* (V)	Grass: *The Tin Drum*
	Layton: *A Red Carpet for the Sun* (V)	
	MacLennan: *The Watch that Ends the Night* (P)	
	Raddall: *At the Tide's Turn and other stories* (P)	
	Richler: *The Apprenticeship of Duddy Kravitz* (P)	
	Savard: *Le barachois* (P, V)	
	J. Simard: *Les sentiers de la nuit* (P)	
	Sheila Watson (1909–98): *The Double Hook* (P)	
1960	Margaret Avison (b. 1918): *Winter Sun* (V)	Jean Lesage becomes Premier of Quebec; beginnings of 'Quiet Revolution'
	Bessette: *Le libraire* (P; tr. as *Not for Every Eye*)	Charles Comfort succeeds Alan Jarvis as Director of the National Gallery
	Blais: *Tête blanche* (P)	
	Patricia Blondal (1926–59): *A Candle to Light the Sun* (P)	Kenojuak: 'The Enchanted Owl' (print)
	Jean-Paul Desbiens (b. 1927): *Les insolences du Frère Untel* (P; tr. as *The Impertinences of Brother Anonymous*)	Passenger jet service links Vancouver and Toronto
		Est. of *Alphabet* (to 1971)

Date	Author and Title	Event

Gélinas: *Bousille et les justes* (D)
P.-M. Lapointe: *Choix de poèmes-arbres*
(V)
Margaret Laurence (1926–87): *This Side
Jordan* (P)
Maclennan: *Scotchman's Return and other
essays* (P)
Claire Martin (b. 1914): *Doux-amer* (P)
B. Moore: *The Luck of Ginger Coffey* (P)
Thériault: *Ashini* (P)
Gérard Tougas: *Histoire de la littérature
canadienne-française* (P)
Frank Underhill (1889–1971): *In Search of
Canadian Liberalism* (P)
Gilles Vigneault (b. 1928): *Contes sur le
pointe des pieds* (P)
Voaden: *Emily Carr* (D)
David Walker (1911–92): *Where the High
Winds Blow* (P)
Robert Weaver: *The Oxford Book of
Canadian Short Stories* (A; three further
series followed)
Wilkinson: *Swann and Daphne* (P)

Robert Duncan: *The Opening of the
Field*

1961 Pierre Berton (b. 1920): *The Secret
World of Og* (P)
Bessette: *Les pédagogues* (P)
Sheila Burnford: *The Incredible
Journey* (P)
L. Cohen: *The Spice Box of Earth* (V)
Diane Giguère (b. 1940): *Le temps des jeux*
(P; tr. as *Innocence*)
Jacques Hébert (b. 1923) and Pierre
Elliott Trudeau (1919–2000): *Deux
innocents en Chine rouge* (P)
Daryl Hine (b. 1936): *The Prince of
Darkness & Co.* (P)
Laurence: *The Stone Angel* (P)
Layton: *The Swinging Flesh* (V)
Jean Le Moyne (1913–96): *Convergences* (P)
Lowry: *Hear Us O Lord from Heaven Thy
Dwelling Place* (P)
MacLennan: *Seven Rivers of Canada* (P)
W.L. Morton (1908–81): *The Canadian
Identity* (P)
Yves Préfontaine (b. 1937): *Pays sans
parole* (V)
John Reeves: *A Beach of Strangers* (D)
G. Roy: *La montagne secrète* (P)
Wilson: *Mrs Golightly and Other Stories*
(P)

Est. of *Livres et auteurs canadiens*
(changed to '... auteurs québécois'
in 1969)
Est. of *Tish* (to 1969)

Date	Author and Title	Event
1962	Ralph Allen (1913–66): *Ask the Name of the Lion* (P) Birney: *Ice Cod Bell or Stone* (V) Coulter: *Riel* (D) Dantin: *Poèmes d'outre-tombe* (V) Kildare Dobbs (b. 1923): *Running to Paradise* (P) George Elliott: *The Kissing Man* (P) Jacques Ferron (1921–85): *Contes du pays incertain* (P) Arthur Hailey: *In High Places* (P) Hénault: *Sémaphore* (V) Hugh Hood (1928–2000): *Flying a Red Kite* Jacques Languirand (b. 1931): *Les insolites* (D) Gatien Lapointe (1931–83): *L'ode au St. Laurent* Lowry: *Selected Poems* (V) Marshall McLuhan (1911–80): *The Gutenberg Galaxy* (P) Gilles Marcotte: *Une Littérature qui se fait* (P) Martin: *Quand j'aurai payé ton visage* (P) W.O. Mitchell: *Jake and the Kid* (P); *The Kite* (P) Eric Nicol (b. 1919): *A Herd of Yaks* (P) Al Purdy (1918–2000): *Poems for All the Annettes* (V) Reaney: *The Killdeer and other plays* (D) Wilfred Watson: *Cockcrow and the Gulls* (D) Phyllis Webb (b. 1927): *The Sea Is Also a Garden* (V) George Whalley: *The Legend of John Hornby* (P) Rudy Wiebe (b. 1934): *Peace Shall Destroy Many* (P) Woodcock: *Anarchism* (P)	Lesage election slogan 'maîtres chez nous' Completion of Trans Canada Highway COMPAC telephone cable links Vancouver Island with Australia and New Zealand Opening of Trans-Canada Highway Canada's first communications satellite, Alouette I, launched in California Shaw festival begins at Niagara-on-the-Lake Neptune Theatre opens, Halifax Michael Snow: 'Walking Woman' series (painting) Jamaica becomes independent Crick and Watson determine the structure of DNA Discovery of Quasars
1963	M. Callaghan: *That Summer in Paris* (P) L. Cohen: *The Favorite Game* (P) Frye: *The Educated Imagination* (P) Garner: *Hugh Garner's Best Stories* (P) Laurence: *The Tomorrow-Tamer* (P); *The Prophet's Camel-Bell* (P; Am. title: *New Wind in a Dry Land*) Layton: *Balls for a One-Armed Juggler* (V)	Jacques Ferron founds Rhinoceros Party Est. of *Parti pris* (to 1968) J. Tuzo Wilson posits 'hot spot' theory of continental drift Discovery of *Contes d'Acadie* manuscript Est. of Charlottetown Festival Bill Bissett issues *blew ointment* (to 1968)

Date	Author and Title	Event
	Gwendolyn MacEwen (1941–87): *Julian the Magician* (P)	US President John Kennedy assassinated
	Louis Maheux-Forcier (b. 1929): *Amadou* (P)	Roy Thomson becomes Baron Thomson of Fleet
	Suzanne Martel: *Quatre Montréalais en l'an 3000* (P; tr. as *The City Underground*)	Stegner: *Wolf Willow* Robbe-Grillet: *Pour un nouveau roman*
	Farley Mowat (b. 1921): *Never Cry Wolf* (P)	
	Richler: *The Incomparable Atuk* (P; Am. title: *Stick Your Neck Out*)	
	George Ryga (1932–87): *Hungry Hills* (P)	
	Trottier: *Mon Babel* (P)	
1964	Birney: *November Walk Near False Creek Mouth* (V)	Don Owen: *Nobody Waved Good-bye* (film)
	Roch Carrier (b. 1937): *Jolis deuils* (P)	Maple leaf flag adopted
	Paul Chamberland (b. 1939): *L'afficheur hurle* (V)	'Beatlemania' reaches North America
	L. Cohen: *Flowers for Hitler* (V)	
	Gallant: *My Heart Is Broken* (P; Eng. title: *An Unmarried Man's Summer*)	
	Haig-Brown: *Fisherman's Fall* (P)	
	Claude Jasmin (b. 1930): *Ethel et le terroriste* (P)	
	Layton: *The Laughing Rooster* (V)	
	Le Pan: *The Deserter* (P)	
	McLuhan: *Understanding Media* (P)	
	Eli Mandel (1922–92): *Black and Secret Man* (V)	
	Suzanne Paradis (b. 1936): *Pour les enfants des morts* (V)	
	Jacques Renaud (b. 1943): *Le cassé* (P)	
	Jane Rule (b. 1931): *Desert of the Heart* (P)	
	F.R. Scott: *Signature* (V)	
	Souster: *The Colour of the Times* (V)	
	Van Schendel: *Variations sur la pierre* (V)	
1965	Hubert Aquin (1929–77): *Prochain épisode* (P)	Nicole Brossard est. *La barre du jour* (becomes *La nouvelle barre du jour* in 1977)
	Bessette: *L'incubation* (P)	Stan Bevington founds Coach House Press
	Blais: *Une saison dans la vie d'Emmanuel* (P)	Citadel Theatre opens, Edmonton
	Jacques Brault (b. 1933) *Mémoire* (V)	Gilles Carle: *La vie heureuse de Léopold Z.* (film)
	Diane Giguère: *L'eau est profonde* (P; tr. as *Whirlpool*)	
	Jacques Godbout (b. 1933): *Le couteau sur la table* (P)	
	Grant: *Lament for a Nation* (P)	

Date	Author and Title	Event

Carl Klinck (1908–90): *Literary History of Canada* (2nd edn, 1976)

F. Loranger: *Une maison, un jour* (D)

Lowry: *Selected Letters* (P)

Martin: *Dans un gant de fer* (P)

B. Moore: *The Emperor of Ice-cream* (P)

Mavor Moore, Donald Harron & Norman Campbell: *Anne of Green Gables* (D; musical adaptation of Montgomery)

Claude Péloquin (b. 1942): *Les mondes assujettis* (V)

John Porter: *The Vertical Mosaic* (P)

Purdy: *Cariboo Horses* (V)

Francis Sparshott (b. 1926): *A Divided Voice* (V)

Vigneault: *Quand les bateaux s'en vont* (V)

Joe Wallace (1890–1975): *A Radiant Sphere* (V)

Webb: *Naked Poems* (V)

1966

Margaret Atwood (b. 1939): *The Circle Game* (V)

Avison: *The Dumbfounding* (V)

L. Cohen: *Beautiful Losers* (P)

Ramsay Cook (b. 1931): *Canada and the French-Canadian Question* (P)

Coulter: *Deirdre* (D)

Réjean Ducharme (b. 1942): *L'avalée des avalés* (P)

Raoul Duguay: *Ruts* (V)

Madeleine Ferron (b. 1922): *Coeur de sucre* (P)

Finch: *Silverthorn Bush* (V)

Christie Harris (1907–2002): *Raven's Cry* (P)

Harold Horwood (b. 1923): *Tomorrow Will Be Sunday* (P)

Laurence: *A Jest of God* (P)

MacEwen: *A Breakfast for Barbarians* (V)

Martin: *La joue droit* (P)

Richard Outram (b. 1930): *Exultate, jubilate* (V)

G. Roy: *La route d'Altamont* (P)

Paul St Pierre: *Breaking Smith's Quarter Horse* (P)

Tremblay: *Contes pour buveurs attardés* (P)

Vigneault: *Contes du coin de l'oeil* (P)

Event (1966):

First volume of *Dictionary of Canadian Biography/Dictionnaire biographique du Canada* published

Medicare legislation passed (all provinces join scheme by 1972)

Barth: *Giles Goat-Boy*

Date	Author and Title	Event
1967	Austin Clarke (b. 1932): *The Meeting Point* (P) Eugène Cloutier: *Le Canada sans passeport* (P) George Clutesi (1905–88): *Son of Raven, Son of Deer* (P) Coulter: *The Trial of Louis Riel* (D) Ducharme: *Le nez qui voque* (P) Dudek: *Atlantis* (V) Bernard Epps (b. 1936): *Pilgarlic the Death* (P) Jean Ethier-Blais: *Signets* (P) Timothy Findley (1930–2002): *The Last of the Crazy People* (P) Frye: *The Modern Century* (P) Godbout: *Salut Galarneau!* (P) Dave Godfrey (b. 1938): *Death Goes Better with Coca-Cola* (P) Eldon Grier (1917–2001): *Pictures on the Skin* (V) Robert Gurik (b. 1932): *Le pendu* (D) John Herbert (1926–2001): *Fortune and Men's Eyes* (D) Hiebert: *Willows Revisited* (P) Hood: *Around the Mountain* (P) Layton: *Periods of the Moon* (V) Livesay: *The Unquiet Bed* (V) MacLennan: *Return of the Sphinx* (P) Mandel: *An Idiot Joy* (V) Page: *Cry Ararat!* (V) Péloquin: *Manifeste infra suivis des Emissions parallèles* (V) Peterson: *The Great Hunger* (D) Heather Spears: *The danish portraits* (V) Scott Symons (b. 1933): *Place d'Armes* (P) Audrey Thomas (b. 1935): *Ten Green Bottles* (P) Vigneault: *Les gens de mon pays* (V)	Report of the Bilingualism and Biculturalism Commission Est. of *Voix et images* Est. of House of Anansi by Dave Godfrey & Dennis Lee Centennial celebrations (Expo 67) Harry Somers: *Louis Riel* (opera; lyrics by Mavor Moore and Jacques Languirand) Paul Almond: *Isabel* (film) First human heart transplant
1968	Aquin: *Trou de mémoire* (P) Blais: *Les manuscrits de Pauline Archange* (P) George Bowering (b. 1935): *Rocky Mountain Foot* (V) Buckler: *Ox Bells and Fireflies* (P) Carrier: *La guerre, yes sir!* (P) L. Cohen: *Songs of Leonard Cohen* (with music) J. Ferron: *Contes anglais et autres* (P); *Contes inédites* (P); *La charrette* (P)	Pierre Elliott Trudeau becomes prime minister (holds, power, with short interruption, to 1984) Death of composer Healey Willan (b. 1880) Theatre Passe-Muraille opens, Toronto Robert Fulford (b. 1932) becomes editor of *Saturday Night* (to 1987) Est. of Radio-Québec

Date	Author and Title	Event
	Garner: *Cabbagetown* (P; unexpurgated edition)	Opening of Rochdale College (closes 1975)
	Gélinas: *Hier les enfants dansaient* (D)	Joyce Wieland: 'Reason Over Passion'
	Grandbois: *Alain Grandbois* (A)	(art work)
	Gurik: *Hamlet, prince du Québec* (D)	European student riots
	Don Gutteridge (b. 1937): *Riel* (V)	
	Red Lane (1936–64): *Collected Poems of Red Lane* (V)	
	Lowry: *Dark as the Grave Wherein My Friend Is Laid* (P)	
	Jack Ludwig (b. 1922): *Above Ground* (P)	
	Alice Munro (b. 1931): *Dance of the Happy Shades* (P)	
	Alden Nowlan (1933–83): *Miracle at Indian River* (P)	
	Paradis: *L'oeuvre de Pierre* (V)	
	R.M. Patterson (1898–1984): *Finlay's River* (P)	
	Jean-Guy Pilon (b. 1930): *Comme eau retenue* (V)	
	S. Ross: *The Lamp at Noon and other stories* (P)	
	W.W.E. Ross (1894–1966): *Shapes and Sounds* (V)	
	Adrien Thério: *Soliloque en hommage à une femme* (P)	
	Michel Tremblay (b. 1942): *Les belles-soeurs* (D)	
	Pierre Vallières (b. 1937): *Nègres blancs d'Amériques* (P)	
	Woodcock: *The Doukhobors* (P)	
1969	Milton Acorn (1923–86): *I've Tasted My Blood* (V)	Canadian Official Languages Act
	Aquin: *L'Antiphonaire* (P)	Neil Armstrong becomes first man on moon
	Atwood: *The Edible Woman* (P)	Woodstock concerts
	Elizabeth Brewster (b. 1922): *Passage of Summer* (V)	Violent anti-Vietnam protests
	Carrier: *Floralie, où es-tu* (P)	American draft-dodgers continue to emigrate to Canada
	Ducharme: *La fille de Christophe Colomb* (V)	
	J. Ferron: *Le ciel de Québec* (P; tr. 1985 as *The Penniless Redeemer*)	
	Marya Fiamengo (b. 1926): *Overheard at the Oracle* (V)	
	Findley: *The Butterfly Plague* (P)	
	Joan Finnigan (b. 1925): script for film *The Best Damn Fiddler from Calabogie to Kaladar*	

Date	Author and Title	Event

R.A.D. Ford (1915–98): *The Solitary City* (V)
Lawrence Garber (b. 1937): *Garber's Tales from the Quarter* (P)
Kent Gooderham: *I Am an Indian* (A)
Phyllis Gotlieb (b. 1926): *Ordinary, moving* (V)
Grant: *Technology and Empire* (P)
Ralph Gustafson (1909–95): *Ixion's Wheel* (V)
Robert Kroetsch (b. 1927): *The Studhorse Man* (P)
Michèle Lalonde: 'Speak White' (V)
Laurence: *The Fire-Dwellers* (P)
Livesay: *Plainsongs* (V)
MacEwen: *The Shadow-Maker* (V)
Ruth Nichols (b. 1948): *A Walk Out of the World* (P)
Zebedee Nungak & Eugene Arima: *Stories from Povungnituk, Quebec* (A)
Laurence J. Peter (1919–90) and Raymond Hull (1919–85): *The Peter Principle* (P)
Jacques Poulin (b. 1937): *Jimmy* (P)
Reaney: *Colours in the Dark* (D)
Beverley Simons (b. 1938): *Crabdance* (D)
Ray Smith (b. 1941): *Cape Breton is the Thought Control Center of Canada* (P)
Waddington: *Say Yes* (V)
Wilfred Watson: *Let's Murder Clytemnestra, According to the Principles of Marshall McLuhan* (D)

1970	Atwood: *The Journals of Susanna Moodie* (V)	'October Crisis' (FLQ bombings; kidnapping and murder of Pierre Laporte; War Measures Act)
	Monique Bosco (b. 1927): *La femme de Loth* (P)	Ken Gass establishes Factory Theatre Lab in Toronto
	Davies: *Fifth Business* (P)	Formation of the sound poetry performance group The Four Horsemen
	J. Ferron: *L'amélanchier* (P)	
	Alan Fry: *How a People Die* (P)	
	John Glassco (1909–81): *Memoirs of Montparnasse* (P); *The Poetry of French Canada in Translation* (A)	Don Shebib: *Goin' Down the Road* (film)
	Godfrey: *The New Ancestors* (P)	Report on the Status of Women in Canada
	Jacques Grand'Maison (b. 1931): *Nationalisme et religion* (P)	Germaine Greer: *The Female Eunuch*
	Anne Hébert: *Kamouraska* (P)	
	Percy Janes (b. 1922): *The House of Hate* (P)	

Date	Author and Title	Event

George Jonas (b. 1935): *The Happy Hungry Man* (V)
D.C. Jones: *Butterfly on Rock* (P)
Naim Kattan (b. 1928): *Le réel et le théâtral* (P)
Laurence: *A Bird in the House* (P)
André Laurendeau (1912–68): *Ces choses qui nous arrivent* (P)
Levine: *From a Seaside Town* (P)
Lowry: *October Ferry to Gabriola* (P)
Markoosie (Markoosie Patsauq, b. 1942): *Harpoon of the Hunter* (P)
John Metcalf (b. 1938): *The Lady Who Sold Furniture* (P)
Gaston Miron (1928–94): *L'homme rapaillé* (V; tr. in part as *The Agonized Life* and as *Embers and Earth*)
bp Nichol (1944–88): *The Cosmic Chef* (V)
Nowlan: *Playing the Jesus Game* (V)
Michael Ondaatje (b. 1943): *The Collected Works of Billy the Kid* (V)
Fernand Ouellette (b. 1930): *Les actes retrouvés* (P)
G. Roy: *La Rivière sans repos* (P; tr. as *Windflower*)
Rule: *This Is Not for You* (P)
Bertram Warr (1917–43): *Acknowledgment to Life* (V)
Woodcock: *Canada and the Canadians* (P)
Richard Wright (b. 1937): *The Weekend Man* (P)

1971

Berton: *The National Dream* (P)
Bessette: *Le cycle* (P)
Birney: *Rag and Bone Shop* (V)
Bill Bissett (b. 1939): *Nobody owns the earth* (V)
Michael Bullock (b. 1918): *Green Beginning, Black Ending* (P)
Carrier: *Il est par là le soleil* (P; tr. as *Is It the Sun, Philibert?*)
A. Clarke: *When He Was Free and Young and He Used to Wear Silks* (P)
Dudek: *Collected Poetry* (V)
Frye: *The Bush Garden* (P)
Gauvreau: *Oeuvres créatrices complètes* (D); *Les oranges sont vertes* (D)
Glassco: *Selected Poems* (V)
Hood: *The Fruit Man, The Meat Man and the Manager* (P)

Est. of *Canadian Fiction Magazine*
Tarragon Theatre opens, Toronto
D. of theatre critic Nathan Cohen (b. 1923)
William French becomes literary editor of the Toronto *Globe*
Claude Jutra: *Mon oncle Antoine* (film)
Founding of Inuit Brotherhood (later Tapirisat)

Date	Author and Title	Event

P.-M. Lapointe: *Le réel absolu* (V)
MacEwen: *King of Egypt, King of Dreams*
(P)
George McWhirter (b. 1939): *The Catalan Poems* (V)
Antonine Maillet (b. 1929): *La sagouine*
(D)
Munro: *Lives of Girls and Women* (P)
Martin Myers (b. 1927): *The Assignment*
(P)
Pitseolak: *Pictures Out of My Life* (P)
Richler: *St. Urbain's Horseman* (P)
Ryga: *The Ecstacy of Rita Joe and other plays* (D)
Chris Scott (b. 1945): *Bartleby* (P)
Leo Simpson (b. 1934): *Arkwright* (P)
Ronald Sutherland (b. 1933): *Snow Lark*
(P); *Second Image* (P)

1972

Acorn: *More Poems for People* (V)
Atwood: *Survival* (P); *Surfacing* (P)
Alfred Bailey (1905–97): *Culture and Nationality* (P)
Victor-Lévy Beaulieu (b. 1945): *Un rêve québécois* (P)
Carol Bolt (1941–2000): *Buffalo Jump*
(D)
Juan Butler (1942–81): *The Garbage-man* (P)
Carr: *Fresh Seeing* (P)
Matt Cohen (1942–99): *Columbus and the Fat Lady* (P)
Davies: *The Manticore* (P)
J. Ferron: *Le Saint-Elias* (P); *La chaise du maréchal ferrant* (P)
David Freedman (b. 1947): *Creeps* (D)
Gustafson: *Selected Poems* (V)
Robert Harlow (b. 1923): *Scann* (P)
David Helwig (b. 1938): *The Best Name of Silence* (V)
Hénault: *Signaux pour les voyants* (V)
Ann Henry (b. 1914): *Lulu Street* (D)
Houston: *Songs of the Dream People* (P)
George Johnston (b. 1913): *Happy Enough* (V)
Harold Sonny Ladoo (1945–73): *No Pain Like This Body* (P)
A. Langevin: *L'élan d'Amérique* (P)
Rina Lasnier (b. 1915): *Poèmes I & II* (V)

Anik I inaugurates Canadian communications satellite system
Barry Callaghan founds *Exile*
Founding of Green Thumb Theatre for Young People, Vancouver
Gilles Carle: *Le vraie nature de Bernadette* (film)
Est. of Lennoxville Festival (to 1982)
Est. of a federal ministry responsible for Multiculturalism

Date	Author and Title	Event

Layton: *Engagements* (P; ed. Seymour Mayne)
Dennis Lee (b. 1939): *Civil Elegies and other poems* (V)
Livesay: *Collected Poems* (V)
MacEwen: *Noman* (P)
Maillet: *Rabelais et les traditions populaires en Acadie* (P); *Don l'Orignal* (P)
Metcalfe: *Going Down Slow* (P)
John Mills (b. 1930): *The Land of Is* (P)
B. Moore: *Catholics* (P)
Nichol: *The Martyrology* (V; further volumes in the continuing series appeared in 1976, 1982, 1983)
Ouellette: *Poésies* (V)
Joe Rosenblatt (b. 1933): *Bumblebee Dithyramb* (V)
Andreas Schroeder (b. 1946): *The Late Man* (P)
Sparshott: *Looking for Philosophy* (P)
John Sutherland (1919–56): *Essays, controversies and poems* (P, V; ed. Miriam Waddington)
Thériault: *N'Tsuk* (P)
Trottier: *Sainte-Mémoire* (V)
Waddington: *Driving Home* (V)
David Watmough (b. 1926): *Ashes for Easter and other monodramas* (D)
J. Michael Yates (b. 1938): *The Abstract Beast* (P, D)

| 1973 | Atwood: *Power Politics* (V) | Est. of Writers Union of Canada |

Atwood: *Power Politics* (V)
Constance Beresford-Howe (b. 1922): *The Book of Eve* (P)
Clark Blaise (b. 1940): *A North American Education* (P)
Maria Campbell (b. 1940): *Halfbreed* (P)
Lovat Dickson (b. 1902): *Wilderness Man* (P)
Wayland Drew (b. 1932): *The Wabeno Feast* (P)
Calixte Duguay (b. 1939): *Les stigmates du silence* (V)
J. Ferron: *Cotnoir* (P)
Gallant: *The Pegnitz Junction* (P)
Roland Giguère (b. 1929): *La main au feu* (V)
Réshard Gool (1931–89): *Price* (P)
Gutteridge: *Coppermine* (V)

Est. of Writers Union of Canada
R. Murray Schafer: 'North White' (chamber music)
Claude Jutra: *Kamouraska* (film)
Watergate hearings

Date	Author and Title	Event
	Herschel Hardin (b. 1936): *Esker Mike and His Wife Agiluk* (D)	
	Kroetsch: *Gone Indian* (P)	
	William Kurelek (1927–77): *A Prairie Boy's Winter* (P)	
	Maillet: *Mariaagélas* (P)	
	Sid Marty (b. 1944): *Headquarters* (V)	
	Fredelle Bruser Maynard (1922–90): *Raisins and Almonds* (P)	
	Judith Merril (1923–97): *Survival Ship and other stories* (P)	
	W.O. Mitchell: *The Vanishing Point* (P)	
	Nowlan: *Various Persons Named Kevin O'Brien* (P)	
	Reaney: *Apple Butter and other plays for children* (D)	
	Stephen Scobie (b. 1943): *The Birken Tree* (V)	
	J. Simard: *Un façon de parler* (V)	
	Peter Such (b. 1939): *Riverrun* (P)	
	John Thompson (1938–76): *At the Edge of the Chopping There Are No Secrets* (V)	
	Tremblay: *A toi pour toujours, ta Marie-Lou* (D); *Hosanna* (D)	
	Wiebe: *The Temptations of Big Bear* (P)	
	Helen Weinzweig (b. 1915): *Passing Ceremony* (P)	
	Yates: *Nothing Speaks for the Blue Moraines* (V)	
	Robert Zend (1929–85): *From Zero to One* (V)	
	Dale Zieroth (b. 1946): *Clearing* (V)	
1974	Aquin: *Neige noire* (P; tr. as *Hamlet's Twin*)	Est. of *Essays on Canadian Writing*
	Jean Barbeau (b. 1945): *Citrouille* (D)	Est. of Studio D (women's production studio), National Film Board
	Yves Beauchemin (b. 1941): *L'enfirouâpé* (P)	F.R. Crawley: *The Man Who Skied Down Everest* (film)
	V.-L. Beaulieu: *Don Quichotte de la démanche* (P)	Richler's screenplay for film version of *The Apprenticeship of Duddy Kravitz*
	Bolt: *Red Emma* (D)	
	Nicole Brossard (b. 1943): *Mécanique jongleuse suivi de masculin grammaticale* (V; tr. 1980 as *Daydream Mechanics*)	Michel Brault: *Les ordres* (film dramatisation of the October Crisis; Cannes Festival first prize)
	John Robert Colombo (b. 1936): *Translations from the English: Found Poems* (V); *Colombo's Canadian Quotations* (A)	Twelve new subatomic particles discovered between 1974 and 1977

Date	Author and Title	Event

Michael Cook (1933–94): *The Head, Guts and Sound Bone Dance* (D)
Frank Davey (b. 1940). *The Clallum* (V)
Michel Garneau (b. 1939): *Quatre à quatre* (D)
Gustafson: *Fire on Stone* (V)
Hardin: *A Nation Unaware* (P)
Joy Kogawa (b. 1935): *A Choice of Dreams* (V)
A. Langevin: *Une chaîne dans le parc* (P)
Laurence: *The Diviners* (P)
Lee: *Alligator Pie* (V)
Macpherson: *Welcoming Disaster* (V)
André Major (b. 1942): *L'épouvantail* (P; tr. as *The Scarecrows of Saint-Emmanuel*)
Daphne Marlatt (b. 1942): *Steveston* (V)
Munro: *Something I've Been Meaning to Tell You* (P)
Ouellette: *Journal dénoué* (P)
Sharon Pollock (b 1936): *Walsh* (D)
David Adams Richards (b. 1950): *The Coming of Winter* (P)
S. Ross: *Sawbones Memorial* (P)
Ray Smith: *Lord Nelson Tavern* (P)
Peter Stevens (b. 1927): *And the Dying Sky Like Blood* (V)
Anne Szumigalski (b. 1926): *Woman Reading in bath* (V)
Thomas: *Blown Figures* (P)
Kent Thompson (b. 1936): *Across from the Floral Park* (P)
Tremblay: *Bonjour là, bonjour* (D)
Wiseman: *Crackpot* (P)

| 1975 | Acorn: *The Island Means Minago* (V)
 Hrant Alianak (b. 1950): *The Return of the Big Five* (D)
 Birney: *Collected Poems* (V)
 J. Brault: *Poèmes des quatre côtés* (V)
 Pierre Châtillon (b. 1939): *Le fou* (P)
 Cook: *Qiller* (D); *Jacob's Wake* (D)
 Davies: *World of Wonders* (P)
 Gutteridge: *Borderlands* (V)
 Anne Hébert: *Les enfants du sabbat* (P)
 Hood: *The Swing in the Garden* (P; first of the continuing 12-vol. *New Age* cycle)
 Kattan: *Adieu, Babylon* (P)
 Kroetsch: *Badlands* (P)
 Lampman: *Lampman's Kate: the love poems of Archibald Lampman* (V) | Greg Gatenby becomes co-ordinator of Harbourfront Readings in Toronto
 Ann Mortifee: *Klee Wyck* (ballet)
 T.H.B. Symons Report: *To Know Ourselves* |

Date	Author and Title	Event

Levine: *Selected Stories* (P)
Livesay: *Ice Age* (V)
Lowry: *Psalms and Songs* (P)
Florence McNeil (b. 1937): *Emily* (V)
A. Major: *L'épidémie* (P; tr. as *Inspector Therrien*)
J. Marshall: *A Private Place* (P)
Metcalf: *The Teeth of My Father* (P)
Miron: *Contrepointes* (V)
B. Moore: *The Great Victorian Collection* (P)
Pierre Morency (b. 1942): *Le temps des oiseaux* (V)
Peter C. Newman (b. 1929): *The Canadian Establishment* (P)
Reaney: *Selected Shorter Poems* (V)
Richler: *Jacob Two-Two Meets the Hooded Fang* (P)
G. Roy: *Un jardin au bout du monde* (P; tr as *Garden in the Wind*)
Rule: *Lesbian Images* (P); *Themes for Diverse Instruments* (P)
W.D. Valgardson (b. 1939): *God Is Not a Fish Inspector* (P)
Stephen Vizinczey (b. 1933): *In Praise of Older Women* (P)
Bryan Wade (b. 1950): *Underground* (D)
Tom Wayman (b. 1945): *Money and Rain: Tom Wayman Live!* (V)
Woodcock: *Gabriel Dumont* (P); *Notes on Visitations* (V)
Yates: *The Qualicum Physics* (V)

1976   Susan Allison (1845–1937): *A Pioneer Gentlewoman in British Columbia* (P; ed. Margaret Ormsby)
Walter Bauer (1904–76): *A Different Sun* (V; tr from German by Henry Beissel)
Louky Bersianik (Lucile Durand, b. 1930): *L'Euguélionne* (P)
Ducharme: *Inès Pérée et Inat Tendue* (D)
Marian Engel (1933–85): *Bear* (P)
Gary Geddes (b. 1940): *War Measures and other poems* (V)
Margaret Gibson (Gilboord) (b. 1948): *The Butterfly Ward* (P)
Godfrey: *I Ching Kanada* (P)
Gotlieb: *O Master Caliban!* (P)

René Lévesque and Parti Québécois win power in Quebec
Est. of *Studies in Canadian Literature*
Jean Beaudin: *J.-A. Martin, photographe* (film)
White: *A Fringe of Leaves*

Date	Author and Title	Event

Jack Hodgins (b. 1938): *Spit Delaney's
Island* (P)
Hood: *Dark Glasses* (P)
Layton: *For My Brother Jesus* (V)
Leslie McFarlane (1903–77): *Ghost of the
Hardy Boys* (P)
Alistair MacLeod (b. 1936): *The Lost Salt
Gift of Blood* (P)
A. Major: *Les rescapés* (P)
Ken Mitchell (b. 1940): *Cruel Tears* (D)
Nichols: *Song of the Pearl* (P)
Ondaatje: *Coming Through Slaughter* (P)
Reaney: *The Donnellys* (D, pts. I & II;
pt. III appeared in 1977)
Rosenblatt: *Top Soil* (V)
Rick Salutin (b. 1942): *1837: The Farmers'
Revolt* (D)
Carol Shields (b. 1935): *Small
Ceremonies* (P)
Andrew Suknaski (b. 1942): *Wood
Mountain Poems* (V)
Tremblay: *Sainte Carmen de la Main* (D)
R. Wright: *Farthing's Fortunes* (P)
Yates: *Fazes in Elsewhen* (P)

| 1977 | Bessette: *Les anthropoïdes* (P) | Charte de la langue française |

Bessette: *Les anthropoïdes* (P)
Blaise & MukHerjee: *Days and Nights
in Calcutta* (P)
G. Bowering: *A Short Sad Book* (P)
Louis Caron (b. 1942): *L'Emmitouflé*
(P; tr. as *The Draft-dodger*)
Jean Charlebois (b. 1945): *Hanches
neige* (V)
François Charron (b. 1952): *Propagande*
(V)
Findley: *The Wars* (P); *Can You See Me
Yet?* (D)
David French (b. 1939): *Leaving Home* (D)
Gustafson: *Corners in Glass* (V)
Hodgins: *The Invention of the World* (P)
Jones: *Under the Thunder the Flowers Light
Up the Earth* (V)
George Kenny (b. 1952): *Indians Don't Cry*
(P; rev. 1982)
W.P. Kinsella (b. 1935): *Dance Me Outside*
(P)
Myrna Kostash (b. 1944): *All of Baba's
Children* (P)
Lee: *Garbage Delight* (V)

Charte de la langue française
(French becomes sole official
language of Quebec)
Est. of Union nationale des écrivains
québécois)
Berger Commission Report,
Northern Frontier, Northern Homeland

Date	Author and Title	Event

Livesay: *Right Hand Left Hand* (P); *The Woman I Am* (V)
Pat Lowther (1935–75): *A Stone Diary* (V)
Mandel: *Another Time* (P); *Out of Place* (V)
Marlatt: *Zócalo* (P)
K. Mitchell: *Everybody gets Something Here* (P)
John Newlove (b. 1938): *The Fat Man* (V)
Sheldon Rosen (b. 1943): *Ned and Jack* (D)
G. Roy: *Ces enfants de ma vie* (P)
Salutin: *Les Canadiens* (D)
F.R. Scott: *Essays on the Constitution* (P)
Josef Skvorecky (b. 1924): *The Bass Saxophone* (P)
Smart: *The Assumption of Rogues and Rascals* (P)
Thomas: *Ladies and Escorts* (P)
Tremblay: *Damnée Manon, sacré Sandra* (D)
Vigneault: *Gilles Vigneault* (songs)
George F. Walker (b. 1947): *Zastrozzi* (D)
Wiebe: *The Scorched-Wood people* (P)

1978   V.-L. Beaulieu: *Monsieur Melville* (P)   Est. of Social Sciences and Human-
Birney: *Fall by Fury* (V)   ities Research Council of Canada
Denise Boucher (b. 1935): *Les fées*   Asian immigration to Canada
ont soif (D)   increases
Caron: *Bonhomme sept-heures* (P)   Home computers begin to become
Cécile Cloutier (b. 1930): *Chaleuils* (V) common
Ann Copeland (pseud., b. 1932): *At Peace* (P)
George Faludy (b. 1910): *East and West* (V)
Larry Fineberg (b. 1945): *Stonehenge* (D)
Godfrey: *Dark Must Yield* (P)
Hood: *Selected Stories* (P)
Basil Johnston (b. 1929): *Moose Meat and Wild Rice* (P)
Kroetsch: *What the Crow Said* (P)
Gilbert Langevin (b. 1938): *Mon refuge est un volcan* (V)
Maheux-Forcier: *Appassionata* (P)
Kevin Major (b. 1949): *Hold Fast* (P)
Marty: *Men for the Mountains* (P)
Robin Mathews (b. 1931): *Canadian Literature: Surrender or revolution* (P)
Munro: *Who Do You Think You Are?* (P; Eng. & Am. title: *The Beggar Maid*)
Ouellette: *Tu regardais intensément, Geneviève* (P)

Date	Author and Title	Event

Al Pittman (b. 1940): *Once When I was Drowning* (V)
Pollock: *The Komagata Maru Incident* (D)
Purdy: *Being Alive* (V)
Richards: *Dancers at Night* (P)
G. Roy: *Fragiles lumières de la terre* (P)
A.J.M. Smith: *The Classic Shade* (V)
John Thompson: *Stilt Jack* (V)
Michel Tremblay: *La grosse femme d'à côté est enceinte* (P)
George Walker: *Three Plays ...* (D)
Watmough: *No More Into the Garden* (P)
Wiseman: *Old Woman at Play* (P)
Yates: *Esox Nobilior Non Esox Lucius* (V)

1979

Bersianik: *Le pique-nique sur L'Acropole* (P)
Bessette: *Le semestre* (P); *Mes romans et moi* (P)
Carrier: *Les enfants du bonhomme dans la lune* (P; tr. as *The Hockey Sweater*)
M. Cohen: *The Sweet Second Summer of Kitty Malone* (P)
Gallant: *From the Fifteenth District* (P)
Dave Godfrey & Douglas Parkhill: *Gutenberg Two* (P)
John Hare: *Anthologie de la poésie québécoise du XIXe siècle* (A)
Wacław Iwaniuk (b. 1915): *Dark Times* (V)
Kattan: *Le rivage* (P)
Pat Lane (b. 1939): *Poems New and Selected* (V)
P.-M. Lapointe: *Écritures* (V)
Maillet: *Pélagie-la-charrette* (P; wins Prix Goncourt)
Erin Mouré (b. 1955): *Empire, York Street* (V)
Ondaatje: *There's a Trick with a Knife I'm Learning to Do* (V)
Madeleine Ouellette-Michalska (b. 1935): *La femme de sable* (P)
Paradis: *Miss Charlie* (P)
Reaney: *Wacousta!* (D)
André Roy (b. 1944): *Les passions du samedi* (V)
Vigneault: *Silences* (V)
Sheila Watson: *Four stories* (P)
Wayman: *A Planet Mostly Sea* (V)
Ludwig Zeller (b. 1927): *In the Country of the Antipodes* (V)

John Beckwith: *The Shivaree* (opera; lyrics by James Reaney)
Anne Claire Poirier: *Mourir à tue-tête* (film)

Date	Author and Title	Event
1980	Bersianik: *Maternative* (V)	Quebec Referendum on 'Sovereignty-Association'
	Bessette: *Le garden-party de Christophine* (P)	'O Canada' becomes official national anthem
	G. Bowering: *Burning Water* (P)	
	Marilyn Bowering (b. 1949): *Sleeping with Lambs* (V)	
	Mary di Michele (b. 1949): *Mimosa and Other Poems* (V)	
	David Donnell (b. 1939): *Dangerous Crossings* (V)	
	David Fennario (b. 1947): *Balconville* (D)	
	Kristjana Gunnars (b. 1948): *One-eyed Moon Maps* (V)	
	Hodgins: *The Resurrection of Joseph Bourne* (P)	
	Margaret Hollingsworth (b. 1940): *Alli Alli Oh* (D)	
	Hood: *None Genuine Without This Signature* (P)	
	Kinsella: *Shoeless Joe Jackson Comes to Iowa* (P)	
	Kroetsch: *The 'Crow' Journals* (P)	
	Gilbert LaRocque (1941–84): *Les masques* (P)	
	David McFadden (b. 1940): *A Trip Around Lake Erie* (P)	
	MacLennan: *Voices in Time* (P)	
	Maheux-Forcier: *En toutes lettres* (P)	
	Joyette Marchessault (b. 1938): *Tryptique lesbien* (P)	
	Marlatt: *What Matters* (A)	
	Tom Marshall: *The Elements* (V)	
	Metcalf: *General Ludd* (P)	
	John Murrell (b. 1945): *Waiting for the Parade* (D)	
	Ouellette: *La mort vive* (P)	
	Duke Redbird (b. 1939): *We Are Métis* (P)	
	Richler: *Joshua Then and Now* (P)	
	Erika Ritter (b. 1948): *Automatic Pilot* (D)	
	Leon Rooke (b. 1934): *Fat Woman* (P); *Cry Evil* (P)	
	Rule: *Contract with the World* (P)	
	Scobie: *McAlmon's Chinese Opera* (V)	
	Tremblay: *L'impromptu d'Outremont* (D); *Thérèse et Pierrette à l'école des saints-anges* (P)	
	Webb: *Wilson's Bowl* (V)	
	Derk Wynand (b. 1944): *One Cook, Once Dreaming* (P)	

Date	Author and Title	Event
1981	Edna Alford (b. 1947) *A Sleep Full of Dreams* (P)	Studio D, NFB: *Not a Love Story* (film)
	Atwood: *Bodily Harm* (P); *True Stories* (V, P)	Gilles Carle: *Les Plouffe* (film)
	A. Bailey: *Miramichi Lightning* (V)	
	Y. Beauchemin: *Le matou* (P; tr. 1986 as *The Alley Cat*)	
	Michel Beaulieu (1941–85): *Visages* (V)	
	Anne Cameron (Cam Hubert; b. 1938): *Daughters of Copper Woman* (P)	
	Carrier: *Cirque Noir* (D)	
	Davies: *The Rebel Angels* (P)	
	Findley: *Famous last Words* (P)	
	Gallant: *Home Truths* (P)	
	Godbout: *Les têtes à Papineau* (P)	
	John Gray (b. 1946): *Billy Bishop Goes to War* (D)	
	Gunnars: *Wake-pick Poems* (V)	
	Ray Guy: *Beneficial Vapours* (P)	
	Hodgins: *The Barclay Family Theatre* (P)	
	Kogawa: *Obasan* (P)	
	Gordon Korman (b. 1963): *I Want to Go Home!* (P)	
	Rachel Korn (1898–1982): *Generations* (V)	
	Kreisel: *The Almost Meeting* (P)	
	Kroetsch: *Field Notes* (V)	
	Robert Lalonde (b. 1947): *La belle épouvante* (P)	
	G. Lapointe: *Corps et graphies* (V)	
	Maillet: *Cent ans dans les bois* (P)	
	Marilú Mallet (b. 1945): *Les compagnons d'horloge-pointeuse* (P)	
	Mandel: *Dreaming Backwards* (V)	
	Marchessault: *La saga des poules mouillées* (D)	
	Marriott: *The Circular Coast* (V)	
	Seymour Mayne (b. 1944): *The Impossible Promised Land* (V)	
	W.O. Mitchell: *How I Spent My Summer Holidays* (P)	
	Ouellette: *En la nuit, la mer* (V)	
	Page: *Evening Dance of the Grey Flies* (V, P)	
	Alice Parizeau (1930–90): *Les lilas fleurissent à Varsovie* (P)	
	Pollock: *Blood Relations* (D)	
	Duke Redbird: *Loveshine and Red Wine* (V)	
	Richards: *Lives of Short Duration* (P)	
	Rooke: *Death Suite* (P); *The Magician in Love* (P)	

Date	Author and Title	Event
	F.R. Scott: *Collected Poems* (V) Elizabeth Spencer (b. 1921): *The Stories of Elizabeth Spencer* (P) Thériault: *La femme Anna et autres contes* (P) Thomas: *Real Mothers* (P) Sean Virgo (b. 1940): *White Lies and other fictions* (P) Fred Wah (b. 1939): *Breathin' My Name with a Sigh* (V) George Walker: *Theatre of the Film Noir* (D) Zieroth: *Mid-river* (V)	
1982	Sandra Birdsell (b. 1942): *Night Travellers* (P) Blais: *Visions d'Anna ou le vertige* (P) Roo Borson (b. 1952): *A Sad Device* (V) Robert Bringhurst (b. 1946): *The Beauty of the Weapons* (V) Brossard: *Picture Theory* (P) Pier Giorgio di Cicco (b. 1949): *Flying Deeper into the Century* (V) Keath Fraser (b. 1944): *Taking Cover* (P) Frye: *The Great Code* (P); *Divisions on a Ground* (P) Gallant: *What Is to be Done* (D) Graeme Gibson (b. 1934): *Perpetual Motion* (P) Haig-Brown: *Writings and Reflections* (P) Anne Hébert: *Les fous de Bassan* (P; tr. as *In the Shadow of the Wind*) Jasmin: *Maman-Paris, Maman-la-France* (P) Kinsella: *Shoeless Joe* (P) A.M. Klein: *Beyond Sambation: selected essays and editorials 1928–1955* (P) Layton: *A Wild Peculiar Joy* (V) MacEwen: *The T.E. Lawrence Poems* (V) McWhirter: *Coming to Grips with Lucy* (P) Maillet: *Christophe cartier de la noisette dit Nounours* (P) Metcalf: *Kicking Against the Pricks* (P); *Making It New* (A) W.O. Mitchell: *Dramatic W.O. Mitchell* (D) Munro: *The Moons of Jupiter* (P) Susan Musgrave (b. 1951): *Tarts and Muggers* (V)	Applebaum-Hébert Report on cultural policy Constitutional Act 'repatriates' Canadian constitution, replaces BNA Act 'Okanada' Exhibition at Academie der Künste in Berlin

Date	Author and Title	Event

Nowlan: *I might Not Tell Everybody This*
(V)
Ondaatje: *Running in the Family* (P)
Gwen Pharis Ringwood (1910–85):
The Collected Plays ... (D)
Rooke: *The Birth Control King of the*
Upper Volta (P)
S. Ross: *The Race and other stories* (P)
C. Scott: *Antichthon* (P)
David Solway (b. 1941): *Selected Poems*
(V)
Tremblay: *La duchesse et le roturier* (P)
Guy Vanderhaeghe (b. 1951): *Man*
Descending (P)
Wilfred Watson: *Mass on Cowback* (V)
Webb: *Sunday Water: Thirteen Anti-*
Ghazals (V); *The Vision Tree* (V)
Wiebe: *The Angel of the Tar Sands* (P)
Rachel Wyatt (b. 1929): *Foreign Bodies* (P)

1983   V.-L. Beaulieu: *Discours de Samm* (P)
Claude Beausoleil (b. 1948): *Une*
certaine fin de siècle (V)
Blaise: *Lusts* (P)
M. Callaghan: *A Time for Judas* (P)
Chamberland: *Aléatoire instantané &*
Midsummer 82 (V)
Beatrice Culleton: *In Search of April*
Raintree (P)
Christopher Dewdney (b. 1951):
Predators of the Adoration (V)
di Michele: *Necessary Sugar* (V)
M. Ferron: *Sur le chemin Craig* (P)
Lucien Francoeur (b. 1948): *Rockeurs*
sanctifiés (V)
Harlow: *Paul Nolan* (P)
Maria Jacobs (b. 1930): *Precautions*
Against Death (P, V)
Jones: *A Throw of Particles* (V)
A.M. Klein: *A.M. Klein : short stories* (P)
Philip Kreiner: *people Like Us in a Place*
Like This (P)
Kroetsch: *Alibi* (P)
René Lapierre: *Profil de l'ombre* (V)
Layton: *The Gucci Bag* (V)
Nowland: *Nine Micmac legends* (P)
H.R. Percy (b. 1920): *Painted Ladies* (P)
Penny Petrone: *First People, First Voices* (A)
Pratt: *E.J. Pratt: On His Life and Poetry* (A)
Paul Quarrington (b. 1953): *Home Game* (P)

Date	Author and Title	Event

Rooke: *Shakespeare's Dog* (P)
Susan Swan (b. 1945): *The Biggest
Modern Woman of the World* (P)
Wiebe: *My Lovely Enemy* (P)
Woodcock: *Letter to the Past* (P)
Eric Wright (b. 1929): *The Night the
Gods Smiled* (P)

1984   Blais: *Pays voilés/Existences* (V)   Marc Garneau becomes first
        Pierre (P)   Canadian astronaut
        G. Bowering: *Kerrisdale Elegies* (V)   Assassination of Indira Gandhi;
        Brault: *Agonie* (V)   Khalistan independence movement
        Brossard: *Double Impression* (V)
        Carrier: *De l'amour dans la ferraille* (V)
        Jean Charlebois: *Présent!* (V)
        Gilbert Choquette (b. 1929): *La flamme
        et la forge* (P)
        M. Cohen: *The Spanish Doctor* (P)
        Jean-Paul Daoust (b. 1946): *Tax* (V)
        Normand de Bellefeuille: *Le livre du
        devoir* (V)
        Francine Déry (b. 1943): *Le noyau* (V)
        Findley: *Not Wanted on the Voyage* (P)
        Madeleine Gagnon (b. 1938): *La lettre
        infinie* (V)
        Geddes: *The Terracotta Army* (V)
        Paulette Jiles (b. 1943): *Celestial
        Navigations* (V)
        Lionel Kearns (b. 1937): *Convergences* (V)
        Susan Kerslake (b. 1943): *Penumbra* (P)
        Suzanne Lamy (b. 1929): *Quand je lis
        je m'invente* (P)
        La Rocque: *Les masques* (P)
        Michel Leclerc (b. 1952): *Écrire ou la
        disparition* (V)
        Livesay: *Feeling the Worlds* (V)
        Maillet: *Crache à pic* (P)
        W.O. Mitchell: *Since Daisy Creek* (P)
        Pierre Olivier (b. 1943): *Les militaires
        ont envahi Manhattan* (P)
        Ouellette-Michalska: *La maison Trestler* (P)
        Paradis: *Les Ferdinand* (P)
        J. Poulin: *Volkswagen blues* (P)
        Purdy: *Piling Blood* (V)
        Richler: *Home Sweet Home* (P)
        Kevin Roberts (b. 1940): *Nanoose Bay
        Suite* (V)
        G. Roy: *Ely! Ely! Ely!* (P)
        Jacques Savoie (b. 1951): *Les portes
        tournantes* (P)

Date	Author and Title	Event

Skvorecky: *The Engineer of Human Souls* (P)
Thomas: *Intertidal Life* (P)
Tremblay: *Albertine en cinq temps* (D)
Tremblay: *Des nouvelles d'Edouard* (P)
Elise Turcotte (b. 1957): *Navires et guerres* (V)
Louise Warren (b. 1956): *L'amant gris* (V)

1985

Anne-Marie Alonzo (b. 1951): *Blues de mine* (V)
Atwood: *The Handmaid's Tale* (P)
V.-L. Beaulieu: *Steven le hérault* (P)
Neil Bissoondath (b. 1955): *Digging Up the Mountains* (P)
Louise Bouchard (b. 1949): *Les images*
M. Callaghan: *Lost and Found Stories* (P)
Charron: *La vie n'a pas de sens* (V)
Lorna Crozier (b. 1948): *The Garden Going On Without Us* (V)
Davies: *What's Bred in the Bone* (P)
Patrice Desbiens (b. 1948): *Dans l'après-midi cardiaque* (V)
René-Daniel Dubois (b. 1955): *Being at home with Claude* (D)
Engel: *The Tattooed Woman* (P)
Francoeur: *Exit pour nomades* (V)
K. Fraser: *Foreign Affairs* (P)
Jean-Paul Fugère (b. 1921): *Popa moman et le saint homme* (P)
Gallant: *Overhead in a Balloon* (P)
Stephen Guppy (b. 1951): *Another Sad Day at the Edge of the Empire* (P)
Kreisel: *Another Country* (P)
Hollingsworth: *Willful Acts* (D)
Kroetsch: *Advice to My Friends* (V)
Marie Laberge (b. 1923): *Deux tangos pour toute une vie* (D)
Layton: *Waiting for the Messiah* (P)
Paul-Chanel Malenfant (b. 1950): *Les noms du père* (V)
B. Moore: *Black Robe* (P)
Bharati Mukherjee (b. 1942): *Darkness* (P)
Ouellette: *Lucie ou un midi en novembre* (P)
Paradis: *Les Ferdinand* (P)
Paradis: *La ligne bleue* (P)
Maryse Pelletier (b. 1946): *Duo pour voix obstinées* (D)
André Roy: *Action Writing* (V)

The Canadian Encyclopedia
Sandy Wilson: *My American Cousin* (film)
Ted Kotcheff: *Joshua Then and Now* (film)
MacDonald Commission Report on Canada's Economic Future (72 vols)
Air India Crash

Date	Author and Title	Event
	Smart: *Necessary Secrets* (V)	
	Richard Stevenson (b. 1952): *Driving Offensively* (V)	
	Pasquale Verdicchio (b. 1954): *Moving Landscape* (V)	
	Villemaire: *La constellation du Cygne* (P)	
	Wah: *Waiting for Saskatchewan* (V)	
	George Walker: *Criminals in Love* (D)	
1986	Blaise: *Resident Alien* (P)	Denys Arcand: *Le declin de l'Empire américain* (film)
	M. Cohen: *Nadine* (P)	
	Findley: *The Telling of Lies* (P)	John Polanyi wins Nobel prize for chemistry
	Pierre Gravel: *La fin de l'histoire* (P)	
	Highway (b. 1951): *The Rez Sisters* (D)	
	Hood: *The Motor Boys in Ottawa* (P)	
	Munro: *The Progress of Love* (P)	
	R. Smith: *Century* (P)	
	Wilfred Watson: *Poems: collected unpublished new* (V)	
1987	C. Beausoleil (b. 1948): *Extase et déchirure* (V)	Meech Lake Accord
	M-M. Bouchard (b. 1958): *Les feluettes* (D)	
	G. Bowering: *Caprice* (P)	
	Brossard: *Le désert mauve* (P)	
	Gurr (b. 1936): *The Ring Master* (P)	
	Krizanc (b. 1956): *Prague* (D)	
	Lill (b. 1950): *The Occupation of Heather Rose* (D)	
	Mistry (b. 1952): *Tales from Firozsha Baag* (P)	
	Ondaatje: *In the Skin of a Lion* (P)	
	Ouellette (b. 1930): *Les heures* (V)	
	Shields: *Swann* (P)	
	Théoret (b. 1942): *Entre raison et déraison* (P)	
1988	Atwood: *Cat's Eye* (P)	David Suzuki wins UN Environment Program Medal
	W. Gibson (b. 1948): *Mona Lisa Overdrive* (P)	
	Micone (b. 1945): *Déjà l'agonie* (D)	
	Mouawad (b. 1968): *Déjà agonie* (D)	
1989	Barcelo (b. 1941): *Nulle part* (P) begins trilogy	Douglas Cardinal displays architectural design of Canadian Museum of Civilization
	Crate (b. 1953): *Pale as Real Ladies* (V)	
	Kroetsch: *Completed Field Notes* (V)	
	LaRue (b.1948): *Copies conformes* (P)	

Date	Author and Title	Event
	Mojica (b. 1954): *Princess Pocahontas and the Blue Spots* (D) Poulin: *Le vieux chagrin* (P) H. Robinson (1900–90): *Write It on Your Heart* (P) Richler: *Solomon Gursky Was Here* (V)	
1990	S. Lee (b. 1952): *Disappearing Moon Café* (P) A-M. MacDonald (b. 1959): *Goodnight Desdemona (Good Morning Juliet)* (D) Poliquin: *Visions de Jude* (P; retitled *La côte de sable*, 2000)	Gulf War
1991	Coupland (b. 1961): *Generation X* (P) Etienne (b. 1936): *La pacotille* (P) W. Gibson: *The Difference Engine* (P) S. Jacob (b. 1943): *L'obéissance* (P) P. Lane: *Winter* (V) D. McKay: *Night Field* (V) Sweatman (b. 1963): *Fox* (P) Turcotte (b. 1957): *Le bruit des choses vivantes* (P)	Civil Code of Quebec is modernized Jin-Me Yoon 'Souvenirs of the Self' (postcard series) Oka Crisis Charlottetown Accord
1992	Atwood: *Good Bones* (V) M. Ferron (b. 1922): *Adrienne* (P) Heighton (b. 1961): *Flight Path of the Emperor* (P) R. Lalonde (b. 1947): *Sept Lacs plus au nord* (P) Majzels (b. 1950): *Hellman's Scrapbook* (P) Ondaatje: *The English Patient* (P) Steffler (b. 1947): *The Afterlife of George Cartwright* (P) Svendsen (b. 1954): *Marine Life* (P) J. Thompson: *Lion in the Streets* (D) Vassanji (b. 1950): *Uhuru Street* (P) Wah: *Alley Alley Home Free* V) Watson: *Deep Hollow Creek* (P) Zwicky: *Lyrical Philosophy* (V)	Roberta Bondar becomes first Canadian woman to go into space
1993	Adderson (b. 1963): *Bad Imaginings* (P) Armstrong: *Ravensong* (P) Atwood: *The Robber Bride* (P) Blaser (b. 1925): *The Holy Forest* (V) Desjardins: *La Love* (P) Godbout: *Le temps des Galarneau* (P) T. King: *Green Grass, Running Water* (P) Shields: *The Stone Diaries* (P)	NAFTA signed

Date	Author and Title	Event
	Tard (1921–98): *Le bon Dieu s'appelle Henri* (P) Verdecchia (b. 1962): *Fronteras Americanas* (D)	
1994	Chong (b. 1952): *The Concubine's Children* (P) F. Gravel (b. 1951): *Ostend* (P) C. Harris (b. 1937): *Drawing Down a Daughter* (V) Ipellie (b. 1951): *Arctic Dreams and Nightmares* (P) Kokis: (b. 1944): *Le pavillon des miroirs* (P) Lepage (b. 1955): *Sept branches de la rivière Ota* (D) Morency: *Les paroles qui marchent dans la nuit* (V) Munro: *Open Secrets* P) M. Ouellette (b. 1961): *French Town* (D)	Atom Egoyan film *Exotica* wins Critics Prize at Cannes Jack Rabinovitch est. the Giller Prize
1995	Atwood: *Morning in the Burned House* (1995) M-M. Bouchard (b.): *Les muses orphelines* (D; prod. 1989) Chen (b. 1961): *L'ingratitude* (P) Daigle: *1953* (D) B. Fraser (b. 1959): *Poor Super Man* (D) Lepage: *Le polygraphe* (film) A. Major: *La vie provisoire* (P) D. McCormack (b. 1969): *Dark Rides* (P) Lowry: *Collected Letters* (–1996; P), ed. S. Grace McWhirter (b. 1939): *A Staircase for All Souls* (V) Mistry: *A Fine Balance* (1995) J. Savoie (b. 1951): *Le cirque bleu* (P) Wharton (b. 1963): *Icefields* (P)	Quebec Sovereignty Referendum Craig Kielburger est. (Kids Can) Free the Children *Margaret's Museum* (film)
1996	Assiniwi: *La saga des Béothuks* (P) Atwood: *Alias Grace* (P) Bringhurst: *Elements of Typographical Style* (rev; P) d'Amour (b. 1948): *Presque rien* (P) Laferrière: *Pays sans chapeau* (P) Y. Martel (b. 1963): *Self* (P) Panych: *Vigil* (D) Vanderhaeghe (b. 1951): *The English-man's Boy* (P) Wah: *Diamond Grill* (P)	Human Rights Act 'Little Sisters' court case decision Est. of *National Post* Est. of *On Spec* magazine

Date	Author and Title	Event
1997	Bolster (b. 1969): *White Stone* (V) Frenette (b. 1954): *La terre ferme* (P) Jarman (b. 1955): *Salvage King, Ya!* (P) Kiyooka (1926–94), with Marlatt: *Mothertalk* (P) Richler: *Barney's Version* (P) Saul (b. 1947): *Reflections of a Siamese Twin* (P) D. Sears (b. 1953): *Harlem Duet* (D)	Jean-Louis Roux chairs Canada Council
1998	A. Alexis (b. 1957): *Childhood* (P) Archambault: *Les maladresses du coeur* (P) Beausoleil: *Le chant de voyageur* (V) Begamudré (b. 1956): *Laterna Magika* (P) Bock (b. 1964): *Olympia* (P) Brand (b. 1953): *No Language Is Neutral* (V) Carson (b. 1950): *Autobiography of Red* (V) Choy (b. 1939): *Paper Shadows* (P) Crosbie (b. 1963): *Queen Rat* (V) Fleming (b. 1964): *Pool-hopping and other stories* (P) Gowdy (b. 1950): *The White Bone* (P) Highway (b. 1951): *The Kiss of the Fur Queen* (P) Hodgins: *Broken Ground* (P) Hughes (b. 1925): *The Story Box* (P) Lachance (b. 1944): *Le roman de Julie Papineau* (P) Munro: *The Love of a Good Woman* (P) Poliquin: *L'homme de paille* (P) D.A. Richards: *The Bay of Love and Sorrows* (P) G. Soucy (b.1958): *La petite fille qui aimait trop les allumettes* (P) M. Tremblay: *Encore une fois, si vous permettez* (D)	Lise Bissonnette (b. 1945) becomes director of the Grande Bibliothèque du Québec
1999	Babstock (b. 1970): *Mean* (V) Bringhurst: *A Story as Sharp as a Knife* (P) G.E. Clarke (b.): *Beatrice Chancy* (V) M. Cohen: *Elizabeth and After* (P) A. Hébert: *Un habit de lumière* (P) W. Johnston (b. 1958): *Baltimore's Mansion* (P)	Est. of Nunavut Adrienne Clarkson becomes Governor-General Est. of Aboriginal TV channel

Date	Author and Title	Event
	Ray Smith: *The Man Who Loved Jane Austen* (P) A. Thomas: *Isobel Gunn* (P) M. Turner: *The Pornographer's Poem* (P) Wiebe (with Y. Johnson, b. 1961): *Stolen Life* (P)	
2000	Atwood: *The Blind Assassin* (P) G. Bowering: *His Life* (V) Carson: *The Beauty of the Husband* (V) Findley: *Elizabeth Rex* (D) N. Klein (b. 1970): *No Logo* (P) D. McKay: *Another Gravity* (V) Ondaatje: *Anil's Ghost* (P) Purdy: *Beyond Remembering* (V) E. Robinson: *Monkey Beach* (P)	Est. of Charles Taylor Prize 'Y2K fear' d. of Pierre Elliott Trudeau
2001	Bök (b. 1966): *Eunoia* (V) Crummey (b. 1965): *River Thieves* (P) Kwan (1934–2001): *Things That Must Not Be Forgotten* (P) Macfarlane (b. 1952): *The Danger Tree* (P) D. McKay: *Vis a Vis* (P) Redhill (b. 1966): *Martin Sloane* (P) T. Taylor (b. 1963): *Stanley Park* (P) A. Thomas: *The Path of Totality* (P) Wharton: *Salamander* (P)	'9–11' terrorism in New York and Washington Nisga'a Treaty in BC Zacharias Kunuk film *Atanarjuak* (*The Fast Runner*) wins Cannes Camera'd'Or
2002	Cariou (b. 1966): *Lake of the Prairies* (P) A. Clarke: *The Polished Hoe* (P) Coupland: *Souvenir of Canada* (P) Dobozy (b. 1969): *When X Equals Marylou* (P) Gaston (b. 1953): *Mount Appetite* (P) Govier (b. 1948): *Creation* (P) W. Johnston: *The Navigator of New York* (P) L. Moore (b. 1964): *Open* (P) Schoemperlen (b. 1954): *Red Plaid Skirt* (P) Shields: *Unless* (P) Vanderhaeghe: *The Last Crossing* (P)	Financial collapse of General Publishing War in Afghanistan Jubilee year of Elizabeth II George Bowering named Canada's first poet laureate

Further reading

The following list constitutes a selective guide to general book-length works concerned with Canadian writing. Readers should also consult the large number of studies concerned with individual authors and artists, local and regional history, and particular ethnic communities. Articles in scholarly journals provide further critical and biographical information. Among the major journals are the following: *Antigonish Review, ARIEL, Atlantic Provinces Book Review, Atlantis, Australian-Canadian Studies, BC Bookworld, Books in Canada, Canadian Children's Literature, Canadian Literature, Canadian Notes & Queries, Canadian Poetry, Canadian Theatre Review, Capilano Review, Commonwealth, Ellipse, Etudes Canadiennes, Etudes Françaises, Event, Essays on Canadian Writing, Gatherings, Geist, Jeu, Journal of Canadian Studies, Journal of Commonwealth Literature, Lettres Québécoises, Liberté, Livres et Auteurs Québécois, Malahat Review, Mosaic, La Nouvelle Barre du Jour, Open Letter, Prairie Fire, Quill & Quire, Room of One's Own, Studies in Canadian Literature, Theatre History in Canada, Voix et Images, University of Toronto Quarterly, West Coast Line.* Monthly and annual bibliographies of Canadian writing appear in *Bibliographie de Québec, Canadiana, Canadian Periodical Index, Journal of Commonwealth Literature.*

ANTHOLOGIES

Bennett, Donna, and Russell Brown, eds. *A New Anthology of Canadian Literature in English.* Toronto: Oxford, 2003.

Clarke, George Elliott, ed. *Eyeing the North Star: Directions in African-Canadian Literature.* Toronto: McClelland & Stewart, 1997.

Compton, Wayde, ed. *Bluesprint: Black British Columbian Literature and Orature.* Vancouver: Arsenal Pulp, 2001.

Downie, Mary Alice, and Barbara Robertson, eds. *The New Wind Has Wings.* Toronto: Oxford, 1984.

Gerson, Carole, and Gwendolyn Davies, eds. *Canadian Poetry from the beginnings through the First World War.* Toronto: McClelland & Stewart, 1994.

Glassco, John, ed. *The Poetry of French Canada in Translation.* Toronto: Oxford, 1970.

Goldie, Terry, and Daniel David Moses, eds. *An Anthology of Canadian Native Literature in English.* 2nd ed. Toronto: Oxford, 1998.

Hutcheon, Linda, and Marion Richmond, eds. *Other Solitudes: Canadian Multicultural Fictions.* Toronto: Oxford, 1990.

King, Thomas. *All My Relations.* Toronto: McClelland & Stewart, 1990.

Lee, Bennett, and Jim Wong-Chu, eds. *Many-Mouthed Birds: Contemporary Writing by Chinese Canadians.* Vancouver: Douglas & McIntyre, 1991.

Mailhot, Laaurent, and Pierre Nepveu, eds. *La poésie québécoise des origines à nos jours.* Sillery: Presses de l'Université du Québec, 1980.

Maillet, Marguerite, et al., eds. *Anthologie de textes littéraires acadiens.* Moncton: Eds. d'Acadie, 1979.

Marcotte, Gilles, et al., eds. *Anthologie de la littérature québécoise.* 4 vols. Montréal: La Presse, 1978–80.

New, W.H., ed. *Canadian Short Fiction.* 2nd ed. Scarborough, ON: Prentice-Hall, 1997.

Ondaaatje, Michael, ed. *The Long Poem Anthology.* Toronto: Coach House, 1979.

Petrone, Penny, ed. *First People, First Voices.* Toronto: University of Toronto Press, 1983.

Quan, Andy, and Jim Wong-Chu, eds. *Swallowing Clouds: An Anthology of Chinese-Canadian Poetry.* Vancouver: Arsenal Pulp, 1999.

Smith, A.J.M., and F.R. Scott, eds. *The Blasted Pine.* 2nd ed. Toronto: Macmillan, 1967.

Thesen, Sharon, ed. *The New Long Poem Anthology.* 2nd ed. Toronto: Coach House, 2001.

Wagner, Anton, ed. *Canada's Lost Plays.* 4 vols. Toronto: CTR Publications, 1978–.

Wasserman, Jerry, ed. *Modern Canadian Plays.* 4th ed, 2 vols. Burnaby, BC: Talonbooks, 2000–2001.

ART, MUSIC, FILM

Belton, Robert, ed. *Sights of Resistance: Approaches to Canadian Visual Culture.* Calgary: University of Calgary Press, 2001).

Jessup, Lynda, ed. *Antimodernism and Artistic Experience.* Toronto: University of Toronto Press, 2001.

Kallman, Helmut, et al., eds. *The Encyclopedia of Music in Canada.* 2nd ed. Toronto: University of Toronto Press, 1992.

Lord, Barry. *The History of Painting in Canada: Towards a People's Art*. Toronto: NC, 1974.

Morris, Peter. *Embattled Shadows: A History of Canadian Cinema, 1895–1939*. Montreal: McGill-Queen's University Press, 1978.

Morris, Peter. *The Film Companion*. Toronto: Irwin, 1984.

Nemiroff, Diana, Robert Houle, and Charlotte Townsend-Gault, eds. *Land, Spirit, Power*. Ottawa: National Gallery of Canada, 1992).

Reid, Dennis. *A Concise History of Canadian Painting*. 2nd ed. Toronto: Oxford, 1988.

Veronneau, Pierre. *À la recherche d'une identité: renaissance d'une cinéma d'auteur canadien-anglais*. Québec: Musée du Cinéma, 1991.

Veronneau, Pierre, ed. *Histoire du cinéma au Québec*. 2 vols. Québec: Musée du Cinéma, 1979.

CHILDREN'S LITERATURE

Egoff, Sheila, and Judith Saltman. *The New Republic of Childhood*. Toronto: Oxford, 1990.

Saltman, Judith. *Modern Canadian Children's Books*. Toronto: Oxford, 1987.

DRAMA

Brisset, Annie. *A Sociocritique of Translation: Theatre and Alterity in Quebec, 1968–1988*. Tr. Rosalind Gill and Roger Gannon. Toronto: University of Toronto Press, 1996.

Conolly, L.W., ed. *Canadian Drama and the Critics*. Vancouver: Talonbooks, 1987.

Filewod, Alan. *Collective Encounters: Documentary Theatre in English Canada*. Toronto: University of Toronto Press, 1987.

Filewod, Alan. *Performing Canada: The Nation Enacted in the Imagined Theatre*. Textual Studies in Canada 15. Kamloops: University College of the Cariboo, 2002.

Gilbert, Helen, and Joanne Tompkins. *Post-colonial Drama: Theory, Practice, Politics*. London & New York: Routledge, 1996.

Gobin, Pierre. *Le fou et ses doubles: figures de la dramaturgie québécoise*. Montréal: Presses de l'Université de Montréal, 1978.

Godin, Jean-Cléo, and Laurent Mailhot. *Le théâtre québécois*. 2 vols. Montréal: HMH, 1970, 1980.

Johnston, Denis. *Up the Mainstream: The Rise of Toronto's Alternative Theatres*. Toronto: University of Toronto Press, 1991.

Knowles, Richard Paul. *The Theatre of Form and the Production of Meaning: Contemporary Canadian Dramaturgies*. Toronto: ECW, 1999.

Rubin, Don, ed. *Canadian Theatre History: Selected Readings*. Toronto: Copp Clark, 1996.

Rudakoff, Judith, and Rita Much, comps. *Fair Play: 12 Women Speak*. Toronto: Simon & Pierre, 1990.

Ryan, Toby Gordon. *Stage Left*. Toronto: Simon & Pierre, 1981.

Wagner, Anton, ed. *Establishing Our Boundaries: English-Canadian Theatre Criticism*. Toronto: University of Toronto Press, 1999.

Wallace, Robert, and Cynthia Zimmerman, comps. *The Work: Conversations with Canadian Playwrights*. Toronto: Coach House, 1982.

Zimmerman, Cynthia. *Playwrighting Women: Female Voices in English Canada*. Toronto: Simon & Pierre, 1994.

FICTION

Allard, Jacques. *Le roman au Québec: histoire, perspectives, lectures*. Montréal: Québec-Amériques, 2000.

Biron, Michel. *L'absence du maître*. Montréal: Presses de l'Université de Montréal, 2000.

Boucher, Jean-Pierre. *Le recueil de nouvelles*. Montréal: Boréal, 1990.

Falardeau, Jean-Charles. *Notre société et notre roman*. Montréal: HMH, 1967.

Fortin, Nicole. *Une littérature inventée*. Québec: Presses de l'Université de Laval, 1994.

Gauvin, Lise. *Langagement: l'écrivain et la langue au Québec*. Montréal: Boréal, 2000.

Harger-Grinling, Virginia, and Terry Goldie, eds. *Violence in the Canadian Novel Sincer 1960*. St John's: Memorial University, 108–.

Harrison, Dick. *Unnamed Country: The Struggle for a Canadian Prairie Fiction*. Edmonton: University of Alberta Press, 1977.

Imbert, Patrick. *Roman québécois contemporain et clichés*. Ottawa: Eds de l'Université d'Ottawa, 1983.

Jensen, Margaret Ann. *Love's Sweet Return: The Harlequin Story*. Toronto: Women's Press, 1984.

Kertzer, Jonathan. *Worrying the Nation: imagining a national literature in Canada*. Toronto: University of Toronto Press, 1998.

Lemire, Maurice. *Les grands thèmes nationalistes du roman historique canadien-français*. Québec: Presses de l'Université Laval, 1970.

Lynch, Gerald. *The One and the Many: English-Canadian Short Story Cycles*. Toronto: University of Toronto Press, 2001.

Marcotte, Gilles. *Le roman à l'imparfait: essai sur le roman québécois d'aujourd'hui*. Montréal: La Presse, 1976.

Nepveu, Pierre. *Intérieurs du nouveau monde*. Montréal: Boréal, 1998.

Northey, Margot. *The Haunted Wilderness: The Gothic and Grotesque in Canadian Fiction*. Toronto: University of Toronto Press, 1976.

Paradis, Suzanne. *Femme fictive, femme réelle: le personnage féminin dans le roman féminin canadien-français, 1994–1966*. Québec: Garneau, 1966.

Paterson, Janet M. *Moments postmodernes dans le roman québécois*. Ottawa: Presses de l'Université d'Ottawa, 1993.

Polk, James. *Wilderness Writers*. Toronto: Clarke, Irwin, 1972.

Poulin, Gabrielle. *Roman du pays, 1968–1979*. Montréal: Bellarmin, 1980.

Ricou, Laurence. *Vertical Man/Horizontal World*. Vancouver: University of British Columbia Press, 1973.

Shek, Ben-Zion. *Social Realism in the French-Canadian Novel*. Montreal: Harvest House, 1977.

Sirois, Antoine. *Lecture mythocritique du roman québécois*. Montréal: Triptyque, 1999.

Stratford, Philip. *All the Polarities*. Toronto: ECW, 1986.

Sutherland, Ronald. *The New Hero*. Toronto: Macmillan, 1977.

FIRST NATIONS STUDIES

Armstrong, Jeannette, ed. *Looking At the Words of Our People: First Nations Analaysis of Literature*. Penticton, BC: Theytus, 1993.

Cruikshank, Julie, et al. *Life Lived Like a Story*. Vancouver: University of British Columbia Press, 1990.

Cruikshank, Julie, et al. *The Social Life of Stories*. Vancouver: University of British Columbia Press, and Lincoln: University of Nebraska Press, 1998.

Emberley, Julia. *Thresholds of Difference: Feminist Critique, Native Women's Writings, Postcolonial Theory*. Toronto: University of Toronto Press, 1993.

Goldie, Terry. *Fear and Temptation: The Image of the Indigene in Canadian, Australian, and New Zealand Literatures*. Kingston, ON: McGill-Queen's University Press, 1989.

Hoy, Helen. *How Should I Read These: Native Women Writers in Canada*. Toronto: University of Toronto Press, 2001.

Hulan, Renée, ed. *Native North America*. Toronto: ECW, 1999.

King, Thomas, et al., eds. *The Native in Literature*. Toronto: ECW, 1987.

Monkman, Leslie. *A Native Heritage: Images of the Indian in English-Canadian Literature*. Toronto: University of Toronto Press, 1981.

New, W.H., ed. *Native Writers and Canadian Writing*. Vancouver: University of British Columbia Press, 1990.

Petrone, Penny. *Native Literature in Canada: From the Oral Tradition to the Present*. Toronto: Oxford, 1990.

Ruffo, Armand Garnet, ed. *(Ad)dressing Our Words: Aboriginal Perspectives on Aboriginal Literatures*. Penticton, BC: Theytus, 2001.

FOLKLORE

Dupont, Jean-Claude, ed. *Mélanges en l'honneur de Luc Lacourcière: folklore français d'Amérique*. Montréal: Leméac, 1972.

Fowke, Edith. *Folktales of French Canada.* Toronto: NC, 1981.

Fowke, Edith, and Carole H. Carpenter, eds. *Explorations in Canadian Folklore.* Toronto: McClelland & Stewart, 1985.

Thomas, Gerald. *The Two Traditions: The Art of Storytelling amongst French-Newfoundlanders.* St John's: Breakwater, 1993.

GENDER, SEXUALITY, LIFE WRITING

Buss, Helen. *Mapping Our Selves: Canadian Women's Autobiography in English.* Montreal: McGill-Queen's University Press, 1993.

Carrière, Marie J. *Writing in the Feminine in French and English Canada: A Question of Ethics.* Toronto: University of Toronto Press, 2002.

Coleman, Dan. *Masculine Migrations: Reading the Postcolonial Male in 'New Canadian' Narratives.* Toronto: University of Toronto Press, 1998.

Dickinson, Peter. *Here Is Queer: Nationalisms, Sexualities and the Literatures of Canada.* Toronto: University of Toronto Press, 1999.

Dybikowski, Ann, et al., eds. *In the feminine.* Edmonton: Longspoon, 1985.

Godard, Barbara, ed. *Collaboration in the Feminine: Writings on Women and Culture from Tessera.* Toronto: Second Story, 1994.

Howells, Coral Ann. *Private and Fictional Words: Canadian Women Novelists of the 1970s and 1980s.* London: Methuen, 1987.

Irvine, Lorna. *Sub/Version: Canadian Fictions by Women.* Toronto: ECW, 1986.

McMullen, Lorraine, ed. *Re(dis)covering Our Foremothers: Nineteenth-century Canadian Women Writers.* Ottawa: University of Ottawa Press, 1990.

Neuman, Shirely, ed. *Reading Canadian Autobiography.* Special issue of *Essays on Canadian Writing* 60 (1996).

Neuman, Shirley, and Smaro Kamboureli, eds. *A Mazing Space: Writing Canadian Women Writing.* Edmonton: Longspoon/NeWest, 1986.

Rimstead, Roxanne. *Remnants of Nation: On Poverty Narratives by Women.* Toronto: University of Toronto Press, 2001.

Scheier, Libby, et al., eds. *Language in Her Eye: Writing and Gender: Views by Canadian Women Writing in English.* Toronto: Coach House, 1990.

Telling It Book Collective. *Telling It: Women and Language across Cultures.* Vancouver: Press Gang, 1990.

Williamson, Janice. *Sounding Differences: Conversations with Seventeen Canadian Women Writers.* Toronto: University of Toronto Press, 1993.

GENERAL THEORY, CRITICISM, AND BACKGROUND MATERIALS

Atwood, Margaret. *Second Words: Selected Critical Prose.* Toronto: Anansi, 1982.

Atwood, Margaret. *Survival.* Toronto: Anansi, 1972.

Ballstadt, Carl, ed. *The Search for English-Canadian Literature.* Toronto: University of Toronto Press, 1975.

Bayard, Caroline, ed. *100 Years of Critical Solitudes.* Toronto: ECW, 1992.

Beaulieu, Victor-Lévy. *Manuel de la petite littérature du Québec.* Montréal: L'Aurore, 1974.

Bessette, Gérard. *Une littérature en ébullition.* Montréal: Editions du Jour, 1968.

Blodgett, E.D. *Configuration: Essays on the Canadian Literatures.* Toronto: ECW, 1982.

Bourassa, André-G. *Surréalisme et littérature québécoise.* Montréal: Editions L'Etincelle, 1977; tr. Mark Czarnecki as *Surrealism and Quebec Literature.* Toronto: University of Toronto Press, 1984.

Camerlin, Lorraine, et al., comps. *Lectures européennes de la littérature québécoise.* Ottawa: Leméac, 1982.

Cameron, Barry, and Michael Dixon, eds. *Minus Canadian.* Special issue of *Studies in Canadian Literature,* 2 (1977).

Davey, Frank. *Canadian Literary Power.* Edmonton: NeWest, 1994.

Davey, Frank. *Post-national arguments.* Toronto: University of Toronto Press, 1993.

Davey, Frank. *Reading Canadian Reading.* Winnipeg: Turnstone, 1988.

Davey, Frank. *Surviving the Paraphrase.* Winnipeg: Turnstone, 1983.

Davies, Gwendolyn. *Studies in Maritime Literary History, 1760–1930.* Fredericton: Acadiensis, 1991.

de Grandpré, Pierre. *Histoire de la littérature française du Québec.* 3 vols. Montréal: Beauchemin, 1968ff.

Doyle, James. *North of America: Images of Canada in the Literature of the United States 1775–1900.* Toronto: ECW, 1983.

Frye, Northrop. *The Bush Garden: Essays on the Canadian Imagination.* Toronto: Anansi, 1971.

Frye, Northrop. *Divisions on a Ground.* Toronto: Anansi, 1982.

Gerson, Carole. *A Purer Taste: The Writing and Reading of Fiction in English in Nineteenth-Century Canada.* Toronto: University of Toronto Press, 1989.

Glickman, Susan. *The Picturesque and the Sublime: A Poetics of the Canadian Landscape.* Montreal: McGill-Queen's University Press, 1998.

Grace, Sherrill. *Canada and the Idea of North.* Montreal: McGill-Queen's University Press, 2001.

Halpenny, Frances G., ed. *Editing Canadian Texts.* Toronto: Hakkert, 1975.

Harrison, Dick, ed. *Crossing Frontiers.* Edmonton: University of Alberta Press, 1979.

Hébert, Pierre. *Censure et littérature au Québec: le livre crucifié,1625–1919.* Saint-Laurent, QC: Fides, 1997.

Heble, Ajay, et al., eds. *New Contexts of Canadian Criticism.* Peterborough, ON: Broadview, 1997.

Henighan, Stephen. *When Words Deny the World: The Reshaping of Canadian Writing*. Erin, ON: Porcupine's Quill, 2002.

Hutcheon, Linda. *The Canadian Postmodern*. Toronto: Oxford, 1988.

Hutcheon, Linda. *Irony's Edge: The Theory and Politics of Irony*. London & New York: Routledge, 1994.

Hutcheon, Linda. *Narcissistic Narrative: History, Theory, Fiction*. Waterloo, ON: Wilfrid Laurier University Press, 1980.

Hutcheon, Linda. *Splitting Images: Contemporary Canadian Ironies*. Toronto: Oxford, 1991.

Jones, D.G. *Butterfly on Rock*. Toronto: University of Toronto Press, 1970.

Karr, Clarence. *Authors and Audiences: Popular Canadian Fiction in the Early Twentieth Century*. Montreal: McGill-Queen's University Press, 2001.

Keefer, Janice Kulyk. *Under Eastern Eyes: A Critical Reading of Maritime Fiction*. Toronto: University of Toronto Press, 1987.

Keith, W.J. *Literary Images of Ontario*. Toronto: University of Toronto Press, 1992.

Klinck, Carl F., ed. *Literary History of Canada*. 3 vols, 2nd ed. Toronto: University of Toronto Press, 1976. Vol. 4, ed. W.H. New. Toronto: University of Toronto Press, 1990.

Kroetsch, Robert, and Reingard M. Nischik, eds. *Gaining Ground: European Critics on Canadian Literature*. Edmonton: NeWest, 1985.

LaBossière, Camille, ed. *Translation in Canadian Literature*. Ottawa: University of Ottawa Press, 1983.

Lecker, Robert. *Canadian Canons: Essays in Cultural Value*. Toronto: University of Toronto Press, 1991.

Lecker, Robert. *Making It Real: The Canonization of English-Canadian Literature*. Concord, ON: Anansi, 1995.

Lecker, Robert, Jack David, and Ellen Quigley, eds. *Canadian Writers and Their Works*. 24 vols. Toronto: ECW, 1983–91.

Lee, Dennis. *Savage Fields*. Toronto: Anansi, 1977.

Lemieux, Enise, et al., eds. *Traité de la culture*. Saint-Nicolas, QC: IQRC, 2002.

Mandel, Eli. *Another Time*. Erin, ON: Porcépic, 1977.

Mandel, Eli, ed. *Contexts of Canadian Criticism*. Chicago and London: University of Chicago Press, 1971.

Marcotte, Gilles. *Littérature et circonstances*. Montréal: Hexagone, 1989.

Marcotte, Gilles. *Une littérature qui se fait. Essais critiques sur la littérature canadienne-française*. Montréal: HMH, 1969.

Mathews, Robin. *Canadian Literature: Surrender or Revolution*. Toronto: Steel Rail, 1978.

McGregor, Gaile. *The Wacousta Syndrome: Explorations in the Canadian Langscape*. Toronto: University of Toronto Press, 1985.

Metcalf, John. *Kicking Against the Pricks*. Toronto: ECW, 1982.

Moss, John, ed. *Future Indicative: Literary Theory and Canadian Literature*. Ottawa: University of Ottawa Press, 1987.

New, W.H. *Borderlands: How We Talk About Canada.* Vancouver: University of British Columbia Press, 1998.

New, W.H. *Dreams of Speech and Violence: The Art of the Short Story in Canada and New Zealand.* Toronto: University of Toronto Press, 1987.

New, W.H. *Land Sliding: Imagining Space, Presence, and Power in Canadian Writing.* Toronto: University of Toronto Press, 1997.

Parker, George L. *The Beginnings of the Book Trade in Canada.* Toronto: University of Toronto Press, 1985.

Ricou, Laurie. *The Arbutus/Madrone Files: Reading the Pacific Northwest.* Edmonton: NeWest; Eugene: University of Oregon Press, 2002.

Ricou, Laurie. *Everyday Magic: Child Languages in Canadian Literature.* Vancouver: University of British Columbia Press, 1987.

Rousseau, Guildo. *L'image des États-Unis dans la littérature québécoise, 1775–1930.* Sherbrooke: Naaman, 1981.

Sarkonak, Ralph, ed. 'The Language of Difference: Writing in QUEBEC(ois).' Special issue of *Yale French Studies,* no. 65 (1983).

Shouldice, Larry, ed. and transl. *Contemporary Quebec Criticism.* Toronto: University of Toronto Press, 1979.

Tallman, Warren. *Godawful Streets of Man.* Special issue of *Open Letter,* 3.6 (1976–7).

Tougas, Gérard. *Histoire de la littérature canadienne-française.* Paris: Presse Universitaire de France, 1964; tr. Alta Lind Cook as *History of French-Canadian Literature.* Toronto: Ryerson, 1966.

Winks, Robin W. *The Myth of the American Frontier.* Leicester: Leicester University Press, 1971.

Woodcock, George. *Odysseus Ever Returning.* Toronto: McClelland & Stewart, 1970.

Woodcock, George. *The World of Canadian Writing.* Vancouver: Douglas & McIntyre; Seattle: University of Washington Press, 1980.

Woodcock, George. *Northern Spring.* Vancouver: Douglas & McIntyre, 1987.

Wyczynski, Paul, et al. *Archives des lettres canadiennces.* 6 vols. Montréal: Fides, 1969–85.

HISTORY AND SOCIAL COMMENT

Anderson, Kay J. *Vancouver's Chinatown: Racial Discourse in Canada, 1875–1980.* Montreal: McGill-Queen's University Press, 1991.

Berger, Carl. *The Writing of Canadian History.* 2nd ed. Toronto: Oxford, 1987.

Brown, Craig, ed. *The Illustrated History of Canada.* Rev. ed. Toronto: Key Porter, 2000.

Cleverdon, Catherine. *The Woman Suffrage Movement in Canada.* 2nd ed. Toronto: University of Toronto Press, 1974,

Finkel, Alvin, Margaret Conrad, and Veronica Strong-Boag. *History of the Canadian People.* 2 vols. Toronto: Copp Clark, 1993.

Friesen, Gerald. *The Canadian Prairies: A History.* Toronto: University of Toronto Press, 1987.

Friesen, Gerald. *Citizens and Nation.* Toronto: University of Toronto Press, 2000.

Gagnon, Serge. *Quebec and Its Historians.* 2 vols., tr. Jane Brierley. Montreal: Harvest House, 1982, 1985.

Grant, George. *Lament for a Nation.* Toronto: McClelland & Stewart, 1965.

Harris, R. Cole, and John Warkentin. *Canada Before Confederation.* New York: Oxford, 1974.

Ignatieff, Michael. *The Rights Revolution.* Toronto: Anansi, 2000.

Porter, John. *The Vertical Mosaic.* Toronto: University of Toronto Press, 1965.

Reid, Malcolm. *The Shouting Signpainters.* Toronto: McClelland & Stewart, 1972.

Saul, John Ralston. *Reflections of a Siamese Twin.* Toronto: Viking, 1997.

Trudel, Marcel. *L'influence de Voltaire au Canada.* 2 vols. Montréal: Fides, 1945.

Warkentin, John, ed. *Canada: A Geographical Interpretation.* Toronto: Methuen, 1968.

INTERNET WEBSITES

www.nlc-bnc.ca/caninfo [National Library]

www.nlc-bnc.ca/6/3/index-e.html [or f.html for French language discussion; National Library Canadian Literature Research Service]

www.umanitoba.ca/canlit/ [Canadian Literature archive]

www.nwpassages.com [extensive links to organizations, programs, sites]

www.umanitoba.ca/faculties/arts/english/treeline [electronic quarterly; links to sites in art, music, other electronic journals]

www.ucalgary.ca/UofC/faculties/HUM/ENGL/canada/ [Canadian poets online]

www.library.utoronto.ca/canpoetry/ [Canadian poets and poetry]

www.arts.uwo.ca/canpoetry/links.htm [poetry web resources]

www.canadiantheatre.com/ [encyclopedia of research]

www.litterature.org [francophone authors in Quebec]

www.lib.sfu.ca/researchtools/databases/dbofdb.htm [click on Women's Studies, then on Canada's early women writers]

www.slais.ubc.ca/saltman/ccib/home.html [Canadian children's illustrated books in English]

http://clcwebjournal.lib.purdue.edu/library/caneth.html [ethnic minority writing]

www.nlc-bnc.ca/cihm/ [Canadian institute for historical microreproductions]

www.archives.ca/ [National archives]

www.canadiana.org [early Canadiana online, complete texts]
www.track0.com/ogwc/ [online guide to writing in Canada]
http://daryl.chin.gc.ca:8000/BASIS/aich/user/www/sf [anglophone
guide to Canadian art]
http://daryl.chin.gc.ca:8000/BASIS/aich/user/www/SF [francophone
guide to Canadian art]
www.virtualmuseum.ca/ [Canadian museum site]
www.imagescanada.ca/ [Canadian image bank]

MULTICULTURALISM

Balan, Jars, ed. *Identifications: Ethnicity and the Writer in Canada.* Edmonton:
Canadian Institute for Ukrainian Studies, 1982.

Bisztray, George. *Hungarian-Canadian Literature.* Toronto:University of Toronto Press, 1987.

Brand, Dionne. *No Burden to Carry: Narratives of Black Working Women in Ontario, 1920s to 1950s.* Toronto: Women's Press, 1991.

Buchignani, Norman, et al. *Continuous Journey: A Social History of South Asians in Canada.* Toronto: McClelland & Stewart, 1985.

Chao, Lien. *Beyond Silence: Chinese Canadian Literature in English.* Toronto: TSAR, 1997.

Clarke, George Elliot. *Odysseys Home: Mapping African-Canadian Literature.* Toronto: University of Toronto Press, 2002.

Davis, Rocío G., and Rosalía Baena, eds. *Tricks with a Glass: Writing Ethnicity in Canada.* Amsterdam: Rodopi, 2000.

Dorsinville, Max. *Caliban Without Prospero: Essay on Quebec and Black Literature.* Erin, ON: Porcépic, 1974.

Foster, Cecil. *A Place Called Heaven: The Meaning of Being Black in Canada.* Toronto: HarperCollins, 1996.

Greenstein, Michael. *Third Solitudes: Tradition and Discontinuity in Jewish-Canadian Literature.* 1989.

Kamboureli, Smaro. *Scandalous Bodies: Diasporic Literature in English Canada.* Don Mills, ON: Oxford, 2000.

Kamboureli, Smaro. *Making a Difference: Canadian Multicultural Literature.* Toronto: Oxford, 1996.

Pivato, Joseph, ed. *Contrasts: Comparative Essays on Italian-Canadian Writing.* Montreal: Guernica, 1985.

Riedel, Walter, ed. *The Old World and the New: Literary Persepctives of German-speaking Canadians.* Toronto: University of Toronto Press, 1984.

Siemerling, Winfried, ed. *Writing Ethnicity: Cross-cultural Consciousness in Canadian and Québécois Literature.* Toronto: ECW, 1996.

Siemerling, Winfried, and Katrin Schwenk, eds. *Cultural Difference and the Literary Text: Pluralism and the Limits of Authenticity in North American Literatures.* Iowa City: University of Iowa Press, 1997.

Vassanji, M.G., ed. *A Meeting of Streams: South Asian Canadian Literature.* Toronto: TSAE, 1985.

Verduyn, Christl, ed. *Literary Pluralities.* Peterborough: Broadview, 1990.

Wah, Fred. *Faking It: Poetics and Hybridity.* Edmonton: NeWest, 2000.

Wickberg, Edgar, ed. *From China to Canada: A History of the Chinese Communities in Canada.* Toronto: McClelland & Stewart, 1982.

Winks, Robin W. *The Blacks in Canada: A History.* 2nd ed. Montreal: McGill-Queen's University Press, 1997.

POETRY

Barbour, Douglas. *Lyric/Anti-lyric.* Edmonton: NeWest, 2001.

Blais, Jacques. *De l'ordre et de l'aventure. La poésie au Québec de 1934 à 1944.* Québec: Presse de l'Université de Laval, 1975.

Bowering, George. *A Way with Words.* Ottawa: Oberon, 1982.

Collin, W.E. *The White Savannahs.* 1936; rpt. Toronto: University of Toronto Press, 1975.

Cooley, Dennis. *The Vernacular Muse.* Winnipeg: Turnstone, 1987.

Davey, Frank, and Ann Munton, eds. 'Long-liners Conference Issue' [the long poem in Canada']. *Open Letter,* 6th series, 2–3 (Summer-Fall 1985).

Dragland, Stan. *Floating Voice.* Concord, ON: Anansi, 1994.

Kamboureli, Smaro. *On the Edge of Genre: The Contemporary Canadian Long Poem.* Toronto: University of Toronto Press, 1991.

Kushner, Eva, and Michael Bishop, eds. *La poésie québécoise depuis 1975.* Special issue of *Dalhousie French Studies,* 1986.

Lilburn, Tim, ed. *Poetry and Knowing.* Kingston, ON: Quarry, 1995.

Lilburn, Tim, ed. *Thinking and Singing.* Toronto: Cormorant, 2002.

Marcotte, Gilles. *Le temps des poètes. Description critiques de la poésie actuelle au Canada français.* Montréal: HMH, 1969.

Moisan, Clément. *Poésie des frontières.* Montréal: Hurtubise, 1979; English version by the author, *A Poetry of Frontiers.* Victoria, BC: Porcépic, 1983.

Popovic, Pierre. *La contradiction du poème: poésie et discours social au Québec de 1948 à 1953.* Candiac: Editions Balzac, 1992.

Scobie, Stephen. *Signature Event Cantext: Essays.* Edmonton: NeWest, 1989.

Trehearne, Brian. *Aestheticism and the Canadian Modernists.* Montreal: McGill-Queen's University Press, 1989.

Trehearne, Brian. *The Montreal Forties: Modernist Poetry in Transition.* Toronto: University of Toronto Press, 1999.

REFERENCE

Avis, Walter, et al., comps. *A Concise Dictionary of Canadianisms.* Toronto: Gage, 1973.

Belisle, Louis-Alexandre, comp. *Dictionnaire nord-américain de la langue française*. Montréal: Beauchemin, 1979.

Benson, Eugene, and Len Conolly, comps. *Encyclopedia of Post-Colonial Literatures in English*. London & New York: Routledge, 1994.

Benson, Eugene, and Len Conolly, comps. *The Oxford Companion to Canadian Theatre*. Toronto: Oxford, 1989.

Boivin, Aurélien. Québec: Nuit blanche, 1992.

Boivin, Aurélien. *Le conte littéraire québécois au 19e siècle. Essai de bibliographie critique et analytique*. Montréal: Fides, 1975.

Canada: The Printed Record. Ottawa: Canadian Institute for Historical Microreproductions, 1981–; provides access to microfiches of items printed before 1920.

Canadian Books in Print. Toronto: University of Toronto Press, 1972–, annual.

The Canadian Encyclopedia, ed. James Marsh. 2nd ed., 4 vols. Edmonton: Hurtig, 1988. Updated in electronic form and in 1-vol. published version, Toronto: McClelland & Stewart, 1999.

CRELIQ history of literature in Quebec, ongoing series (Québec: Université Laval).

Dean, William G., et al., comps. *Concise Historical Atlas of Canada*. Toronto: University of Toronto Press, 1998.

Dictionary of Canadian Biography/Dictionnaire biographique du Canada. 14 volumes, ongoing. Vols. 1–12 ed. Louis Hamelin and Francess Halpenny, vols. 13–14 ed. Ramsay Cook and Réal Bélanger. Toronto: University of Toronto Press, 1966–. Electronic version released in 2000.

Fowke, Edith, and Carole Carpenter, comps. *A Bibliography of Canadian Folklore in English*. Toronto: University of Toronto Press, 1981.

Hayne, David M., and Antoine Sirois, comps. *Bibliography of Studies in Comparative Canadian Literature*. Sherbrooke: Université de Sherbrooke, 1989.

Ingles, Ernie. *Bibliography of Canadian Bibliographies*. 3rd ed. Toronto: University of Toronto Press, 1994.

Lecker, Robert, and Jack David, eds. *The Annotated Bibliography of Canada's Major Authors*. 10 vols. Downsview, ON: ECW, 1979–.

Lemire, Maurice, ed. *Dictionnaire des oeuvres littéraires du Québec*. 5 vols. Montréal: Fides, 1978–.

'Letters in Canada,' annual review, *University of Toronto Quarterly*, 1936–d.

New, William H., ed. *Encyclopedia of Literature in Canada*. Toronto: University of Toronto Press, 2002.

Story, G.M., et al., comps. *Dictionary of Newfoundland English*. Toronto: University of Toronto Press, 1982.

Stratford, Philip. *Bibliography of Canadian Books in Translation: French to English and English to French*. Ottawa: CCRH, 1977.

Tougas, Gérard, comp. *A Checklist of Printed Materials Relating to French-*

Canadian Literature, 1763–1968. 2nd ed. Vancouver: University of British Columbia Press, 1973.

Toye, William, ed. *The Oxford Companion to Canadian Literature.* 2nd ed. Toronto: Oxford, 1997; concise ed., 2001.

Wagner, Anton, ed. *The Brock Bibliography of Published Canadian Plays in English 1766–1978.* Toronto: Playwrights Press, 1980.

Waterston, Elizabeth, comp. *The Travellers: Canada to 1900.* Guelph: University of Guelph, 1989.

Watters, R.E., comp. *A Check List of Canadian Literature and Background Materials, 1628–1950.* Rev. ed. Toronto: University of Toronto Press, 1972.

Weiss, Allan, comp. *Comprehensive Bibliography of English-Canadian Short Stories, 1950–1983.* Toronto: ECW, 1988.

Index